Vocational Rehabilitation and Supported Employment

edited by

Paul Wehman, Ph.D.
Department of Rehabilitation Medicine
Medical College of Virginia
Virginia Commonwealth University
Richmond

and

M. Sherril Moon, Ed.D.
Rehabilitation Research and Training Center
Virginia Commonwealth University
Richmond

·PAUL·H·
BROOKES
PUBLISHING CO.

Baltimore • London • Toronto • Sydney

Paul H. Brookes Publishing Co.
Post Office Box 10624
Baltimore, Maryland 21285-0624

Copyright © 1988 by Paul H. Brookes Publishing Co., Inc.
All rights reserved.

Typeset by Harper Graphics, Waldorf, Maryland.
Manufactured in the United States of America by
The Maple Press Company, York, Pennsylvania.

Library of Congress Cataloging-in-Publication Data

Vocational rehabilitation and supported employment / [edited by] Paul
   Wehman, M. Sherril Moon.
        p.   cm.
   Bibliography: p.
   Includes index.
   ISBN 0-933716-98-2
   1. Vocational rehabilitation—United States.   2. Handicapped—
Employment—United States.   I. Wehman, Paul.   II. Moon, M.
Sherril, 1952–   .   III. Title: Supported employment.
HD7256.U5V59   1988
362′.0425—dc19   88-7315
                                                            CIP

Contents

v

Contributors

J. Michael Barcus, M.Ed.
Assistant Director of Training
RRTC/Virginia Commonwealth University
VCU Box 2011
Richmond, VA 23284-2011

Roy Beziat, Ph.D.
Director, Center of Rehabilitation and Manpower
  Studies
President, Development and Training Association
Room 3119, Jull Hall
The University of Maryland
College Park, MD 20742

Lisa Brinkman, M.H.A.
Consultant
Training and Research Institute for Adults with
  Disabilities
Boston College
Chestnut Hill, MA 02167

Jay Buckley, Ed.D.
Research Associate in Special Education and
  Rehabilitation
Associate Director of the Employment Network
  Technical Assistance Project in Supported
  Employment
University of Oregon
Division of Special Education and Rehabilitation
Eugene, OR 97403

Joseph F. Campbell, Ed.D.
President, Incentive Community Enterprises, Inc.
441 Pleasant St.
Northampton, MA 01060

Walter A. Chernish, M.B.A.
Executive Director, Louise W. Eggleston Center
780 West 20th St.
Norfolk, VA 23517

Frederick C. Collignon, Ph.D.
President, Berkeley Planning Associates
3200 Adeline St.
Berkeley, CA 94703

Terry Bloom Edelstein, M.P.H.
Executive Director, Connecticut Association of
  Rehabilitation Facilities
West Elm Office Commons
1080 Elm St.
Rocky Hill, CT 06067

Jane M. Everson, M.Ed.
Personnel Preparation Coordinator
RRTC/Virginia Commonwealth University
VCU Box 2011
Richmond, VA 23284-2011

Don Fender, M.S.
Director, Community Living Services for the
  Programs for Individuals with Autism
South Carolina Department of Mental Health
P.O. Box 485
Columbia, SC 29202

Katherine W. Fender, B.S.
Coordinator, Employment Services for the
  Programs for Individuals with Autism
South Carolina Department of Mental Health
P.O. Box 485
Columbia, SC 29202

Karen Flippo, M.R.A.
Project Coordinator, Rehabilitation Employment
  Specialist Training for Direct Service Personnel
University of San Francisco
Rehabilitation Administration Department
Ignatian Heights, CA 94117

Susan Lehmann Griffin, M.S.
Project Coordinator, RRTC—Employment
  Network
RRTC/Virginia Commonwealth University
VCU Box 2011
Richmond, VA 23284-2011

Mark L. Hill, M.S.Ed.
Director, Office of Supported Employment
Virginia Department of Mental Health
Mental Retardation and Substance Abuse Services
P.O. Box 1797
Richmond, VA 23214

Margaret Hutchins, M.Ed.
Coordinator, A.I.M.E.S.—Application of
  Industrial Methods to Employment Services to
  Students with Multiple Handicaps
Department of Special Education
University of Illinois at Urbana-Champaign
288 Education Building
1310 South 6th St.
Champaign, IL 61820

Katherine J. Inge, M.Ed., O.T.R.
Training Associate
RRTC/Virginia Commonwealth University
VCU Box 2011
Richmond, VA 23284-2011

William E. Kiernan, Ph.D.
Director, Training and Research Institute for Adults
  with Disabilities
Boston College
Chestnut Hill, MA 02167

John Kregel, Ed.D.
Associate Professor of Special Education
Research Director
RRTC/Virginia Commonwealth University
VCU Box 2011
Richmond, VA 23284-2011

Jeffrey S. Kreutzer, Ph.D.
Director, Rehabilitation Psychology and
  Neuropsychology
Medical College of Virginia
Box 677
MCV Station
Richmond, VA 23298-0677

David Mank, Ph.D.
Director, Employment Network Technical
  Assistance Project in Supported Employment
Assistant Professor of Special Education and
  Rehabilitation
University of Oregon
Eugene, OR 97403

Pat McCarthy, Ed.D.
State Director of Programs for Individuals with
  Autism
South Carolina Department of Mental Health
P.O. Box 485
Columbia, SC 29202

Robert McDaniel, Ph.D.
Director, Rehabilitation Administration Department
University of San Francisco
Ignatian Heights
San Francisco, CA 94117-1080

Bruce M. Menchetti, Ph.D.
Vocational Education Consultant for the
  Handicapped
School District of Greenville County
301 Camperdown Way
Box 2848
Greenville, SC 29602

M. Sherril Moon, Ed.D.
Associate Professor
Associate Director and Director of Training
RRTC/Virginia Commonwealth University
VCU Box 2011
Richmond, VA 23284-2011

M.V. Morton, M.S.Ed.
Project Consultant, Traumatic Brain Injury Mental
  Health Training Grant
Department of Psychiatry
Medical College of Virginia
P.O. Box 268
Richmond, VA 23298

John H. Noble, Jr., Ph.D.
Professor of Social Work and Rehabilitative
  Medicine
State University of New York at Buffalo
191 Alumni Arena
Amherst, NY 14260

Wendy S. Parent, M.S.
Assistant Coordinator, Transition into Supported
  Employment for Youth with Severe Disabilities
  Project
RRTC/Virginia Commonwealth University
VCU Box 2011
Richmond, VA 23284-2011

Ian Pumpian, Ph.D.
Associate Professor of Special Education
San Diego State University
Special Education Department
6310 Alvarado Court
San Diego, CA 92182

Adelle Renzaglia, Ph.D.
Associate Professor of Special Education
Coordinator, Moderate and Severe Handicaps
  Training Program
University of Illinois at Urbana-Champaign
288 Education Building
1310 South Sixth St.
Champaign, IL 61820

Lynda Richard, M.Ed.
Project Director, Pennsylvania State Task Force
  Supported Employment Project
Eastern Technical Assistance and Monitoring
  Center
Temple University
Developmental Disabilities Center
Ritter Hall Annex #960
Philadelphia, PA 19122

Frank R. Rusch, Ph.D.
Professor of Special Education
Director, Secondary Transition Intervention
  Effectiveness Institute
University of Illinois
Department of Special Education
110 Education Building
1310 South Sixth St.
Champaign, IL 61820

Paul Sale, Ed.D.
Assistant Professor of Special Education
Coordinator, Virginia Commonwealth University's
  Master's Degree Program in Supported
  Employment
RRTC/Virginia Commonwealth University
VCU 2011
Richmond, VA 23284-2011

Robert L. Schalock, Ph.D.
Professor and Department Chairman of Psychology
Hastings College
Program Consultant for Mid-Nebraska Mental
    Retardation Services, Inc.
P.O. Box 1146
Hastings, NE 68901

Michael S. Shafer, Ph.D.
Assistant Director, Research
RRTC/Virginia Commonwealth University
VCU Box 2011
Richmond, VA 23284-2011

Holly Shepard, M.Ed.
Project Director, Educating Students with Severe
    Handicaps in Least Restrictive Environments
University of Southern Mississippi–Mississippi
    University Affiliated Program
Southern Station
Box 5162
Hattiesburg, MS 39406

R. Timm Vogelsberg, Ph.D.
Associate Professor of Psychological Studies at
    Temple University
Director of Training and Habilitation,
    Developmental Disabilities Center
Temple University
RA #949
Philadelphia, PA 19122

Paul Wehman, Ph.D.
Professor of Rehabilitation Medicine
Director, RRTC/Virginia Commonwealth
    University
VCU Box 2011
Richmond, VA 23284-2011

Elizabeth West, M.A.
Program Manager, San Diego Community College
    District Foundation, Inc.
1536 Frazee Rd.
San Diego, CA 92108-1307

Wendy Wood, M.Ed.
School of Education
Virginia Commonwealth University
Richmond, VA 23284-2011

Acknowledgments

This book would not have been possible without the selfless contributions of each of the authors in developing their respective chapters. When we agreed to undertake this book, we did not think, nor do we now, that one or two people have all of the knowledge on vocational rehabilitation and supported employment. It seemed that the only way to provide a comprehensive treatment of the topic was to draw on outside experts. We are deeply grateful to each contributor for sharing his or her opinions and expertise. We believe that the significant effort undertaken by these authors is revealed throughout the book.

We next wish to acknowledge the disabled people themselves, and their families, for their willingness to try real work for the first time. Without this courage and pioneering spirit, there would be no supported employment. Risks involve loss or confusion of government subsidy funds, hassles with transportation, and often less-than-desirable job options. In addition, family schedules can be disrupted significantly at times. In short, no matter how good the local service personnel are in program implementation, families and consumers have to take a chance at something new. This courage is opening the door for others and will open the doors for future generations of people with severe disabilities.

Third, we wish to thank the U.S. Department of Education, Office of Special Education and Rehabilitative Services, for moral and governmental support. Grant funds partially supported our efforts in planning this volume. Obviously, people like Madeleine Will, Tom Bellamy, Dick Melia, Fred Isbister, Mike Herrell, Paul Thompson, Bill Halloran, and Fred Orelove have made a big difference in allowing supported employment and integration activities to move forward.

Finally, we thank Rachel Conrad, Dawn Lorinser, Brenda Robinson, Jan Smith, Steve Hall, and Monique Wiggins for their patience and high-quality contributions in manuscript development and support. This has been a long and challenging project to complete. We are grateful to these people for their measurable help in improving the technical quality of the overall manuscript.

Preface

This book assembles many of the ideas, philosophies, models, concepts, and issues that characterize supported employment as we know it in 1988. Because of the rapidly changing nature of this field, there is little doubt that many of the thoughts in these pages will have been seriously reevaluated 3–5 years from now. We hope that this is the case, since the collective sense of the editors and contributors of this volume is that the knowledge contained here represents only a beginning. This text focuses *exclusively* on supported employment and vocational rehabilitation. The first two sections examine philosophical, regulatory, historical, and general programmatic issues; followed by a review, in Section III, of how community-based programs are responding to the challenge of supported employment; a look at relationships with business and government regulations in Section IV; and finally, in Section V, a discussion of applications with different populations of disabled persons. This latter section was difficult to write, since only limited data are available for a number of the affected groups. It is expected that these data will expand over the next few years.

Supported employment has engendered considerable controversy in the field. Initially, it was viewed by some as the panacea for all of the employment problems of people with disabilities. Others viewed supported employment as some terrible idea lurking around the corner, ready to cause upheaval in local programs. Many human service professionals, however, are finally realizing what supported employment really is: real work with permanent (intermittent or daily) staff support for people historically excluded from the labor force because of the severity of their disability. Supported employment is much like a civil rights movement for forgotten severely disabled people who society has safely put away, out of sight for the most part, in adult day centers and other segregated programs. It is heavily grounded in values of integration and normalization. The excitement of *good* supported employment programs is that these people are finally being afforded the dignity of real work in real business settings. They are taking their place as equals in society.

We hope that readers find this book a useful and stimulating resource on current thinking in supported employment. Certainly that has been the aim of each of the expert contributors to this volume. As we enter the end of the 1980s, we are clearly well on our way to supported employment implementation. But how successful will this implementation be? Will it be with the right population? Will the models expand in number and be more creative? Will data management systems now being put into place provide enough appropriate information to change the funding streams in place? And, finally, will local service programs change their collective emphasis from predominantly on-site special center programs to small, dispersed, off-site employment programs? The answers to these questions will come only with time, but all of us in the field can contribute to their resolution. This remains our challenge.

SECTION I

GENERAL ISSUES RELATED
TO SUPPORTED EMPLOYMENT

Chapter 1

Supported Employment

Toward Zero Exclusion of Persons with Severe Disabilities

Paul Wehman

Within the past 2 decades, astounding progress has been made in learning how to help persons with severe disabilities work productively. Totally deaf and blind persons with severe mental retardation, for example, have demonstrated the ability to assemble complex electronic circuit boards (Gold, 1976); similarly, persons with profound mental retardation have shown they can productively assemble cable harnesses (Hunter & Bellamy, 1977), chain saws (O'Neill & Bellamy, 1978), and various other manufacturing equipment.

The best of this training technology (Moon, Goodall, Barcus, & Brooke, 1986) has been extended to competitive employment placement in food service settings (Sowers, Thompson, & Connis, 1979), laundry settings (Bates & Panscofar, 1983), cleaning (Cuvo, Leaf, & Borakove, 1978), and other service occupations (Vogelsberg, Ashe, & Williams, 1985; Wehman, Hill, et al., 1985) for historically unemployed people with severe disabilities. Similarly, industry-based enclaves (Rhodes & Valenta, 1985), mobile work crews (Bourbeau, 1985), small business arrangements (O'Bryan, 1985), and rehabilitation engineering practices (Sowers, Jenkins, & Powers, 1988) have provided evidence of the competence and employability of many people with severe disabilities. Positive

work experiences have resulted for persons with autism (Smith, 1984), severe mental retardation (Wehman, Hill, Wood, & Parent, 1987), brain injury (Wehman et al., in press), and cerebral palsy (Sowers, Jenkins, & Powers, in press).

Why begin this book with a presentation of the rapid gains that have occurred in demonstrating vocational competence? Simply because it is this progress, these research data, and the accumulating knowledge base that provide the cornerstone of credibility for supported employment. A model of supported employment has dramatic implications for vocational rehabilitation practices as we know them today. Critical issues related to vocational evaluation, eligibility, the 60-day closure, and preplacement work adjustment activity are but a few of the practices that are being increasingly scrutinized by professionals in the field. Supported employment implementation calls into question the merit and validity of some of these practices for persons with truly severe disabilities.

The goal of the editors of this book is to assemble the best thinking on some of the most exciting yet challenging aspects of supported employment and vocational rehabilitation. No longer can supported employment be viewed as a series of isolated research endeavors limited to a handful of prodigious investigators in different universities. From the administrative branch of the federal government (Will, 1984) to the legislative branch (Rehabilitation Act Amendments, October 1986), supported employment is becoming institutionalized in all 50 states as a viable employment alternative for difficult-to-place clients.

The overriding issue facing vocational rehabilitation is how to credibly manage supported employment *implementation*. This will be a difficult task because: 1) only limited financial and training resources are available; 2) there will continue to be an increased push to serve the most difficult clients; and 3) many vocational rehabilitation service personnel will not be convinced of the merits of supported employment. Furthermore, in order to maximize the existing dollars available, rehabilitation managers will have to forge more interagency funding arrangements than ever before. Failure to do this well will almost certainly doom supported employment programs.

SUPPORTED EMPLOYMENT: AN OVERVIEW

Supported employment is paid work that takes place in regular or normal work settings. It may be competitive employment (work that pays minimum wage) or employment with subminimum wages in individualized or group placement situations. The August 14, 1987, federal regulations define supported employment as follows:

> The term "supported employment" contains three elements: (1) Competitive work; (2) an integrated work setting; and (3) the provision of on-going support services. The proposed regulations define "competitive work" to mean "work that is performed on a full-time basis or on a part-time basis, averaging at least 20 hours per week, and for which an individual is compensated in accordance with the Fair Labor Standards Act." The Fair Labor Standards Act allows employers the flexibility to compensate workers with handicaps at a wage level that is: (1) Lower than the minimum wage; (2) commensurate with those wages paid to non-handicapped individuals employed in the same locality and performing the same type, quality and quantity of work; and (3) related to the individual's productivity. The use of these standards is designed to ensure that individuals with severe hand-

icaps under this program receive fair and competitive wages—not just "token" wages such as those received by many individuals with severe handicaps in work activity centers. (*Federal Register*, August 14, 1987)

Ongoing Services

The major implication of this definition for vocational rehabilitation is the provision of ongoing services. Traditionally, vocational rehabilitation has provided only time-limited services; that is, services with a beginning and an end, that are not provided throughout the total duration of the client's employment. These regulations do not mandate or even suggest that rehabilitation agencies are to provide permanent follow-along services. Vocational rehabilitation will provide initial funding of the case, with long-term follow-along provided by other local or state agency sources. The initially proposed federal regulations on supported employment furthermore state:

> The proposed regulations, at 363.7, define "traditionally time-limited post-employment services" as services that are needed to support and maintain an individual with severe handicaps in employment, are based on an assessment by the State of the individual's needs as specified in an individualized written rehabilitation program, and are provided for a period of time not to exceed 18 months before transition is made to extended services provided under a cooperative agreement pursuant to 363.50. The proposed definition defines "time-limited" to mean not more than 18 months of program support by the designated state unit for any one severely handicapped individual. Although 18 months is established as an outside limit, current data indicates that most individuals will progress to extended services in a much shorter time, usually within six to twelve months. Under this program, extended services must be provided to each individual, following termination of time-limited services by the State vocational rehabilitation agency. Extended services must be financed by public funds, other than Title VI, Part C funds, or by funds from private nonprofit organizations. (*Federal Register*, August 14, 1987)

What this provision means for vocational rehabilitation is that, more than ever, there is a necessity for locally driven interagency agreements that culminate in shared funding. Rehabilitation counselors should not authorize services for individual or group placement of clients who are targeted for supported employment *unless* long-term funding has been arranged. Vocational rehabilitation has always had a history of interagency funding. Supported employment initiatives, however, call for this type of planning and leveraging of resources to occur in any locality where supported employment programs are planned.

Integrated Work Settings

A major aspect of supported employment programs is an emphasis on work in *integrated settings. Integrated settings* can be defined as situations where nonhandicapped workers or members of the public at large predominate. This arrangement, which also emphasizes small work arrangements, is a radical departure from large sheltered workshop settings, which have been the major source of long-term vocational services for the majority of mentally and physically disabled persons.

Any model of supported employment opposes large segregated sheltered workshop and day program arrangements. Stemming from the philosophical roots of normalization (Wolfensberger, 1971), integration with nonhandicapped people is seen as a vital element of meaningful and normalizing work. Programmatically, there is also a strong feeling that people with severe disabilities, like people with no disabilities, prefer normal work environments and perform better in them.

The U.S. Department of Education, Office of Special Education and Rehabilitative Services, has proposed the following initial supported employment regulations in this area:

> The regulations propose to define "integrated work setting" by describing three types of job sites that provide for integration of handicapped and nonhandicapped individuals. The definition recognizes that maximum integration in a work setting may not always be feasible for every individual with severe handicaps under this program. The proposed regulations define one kind of integrated work setting as a job site where most co-workers are not handicapped and handicapped individuals are not part of a work group of other handicapped individuals. A second permissible kind of integrated work setting would be a job site where most co-workers are not handicapped and individuals with handicaps are of a small work group of not more than eight individuals, all of whom have

handicaps. However, in this case an individual with severe handicaps must have regular contact with non-handicapped individuals, other than personnel providing on-going support services, in the immediate work setting—since there is no actual integration at the particular job site. The proposed standard limiting a small work group to a maximum of eight handicapped individuals is based on data and information collected from Statewide Supported Employment Demonstration projects funded by the Office of Special Education and Rehabilitative Services in fiscal year 1985. (*Federal Register*, August 14, 1987)

The regulations on integration have been controversial. Proponents of integration feel that these guidelines are too liberal and allow for groups to be too large and subsequently not well integrated. Others believe that the number of persons in a group placement is not as relevant as the pay involved, type of work, and so forth. While this debate is expected to continue, it would appear that large-group placements are not very normalizing and stretch the limits of real integration.

Target Population

Paid employment in integrated work settings with permanent follow-along supervision is a departure from what most severely disabled people in adult day programs have traditionally received (Mank, Rhodes, & Bellamy, 1986). However, what makes a supported employment approach remarkable is the emphasis on working with the difficult-to-place, most severely handicapped population. Indeed, those vocational programs that are presumably engaging in supported employment activity should not only be providing paid employment in real work settings with long-term support but should be focusing upon the *most severely handicapped*. Failure to do so negates a major supposition of supported employment and, in fact, is a perversion of the entire concept.

The initial regulations for supported employment in the August 14, 1987, *Federal Register* indicate the following guidelines for identifying the target population:

> The supported employment program is intended to provide services to individuals who, because of the severity of their handicaps, would not traditionally be eligible for vocational rehabilitation services. Individuals who are eligible for services

under the program must not be able to function independently in employment without intensive ongoing support services and must require these ongoing support services for the duration of their employment.

In reviewing these regulations, this writer feels that these guidelines are too vague and that more specific indications of who should receive supported employment are warranted. Hence, the definition of *target population* for supported employment used in this book is as follows:

> Individuals who are eligible for services under the program must not be able to function independently in employment without intensive, ongoing support services and must require these ongoing support services for the duration of employment. Such individuals typically exhibit significant levels of mental retardation (IQ < 55), severe physical or sensory handicapping conditions, autism, severe traumatic brain injury, and/or a history of chronic mental illness, and must receive the highest priority for supported employment.

Failure to understand who should receive supported employment has been a major pitfall of many otherwise good community-based vocational programs. There has been a strong tendency to admit first those clients who are easiest to work with. This type of thinking and program strategy must change. Responsive programs should try to place all clients regardless of the presenting problems. The power of the supported employment movement resides in the opportunity it presents to help those with the greatest amount of problems. The aim is to "shortcut" the job readiness deficiencies of the client and match him or her to a job that minimizes deficits. As the reader considers the notion of zero exclusion[1] from supported employment, it may help to review the following brief case summaries of persons with highly challenging behaviors. Each person described (real names are not used) could easily be considered a legitimate candidate for supported employment.

1. Jim has been diagnosed as autistic from birth, with an IQ between 32 and 45, depending on the test. When frustrated, he becomes very agitated and rocks rapidly, sometimes shriek-

ing loudly. Modulating his voice has been a problem, plus he cannot stay on task very long. The special education director and teacher are very negative, but parents are hopeful. *Does Jim have an employment outlook?*

2. Doug, age 19, has severe cerebral palsy. He wears a head pointer and can use a computer keyboard. He has been in the Cerebral Palsy Center all of his life. Doug cannot move his arms or legs independently and has significant spasticity in the upper trunk. He is in an electric wheelchair, which he can partially operate. *Does Doug have an employment outlook?*

3. Kelly, age 20, is strapped to a board on a classroom floor. This is to help posture. His records say he has an IQ of 6, and no voluntary arm, leg, or head movement other than eyeblink and swallowing responses. Much of his day involves therapy and self-care maintenance activities. He is subject to frequent seizures. His parents want him at home and not institutionalized. *Does Kelly have an employment outlook?*

4. Larry, age 30, has a measured IQ of 27, periodically head-rocks in a self-stimulative manner, and is totally nonverbal. He can walk, has most self-care skills, but acts socially immature at times. He cannot read, write, count, or use public transportation. Local vocational rehabilitation and the sheltered workshops cannot service him. *Does Larry have an employment outlook?*

5. Marie is 19 years old and is labeled autistic. Videotape observation during classroom activity indicates 65 body-rocks per minute, periodic hand-biting, and shrieking. Marie throws things when she becomes upset, and her parents are concerned about how long they can keep her at home. Her IQ is 24, and she is marginally verbal. *Does Marie have an employment outlook?*

6. Sandra is 23 and is labeled seriously head-injured as a result of a car accident. She has had medical, surgical, and physical rehabilitation for 5 years. She was in a coma for 2 months following the accident. She walks unsteadily, has a history of substance abuse, and cannot usually remember things for longer than 10–15 minutes at a time. She has normal speech, but is socially inappropriate, with swearing, and so on, under stress. *Does Sandra have an employment outlook?*

As it turns out, Jim, Larry, Marie, and Sandra have all worked competitively or are working

[1]*Zero exclusion*, a term taken from Brown and his coworkers (1977), refers to not excluding any disabled persons from services regardless of the level of disability they exhibit.

now. Marie is awaiting replacement after production-related problems in a restaurant setting. Jim works as a lockbox operator in a bank for $5.10 per hour, Larry has worked for almost 8 years in a food service capacity at a local university, and Sandra works on a local surveying team. Doug is still in school and has experienced nonpaid field externships. He is awaiting eventual placement with the help of a rehabilitation engineer. Kelly is the only person of the six for whom there is no immediate employment outlook. A review of the literature does not show profoundly intellectually impaired nonambulatory people employed at this writing. Yet how can one say Kelly will never be employable? Similar statements were made about other persons with severe handicaps only a few years ago.

WHY SUPPORTED EMPLOYMENT?

One question related to supported employment that is being asked by long-time vocational rehabilitation experts is: Why do we need another service when we barely have enough case service dollars now to meet the increasing demand for services? There are several answers to this question. First, most persons with truly severe disabilities will not be able to obtain a real job without professional help. Substantial planning and assistance are needed to overcome transportation difficulties, parental concerns, and employer skepticism, and to locate an appropriate job. A specialized, individualized approach is required to ensure job retention.

A second reason for this approach is that many persons with severe disabilities will be unable to maintain employment without professional support. The amount and nature of support will vary from person to person and, of course, will be influenced by the nature of the disability. For example, one would expect that the amount of support required by an individual with severe cerebral palsy would lessen progressively, reaching a point of very little follow-along. On the other hand, the individual with a history of long-term institutionalization and a dual diagnosis of mental retardation and emotional disturbance would unequivocally require greater periods of long-term support (Anthony & Jansen, 1984).

The inability of many persons with severe disability to transfer those skills learned in special centers to real jobs is a third reason for using a supported employment approach. Although "readiness" is a time-honored concept of vocational preparation in day programs, in reality, it has not held up. Clients do not "flow" from work activity to workshop to competitive employment (Whitehead, 1979); furthermore, studies by Sowers et al. (1979) and Wehman et al. (1985) clearly show that many persons who are purported to not be ready for competitive employment do well with a supported competitive employment approach (Wehman, Hill, Wood, & Parent, 1987).

A fourth rationale for consideration of supported employment is based on the most effective use of limited case service dollars. Setting aside one's professional biases in favor of a particular vocational rehabilitaiton service, the successes of supported competitive employment (see Rusch, 1986, for description of many of these programs; or *Psychology Today*, March 1985) suggest strongly that the outcomes and costs associated with day center nonvocational skill programming, vocational evaluation, or work adjustment should be contrasted with the outcomes and costs related to supported competitive employment. Stated another way, why spend $3,000 on "preemployment" preparation activity for a given client if roughly the same amount can be spent immediately on job coaching services (Wehman & Melia, 1985) in supported competitive employment? These are the types of questions and decisions that rehabilitation management and counselors increasingly will need to confront.

A final rationale for using this specialized placement and training approach is to meet the labor demands and needs of certain businesses and industries. The hotel and restaurant industry and cleaning industry, for example, are two high-growth areas in entry-level service occupations. Similarly, micrographics and entry-level computer skills are growth industries that persons with severe physical disability might be able to enter with support. Previous experiences in the state of Virginia (Shafer, 1986) suggest that business personnel welcome this approach because of training and follow-along components.

Major Outcomes

The variety of positive outcomes associated with working in a real job are too numerous to enumerate in detail in this brief section. Interested readers are referred to Hill, Banks et al. (1987), Rusch (1986), or Wehman (1981). Wages are an important aspect of work and one of the most powerful outcomes tied to supported employment. Decent wages can significantly influence the quality of one's life by providing greater disposable income. Similarly, these dollars are spent in individual communities, thus enhancing the local economy. Employment advancement is also greater in supported employment. Bellamy, Rhodes, and Albin (1986) indicated, for example, that only 2.7% of all work activity employees go to sheltered work, and less than 12% of all sheltered workshop employees advance to nonsheltered competitive work.

An obvious benefit of competitive employment is the chance for the handicapped individual to work with and around nonhandicapped persons. A less obvious but also important outcome of nonsheltered work is the significant increase in independent community skills such as travel competencies, communication skills, and other related behaviors such as use of a vending machine, which occur in the context of real work. Most of the other adult service options provide much more protected environments because the client is not considered "ready" for work.

At least two significant societal benefits should be noted as resulting from supported employment. First, the worker makes an important contribution in state and federal taxes. And second, supported employment removes the expensive ongoing public costs associated with nonemployment or highly limited employment progress. In most states, workshops are subsidized at well over $2,500 per person annually, and activity centers are subsidized at easily over $6,000 annually per client.

Settings for Supported Employment Programs

Supported employment programs are labor intensive, not capital intensive. Therefore, there is not a need for a large physical space to house persons with disabilities during the day, since work with clients takes place directly in business and industry. From a cost standpoint, this is an attractive feature of this vocational option. Many supported employment programs (e.g., Rusch, 1986) are established on this basis.

On the other hand, there is no reason why effective placement and training programs cannot also occur from community-based adult day programs, rehabilitation facilities, schools, and vocational technical centers. If, in fact, there already is an aggregate of professional personnel existing in a given setting, then it may be possible to redeploy some of these persons into supported employment.

In Virginia State there are local rehabilitation facilities that receive rehabilitative service case funds to provide supported competitive employment for at-risk clients (Hill, Hill, et al., 1987). Facilities are licensed to provide transitional and supported employment. Clients with moderate mental retardation usually take 8–12 weeks to become stabilized in their job. At this point, the participating staff and business decide the level of involvement necessary by the supported employment specialist. Follow-along employment support services are then funded by the local mental retardation/mental health services. These costs are typically much less expensive. It appears that this approach is one successful way to implement the program, but it is probably too early to evaluate these efforts. Schools can also be logical settings from which supported employment efforts can occur. With such a major push nationally toward transition from school to work, many schools are experiencing greater pressure to provide job placement for students with severe handicaps before graduation.

In short, we do not know yet which settings are ideal. In all likelihood, all of the ones just described may be appropriate at a given time with the right staff attitudes, funding base, and local economy.

In addressing the issue of which settings are appropriate for initiating supported employment activity, it may be helpful to consider the dilemma that many sheltered workshops and adult activity centers face. Increasingly, activities such as segregated benchwork and those pertaining to personal care skills are being questioned, and off-site integrated employment is being investigated as an alternative. Since there are over 7,000 local center-based programs throughout the country, this issue is at the heart of implementing supported employment activities on a nationwide basis.

Consider, for example, the following case study involving the executive director of a rehabilitation facility. There are no easy answers to the questions she faces. (Some potential solutions are suggested in the Appendix at the end of this chapter.)

Local System Case Study

An executive director for a rehabilitation facility in a medium-sized city (population, 200,000) and her advisory board are concerned about the need for additional services for persons with severe disabilities in their local community. The community is predominantly service-oriented, focusing on the tourist industry. It also has two large prime manufacturing businesses. The facility's program currently services 200 individuals with mild and moderate mental disabilities through a center-based sheltered employment model. The center has a waiting list of 38 persons.

There has been a recent push from parents and advocacy groups to serve more persons with autism and moderate, severe, and profound mental retardation. The local community services board considers the present operations of the facility to be exemplary, and does not have funds available to expand services. The services board is discussing how to procure additional funds to increase the current operating capacity, in order to accommodate those individuals waiting for facility services. There has been discussion about converting existing services to supported employment. After attending several national conferences, the executive director has decided she wants to offer supported employment services within her community.

Management Questions to Consider[2]

1. What strategies could/should the executive director use to convince the services board to consider supported employment?

2. Should the workshop even try to get into the supported employment area?
3. Should the executive director propose conversion of current operations or the addition of supported employment as an option?
4. How would the community determine which supported employment option to implement first, and why?
5. Construct a tentative budget for this activity and a reasonable timeline for implementation.
6. What steps would need to be taken to establish a supported employment option?

SUPPORTED EMPLOYMENT: THE CHALLENGE TO VOCATIONAL REHABILITATION

In reviewing what supported employment means specifically to the day-to-day funding and service operations of vocational rehabilitation, one is struck with the potential impact of such employment on: 1) vocational evaluation, 2) eligibility, 3) work adjustment practices, and 4) the 60- to 90-day closure practices. This section briefly reviews some of these issues.

Vocational Evaluation

The rehabilitation service system is currently designed to give vocational evaluation a preeminent role. Potential clients can rarely get into the service system (i.e., receive vocational rehabilitation sponsorship) without a formal and usually standardized evaluation. Chapter 6 of this book articulates the role of standardized evaluation. However, it bears mentioning here that vocational evaluation, as historically practiced, is not especially useful to either potential clients in supported employment or service providers who must frequently rely on these evaluations.

Why such a strong statement? If one reviews the philosophical roots of supported employment in the classic Department of Education position paper (Will, 1984), it is evident that assessment of job readiness is *not* a precursor to employment. In fact, the premise of an evaluate-train-place model is reversed to a place-

---

[2]See Appendix at the end of this chapter for potential answers to questions 1–4 and 6.

train-follow-along model. In addition to these seeming incompatibilities in the traditional evaluation model, a second problem emerges with supported employment. Most of the persons who are legitimate candidates for supported employment do not respond well or at all to the standardized instruments that psychometric experts have designed. Hence, an immediate conflict arises. Sam, for example, who has an IQ of 30, is nonverbal, engages in self-stimulatory head-weaving, and has limited self-care skills, shows up at the office of the local rehabilitation counselor. The counselor refers him to the local evaluation center, which diagnoses him as mentally retarded and writes the following report (a real excerpt from a vocational evaluation in 1977, with the exception that Sam is not the client's real name):

> Sam is a small mongoloid white man who looks much younger than 21. He is mostly without speech, though it is possible to understand an occasional word in his usually monosyllabic utterances. He is pleasant, smiling, and cooperative, a little given to perseverative and ritualistic behavior.
>
> Measure of intellectual function derived from the FRPV forms A and B yields IQ scores of 27 and 30, respectively. This is in accord with the findings of the school psychologist in 1973. He is in the lower end of the trainable MR range—severely retarded.
>
> Sam is good natured, friendly, and willing, but realistically unemployable. He can, under close supervision, do things like simple household chores and leaf-raking, and he enjoys them, but he is not really employable. Under sheltered workshop conditions, he may be able to sweep or do some other repetitive perseverative operation.
>
> Test results discover a great deal of organic difficulty, one of the prime results of which is his perseveration. Once he starts doing something, he does it over and over again until stopped.
>
> I am sorry I cannot give a more optimistic report. Sam is a very likable fellow.

Once the counselor receives this report, he becomes immediately negative about the prospect of spending limited case service dollars on Sam. Therefore, Sam is refused any help toward employment.

While the foregoing case study simplifies the issues at hand, it highlights the evaluation challenge for vocational rehabilitation personnel. Clearly, not every client should be or is a candidate for supported employment, although Sam

definitely was. Many simply do not need such involved and extended services. Also, it is certain that some type of screening measure ultimately will be necessary to determine the type of service model (enclave, work crew, supported competitive, or small business) in which it might be most appropriate for counselors to invest their funds on behalf of potential clients. A major part of this book, especially Chapters 2, 6, and 11, addresses this need for screening.

Eligibility

The vocational rehabilitation system is not an entitlement for services for all disabled persons. Unlike the special education system, in which services are mandated through Public Law 94-142, rehabilitation does often follow a specific order of selection. Potential clients must show a substantial handicap that necessitates rehabilitative services and must appear to be employable if rehabilitative services are to be provided. Therefore, to use again the case of Sam, he would, in the eyes of many rehabilitation counselors, meet the first criterion of substantial handicap but certainly not the second of possible employability.

During much of the time vocational rehabilitation services have been available, it has been appropriate to exclude certain clients because of the real or perceived difficulty they have presented for employment. A major element influencing those decisions has been, and is, the level and quality of community vocational services with which counselors locally have had to work. Very limited services (i.e. poor-quality vendors for providers) have greatly narrowed the options available to counselors in assisting difficult-to-place clients.

Another, more dominant factor in the eligibility determination process is the common belief that certain clients have no vocational potential. This was true at one time for many clients with very severe disabilities. However, as alluded to at the beginning of this chapter, the knowledge base of how to improve the employability of people with severe disabilities has changed dramatically in the last 15 years. Thus, people who were once seen as ineligible are currently, or should be, viewed as eligible if the *appropriate* local rehabilitative service is found for them. This is another way of saying that if a seeing eye dog is valuable for a visually impaired person to work, or an electric wheelchair is essential for a physically disabled person to return to a job, then an on-site job trainer may also be essential in helping the severely head-injured person be reemployed. In short, the supported employment model is shrinking the pool of people who honestly can be viewed as ineligible.

Work Adjustment

Vocational training, development of work habits, and acquisition of selected social and academic skills before job placement are activities that many mentally and physically disabled clients traditionally receive with vocational rehabilitation funds. These activities, broadly known as work adjustment activities, account for a major chunk of a rehabilitation counselor's case management expenditures. The underlying assumption behind these expenditures has been that severely disabled clients who have significant skill deficits cannot work *until* these deficits are remediated. This approach relies on fundamentally different assumptions than supported employment, which assumes that on-site training can occur while the person is employed. Specific vocational and social deficiencies are thus remediated in the context of the job.

The systematic redirection of work adjustment funds from a posture of preplacement remediation to on-site training and support will probably, over time, yield a far greater number of successful competitive closures. That is, counselors who choose to increasingly spend more and more of their finite resources on employment specialist or job coach services instead of preplacement activity will probably use case service funds more efficiently. Again, the underlying assumption is that preplacement activity does not correlate well with job placement and job retention.

It would appear that work adjustment as a major rehabilitation activity will come under increasing investigation. Managers and counselors alike will have to examine more closely what they are getting for their money. As mentioned earlier, the issues increasingly will turn on "What is the *most* we can get for our money?"

and "How much or what level of preplacement (preparatory) activity is *really* necessary?" The more persons with truly severe disabilities who enter the competitive labor force with the help of supported employment but without work adjustment, the clearer will be the answers to these questions.

The 60- to 90-Day Closure

The relatively rapid closure of cases after 2 to 3 months has worked well with a select number of mildly disabled rehabilitation clients. These are persons who, after a time-limited training intervention and appropriate job placement, adjust to their jobs with increasing independence. Many clients, of course, take more than one placement or longer than 60 to 90 days before absolute closure can occur with a high level of confidence.

Supported employment, obviously, is not consistent with rapid closure. The nature of supported employment is long-term permanent (not time-limited) follow-along. Vocational rehabilitation will need to fund time-limited transitional employment, that is, on-site job training services, until clients become more proficient on the job (Hill, Hill, et al,. 1987). At this point, a closure can be taken, with long-term follow-along (supported employment) given to the client by another local or state agency. The frequency of positive closures may increase through use of supported employment models, but the length of time until closure may also increase significantly.

STRENGTHS OF THE VOCATIONAL REHABILITATION SYSTEM FOR ENHANCING SUPPORTED EMPLOYMENT

Although this chapter's discussion has so far centered heavily on the problems and challenges facing vocational rehabilitation in implementing supported employment programs, at the same time vocational rehabilitation offers a number of strengths that will positively affect supported employment activity. These strengths should not be overlooked and are briefly discussed here.

First, the vocational rehabilitation program is predominantly a federal-state program. The majority of dollar resources come from the federal government, and a strong federal statute and regulations undergird the system. This backing provides for uniformity and standardization of procedures in referral, case management, coordination, and long-term planning. Such a broad national uniformity can be very advantageous in implementing supported employment nationwide.

Second, the Rehabilitation Act of 1973, together with its several amendments over the past 15 years, is an excellent law. It provides a high degree of flexibility for purchase of services, program operation, pilot programming, innovation, and diversity. The strength of the law is that it can work very effectively for disabled consumers, provided the state rehabilitation agency is responsive.

A third positive factor inherent in most vocational rehabilitation programs is a good network of communication with employers in business and industry. Placement counselors, especially, who spend much of their time in businesses, usually have an accurate perception of what the local labor needs are and of the overriding problems facing employers in personnel recruitment and management. As supported employment is clearly a business-oriented service program, these linkages with the private sector can make an enormous difference.

Finally, *employment* is fundamentally what vocational rehabilitation is and always has been about, and is considered by this writer to be an overriding strength of the rehabilitation system. The notion of putting people with truly severe disabilities to work should not be anathema to people working in vocational rehabilitation. The issue probably revolves more on how it can be done, how much it will cost, and who should get services first.

ROLE OF REHABILITATION COUNSELORS IN SUPPORTED EMPLOYMENT

Many rehabilitation counselors, when first learning about supported employment, question what their role should be. There has been some concern that rehabilitation counselors will be thrust exclusively into the position of being a "broker" of community services. As was noted earlier, to a certain extent, this is always true with any case that comes to the counselor. Without a sufficient number and quality of community service vendors, the counselor has limited options to recommend for clients.

A rehabilitation counselor can perform several functions when working with supported employment programs. Identification and verification of capable agencies in the community, both facility-based and nonfacilities, that can provide supported employment is one of the counselor's major roles. In addition, working with these vendors to improve the quality of their services can make a big difference in the long run in terms of how useful the case service dollars can be.

A second role of the counselor involves the careful referral of appropriate clients to supported employment opportunities. If clients who, in reality, do not need long-term support services are referred, then too much money will be spent on an unwarranted service. Similarly, the advantage of having effective supported employment programs available in a community will be negated if persons with truly severe disabilities are not allowed eligibility for these services.

As already alluded to, evaluating the quality of services provided to clients is another very important role of the rehabilitation counselor in supported employment. To monitor quality, however, the counselor must have sufficient information about what supported employment is and what it is not. Therefore, inservice training is essential for many counselors who have been in the field for a long time but away from preservice education experiences. The counselor must be knowledgeable about how many hours should be authorized for employment specialist or job coach services. Knowing when to reduce or expand the number of hours comes only with an understanding of how effective the model is with clients with certain characteristics.

Table 1 summarizes the reasons why rehabilitation counselors should seriously consider authorizing supported employment services. The four points in the table should be a benchmark for decision making on supported employment by counselors and vocational evaluators.

Table 1. Why purchase supported work/competitive employment services?

1. Many severely disabled clients cannot gain employment without the service.
2. Many severely disabled clients will be terminated from employment without support.
3. Most severely disabled clients respond best to training that takes place in the natural community environment.
4. Rehabilitation case funds can be directly channeled into real employment without intermediate "get-ready" steps.

CONCLUSION

In summary, this chapter has emphasized several points about supported employment, including:

1. Viable supported employment programs focus on offering services to persons with substantial disabilities who would be unable to work without ongoing support.
2. Supported employment programs are characterized by on-site training by staff of clients who are usually not "job-ready" at the time of placement.
3. Staff working as supported employment specialists usually need to work flexible hours and be prepared to spend the majority of their work time at a job site in business or industry.
4. Many of the preplacement vocational activities engaged in by professionals on behalf of clients with severe disabilities are not necessary or useful in competitive employment. An on-site trainer can actually be much more helpful in specifically targeting the behaviors that need development.

The remaining chapters in this book address a wide range of topics on supported employment and vocational rehabilitation. The thrust of this text is to demonstrate how vocational rehabilitation can play a major role in facilitating and implementing supported employment programs.

REFERENCES

Anthony, W. A., & Jansen, M. A. (1984). Predicting the vocational capacity of the chronically mentally ill: Research and policy implications. *American Psychologist, 39*(5), 537–544.

Bates, P., & Panscofar, E. (1983). Project Earn: A competitive employment training program for severely disabled youth in the public school. *British Journal of Mental Subnormality, 19*(2), 97–103.

Bellamy, G. T., Rhodes, L. E., & Albin, J. M. (1986). Supported employment. In W. E. Kiernan & J. A. Stark (Eds.), *Pathways to employment for adults with developmental disabilities* (pp. 129–138). Baltimore: Paul H. Brookes Publishing Co.

Bourbeau, P. (1985). Mobile work crews: An approach to achieve long-term supported employment. In P. McCarthy, J. M. Everson, M. S. Moon, & J. M. Barcus (Eds.), *School-to-work transition for youth with severe disabilities* (Monograph, pp. 168–182). Richmond: Virginia Commonwealth University, Project Transition into Employment, Rehabilitation Research and Training Center.

Brown, L., Nietupski, J., & Hamre-Nietupski, S. (1976), Criterion of ultimate functioning. In M. Thomas (Ed.), *Hey, don't forget about me!* Reston, VA: Council on Exceptional Children.

Cuvo, A. J., Leaf, R. B., & Borakove, L. S. (1978). Teaching janitorial skills to the mentally retarded: Acquisition, generalization, and maintenance. *Journal of Applied Behavior Analysis, 11*, 34–35.

Elder, J. (1984). Job opportunities for developmentally disabled people. *American Rehabilitation, 10*(2), 26–30.

Federal Register. (1987, August 14). Washington, DC: U.S. Government Printing Office.

Gold, M. W. (1976). Task analysis of a complex assembly task by the blind. *Exceptional Children, 43*, 78–84.

Hill, M. L., Banks, P. D., Handrich, R. R., Wehman, P. H., Hill, J. W., & Shafer, M. S. (1987). Benefit-cost analysis of supported competitive employment for persons with mental retardation. *Research in Developmental Disabilities, 8*(1), 71–89.

Hill, M., Hill, J., Wehman, P., Revell, G., Dickerson, A., & Noble, J. (1987). Supported employment: An interagency funding model for persons with severe disabilities. *Journal of Rehabilitation, 53*(3), 13–21.

Hunter, J., & Bellamy, G. T. (1977). Cable harness construction for severely retarded adults: A demonstration of training technique. *AAESPH Review, 1*(7), 2–13.

Mank, D. M., Rhodes, L. E., & Bellamy, G. T. (1986). Four supported employment alternatives. In W. E. Kiernan & J. A. Stark (Eds.), *Pathways to employment for adults with developmental disabilities*, (139–153). Baltimore: Paul H. Brookes Publishing Co.

Moon, S., Goodall, P., Barcus, M., & Brooke, V. (Eds.) (1986). *The supported work model of competitive employment for citizens with severe handicaps: A guide for job trainers* (rev. ed.). Richmond: Virginia Commonwealth University, Rehabilitation Research and Training Center.

O'Bryan, A. (1985). The STP benchwork model. In P. McCarthy, J. M. Everson, M. S. Moon, & J. M. Barcus (Eds.). *School-to-work transition for youth with severe disabilities* (Monograph, pp. 184–199). Richmond: Virginia Commonwealth University, Project Transition into Employment, Rehabilitation Research and Training Center.

O'Neill, C., & Bellamy, G. T. (1978). Evaluation of a procedure for teaching chain saw assembly to a severely retarded woman. *Mental Retardation, 16*(1), 37–41.

Rhodes, L. E., & Valenta, L. (1985). Industry-based supported employment: An enclave approach. *Journal of the Association for Persons with Severe Handicaps, 10*(1), 12–20.

Rusch, F. R. (Ed.). (1986). *Competitive employment issues and strategies*. Baltimore: Paul H. Brookes Publishing Co.

Shafer, M. S. (1986). Utilizing co-workers as change agents. In F. R. Rusch (Ed.), *Competitive employment issues and strategies* (pp. 215–224). Baltimore: Paul H. Brookes Publishing Co.

Smith, M. D. (1984). *Community and vocational rehabilitation of the severely handicapped*. Washington, DC: U.S. Department of Education, National Institute of Handicapped Research, Office of Special Education and Rehabilitative Services.

Sowers, J., Jenkins, C., & Powers, L. (1988). The training and employment of persons with severe physical disabilities. In R. Gaylord-Ross (Ed.), *Vocational education of persons with special needs* (pp. 387–416). Palto Alto, CA: Mayfield Publishing Co.

Sowers, J., Thompson, L. E., & Connis, R. T. (1979). The food service: Vocational training program. In G. T. Bellamy, G. O'Conner, & O. C. Karan (Eds.), *Vocational rehabilitation of severely handicapped persons*. Baltimore: University Park Press.

Vogelsberg, R. T., Ashe, W., & Williams, W. (1986). Community-based service delivery in rural Vermont: Is-

sues and recommendations. In R. H. Horner, L. H. Meyer, & H. D. B. Fredericks (Eds.), *Education of learners with severe handicaps: Exemplary service strategies* (pp. 29–59). Baltimore: Paul H. Brookes Publishing Co.

Wehman, P. (1981). *Competitive employment: New horizons for severely disabled individuals*. Baltimore: Paul H. Brookes Publishing Co.

Wehman, P., Hill, M., Hill, J., Brooke, V., Pendleton, P., & Britt, C. (1985). Competitive employment for persons with mental retardation: A follow-up six years later. *Mental Retardation, 23*(6), 274–281.

Wehman, P., Hill, J., Wood, W., & Parent, W. (1987). A report on competitive employment histories of persons labeled severely mentally retarded. *Journal of the Association for Persons with Severe Handicaps, 12*(1), 11–17.

Wehman, P., Kreutzer, J., Wood, W., Stonnington, H., Diambra, J., & Morton, M.V./Helping Traumatically brain injured patients return to work: Three case studies. *Archives of Physical Medicine of Rehabilitation*.

Wehman, P., & Melia, R. (1985). The job coach: Function in transitional and supported employment. *American Rehabilitation, 11*(2), 4–7.

Whitehead, C. W. (1979). Sheltered workshops in the decade ahead: Work and wages, or welfare. In G. T. Bellamy, G. O'Connor, & O. C. Karan (Eds.), *Vocational rehabilitation of severely handicapped persons* (pp. 66–92). Baltimore: University Park Press.

Will, M. C. (1984). *Supported employment for adults with severe disabilities: An OSERS program initiative*. Washington, DC: U.S. Department of Education.

Wolfensberger, W. (1971) (Ed.). *The principle of normalization in human service*. Toronto: National Institute on Mental Retardation, York University Campus, Downsview.

Appendix

Possible Solutions to Questions Posed in Local System Case Study

Question 1–4 and 6 correspond to those in the text.
Question 5 in the text is not dealt with here.

1. What strategies could/should the executive director use to convince the services board to consider supported employment?
   —Review the locality's current philosophy.
   —Review literature on supported employment and transition.
   —Observe and review model-supported competitive employment programs.
   —Observe and review the current program(s) in the locality.
   —Define what supported employment will mean to the system.
   —Define what transition will mean to the system.

2. Should the workshop even try to get into the supported employment area?
   —Federal and state initiatives have identified employment for persons with severe disabilities as a priority.
   —Research and demonstration results nationally support the employment potential of persons with severe disabilities.
   —There has been a federal and state redirection of existing resources toward supported employment.
   —There is growing pressure from parents and consumers to have community-based employment services as an alternative.

3. Should the executive director propose conversion of current operations or the addition of supported employment as an option?
   With respect to this decision, there are several issues to be considered:
   —How will/would decisions be made regarding placement?
   —Can consumers benefit from a multiservice approach?
   —How will resource priorities be set?
   —Could negative impacts result from operating both options in the same agency?
   —How will checks and balances assure compatibility between the two programs?
   —Is there a way to construct the two approaches into a system?
   —What are the views of parents, advocates, and so forth?
   —Is the operation of both alternatives to be temporary until supported employment proves its value?

4. How would the community determine which supported employment option to implement first, and why?
   —Conduct a general screening for potential jobs.
   —List local industry position types available.
   —Conduct an environmental analysis of the representative job types in the community.
   —Review the job types to determine which option (one on one, enclave, work-crew) would be appropriate for the majority of available jobs.

5. What steps would need to be taken to establish a supported employment option?
   —Identify proposed change.
   —Develop a longitudinal plan for implementation. Things to consider when developing the plan:
      What is the desired result?

Do organization personnel agree? How will personnel be affected?

Who has been identified as the change agent? What are this person's responsibilities?

What methods will be used to communicate the process to staff?

What methods are in place for staff input?

List measurable goals and objectives to accomplish change.

How will these goals and objectives be measured?

List those responsible to accomplish goals and the time frame.

What methods will be used to reduce the negative effects of system change on staff?

Identify available resources.

Establish administrative policies (logistical, service delivery, and staff development).

Implement plan for change.

Chapter 2

Supported Employment Service Delivery Models

M. Sherril Moon and Susan Lehmann Griffin

As was observed in Chapter 1, supported employment is a relatively new concept. Few service delivery models have been developed that fully meet the 1987 federal criteria, including service to citizens with severe handicapping conditions, decent wages, at least 20 hours of work per week, integration with workers who are not handicapped, and ongoing follow-along assistance to ensure job retention. As more and more persons with a variety of disabling conditions become involved in supported employment, the types of supported employment options available will increase. At present, however, four primary service delivery models appear to have been replicated throughout the country. These are the individual placement model, the enclave, mobile work crews, and small business arrangements. It is important to note that these models are currently being modified and will continue to be modified and adapted according to business and economic conditions. Over the next decade many more creative and alternative supported employment models will be developed through the efforts and ingenuity of local service workers.

INDIVIDUAL PLACEMENT MODEL

The individual placement model, also variously referred to as the supported work model of competitive employment, the supported competitive approach, the supported jobs model, and job coaching, is considered by many to be the least restrictive or most normalizing of all the service delivery models (*Rehab Brief*, 1986). Using this model, an employment specialist (the terms *job coach* or *job trainer* are often used synonymously with *employment specialist*) places and trains a worker in a community job and provides as much training and follow-along as is necessary to keep the individual in that position (Mank, Rhodes, & Bellamy, 1986; Moon, Goodall, Barcus, & Brooke, 1985, Wehman, 1981; Wehman & Kregel, 1985). There is one trainer for each worker, and it is assumed that over time, the type and amount of assistance provided by the trainer will be reduced, although some type of follow-along will be provided permanently. The jobs targeted for individual placement include any regular community-based positions. Of course, the nature of the local labor market and the preference and previous experience of the worker are major determining factors in the specific placements made (Wehman, 1986).

This approach is often compared to more traditional rehabilitation job placement methods, but there are several key differences, as described by Wehman and Kregel (1985). First, this model does not require that a person be "job ready" before placement can occur. A comprehensive training approach is provided after job placement, involving instruction in work, social, self-care, and community access skills. This training eliminates the need for extensive "preplacement" training. Second, this approach is *not* a transitional or time-limited procedure and assures long-term support in whatever ways are needed for the individual worker, so long as the support is specifically job related. A third distinguishing factor is that this model typically uses a single professional known as an employment specialist, job coordinator, job trainer, or job coach, who is responsible for all facets of the process including job development, placement, training, and follow-along.

Key Components

The phases of the individual placement model can be delineated as: 1) job development and consumer assessment, 2) job-site training and advocacy, and 3) ongoing assessment and follow-along. Each of these phases is briefly described here.

Job development and consumer assessment are typically conducted simultaneously so that the right job can be matched to the worker's interests, prior training, transportation possibilities, and physical requirements. The placement process begins by surveying the community labor market to identify the types of jobs likely to have vacancies or high turnover rates and that appear to be within the capacity of potential clients. After specific jobs have been identified, an analysis of work environment requirements must be completed. This process has been variously referred to as a job inventory (Belmore & Brown, 1978) or job analysis (Vandergoot & Worrell, 1979). It is critical that adequate details be provided in terms of job requirements, characteristics of the work environment, and other features that may influence job retention.

Initial consumer assessment is conducted concurrently with the job development and analysis activities. Information is obtained concerning the client's adaptive behaviors, parent/caregiver attitudes, transportation possibilities, the consumer's expressed willingness to work, and other relevant factors. In addition, the assessment will determine the consumer's current ability to perform vocational skills required in the targeted job area. An inability to perform a large number of these skills does not preclude a consumer from supported work services, since a major strength of the supported work model is its ability to place individuals who do not possess all the work skills needed for immediate job success. However, assessment information will help the employment specialist to best match a consumer to a specific job.

The major forms of consumer assessment that are useful to a job trainer include: 1) *interviews and informal observations* with consumers, primary caregivers, and current or past work or school supervisors; 2) *the interpretation of formal evaluations* in the educational, vocational, social, psychological, and medical areas; and 3) *behavioral assessment* in a real work setting of a consumer's abilities, through observational assessment of skills identified in the environmental analysis.

A job placement is made by matching a job's requirements to a worker's characteristics. This process involves evaluating job analysis data and consumer assessment information to determine who in the referral pool appears most suitable for a particular job opening. Several individuals from the referral pool are identified through a preliminary screening in which the essential requirements of the job are checked against the needs of each potential worker. For example, if weekend work is required, one must know whether the individual is willing and able to work on weekends. Furthermore, it is necessary to establish how the person will get to work and whether or not the family will be supportive of these working hours. Analyzing certain key factors such as these helps identify potential candidates. A more detailed analysis of consumer factors and job characteristics, which has been referred to as the job/worker compatibility analysis (Moon et al., 1986) will further help to identify the best candidates for a particular job. Once a consumer has been chosen for placement in a specific job, the job trainer must be prepared to introduce him or her to the employer through a formal job interview and/or an informal job site visit. The job trainer plays an active role in placing an individual worker and coordinating transportation, clothing, Social Security needs, and other job placement needs.

Job-site training and advocacy involve direct, systematic instruction of job tasks and related behavioral skills such as communication, on-task behavior, transportation, and appropriate use of mealtimes and breaktimes. Job-site training begins the first day of employment and can last from several weeks to several months, depending on the skill level of the employment specialist, the skill level of the worker, and the complexity of the job. The phases of job-site training have been identified by Barcus, Brooke, Inge, Moon, and Goodall (1987) as job orientation and assessment, initial training and skill acquisition, stabilization, and advocacy. Table 1 indicates some of the procedures that are likely to be involved in the various phases of job-site training for workers who have developmental disabilities.

Ongoing assessment of a worker's job performance begins the day he or she is placed on the job and training begins. Daily feedback from behavioral training data, observations, and interactions with the employer, family members, and coworkers indicates immediately and continually whether or not the worker is adapting to job demands. It is critical that the job trainer devise a method to regularly assess a worker's progress after the trainer has faded from the job site. This period, known as follow-along, allows a job trainer to monitor a worker without being on the job site on a daily basis, and can last for an indefinite period of time. Incorporating this follow-along period into job-training programs assures both the employer and employee that help is available should a problem arise. Without this assurance of the availability of continued job-site intervention, the worker could be terminated owing to a small change in the work environment.

Some of the factors that influence the stability of a person's job include the introduction of new management, new coworkers, changes in the daily work schedule, and problems within the family structure. The job trainer should be aware of when such changes occur and be prepared to intervene if any of them affects the person's work performance. Methods of evaluating worker progress and of determining intervention strategies include: periodic employee evaluations; progress reports; parent/guardian questionnaires; on-site visits; and telephone contacts with employers and family members or group home staff.

One of the most commonly asked questions about this model is, "Who will provide permanent funds?" One approach that has worked well involves the use of state rehabilitation funds for the initial job placement and job-site training costs, with the less expensive follow-along paid for by local and state developmental disabilities or other adult service case management funds (Hill, Hill, et al., 1987). Fees for services agreements and vendorship agreements enable funding agencies to contract for a specified number of hours or costs per year. Chapter 3 elaborates more on funding possibilities.

Advantages of This Model

This model has the most potential for providing competitive wages to workers because it places workers in existing job opportunities within their communities. It not only meets the needs of workers who have traditionally received no pay or very little remuneration in sheltered settings but also meets the labor demands of businesses in a particular community (Wehman, 1986).

This approach has also been shown to be cost-effective in the use of limited case service dollars. Repeated demonstrations (Hill, Banks, et al.,1987; Rusch, 1986; Vogelsberg, 1985) have shown that placement and training in a "real" job can cost less than training in nonvocational programs, work adjustment, or long-term sheltered employment, which usually do not result in regular paid employment. In addition, when workers are placed in jobs that pay at least minimum wage, they become contributing taxpayers or full citizens who are also eligible for retirement benefits.

ENCLAVE

Enclaves, along with work crews and small businesses, are group supported employment options that typically provide permanent, full-time, on-site supervision to their workers with handicaps. An *enclave* can be defined as a group of individuals, usually three to eight, who work

Table 1. Some of the procedures involved in job-site training for workers with developmental disabilities

Orientation and Assessment

First Day of Work

Drive worker to work (postpone travel training until second day).
Arrive at the job site 30 minutes early.
Show worker the location of restroom, telephone, employee lounge, supervisor's office.
Assign the worker to a job task that he or she can complete independently or without total supervision.
Reinforce the worker frequently for ''hanging in there'' and performing the job duties.

Orientation Training to the Work Environment

Have the worker follow the same route from home to the job site each day.
Enter and exit the building using the same doors each day.
Help the worker locate his or her primary work station in relation to the other work environments (e.g., while in the lunchroom, ask the worker to locate the work stations).
Have the employee locate other work environments (restrooms, work supplies, break areas, lunch area, supervisor's office, emergency exits, etc.) in relationship to the primary work station.

Orientation to the Community

Determine transportation options.
Discuss with the worker and family the pros and cons of each option.
Mutually select the most feasible option.
Design transportation training program prior to first day of work.
Implement travel training on day 2 of the job.

Assessment of Job/Worker Compatibility

Identify major job tasks/duties.
Note approximate time of day each major duty is performed and approximate time taken to perform each major duty.
Sequence major job duties according to when they are performed during the workday.
Identify changes in the schedule on a day-to-day basis.
Complete a job duty analysis.
Identify major skills that are necessary to perform each job duty.
Field-test the job duty (task) analysis by observing a coworker.
Have final job duty analysis approved by the supervisor.
Give a copy of the job duty analysis to the supervisor.
Have the employer or floor supervisor complete an employee evaluation 2 weeks after the first day at work.
Prepare a progress report based on the first work evaluation.
Review progress report with the worker, worker's family, or group home counselors.
Have the employer complete an evaluation 1 month from the first day of work.
Prepare a progress report based on the second work evaluation.
Review progress with the worker, worker's family, or group home counselor.

Job Compatibility

Utilize the sequence of job duties, job task analysis, and employee evaluation information gathered during the first 2 weeks to identify critical job skills areas that may be potential problems. Compare with consumer assessment information.
For potential problems identified after 2 weeks of being on the job:
    Determine if the job skill can be adapted.
    Determine if the job skill can be modified.
    Design and implement a systematic instructional program to train the job skill.
    Evaluate the worker's progress.

Initial Training/Skill Acquisition

Training Schedule

Review the sequence of job duties and job duty analysis.
Identify the major job duties to be trained.
Establish the time of day instruction will occur on each job duty (initial training schedule).

Job Duty Task Analysis (TA)

Observe coworker(s) performing the job.
Identify each step performed.
Record each step, in sequence, on a task analytic recording sheet.
Using the task analysis, perform the job duty yourself.
Revise the job duty task analysis by adding or deleting steps.

Initial Job Performance

(continued)

Table 1. *(continued)*

Write the individualized job duty task analysis on a task analytic recording sheet.

Collect probe data before instruction begins.

Systematic Instructional Program

Establish a written instructional plan, making sure it includes:
   Training schedule
   Individualized job duty task analysis
   Reinforcement procedures
   Instructional techniques
   Training procedures
   Data collection procedures with:
      Schedule for collecting prompt data
      Schedule for collecting probe data

Implement Systematic Training

   Implement instructional program (as written).
   Collect probe data according to the schedule established in the instructional program.
   Collect prompt data according to the schedule established in the instructional program.
   Graph and review data weekly.
If probe data indicate that the percentage of steps independently completed is increasing, continue the program.
   When the employee is performing 80% of the TA steps independently and 20% with a verbal prompt, move 3 feet away from the employee.
   Maintain this distance until the employee performs the task for 2 consecutive days with no more than 20% of task requiring verbal prompts.
   Increase distance from the employee to 6 feet.
   Maintain distance of 6 feet until the employee performs the task for 2 consecutive days with no more than 10% of the task requiring verbal prompts (90% independent).
   Increase distance from the employee to across the room. Maintain this distance until the employee performs the task 100% independently on three consecutive probes.
   Leave the immediate work area for increasing periods of time.
   Continue to probe; if skills regress, begin training again.
If probe data indicate no increase in independent job performance, but a review of the prompt data shows a decrease in the level of prompts, continue the instructional program.
If the prompt data show no decrease in the level of prompts, continue the instructional program for three training sessions.
If, at the end of three training sessions, the level of prompts is decreasing, continue the program.
If the data show no decrease in the level of prompts, change the level of reinforcement or the schedule of reinforcement.
If, after three training trials, the level of prompts necessary is decreasing, continue the program.
If the level of prompts shows no decrease, break the steps of the job duty task analysis into smaller steps.
Implement the least intrusive prompting procedures with the new task analysis.
If, at the end of three training trials, the level of prompts is decreasing, continue the program.
If the data show no decrease, review all the data and consider changing instructional techniques and/or modifying response cues or response prompts.
If, at the end of three training trials, the level of dependency on prompts is decreasing, continue the program.
If, at the end of three training trials, the data show no decrease in the level of dependency on prompts, consider modifying the job.

Job Modification

Review the prompt data to determine the specific problem area(s).
Evaluate the job environment by asking:
   Can simple adaptations be made to existing equipment to enable the employee to perform the job?
   Are there coworkers who could share the job duty with the employee?
   Are there coworker job duties of equal responsibility and duration that the employee could perform while the coworker performs the duties that are difficult for the employee?
Determine the alternatives and outline strategies for modifying the specific job duty in question.
Review alternatives/strategies with the employer and come to a mutual agreement on the best job modification option.
Explain to the employee that he or she must improve work skills or will lose the job.
Implement the job modification.
Provide systematic instruction.
Collect data (probe and prompt).
If the percentage of steps performed independently increases, continue the program.
If, after job modification and retraining, the percentage of steps performed independently shows no significant increase, recommend that the employee resign from this position.

(continued)

Table 1.   *(continued)*

Intervention Time

Record employment specialist intervention time with each worker on a daily basis.

Employee Evaluation

Have the employer complete an evaluation 2 weeks from the first day of work.
Prepare a progress report based on the employee evaluation.
Review progress with the employee and the employee's family or group home.
Have the employer complete an evaluation 1 month from the first day of work.
Prepare a progress report.
Review progress with the employee and the employee's family or group home staff.
Have the employer complete an evaluation 2 months from the first day of work.
Prepare a progress report.
Review progress with the employee and the employee's family or group home staff.

Stabilization

Increasing Employee Production Rate to Company Standards

Verify company production standards.
Determine employee's current production level.

Implement Stabilization Procedures

Implement procedures to increase production rate when the employee performs 100% of the steps of the task analysis
   for the major job duty initially targeted for training over three consecutive probes.
Select instructional methods to increase production rate by doing one or more of the following:
   Program natural cues.
   Program natural consequences.
   Program natural reinforcers.
   Expand performance across supervisors.
   Expand performances across job situations.
   Utilize coworker facilitator.
   Train self-management.
Design and implement program to increase production rate to company standards.

Expand Performance across Job Duties

Record probe data on established schedule.
Record production data on established schedule.
Review data weekly.
If production rate is increasing, continue program.
If production rate is not increasing, modify the program.
At the same time, identify the next major duty to be trained.
Design and implement skill acquisition program.
Check on-task/attending behavior for skills performed independently.
Repeat this process until all duties are being performed independently under natural worksite conditions.

Procedures for Fading from the Job Site

Discuss the fading schedule with the employer; agree on a day to begin.
Inform the employee that you are leaving the job site.
Inform the employer and coworkers that you are leaving and provide them with your telephone number.
Leave for no more than half a day the first time.
Continue to record on-task/attending and production data on established schedule.
Record the probe data so that all major duties are probed a minimum of once per week.
Review the data.
Continue fading your presence from the job site so long as the employee continues to perform all duties at company
   standards.
Continue to collect employee evaluations on established schedule.
Continue to complete progress reports on established schedule.

Source: Adapted from Barcus et al. (1987).

in a special training group within a regular, community-based industry (Rhodes & Valenta, 1985a). This business is called the "host" company. It is similar to earlier work stations in industry models (McGee, 1975), except that the goal of a supported employment enclave may not necessarily be to move all workers into the regular work force without support. Many experts consider an enclave to be an alternative to the individual placement approach for persons who have more severe disabilities and need more supervision (Rhodes & Valenta, 1985a). A good enclave provides pay that is commensurate to that of other workers in the host company who are producing the same amount of work, and it provides the same working conditions, including hours, breaks, benefits, and incentives (Mank et al., 1986). Enclaves can be structured so that the supervisor/trainer and employees can be paid at least in part by a service agency or not-for-profit company or the host company. Workers may be employees either of the host company or of the not-for-profit support company. The enclave supervisor is usually employed by the support company.

Key Components

Rhodes and Valenta (1985b) outlined a model for organizing enclaves that includes five areas: 1) developing the work situations, 2) meeting work requirements, 3) integrating employees, 4) coordinating services, and 5) providing ongoing support. Readers should refer to this article for more complete details on these procedures, but highlights of each component are provided here.

Finding a host company that will provide the enclave the opportunity to work can be a challenge. Rhodes and Valenta (1985b) suggest that a larger company may be better because it provides more opportunity for integration, draws less attention to a "special training production line," and may limit chances for layoffs. A company with a positive community image is also preferable because it is more dedicated to its employees. A company committed to planning and willing to take about 6 months to plan the requirements and responsibilities is also important.

Work requirements are met when the enclave supervisor delivers effective instruction in skill acquisition and work productivity and the host company makes some adaptations in its production system. Behavioral training is essential, and the supervisor must be able to guarantee a certain amount of productivity and quality. A model worker can be provided by the host company to help increase skill development and rate

of performance. It is also possible to gradually increase the number of workers so that each can receive more individualized attention in the initial training phase.

Integration of employees should be actively pursued by the enclave supervisor, but the degree of supervision will depend largely on company characteristics. It should occur naturally as part of using public transportation, taking breaks and eating meals, or participating in company recreation activities (Mank et al., 1986).

Workers' pay can be provided either directly or indirectly. With direct pay, the host company provides a regular paycheck to the clients, with no third-party agency. With indirect pay, on the other hand, the host company pays a sponsoring agency or organization, which in turn pays the enclave member. Most enclaves appear to be following an indirect pay route, although as training and technology become more sophisticated, direct pay may occur more rapidly.

Coordinating services and providing ongoing support are continuing processes for the agency or not-for-profit company starting the enclave. Negotiations must be formalized to ensure adequate pay, integration opportunities, and advancement when appropriate. For example, in one of the most well-publicized and successful enclaves in the country—Trillium, at Physio Control in the state of Washington—employees of the enclave become regular, fully paid and benefited employees of the host company once they reach 65% productivity (Mank et al., 1986).

Quality Characteristics

Rhodes and Valenta (1985b) delineated 10 key program characteristics for enclaves on a scale of less to more desirable (see Table 2). This type of information can be valuable in evaluating the appropriateness of a supported employment enclave or in establishing a new one.

Advantages of This Model

The enclave can provide more permanent support than an individual placement model and thus can offer employment for persons who may never function adequately in a regular community job. Enclaves also have the initial advantage of providing employment to several people simultaneously while engaging only one

Table 2. Quality characteristics of an industry-based model

Characteristics	Less desirable ←		→ More desirable
1. Enclave employees		Employees require intensive, ongoing support to meet job and/or social requirements of the work setting.	
2. Physical space	Employees are physically separated from coworkers by walls or other barriers.		Employees are located in physical proximity to coworkers; coworkers work on same production line as enclave employees.
3. Type of work	Work performed is not typically done by coworkers.		Work performed is typical of work done by coworkers.
4. Personnel status	Employees are legally employed by a third-party support organization.		Employees are legally employed by the host company.
5. Pay, benefits		Pay and benefits are based upon productivity, commensurate with wages/benefits received by coworkers.	
6. Transportation	Arrive via segregated bus for people with disabilities.		Arrive via carpools with coworkers; public or company transportation.
7. Number in enclave	Larger numbers (more than 8); in smaller companies (fewer than 100 employees).		Enclave represents approximately 1% or less of total work force.
8. Work routines (e.g., hours worked, days worked, breaktimes and lunchtimes)	Different from routines of coworkers.		Same as those of coworkers.
9. Staff supervision	Low skills in industry practices and in training/supervising persons with disabilities. Supervisor is employed by third-party support organization.	Supervisor is employed directly by company.	Understands relevant company procedures and brings training/supervision skills to company.
10. Support organization	Is highly visible within the host company in operating the enclave.		Maintains low visibility, but intervenes when necessary to maintain and support employment (e.g., training other company employees, providing behavior management consultation, identifying referrals, maintaining labor certificates).

Source: Rhodes and Valenta (1985b).

supervisor. However, this advantage may diminish over time, owing to the lack of fading of the supervisor. However, as employees move from the enclave to the regular host company payroll or to an individual placement, other workers can continually move into the enclave. With an enclave, there is also a good potential for employees to receive decent pay and benefits, depending upon the negotiations with the host company.

MOBILE WORK CREW

The mobile work crew is a group supported employment option, usually with three to eight workers and one or two supervisors. A mobile crew travels through a community performing specialized contract services, and typically operates from a van. Custodial and groundskeeping services have been a primary source of contracts for mobile crews. This is not a new model (Jacobs, 1974), and several rehabilitation facilities have operated work crews for a long time.

Mank et al. (1986) stated that work crews are good options for communities such as rural areas or small towns with small service needs or not much industry or in places where there is readily available short- or long-term contract work including janitorial work, snow removal, landscaping, farm labor, plant care, or painting. A crew can be operated from another agency or run as a small business. Generally, a crew is established as a not-for-profit business. This is due to the inability of all workers to produce at full productivity, which requires extra costs, more supervision, and the use of some public funding. Mobile crews are different from enclaves because they typically operate from several contracts and move regularly from site to site.

A mobile crew supervisor must be adept at being both a businessperson and a trainer of persons with severe handicaps. Contract procurement is tedious and difficult, and is a regular part of supervising a crew, along with meeting U.S. Department of Labor certification requirements, purchasing equipment, maintaining a vehicle, obtaining insurance, and making sure that the quality of work is up to par (Bourbeau, 1985).

Key Components

Bourbeau (1985) has delineated a number of areas that must be accounted for in operating a work crew. Table 3 summarizes these recommendations.

Advantages of This Model

Some of the advantages of operating crews have been stated earlier, including the fact that they can be set up in small communities that do not have lots of industry or a significant number of citizens with disabilities. Another advantage is that they can operate flexibly, depending on the community needs. The fact that workers can travel to a variety of places in the community, such as lunch stops and break areas, allows for integration opportunities. Crews are typically very visible, so that the public at large can observe the working potential of its citizens with disabilities. Crews can also be run cost-efficiently, because after initial start-up and purchases, there should be little overhead costs and revenue generated can largely cover operating expenses once wages are paid (Bourbeau, 1985).

SMALL BUSINESS OPTION

The final model described here is a small business or entrepreneurial alternative, which can be a manufacturing service or a subcontract operation hiring *eight or fewer workers* with handicaps as well as some workers who are not handicapped. One of the first small business ventures was the Specialized Training Program (STP) benchwork model, which involved a network of small electronics assembly businesses across the country (Boles, Bellamy, Horner, & Mank, 1984; Mank et al., 1986; O'Bryan, 1985). A supported employment small business would be homogeneous in nature, providing one type of product or service. Boles et al. (1984) suggest that this option should be used for workers with the most severe handicaps, who will constantly need behavioral training. The small business model differs markedly from traditional sheltered workshops in two ways. First, it is very small, usually serving, as just mentioned, eight or fewer workers. Second, the focus is on the *most* severely disabled people, who traditionally would never be accepted into a sheltered workshop because of their low productivity. Third, long-term and small-parts contracts reduce overhead costs (O'Bryan, 1985).

This model can be an appropriate placement for workers who exhibit severe social or behavioral deficits, are very slow, or have limited self-care skills. In fact, this model takes major credit for demonstrating to a skeptical professional community that persons with very severe and profound handicaps can work productively. The success of a small business will depend on its

Table 3. Components of operating a mobile work crew

I. Preimplementation considerations
  A. Market Analysis
  B. Contract Bidding
  C. Purchase of equipment and supplies
  D. Transportation
    1. Purchase of vehicles
    2. Adaptation of vehicle
  E. Insurance
    1. Purchase of insurance or bonding
  F. Staffing
    1. Larger business with several crews has manager and several supervisors. Manager will do job procurement, bidding, contracting, inventory, billing, and payroll, while supervisors do day-to-day operations and training.
    2. Small business with single crew has supervisor who performs all functions.
  G. Delineating Supervisor's duties
    1. Provide vocational training and job supervision for five workers; develop and implement individualized program plans; collect and summarize daily behavioral and performance data.
    2. Provide training in community skills for all workers on the crew.
    3. Locate potential jobs, analyze for suitability, submit bids, and contract for work to be done.
    4. Purchase required equipment and supplies, manage inventory, and maintain equipment in good working order.
    5. Conduct time studies as required by regulations.
    6. Compute payroll for workers.
    7. Collect and summarize data, maintain records, and compile reports.
    8. Assure the quality of work performed by the crew and maintain community relations.
    9. Transport workers.
II. Daily program operations
  A. Job analysis
    1. Select appropriate sites.
    2. Bid the work accurately.
    3. Structure job according to tasks, time, equipment.
    4. Assign tasks to crew members.
  B. Work assignment
    1. Assign work according to interest and ability levels.
    2. Document work quality and rate for training, payroll, and management purposes.
  C. Training
    1. Make sure all members complete assignments.
    2. Provide specific training to individuals.

Source: Adapted from Bourbeau (1985).

ability to attract customers or, in some cases, contracts. For any social integration to occur, the business must be located close to other businesses, stores, restaurants, and easily accessible recreation sites. Workers will usually be paid on a productivity basis, so care must be taken to provide enough work and to train to enhance production rates.

Key Components

Like any successful business, the entrepreneurial model must include astute management, financial, and commercial operations. The other component that the owners and managers must assure is a high quality of training for the employees, in much the same manner as provided by other models. Furthermore, procedures for marketing, sales, production, documentation, quality control, wage differential, and cost anal-

ysis must be developed (Boles et al., 1984; O'Bryan, 1985).

Mank et al. (1986) remind us that agencies interested in this model must ask two questions. First, is this most restrictive of all the models really necessary for persons with disabilities in a given community? And second, is there a need for another business, and can another business provide enough work for its employees? By most accounts, this model is just as expensive as most traditional day programs, requiring $15,000 to $25,000 in start-up capital.

COMMONLY ASKED QUESTIONS ABOUT THE SERVICE DELIVERY MODELS

As service providers, parents, the business community, and consumers make decisions about the most feasible supported employment options in a given community, many questions arise. Some of the most often expressed concerns are delineated here. Readers should note that although the responses provided are typical or possible solutions, most questions can only be answered after considering factors such as the local economy, interagency funding arrangements, school vocational training programs, and family support.

Do the four supported employment options represent a continuum of services, and should workers be moved from one to the other as skill levels change?

The options were designed to be permanent employment situations, with the individual placement model being, in many cases, the least restrictive alternative as well as the most normalized option. It is certainly desirable to move a worker from one job or model to another when a particular option is less restrictive, provides better outcomes such as wages, integration, or benefits, or when a worker wishes to make a job change based on sound reasoning. Very few communities have a *range* of truly acceptable supported employment options. Therefore, a worker is often not placed and trained with the particular model that is the ideal option for that individual.

As Bellamy, Rhodes, and Albin (1986) have stated:

> There is a nearly infinite array of supported employment strategies and structures, each of which combines a particular kind of work opportunity with a particular method of ongoing support. Each, no doubt, has advantages and drawbacks in terms of generating real employment outcomes while overcoming barriers to employment experienced by the individuals with disabilities. No single alternative is ideal, and none fits all situations. Community development of supported employment programs requires adaptation to local employment opportunities and individual service requirements.
>
> Employment models are needed that result in valued work outcomes for individuals with severe handicaps, yet vary enough to provide employment solutions in varied local communities. At the individual level, each supported employment alternative should be assessed as to whether or not it is the least restrictive alternative. (p. 40)

If no supported employment options exist in a community, which would be best to initiate first?

This will depend on several factors, most importantly the skill level and support needs of the workers who have been targeted and the business base and economic health of the community. The funding base of the company or agency providing the service will also be a factor, since an option such as the small business or mobile work crew will require more capital to meet initial start-up costs.

Most cities and towns will be able to support several individual placements across industries. Because the individual placement model can typically provide at least minimum wage and immediate company benefits when employees are hired on a full-time basis, it is logical to implement this model whenever possible. Some argue that doing this will limit the number of workers who can be placed, since the model requires one trainer with one worker on a full-time basis until the worker starts performing at company standards. However, the trainer does gradually fade from the site and can then begin training another worker. In the group models the trainer or supervisor does not fade. Thus, over a one-year period approximately the same number of workers (three to eight) can be served using one trainer with the individual model as with one group model.

Does one model more naturally enhance integration?

There is not sufficient data as yet to indicate that one model typically provides more opportunities for consistent integration of handicapped and nonhandicapped workers. The amount and quality of integration will depend on many variables, including the location of the job; the type of work; the general makeup of the work force; the motivation, social skills, and verbal ability of the disabled worker; and probably most critically, the efforts of the employment specialist or supervisor to advocate for integration. Some experts who have experience with several models believe that the individual placement approach and enclaves provide more continuous integration than the mobile crew or the small business (Mank et al., 1986).

Regardless of the wages earned, hours worked, or long-term support provided, a job placement cannot be technically considered supported employment unless opportunities for integration are present.

Which models are best for citizens with the most severe disabilities?

Selection of any of these models is dependent upon the characteristics of both the individual and the particular job and a careful match between the two. Hypothetically, these models are appropriate for persons whose handicaps are so severe that traditional rehabilitation methods will not be successful. If a consumer can be served by a less intensive placement model, then supported employment options should be reserved for those with more significant disabilities. It is not true that persons with milder disabilities have more success maintaining jobs when placed and trained through supported employment programs (Hill, Wehman, Hill, & Goodall, 1986).

Can persons with severe disabilities other than mental retardation be served by any or all of the service delivery models?

Although there is more longitudinal data indicating the success of the supported employment models with persons with mental retardation (Wehman, Hill, Wood, & Parent, 1987) as opposed to other severe disabilities, all these models and variations of them are now being used to serve individuals with a variety of handicapping conditions. These include autism, chronic mental illness, multiple sensory handicaps (deafness and blindness), severe physical disabilities, and head injury. Later chapters in this book describe how supported employment options can be implemented for persons with a variety of disabling conditions. Only repeated applications and the regular, longitudinal tracking of data will indicate which models are most adaptable.

Regardless of the type of disability or model being considered, two questions should be asked before implementing a training program: 1) Is the degree of disability truly severe enough to warrant supported employment? 2) Are the expected outcomes of employment quality ones such as a decent wage, good benefits, and integration with workers who are not disabled?

What type of organization can best implement supported employment?

Supported employment options can be initiated by sheltered workshops, day activity or developmental disability centers, schools, or private companies. Most sources to this point have been not-for-profit organizations, which can qualify for special monetary matching funds, contributions, or grants from civic and government sources and can obtain U.S. Department of Labor permission to pay subminimum wages when necessary, based on production rates. However, there is no reason why for-profit companies could not initiate supported employment programs, so long as such companies can provide decent wages and integration opportunities and meet the long-term support needs of the workers with severe disabilities.

Any organization that already runs other employment or vocational training programs must ensure that its supported employment options maintain separate and specific operations. For example, supported employment staff should not be involved in other organizational activities, and any profits acquired by the group models should be used to boost worker salaries, not to support other organizational activities.

Regardless of the type of sponsoring organization, a supported employment program requires the following: a survey of local business to determine what types of employment models are needed; a service delivery system that is totally community-based; workers with truly severe disabilities and who really need this kind of intensive support; the commitment of some funding source to support continuous follow-along services; adequately trained staff; and methods for evaluating the appropriateness of the program. The remaining chapters in this book provide information on these factors.

SUMMARY

Although four major supported employment service delivery models currently predominate, these are undergoing changes to meet the needs of workers with disabilities and the conditions of local labor markets. There is no one "best" supported employment model; rather, any of the models may be found most suitable to a particular individual at a given time in a certain local economy. Persons with severe disabilities, human service providers, families, advocates, and local businesspersons must work together to create a variety of employment opportunities in every community.

Each supported employment placement, regardless of the model, must be evaluated across several criteria, including: whether or not the worker is being paid the maximum wage possible and is working a relatively normal amount of time (20 to 40 hours per week); and whether or not the worker is in a situation that is opti-

mally integrated and the least restrictive according to his or her needs. In addition, the program needs to answer adequately the following questions: First, does the program serve only those persons who could not retain employment without the intensive training and continuous follow-along services? Second, has the provider working with the client, family, support agencies, and employer, arrived at a cost-effective way to provide the full range of support that is necessary? Finally, have the needs and desires of the individuals requiring supported employment been matched to the needs of local businesses, so that a true partnership between industry and human service providers is accomplished?

REFERENCES

Barcus, M., Brooke, V., Inge, K., Moon, S., & Goodall, P. (1987). *An instructional guide for training on a job site: A supported employment resource.* Richmond: Virginia Commonwealth University, Rehabilitation Research and Training Center.

Bellamy, G. T., Rhodes, L. E., & Albin, J. M. (1986). Supported employment. In W. E. Kiernan & J. A. Stark (Eds.), *Pathways to employment for adults with developmental disabilities* (pp. 129–138). Baltimore: Paul H. Brookes Publishing Co.

Belmore, K., & Brown, L. (1978). Job skills inventory strategy for use in public school vocational training programs for severely handicapped potential workers. In N. Haring & D. Bricker (Eds.), *Teaching the severely handicapped* (Vol. 3.). Columbus, OH: American Association for the Education of the Severely and Profoundly Handicapped.

Boles, S. M., Bellamy, G. T., Horner, R. H., & Mank, D. M. (1984). Specialized training program: The structured employment model. In S.C. Paine, G. T. Bellamy, & B. Wilcox (Eds.), *Human services that work: From innovation to standard practice* (pp. 181–205). Baltimore: Paul H. Brookes Publishing Co.

Bourbeau, P. E. (1985). Mobile work crews: An approach to achieve long-term supported employment. In P. McCarthy, J. Everson, S. Moon, & M. Barcus (Eds.), *School to work transition for youth with severe disabilities.* Richmond: Virginia Commonwealth University, Rehabilitation Research and Training Center.

Hill, J., Banks, D., Hill, M., & Wehman, P. (in press). Individual characteristics and environmental effects on the competitive employment of workers with mental retardation. *American Journal of Mental Deficiency.*

Hill, J. W., Wehman, P., Hill, M., & Goodall, P. (1986). Differential reasons for job separation of previously employed persons with mental retardation. *Mental Retardation* 24(6), 347–351.

Hill, M. L., Banks, P. D., Handrich, R. R., Wehman, P. H., Hill, J. W., & Shafer, M. S. (1987). Benefit-cost analysis of supported competitive employment for persons with mental retardation. *Research in Developmental Disabilities*, 8(1), 71–89.

Hill, M., Hill, J., Wehman, P., Revell, G., Dickerson, A., & Noble, J. (1987). Supported employment: An interagency funding model for persons with severe disabilities. *Journal of Rehabilitation*, 53 (3), 13–21.

Jacobs, J. W. (1974). Retarded persons as gleaners. *Mental Retardation*, 14(6), 42–43.

Mank, D. M., Rhodes, L. E., & Bellamy, G. T. (1986). Four supported employment alternatives. In W. E. Kiernan & J. A. Stark (Eds.), *Pathways to employment for adults with developmental disabilities* (pp. 139–153). Baltimore: Paul H. Brookes Publishing Co.

McGee, J. (1975). *Work stations in industry.* Omaha: University of Nebraska.

Moon, S., Goodall, P., Barcus, M., & Brooke, V. (Eds.). (1986). *The supported work model of competitive employment for citizens with severe handicaps: A guide for job trainers* (rev. ed.). Richmond: Virginia Commonwealth University, Rehabilitation Research and Training Center.

O'Bryan, A. (1985). The STP benchwork model. In P. McCarthy, J. M. Everson, M. S. Moon, & J. M. Barcus (Eds.), *School-to-work transition for youth with severe disabilities* (Monograph, pp. 183–194). Richmond: Virginia Commonwealth University, Project Transition into Employment, Rehabilitation Research and Training Center.

Rehab Brief. (1986). Supported Employment, 10(1). Washington, DC: U.S. Department of Education, National Institute on Disability and Rehabilitation Research, Office of Special Education and Rehabilitative Services.

Rhodes, L. E., & Valenta, L. (1985a). Industry-based supported employment: An enclave approach. *Journal of the Association for Persons with Severe Handicaps*, 10(1), 12–20.

Rhodes, L. E., & Valenta, L. (1985b). Enclaves in industry. In P. McCarthy, J. M. Everson, M. S. Moon, & J. M. Barcus (Eds.), *School-to-work transition for youth with severe disabilities* (Monograph, pp. 129–149). Richmond: Virginia Commonwealth University, Project Transition into Employment, Rehabilitation Research and Training Center.

Rusch, F. R. (Ed.). (1986). *Competitive employment issues*

and strategies. Baltimore: Paul H. Brookes Publishing Co.

Vandergoot, D., & Worrell, J. (1979). *Placement in rehabilitation: A career development perspective*. Baltimore: University Park Press.

Vogelsberg, R. T. (1985). Competitive employment programs for individuals with mental retardation in rural areas. In S. Moon, P. Goodall, & P. Wehman (Eds.), *Critical issues related to supported competitive employment: Proceedings from the first RRTC symposium on employment for citizens who are mentally retarded* (pp. 57–81). Richmond: Virginia Commonwealth University, Rehabilitation Research and Training Center.

Wehman, P. (1981). *Competitive employment: New horizons for severely disabled individuals*. Baltimore: Paul H. Brookes Publishing Co.

Wehman, P. (1986). Competitive employment in Virginia. In F. R. Rusch (Ed.), *Competitive employment issues and strategies* (pp. 23–33). Baltimore: Paul H. Brookes Publishing Co.

Wehman, P., Hill, J. W., Wood, W., & Parent, W. (1987). A report on competitive employment histories of persons labeled severely mentally retarded. *Journal of the Association for Persons with Severe Handicaps*, *12*(1), 11–17.

Wehman, P., & Kregel, J. (1985). A supported work approach to competitive employment of individuals with moderate and severe handicaps. *Journal of the Association for Persons with Severe Handicaps*, *10*(1), 3–11.

Chapter 3

Supported Competitive Employment

An Interagency Perspective

Mark L. Hill

"Normalization," "integration," and "real work for real pay" are but a few of the concepts that have sparked recent changes in the way employment programs for persons with severe disabilities are being viewed. Federal legislation now firmly supports services that promote independence to the greatest extent possible in natural environments (PL 98-527, 1984). Policy statements regarding employment for persons with disabilities promote integrated, normalized job placement and maintenance as positive values (Elder, 1984; Will, 1984).

In this time of rapid conceptual and technological change, the need for answers to increasingly complex questions places great emphasis on effective resource utilization. One method for helping managers and leaders to make difficult decisions is benefit/cost analysis.

The commitment to and the level of funding for supported competitive employment (SCE) is inherently connected to the benefits and costs associated with the provision of these new services. Given current budgetary constraints and the development of congressional deficit reduction strategies, the present focus on financial outcomes and cost-effectiveness will have a long-lasting effect on the development and maintenance of employment programs for persons with disabilities. The cost dilemma is a real concern to adult service providers. Decisions to allocate sparse funding are made daily.

Programs that justify their existence with positive financial and qualitative outcomes are more likely to survive and prosper in the future. Lippitt, Langseth, and Mossop (1986) indicate that planned organizational changes take place in part because of the need to improve morale or productivity, or to institute desirable new procedures. If planned change is to become a reality, leaders must review the present systems' outcomes, develop strategic innovations for improvement, and modify the systems to foster utilization of improved technology.

First impressions of a supported competitive employment program might lead one to question the ultimate feasibilty of such an operation due to its high costs. Supported competitive employment has been characterized in the previous two chapters as utilizing professional staff who provide individualized and intensive assistance to consumers in: 1) making a job placement, 2) providing job-site training and assessment,

Acknowledgments: There are numerous contributors to the content, research, and philosophy espoused in this chapter. There is not room to list all contributors, many of whom are cited in the references at the end of the chapter. However, I would like to acknowledge here individuals whose input was significant: Dave Banks, Altamont Dickerson, Rita Handrich, Janet Hill, Helen Metzler, John Noble, David Pitonyak, Grant Revell, Martha Rice, and Craig Thornton.

and 3) engaging in long-term follow-along support as needed. These characteristics would lead one to believe that provision of supported competitive employment is expensive in comparison to more traditional preemployment training where the mode of operation is usually staff training and supervising of groups of consumers.

This chapter examines the benefits and costs of supported competitive employment and presents a variety of interagency financial arrangements that make the provision of supported employment possible. The chapter is divided into two parts. The first part presents the supported competitive employment model to illustrate a habilitation program that allows greater monetary returns to society and to persons with severe disabilities than other more traditional adult service programs. A benefit-cost analysis of a supported competitive employment program in Virginia, from 1978 to 1986, is discussed from two perspectives: that of the consumer (i.e., the adult with severe disabilities) and that of the taxpayer. The second part of the chapter discusses the implementation of supported competitive employment in Virginia as a model to demonstrate the interagency collaboration necessary for the initial and ongoing service components. Suggestions relating to implementation plans are provided and sources of funding are identified and examined.

BENEFITS AND COSTS OF SUPPORTED COMPETITIVE EMPLOYMENT

Program evaluation based upon the analysis of economic or financial outcomes is typically referred to as benefit-cost analysis. Economics has been defined by Conley (1973) as "the study of the allocation of scarce resources among competing uses" (p. 2). Benefit-cost analysis is the formal analytical procedure used to assess the financial outcomes of providing a service. For example, in the case of supported competitive employment, the benefit-cost analysis delineates the benefits (i.e., monetary returns to society) and costs (i.e., additional expenses incurred as a result of a program) involved in the provision of supported competitive employment

services. Benefit-cost analyses help taxpayers, consumers, and governmental agencies involved with supported employment initiatives to identify: 1) what financial outcomes may be associated with these services; 2) what the related costs of these services are; and 3) how these costs compare with other services (e.g., segregated sheltered work and adult day activity centers.)

This section's analysis of program costs and benefits is presented from the perspectives of both the individual receiving SCE services—the consumer—and the taxpayer who must bear the relative costs and benefits accrued at the government or systems level. From the consumer's perspective, concerns revolve around the relative financial gains of paid supported competitive employment. Are people better off financially when they are employed competitively, or do they lose more than they gain? From the taxpayer's perspective, the issues concern costs associated with developing programs that provide SCE services. Are the benefits associated with SCE worth the costs of developing the service?

Benefit-Cost Analysis: An Introduction

The analysis provided in this chapter is based upon a post hoc evaluation of services provided by the Rehabilitation Research and Training Center (RRTC) in Richmond, VA, during a *consecutive 8-year period* at Virginia Commonwealth University (VCU) to persons with severe mental disabilities in several predominantly urban areas of Virginia.

As presented in Table 1, the majority of the 214 consumers placed into supported competitive employment during the analysis period were described as moderately mentally retarded. The most frequent types of jobs in which these consumers were employed consisted of entry-level, nonskilled service occupations such as janitors or dishwashers. Approximately 70% of all consumers placed into supported competitive employment remained employed for at least 6 months. The average length of time that consumers have been employed during the study period is 21 months. This employment retention figure is a critical reference point for interpreting

Table 1. Demographic information for consumers placed in supported competitive employment, July 1978–August 1986 [a]

Functioning level
  Severe MR: 5%
  Moderate MR: 51%
  Mild MR: 34%
  Borderline MR: 10%

Types of jobs consumers perform
  Food service: 41.5%
  Janitorial: 41%
  Laborer: 1.5%
  Laundry: 11%
  Industrial: 5%

Types of companies hiring consumers
  Food: 33%
  Health care: 10%
  Janitorial: 5%
  Services: 18%
  Education: 9%
  Industrial: 3%
  Commercial: 14%
  Lodging: 8%

Company affiliations
  Private-profit: 60%
  Local government: 10%
  Federal government: 2%
  Nonprofit: 23%
  State government: 5%

[a] Based on 214 consumers placed in competitive employment positions. Seventy percent of consumers retained their positions 6 months after placement. Average consumer income prior to placement was reported at $18 per month, with 19% of consumers reporting annual salaries in excess of $200. Average monthly consumer income after placement in competitive employment was $435.60, with average hourly wage at $3.53 (hourly wage ranged from $3.35 to $5.07).

a longitudinal benefit-cost analysis. For example, in the study presented, the total benefits or costs over 94 months can be divided by the mean months employed to calculate the average monthly figures.

The general analytical procedures used in this report were adapted from Thornton's (1985) accounting model. This procedure provides a factual presentation of economic benefits and costs as opposed to the more common prediction-oriented benefit-cost analysis. The analysis presented is based on actual monetary outcomes incurred from an intervention (i.e., supported competitive employment), which were identified from permanent records and information supplied by cooperating agencies. These outcomes were then conceptualized by their effect on governmental expenditures and consumer outcomes. Due to the lengthy period of this analysis, the effects of varying economic factors, such as inflation and discounting, were considered (Thornton, 1985). Brief explanations of the procedures used to account for inflation and discounting follow.

Inflation   In order to account for the changing value of money across the 8-year (94 months) time period, all dollar figures were converted to constant dollars expressed in 1986 (Quarter 1) figures as provided by the U.S. Department of Commerce (1986). This conversion was accomplished by applying the gross national product (GNP) implicit price deflator to actual dollar amounts expended during the 94 months of the programs' operation. These figures, as pointed out by Thornton (1985), are believed to actually reflect the monetary value changes in the wide range of products and services used by social service programs.

Discounting   *Discounting* is a term used by economists to represent the manner in which dollars, over time, change in value. In benefit-cost analyses, all future benefits and costs must be discounted to present value. Present value represents the price one would be willing to pay for a future benefit, *or* in other words, how much one must set aside now to meet a future cost.

Discounting is applied to both benefits and costs in this analysis. Economists recommend the application of differing discount rates "to evaluate the sensitivity of the results to the interest rate chosen, and partly to reflect divergent views on which rate is appropriate" (Conley, 1973, p. 264). A 5% discount rate was applied to all figures in this study, but 3% and 10% discounting rates were also applied to determine the effects of lower and higher levels of discounting on the outcome. Varying the discount rate between 3% and 10% had a negligible impact on the results.

Several variables were used to complete the benefit-cost analysis. These variables are listed in the subheadings of Table 2 and are described in the paragraphs following. Financial benefits (Part I of Table 2) are discussed first, followed by costs and expenditures (Part II of Table 2).

Table 2. Financial outcomes of a supported competitive employment program

I. Financial benefits

		Financial perspective	
		Consumer benefits	Gov't. agency/ taxpayer savings
A.	Increased revenue		
	1. Total consumer income	$12,013	$ 0
	2. Fringe benefits	1,802	0
	3. Taxes paid/collected	0	2,763
	4. Targeted job tax credit (TJTC)	0	1,184
B.	Decreased service expenditures (For public schools, sheltered workshops, and activity centers due to placement of consumer into employment)	0	8,985
C.	Decreased government subsidies		
	1. Decreased Supplemental Security Income payments	0	2,350
	Total benefits per consumer	$13,815	$15,282[a]

II. Costs/expenditures

		Financial perspective	
		Consumer costs	Gov't. agency/ taxpayer costs
A.	Operational costs		
	1. Federal demonstration	$ 0	$ 6,987
B.	Lost workshop earnings	1,887	0
C.	Decreased government subsidy		
	1. Reduced SSI check	2,350	0
D.	Taxes paid/credited		
	1. Paid by consumer	2,763	0
	2. Credited to employer	0	1,184
	Total costs/expenses per consumer	$ 7,000	$ 8,171

III. Summary/balance

Total benefits	$	13,815	$	15,282
− Total costs		7,000		8,171
= Per consumer net savings (94 months of program operation)	$	6,815[a]	$	7,111[a]
Group value (N = 214; 94 months)		$1,458,410		$1,521,754
Yearly benefit per consumer	$	3,894[b]	$	4,063

[a] Mean months employed for study population = 21 months.
[b] Yearly benefit per consumer = (net savings / mean months employed) × 12.

Increased Revenue

Increased revenue refers to those aspects of supported employment that provide monetary benefits from both the consumer and taxpayer. It is composed of total consumer income, fringe benefits, taxes paid/collected, and employer tax credits.

Total Consumer Income   Total consumer income represents the sum total income earned by all consumers, divided by the number of consumers in the study (214), to arrive at the average individual consumer income through supported competitive employment. Per consumer income ($12,013) represents a benefit to the consumer (see Table 2).

Fringe Benefits   Fringe benefits represent an estimate of the monetary value of the fringe benefits (health insurance, social security, sick leave, vacation time, etc.) received by the consumer placed into supported employment. This figure is calculated at 15% of each consumer's gross income, as suggested by the U.S. Department of Labor (1980) for low-income wage earners. Fringe benefits ($1,802) also represent a benefit to the consumer (see Table 2).

Taxes Paid/Collected This figure is an estimate of taxes (income, payroll, sales, and excise) paid by the consumers who are placed into supported competitive employment, and is calculated at 23% of each consumer's gross income, a figure reported by Pechman and Okner (1974) as an effective tax rate for low-wage earners. The resulting figure of $2,763 represents the average estimate of taxes paid by each consumer, based upon individual gross earnings. These taxes are *paid* by the consumer, and *collected* by the taxpayer. Thus, taxes collected represent a benefit to the taxpayer (see Table 2).

Targeted Job Tax Credit (TJTC) Employer tax credits represent an amount of money deducted from the employer's tax debt for hiring an individual with mental retardation (or other disabilities). Targeted job tax credits essentially provide a rebate to the employer for the first 2 years a disabled person is employed. Specifically, TJTC provides one-half of the consumer's income for the first year, which may not exceed $3,000. The figure presented in Table 2 ($1,184) represents an average of the amount rebated to employers for hiring the individuals in the sample population. The rebate through the TJTC program represents a benefit to the employer-taxpayer. In this case, although the tax credit is a benefit, it is a *transfer* from all taxpayers to a subgroup of taxpayers (i.e., employers), and thus the tax credit is also discussed later as a cost. In January 1987, the TJTC program was changed to a maximum benefit of $2,400, and second-year benefits were eliminated.

Decreased Service Expenditures

Decreased service expenditures represent the decrease in costs to governmental service agencies as consumers are transferred from alternative programs (i.e., sheltered workshops, day activity centers, or public schools) into supported employment.

Sheltered Workshop and Day Activity Program Costs Noble (1985) provided estimates for sheltered workshop ($3,744) and day activity program ($5,916) costs in Virginia for

1985. Estimates of sheltered workshop and day activity center costs for the remainder of the analysis period were calculated by applying the effects of inflation to the figures provided by Noble (1985).

Public Education Costs Actual individual student costs for public education in Virginia were provided by the National Education Association (NEA) for the entire length of the analysis period. While no figures are available on the state or federal level for the costs of special education, special education costs have been estimated at two to three times the cost of public education (Kakalik, Ferry, Thomas, & Carney, 1981). The figures provided by the NEA were multiplied by two (the more conservative estimate) to obtain individual student costs for special education in Virginia.

The "decreased service expenditure" figure presented in Table 2 ($8,985) represents the average savings in alternative program costs per consumer based on the most recent alternative program and the number of months employment lasted.

Decreased Government Subsidies

Decreased governmental subsidies are financial outcomes realized when consumers placed in supported employment receive systematic reductions in Supplemental Security Income (SSI) payments.

Supplemental Security Income The SSI payments in this study were derived by computing actual SSI reductions to each consumer's earned income over the period of his other employment. Pay raises, periodic SSI inflation rate adjustments, and consumers' living arrangement all affect the SSI payment on a month-to-month basis and have been included in each consumer's SSI computation. The figure presented in Table 2 ($2,350) depicts the average amount of SSI lost by the consumer owing to increased income from supported employment, and thus represents a benefit to the taxpayer.

Summary of Consumer and Taxpayer Benefits

Increased revenue, decreased service expenditures, and decreased government subsidy, as just outlined, comprise the benefits to the consumer and taxpayer in this analysis. The figures representing total benefits per consumer are summations of the consumer benefits column ($13,815) and the government agency/taxpayer savings column ($15,282), and are discussed in a later section.

Part II of Table 2 presents costs and expenditures involved in the benefit-cost analysis. Costs and expenditures of the supported competitive employment program include: operational costs, lost workshop earnings, decreased government subsidy, and taxes paid and credited. Each of these "cost" categories is defined and described next.

Operational Costs

Operational costs refer to the governmental agencies that fund supported competitive employment services. The total program costs ($1,495,162) required during the 94 months of program operation were divided by the number of consumers placed into supported competitive employment (214) to determine program costs per consumer. The figure of $6,987 represents the average cost per consumer. Since the project was federally funded using tax dollars, the $6,987 is conceptualized as a cost to the taxpayer. It should be noted that this $6,987 is not an annual cost per consumer. These are average costs incurred for all individuals, those placed very recently as well as individuals placed in 1978. A discussion of annual cost interpretation follows in "Consumer Outcome Summary" section.

Lost Workshop Earnings

Lost workshop earnings refer to the income consumers lost as a result of being placed into supported competitive employment. Noble (1985) estimated the average income per consumer employed in sheltered workshop settings at $1,246 in 1985. Estimations of sheltered workshop income for other years in the analysis period were computed by applying appropriate inflation rates. Yearly income figures were divided by 12 to obtain average monthy income. The resulting figures were then multiplied by the number of months each consumer had been competitively employed, *only* for those consumers who had been employed by a sheltered workshop just

prior to their placement into supported competitive employment. Since consumers are no longer receiving sheltered workshop income as a result of being involved in supported employment, the $1,887 "lost workshop earnings" figure is conceptualized as a cost to the consumer.

Decreased Government Subsidy

As explained earlier, decreased government subsidy refers to the manner in which the SSI payments of consumers placed into supported competitive employment are systematically reduced. Although SSI reductions were conceptualized as a *benefit to the taxpayer* earlier, this part of the analysis is now examining the impact of supported competitive employment from a cost perspective. In this case, since the consumer receives lower SSI payments, the reduction in monies received ($2,350) represents a cost to the consumer.

Taxes Paid/Credited

Taxes paid and credited refer to an estimate of all taxes paid by consumers placed into supported competitive employment. This estimate is derived by multiplying the total consumer income ($12,013) by 23%, an effective tax rate for low-income earners (Pechman & Okner, 1974).

Taxes Paid by Consumer Earlier in this chapter, the taxes paid by the consumer were discussed as a benefit to the taxpayer. From the perspective of costs, however, the consumer is paying income and other taxes due to an increased income as a result of placement into supported competitive employment. Therefore, when assessing costs, the $2,763 average tax payment is viewed as a cost to the consumer.

Taxes Credited to Employer Taxes are credited to employers through TJTC as an incentive to hire workers with disabilities. Earlier in this discussion, these tax incentives were conceptualized as rebates, which were benefits to the employer-taxpayer. However, from the perspective of costs associated with supported competitive employment, these tax credits reduce government revenue, and therefore the $1,184 represents a cost to taxpayers as well.

Summary of
Consumer and Taxpayer Costs

Operational costs, lost workshop earnings, decreased government subsidy, and taxes paid and credited comprise the costs to the consumer and the taxpayer in this analysis. The figures representing total costs are merely summations of the consumer costs column ($7,000) and the government agency/taxpayer column ($8,171) and are discussed in the "Consumer Outcome Summary" and "Taxpayer Outcome Summary" sections.

PROCEDURES FOR COMPLETING
THE OUTCOME ANALYSIS

Based upon the preceding discussion of the benefits and costs associated with supported competitive employment, it is important to realize that a study of program benefits and costs is highly dependent upon the reference perspective. For example, some variables (specifically, taxes paid/collected and decreased Supplemental Security Income payments) are considered a cost from the consumers' perspective, while simultaneously considered a benefit from the taxpayers' perspective. Each perspective must be reviewed separately.

Consumer Perspective

Benefits to the Consumer Financial outcomes of supported employment that were conceptualized as benefits to the consumer include total consumer income ($12,013) and fringe benefits ($1,802). By combining consumer income and fringe benefits, one arrives at the average financial benefit received by RRTC consumers ($13,815).

Health costs to consumers were not considered in this analysis, because, in the study sample, individuals who did not receive health insurance as a fringe benefit of employment had not been removed from Medicaid during the analysis period. Sections 1619*a* and *b* of the Social Security Act of 1987 allowing for continued Medicaid coverage have been instrumental. It is anticipated that loss of Medicaid coverage will occur as salaries and length of employment increase. Future analyses may include costs associated with health and Medicaid services.

It is important to note that the figure of $13,815 represents an average income figure for the 94-month analysis period; obviously, wide variations in consumer benefits will be discovered when benefits are assessed on an individual consumer by consumer basis.

Costs to the Consumer Financial outcomes of supported employment that were conceptualized as costs to the consumer consist of lost workshop earnings ($1,887), reductions in SSI checks ($2,350), and finally, taxes paid ($2,763). These outcomes represent lost financial income (or increased expenditures) realized by each consumer as a result of obtaining supported competitive employment positions. By adding the monetary values associated with each of the preceding variables, the average financial cost per consumer amounts to $7,000.

Consumer Outcome Summary

Total consumer income and fringe benefits were combined in the study to arrive at an average gross income figure per client ($13,815). Also combined were increased financial expenditures (i.e., costs) for each consumer that occurred as a result of being involved in supported competitive employment ($7,000). By subtracting the total financial losses ("costs") from consumer gross income ("benefits"), a net income figure (i.e., net benefit) of $6,815 is arrived at for each consumer. In other words, placement into supported employment resulted in an average increase of $6,815 in financial income per consumer. When this figure is summed for all 214 consumers served during the period of analysis, the total benefit for all consumers is $1,458,410 (see Table 2, Part III).

The per-consumer benefit of $6,815 represents the average increase in income per consumer, based upon tenure in the competitive employment market. This is not an annual income increase per consumer. To assist in clarifying consumer benefits, an estimate of the average annual benefit per consumer is presented.

An annual benefit per consumer (i.e., average annual increase in income) is obtained by dividing the total benefit per consumer ($6,815) by the mean number of months they were employed (21). The resulting figure, representing monthly income increases for each consumer ($324.50), is then multiplied by 12 months (1 year) to represent an annual benefit per consumer. The average annual increase in income for RRTC consumers, therefore, is extrapolated to total $3,894.

Overall, from the consumers' perspective, the RRTC program of supported competitive employment is a financially prosperous venture. Consumers gained an average of $3,894 per year in net gain as a result of their placement and training in supported competitive employment. The financial efficacy of supported competitive employment from the taxpayers' perspective is discussed next.

Taxpayer Perspective

Financial outcomes from the taxpayer's perspective have also been discussed earlier and are presented in Table 2. When a benefit-cost analysis is conducted from a governmental or taxpayer perspective, the primary concern is to determine whether adoption of alternative services will result in an increase or decrease in governmental expenditures. A study of benefits and costs from a taxpayer's perspective will assess increases in governmental expenditures (i.e., increased costs) and subtract from those expenditures any decrease in expenses (i.e., benefits) associated with the program at hand, in this case, a program of supported competitive employment.

Benefits to the Taxpayer Government agencies/taxpayers reap a number of benefits from supported competitive employment. In addition to the increased tax revenue already described ($2,763), the taxpayer-employer receives targeted job tax credits ($1,184) for hiring persons with disabilities; decreases occur in alternative programming funds (sheltered workshops, day activity centers) ($8,985); and the amount of SSI payments is reduced ($2,350). Adding the figures presented in Table 2 as benefits to "government agency/taxpayer savings" results in a total benefit of $15,282 per consumer during the 94 months of program operation. Bas-

ically, for each consumer served by the RRTC during the 94 months, governmental agencies and taxpayers collectively realized a savings of $15,282.

Costs to the Taxpayer The adoption of supported competitive employment services results in two additional expenditures by government agencies: the funding support necessary to provide these services ($6,987), and the lost tax revenue realized by the TJTC program ($1,184). Adding these two figures together results in the total per consumer expenditures (i.e., costs) of the RRTC program from a government agency/taxpayer perspective ($8,171).

Taxpayer Outcome Summary

Total taxpayer benefits of supported competitive employment, arrived at by adding increased tax revenue ($2,763), TJTC ($1,184), decreases in alternative program costs ($8,985), and deductions in SSI payments ($2,350), equal $15,282 per consumer. Total costs for the taxpayer, as described earlier, total $8,171. When the financial expenditures realized by the government agency/taxpayer ($8,171) are subtracted from the financial savings associated with supported competitive employment ($15,282), the net benefit of these services, as presented in Table 2, Part III, is $7,111 for each consumer served during this analysis period. When the net benefit per consumer ($7,111) is multiplied by the total number of consumers served (214), the total net benefit of this supported competitive employment program is $1,521,754.

Again, this figure of $1,521,754 does not represent an *annual* savings from a taxpayer's perspective, but a cumulative savings during the 94 months of program operation.

In order to determine a yearly net benefit, the net savings per consumer figure ($7,111) was divided by the mean number of months a consumer was employed (21), and multiplied by 12 to achieve an annual figure. The resulting figure ($4,063) represents the annual savings to governmental agencies for each consumer served by this supported competitive employment project.

BENEFIT-COST RATIOS FOR TAXPAYERS AND CONSUMERS

In Tables 3, 4, and 5 the data base is used to compute benefit-cost ratios for each year that the Virginia project was in operation.

Tables 3, 4, and 5 show the figures used to determine the taxpayer, consumer, and earnings productivity benefit-cost analyses, respectively.

Benefit-Cost (B/C) Taxpayer Index

Table 3 presents the monetary outcomes for taxpayers for each year of the supported competitive employment program at the RRTC. Total taxpayer benefits (Taxes Paid + SSI Reduction + Alternate Program Cost) are divided by total taxpayer costs (TJTC Cost + Project Expenses) to find the taxpayer's benefit cost ratio. For example, in 1985 every $1 dollar in costs was matched by an average gain of $2.97 in taxpayer benefits for each of the 104 consumers served during that year. *In other words, for each $1 of taxpayer money expended in program costs, the taxpayer actually recouped $2.97 in savings.*

Benefit-Cost (B/C) Consumer Index.

Table 4 presents the monetary outcomes for consumers for each year of the supported competitive employment program at the RRTC. Total consumer benefits (Gross Wages + Fringe Benefits) are divided by total consumer costs (SSI Reduction + Foregone Sheltered Workshop Wages + Taxes Paid) to find the consumer's benefit cost index. For example, *in 1985 for every $1 dollar of net income the consumer had*

Table 3. Taxpayer benefit-cost analysis[a]

Year ending June	Consumers served	Taxes paid	+	SSI reduction	+	Alternate program cost	/	TJTC[b] cost	+	Project expenses	=	Taxpayer's B/C index
1979	16	$ 10,408		$ 0.000		$ 33,578		$ 0.000		$ 230,391		0.19
1980	41	53,468		7,482		145,428		21,679		239,013		0.79
1981	59	73,630		45,070		202,578		36,485		209,708		1.30
1982	72	76,314		55,887		244,730		35,867		194,170		1.64
1983	86	88,807		72,557		280,349		58,135		182,652		1.83
1984	99	104,215		100,770		339,340		43,907		174,572		2.49
1985	104	96,027		113,409		344,415		49,149		137,384		2.97
1986[c]	112	88,408		107,628		332,388		52,873		127,271		2.93
Cumulative Total	214	$591,278		$502,804		$1,922,806		$298,096		$1,495,162		1.68

[a] Inflation corrected to first quarter of 1986; discount rate = 5%.
[b] TJTC = targeted job tax credit.
[c] Based on only 10 of 12 months.

Table 4. Consumer benefit-cost analysis[a] year

Year ending June	Consumers served	Gross wages	+	Fringe benefits	/	SSI reduction	+	Foregone sheltered workshop wages	+	Taxes paid	=	Consumer B/C index
1979	16	$ 45,252		$ 6,788		$ 0.000		$ 4,234		$ 10,408		3.55
1980	41	232,469		34,870		7,483		25,466		53,468		3.09
1981	59	320,131		48,020		45,070		37,286		73,630		2.36
1982	72	331,798		49,770		55,887		48,554		76,314		2.11
1983	86	386,119		57,918		72,557		57,137		88,807		2.03
1984	99	453,110		67,966		100,770		77,361		104,215		1.85
1985	104	417,510		62,626		113,409		80,966		96,027		1.65
1986[b]	112	384,385		57,658		107,628		72,787		88,408		1.64
Cumulative Total	214	$2,570,772		$385,616		$502,804		$403,790		$591,278		1.97

[a] Inflation corrected to first quarter of 1986; discount rate = 5%.
[b] Based on only 10 of 12 months.

before supported employment, each of the 104 consumers actually received an average of $1.65 in net income. During the first years of program operation, the consumer benefit-cost ratio was higher and has gradually declined over time. This is primarily because of the decrease in SSI benefits, which accompanies the increase in consumer earnings and fringe benefits. This figure is beginning to show stabilization and, with current Social Security regulations, is unlikely to ever drop below $1.

Earnings Productivity Index

Table 5 lists the earnings productivity index *for each year* of program operation. Gross wages earned are divided by project expenses to find the earnings productivity index. For example, *in 1985 every $1 spent in program costs produced a gain of $3.04 in consumer earnings.* During the first years of program operation, the earnings productivity index was much lower; in 1980 for every $1 spent, earnings were only 97¢. This is because of the higher program costs that are required to initially stabilize individuals in employment. In other words, the number of people maintained over time increases in relationship to the program costs.

Overall, during the 94 months of RRTC operation, government agency/taxpayers realized a benefit of $15,282 per consumer and a cost of $8,171 per consumer. That is, from the taxpayer/government agency perspective, for every $1 expended, $1.87 was accumulated in benefits. From the consumers' perspective, during the 94 months of RRTC operation, an average

benefit of $13,815 was accrued, and additional losses (costs) of $7,000 were realized. For consumers then, for every $1 relinquished (i.e., in taxes, SSI, and workshop earnings), $1.97 was received in increased income.

The results of this analysis would encourage a major redistribution of adult service tax dollars to supported competitive employment programs. This study's method of analysis includes all start-up costs and indicates that over time (94 months in this case), significant gains are predictable for consumer and taxpayer. Assuming that there are significant qualitative benefits of providing SCE, resource management logic alone would support substantial investment in this innovation.

It is indeed rare for consumers and taxpayers alike to prosper financially through the implementation of a social program. The placement of persons with developmental disabilities into nonvocationally oriented day centers without the option of the more integrated SCE service is not optimally beneficial to the consumer or the taxpayer. For a similar or reduced amount of money expended by taxpayers, many adults with severe disabilities can be competitively employed rather than attend segregated day centers. The challenge to social service professionals to provide financially efficient programs to consumers and taxpayers alike is irrefutable. The question remaining is not whether the services *should* be provided, but how to provide them in an efficient and fiscally sound manner.

The next section of this chapter examines ways to fund supported employment.

Table 5. Earnings productivity benefit-cost analysis[a]

Year ending June	Consumers served	Gross wages earned	/	Project expenses	=	Earnings productivity index
1979	16	$ 45,252		$ 230,391		0.20
1980	41	232,469		239,013		0.97
1981	59	320,131		209,708		1.53
1982	72	331,798		194,170		1.71
1983	86	386,119		182,652		2.11
1984	99	453,110		174,572		2.60
1985	104	417,510		137,384		3.04
1986[b]	112	384,385		127,271		3.02
Cumulative Total	214	$2,570,772		$1,495,162		1.72

[a] Inflation corrected to first quarter of 1986, discount rate = 5%.
[b] Based on only 10 of 12 months.

INTERAGENCY FUNDING MODELS FOR SUPPORTED EMPLOYMENT

A major failure of many program initiatives in education and human services has been local and state programs' total dependency on federal grants. When these funds were removed, programming ceased.

In order to ensure successful supported employment initiatives, programs that result in low-quality employment outcomes must be converted to programs that result in high-quality employment outcomes. This can be accomplished by using dollars already present in the system.

If a major premise of supported employment is that existing funds should be redirected into higher-quality employment outcomes, two conditions must be met. First, there must be a viable, on-going funding stream for service provision behind a given consumer. Second, numerous local and/or state agencies will need to share funding resources in order to provide for initial permanent and ongoing employment support.

The establishment of funding mechanisms to better meet the long-term commitment of competitive supported employment requires an analysis of crucial service strategies (Hill, 1988). Those major design strategies associated with SCE address the following:

1. *Where the service is provided*: The service must be provided in the most natural environment possible, and must promote social interactions with nonhandicapped individuals.
2. *When the service is provided*: Services must be provided *at and after* the consumer is placed in the work environment, for so long as the consumer requires assistance.
3. *What type of service is provided*: Staff intervention time must be provided for the consumer, using precision instruction methods, and must be related specifically to the tasks required in the consumer's existing and ongoing environment.

There is a critical distinction under the supported work model between the traditional purchase of *pre*employment services and the use of funds to purchase community-based *post*employment services. Pre-employment services are designed to deal with an unknown environment of the future. The provision of postemployment services allows consumers to be placed in paid settings where training is provided in skills needed for the existing work and living environments. When the focus is on teaching consumers the skills required in existing environments, the validity of the curriculum is maximized and the efficiency of the service system is improved.

Developing Cooperative Agreements

Efforts between agencies can help redistribute funds from low-outcome services to high-outcome services, a major goal of the supported employment initiative. For vocational rehabilitation agencies, this means careful evaluation of the dollars now earmarked for work adjustment, evaluation, and extended sheltered employment, or in other words *pre*employment expenditures, in reference to consumer outcomes. Services that have the greatest positive effect on consumer outcomes such as net income and the achievement of integration and independence must be utilized. To ensure this connection of services to consumer outcomes, measurement of these outcomes must become part of the evaluation of various services.

*Post*employment services, such as job coach services for consumers in paid integrated settings, have been shown to provide immediate and concrete gains in these consumer employment outcomes (Hill et al., 1987). Programs offering alternative adjacent strategies should provide comparable outcome analysis.

Agencies such as the departments of mental health and mental retardation and other day program support agencies need to redistribute a portion of the funds slotted for adult day center and sheltered employment to higher-outcome services for individuals requiring *ongoing* support in paid integrated settings, such as postvocational rehabilitation training and stabilization on the job.

Promoters of supported employment should not advocate *defunding* some organizations while expanding others. Rather, they should aggressively advocate that all organizations that provide service to consumers with disabilities emphasize employment in *paid integrated* settings (i.e., in the regular workplace with non-disabled workers).

The case for reallocating funds is developed here in three sections. First, an enhanced, restructured service system is described. Second, implementation guidelines within the existing constraints of resouces and funding authority are provided. Finally, specific service provision funding issues are addressed.

Service System Enhancement

In 1978, with innovation and expansion monies from the federal government, the Virginia Department of Rehabilitation Services funded Project Employability. This project, implemented by Virginia Commonwealth University, demonstrated that integrated competitive employment for the severely disabled/mentally retarded population is not only possible but attractive to the consumer. In May of 1983 the National Institute of Handicapped Research (NIHR) established the already-mentioned Rehabilitation Research and Training Center (RRTC) at VCU. In July of 1984, the RRTC was approved as a vendor to the Virginia Department of Rehabilitation Services for time-limited community employment services or job-coach training services. In addition, the RRTC facilitated the provision of follow-up and maintenance support by enlisting local community service boards (CSBs), who derive most of their financial support from the Virginia State Department of Mental Health and Mental Retardation and Substance Abuse.

For local program initiators to be effective in making supported employment a reality in their community, three funding sources can be accessed. One source is called discretionary funding. These funds are time-limited and are usually distributed as contracts or grants for specific targeted initiatives. Many federal, state, and private agencies expend "discretionary" dollars for demonstrations in the field. *Discretionary funds unfortunately do not guarantee ongoing commitments from existing established service systems.* Within the existing service system are the other two key funding sources. They are the vocational rehabilitation (VR) system as guaranteed and funded through the Rehabilitation Act of 1973 and amended in 1986 to include supported employment. The third major funding source is state offices for persons with developmental disabilities, mental illness, and problems associated with substance abuse.

Discretionary funding sources are both public and private, and are distributed at the discretion of agencies such as the U. S. Department of Education, Goodwill Industries, and private corporations. The funding they supply may come in the form of gifts, grants, or contracts in response to proposals submitted.

Table 6 briefly outlines potential funding sources for supported employment.

Discretionary money can be one source of seed funding for an agency to begin operation and perhaps sustain itself for 2 to 3 years. But what if discretionary money is not awarded in response to a grant proposal? This does not mean the existing service systems cannot be modified and restructured to begin implementation of supported employment services; the other two sources of funds may be sufficient to begin supported employment services.

The discussion and presentation of the model that follows emphasizes the utilization of continuous funding streams. The model is based on the ongoing development of services in Virginia.

IMPLEMENTATION GUIDELINES: FUNDING TIME-LIMITED AND ONGOING SERVICES UNDER A PROGRAM OF SUPPORTED EMPLOYMENT

Using the expanded array of employment services as described in Chapters 1 and 2, the rehabilitation agency can use case service dollars to support the initial training and stabilization of a person with severe disabilities in an integrated employment setting.

The rehabilitation counselor, when given a wider variety of alternative outcome options (i.e., enclaves, mobile work crews, competitive jobs), is able to increase the quality and success of programming for each individual consumer. The increased potential for job/consumer compatibility results from an expanding number of in-

Table 6. Funding sources for supported employment

Funding source	Agency capability
State developmental disabilities planning council	1. Start-up activities 2. Model supported employment demonstration projects, 3. Training grants, or 4. Evaluation projects
State special or vocational education programs	1. Model demonstration 2. Employment-directed programs for transition-age youth
State vocational rehabilitation	1. Start-up activities 2. Time-limited initial training services 3. Model demonstrations
Joint training partnership act, programs (JTPA), private industry council	1. Job placement 2. Job-site training 3. Follow-along services
State mental health/mental retardation/human resources	1. Start-up activities 2. Stabilization 3. Long-term follow-along employment 4. Model demonstration
Federal Departments of Education, Labor, and Health and Human Sevices	1. Model demonstrations 2. Start-up activities 3. Time-limited funding

tegrated environments and service configurations from which to choose. This enlarged service array is a major avenue to greater integration and pay for persons with severe disabilities.

The proposed model suggests that the state rehabilitation agency provide the resources for the initial site training until the support required for job maintenance levels off and becomes static and the individual is stable, although not completely independent, at the employment site. Additional agencies able to provide funding for supported employment are included in the interagency model.

Vocational Rehabilitation Time-Limited Funding Options

State rehabilitation agencies can finance a time-limited component of supported employment in three ways. The first is to provide the service with their own staff, the second is by vendor fee for services rendered, and the third is by providing a contract for the service.

Whichever method is used, it should require extensive rehabilitation counselor involvement. The rehabilitation counselor can take the lead in ensuring services for job placement, initial training, and intervention toward consumer stabilization. Although such a program tends to be extended, it is still time-limited. Once a partic-

ipant *stabilizes*, that is, requires a consistent level of staff intervention time, he or she would then require follow-along services; the vocational rehabilitation case would be closed after it had been transferred to a cooperating, continuous funding follow-up and maintenance agency such as a department of mental health and mental retardation or community service board.

Reopening a vocational rehabilitation case would be no different than for other rehabilitation consumers. For example, a consumer who becomes unemployed may need additional placement and training at a new employment setting. As mentioned previously, the case is only closed with respect to time-limited employment. Follow-up and maintenance services would continue through the on-going service agency.

Ongoing Follow-Along/Follow-Up Services

A major component in the success of integrated employment for persons with severe disabilities is the long-term follow-up provided in the on-going service phase. For this to happen, interagency cooperation is imperative.

Public and private agencies, which provide the funding for day activity programs and workshops, currently supply long-term follow-along services to disabled persons who participate. Although these services are often restricted to segregated settings, such agencies have a clear precedent for funding long-term follow-along services and could well apply the funding to extended support services in integrated community employment settings. Many ongoing service agencies have begun to provide integrated services. Vocational rehabilitation agencies have a mandate to support these efforts financially. Cooperative efforts then can become less expensive for all members of the cooperative.

If state rehabilitation agencies withdraw at the end of time-limited service phases, other state or local agencies must provide the long-term follow-up support essential to the success of the consumer. Again, these services can range from extensive and ongoing interventions to those that are only minimal and infrequent, depending on the consumer. In any case, individuals requiring a high degree of job coach intervention would likely be attending a day program if they were not employed. What is proposed here is that funds for day programming or a portion of these monies be used for continuous service in integrated employment settings. Developmental disability programs, mental health/mental retardation departments, and other social service agencies are electing to redesign their service structure to accommodate the new federal initiative to provide ongoing supported employment services (*Federal Register*, 1984).

Interagency Case Management

Interagency staffing for consumers of supported employment services potentially includes a consumer and/or consumer advocate, the rehabilitation counselor, personnel representing the agency to provide the ongoing services, and any potential vendor from the array of local employment service organizations. Representatives of the various agencies coordinate transfer of service and/or financing responsibilities among agencies, based upon a cooperative agreement. The follow-up and maintenance agency monitors the individual participant's job placement and progress. Ample prior notice is given of the anticipated date of the termination of time-lim-

ited services, and all parties should agree to the process of transfer from time-limited to ongoing employment services. Written agreements are likely to be necessary to ensure appropriate cooperation.

The key person in the *initial* success of this model is the rehabilitation counselor. The counselor must decide whether to purchase services for a given consumer, what the nature of the services will be, and determine when a consumer is stabilized in order to transfer him or her to ongoing funding and monitoring of the case. These decisions are based on the best evaluation data at the counselor's disposal. To assist the counselor in these decisions, outcome measures should be provided by the service providers. These measures may include written evaluations by employers; reports on amount of intervention time needed and for what targeted behaviors; data from direct observational assessment; reports of any critical incidents on the job site; consumer progress data on skill acquisition and production rate; wages earned; hours worked; and level of social presence and participation. Additional outcomes may need identification at the local implementation level.

An interagency team as implemented in Virginia suggests that change in a participant's status from time-limited to ongoing services be based on the stabilization of staff time needed to keep the consumer employed. When the staff time required to maintain persons in their positions is moving from intensive to a stabilized amount of time, it is considered part of the time-limited service component. Once the staff intervention time stabilizes, the consumer enters the *ongoing follow-up/maintenance service* phase. This is the dividing line for shifting funding responsibility to another agency and for ending service provision from the state vocational rehabilitation agency to that of a long-term state or local agency for follow-along and maintenance services. Figure 1 illustrates this model process.

Cooperative agreements drawn up among agencies attempting to implement this model must develop their own specific guidelines for funding. The actual length of the stabilization period may vary for individual consumers. Employer satisfaction with the client's job perfor-

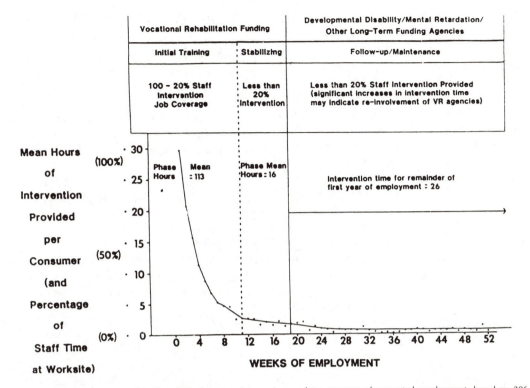

Figure 1. An interagency model: Time-limited to on-going services under a program of supported employment, based on 206 consumers, 315 positions. (Source: Rehabilitation Research and Training Center, May, 1978 to December, 1985.) (*Note*: Researchers are cautioned that the intervention time presented in this graph represents averages, and considerable variability exists among individual consumers. These figures should in no way be used as cut-off scores for success or upper limits for authorizing services.)

mance, based in part on a commitment to ongoing job-coach support, is a key consideration in identifying the timing for a VR case closure. Funding transfer guidelines will require local adjustment and agreement between agencies. The general guidelines presented here are suggestions for interagency cooperation when making individual site placements.

The ongoing follow-along component of this model is equally as critical for employment success. The retention-oriented phase has been underemphasized in the past and has contributed to the current inadequate service system. Ironically, this undersupported component is the *least expensive* in terms of staff time and yet *most productive* in terms of job duration and retention (Hill & Wehman, 1983). The amount of staff intervention required to maintain a person in a job is much less than the time required in initial training on a daily basis. Services in this phase must, however, continue indefinitely based upon the consumer's need. Funding for this phase is provided by agencies such as the local and state departments of mental health and mental retardation, state and local developmental disability agencies, and any other organizations that typically support ongoing day programs.

INTERAGENCY RATIO OF SUPPORT SHIFTS

As one agency (Department of Rehabilitative Services [DRS] in Virginia's case) stabilizes consumers in integrated employment settings, the follow-along costs for other agencies will expand as the pool of persons for stabilized integrated employment settings is increased. For example, as depicted in Table 7, in the first 12 months the funding ratio might be 80% VR and 20% from a local community service board (CSB) or other cooperating long-term service organization. The funding ratio for the second year might be DRS 66% and cooperating CSB 34%. In the third year, given an estimated two placements per month and a 65% success rate, the funding ratio would be DRS 56% and cooperating CSB 44%. Proportionately, VR will contribute a smaller portion of the funds for supported employment in each successive year. This ratio will continue to shift indefinitely until all follow-along cases for whom supported employment is appropriate have been accommodated, assuming ongoing movement of persons with severe disabilities from segregated settings into integrated work. Table 7 depicts this shifting ratio and estimates the persons placed and maintained based on the experiences of service providers in Virginia. In addition, the estimated total cost is provided for each agency (inflation and cost of living held constant). From vocational rehabilitation's perspective, the vocational rehabilitation agency uses its dollars to bring other agencies into employment initiatives. From the ongoing agencies' perspective, vocational rehabilitation assists with the initial phases of providing a more normalized life for consumers. It should be apparent that in this case cooperation is beneficial to all parties.

FINANCIAL

Rate-Setting Structure

An appropriate method for funding and/or monitoring services of community-based service providers must be established, especially if private profit or nonprofit vendors are utilized. Community-based operations are dependent on the employer's willingness to allow training "on site"; also, on-site training is likely to vary greatly in response to employment and consumer needs. Thus, an alternative to the traditional "daily rate" payment/monitoring structure is suggested.

Staff Intervention Time/Units of Service

Since consumers in supported employment programs do not attend a standard "day" program, the service model should be measured in accumulated staff intervention time.

Intervention time can be expected to differ according to the local employment situation, the number of hours per week the consumer works, and the degree of compatibility of the client to the job.

An intervention time recording sheet used by vendors of SCE in Virginia is provided in Appendix A.

Vocational Rehabilitation Financing Options

A vocational rehabilitation agency can provide for SCE in three basic ways, as follows:

1. VR contracts for the service. A predetermined level of funding is established and given in regular payments to a provider of SCE; the provider's expenditures would be accounted for at the end of the contract.
2. A provider is authorized to provide service to consumers, after which reimbursement is paid to the provider (a sample hourly rate accounting formula is provided in Appendix B).
3. The VR agency's own staff can offer the job-coaching service for initial training to stabilization.

Each of these methods has advantages and disadvantages, as described next.

Contract for Service   There are numerous advantages to using a contract-for-service approach. These include:

Table 7. Example of shifting interagency support (estimated interagency funding levels)[a]

	Vocational rehabilitation agency			DMHMR, DD or comparable agency [b]		
Year	% total funding	# persons placed	Cost[c]	% funding	# persons followed	Cost[c]
1	80	15–30	$80,000	20	14	$ 20,000
2	66	15–30	80,000	34	28	40,000
3	57	15–30	80,000	43	42	60,000
4	50	15–30	80,000	50	56	80,000
5	44	15–30	$80,000	56	70	$100,000

[a] Based on experiences of service providers in Virginia, 1982–1987. See text for additional explanation of data.
[b] Any organization that provides follow-along funds can be considered here under "comparable" (e.g., United Way, state legislative set-aside funds, Association for Retarded Citizens).
[c] Inflation and cost of living are held constant.

1. Provides more security to provider agency, reducing costly staff turnover and promoting organizational growth.
2. Individual rehabilitation counselors are less responsible for the ongoing funding needs of a provider.
3. The level of service is predictable; the provider's capacity for offering a service is predetermined.
4. In a contract for service, individual rehabilitation counselors would spend less time dealing with red tape and paperwork.
5. Retention rates for consumers may be higher when job coaches have more flexibility and freedom to provide service "as necessary."
6. There is likely to be less stress on and between providers and the rehabilitation counselor when funding is less of an issue in the relationship.

Disadvantages include:

1. Consumer outcomes may be reviewed infrequently and are prone to aggregate data review instead of individual consumer analysis.
2. Costs for individual consumers are hard or impossible to determine.
3. If increased service capacity is needed, a new contract would have to be negotiated.

In sum, several recommendations can be drawn from this discussion. First, in a contract, specifics on services provided to consumers should be well documented. Second, review of provider activities should be frequent and oriented around individual consumer outcomes. Third, recording and submission of intervention time or other unit of service provided to the individual consumer should be required. Finally, future contracts should be given to providers based on their ability to meet expected outcomes.

Reimbursement Method There are also several advantages to the hourly or daily reimbursement method of payments. These include:

1. Funds expended can be easily tracked to individual clients.
2. Authorizations and reauthorizations by rehabilitation counselors provide a regular forum for communication with the provider.

3. The vocational rehabilitation agency is not committed to expending funds except in small increments (i.e., approving a vendor for reimbursement requires much less risk than contracting large sums of money to a provider).
4. Funding can be increased or decreased according to the VR agency's need for service.

Disadvantages include:

1. The provider has little security and may not be able to predict the yearly level of funding, contributing to a less stable organization.
2. Providers are financially dependent on the rehabilitation counselor's commitment to individual consumers.
3. Each authorization from VR counselors would require negotiation, increasing the costs or amount of time not directly related to the consumer's employment training needs.
4. During the start-up activities, actual costs cannot be met by hourly rate reimbursements based on consumer-specific intervention time.

Recommendations regarding this mode of payment include, first, that cost reimbursement during start-up activities should not be based on an estimated hourly rate; actual costs should be identified and provided. Once intervention time stabilizes and becomes predictable, the hourly rate reimbursement method can be instituted. Second, sufficient preauthorization commitments by the VR counselor are necessary to ensure that the consumer receives a situational screening and full-time training coverage at the job site during the critical first weeks. Third, and finally, individual consumer requirements will fluctuate, and wide variations in needed staff time should be expected. Additional authorizations of needed staff time should be provided as required.

VR Staff Provides Job Coach Service
Advantages of using the VR staff include:

1. The VR agency is in direct control of the initial service activity provided to consum-

ers, and stabilization is determined by VR staff.

2. The capacity for service is predictable and predetermined by the level of staffing for these positions.
3. Individual job-coach security is increased.

Disadvantages include:

1. The transfer of funding for post–VR services would require different staff to follow the consumer than those who provided the initial training.
2. Geographical or logistical problems may prevent efficient operation.

Recommendations regarding this method of payment include:

1. Job-coach staff should be assigned to consumer-specific placement and postplacement activities only. The level of intervention should be based on consumer and employer need, rather than job-coach case-load levels.
2. The pay and status of the job-coach staff should be on a par with that of the rehabilitation counselor. The job-coach position requires a high degree of professionalism and specialized skill.

Whatever method is selected, providers must receive real cost support. All parties benefit from properly funded programs, and organizational success is dependent on fiscally sound policies.

In addition, regardless of the cost and service accounting method, it is recommended that an employment situational assessment and initial training period be authorized by the vocational rehabilitation counselor to allow for immediate placement should an appropriate position be identified. Authorizations should be generous in the first critical weeks after job placement to ensure full support of the consumer. Individual requirements will fluctuate, and should be monitored closely. Reauthorization of needed staff time can be negotiated at regular intervals. The authorization procedure should furthermore guarantee counselor/case manager interaction and ongoing communication regarding consumer progress.

The costs paid per individual take into account only successful job retention. Thus, intervention hours are accumulated and paid for consumers who continue to work. As a consequence, funds for supported employment can only be spent on endeavors that are currently succeeding.

Establishing an appropriate amount for contracts to provide time-limited and ongoing services can be done by calculating the annual costs per job coach, projecting the number of direct service staff needed to accommodate persons placed and retained in the employment settings, and then multiplying the number of direct service staff needed by the annual staff cost. Again, it must be emphasized that this figure should include all costs, supervision, travel, office supplies, office space, telephone salary, fringe benefits, and other related costs.

SUMMARY

This chapter has reviewed problems associated with the current employment service system for persons with severe disabilities and has recommended provision of an expanded array of services. Emphasis has been placed on interagency cooperation and the redistribution of existing resources to implement time-limited and ongoing services under a program of supported employment.

The key requirements for improving employment services for persons with severe disabilities are:

1. Establishing mechanisms for agencies to reallocate funds to enhance employment outcomes for persons with disabilities and fostering an array of employment services that are more responsive to individual needs.
2. Providing ongoing consumer support at employment sites, based on the consumer's need for intervention to retain employment.
3. Effecting smooth transition of responsibility for consumers support from time-limited service provided by the state vocational rehabilitation agency to ongoing support from agencies that traditionally provide supported day activity programs and sheltered workshops.

4. Establishing appropriate intervention service rates for service providers and promoting an appropriate financial accounting system that delineates specific costs for each participant.

5. Evaluating programs by reviewing their impact on consumer outcomes such as net income, level of independence, and level of social presence and participation with persons without disabilities.

REFERENCES

Conley, R. W. (1973). *The economics of mental retardation*. Baltimore: Johns Hopkins University Press.

Elder, J. (1984). Job opportunities for developmentally disabled people. *American Rehabilitation, 10*(2), 26–30.

Federal Register. (1984, September 25). *Employment of handicapped clients in sheltered workshops*. Report 98-1074, Chapter V, Part 525, Section 102[11][F], 17509. Washington, DC: U.S. Government Printing Office.

Hill, M. L. (1988). *Interagency vendorization: Expanding supported employment services*. Richmond: Virginia Commonwealth University and Virginia Department of Mental Health, Mental Retardation, and Substance Abuse Services.

Hill, M., Banks, P., Handrich, R., Wehman, P., Hill, J., & Shafer, M. (1987). Benefit cost analysis of supported competitive employment for persons with mental retardation. *Research in Developmental Disabilities, 8* (1), 71–89.

Hill, M. L., & Wehman, P. H. (1983). Cost benefit analysis of placing moderately and severely handicapped individuals into competitive employment. *Journal for the Association of the Severely Handicapped, 8*, 30–38.

Kakalik, J. S., Ferry, W. S., Thomas, M. A., & Carney, M. F. (1981). *The cost of special education*. Santa Monica CA: RAMP. Prepared for the U.S. Department of Education.

Lippitt, G., Langseth, P., & Mossop, J. (1986). *Implementing organizational change*. San Franscisco. Jossey-Bass.

Noble, J. (1985,). *The benefits and costs of supported employment and impediments to its expansion*. Paper presented at the Policy Seminar on Supported Employment, Virginia Institute for Develomental Disabilities, Richmond.

O'Neill & Associates. (1984). *Competitive employment summary update of placements made from adult day programs*. Seattle: State of Washington Office of Developmental Disabilities.

Pechman, J., & Okner, B. (1974). *Who bears the tax burden?* Washington, DC: Brookings Institute.

PL 98-527. Developmental Disabilities Act Amendment of 1984. *Federal Register, 53*(4), May 4, 1988.

Rusch, F. R. (ed.). (1986). *Competitive employment issues and strategies*. Baltimore: Paul H. Brookes Publishing Co.

Thornton, C. (1985). Benefit-cost analysis of social programs. In R. H. Bruininks & K. C. Lakin (Eds.), *Living and learning in the least restrictive environment*. Baltimore: Paul H. Brookes Publishing Co.

U.S. Department of Commerce. (1986). *Survey of current business*. Washington, DC: U.S. Department of Commerce, Bureau of Economic Analysis.

U.S. Department of Labor. (1980). *Employee compensation in private non-farm economy, 1977* (pp. 80–85). Washington, DC: U.S. Department of Labor, Bureau of Labor Statistics Summary.

Wehman, P., & Hill, J. (Eds.). (1985). *Competitive employment for persons with mental retardation: From research to practice* (Vol. 1). Richmond: Virginia Commonwealth University, Rehabilitation Research and Training Center.

Will, M. C. (1984). *Supported employment for adults with severe disabilities: An OSERS program initiative*. Washington, DC: U.S. Department of Education.

Appendix A

Consumer-Specific Intervention Time Recording Sheet

Directions for completing form follow.

Consumer's name: _____   Staff member's name: _____

SSN: __ __ __/ __ __/ __ __ __ __   ID code: _____

Recording period: __ __/__ __   Case managers; DRS:_____
             mo. yr.

MHMR: _____

Date (month/day)							
Intervention Time Directly Related To Job-Skills Training (hour:minutes) 1. Active (consumer and job coordinator at job site)							
2. Inactive (between periods of active intervention)							
Intervention Time Indirectly Related To Job Skills Training (hours:minutes) 1. Travel/transport							
2. Consumer training							
3. Program development (task analysis and behavioral and intervention programs)							
4. Direct employment advocacy (worksite related, includes consumer-specific job development)							
5. Indirect employment advocacy (nonworksite related)							

Date (month/day)							
6. Screening and evaluation (screening consumer for service eligibility)							
TOTAL (daily)							

General Definitions

Enter name and Social Security number (SSN), or affix preprinted label, of the consumer in the space provided. Also enter the name and I.D. number of the employment specialist who actually provided the intervention time recorded on this sheet.

Intervention Time Directly
Related to Job-Skills Training

1. Time active: Time at job site actually spent working with consumer, including active observation. Includes *anything done to actively train the consumer.*

2. Time inactive: Time spent on the job site between periods of active intervention. This is time during which *you have removed yourself from active involvement with and/or active observation of the consumer.*

Intervention Time Indirectly
Related to Job-Skills Training

1. Travel/transport: Time used in traveling to a job site, to a meeting *about a consumer, to the consumer's home, or in transporting a consumer anywhere.*

2. Consumer training: Time spent *training the consumer in other than directly related job skills* while he or she is *not at work.* Examples are: money handling, grooming, counseling, bus training, family matters, and so forth.

3. Consumer program development: This is time spent developing appropriate instructional plans (*Writing task analyses and behavioral intervention programs*). Consumer-specific job development is *not* included here.

4. Direct employment advocacy: Time spent *advocating* for the consumer *with job site personnel for purposes directly related to employment.* These persons would include *employers, supervisors, coworkers, and customers.* Consumer-specific job development is also included here.

5. Indirect employment advocacy: Time spent *advocating with persons not directly affiliated with the employment site.* These persons would include *bus drivers, school personnel, landlords, case managers, bank personnel, parents, and so forth.*

6. Screening/evaluation: Time spent *screening consumer referrals* to determine eligibility for services or evaluating eligible consumers. Any time spent analyzing any information relevant to a consumer's employment potential is included here. The following, when *done for purposes of screening or evaluation would be included here: reviewing consumer records; consumer interview; communication with parents/ guardians or involved agencies; observation of consumer in real or simulated work settings.*

Note: If intervention indirectly related to job-skills training (for example, calling the employer of another consumer, or program development) is performed while inactive on the job site, *do not* record the time in both places, even if it was for two different consumers. Record the time as indirectly related to job-skills training (in the appropriate category), rather than inactive time directly related to job-skills training, even though you are at the job site.

Appendix B

Sample Hourly Rate Accounting Formula

HOURLY UNIT RATE COMPUTATION FOR TIME-LIMITED AND ONGOING SERVICES UNDER A PROGRAM OF SUPPORTED EMPLOYMENT (1/87)

The following rate strategy was developed in 1984 by the RRTC (Hill, 1988) to provide an appropriate means for providers of competitive supported employment to recover the costs of delivering service. The actual dollars reported in the formula are those used in the 1987 contract negotiation with the Virginia Department of Rehabilitative Services (DRS). In this program individual consumer intervention needs vary greatly and are dependent on the specific assets and barriers associated with each consumer and each employment position. That is, job/consumer compatibility varies and thus intervention levels also vary accordingly. It is suggested that an *hourly* service unit for intervention is appropriate for tracking the services provided to a consumer by a job coach.

There are two basic ways that a unit of service can be used to financially support a provider of "service." Units can be authorized by the service purchaser for individual consumers, or a *contract* for service can be negotiated for a group of consumers (preagreed aggregate of service units).

The formula below is an estimate of component costs for an hourly unit of service. Annual budget extrapolations are made in the final summary table. The hourly unit of service system requires close monitoring to ensure appropriate financial support to service providers.

The following is an itemized breakdown of component costs within the unit rate that are necessary to operate an agency providing competitive supported employment.

Personnel

Direct service name/position	Hrs. per week/full-time equivalent	Salary ($)	Fringe benefits (%)	Hourly rate ($)	Total ($)
	40/1	18,300	27	11.17	23,241
	40/1	18,300	27	11.17	23,241
	40/1	18,300	27	11.17	23,241
	40/1	18,300	27	11.17	23,241
	40/1	18,300	27	11.17	23,241
	40/1	18,300	27	11.17	23,241
	40/1	18,300	27	11.17	23,241
	40/1	20,020	27	12.22	25,425
	40/1	21,889	27	13.36	27,799
	20/.5	8,000	—	—	8,000
	20/.5	8,000	—	—	8,000
	40/1	8.43 per hr.	7.05	9.08	16,704
Total					248,615

Developed by Mark Hill, director of Information Systems, Rehabilitation Research and Training Center, Virginia Commonwealth University.

Mean Job Coach (JC) Yearly cost = Total/Number of job coaches (FTE): $248,615. / 11 = $22,601

In Hill's formula it is estimated that 65% of a job coach's time can be spent directly "intervening" with consumers. When annual, sick, and holiday leave is considered, the annual available hours of intervention is 1,196. The formula for computing this follows:

(52 − 6 weeks = 46 weeks available to provide intervention per job coach) (2 weeks for annual leave, 2 weeks for sick leave, and 2 weeks for holiday leave) (46 × 40-hr wk. = 1,840 × 65% time = 1,196 staff hours available for client-specific intervention time)

Direct service personnel component cost of hourly rate = Mean JC cost/mean intervention hours:

$$\$22,601/1,196 \text{ hrs.} = \$18.90$$

Although the RRTC estimates that 65% of a job coach's work time can be spent intervening, startup lag time, lack of referrals, and other varying conditions may prevent this level of reimbursement from occurring. If a provider agency is not provided reimbursement for 65% of the direct service staff's time, there will be insufficient funds for that agency to operate. Procedures for providing supplemental funding to cover actual costs are discussed in a 1986 research report from the Stout Vocational Rehabilitation Institute, University of Wisconsin, titled: *Fee for Services: Principles and Practices Among State Vocational Rehabilitation Agencies and Facilities* (Menomonie, WI 54751).

Nondirect Service Support Personnel

Administration

Principal investigator	5% time, wage, and fringe =	$ 2,337
Employment services division director	50% time, wage, and fringe =	21,590
ESD assistant director	60% time, wage, and fringe =	17,907
Bookkeeper	15% time, wage, and fringe =	3,200
Clerical/data entry	100% time, wage, and fringe =	19,050
Total nondirect personnel	=	$64,084

Component cost of hourly rate = Total/number of JCs/mean intervention hours:
$$\$64,084./11 \text{ JCs}/1,196 = \$4.87$$

Occupancy Costs

Rent, utilities, and maintenance for all project staff is used to calculate occupancy cost.
13.65 persons in vendor services (total staff FTE)
13.65 × $840 (estimate per person) = 11,466 rent, utilities, and maintenance

$$\$11,466/11 \text{ JCs} = \$1,042.$$

Occupancy component cost of hourly rate = JC mean cost/mean intervention hours

$$\$1,042/1,196 = \$0.87$$

Support Costs

Telephone per person	$ 220
Postage per person	267
Office supplies per person	166
Technical assistance	1,455
Total	$2,108

Support component cost of hourly rate = Total/Mean intervention hours:

$$\$2,108/1,196 = \$1.76$$

Transportation Costs

Average miles per JC = 252 miles @ .205 per mile = $51.66
51.66 × 12 = $619.92 est. yearly average
Transportation component cost of hourly rate = Mean travel/mean intervention hours:
$$\$619.92/1,196 = \$0.52$$

Summary Hourly Rate Components

Component type	% of hourly rate	Component rate ($)
Personnel (88%)		
Direct service...................................	70%	18.90
Nondirect service............................	18%	4.87
Occupancy.....................................	3%	0.87
Support costs	7%	1.76
Transportation	2%	0.52
Totals		Hourly 26.92
Total units of service (annual) available per direct service staff...		1,196 Hours of intervention

Chapter 4

Supported Employment in Perspective

Traditions in the Federal-State Vocational Rehabilitation System

Michael S. Shafer

An alliance between the state and federal levels of government has jointly operated programs to rehabilitate American citizens since 1918. The vocational rehabilitation system in this country was originally developed to maintain a healthy and productive labor force; employees who became disabled on the job and veterans who were disabled at war were the original recipients of services. Throughout the ensuing years the system has repeatedly been called upon to expand its range of clientele and serve persons experiencing chronic disabling conditions. Legislative charges to extend services to persons with severely handicapping conditions have been most notable in the past 15 years as the nation has depopulated its institutions for persons with mental retardation and mental illness. The displacement from institutions of thousands of individuals with handicaps has put a tremendous strain upon ill-operated and poorly coordinated community services such as residential, educational, day, and vocational services.

The responsiveness of the vocational rehabilitation system to the needs of persons with severe handicaps who were deinstitutionalized has received mixed reviews. While it may be said that the system at least has attempted to respond to the needs of these individuals (cf., Vocational Rehabilitation Act of 1973, as amended), the vast majority of persons with severe handicaps continue to go unserved by the system (Bellamy, Rhodes, & Albin, 1986). The failure to more adequately serve persons with severe handicaps reflects an uneven and often inconsistent policy regarding rehabilitation. While the system has been repeatedly instructed to serve more persons with severely handicapping conditions, it has rarely been authorized to provide the services that these individuals have required.

The degree to which supported employment will be accepted by the federal-state rehabilitation system represents a critical issue. This new service contrasts sharply with the traditional values and philosophy of the federal-state system. This chapter discusses the provisions of the 1986 amendments of the Vocational Rehabilitation Act (PL 99-506) in relation to the historical traditions of the public rehabilitation system.

Preparation of this chapter was supported by Grant Nos. GO28301124 and GO8430106 from the National Institute of Disability and Rehabilitation Research, U.S. Department of Education. The opinions expressed in this chapter are those of the author, and no official endorsement by the department should be inferred. Appreciation is extended to Fred Orelove and Jane Everson for comments made on an earlier draft of this chapter.

LEGISLATIVE HISTORY OF FEDERAL VOCATIONAL REHABILITATION SERVICES

Legislative Enactments of 1920 and 1943

As previously mentioned, the legislative history of vocational rehabilitation (VR) services for citizens with disabilities spans approximately 70 years. Federally sponsored rehabilitative services for World War I veterans were initially authorized in 1918. Services to nonmilitary persons with disabilities were first authorized in 1920 with the passage of the Smith-Fess Act (Braddock, 1987). This act authorized rehabilitative services only for persons with physical handicaps.

In 1943, the Barden-LaFollette Act extended the reimbursement arrangement for services to persons with mental illness and mental retardation as well (LaVor, 1975). However, the number of persons with mental handicaps who received rehabilitative services was extremely small with regard to the total population of persons with mental handicaps as well as the total number of persons served under the VR system. In 1945, 106 persons with mental retardation were served by the VR system, representing less than 1% of the entire case load for that fiscal year (Braddock, 1987). During this same time, an estimated 1.5 million people experienced handicapping conditions severe enough to affect their employment (Wright, 1980).

Hill-Burton Act of 1954

The Rehabilitation Act Amendments of 1954, also known as the Hill-Burton Act, divided the U.S. Office of Vocational Rehabilitation into three separate funding streams: Basic State Grant Programs, Extension and Improvement Programs, and Special Projects. The Basic State Grant Program represented the largest funding stream and provided for the basic services that were authorized through the act. Authorized services provided under this program were reimbursed by the federal government at 75% of the service costs.

The amendments of 1954 allowed research, training, and demonstration programs to help upgrade the total scope of the rehabilitation system (LaVor, 1975). Extension and Improve-ment grants provided revenue for the construction and maintenance of rehabilitation facilities that were operated by the states and their service providers. These grants represented the first authorization by the federal government to pay directly for the construction of rehabilitation facilities such as sheltered workshops and evaluation and work activity centers (Wright, 1980). The basic services that states were authorized to provide were supplemented by 41 grants and contracts between 1955 and 1957 that were authorized by Special Projects (Braddock, 1987). These projects were indicative of a new emphasis upon service innovation and expansion that was designed to increase the number of persons served by the system, and signaled the initiation of extensive federal financial assistance for the provision of vocational services.

Public Law 89–333

The enactment of Public Law 89-333 in 1965 provided authorization for extended evaluation of the rehabilitation potential of clients for whom clear determination of eligibility could not be determined. This authorization allowed for funded evaluations of up to 18 months, and would become a common avenue for persons with developmental disabilities to receive rehabilitative services. In addition, the 1965 amendments provided federal funds to improve and expand local sheltered workshop facilities, furthering a workshop orientation that permeated service considerations for persons with developmental disabilities or severe handicaps.

Rehabilitation Act of 1973

The passage of the Vocational Rehabilitation Act of 1973 (PL 93-112) represented a major rewrite of the entire federal statute authorizing rehabilitative services. This act introduced a number of key concepts regarding equal opportunity and nondiscrimination for persons with disabilities. In particular, the act recognized that most persons with severely handicapping conditions were unserved by the federal-state rehabilitation system or other federally supported agencies. The act expressly forbade discrimination on the basis of handicapping conditions in employment and in the delivery of federally supported services. Section 503 required government contractors to institute affirmative action plans to enhance recruitment and employment of qualified workers who were handicapped. This section also provided specific administrative and legal remedies for workers who had experienced discrimination in the workplace. Section 504 prohibited discrimination on the basis of handicap by any agency in receipt of federal financial assistance. This section specifically stated:

No otherwise qualified handicapped individual in the United States, as defined in section 7(6) shall, solely by reason of his/her handicap, be excluded from participation in, be denied the benefits of, or be subject to discrimination under any program or activity receiving federal financial assistance. (29 USC 794).

Collectively, these two statutes have resulted in more controversy and judicial action than any other part of the act. As a direct consequence of Section 504, the Architectural and Transportation Barriers Compliance Board was created to assure that the construction and design of federally financed buildings and transportation systems did not discriminate against people with handicaps.

The 1973 act also required states to give priority to services for people with severe handicaps, who frequently had been denied services in the past. Ironically, the same act that contained Section 504 and required states to serve more severely handicapped people continued to legitimize service denial procedures. The act required all applicants to be determined to be employable prior to the provision of services. Employability was defined as:

a determination that the provision of vocational rehabilitation services is likely to enable an individual to enter or retain employment consistent with his or her capacities and abilities in the competitive labor market; the practice of a profession; self-employment; homemaking; farm or family work (including work for which payment is inkind rather than in cash); sheltered employment; and other gainful activity. (29 U.S.C. 706(7)).

The method by which employability was determined relied upon projective techniques and psychometric procedures developed for use with less impaired populations (Fry, 1986). The process of eligibility typically resulted in service denial for persons who were severely handicapped and who failed to display any employ-

ment potential as a result of these evaluations (Whitehead, 1981).

In spite of the shortcomings of the 1973 act, the mandate for individualized written rehabilitation programs (IWRP) represented a significant breakthrough in the delivery of more appropriate services. Such programs were to be jointly developed by a rehabilitation counselor and the client and were to provide: 1) a statement of the long-range rehabilitation goals for the individual and intermediate rehabilitation objectives related to the attainment of such goals; 2) a statement of the specific rehabilitation services to be provided; 3) a projected date for the inititiation and expected duration of services; and 4) objective criteria and evaluation procedures.

The requirement of IWRPs had a significant effect on the evolution of rehabilitative services for three essential reasons. First, the IWRP provided some degree of accountability for evaluating the services provided to an individual. Previously, there had been limited ability to monitor or assess services. Second, the IWRP reoriented the direction of service delivery so that the client became a "team member" in the rehabilitation planning and delivery process, with specific procedural rights and responsibilities. The act provided for client input in the formulation of a rehabilitation plan as well as in the revision or alteration of that plan. Third, the IWRP was representative of a basic philosophical shift from a medical to an educational service orientation.

Unquestionably, the 1973 act embodied the most sweeping changes in the federal-state rehabilitation system since its inception in 1918. With these amendments, Congress clearly specified the legislative intent to serve people with severe disabilities. The former executive chairman of the National Rehabilitation Association remarked that "in almost every major section of the Act, including sections dealing with research, special projects, and training of rehabilitation personnel, expansion and improvement of services for severely handicapped individuals are stated among the objectives of such programs" (Whitten, 1974, p. 2). Unfortunately, the act failed to authorize any additional programs to serve severely handicapped individuals

(Wright, 1980). Furthermore, the eligibility process continued to require a determination that full-time competitive employment was within the abilities of the applicant. As a result, the vast majority of persons identified as severely handicapped continued to be excluded from vocational rehabilitation services because they did not display the potential to benefit from the services authorized.

Rehabilitation Act Amendments of 1978

The passage of the Rehabilitation, Comprehensive Services, and Developmental Disabilities Amendments of 1978 (PL 95-602) constituted the first major attempt to serve persons with severe handicaps. These amendments authorized independent living services to persons with severe handicaps and clarified the legislative intent of the term *severely handicapped* by using a more functional definition.

Severely Handicapped Definition   The amendments of 1978 identified an individual with severe handicaps as one:

(1) who has a severe physical or mental disability which seriously limits one or more functional capacities (mobility, communication, self-care, self-direction, work tolerance, or work skills) in terms of employability; and,

(2) whose vocational rehabilitation can be expected to require multiple services over an extended period of time; and

(3) who has one or more physical or mental disabilities resulting from amputation, arthritis, blindness, cancer, cerebral palsy, cystic fibrosis, deafness, heart disease, hemiplegias, hemophilia, respiratory or pulmonary dysfunction, mental retardation, mental illness, multiple sclerosis, muscular dystrophy, musculo-skeletal disorders, neurological disorders (including stroke and epilepsy), paraplegia, quadriplegia, and other spinal conditions, sickle cell anemia, specific learning disability, and end stage renal disease, or another disability or combination of disabilities determined on the basis of an evaluation of rehabilitation potential to cause comparable substantial functional limitation. (*Federal Register*, January 19, 1981, pp. 5526)

This definition emphasized the extended service needs of persons with severe handicaps to achieve a rehabilitation outcome. In addition, the definition represented an initial shift toward a more functional approach of identifying handicapping conditions and away from the categorical strategies employed in the past.

Independent Living Programs   The authorization for independent living programs may be viewed as the first mandate to provide additional services to persons failing to meet the eligibility criteria of the Basic State Grant Program. These services were to be directed toward "individuals who in all likelihood would never become wage earners" (Wright, 1980, p. 154). At long last, enabling legislation was authorized to increase the range of service options available to severely handicapped individuals. These services had originally been proposed in the 1973 rewrite of the Vocational Rehabilitation Act, but were ultimately deleted, owing to budgetary concerns and the threat of a veto from the White House. In fact, the National Rehabilitation Association had originally lobbied in 1965 for the provision of independent living services for persons not meeting eligibility criteria (Whitten, 1966). The authorization for these services was accomplished by the addition of Title 7 to the act, which provided separate funding for comprehensive services of independent living, including formation of state independent living councils, funding for independent living centers, and independent living programs for older blind individuals. Independent Living Services, as defined by the amendments of 1978, meant:

Any appropriate vocational rehabilitation service (as defined by Title I of this Act) and any other service that will enhance the ability of a handicapped individual to live independently and function within his family and community and, if appropriate, secure and maintain appropriate employment. Such services may include any of the following: counseling services, including psychological, psychotherapeutic, and related services; housing incidental to the purpose of this section (including appropriate accommodations and modification of any space to serve handicapped individuals); appropriate job placement services; transportation; attendant care; physical rehabilitation; therapeutic treatment; needed prostheses and other appliances and devices; health maintenance; recreational activities; services for children of preschool age, including physical therapy, development of language and communication skills and child development services; and appropriate preventive services to decrease the needs of individuals assisted under the program for similar services in the future. (29 USC 796a)

These provisions specified a basic reorientation in the services to be provided and the clientele to be served by the system. Individuals of all ages were appropriate consumers of services under this part of the act and were granted access to services not necessarily related to the attainment of a vocational outcome. Furthermore, access to these services was not contingent upon the determination of employability as mandated by the requirements of Title I of the act. Service priority under this part of the act was given to persons "whose disabilities are so severe that they do not presently have the potential for employment but may benefit from vocational rehabilitation services which will enable them to live and function independently" (Rehabilitation, Comprehensive Services, and Developmental Disabilities Amendments of 1978, 29 USC 796b).

The 1978 amendments also identified 11 forms of individualized services that were to be authorized for provision under the Basic State Grant Program (Title 1). These services ranged from vocational evaluation to reader services for the blind and continued to reflect an orientation toward services that typically would not successfully result in remunerative activity within an integrated worksite by persons with severely handicapping conditions.

Vocational Rehabilitation Act Amendments of 1986: PL 99-506

On October 21, 1986, President Ronald Reagan signed into law the Vocational Rehabilitation Act Amendments of 1986. These amendments repeatedly refer to supported employment in determining eligibility (Title I), authorizing personnel preparation projects and demonstration programs (Title III), authorizing new and innovative projects (Title VI), and permitting states to use funds from the Basic State Grant Program (Title I) to fund supported employment.

Supported Employment Definition The 1986 amendments define supported employment as competitive work in integrated work settings:

(A) for individuals with severe handicaps for whom competitive employment has not traditionally occurred, or

(B) for individuals for whom competitive employment has been interrupted or intermittent as a result of a severe disability, and who, because of their handicap, need on-going sup-

port services to perform such work. Such term includes transitional employment for individuals with chronic mental illness. (PL 99-506, Title I, Sec. 103,i)

Title VI, Part C The 1986 amendments added a separate part to the act in order to include specific and separate authorizations for supported employment projects. Title VI, Part C was established to:

authorize grants (supplementary to grants for vocational rehabilitation services under Title 1) to assist states in developing collaborative programs with appropriate public agencies and nonprofit private organizations for training and short-term post employment services leading to supported employment for severely handicapped individuals. (PL 99-506, Title VI, Part C, Sec. 631)

This part of the act was established to develop supported employment services in addition to services authorized under the Basic State Grants Program (Title I). The establishment of Part C came in response to concerns raised by officials of vocational rehabilitation programs and representatives of traditional rehabilitation consumer groups that increasing training and services to persons with severe disabilities which tend to be more costly, would deplete existing resources that were already inadequate to appropriately serve all clients eligible for vocational rehabilitation services (Noble, Conley, & Elder, 1986). The addition of Part C to Title VI was intended to supplement rather than supplant existing supported employment services already provided under Title I by some states. In fact, the bill provided that "a State is not restricted from providing training and time-limited post-employment services leading to supported employment through the State allotment under Title I of the Act" (*Senate Report 99-388*, p. 25).

Interagency Cooperation One of the more significant implications of supported employment is the tacit acceptance of clients with severe handicaps who typically require extended services. While the Vocational Rehabilitation Act has historically defined that the vocational rehabilitation of persons with severe handicaps can be expected to "require multiple vocational rehabilitation services of an extended period of time" (34 CFR 361.1), the inclusion of supported employment represents the first legislative authority to provide vocational services to these individuals for an extended period of time. However, these amendments do not require state agencies to provide these extended services. Rather, the amendments are designed to provide a "time-limited entry into supported employment through the State rehabilitation agency with the expectation that other State agencies and organizations will be responsible for the long-term support" (*Senate Report 99-388*, p. 24).

Employability Redefined As noted previously, the eligibility requirements for vocational rehabilitation have traditionally resulted in the denial of services to persons with severe handicaps. Whitehead (1981) noted that persons with developmental disabilities had a higher-than-average rate of rejection or service denial from vocational rehabilitation agencies.

To enhance the access of rehabilitative services to persons with severe handicaps, the 1986 amendments made significant changes in the manner in which clients are determined to be eligible for rehabilitative services. In particular, these amendments redefined the concept of employability as:

a determination that, with the provision of vocational rehabilitation services, the individual is likely to enter and retain, as a primary objective, full-time employment, and when appropriate, part-time employment, consistent with the capacities and abilities of the individual in the competitive labor market or any other vocational outcome the Secretary may determine consistent with this Act. (PL 99-506, Sec. 103[6]).

The most significant changes in the definition are the inclusion of part-time employment and the open-ended acceptance of "any other vocational outcome." These revisions were intended to "emphasize that for individuals for whom part-time employment is an appropriate outcome, the client may not be denied services on that basis" (*Senate Report 99-388*, p. 7).

The inclusion of the phrase "any other vocational outcome the Secretary may determine consistent with this Act" appears to be an attempt to indirectly link employability determination with supported employment. That is, full- or part-time employment in a supported em-

ployment alternative would be sufficient to consider someone eligible for services. While this section of the act does not specifically discuss supported employment, language elsewhere in the act does. In Section 7, these amendments state: "For the purpose of this Act, supported employment, as defined in this paragraph, may be considered an acceptable outcome for employability" (PL 99-506, Title I, Sec. 7[18,b]).

Expansion of the IWRP The 1986 amendments provide for the expansion and elaboration of the IWRP to support the concept of individualization in service planning. The intent of the U.S. Congress in expanding the scope of the IWRP was to "most strongly reaffirm the concept of 'individualization' which is inherent in the Rehabilitation Act" (*Senate Report 99-388*, p. 12). The 1986 revisions to the IWRP clearly reflect an attention to individual needs and to the implications of supported employment services. In addition to the original requirements for the IWRP, the new amendments require the IWRP to:

(a) be developed on the basis of a determination of employability designed to achieve the vocational objective of the individual,

(b) specify the provision of rehabilitation engineering services where appropriate, and

(c) assess and re-assess the need for post-employment follow-along services after case closure and to provide a statement detailing how these services will be provided or arranged through agreements with cooperative agencies (PL 99-506, Title I, Sec. 102, b, 100 STAT. 1815).

TRADITIONS IN VOCATIONAL REHABILITATION

The legislative history of the federal state VR system has produced a system and process rich in tradition. Many of these traditions have been affected by the authorization of supported employment. The following two sections review these traditions and discuss the challenges presented by supported employment.

Underlying Philosophy

By definition, vocational rehabilitation is concerned with rehabilitating people for vocational activity. As defined by Jaques (1970), *rehabil-*

itation refers to a readaptation process following an injury or a disorder. Vocational rehabilitation has historically concerned itself only with those individuals who had acquired a disabling condition, either through an industrial mishap, an automobile accident, armed conflict, disease, or some other means. This early orientation shaped a rehabilitation philosophy that emphasized productivity and self-sufficiency. The orientation toward productivity and self-sufficiency is most pervasive in the eligibility requirements of the system. These requirements have historically mandated that applicants display the potential for full-time competitive employment and the potential that they could become self-sufficient and productive members of the labor force following rehabilitative services.

Public vocational rehabilitation can be characterized by three essential principles (Bitter, 1979). First, vocational rehabilitation supports equality of opportunity, particularly in the workplace. As such, vocational rehabilitation services to persons with disabilities are justified on the basis that these services will enhance individuals' ability to experience the same opportunities for financial enrichment, career advancement, and self-enhancement that are available to able-bodied working individuals. Second, vocational rehabilitation assumes a holistic approach to treating clients. Services cannot be appropriately provided when they are not coordinated. Effective rehabilitation requires that the whole person be dealt with in a unified fashion that addresses all major facets of living. The third principle is an orientation toward individuality. In essence, this principle assumes that services are designed and provided to individuals on the basis of their unique and individual needs.

The Rehabilitation Process

The rehabilitation process that most clients encounter consists of four basic steps: evaluation, planning, treatment, and termination (Rubin & Roessler, 1983). This process is an orderly and systematic sequence of activities that must be followed according to federal and state regulations. All clients applying to the system must first receive some form of evaluation before re-

ceiving services. This evaluation may be an informal process in which the counselor discusses vocational interests with the client. Conversely, such an evaluation may represent a formal referral to a vocational evaluation center where the client may be seen for a period of up to 18 months before actual services are initiated. Regardless of the formality or duration of this evaluation, all clients applying for services must receive some form of evaluation, and all counselors must report that they provided some form of evaluation before actual services can be received.

One of the most comprehensive discussions of the sequential nature of the rehabilitation process was provided by Bitter (1979). Bitter's description is noteworthy because it discusses the rehabilitation process within the context of the case reporting system employed by the Rehabilitation Services Administration and each of the state vocational rehabilitation agencies. This system uses a series of status codes to represent various steps within the rehabilitation process as well as different services provided by the process. Status codes can be divided into four major types: referral processing (status codes 00 to 08), preservice (status codes 10 to 12), inservice (status codes 14 to 24 and status code 32), and finally, closure of active services (status code 26).

Referral Processing The referral process begins with a client applying for services from the state agency. Upon application, the client is assigned to a particular counselor who generally conducts an intake interview and attempts to make an initial determination that the client is eligible to receive vocational rehabilitation services. This determination is dependent upon the counselor's decision that the client exhibits a handicap that impedes employment potential and that the client can be reasonably expected to experience improved vocational potential as a result of receiving rehabilitation services. If the counselor is unable to make such a determination, the client may be referred for evaluation services for a period of up to 18 months. When a counselor makes a determination that a client is not eligible to receive services, the client's case is terminated as an ineligible case closure (status 08). None of the activities conducted during this phase of the rehabilitation process is considered a service to the client.

Preservice   This phase of the rehabilitation process begins once the client has been determined eligible to receive vocational rehabilitation services. Major activities that occur during this phase of the process include the development of an individualized written rehabilitation program and the arrangement of services to be provided to the client as identified by the IWRP.

Once the IWRP has been developed, the counselor may begin to arrange for services to the client. Typically, these services are provided by rehabilitation service providers other than the rehabilitation counselor. These providers may include a host of rehabilitation facilities such as work adjustment centers, vocational evaluation centers, sheltered workshops, and job placement agencies. Counselors generally refer clients to these agencies and authorize a specified type, amount, or duration of service. These specifications are usually expressed in a unit service formula, with the service provider receiving a fixed amount of revenue from the state agency for each unit of service.

Inservice   The inservice phase of the rehabilitation process refers to the period during which clients actually receive vocational rehabilitation services designed to help them achieve their vocational objectives. Three basic types of services may be provided during this period: counseling, restoration, and vocational training. According to Bitter (1979), counseling (status 14) refers to counseling and guidance only and (possibly) placement services for preparing the client for employment. Restoration (status 16) includes medical, surgical, psychiatric, or therapeutic treatment, and/or the fitting of a prosthetic appliance. Finally, training (status 18) refers to "any sort of learning situation, including school training, on-the-job training, work adjustment, tutoring, and training by correspondence" (Bitter, 1979, p. 38). These services are provided either individually or in combination until the client is considered ready for employment.

Once the client is considered "job-ready," placement into employment may be made. Once this occurs, the client's status is considered to be in "trial employment" (status 22). The client must remain in this status for at least 60 days before case closure can occur. A final form of service that can be provided to clients is referred to as "postemployment." Postemployment refers to services provided to employed clients whose cases have already been closed, but who are in need of additional services to maintain their employment. Clients may receive these services without having to reenter the rehabilitation system through the standard application and eligibility determination process.

Closure of Active Cases   Rehabilitation counselors may successfully "close" (status 26) the cases of clients who have maintained stable employment for 60 continuous days. Following case closure, the client is considered rehabilitated and the counselor will no longer provide or monitor services except in the unique situation of postemployment services, as previously discussed. In addition to status 26 closures, rehabilitation counselors may also terminate services to clients through two other closure codes. Status 30 closures refer to clients who were denied services and had their cases closed before the services were provided. These clients were either evaluated to be ineligible for services or had been evaluated as eligible and had an IWRP developed, but did not subsequently receive services. Status 28 closures represent clients who have received services but who failed to become successfully employed.

Rehabilitation Counselors

Rehabilitation counselors represent a critical link in the rehabilitation process, as they serve as the liaison between clients and the rehabilitation system. These individuals are responsible for monitoring, arranging, and managing all facets of the rehabilitation process. Due to their global functions within the rehabilitation process, rehabilitation counselors have been characterized by some as the most important staff members in the rehabilitation process (Wright, 1980).

As implied by their title, rehabilitation counselors are employed to counsel their clients. While counseling per se generally connotes psychotherapeutic interchange, vocational rehabilitation counselors employed within the federal-state rehabilitation system generally engage in much more than simply counseling their clients. They are involved in all facets of the rehabilitation process, from intake interviewing to case closure on an individual client basis. The specific functions they perform depend upon the needs of the client, the nature and demands of the agency for whom they are employed, and the requirements of the community (Riggar, Maki, & Wolf, 1986). However, a sample of activities that these counselors typically perform includes: determining whether applicants are eligible and feasible, planning with clients the objectives and strategies for their rehabilitation, managing and arranging for necessary services, making client referrals to other agencies, providing ongoing counseling, keeping in contact with the client's family, and conducting or participating in job placement (Greenwood, 1982; Wright, 1980).

Recent discussion of rehabilitation counselor functions has emphasized the importance of case management and case-load management (Emener & Rubin, 1980; Emener & Spector, 1985; Matkin, 1983; Rubin et al., 1984). *Case management* may be defined as: "the counselor's managerial activities that facilitate the movement of each rehabilitant through the service process." In contrast, *case-load management* may be defined as "the responsiblity of the counselor for the progress of a whole group of clients who constitute the counselor's case load" (Wright, 1980, p. 170). Regardless of the definitions applied to these terms, case management and case-load management entail significant management, coordination, and planning skills on the part of rehabilitation counselors (Cox, Connolly, & Flynn, 1981).

THE CHALLENGES OF SUPPORTED EMPLOYMENT

The 1986 amendments provided for dramatic changes in the federal-state rehabilitation system and significantly restructured the rehabilitation process. These amendments highlight a number of issues that must be dealt with as supported employment becomes integrated with the federal-state rehabilitation system.

Integration versus Segregation of Supported Employment

A major issue that will ultimately affect the institutionalization of supported employment services is the degree to which state rehabilitation agencies will integrate the provision of supported employment with the array of services that they already provide under Title I of the Vocational Rehabilitation Act. Some observers have expressed concern that, owing to the separate funding under Title VI, Part C, supported employment may be established within state agencies in a manner comparable to the separate administration of independent living services.

The critical issue regarding administrative integration of supported employment is the ability of rehabilitation counselors to readily purchase these services in the same manner by which they make use of other rehabilitation services such as work adjustment, vocational evaluation, and job placement services. Typically, these services can be purchased for clients from public and private not-for-profit rehabilitation facilities and providers through the expenditure of case management dollars. If rehabilitation counselors are to use supported employment, they must be able to do so in a fashion with which they are familiar.

State agencies need to implement policies that will allow rehabilitation counselors to access supported employment services. In Virginia, for example, supported employment has been integrated within the state system, and counselors can purchase these services for their clients from approved vendors, in the same fee-for-service arrangement in which other rehabilitative services are secured.

Determining Eligibility

Eligibility for vocational rehabilitation was altered dramatically by the 1986 amendments to include part-time employment and supported employment as reasonable case closure alternatives. A lingering and as yet unanswered issue involves the guidelines by which rehabilitation counselors can determine that clients are appropriate candidates for supported employment. That is, what client characteristics should counselors look for when deciding to refer a client for supported employment? The amendments partially address this issue when defining *supported employment*. According to this definition, people who are appropriate for supported employment may be:

1. Severely handicapped with little or no history of competitive employment;
2. Severely disabled with interrupted or intermittent exposure to competitive employment;
3. Chronically mentally ill (employment history not specified); or
4. In need of ongoing support services to perform competitive employment.

Most individuals would agree that supported employment is intended for those individuals with the most severe levels of functional limitations who have historically been denied access to traditional vocational rehabilitative service because of their perceived lack of vocational potential. Further clarification is needed to guard against counselors referring inappropriate clients for supported employment. In particular, counselors may make supported employment referrals for "guaranteed closures" by referring individuals who would in all likelihood realize remunerative employment through less intensive service arrangements.

Regulations have been published by the Rehabilitation Services Administration regarding the supported employment authorizations (*Federal Register*, August 14, 1987). However, these regulations fail to address changes in the eligibility determination process that must be dealt with as supported employment services are implemented systemwide.

Rehabilitation Process

Rehabilitation counselors are accustomed to a standard process through which their clients proceed in an orderly and timely fashion. As previously noted, this process typically consists of four components: evaluation, planning, treatment, and termination. The process is heavily regulated and requires that counselors use the case service status report system. The addition

of supported employment services presents two special challenges to this system.

First, supported employment is both a service and a placement. The current case service status system requires that clients first receive some form of rehabilitation service (counseling, restoration, or vocational training) before being placed into employment. Changes in the regulations regarding this service-placement sequence are necessary so that supported employment can be viewed as a separate service-placement provision not requiring the traditional sequence.

A second challenge that supported employment presents is the recording and evaluation of these services within the case management report system that the Rehabilitation Services Administration currently maintains. As discussed previously, this system consists of four sets of status codes used by rehabilitation counselors to report the sequential progress of their clients. This report system needs to be altered so that supported employment may be evaluated separately from other services provided by the VR system. It is important that alterations be made to this report system that allow for separate evaluation of supported employment. Otherwise, it will not be feasible to demonstrate the effectiveness of supported employment on a systemwide basis.

Supported Employment and Traditional Values

Supported employment represents a significant break with traditional rehabilitation values regarding productivity and self-sufficiency. Specifically, supported employment implicitly accepts individuals who will require repeated and extended services. This contrasts sharply with the values of the federal-state rehabilitation system, which has traditionally emphasized the provision of services on a time-limited basis prior to placement into employment.

Extensive efforts are needed to modify the values and philosophy that rehabilitation professionals, and in particular rehabilitation counselors, apply to the rehabilitation process. These efforts must address the commonality of goals between traditional vocational rehabilitation and supported employment. Both orientations obviously value meaningful and remunerative employment outcomes. However, these efforts must also address the ability of the system to achieve these outcomes while continuing to provide support services.

Interagency Cooperation

The supported employment authorization requires a great degree of interagency cooperation and collaboration. State agencies are required to coordinate with other state service agencies to provide funding for extended follow-along services in supported employment. This requirement places new demands upon state agencies as well as upon rehabilitation counselors. At the agency level, cooperation and collaboration must be initiated and supported by top administrators and commissioners. Similarly, at the counselor level, interaction and cooperation with professionals from different agencies and with different philosophical orientations must occur.

In most states, this interagency cooperation is already occurring. However, the lack of identified service agencies for certain disability groups (e.g., traumatically brain-injured people) seriously restricts access to supported employment. As such, alternative strategies for providing extended follow-along support services must be developed.

Rehabilitation Counselors in Supported Employment

A final issue raised by the authorization for supported employment is the role of rehabilitation counselors in the supported employment process. Recently, a great deal of attention has been focused upon the role and function of the rehabilitation counselor in supported employment (Revell & Arnold, 1984; Szymanski, 1987; Tooman, Revell, & Melia, 1988). Tooman et al. (1988) identified four specific functions for rehabilitation counselors: 1) assisting eligible clients in gaining access to and continuing to use supported employment services; 2) providing some of the direct employment services;

3) purchasing or assisting in arranging services with a supported employment service provider; and 4) arranging for client retraining from a supported employment service provider by using traditional postemployment services. Generally, literature on the role of rehabilitation counselors in supported employment has discussed the divergent functions of service provider and case manager. In most state agencies, the typical size of rehabilitation counselors' case loads will severely restrict their ability to effectively or reliably serve as direct service providers. As noted in Chapter 1, the most efficacious roles for rehabilitation counselors in the supported employment process appear to be those of case management and monitoring, functions with a strong tradition in the federal-state system.

SUMMARY

Supported employment presents new and unique challenges to the federal-state rehabilitation system. This system has a rich and varied history that, over the years, has developed many valued traditions. Among these traditions, the orientations toward attaining independence and productivity for consumers of the rehabilitation process represent two of the more challenging aspects confronted by supported employment. Many view supported employment's implicit acceptance of persons with limited vocational potential and the provision of extended services as incompatible with these traditions.

The challenge of supported employment is to redefine concepts such as independence and productivity. These terms must be approached in relation to the individuals for whom they are to be applied and the environments in which they are found. As such, independence and productivity for the industrially injured consumer must be viewed drastically differently from the way they are perceived for the developmentally disabled consumer. While supported employment may challenge traditional values such as independence and productivity, it supports and extends the essential value of public rehabilitation, which is paid employment for all Americans with disabilities.

REFERENCES

Bellamy, G. T., Rhodes, L., & Albin, J. (1986). Supported employment. In W. E. Kiernan & J. A. Stark (Eds.), *Pathways to employment for adults with developmental disabilities* (pp. 129–138). Baltimore: Paul H. Brookes Publishing Co.

Bellamy, G. T., Sheehan, M., Horner, R., & Boles, S. (1980). Community programs for severely handicapped adults: An analysis. *Journal of the Association for Persons with Severe Handicaps, 5*(4), 307–324.

Bitter, J. A. (1979). *Introduction to rehabilitation*. St. Louis: C. F. Mosby.

Braddock, D. (1987). *Federal policy toward mental retardation and developmental disabilities*. Baltimore: Paul H. Brookes Publishing Co.

Cox, J. G., Connolly, S. G., & Flynn, W. G. (1981). Managing the delivery of rehabilitation services. In R. M. Parker & C. E. Hansen (Eds.), *Rehabilitation counseling foundations-consumers-service delivery* (pp. 295–324). Boston: Allyn & Bacon.

Emener, W. G., & Rubin, S. E. (1980). Rehabilitation counselor roles and functions and sources of role strain. *Journal of Applied Rehabilitation Counseling, 11*(2), 57–69.

Emener, W. G., & Spector, P. E. (1985). Rehabilitation case management: An empirical investigation of selected rehabilitation counselor job skills. *Journal of American Rehabilitation, 16*(2), 11–21.

Federal Register, 46(12), (1981, January 19), 5526. Washington, DC: U.S. Government Printing Office.

Federal Register, 52(157), (1987, August 14), 30546–30552. Washington, DC: U.S. Government Printing Office.

Fry, R. (1986). *Work evaluation and adjustment: An annotated bibliography*. Menomonie, WI: University of Wisconsin-Stout.

Greenwood, R. (1982). Systematic management. In R.J. Roessler & S.E. Rubin (Eds.), *Case management and rehabilitation counseling* (pp. 227–258). Baltimore: University Park Press.

Jaques, M. E. (1970). *Rehabilitation counseling: Scope and services*. Boston: Houghton Mifflin.

LaVor, M. (1975). Federal legislation for exceptional persons: A history. In F. Weintraub, A. Abeson, J. Ballard, & M. LaVor (Eds.), *Public policy and the education of exceptional children* (pp. 96–111). Reston, VA: Council for Exceptional Children.

Matkin, R. F. (1983). The roles and functions of rehabilitation specialists in the private sector. *Journal of Applied*

Rehabilitation Counseling, 14(1), 14–27.

Noble, J. M., Conley, R. W., & Elder, J. K. (1986). Where do we go from here? In J. A. Stark & W. E. Kiernan (Eds.), *Pathways to employment for adults with developmental disabilities* (pp. 85–100). Baltimore: Paul H. Brookes Publishing Co.

Rehabilitation, Comprehensive Services, and Developmental Disabilities Amendments. Public Law 95–602, 1978.

Revell, W.F., & Arnold, S.M. (1984). The role of the rehabilitation counselor in providing job oriented services to severely handicapped mentally retarded persons. *Journal of Applied Rehabilitation Counseling, 15*(1), 22–27.

Riggar, T. F., Maki, D. R., & Wolf, A. W. (1986). *Applied rehabilitation counseling*. New York: Springer-Verlag.

Rubin, A. E., Matkin, R., Ashley, J., Beardsley, M., May, V., Onstott, K., & Puckett, F. D. (1984). Roles and functions of certified rehabilitation counselors. *Rehabilitation Counseling Bulletin, 27*(4), 199–224.

Rubin, S. E., & Roessler, R. T. (1983). *Foundations of the vocational rehabilitation process*. Baltimore: University Park Press.

Senate Report 99-388. (1986). Washington DC: U.S. Government Printing Office.

Szymanski, E. M. (1987). *Supported and transitional employment: New options for rehabilitation counselors*. Utica, NY: New York Office of Vocational Rehabilitation.

Tooman, M. L., Revell, W. G., & Melia, R. P. (1988). The role of the rehabilitation counselor in the provision of transition and supported employment programs. In S.E. Rubin & N.M. Rubin (Eds.), *Contemporary challenges to the rehabilitation counseling profession* (pp. 77–92). Baltimore: Paul H. Brookes Publishing Co.

Vocational Rehabilitation Act. Public Law 93–112, 1973.

Vocational Rehabilitation Act Amendments. Public Law 89–333, 1965.

Vocational Rehabilitation Act Amendments. Public Law 99–506, 1986.

Whitehead, C. (1981). *Final report: Training and employment services for handicapped individuals*. Washington, DC: Department of Health and Human Services.

Whitten, E. B. (1966). The challenge of PL 89-333. *Journal of Rehabilitation, 32*(1), 2.

Whitten, E. B. (1974). The Rehabilitation Act of 1973 and the severely disabled. *Journal of Rehabilitation, 40*(4), 39–40.

Wright, G. N. (1980). *Total rehabilitation*. Boston: Little, Brown.

Chapter 5

An Analysis of Federal and State Policy on Transition from School to Adult Life for Youth with Disabilities

Jane M. Everson

Transition from school to adult life for youth with disabilities is becoming an increasingly shared concern among federal and state policymakers. Transition as a concept was conceived in federal policy and legislation dating to the early 20th century and received intensified emphasis in the 1960s and 1970s during periods of often open confrontation between individual human rights and societal rights. By the early 1980s, transition had been established as a specific social policy need and was declared a national priority by the Office of Special Education and Rehabilitative Services (OSERS) within the U. S. Department of Education (Will, 1984b). Since 1984, transition has evolved from a theoretical and philosophical framework for education and adult service coordination developed by federal policymakers and academicians into an issue that demands a complex and introspective assessment of current services and outcomes by state and local policymakers (Wehman, Moon, Everson, Wood, & Barcus, 1988).

This chapter's purpose is twofold: first, to analyze the major political, societal, and economic events that led to OSERS' 1984 initiative on transition; and second, to discuss the emergence of transition as a state and local policy issue that has widespread implications for the way educational and adult services are administered in numerous states and localities. The first part of the chapter traces the federal response to the needs of transition from early 20th century legislation and policy identifying the problem through the signing of the Education for All Handicapped Children Act (PL 94-142) in 1975, the 1984 OSERS initiative on transition, and the most recent amendments of the Education of the Handicapped Act in 1986, PL 99-457 (Section 626). The second part of the chapter discusses the evolution of transition demonstration efforts, interagency planning efforts, and transition legislation at the state and local levels across the United States.

PHASES OF SOCIAL POLICY

Policy science experts agree that policy progresses through a sequence of phases, from the initial articulation of a need through the implementation and evaluation of services and resources. Gil (1976), for example, described three distinct stages: 1) development of life-sustaining and life-enhancing services; 2) division of labor or allocation of status within society; and

The development and dissemination of this chapter was partially supported by Grant No. G00B430056 from the U.S. Department of Education.

3) distribution of rights to resources, goods, and services through entitlements, rewards, and constraints. Brewer (1974) established editorial direction for the journal *Policy Sciences* by envisioning a broader six-phase model through which policy passes over time: 1) invention/initiation of a problem; 2) estimation or predetermination of risks, costs, and benefits of a policy; 3) selection or decision making related to proposed policies; 4) implementation or execution of a selected policy option; 5) evaluation of the implemented policy; and 6) termination or adjustment of policies that have become dysfunctional, redundant, outmoded, or unnecessary.

The history of transition policy can be traced through a similar series of phases. Initial recognition or identification of the transition problem was a role assumed by the federal government. Recognition reached its peak in 1983–1984, although, as the following section demonstrates, numerous federal legislative actions throughout the early 20th century both directly and indirectly served as catalysts for the emergence of transition as a 1980s buzzword. Federal initiatives and legislation in 1983–1984 laid the foundation for states and localities to begin to estimate, select, implement, and evaluate transition policy. Currently, in 1987, individual states are at various phases in their establishment of transition policy. As described in a later section, some states appear to have leaped ahead to implementation and evaluation phases without progressing through an estimation phase. A few states have yet to progress beyond the invention/initiation phase; and still others are cautiously estimating risks, costs, and benefits associated with transition planning and implementation.

FEDERAL ROLE IN TRANSITION POLICY

Early 20th-Century Influences

Federal endorsement of employment as an expected outcome of public education was first supported by the Smith-Hughes Act of 1917, which authorized grants to states for vocational education. In 1918, a push to rehabilitate World War I soldiers encouraged the passage of the nation's first rehabilitation act; in 1920, services were extended to all civilians needing rehabilitation services through the Smith-Fess Act. These early federal efforts at vocational education and vocational rehabilitation were targeted primarily ulation with developmental disabilities. Nevertheless, the measures provided a common ''life-enhancing'' (Gil, 1976) thrust to national social policy of the early 20th century.

American social policy at that time that promoted life enhancement was also likely to be thinly veiled in cost-effective, or perceived as cost-effective, programs. The early vocational education and vocational rehabilitation programs were no exception. They laid the foundation for three federal policy assumptions that would later translate into federal support of transition policy by: 1) supporting a national work ethic; 2) providing financial assistance to future workers with defined potential and need; and 3) establishing employment as a perceived cost-effective outcome of vocational preparation and training programs.

In 1943, with the enactment of the Barden-LaFollette Act, federal policy regarding employment training for persons with disabilities made a significant step toward enhancing the lives of persons with developmental disabilities. The Barden-LaFollette Act amended the original vocational rehabilitation act to authorize provisions for clients with mental disabilities. These amendments represented a shift from a belief in only *rehabilitation* to the inclusion of a belief in *habilitation*—a major shift because they extended the expectation of employment as a service outcome for individuals who had not previously proven themselves with a work history.

Although the first federal efforts at establishing a national Social Security system were initiated in 1935, it was not until 1950 that persons with disabilities were entitled to a state-federal matching program of financial assistance through the Aid to the Permanently and Totally Disabled (APTD) program. Prior to this program, persons with disabilities were eligible for services under state and locally funded General Assistance programs.

The establishment of the APTD program represented the beginning of a federal flux that continues today between life-sustaining and life-enhancing policies and the conflicting policies of funding for Social Security, Medicaid, and vocational rehabilitation. Vocational rehabilitation programs continued to provide employment training to persons who, although disabled and unable to show a work history, could still demonstrate potential to work. The vast majority of individuals with more severe disabilities were channeled into the APTD program and were provided ongoing financial support because they were deemed to have permanent disabilities and therefore unable to obtain and maintain employment. The APTD program also laid the foundation for the eligibility versus feasibility debate that rages today in vocational rehabilitation agencies. This debate revolves around the belief that persons with more severe disabilities cost more to habilitate and to maintain in employment and, therefore, offer a smaller return on an investment than do less disabled Americans and those with a proven work history.

As Coudroglou and Poole (1984) have concluded, all social policy in the United States is predicated on two questions: 1) Is the origin of an individual's disability related to employment? and 2) Is the disabled person an injured veteran or a disabled worker? Coudroglou and Poole (1984) observed that these questions have led American policymakers to view disabled workers either as past contributors to our economic system, and thus deserving of a chance for future active economic involvement, or as outside our economic system and thus deserving of charity and financial support.

Throughout the 1940s and 1950s, the duality of the nation's social policies and the fragmentation of disability services continued to intensify. Berkowitz, Johnson, and Murphy (1976) have noted that American service programs were designed to serve specific needs and specific populations and that each program is governed by a different set of eligibility rules. Federal support for education, income support, medical support, and vocational rehabilitation programs continued to grow throughout the 1950s with

the establishment of formal parent groups (Braddock, 1987; Everson, 1985). By the close of the 1950s, largely as a result of parent advocacy groups, the federal government had begun to recognize its responsibility for both policy leadership and fiscal support.

Federal Executive Initiatives and Legislation in the 1960s

The 1960s ushered in a decade of federal policies that focused more on civil rights of all Americans and less on specific services to individuals with disabilities. This focus prompted federal social policy regarding individuals with disabilities to move dramatically from Gil's (1976) first stage of life-sustaining and life-enhancing services toward the second stage of division of labor or allocation of status within society. The two most important federal activities of the 1960s, which would later fuel a response to the identification of a transition problem in the 1980s, were: 1) the establishment of the President's Panel on Mental Retardation (PPMR) in 1961; and 2) the passage of the Civil Rights Act (PL 88-352) in 1964.

President John F. Kennedy's support of a comprehensive interagency and interdisciplinary task force to address the problems of Americans with mental retardation was the first attempt by the federal executive branch to coordinate the dual service systems that had so far characterized the 20th century. Kennedy's attempts to organize policy previously under the aegis of the legislative branch of the federal government was spurred by his personal experience of having a family member with mental retardation as well as by concern for the disjointed service systems nationally. Political ideology of the 1960s further encouraged federal policymaking toward Americans with disabilities. Castellani (1987) noted three beliefs that guided policymakers: 1) civil rights issues; 2) normalization philosophy; and 3) the principle of least restrictive alternatives.

As Braddock (1987) has observed, the 95 recommendations of the PPMR form the foundation of current federal assistance programs for Americans with disabilities (e.g., the enactment of the Maternal and Child Health and Mental

Retardation Planning Amendments of 1963 (PL 88-156), the Mental Retardation Facilities and Community Mental Health Centers Construction Act of 1963 (PL 88-164), the expansion of the Social Security Act in 1962 to encourage the use of federal funds to deinstitutionalize mental health clients, and the establishment of a Division on the Education of Handicapped Children in the U.S. Office of Education).

The Civil Rights Act of 1964, although not focused specifically on individuals with disabilities, laid the groundwork for future legal and legislative action by prohibiting discrimination in education and other federally supported programs on the basis of race and national origin.

Education and Rehabilitation Legislation of the 1970s

The 1970s saw the continued development of federal policy related to individuals with disabilities, which attempted to fulfill Gil's (1976) second phase of policy development: division of labor and allocation of resources, goods, and services.

The two most important federal activities of the 1970s related to identification of the transition problem were Section 504 of the Vocational Rehabilitation Act of 1973 (PL 93-112) and the enactment of the Education for all Handicapped Children Act (PL 94-142) in 1975. Section 504 of the Rehabilitation Act of 1973 guaranteed civil rights to Americans with disabilities by prohibiting discrimination, primarily in the area of employment, by any agency, activity, or program receiving federal funds. PL 94-142 secured free and appropriate education for all students aged 3 through 21 regardless of the type or severity of disability.

The year 1975 also witnessed the birth of the career education movement when U.S. Office of Education Commissioner Sidney P. Maryland stated that "all education is career education, or should be . . . anything else is dangerous nonsense" (cited in Hoyt, 1975). The Vocational Education Amendments of 1976 (PL 94-482) required states to match federal funds for vocational education for students with disabilities and to cooperate with PL 94-142 procedural safeguards. Each of these acts attempted to establish guidelines for the allocation of ed-

ucation and other federally supported resources to Americans who had not traditionally gained access to these resources. In addition, both acts encouraged the identification of transition as a policy issue in the 1980s by extending a belief in the benefits of education and employment services to Americans with disabilities, including those with the most severe disabilities.

Transition Legislation and Initiatives of the 1980s

Although transition from school to adult life was not defined or addressed as a specific policy issue until the early 1980s, it can be argued that the problems associated with the movement of youth from special education programs to adult life are a natural outgrowth of the mandates of PL 94-142. Mandated public education for all students, regardless of the existence of a handicapping condition, ushered a new generation of students into the nation's public school systems. In 1984, OSERS estimated that between 250,000 and 300,000 students were exiting special education programs each year (Will, 1984b).

The premise so far in this chapter has been that an implied outcome of American public education is employment; therefore, employment can be viewed as one measure of the effectiveness of educational preparation and transition planning. Federal social policy throughout the 20th century has supported this expectation. In 1983, however, the U.S. Commission on Civil Rights estimated that between 50% and 75% of Americans with disabilities were unemployed. Data from a Harris (Harris, 1986) telephone survey conducted in 1985 and cited at the 1986 reauthorization hearings on the Education for All Handicapped Children Act showed little improvement, with the conclusion that 67% of Americans with disabilities were unemployed and that employees with disabilities were 75% more likely to be employed part-time. Follow-up studies of transition-aged youth with disabilities who had exited special education programs in the early 1980s revealed similar startling results: 58% of a sample of 300 students with mental retardation leaving school in Virginia were unemployed (Wehman, Kregel, & Seyfarth, 1985); 37% of 462 former students in a cross-categorical sample in Vermont were unemployed (Hasazi, Gordon, & Roe, 1985); and 37% of 234 graduates in a cross-categorical sample in Colorado were unemployed (Mithaug, Horiuchi, & Fanning, 1985). Also, in the Colorado study, of the 63% of the graduates who were working, only 32% were reported to be working full-time, and 43% earned less than $3 per hour.

Another implied outcome of American public education is independence, or, at least, decreased dependence on federal and state social service programs. As has been described throughout this chapter, the evolution of dual systems of income and medical support for individuals with disabilities has meant that much 20th-century social policy has been at odds with this assumption. Will (1984a) cited a White House Task Force on Disability Policy that indicated that 8% of the nation's gross national product is spent each year on disability programs. Will and the task force shared a concern that the large majority of this money funds programs that support dependence rather than encourage independence. Furthermore, the President's Committee on Employment of the Handicapped has estimated that of the approximately 650,000 youth with disabilities who leave high school programs each year, 40% will be underemployed and live at the poverty level and 26% will live on welfare (cited in Corthell & VanBoskirk, 1984). In 1976, Hoyt estimated that of 2.5 million students with disabilities who were targeted to leave school between 1976 and 1980, 75,000 (3%) would be totally dependent and live in institutions and 200,000 (8%) would live in their local communities and remain idle much of their time.

The Western Regional Resource Center (WRRC), in a topical update on transition (1985), summed up the feelings of parents, policy makers, and professionals on the inability of PL 94-142 to ensure employment and independent living outcomes for special education students:

> Since the inception of Public Law 94-142, the Education for All Handicapped Children Act, society has developed the expectation, especially among parents and the students themselves, that a brighter future was ensured for these students following graduation. That brighter future has been dimmed somewhat by a lack of procedures for planning, lack of services, and lack of opportun-

ities for these young adults. The result has broken the implicit promise of 94-142—that promise being individuals' equal right to independence, integration, and productive work. (p. 2)

During the reauthorization of the Education of the Handicapped Act in 1983, the U.S. Senate Subcommittee on the Handicapped for the first time provided a federal response to the transition problem. The 1983 amendments (PL 98-199, Sec. 626) articulated the transition problem as follows:

> The subcommittee recognizes the overwhelming paucity of effective programming for these handicapped youth, which eventually accounts for unnecessarily large amounts of handicapped adults who become unemployed and therefore dependent on society. These youth historically have not been adequately prepared for the changes and demands of life after high school. In addition, few, if any, are able to access or appropriately use traditional transitional services. Few services have been designed to assist handicapped young people in their efforts to enter the labor force or attain their goals of becoming self-sufficient adults, and contributing members to our society. (PL 98-199, Section 626, 1983)

Section 626 authorized more than 6 million dollars each year during fiscal years 1984, 1985, and 1986 to address the transition problem. During the next 3 years, these funds were awarded to educational and rehabilitation institutions in more than 40 states to encourage the development of secondary education services, postsecondary services, and personnel development services related to transition from school to adult life planning (DeStefano, 1987).

In 1984, OSERS, under the leadership of Madeleine Will, issued a position paper that defined transition and established it as a national priority:

> The transition from school to working life is an outcome-oriented process encompassing a broad array of services and experiences which lead to employment. Transition is a period that includes high school, the point of graduation, additional post-secondary education or adult services, and the initial years in employment. Transition is a bridge between the security and structure offered by the school and the opportunities and risks of adult life. (Will, 1984b, p. 2)

Building upon a history of federal support of preparation for employment by the nation's public schools, OSERS clearly stated that youth

receiving special education services were not to
be excluded from this expectation:

> Sustained employment represents an important
> outcome of education and transition for all Amer-
> icans. The goal of OSERS programming for tran-
> sition is that individuals leaving the school system
> obtain jobs, either immediately after school or after
> a period of post-secondary education or vocational
> services. Employment is a critical aspect of the
> lives of most adults in our society. (Will, 1984b,
> p. 3)

The OSERS definition of transition clearly
applied two historically documented federal assumptions related to employment to the newly
defined policy area of transition planning:
1) employment is *the* desired outcome of education and transition planning and is consistent
with a national work ethic for all Americans; and
2) employment is a cost-effective outcome that
will increase an individual's productivity and
worth to society while decreasing his or her
dependence on social service programs. The
transition initiative broadened earlier federal
policy by extending the employment expectation to all Americans with disabilities regardless
of the severity of their disability and regardless
of a previous work history.

Although significant changes in federal legislation and policy related to income and medical support for Americans with disabilities have
occurred during the 1980s, (e.g., the Omnibus
Reconciliation Act of 1981, PL 97-35; and the
Employment Opportunities for Disabled Americans Act of 1986, PL 99-643), a pressing need
still remains to address the conflict between life-
sustaining and life-enhancing policies affecting
Social Security, medical support, and vocational rehabilitation programs. As Gettings (1980)
noted, "The preponderance of federal dollars
currently expended on behalf of mentally retarded clients are funneled through income
maintenance, medical, and public assistance
programs" (p. 4).

Although OSERS' position is clearly consistent with 20th-century federal policy, numerous
critics have challenged the model for its sug-
gestion that "the nonvocational dimensions of
adult adjustment are significant only in so far
as they contribute to the ultimate goal of employment" (Halpern, 1985, p. 480). As is discussed in the following section, state
policymakers, for the most part, however, have
accepted the federal emphasis on employment
outcomes in their early efforts in transition planning.

STATE AND LOCAL
EFFORTS IN TRANSITION PLANNING

The OSERS priority on national transition planning, accompanied by the funding authorizations of PL 98-199, established transition as a
service priority area in nearly every state department of education and rehabilitation services across the United States. In 1986, federal
funding for transition services was extended for
another 3 years through the most recent amendments to the Education of the Handicapped Act
(PL 99-457).

The second part of this chapter assesses the
current status of transition policies in selected
states across the country using Brewer's six-
phase model of policy development as a framework (Brewer, 1974). Although, as stated earlier, states are at varying degrees in the
development of transition policy, by early 1987
nearly every state in the nation had begun to
address transition policy at a state and/or local
level. A survey conducted by the Northeastern
Regional Resource Center (NRRC, n.d.) of 18
states yielded the following conclusions:

> First of all, the states are at different points on the
> continuum of change. Second, many of the staff
> members indicate that their state is at the beginning
> stages of its endeavor. Third, most of the efforts
> to strengthen transitional services are supported by
> federal funds through grants, contracts or person-
> nel development funds. Fourth, the most common
> activities pursued are creating state level task forces
> training development of model transition programs
> and attempting to pass legislation. Fifth, in the
> activities of all states there is an emphasis on co-
> ordination from membership on task forces. Sixth,
> some states are developing a rational model with
> great involvement of all stakeholders, while others
> are striving for an incremental approach. Seventh,
> some states are utilizing mechanisms which pro-
> vide a greater assurance of their efforts (to) a vast
> number of constituents. (p. 2)

The federal government served as the catalyst
for state recognition and initiation of transition
planning, but there is currently no specific fed-

eral policy prescribing guidelines to individual states for specific transition planning and implementation. Instead, state policymakers have often adopted and/or adapted philosophical and frequently untested academic models.

Legislation enacted in various states that is related to transition generally falls into two broad categories: 1) legislation that strengthens provisions for release of school records and hastens the referral process to adult services; and 2) legislation that specifically targets transition planning, either at a state, community, or individual student level. Examples of this legislation as well as other less formal methods of transition planning and implementation are discussed in the remainder of this chapter.

Phase One:
Invention/Initiation
of the Transition Problem

Of all the states, California has so far passed legislation that comes closest to *entitling* all referred clients who qualify for disability services to such services. As early as 1976, prior to the federal flurry of activity related to transition, California legislators enacted the Lanterman Developmental Disabilities Services Act. The purpose of the act was to provide continuity of services between the public schools and adult services for students with developmental disabilities. It provided funding for 21 private, nonprofit regional centers, which provide a range of services to persons with disabilities. Individuals who are referred to one of the regional centers are entitled to an evaluation and assessment report, ongoing case management, and any services that have been written into their individualized program plan (IPP). Since regional centers must remain within their allocated budgets, however, it appears that services are written into a client's IPP only if regional funds are available to provide the services (Nettekoven & Ramsey, 1985).

The most prescriptive component of Section 626 of PL 98-199 required states to collect information on the number of students exiting special education programs each year. In 1986, McDonnell, Wilcox, and Boles, reporting on their frustrated efforts to obtain accurate data from all 50 states and the District of Columbia

on the service needs of transition-aged youth, posed the question, "Do we know enough to plan for transition?" Their frustration was not surprising to many state policymakers. Bates, Suter, and Poelvoorde (1986), in commenting on efforts to follow up former special education students in Illinois, summarized the concerns of administrators in many states:

> Human services professionals do not have followup data on persons who have exited special education from which they are able to evaluate the effectiveness of specific services or determine existing and future needs and development. At present we have very little information in Illinois regarding the post-school employment and residential status of handicapped youth following high school. (p. 32)

In 1983, Massachusetts became the first state to pass legislation related specifically to transition planning (Executive Office of Human Services [EOHS], 1984). The legislation, also known as Chapter 688 or popularly as the "Turning 22 Law," established a statewide Bureau of Transitional Planning (BTP) within the Executive Office of Human Services. The law does not entitle eligible youth for employment or other adult services; it simply entitles them to the development of an individualized transition plan (ITP). Walsh (1985) has noted, "[Chapter 688] is not intended for the many students who have received special education services and are now able to enter competitive work situations and lead independent lives as adults" (p. 72). Instead, eligibility is based upon receipt of Supplemental Security Income (SSI) and/or registration at the Massachusetts Commission for the Blind. In addition, the bill stipulates that eligible students must be evaluated as unable to work competitively for 20 or more hours per week. The school system, student, and/or family member may initiate a Chapter 688 referral 2 to 3 years prior to the student's targeted date for leaving school.

Chapter 688 represented an attempt by Massachussetts policymakers to fulfill Gil's (1976) final stage of social policy development—a distribution of rights and resources through an entitlement policy. Further, it advanced state policy on transition from an initiation phase to an implementation phase, with minimal effort spent on predetermining risks or selecting proposed actions from alternative policies. Most importantly, Chapter 688 provided a model for other states across the country.

In 1985, the Indiana state legislature also recognized the need to formalize transition planning services by strengthening the referral process between the public schools and adult services through the enactment of PL 28. Under this law, public schools are required to identify students who are likely to benefit from adult services before November 1st of the students' last year in school. At each identified student's annual case review meeting, the school is to invite a local rehabilitation counselor to participate in the meeting, and is to give the parents an information release form to allow records to be transferred to the departments of vocational rehabilitation and mental health. If release forms are signed and returned to the school, each student's records are then transferred to the department of vocational rehabilitation for eligibility determination, and finally to the department of mental health for eligibility determination. The department of mental health returns the eligibility decision to the department of vocational rehabilitation, which is then responsible for notifying the student, parents, and school of the eligibility decision within 180 days.

The Association for Retarded Citizens of the United States (ARC–US) obtained funding from the Administration on Developmental Disabilities (ADD) of the U.S. Department of Health and Human Services to establish and support a national system of Transitional Service Centers (ARC, 1986). In 1985, 10 sites were selected from over 60 applications to assist localities with coordinating school to adult life transition. According to the Association for Retarded Citizens (ARC, 1986), the broad purposes of the Transitional Services Centers are to:

1. Assist in the location of and access to the most appropriate combination of services and resources;
2. Systematically collect, maintain, and disseminate information on services and resources available;
3. Assist in the development and support of relationships among agencies; and
4. Assist in the development of new programs and services for students or clients (pp. 7–8)

Although these initial efforts in transition planning in California, Massachusetts, Indiana, and ARC should be applauded because of their leadership in addressing the transition problem, they have been hindered, to some extent, by a lack of accurate data, financial resources, trained personnel, and, most critically, clearly defined goals for transition planning. As Brewer (1974) observed, "This phase emphasizes sharpened redefinition of the problem. It refers to the fragile business of reconceptualizing a problem, laying out a range of possible solutions, and then beginning to locate potentially 'best' choices within that range" (p. 240).

It has become increasingly clear that state-mandated transition planning alone will not automatically assure optimal transition outcomes for youth with disabilities. Since the enactment of Chapter 688 in 1983, over 3,000 referrals have been made to the Bureau of Transitional Planning (BTP), averaging between 600–800 each year (Northeast Regional Resource Center, n.d.). In California and in Massachusetts, *optimal* services are not always available even though clients are referred and deemed eligible. A parent of a 21-year-old young man with severe disabilities expressed the concerns of many parents and service providers in describing transition in Massachusetts as a myth rather than the reality (in Nettekoven & Ramsey, 1985).

Phase Two: Estimation or Predetermination of Risks, Costs, and Benefits of Transition Policy

Most states have reacted less quickly and more cautiously to the transition problem than California, Massachusetts, and Indiana's earliest efforts. Florida, Illinois, Kentucky, Minnesota, and Virginia, for example, have supported the development of state-level interagency task forces and/or state conferences to explore the needs of transition-aged youth in their respective states before committing resources to statewide transition planning and implementation efforts.

In 1985, the Florida State Legislature appropriated funds for a statewide study of special education students in transition to be reported specifically to the Florida legislature, department of education, department of health and rehabilitative services, and the department of labor. The final report (Project Transition, 1986) included three main components: 1) a survey of 5,000 parents of former special education students to determine their son's or daughter's employment status; 2) a proposed state transition model; and 3) conclusions and recommendations. Highlights of recommendations contained in the report include:

1. Enact additional legislation requiring the implementation of a transition process within each school district;
2. Create the position of State Transition Coordinator within the Department of Education;
3. Form a statewide task force that will address the needs and make recommendations on the problem of dropouts in exceptional education;
4. Strengthen coordination efforts between exceptional education and vocational education in each county and emphasize the need for more vocational work experiences, and work study classes for students with handicaps;
5. Increase employment and supported employment options;
6. Develop standards for Exceptional Adult Basic Education programs;
7. Develop vocational education as another viable option for handicapped students and adults; and
8. Increase substantially the funding level for Health and Rehabilitative Services Developmental Services programs. (pp. 103–104)

Project Transition's final report was a well-conceived attempt to assess the benefits of adopting a statewide transition policy. The project staff noted that it was beyond the scope of the study, however, to analyze the costs of the transition policy, and instead:

> Recommended for the future a comparative cost analysis study to determine funding required to put a transition process into place statewide. This study should also examine benefits to Florida of placing a student into agency services or employment following graduation versus the costs of re-training a student after a lapsed period of time. (p.4)

In 1985, the Illinois State Legislature also passed legislation, HB 892 (Illinois Transition Statute, 1985), to develop a statewide plan for the identification, assessment, evaluation, and referral of all special education students during their transition years. Members of the task force created to develop the statewide plan noted three implicit assumptions of the legislation:

> One, such a plan must address the adequacy of existing secondary services related to transition

outcomes. Two, the state plan must operationalize a transition planning process for bridging the gap between school and post-school service agencies. Finally, this plan needs to encourage the expansion of post-school program options that assure meaningful work and community participation opportunities for all citizens. (Bates et al., 1986)

The final report submitted by the Governor's Planning Council on Developmental Disabilities (GPCDD) to the Illinois State Legislature in the summer of 1986 made several recommendations:

1. Create a Transition Assistance Committee (TAC) within the GPCDD for the purpose of operationalizing and coordinating an ongoing commitment of interagency resources for the improvement of school and post-school transition services.
2. The TAC . . . should develop a transition planning and needs assessment data system that identifies student characteristics, projected employment and independent living goals, and needed secondary/post-secondary services.
3. The TAC . . . should develop a post-school follow-up survey . . . .
4. Formal transition planning should be initiated by the public schools in conjunction with the students' IEP meetings. Transition plans should be developed for students several years (2–6) prior to exit.
5. Transition planning and coordinating committees (TPCCs) should be established in local communities . . . .
6. A statewide information campaign regarding transition related services . . . should be directed at parents.
7. Technical assistance and inservice activities should be initiated . . . .
8. Competencies need to be identified for professional and paraprofessional roles associated with . . . transition.
9. The participating agencies within the TAC should identify transition related outcome measures.
10. Services in the community should be available to all Illinois citizens that [and should] focus on enhanced employment outcomes and increased community participation. (Bates et al., 1986, pp. 29–45)

Similar to the caveat issued by Project Transition in Florida, Bates et al. (1986) noted an inability to make final cost projections and analyses for statewide implementation of their recommendations. The state was, however, able to set guidelines for the initial funding of the recommendations by requesting $75,000 to support staff and necessary activities of the TAC for the following year.

Florida's and Illinois's efforts to determine risks, costs, and benefits associated with statewide transition planning and implementation represent leadership efforts in each state beyond the invention/initiation phase. As Brewer (1974) observed:

> The objective of estimation is to narrow the range of plausible policy solutions by excluding the infeasible or the truly exploitative for instance, and to order the remaining options according to well-defined scientific and normative criteria. (p. 240)

Phase Three:
Selection of Transition Policy

Phase three requires an individual or, in most instances, a group of individuals, to select transition policy on the basis of identified needs and recommendations as well as the estimated costs and benefits of the proposed policy options. In the examples of Florida and Illinois, each state's decision makers (in each case, the state legislative body) had the authority to accept, revise, or reject the policy recommendations presented in the final reports. In each case (Bates, 1987; J. Rollin, personal communication, January 1987), the decision makers accepted, with some revisions, the proposed recommendations for a statewide policy.

Minnesota, through the efforts of the Interagency Office on Transition Services (IOTS) and the State Interagency Transition Committee (STIC), has taken a leadership role in statewide transition policy. In 1987 two pieces of legislation were passed related to transition planning. The first, similar to legislation in Massachusetts, Indiana, and Kansas, entitles all special education students from age 14 on to the development of an ITP. The second piece of legislation mandates the development of community transition committees. These local interagency committees have two major responsibilities: 1) to identify current services and programs; and 2) to develop community action plans with suggestions for changes. The IOTS estimates that approximately 100 community teams will be developed (B. Troolin, personal communication, August 5, 1987). Minnesota has selected a com-

prehensive transition policy that incorporates statewide systems change at a state, community, and individual student level (Wehman et al., 1988).

Phase Four:
Implementation of Transition Policy

Implementation, as defined by Brewer (1974), refers to "executing a selected option" (p. 240). Implementation enables the policy's stakeholders to find "out what is actually happening and how reality differs from what was intended or implied by those more responsible for the selection phase of the decision" (Brewer, 1974, p. 241).

Kansas is an example of a state that has plunged ahead to an implementation phase of policy development. In 1986, the Kansas State Legislature passed HB 2300, which authorized funds and other resources for the development of local transition planning in two pilot communities, Salina and Hayes. HB 2300 entitles a defined target population of students within each of the pilot sites to the development of "transitional plans."

North Carolina has also begun to implement a statewide transition policy. In January 1986, the state department of education awarded minigrants to eight school districts across the state for transition planning and development (NRRC, n.d.). The state department of education has also assumed an active leadership role with the funded localities and other localities across the state through the provision of inservice workshops, interagency team meetings, and dissemination of project results.

Oregon is another state that has also begun to implement a statewide transition policy, but only after carefully progressing through a policy development process similar to that described by Brewer (1974). In 1984, the state department of education contracted with the Universities of Oregon and Washington to conduct follow-up studies of the postsecondary needs of special education students with a complete range of disabilities. These studies yielded the data and support for the development of a statewide task force, which developed and distributed a series of policy recommendations to state directors of agencies and organizations who provide services to transition-age youth. Using these recommendations as a foundation, five interagency task forces were developed to address five target areas: 1) curriculum and instruction; 2) transition planning; 3) interagency coordination; 4) documentation of individual transition plans; and 5) certification and training issues (NRRC, n.d.). The efforts of these task forces resulted in the development of a comprehensive state plan for the implementation of transition procedures. In January 1986, implementation of the state plan was initiated through a request for proposal process; 12 "model" sites were selected for initial implementation of the plan.

Phases Five and Six: Evaluation and Termination

The need for an evaluation phase of transition policy has been recognized by nearly every state that has begun to plan and implement policy (e.g., Bates et al., 1986; J. Lambrou, personal communication, January 1987; NRRC, n.d.; Project Transition, 1986). Because transition policy implementation is relatively recent, however, few, if any, states have more than preliminary information on the effectiveness of the policy within their given states. Perhaps the most promising effort in this area is the research being conducted by the federally funded Secondary Transition Intervention Effectiveness Institute at the University of Illinois at Urbana-Champaign. This project was funded to evaluate the impact of the OSERS initiative on state transition policy (DeStefano, 1987).

During the next few years, as more and more states begin to assume responsibility for transition planning and implementation, human service professionals must seek out information on the effectiveness of the various policies adopted by different states. Many of transition's strongest supporters have rallied around the concept with only a vague idea of its intended goals and even a vaguer idea of mechanisms for evaluating the goals' effectiveness. As Brewer (1974) has noted, "evaluation is a scarce commodity, but it is essential, and it is a necessary ingredient to the next and final (termination) phase of the process" (p. 241).

Termination is defined by Brewer (1974) as "the adjustment of policies and programs that have become dysfunctional, redundant, outmoded, unnecessary, and so forth" (p. 241). Conceptually, this phase of policy development is less clearly defined than any of the other phases. Arguably, termination of transition policy may occur before or after any of the other phases, depending upon decisions made (or not made!) by the policy's supporters or opponents. For example, defeat of legislation requiring mandated transition plans, or reduced fiscal support for adult services, are policy decisions that are frequently made by decision makers before formal or informal policy has progressed through any or all of its stages of development.

Brewer (1974) suggested that several questions must be considered in relation to termination of a policy. One question has particular importance for transition policy in view of recent federal support of early intervention programs, in effect, transition from home to school: "What might be learned in the termination process that will inform the initiation and invention of new policies? " (p. 241). The problems associated with transition are not new; for the most part, they are the result of shortsightedness on the part of professionals and policymakers throughout the 20th century. As Madeleine Will (1984a) has commented, "Let us pause and reflect—but not too long."

REFERENCES

Association for Retarded Citizens of the United States. (1986). *Transitional service centers. Assisting students with developmental disabilities into employment and community life: A procedural handbook*. Arlington, TX: Author.

Barden-LaFollette Act. Public Law 113, 1943.

Bates, P. (1987, February). *Transition in Illinois—Where we are, where we're going*. Paper presented during panel discussion at Northwestern Illinois Association Workshop on Transition, Rockford.

Bates, P., Suter, C., & Poelvoorde, R. (1986). *Illinois transition project: Transition plan development for special education students in Illinois public schools. Final report*. Chicago: Governor's Planning Council on Developmental Disabilities.

Berkowitz, M., Johnson, W., & Murphy, E. (1976). *Public policy toward disability*. New York: Praeger.

Braddock, D. (1987). *Federal policy toward mental retardation and developmental disabilities*. Baltimore: Paul H. Brookes Publishing Co.

Brewer, G. (1974). The policy sciences emerge: To nurture and structure a discipline. *Policy Sciences, 5*, 239–244.

Castellani, P. J. (1987). *The political economy of developmental disabilities*. Baltimore: Paul H. Brookes Publishing Co.

Corthell, D., & VanBoskirk, C. (1984). *Continuum of services: School to work*. Menomonie, WI: University of Wisconsin-Stout, Stout Vocational Rehabilitation Institute, Research & Training Center.

Coudroglou, A., & Poole, D. (1984). *Disability, work, and social policy*. New York: Springer-Verlag.

DeStefano, L. (1987, February). *Model transition programs throughout the United States*. Paper presented at Northwestern Illinois Association Workshop on Transition, Rockford.

Education for All Handicapped Children Act. Public Law 94–142, 1975.

Education of the Handicapped Act. Public Law 99–457, 1986.

Education of the Handicapped Act Amendments. Public Law 98–199, 1983.

Employment Opportunities for Disabled Americans. Public Law 99–643, 1986.

Everson, J.M. (1985). *A history of parent organizations in the United States: From fund raisers to policy makers*. Unpublished manuscript, Virginia Commonwealth University, Richmond.

Executive Office of Human Services (1984). Chapter 688. *(The "Turning 22 Law") implementation: Guidelines and instructions for local school districts*. Boston, MA.

Gettings, R. (1980, October). *Federal financing of services to mentally retarded persons: Current issues and policy options*. Alexandria, VA: National Association of State Mental Retardation Program Directors.

Gil, D. (1976). *Unravelling social policy*. Cambridge, MA: Schenkman.

Halpern, A. (1985). Transition: A look at the foundations. *Exceptional Children, 51*(6), 479–486.

Harris, Louis and Associates. (1986). *Survey of disabled Americans: Bringing disabled Americans into the mainstream*.

Hasazi, S., Gordon, L. R., & Roe, C. A. (1985). Factors associated with the employment status of handicapped youth exiting high school from 1979–1983. *Exceptional Children, 51*(6), 455–469.

Hoyt, K. (1975). Career education: Contributions to an evolving concept. Salt Lake City: Olympus.

Hoyt, K. (1976). *Refining the career education concept*. Washington, DC: U.S. Department of Health, Education & Welfare, Department of Education.

Illinois Transition Statute. (1985). *HB 892*. Illinois State Legislature.

Indiana Transition Legislation. Public Law 28, 1985.

Lanterman Developmental Disabilities Services Act. California statute, 1976.

McDonnell, J., Wilcox, B., & Boles, S. M. (1986). Do we know enough to plan for transition? A national survey of state agencies responsible for services to persons with severe handicaps. *Journal of the Association for Persons with Severe Handicaps, 11*(1), 53–60.

Mithaug, D., Horiuchi, C., & Fanning, P. (1985). A report on the Colorado statewide follow-up survey of special education students. *Exceptional Children, 51*, 397–401.

Nettekoven, L., & Ramsey, E. (1985). Entitlements: One solution to the transition dilemma? In M. Gould & G.T. Bellamy (Eds.), *Transition from school to work and adult life* (pp. 24–56). Eugene, OR: University of Oregon, Center on Human Development, Specialized Training Program.

Northeastern Regional Resource Center (NRRC). (n.d.). *A guide to the efforts of selected state education agencies to improve transitional services*. Burlington, VT: Trinity College, Northeastern Regional Resource Center.

Omnibus Reconciliation Act. Public Law 97–35, 1981.

Project Transition. (1986, June). *Florida's exceptional students in transition from school to community. Final report*. Tallahassee, FL: Project Transition.

Smith-Fess Act. Public Law 236, 1920.

Smith-Hughes Act. (U.S. statutes at large, volume 39), 1917.

United States Commission on Civil Rights. (1983). *Accommodating the spectrum of individual disabilities*. Washington, DC: Author.

Vocational Rehabilitation Act. Public Law 93–112, 1973.

Walsh, M.A. (1985, May). Individual transition plans. In *Proceedings document. Preparation for Life: A Conference on Transition from School to Work* (pp. 72–84). Des Moines: Mountain Plains Regional Resource Center, Drake University.

Wehman, P., Kregel, J., & Seyfarth, J. (1985). Transition from school to work for individuals with severe handicaps: A follow-up study. *Journal of the Association for Persons With Severe Handicaps, 10*(3), 132–136.

Wehman, P., Moon, M. S., Everson, J. M., Wood, W., & Barcus, J. M. (1988). *Transition from school to work: New challenges for youth with severe disabilities*. Baltimore: Paul H. Brookes Publishing Co.

Western Regional Resource Center. (1985, May). *Parents and transition*. Eugene, OR: University of Oregon, Western Regional Resource Center.

Will, M. (1984a). Let us pause and reflect—but not too long. *Exceptional Children, 51*(1), 11–16.

Will, M. (1986b). *OSERS programming for the transition of youth with disabilities: Bridges from school to working life*. Washington, DC: U.S. Department of Education, Office of Special Education and Rehabilitative Services.

Chapter 6

Vocational Evaluation and Eligibility for Rehabilitation Services

Bruce M. Menchetti and Frank R. Rusch

The rehabilitation process, consisting of intake, referral, evaluation, individualized planning, treatment, training, placement, and closure, is designed both to determine the eligibility for service of individuals with handicaps and to provide appropriate service to those who are eligible. Two criteria are used by state vocational rehabilitation personnel to determine an individual's eligibility to receive services: 1) the applicant must have a physical or mental disability that interferes with his or her employment; 2) a reasonable possibility must exist that rehabilitative services will result in gainful employment.

Vocational evaluation is pivotal to the rehabilitation process. In conjunction with intake and referral information, evaluation data are used to identify disabilities and to determine whether or not an individual has a reasonable chance of getting and keeping a job. As a result, vocational evaluation has played a key role in determining eligibility for rehabilitation services, and thus has become the component of the rehabilitation process with the most direct impact upon persons seeking employment services.

For some applicants of vocational rehabilitation services, the connection between evaluation and eligibility is straightforward. For instance, medical evaluations are frequently useful to identify the medical or psychiatric treatment needed to reduce an individual's disability. Once the applicant has been determined to be eligible and appropriate services have been identified, the rehabilitation process can progress toward job placement and eventual closure. For many vocational rehabilitation applicants, however, evaluation practices do not always result in such precise eligibility and service outcomes. For individuals with severe disabilities such as mental retardation, cerebral palsy, and autism, vocational evaluation often results in ineligibility.

Given the supported employment mandate of the Rehabilitation Act amendments (PL 99-506), professionals in vocational rehabilitation, developmental disabilities, mental health and retardation, and special education will have to reexamine their vocational evaluation practices. Evaluation procedures that do not provide meaningful information related to planning effective programs for persons with severe handicaps will be of no help to these practitioners in facing the challenge of supported employment. When testing procedures do not result in training-related information, evaluation becomes nonfunctional in the larger rehabilitation process.

This chapter has three purposes: to describe the evolution of current evaluation procedures, to address the utility of current practices in the development of effective supported employment programs, and to recommend changes in evaluation and eligibility procedures. It is the authors' intent to provide readers with helpful suggestions in planning vocational evaluation activities that are closely related to supported employment training. These writers believe that vocational evaluation should remain an integral and useful part of the rehabilitation process.

EVOLUTION OF CURRENT VOCATIONAL EVALUATION PROCEDURES

Service providers can choose from a wide variety of evaluation procedures to identify the employment training needs of persons with disabilities, including measures of general intelligence, educational achievement, motor dexterity, mechanical aptitude, occupational interest, personality traits, and work habits. Many of these procedures have been adapted from methods developed by early researchers in vocational evaluation. Current practice, therefore, cannot be adequately understood without examining the history of vocational evaluation.

Standardized intelligence, achievement, and aptitude tests have been used for vocational evaluation since World War I. It was not until World War II, however, that these measures gained widespread use, when approximately 14 million men underwent some form of achievement or aptitude testing to evaluate their suitability for various military jobs. The work of Robert L. Thorndike, the psychologist largely responsible for the development and administration of the Aviation Psychology Program of the Army Air Force during World War II, shaped the field of vocational evaluation, and his influence is still felt today.

Thorndike defined the goal of personnel testing as "selecting certain individuals from among the applicants for a job, or determining for which of two or more possible job categories a particular individual shall be assigned" (Thorndike, 1949, p. 4). This form of evaluation challenged the personnel psychologist to derive "insights and hypotheses as to the psychological functions required for success on the job" (p. 12). To accomplish this, Thorndike suggested a rigorous method consisting of job analysis, selection and invention of test procedures, combination of tests into a battery, and finally, systematic administration of the testing program. Thorndike's ap-

proach to vocational evaluation was analytical, objective, and empirical. He wrote:

> The feature that distinguishes reputable work in personnel selection from that of the mass of self-styled "psychologists," "personnel experts," and other quacks is that the reputable worker in the field is continuously concerned with testing, re-verifying, and improving the adequacy of his procedures. (p. 2)

Some of the psychological functions that Thorndike and his colleagues identified as prerequisites for successful Air Force pilots were an understanding of mechanical principles, knowledge of general information, complex coordination, instrument comprehension, and arithmetic reasoning.

Thorndike's approach to vocational evaluation was highly empirical. The procedures he used to develop, select, validate, and combine tests became known as the process of standardization (Neff, 1966). Because many of the characteristics Thorndike measured were related to both general and specialized psychological functions, Neff (1966) labeled this evaluation model the mental testing approach.

The Mental Testing Approach in the Private Sector

The mental testing approach to vocational evaluation developed and refined by Thorndike for the military was eventually adopted by business and industry, where prospective employees were evaluated with batteries of aptitude and achievement tests.

Test authors like George K. Bennett developed instruments designed to measure general vocational aptitudes. The Test of Mechanical Comprehension, Form AA (Bennett, 1947) became one of the most widely used instruments for testing job applicants. The major purpose of this testing was to measure the applicant's ability to perceive and understand physical laws and practical mechanical relationships. Bennett claimed that this aptitude was important for a wide variety of jobs. With this assertion, the field of vocational evaluation, which had originated to select individuals for highly specialized jobs such as piloting aircraft, became oriented toward the prediction of general vocational success.

The vocational evaluation model that employed standardized tests for predicting general vocational ability gained strength in the post–World War II era. Business and industry utilized a wide range of evaluation instruments to screen prospective employees for a variety of jobs. Many of these instruments, however, were a compilation of techniques used by the military to test ability for specialized jobs (Cronbach, 1960). For example, the Flanagan Aptitude Classification Tests were a battery of 21 tests, suggested by Air Force studies, that included measures of scale reading, carving skill, and tapping ability. The Guilford-Zimmerman Aptitude Survey, published in 1947, also contained measures found useful in Air Force classification (Guilford, 1947). Perhaps owing to its adoption by business and industry, the mental testing approach became the preeminent model of vocational evaluation. When education and rehabilitation professionals became involved in vocational evaluation, the mental testing approach was the methodology they selected.

The Mental Testing Approach in Education and Rehabilitation

The mental testing approach has been characterized as standardized testing to *predict* general vocational ability (Cobb, 1972; Gold, 1973; Halpern, Lehmann, Irvin, & Heiry, 1982; Neff, 1966). The mental testing model with its prediction orientation has been applied to the vocational evaluation of individuals in educational and rehabilitation settings, and many of the evaluation techniques in use throughout the country reflect this approach.

One of the first instruments developed for use in educational settings was the Differential Aptitude Tests (DAT) (Bennett, Seashore, & Wesman, 1947). Linn (1978) has called the DAT the Cadillac of multiple aptitude batteries. The DAT battery consists of eight tests, including verbal reasoning, numerical ability, abstract reasoning, clerical speed and accuracy, mechanical reasoning, space relations, spelling, and language usage. The DAT tests were designed to assist high school vocational guidance counselors in advising students on career choices. Several reviewers have suggested that the DAT is one of the most thoroughly validated instruments of its kind (Cronbach, 1960; Linn, 1978; Mastie, 1976). Although disabled persons were not included in the DAT standardization sample, the instrument is characteristic of the mental testing approach to vocational evaluation. In fact, the evaluation methodology and prediction orientation used by the DAT have been incorporated into many current systems used by education and rehabilitation professionals, including both the multiaptitude batteries and the popular work sample systems used in many vocational evaluation programs.

The U.S. Employment Service (USES) has developed the Nonreading Aptitude Test Battery (NATB) for vocational evaluation of "educationally deficient" individuals. The NATB is a nonreading version of the most widely used multiaptitude battery, the USES General Aptitude Test Battery or GATB (Borgen, 1983). The NATB subtests correspond closely to those of the DAT and include verbal ability, numerical ability, manual dexterity, clerical perception, form perception, spatial perception, general learning ability, motor coordination, and finger dexterity. The similarities between the NATB, revised in 1981, and the DAT (developed in 1947) are striking; in fact, even some of the more work-oriented vocational evaluation systems in the NATB still closely resemble those in the DAT.

Another instrument, the VALPAR Component Work Sample System, comprises 16 subtests (Botterbusch, 1980), many of which resemble subtests of the DAT. VALPAR subtests include independent problem solving, numerical sorting, money handling, clerical comprehension and aptitude, simulated assembly, size discrimination, electrical circuitry and print reading, small tools, upper extremity range of body motion, multilevel sorting, whole range of body motion, trilevel measurement, eye-hand-foot coordination, soldering and inspection, integrated peer performance, and drafting. Many of the VALPAR subtests focus on general work aptitudes, which is a defining feature of the mental testing approach to vocational evaluation.

Two extremely popular and widely used vocational evaluation techniques, the multiaptitude test battery (e.g., NATB) and the work sample system (e.g., VALPAR) are directly related to the mental testing approach. Some similarities between current evaluation techniques and the traditional mental testing approach include: 1) a focus on general work abilities that are presumably elements of successful vocational adjustment, 2) a prediction orientation and purpose, and 3) a heavy reliance on standardized instruments. The aptitude, achievement, and work sample methods have advanced to the forefront of education and rehabilitation evaluation programs (Brolin, 1982; Phelps & McCarty, 1984). Proponents of the approach have suggested that the behaviors measured with aptitude and achievement batteries may be related to an individual's employability. For example, Brolin (1982) has said, "Academic skills in the areas of reading, writing, and mathematics play an important role in the determination of vocational potential" (p. 91). The capability of mental testing techniques, most of which were originally designed to screen nonhandicapped persons for highly specific jobs, to predict the general employment potential of persons with handicaps has been questioned repeatedly (Cobb, 1972; Gold, 1973, Menchetti, Rusch, & Owens, 1983; Schalock & Karan, 1979; Wolfensberger, 1967). Given the continuing debate, the utility of the mental testing approach in vocational evaluation must be examined critically by education and rehabilitation professionals.

UTILITY OF CURRENT VOCATIONAL EVALUATION PRACTICES

The mental testing approach has gained widespread acceptance in the vocational evaluation of individuals with disabilities, for several reasons. Aptitude batteries, achievement tests, and work sample systems have been marketed aggressively by publishers. Many of the current vocational evaluation instruments have reported elaborate standardization and validation data (Field, Sink, & Cook, 1978; Flenniken, 1975; Hull & Halloran, 1976; Jones & Lassiter, 1977). These reports, however, have not served to persuade the critics of the mental testing approach or of similar instruments used in evaluating persons with handicaps.

Neff (1966) has pointed out that although the mental testing approach "seems like a triumph of empirical logic, one may be almost astonished to discover that even the most impeccably developed tests have respectably high reliabilities but disappointingly low predictive validity" (p. 55). Other researchers have pointed out that many of the standardized measures used for vocational evaluation of persons with handicaps have not been sufficiently validated for this purpose (Gold, 1973; Wolfensberger, 1967). Finally, some critics have suggested that the purpose of many vocational evaluation programs, namely the prediction of general employability, may be unrelated to the more relevant goal of identifying the specific training needs of persons with handicaps (Cobb, 1972; Halpern et al., 1982; Menchetti et al., 1983; Schalock & Karan, 1979). The paragraphs following further examine current vocational evaluation practice for supported employment in light of these and other criticisms.

Many professionals have pointed out a lack of empirical evidence, showing that scores on instruments currently used in vocational evaluation programs are related significantly to the employability of persons with handicaps (Browning & Irvin, 1981; Cobb, 1972; Gold, 1973; Menchetti et al., 1983; Schalock & Karan, 1979; Wolfensberger, 1967). Some of these individuals have criticized the validation research, whereas others have questioned the evaluation methodology and purpose.

Twenty years ago, Wolfensberger (1967) criticized the validation research for several reasons, including poor methodology, lack of cross-validation studies, failure to analyze training variables, and the assumption that the criteria defining successful employment were the same for all persons. Wolfensberger's criticisms emphasized that training variables play a critical role in assessing the employability of persons with handicaps. These variables are typically not taken into account by current evaluation techniques, which has suggested to many in the field that a vocational evaluation approach that predominantly measures general abilities, achievement, aptitudes, and other manifestations of prior learning is nonfunctional. This belief has led to an attempt to shift the purpose and orientation of vocational evaluation for persons with handicaps.

In an important work titled *The Forecast of Fulfillment*, Cobb (1972) stated that there are two basic orientations to vocational evaluation, the prediction orientation and the counseling orientation. A major goal of evaluation approaches with a *prediction* orientation is the measurement of variables that presumably forecast future employment potential. Approaches with a *counseling* orientation attempt to measure variables that can be used to identify the specific training needs of persons with handicaps. Techniques of evaluation with a counseling orientation can be used for the curriculum development and instructional planning needed to improve vocational training opportunities for individuals with handicaps. Many professionals have suggested that Cobb's counseling orientation is the only relevant vocational evaluation approach.

Gold (1973) criticized evaluation techniques designed primarily to predict a person's potential for employment, suggesting that the validity of instruments with a prediction orientation was statistically significant in a research context but was lacking in practical applicability. Gold was referring to the numerous studies that correlated scores on newly developed aptitude batteries and work samples with measures on other, more established instruments (such as studies by Distefano, Ellis, & Sloan, 1958; Tobias, 1960; Wagner & Hawver, 1965).

Gold (1973) pointed to three serious problems with this approach to validation. First, many of the criteria measures, that is, the scores on the more established tests, had not established their own validity and reliability with handicapped populations. Gold also pointed out that any validation study that correlated scores on a newly developed test with current scores on similar, but more established, tests was investigating concurrent validity. Cronbach (1960) suggested that concurrent validation data have limited generality when tests are used to make predictions regarding potential performance. Finally, Gold reemphasized that vocational evaluation with a prediction orientation has little relevance to the training needs of individuals with handicaps. For example, determining that a person with mental retardation has a low IQ, or low scores on a general aptitude battery, Gold argued, reveals nothing about how to plan an appropriate course of vocational training for that individual. In fact, the poor performance on aptitude tests by persons with handicaps is often used to justify their exclusion from the very training they require. Like Wolfensberger (1967), Gold (1973) called for a shift in the focus of vocational evaluation away from a prediction orientation and toward a training facilitation orientation.

The professional call for a change in the focus of evaluation continued. Schalock and Karan (1979) advocated an approach that emphasized a close, interactive relationship between evaluation and training activities, an approach they termed *edumetric* because its focus is on the measurement of education and training needs. Halpern et al. (1982) differentiated between traditional and contemporary evaluation approaches and suggested that traditional measures are useful when the goal is to identify prior learning such as aptitudes, interests, and traits. Halpern et al. (1982) pointed out, however, that when one is evaluating the vocational needs of persons with handicaps, traditional information is often redundant. A contemporary evaluation approach that measures applied work performance and social behavior in the context in which such performance is expected would better facilitate identification of an individual's training needs and increase his or her access to training opportunities. Halpern et al. (1982) suggested the emergence of contemporary evaluation techniques as the most functional approach to vocational evaluation. Most recently, Kokaska and Brolin (1985) stated that

> norm-referenced tests that compare a student's performance against the norm are not the most appropriate method of assessment to ascertain the individual's competence. In our opinion, a type of criterion-referenced test that assesses the student's mastery or competence in specific areas is more useful. (p. 281)

SUPPORTED EMPLOYMENT: NEW CHALLENGES FOR VOCATIONAL EVALUATION

General agreement is emerging among professionals that vocational evaluation services for persons with handicaps should emphasize the identification of individual training needs over measurement of prior learning (e.g., achievement, general aptitudes, work habits). Evaluation techniques that focus on prior learning highlight the limitations of the individual. Proponents of supported employment have collected data suggesting that the difficulties experienced by many persons with severe handicaps when seeking competitive employment cannot be solely attributed to their limitations (Bates, 1986; Bellamy, Rhodes, Bourbeau, & Mank, 1986; Rusch & Mithaug, 1980; Vogelsberg, 1984; Wehman, 1981). Instead, these professionals have pointed out that the employment problems faced by these persons are, in part, a result of ineffective services and the larger societal employment context. The concept of supported employment is based upon research findings that corroborate this position. First, researchers have pointed to national studies of the outcomes attained by sheltered work programs, which serve the majority of persons with handicaps (General Accounting Office, 1980; Greenleigh Associates, 1975; U.S. Department of Labor, 1977, 1979; Whitehead, 1981). These studies have shown that sheltered services have been largely ineffective in providing reasonable wages for their workers, in moving them to higher levels of productivity, and in enabling them to enter the competitive labor force. Second, supported employment proponents have indicated that there is conclusive evidence of the productive capacity of individuals with severe handicaps. Using behavioral training techniques and a systematic approach to working with community employers, researchers have demonstrated that persons with handicaps can learn the skills needed to earn wages significantly above the sheltered workshop average (Rusch, 1986). Based on these data, supported employment programs have proliferated. All of these programs assume that persons with handicaps can become productive members of society.

Many of the empirically based tenets of supported employment have had a direct impact upon vocational evaluation. Given the emphasis on systematic training, supported employment evaluation efforts have been designed to identify needed training resources and individual training objectives. Furthermore, with the concentration on community employment alternatives, vocational evaluators have focused their mea-

sures toward community expectations, as these evaluations bear a close relationship to the needs of local labor markets (Pancsofar, 1986). Finally, vocational evaluation efforts have facilitated the data-based instructional decisions used in behavioral training programs. The relationship of these supported employment tenets to vocational evaluation is summarized in Table 1.

Some of the guiding tenets of supported employment have begun to be incorporated into vocational evaluation policy. The Vocational Evaluation and Work Adjustment Association (VEWAA) has suggested that vocational evaluation must benefit both the service provider and the client by providing information that facilitates the development of a plan of action (Schneck, 1981). Recent legislation (e.g., PL 99-506 and the Carl D. Perkins Vocational Education Act of 1984) has placed demands on local rehabilitation and education agencies to conduct evaluation that results in both identification of the vocational needs of persons with handicaps and increased access to needed services. Kokaska and Brolin (1985) have suggested that the only reasonable purpose for vocational evaluation is to facilitate the career development of the individual. According to these authors, the major function of evaluation is that ''the individual's strengths and weaknesses can be discerned so that the IEPs and the Individualized Written Rehabilitation Plans (IWRPs) can be planned, and individual and group progress can be monitored'' (p. 281). The remainder of this chapter addresses the need for evaluation techniques to meet the challenges presented by supported employment.

Table 1.   Tenets of the supported employment movement related to vocational evaluation

The relationship of the tenets of supported employment to vocational evaluation may be summarized as follows:

- The purpose of evaluation is to facilitate the identification of individual training needs and resources.
- Measures should be community-referenced and interpretation of performance must assist instructional decision making.
- Successful vocational adjustment is related to training variables and the employment context.

EVALUATION IN SUPPORTED EMPLOYMENT

For many years, the multiaptitude battery and work sample techniques have dominated the field of vocational evaluation. Although these techniques have been used to measure a variety of general aptitudes and skills, the relationship of these variables to the successful vocational adjustment of individuals with handicaps has not been established empirically. In fact, recent research has suggested that productivity is more closely associated with service provision. Services, including systematic instruction, frequent contact with employers, and the availability of long-term support, have defined supported employment. Education and rehabilitation professionals interested in developing supported employment programs must adapt their current evaluation and eligibility procedures to the outcome-oriented approach of supported employment.

Certain features of supported employment will require the use of unique vocational evaluation methods. Given the behavioral orientation of supported employment, evaluation efforts must result in information that can be used to plan individual training programs, suggest alternative training approaches, and determine whether outcomes are within an acceptable range of performance. The community employment focus of supported employment will also have direct implications for vocational evaluation. In order to facilitate community job placement, vocational evaluation measures must be community referenced; that is, the instruments should be closely related to local labor market needs. Finally, the long-term follow-up services associated with supported employment will require evaluation techniques that are continuous, in order to ensure that retraining can be provided when needed *and* that employer satisfaction is documented and monitored.

Ecological Analysis

One evaluation technique that has been very useful in supported employment programs is ecological analysis. Applied to vocational evaluation, ecological analysis is the identification and measurement of actual skills required for employment. Wehman, Renzaglia, and Bates (1985) have defined ecological analysis as a systematic approach to identifying skills that have a high priority for a person to learn. In employment settings, ecological analysis has also been called job analysis (Rusch & Mithaug, 1980; Schutz & Rusch, 1982). In supported employment, job analysis has been used as a strategy for conducting an empirical analysis of the employment ecology.

One example of an empirical approach to identification of high priority employment skills is the Job Skills Inventory (Belmore & Brown, 1978). The Job Skills Inventory analyzes the employment ecology with a three-step strategy or process. First, the general vocational and social skill requirements of a specific job are identified. Second, workers employed in the target job are directly observed and each previously identified skill is broken down into its component behaviors, a technique known as task analysis. Finally, critical factors such as an individual's transportation and independent living skills are identified. These factors are important to long-term job success and must be evaluated so that skill training and supportive services can be provided when necessary.

The information obtained using the Job Skills Inventory is particularly relevant to supported employment. The work, social, and community skills identified can be easily translated into training objectives. Using behavioral observation techniques and evaluation of individual performance, a method for determining intervention effectiveness and planning needed program adjustments can be designed. Task analysis data collected during the inventory process can be used to establish normal levels and rates of worker productivity. This information is important because it allows evaluators and trainers to judge when a target employee's work performance is acceptable. The job inventory strategy assures that skills are referenced to the local labor market and that they have a high probability of being valued by community employers. Finally, the job inventory process can be used to develop evaluation instruments such as skill checklists for continuous measurement of worker performance. The inventory process represents a promising technique for supported employment.

Table 2 delineates the steps in the job inventory process, culminating in the development of an individualized training plan.

Another evaluation instrument based upon an ecological analysis of employment opportunities is the Vocational Assessment and Curriculum Guide or VACG (Rusch, Schutz, Mithaug, Stewart, & Mar, 1982). The VACG includes a variety of general work and social skills based on an empirical analysis of job demands. Rusch, Schutz, and Agran (1982) surveyed employers in service and light industries to determine the skill demands of their entry-level jobs. The results of this survey provided the item pool for the VACG.

The VACG has been designed as a behavior-rating scale that provides a measure of the vocational and social skills of persons with handicaps. The VACG comprises ten domains: attendance/endurance, independence, production, learning, behavior, communication, social skills, grooming/eating, reading/writing, and mathematics. There are 66 items on the VACG, each beginning with the phrase, "Does the worker," followed by a description of the behavior being assessed. Several possible responses are provided that indicate levels of performance displayed by the worker, and raters are instructed to select the phrase that best describes the individual's current level of functioning. The VACG was designed to be used by classroom teachers, rehabilitation counselors, adult service providers, parents, and paraprofessionals to determine an individual's general skill level in relation to standards suggested as important for success in such occupations as the food service industry, janitorial work, and light industrial occupations. The pri-

mary purpose of the instrument is to assist in the job inventory process by providing a starting point for the development of a supported employment program in the occupation areas just mentioned. The measure also provides functional training objectives for school-aged students with handicaps as they move toward competitive employment opportunities. The VACG has proven to be a useful evaluation instrument in ongoing supported employment programs.

Vogelsberg (1986) has described the role of the VACG in supported employment evaluation in Vermont. (The VACG is one of two instruments utilized in the evaluation phase of the Vermont program; the other is a locally developed tool, the Individual Skill Inventory.) The VACG is administered to provide curriculum recommendations for individuals who cannot be immediately employed. The recommendations, in the form of specific training objectives, are forwarded to adult service and local education agencies for incorporation into an individual's program plan. The Individual Skill Inventory provides the structure for completing the job inventory process for specific positions in the community. Vogelsberg (1986) has stressed that factors such as transportation, parental support, and agency cooperation are also evaluated and play an important role in identifying the best candidates for supported employment.

Menchetti and Rusch (1987) have investigated selected psychometric properties of the VACG. These included reliability issues of score stability, internal consistency, and interrater agreement. The capability of VACG domain scores to discriminate between groups of handicapped and nonhandicapped workers was also examined as a validity concern. The reliability data obtained by Menchetti and Rusch indicated that the VACG provides stable, consistent, and accurate measurement of skills. The reliability data also compared favorably with similar information reported for other vocational rating scales. The VACG validation data indicated that domain scores differentiate between groups of workers with handicaps employed in sheltered settings and groups of handicapped and nonhandicapped workers employed in service occupations.

Table 2. The job inventory process

Steps in the job inventory process may be summarized as follows:

1. Identify the general work and social skill requirements of a community job.

2. Observe worker performance to analyze the component tasks of the job and establish normal levels of productivity.

3. Determine the need for additional community support services—for example, transportation and independent living.

4. Develop an individualized training program and plan continuous evaluation procedures.

Studies investigating the psychometric properties of instruments with an ecological analysis orientation are important for a number of reasons. Research of this kind signals a return to the rigorous scientific regimen of test development and validation suggested by pioneers in the field such as R.L. Thorndike. Renewed emphasis on empiricism will enhance the field of vocational evaluation and improve the adequacy of measurement techniques.

The job inventory process and instruments such as the VACG, which are based on an empirical analysis of the employment ecology, provide a strategy for the development of useful evaluation procedures. Professionals interested in providing effective supported employment services must use this strategy in their evaluation programs.

Recommendations for Vocational Evaluation in Supported Employment

Meeting the challenge of supported employment will require an evaluation program that is designed to meet the needs of local labor markets *and* the individual seeking a job. Several steps must be followed by evaluators to ensure that the data they obtain are functionally related to community work opportunities and to the employment needs of individuals with handicaps. These include: evaluating local labor markets, evaluating potential employees' vocational and related skill needs, developing individualized training plans, continuously monitoring program efforts, and evaluating employer satisfaction on a regular basis.

Evaluating Local Labor Markets An initial step in the development of supported employment evaluation programs should be the identification of the needs of community employers. Evaluators can utilize techniques such as employer surveys and job analysis (Martin, 1986) to assess target work environments (e.g., restaurants, factories, offices.) The information obtained can be used to specify both general and specific skill requirements of locally available jobs. If this step is not practical at the local level, instruments such as the VACG will provide useful information about the skill requirements of service and light industrial occupations.

Evaluating Individual Needs After obtaining information about marketable community work skills, the evaluator must turn his or her attention to the individual. Evaluators should determine a potential employee's current skill level in relation to the community-referenced standards identified with locally developed surveys or with the VACG. In addition, employment-related factors, such as transportation, medical needs, or economic considerations must be assessed. Usually, prior assessment summaries or school records will contain this information.

Planning Individual Training Training objectives must be specified for each individual seeking supported employment. Many school programs have begun writing individualized transition plans (ITPs) for high school students. Vocational rehabilitation professionals utilize an individualized written rehabilitation plan (IWRP) to specify services. The ITP and IWRP provide vehicles for specifying training objectives related to supported employment. Vocational evaluators can write training objectives for each of the skills included on a locally developed skill checklist or use the curriculum guide portion of the VACG to target objectives for inclusion on an individual's program plan.

Continuously Monitoring Progress In supported employment programs, the evaluator's role does not end with the development of a program plan. Planning and training efforts must be closely connected and mutually beneficial. Individualized program plans (i.e., ITPs, IWRPs) should include recommendations for continuous monitoring of worker performance. Behavioral observation techniques and repeated-measures experimental designs such as the multiple baseline and changing criterion are useful tools for analyzing work behavior (Agran, 1986). Vocational evaluators must be familiar with these techniques in order to facilitate the provision of effective services. A discussion of behavioral assessment methodology is beyond the scope of this chapter, but readers may consult a number of excellent references on this topic: e.g., Agran (1986); Bates & Hanson (1983); Kazdin (1982); Kratochwill (1978); Rusch & Mithaug (1980); Wehman (1981). Continuous assessment of worker performance is needed to facilitate supported employment decisions such as the need to provide retraining and the appropriate time to withdraw intervention procedures. Such evaluation is crucial to the success of supported employment programs.

Evaluating Employer Satisfaction   The final step in evaluation should be an assessment of the employer's satisfaction with supported employment. Employers are important participants in supported employment, and the most successful programs have evaluated employers' perceptions of training goals, procedures, and outcomes. Information regarding employer satisfaction enables programs to be responsive to the needs of the local labor market and increases the likelihood that these markets will be accessible to persons with handicaps.

SUMMARY

This chapter has built a case for change in current rehabilitation and education evaluation procedures. In addition, recommendations and examples of more functional approaches to vocational evaluation of persons with handicaps have been presented. There is no doubt that, once put into widespread practice, these functional evaluation techniques will also replace traditional ideas about eligibility for employment services. In summary, the authors suggest the following changes in the current procedures used to determine whether or not an individual has potential for gainful employment:

1. Vocational evaluation techniques must move away from methods that measure general aptitudes and work habits that have never been shown to be related to the successful vocational adjustment of individuals with handicaps.

2. Service providers must abandon eligibility procedures that are based upon invalid predictions of general employment potential.

3. Vocational evaluation techniques must be based upon an empirical analysis of the local labor market. Techniques and instruments such as a job inventory and the VACG may prove useful.

4. Vocational evaluation efforts must result in information that facilitates program planning, is community-referenced, and assists in instructional decision making. Evaluation in supported employment programs must be continuous to assure that retraining can be provided when needed and that employer satisfaction can be measured.

5. Service providers must base eligibility determination for supported employment programs on job inventory data, job availability, presence of supportive family members, transportation factors, and the economic consequences of community employment on the target individual.

6. Vocational evaluation professionals must rediscover the rigorous empirical methods suggested by the pioneers in the field, to develop new techniques for use with handicapped persons.

REFERENCES

Agran, M. (1986). Analysis of work behavior. In F.R. Rusch (Ed.), *Competitive employment issues and strategies* (pp. 153–164). Baltimore: Paul H. Brookes Publishing Co.

Bates, P.E. (1986). Competitive employment in southern Illinois: A transitional service delivery model for enhancing competitive employment outcomes for public school students. In F.R. Rusch (Ed.), *Competitive employment issues and strategies* (pp. 51–64). Baltimore: Paul H. Brookes Publishing Co.

Bates, P.E., & Hanson, H.B. (1983). Behavioral assessment. In J.L. Matson & S.E. Breuning (Eds.), *Assessing the mentally retarded* (pp. 27–63). New York: Grune & Stratton.

Bellamy, G.T., Rhodes, L.E., Bourbeau, P.E., & Mank, D.M. (1986). Mental retardation services in sheltered workshops and day activity programs. In F.R. Rusch

(Ed.), *Competitive employment issues and strategies* (pp. 257–273). Baltimore: Paul H. Brookes Publishing Co.

Belmore, K., & Brown, L. (1978). A job skill inventory strategy designed for severely handicapped potential workers. In N.G. Haring & D.D. Bricker (Eds.), *Teaching the severely handicapped* (Vol. 3, pp. 223–262). Columbus, OH: Special Press.

Bennett, G.K. (1947). *Test of Mechanical Comprehension, Form AA manual.* New York: Psychological Corp.

Bennett, G.T., Seashore, H.G., & Wesman, A.G. (1947). *Differential Aptitude Tests manual.* New York: Psychological Corp.

Borgen, F.H. (1983). A review of the USES General Aptitude Battery. In J.T. Kapes & M.M. Mastie (Eds.), *A counselor's guide to vocational guidance instruments* (pp. 42–46). Falls Church, VA: American Personnel and Guidance Association.

Botterbusch, K.F. (1980). *A comparison of commerical vocational evaluation systems*. Menomonie, WI: Stout Vocational Rehabilitation Institute, University of Wisconsin-Stout.

Brolin, D.E. (1982). *Vocational preparation of persons with handicaps* (2nd ed.). Columbus, OH: Charles E. Merrill.

Browning, P., & Irvin, L.K. (1981). Vocational evaluation, training, and placement of mentally retarded persons. *Rehabilitation Counseling Bulletin, 25*, 374–408.

Carl D. Perkins Vocational Education Act. Public Law 98–524. Criteria for Services for the Handicapped and for the Disadvantaged. 20 U.S.C.

Cobb, H.V. (1972). *The forecast of fulfillment*. New York: Teachers College Press.

Cronbach, L.J. (1960). *Essentials of psychological testing*. New York: Harper & Row.

Distefano, M.K., Ellis, N.R., & Sloan, W. (1958). Motor proficiency in mental defectives. *Perceptual and Motor skills, 8*, 231–234.

Field, T.F., Sink, J.M., & Cook, P. (1978). The effects of age, IQ, and disability on performance on the JEVS system. *Vocational Evaluation and Work Adjustment Bulletin, 11*, 14–22.

Flanagan, J. C. (1953). *Flanagan aptitude classification tests*. Chicago, IL: Science Research Associates.

Flenniken, D. (1975). Performance on the 1973 revised Philadelphia JEVS work sample battery. *Vocational Evaluation and Work Adjustment Bulletin, 8*, 35–47.

General Accounting Office (1980). *Better reevaluations of handicapped persons in sheltered workshops could increase their opportunities for competitive employment*. Washington, DC: General Accounting Office.

Gold, M. (1973). Research on the vocational rehabilitation of the retarded: The present, the future. In N. Ellis (Ed.), *International review of research in mental retardation* (Vol. 6, pp. 97–147). New York: Academic Press.

Greenleigh Associates. (1975). *The role of the sheltered workshop in the rehabilitation of the severely handicapped*. Report to the Department of Health, Education, and Welfare, Rehabilitation Services Administration, New York. New York: Author.

Guilford, J.P. (1947). *Printed classification tests*. Washington, DC: U.S. Government Printing Office.

Halpern, A.S., Lehmann, J.P., Irvin, L.K., & Heiry, T.J. (1982). *Contemporary assessment for mentally retarded adolescents and adults*. Baltimore: University Park Press.

Hull, M., & Halloran, W. (1976). The validity of the Nonreading Aptitude Test Battery for the mentally handicapped. *Educational and Psychological Measurement, 36* 547–552.

Jones, C., & Lassiter, C. (1977). Worker non-worker differences on three VALPAR component work samples. *Vocational Evaluation and Work Adjustment Bulletin, 10*, 23–27.

Kazdin, A.E. (1982). *Single-case research designs*. New York: Oxford University Press.

Kokaska, C.J., & Brolin, D.E. (1985). *Career education for handicapped individuals* (2nd ed.). Columbus, OH: Charles E. Merrill.

Kratochwill, T.R. (Ed.) (1978). *Single-subject research: Strategies for evaluating change*. New York: Academic Press.

Linn, R. L. (1978). Review of the differential aptitude tests. In O.K. Buros (Ed.), *The eighth mental measurements yearbook* (pp. 659–661). Highland Park, NJ: Gryphon Press.

Martin, J.E. (1986). Identifying potential jobs. In F.R. Rusch (Ed.), *Competitive employment issues and strategies* (pp. 165–185). Baltimore: Paul H. Brookes Publishing Co.

Mastie, M.M. (1976). Test review: Differential Aptitude Tests, Forms S and T, with career planning program. *Measurement and Evaluation in Guidance, 9*, 87–95.

Menchetti, B.M., & Rusch, F.R. (1987). *Reliability and validity of the Vocational Assessment and Curriculum Guide*. Manuscript submitted for publication.

Menchetti, B.M., Rusch, F.R., & Owens, D.M. (1983). Vocational Training. In J.L. Matson & S.E. Breuning (Eds.), *Assessing the mentally retarded* (pp. 247–284). New York: Grune & Stratton.

Neff, W.S. (1966). Problems of work evaluation. *Personnel and Guidance Journal, 44*, 682–688.

Pancsofar, E.L. (1986). Assessing work behavior. In F.R. Rusch (Ed.), *Competitive employment issues and strategies* (pp. 93–102). Baltimore: Paul H. Brookes Publishing Co.

Phelps, L.A., & McCarty, T. (1984). Student assessment practices. *Career Development for Exceptional Individuals, 7*, 30–39.

Rehabilitation Act Amendments of 1986. Public Law 99–506, 20 U.S.C.

Rusch, F.R. (Ed.). (1986). *Competitive employment issues and strategies*. Baltimore: Paul H. Brookes Publishing Co.

Rusch, F.R., & Mithaug, D.E. (1980). *Vocational training for mentally retarded adults: A behavior analytic approach*. Champaign, IL: Research Press.

Rusch, F.R., Schutz, R.P., & Agran, M. (1982). Validating entry level survival skills for service occupations: Implications for curriculum development. *Journal of the Association for the Severely Handicapped, 8*, 32–41.

Rusch, F.R., Schutz, R.P., Mithaug, D.E., Stewart, J.E., & Mar, D.W. (1982). *Vocational Assessment and Curriculum Guide*. Seattle: Exceptional Education.

Schalock, R.L., & Karan, O.C. (1979). Relevant assessment: The interaction between evaluation and training. In G.T. Bellamy, G. O'Connor, & O.C. Karan (Eds.), *Vocational rehabilitation of severely handicapped persons* (pp. 33–54). Baltimore: University Park Press.

Schneck, G.R. (1981). Program improvement in vocational assessment for the handicapped. In R.A. Stodden (Ed.), *Vocational assessment: Policy paper series: Document 6* (pp. 1–25). Urbana-Champaign: University of Illinois, Leadership Training Institute.

Schutz, R.P., & Rusch, F.R. (1982). Competitive employment: Toward employment integration for mentally retarded persons. In K.P. Lynch, W.E. Kiernan, & J.A. Stark (Eds.), *Prevocational and vocational education for special needs youth: A blueprint for the 1980s* (pp. 133–159). Baltimore: Paul H. Brookes Publishing Co.

Thorndike, R.L. (1949). *Personnel selection: Test and measurement techniques*. New York: John Wiley & Sons.

Tobias, J. (1960). Evaluation of vocational potential of mentally retarded young adults. *Training School Bulletin, 56*, 122–135.

U.S. Department of Labor (1977). *Sheltered workshop study: A nationwide report on sheltered workshops and their employment of handicapped individuals* (Vol. 1). Washington, DC: Author.

U.S. Department of Labor (1979). *Study of handicapped clients in sheltered workshops* (Vol. 2). Washington, DC: Author.

Vogelsberg, R.T. (1984). Competitive employment programs for individuals with mental retardation in rural areas. In P. Wehman (Ed.), *Proceedings from the national symposium on employment of citizens with mental retardation*. Richmond: Virginia Commonwealth University.

Vogelsberg, R.T. (1986). Competitive employment in Vermont. In F.R. Rusch (Ed.), *Competitive employment issues and strategies* (pp. 35–49). Baltimore: Paul H. Brookes Publishing Co.

Wagner, E.E., & Hawver, D.A. (1965). Correlations between psychological tests and sheltered workshop performance for severely retarded adults. *American Journal of Mental Deficiency, 69*, 685–691.

Wehman, P. (1981). *Competitive employment: New horizons for severely disabled individuals*. Baltimore: Paul H. Brookes Publishing Co.

Wehman, P., Renzaglia, A., & Bates, P.E. (1985). *Functional living skills for moderately and severely handicapped individuals*. Austin, TX: PRO-ED.

Whitehead, C. (1981). Final report: *Training and employment services for handicapped individuals in sheltered workshops*. Washington, DC: U.S. Department of Health and Human Services, Office of Social Services Policy, Office of the Assistant Secretary for Planning and Evaluation.

Wolfensberger, W. (1967). Vocational preparation and occupation. In A.A. Baumeister (Ed.), *Mental retardation* (pp. 232–273). Chicago: Aldine.

Chapter 7

A Community-Referenced Approach to Preparing Persons with Disabilities for Employment

Adelle Renzaglia and Margaret Hutchins

An individual's worth is often judged by his or her contribution to society and employment has evolved to become a major factor in evaluating this worth (Kiernan & Stark, 1986). Perhaps such a philosophy partially explains the increasing determination with which persons with disabilities are seeking appropriate and challenging employment opportunities. Because of the relentless pursuit of this goal by persons with disabilities, their advocates, and families, the demands and challenges faced by special education and rehabilitation personnel are numerous. Traditional vocational training and service delivery models must be evaluated to ensure that they provide the services needed to prepare persons with disabilities for productive job placements.

To be successful, direct service providers in special education and vocational rehabilitation must be able to: 1) identify potential employment opportunities, 2) functionally assess the student or client, 3) design an individualized vocational curriculum, 4) select the most appropriate training experiences and placements with respect to the abilities and needs of the individual and the prospective employer, and 5) effectively instruct, using sound methodological procedures, persons with disabilities to successfully perform all necessary job responsibil-

ities to the satisfaction of an employer or supervisor. Vocational service systems must design or adopt implementation models to support each of these activities to facilitate long-term placements and movement from traditional sheltered employment and day activity settings to integrated work sites.

A brief historical perspective of the vocational service delivery system and components related to vocational preparation and training may offer insight into the rationale for initiating change in assessment strategies, curriculum design and implementation, rules for selecting job opportunities and placements, and direct training strategies and formats. Early programmatic models that provided vocational training to individuals with disabilities who were not "job ready" were designed as a continuum of services, with the intent to move clients through increasingly more demanding work experiences while building "work adjustment" skills (e.g., attention to task, positive work attitude, acceptable productivity) to a satisfactory level. "Work adjustment" programs were most typically found in sheltered workshops and day or work activity centers. This continuum of services model purported to offer a method for an individualized progression through the system, preparing clients for employment.

Common characteristics may be identified across many work adjustment training programs in the areas of assessment procedures, curricula, training, and evaluation procedures. Traditional assessment procedures include a battery of diverse vocational tests to evaluate the vocational potential of clients receiving services (Revell, Kriloff, & Sarkees, 1980). By assessing achievement, aptitude, dexterity, fine and gross motor skills, and other abilities, professionals are expected to be able to pinpoint and predict an individual's employment potential. Typically, assessments are not related to the actual demands of any particular job, and if job samples are evaluated, they are often restricted to work that is available within the facility and permit a minimal instructional period (Revell et al., 1980).

Vocational curricula for individuals with disabilities who are receiving work adjustment or prevocational services usually emphasize work skills for the areas of employment within the service facility and broad generic behaviors, rather than specific skills required by specific jobs in the community. Habilitation plans often include numerous objectives and training goals reflecting abstract and affective worker characteristics such as attitude, attending to task, motivation, work habits, and so forth. Many of these attributes are perceived as personally intrinsic and unlikely to be modified using management or systematic instructional programs. The lack of progress in such curricular areas often prevents client movement into a community-based employment site.

Decision rules and procedures for selecting skill training and work sites frequently are not systematic and may not include an individual analysis to promote job matches that will be the most meaningful for employers and individual future employees. Skill training is often minimized for the worker who is disabled with the expectation that work habits, behaviors, and skills will easily generalize from experience to experience and that a paycheck will motivate maximum work performance. However, little evidence has been provided to support the notion of skill generalization. In fact, researchers suggest that service providers should not expect persons with moderate and severe handicaps to generalize (Bellamy, Rhodes, & Albin, 1986; Brown, Nietupski, & Hamre-Nietupski, 1976). Therefore, skills having immediate and direct relevance should be trained in the context and settings in which they will ultimately be required.

The characteristics of traditional vocational training programs and work adjustment services necessitated further investigation when professionals began to probe the actual outcomes of the service delivery system and explore alternative vocational training practices. Bellamy and his colleagues (1986) suggested that movement through the continuum of vocational services to higher-level employment training options or actual community-based employment has been minimal. The authors cited studies revealing that fewer than 5% of the clients advanced through the system per year. Two possible explanations for these outcomes are that the individuals were either incapable of performing more sophisticated work or the service delivery system was ineffective. Yet, an historical review illustrates that persons with more severe handicaps who were not employed could acquire work skills and produce at acceptable rates (e.g., Gold, 1972, 1974, 1976; Hunter & Bellamy, 1976; Renzaglia, Wehman, Schutz, & Karan, 1978; Spooner & Hendrickson, 1976). Further demonstrations of employability within competitive work settings (e.g., Sowers, Thompson, & Connis, 1979; Wehman & Hill, 1979, 1982) and increasing support for the use of a community-based approach that emphasizes conducting ecological assessments (Brown et al., 1976), training in the natural environment (e.g., Rusch & Mithaug, 1980; Wehman, Hill, & Koehler, 1979), and systematic teaching of work skills validated in the community (Renzaglia, Bates, & Hutchins, 1981; Rusch, 1986) offer justification for the design and implementation of vocational training models that have an alternative focus on program components. A community-referenced approach provides a stronger, more functional relationship between service delivery and the targeted outcome and takes a more proactive role in providing optimal employment opportunities for clients with disabilities.

This chapter identifies and describes the critical components of a community-referenced vocational training program. Considerations and issues related to each program characteristic are provided. An evaluation of current service delivery system practices in comparison to those presented in the proposed model should offer direction for program design and development as well as confirm positive changes in current program practice.

A COMMUNITY-REFERENCED APPROACH TO VOCATIONAL TRAINING

With the growing body of research documenting the lack of progress of persons with disabilities who are being serviced by traditional "work adjustment" models and the successes of alternative approaches even with persons with severe handicaps, the need for redirecting efforts in providing services is becoming more evident. The traditional prevocational/work adjustment model must be abandoned, and a community-referenced approach adopted. From the onset of training, trainers must target skills required for performance of real jobs in actual employment sites. In addition, training on real work skills should be initiated at young ages and must be a collaborative effort between public schools and adult service providers, including vocational rehabilitation professionals (Schalock, 1986). This will maximize the potential for all persons to be served regardless of handicapping conditions to be gainfully employed in integrated community settings.

Although a community-referenced model and a traditional work adjustment model include the same major components, the specific strategies and procedures (the focus) for providing services within those components differ. Table 1 compares the traditional and community-

Table 1. Comparison of traditional and community-referenced approaches to vocational training

Traditional	Community-referenced
Assessment	
• Uses standardized and/or formal assessment instruments and techniques • Results used to predict vocational potential • May not be a direct relationship between results and community employment opportunities • Screens out individuals for employment	• Provides information about employment opportunities in the community • Identifies areas of needed training • Uses informal procedures (nonstandardized) • Targets community-based employment for all persons evaluated
Curriculum	
• Generic • Trains work in the context of simulated jobs • Emphasizes "work adjustment" skills • No method of selecting appropriate curriculum for the individual	• Directly derived from specific community job opportunities • Individualized • Emphasizes using methods to systematically select skill training areas • Socially valid with respect to individual job types
Training/training settings	
• Unstructured training • Training minimally provided prior to placement • Preplacement training provided in simulated settings • Relies upon employment site to train when placed on a job	• Systematic training procedures used • Training provided in natural environments reflecting actual employment opportunities • Intensive training provided prior to placement, after placement, or both
Placement and follow-up	
• Job opening determines placement • Follow-up is time-limited	• Placement systematically determined by matching needs of individual and parameters of business including potential for job opening • Ongoing support provided after placement is made • Length of time support is given is determined by individual need

referenced approaches across major program components, including assessment, curriculum, training, training settings, and placement and follow-up services. The remainder of this chapter addresses these components (in an order that varies somewhat from the foregoing list) as incorporated into a community-referenced approach to training.

Populations Targeted for Services

Since financial independence is a societal expectation for adults, persons with disabilities should be given opportunities to meet these expectations as well. Therefore, practicing a vocation resulting in gainful employment is very important for all persons, including people with disabilities regardless of the degree of handicapping condition.

In our society few individuals should be exempt from the expectation of employment. Persons who are independently wealthy always have the choice of whether or not to work. In addition, persons who are so medically fragile that work would be life threatening, as well as those who have reached retirement age, are not expected to work, and in fact, are provided for within the current system. In most other cases, persons with disabilities should have the right to paid work and should be expected to contribute to their communities as productive citizens.

Vocational training should be initiated at young ages as a part of public school programs. Although public school personnel will have the major responsibility for providing services to students under the age of 21 years, the effort to provide services should be collaborative. If public school personnel initiate contacts with adult service providers prior to student graduation, the likelihood of successful transition from school to employment and postschool support services increases.

By 16 years of age, students with disabilities should have been introduced to the adult service agencies that will be responsible for services after graduation from public school. In addition, although involvement may be minimal at first, vocational rehabilitation services should be initiated with all students at 16 years of age. As students grow older, the level and type of involvement of vocation rehabilitation counselors will change until total responsibility rests on the counselors in collaboration with other adult service providers when students graduate.

Assessment

The first step in establishing a community-referenced vocational training model is assessment. Assessment activities address two major questions: 1) What employment and training opportunities are available in the community? and 2) How do a trainee's skills compare to those needed for employment in specific jobs in the the community?

Community Assessment The purpose of community assessment is to identify potential employment opportunities characteristic of the specific community in which individuals receiving training will eventually seek jobs (Hutchins, Renzaglia, Stahlman, & Cullen, 1986; Rusch & Mithaug, 1980; Wehman, Renzaglia, & Bates, 1985). Information gathered from this type of assessment can be used by vocational trainers when deciding on the skills to target for training. A community assessment assists in identifying those skills required for performance on real jobs in actual employment sites.

Since a community assessment is usually a large undertaking, service providers should collect the information cooperatively. Information gathered through a community assessment is pertinent to all service providers training vocational skills to persons with disabilities. Therefore, both public school and adult service agency staff should participate in collecting the community employment information (Hutchins et al., 1976). If public school personnel and adult service providers participate collaboratively in surveying the community, the task is more manageable and may result in community-referenced programs for trainees with disabilities at all age levels. In addition, the programs naturally build on one another to promote productive employment.

In order to effectively assess a community for potential jobs, a systematic plan and procedure must be employed. Since even the smallest communities are too large to haphazardly assess with any assurance that all employment sites have been evaluated, a method for approaching segments of the community or representative employers should be developed. The first step in systematically surveying a community involves *generating a list of local businesses*. This can be done by grouping businesses into geographic areas or by job type (e.g., janitorial, industrial).

Once this list is complete, vocational program developers should *initiate contacts with employers*. However, rather than contacting all employers on the list at one time, employers should be telephoned or sent letters systematically by geographic area or job type. In so doing, program developers avoid a situation in which an employer is initially contacted to introduce the purpose of the interaction and then not recontacted to obtain relevant program information for months afterward. Initial contacts should be introductory in nature, with vocational program developers explaining the purpose of the contacts (present and future), the nature of the vocational training program being developed, and the timeline for future interactions.

Following the initial contact, an *employer interview* should be conducted to identify: 1) the employer's willingness to hire persons with moderate and severe handicaps, 2) the employer's willingness to allow on-the-job training in the employment site, 3) the types of jobs available in the employment site, 4) the desirability of the jobs available (e.g., wages, benefits, hours, schedule), and 5) the number of persons hired in the business and the turnover rate. All of this information has implications for 1) program development, 2) developing the content of training programs, and 3) making effective job matches for individual trainees. A file should be established for each business contacted, and all relevant information should be kept there for future reference when a trainer is making training or placement decisions for individual trainees.

The information obtained through the employer interviews provides trainers with only a portion of the information needed for training. Employer interviews help trainers to identify the job types that are available and the desirability of jobs in the community. Additional information about the skills required to adequately perform a job in a specific business and the work-related skills considered necessary for employment in the business should be obtained prior

to establishing vocational training programs (Hutchins et al., 1986; Rusch & Mithaug, 1980; Wehman et al., 1985). This information is directly related to curricular content for training programs in specific job types.

A *job analysis* should be conducted to identify requisite work and work-related skills. Although a job analysis can be conducted through employer or employee interviews, the recommended and most accurate method of completing a job analysis is to directly observe employees performing a targeted job. While observing the employee working, the individual conducting the job analysis should record the specific tasks required to adequately perform the job (e.g., wiping table, scraping trays, mopping floors may be required of a bus person in a cafeteria). Methods for conducting job analyses have been described by a number of experts in vocational training (e.g., Hutchins et al., 1986; Rusch & Mithaug, 1980; Wehman, 1981; Wehman et al., 1985). These methods have been as open-ended as narrative recordings of the tasks engaged in by employees (i.e., Rusch & Mithaug, 1980) to a more precise method of checking off skills on a master checklist of skills identified by job type (i.e., Hutchins et al., 1986). Persons conducting job analyses should select the method best suited to them. Figure 1 is an example of a format for checking off skills on a master checklist. The checklist was developed by conducting repeated observations of employees hired in a specific job type (i.e., laundry worker) across businesses. The items that at least 50% of the employment sites required of persons hired in that job type were included in the master checklist (Hutchins et al., 1986).

An analysis of required work-related skills may not always be possible through direct observation, since many of the skills required may not be easily observed at any given time. Work-related skills include language, self-help, mobility, and functional academic skills in addition to skills that relate to being a responsible worker (e.g., is on time to work, frequency of being absent), an independent worker (e.g., level of supervision provided), and the absence of maladaptive behaviors. The work-related skills required for a specific job can be assessed through a paper-and-pencil survey or employer inter-

Laundry Worker Observations Checklist

Site _____   Date _____   Observer _____

V	H	Sp	Skill	Required frequency*		Materials and equipment	Comments
			I. Laundering of items				
			A. Launders dirty items				
			sheets, pillowcases				
			towels, washcloths				
			bathmats				
			bedspreads				
			blankets				
			pillows				
			shower curtains				
			drapes, curtains				
			mattress pads				
			rags				
			tablecloths				
			napkins				
			pants				
			smocks				
			dresses				
			shirts				
			overcoats				
			aprons				
			II. Preparation of items for wash cycle				
			A. Sorts dirty laundry			__ from a chute	
			Sorts by item type			__ from a bin	
			Sorts by color			__ from bags	
			Sorts by size				
			Places in separate pile if badly stained				
			B. Treats stained/soiled laundry				
			Makes up soaking solution				
			Puts them into soaking solution				
			Puts stain remover directly on spot/stain				
			Puts aside for supervisor to check				
			C. Puts torn laundry in appropriate places				
			Discards torn items				

*Frequency Code:
1—as needed   3—once a week   5—once a month
2—2 to 4 times a week   4—twice a month   6—less than once a month

Figure 1. Sample format for master checklist for laundry worker, used to conduct a job analysis. (From Hutchins, M., Renzaglia, A., Stahlman, J., & Cullen, M. [1986]. *Developing a vocational curriculum for students with moderate and severe handicaps.* Charlottsville, VA: University of Virginia; reprinted by permission) (Project CO-OP, University of Virginia, Contract No. 300-82-0359.) (V, H, and Sp refer to need for vision, hearing, or speech to complete job task.)

view. A number of instruments have previously been developed to assist vocational trainers in assessing work-related skills (e.g., *Vocational Assessment and Curriculum Guide [Rusch, Schutz, Mithaug, Stewart, & Mar, 1982]; Work-Related Skills Survey* [Hutchins et al., 1986]). Therefore, those persons initiating job analyses need not develop new procedures. Figure 2 provides an example of the format and type of questions included in the Work-Related Skills Survey.

Once employer interviews and job analyses are complete, vocational trainers have the information necessary to make decisions regarding the types of vocational experiences that seem most relevant to potential future employment and the specific skills that should be targeted for training within job types selected for instruction. By maintaining all of the information obtained through the community assessment in the earlier-mentioned organized file (e.g., employers by job type), vocational trainers can refer to the information regularly when making training and placement decisions. This ensures that training programs are community referenced and that trainees are instructed either in skills required in current placements or in skills that have a high likelihood of being used in future employment for persons receiving training prior to placement.

Assessing Trainee Skills   The information gathered from the community assessment, interviews, and job analyses should serve as a basis for structuring the assessment process for individual trainees. The purpose of trainee assessment in a community-referenced approach is not to predict employability or potential. Instead, the individual assessment process should be formative rather than summative and serve as a guideline for instruction. Therefore, the traditionally used standardized assessment procedures are not recommended as part of this process. Although the community-referenced approach is much like the traditionally used situational assessment (Revell et al., 1980), the conclusions drawn from assessment results are different. Rather than making global statements about trainee skills based on performance, the community-referenced approach uses the information to identify skills needing instruction in the vocational training process.

The skills identified as required for success on community jobs should be the same skills on which trainees are assessed. Both work and work-related skills should be considered in relationship to actual jobs available in the community (Hutchins et al., 1986). Initial assessment procedures might involve using the skills identified in the community assessment by job type in a checklist format. Through direct observation of trainee skills or through past experiences, the skills on the checklist can be systematically evaluated to determine those that have been mastered and those needing further, in-depth evaluation.

Following these initial assessment procedures, the skills identified as needing instruction should be further evaluated through specific, systematic assessment procedures. The situational assessment technique, in which the trainee is placed in a real job situation over time (Revell et al., 1980), can be used to evaluate specific trainee skills in depth. However, rather than selecting work settings for evaluation based on availability alone (e.g., evaluating skills in a sheltered workshop or in a local cafeteria because they are convenient), the evaluator/trainer should place the trainee in a work setting in which the skills specific to the job type being evaluated naturally occur. Specific assessments can also be conducted in on-the-job training sites.

Systematic assessment procedures involving direct observation over time should be utilized to identify where the trainee's skills break down and where instruction should begin (Bellamy, Horner, & Inman, 1979; Wehman et al., 1985). Task analyses should be developed to represent the steps involved in successfully performing the tasks required of the job being evaluated. The task analyses can then be used to structure assessment procedures in which the trainer observes a trainee performing the job. Correct responses and errors should be recorded in a task analytic assessment, documenting the steps of the task that have been mastered by the trainee and those needing further instruction (Bellamy et al., 1979; Wehman et al., 1985). Figure 3 provides an example of a task analytic assessment procedure for wiping tables, as performed in a cafeteria table busing job. The steps in the task are listed along the left side of the data

Business: _____ Job type: _____

Respondent's position: _____ Date completed: _____

Instructions:

1. Please rate the skill areas as they apply to an individual seeking employment within your facility. For some skill items, you need to select the minimal standard of performance that would be mandatory.

    Example A: Client can: (choose one—minimal standards)

        a. Walk unassisted
        (b.) Walk assisted (cane, crutches, etc.)
        c. Manipulate self in a wheelchair
        d. Be pushed in wheelchair by another employee

    The exemplified response indicates that the building is not barrier free and is inaccessible to wheelchairs. Any client employed in this facility would have to be mobile without the use of a wheelchair.

    For other skill items, responses need to be rated using the response measures that follow.

    Example B: Individual has full use of:

a.	Shoulders	1	2	3	④
b.	Arms	1	2	3	④
c.	Hands/fingers	1	2	③	4
d.	Legs	①	2	3	4
e.	Feet	①	2	3	4

    The responses represented here indicate that the job or task requires use of arms, shoulders, and hands but not legs or feet.

    The response measures used to rate the items are defined as:

1—Irrelevant:	Is not considered when evaluating an individual for employment: does not apply.
2—Minimally important:	Is considered when evaluating an individual for employment but would not be a deciding factor.
3—Important:	Is heavily weighed in the evaluation of an individual for admittance into the program and could be a deciding factor; possibly an area or skill for which less than optimal ability would be tolerated but that would need some improvement or progress.
4—Mandatory:	Is necessary without exception, for employment.

2. Please identify priority skill areas that you consider to be most critical for employment by simply placing a check mark (✔) beside 10 of the items listed in the survey.

                                      * * * * *

15. Identifies upon request:

a.	Full name	1	2	3	4
b.	Home address	1	2	3	4
c.	Telephone number	1	2	3	4
d.	Age	1	2	3	4
e.	Name of employer	1	2	3	4
f.	Address of employer	1	2	3	4

16. Is able to communicate such basic needs as:

a.	Thirst	1	2	3	4
b.	Hunger	1	2	3	4
c.	Sickness	1	2	3	4
d.	Pain	1	2	3	4
e.	Toileting necessities	1	2	3	4

17. Responds appropriately to safety signals when given:

a.	Verbally	1	2	3	4
b.	Through signs	1	2	3	4
c.	From signals (buzzers, bells, etc.)	1	2	3	4

18. Initiates contact with fellow worker when he or she:

a.	Needs help on task	1	2	3	4
b.	Needs task materials from fellow worker	1	2	3	4
c.	Needs evaluation of work completed	1	2	3	4

(continued)

Figure 2. Sample items from Work-Related Skills Survey, used in conducting job analyses. (From Hutchins, M., Renzaglia, A., Stahlman, J., & Cullen, M. [1986]. *Developing a vocational curriculum for students with moderate and severe handicaps.* Charlottesville, VA: University of Virginia; reprinted by permission.)

19. Initiates contact with supervisor when he or she:
    a. Cannot do job   1 2 3 4
    b. Runs out of materials to do job   1 2 3 4
    c. Finishes job   1 2 3 4
    d. Feels too sick or tired to continue working 1 2 3 4
    e. Needs drink of water or to go to restroom 1 2 3 4
    f. Makes a mistake on the job   1 2 3 4
20. Follows: (choose one—minimal standards)
    a. 1-step instructions
    b. 2-step instructions
    c. More than 2-step instructions
21. Follows instructions with: (choose one—minimal standards)
    a. Two or more reminders
    b. One reminder
    c. Two reminders

University of Virginia
Grant No. G008001912

Figure 2. (continued)

sheet, and the instructions for conducting the assessment are at the bottom of the data sheet.

Specific assessments should be conducted across days, in a consistent, systematic manner. If procedures are written so that any trainer can follow them, consistency will be obtained within and across trainers, reflecting a true picture of a trainee's skills. As stated previously, these indepth analyses of trainee skills can serve as guidelines for where to begin instruction, and ongoing evaluation using these procedures will assist trainers in assessing trainee progress and program success.

Curriculum

Selecting target skills (curriculum) for training should be a direct outcome of community and individual assessment procedures. The skills required of community employment sites comprise the curriculum for training. However, the

Training Session Dates

Task components	Trainer: _____ Trainee: _____ Date: _____ Environment: _____ Instructional cue: "Wipe the tables."														
	1. Find damp cleaning rag.														
	2. Go to empty table with rag.														
	3. Move objects from table.														
	4. Fold rag to hand-size.														
	5. Place rag on table with hand on top and fingers spread apart.														
	6. Wipe entire surface of table.														
	7. Scrub any messy areas.														
	8. Place objects back on table.														
	9. Go to next table.														

Assessment procedures: Observe trainee in dining area. Give cue "Wipe the tables" and allow 5 seconds for independent initiation of Step 1 in task analysis. If trainee correctly responds, record (+) and proceed to Step 2, 3, and so forth. If trainee incorrectly responds, performs a step out of sequence, or does not respond in 5 seconds, record (−) and discontinue the assessment. Record all remaining steps as incorrect (−). Do not prompt or reinforce.

Figure 3. Sample task analytic assessment procedure and data sheet for table wiping in a cafeteria table busing job.

considerations for curriculum selection for individual trainees include the age and past experiences of the trainee.

When students are young (under 18 years of age), identification of the specific business for future employment may be difficult. Such identification could limit a student's opportunities and possibilities for securing more desirable employment alternatives. Therefore, the goal of vocational programming at young ages is to provide students with a variety of work experiences across job types and to progressively narrow the number of job types that seem viable as the trainee grows older. This sampling of job types will provide trainers with information regarding students' preferences, differential skills, potential for progress, and so forth, that is relevant to future selection of a placement site.

Because young students will be given a variety of experiences, selecting skills for training that have generic value to the range of community jobs in one job type is very important. This is what Hutchins et al. (1986) refer to as a core skill approach to curriculum. Core skills are skills identified as being required by the majority of employers hiring employees in a particular job type (e.g., wiping tables is likely to be a core skill for a bus person position across employment sites). The core skills identified for each job type should be directly derived from the community assessment job analyses.

The procedure used by Hutchins et al. (1986) to establish core skills for each job type, as determined relevant in the community in which trainees were to be employed, first involved identifying a minimum of 10 businesses in the community for each job type. The businesses were contacted and observations were made (using the master checklists described previously in community assessment) to identify the work and work-related skills required for successful performance of the job type. Those skills required by at least 70% of the 10 or more employers were considered core skills of the job type.

Table 2 includes a list of the core skills identified by Hutchins et al. (1986) for the laundry worker job type. The core skills are organized by category of skill. Those skills listed under the general skill column are the core skills identified by 70% or more of the businesses observed. The specific skills column details the ways in which the general skill is performed. Next to the specific skills are the percentages of the businesses requiring the general skill that also require the specific skill. Those core skill lists, including specific skills, should provide trainers with a community-referenced curriculum that increases the likelihood of a trainee learning skills that are relevant to employment in real jobs.

As stated earlier, as a trainee grows older, the number of job types in which he or she receives training should be narrowed. When trainees reach 19 years of age, vocational trainers should be considering specific placements. When a specific placement has been selected for a trainee, the skills targeted for instruction no longer need to have generic value to all positions in a job type. Instead, the skills should be identified through a specific job analysis of the position targeted for employment in the placement site. The employer interviews and job analyses conducted previously will assist trainers in identifying the skills required in a specific placement site.

The progression described, from varied experiences in which core skills are taught to specific placements in which job specific skills are taught, should facilitate meaningful vocational training. In fact, the early training experiences will provide a foundation for future placement. With this approach, training at all levels will be community referenced and will have longitudinal value.

Selecting Work Experiences and Job Placements

A critical component of any vocational service delivery program is a systematic process for selecting work experiences and/or job placements for individuals with disabilities (Hutchins et al., 1986; Pietruski, Everson, Goodwyn, & Wehman, 1985). To facilitate successful long-term employment, careful consideration must be given to the work skills selected for instruction and the types of job training in which an individual participates. Variables must be identified that can assist special education and rehabilitation professionals in making the right choices and

Table 2.   Core skill list for businesses hiring employees in the laundry worker job type [a]

Laundry Worker Core Skill List

Category	General skill	Specific skill	(%)
I. Laundering of items	Launders dirty items	sheets, pillowcases	100
		towels, washcloths	100
		bathmats	100
		bedspreads	70
		blankets	90
		pillows	10
		shower curtains	80
		drapes, curtains	10
		mattress pads	90
		rags	100
		tablecloths	60
		napkins	60
		pants	40
		smocks	50
		dresses	30
		shirts	30
		overcoats	20
		aprons	30
		lab coats	10
		dust mop heads	10
II. Preparation of items for wash cycle	Sorts dirty laundry	Sorts by item type	100
		Sorts by color	30
		Places in separate pile if badly stained	100
	Treats stained/soiled laundry	Makes up soaking solution	10
		Puts them into soaking solution	70
		Puts stain remover directly on spot/stain	10
		Puts aside for supervisor to check	30
	Puts torn laundry in appropriate places	Discards torn items	33
		Records what item is discarded in/on inventory book/sheet	33
		Puts into box for use as rags	56
		Gives to supervisor	56
	Loads washing machine	Loads machine full	90
		Puts in specific number of items	10
		Puts in weighed pile	10
		Launders items in shortest supply first	10
III. Washing machine operation	Sets wash cycle on machine	Sets dial for wash time	20
		Sets dial for fabric type	20
		Presses button(s) to set cycle	40
		Inserts computer card for appropriate item	20
		Presses destainer button	20
		Refers to chart with linen types for cycles to use	40
		Sets dials on side of machine to correct items	40
		Pushes emergency button to off while setting	10
	Adds detergents to machine	Measures out needed amount	22
		Checks supply of automatically released detergent	78
		Changes/refills containers for automatic release	67
		Pours detergent into machine	22
		Pours water into soap box after adding detergent	11

(continued)

Table 2. *(continued)*

	Laundry Worker Core Skill List		
Category	General skill	Specific skill	(%)
		Adds softeners/brighteners to machine at beginning of cycle	67
		Adds softeners/brighteners to machine during wash cycle	33
	Turns machine on/off	Turns machine to on/start	100
		Turns machine to off when cycle ends	80
	Unloads washer	Loads wet laundry from machine into bins	100
		Leaves washers loaded at end of shift/day	20
IV. Dryer operation	Readies items for dryer	Pushes cart of wet items to dryer	100
		Sorts washed items before drying	22
	Loads dryer	Loads about half way	80
		Puts specified number of items into dryer	30
		Untangles sheets first	10
	Sets cycles on dryer	Sets drying time	100
		Sets to correct temperature	60
		Sets to correct fabric setting	20
		Sets cooling time	90
		Uses reference chart to note correct dryer settings	30
	Unloads dryer	Unloads laundry into bins	100
		Unloads laundry and lays across bin or table	70
		Redries any items still wet	100
		Places clean rags in storage bin	10
V. Folding, stacking and storing of clean laundry	Folds clean laundry by hand	Folds 1st sheet as 2nd goes through mangle	10
		Re-marks labels as needed	10
	Stacks clean laundry	Stacks with same edges together	100
		Stacks by color	40
		Stacks with top and bottom sheets and pillowcases bundled	20
		Stacks with a specific number in a pile (i.e., 10 sheets in a pile)	30
		Stacks by department	10
		Stacks by size	20
		Stacks by quality	10
		Stacks by border type	10
	Stores clean laundry	Brings to separate storage room	20
		Stores on shelves in laundry room	80
		Records amount of linens stored	10
		Counts items for inventory	10
		Puts in bins to be delivered	10
VI. General duties	Cleans laundry room	Wipes surfaces	80
		Sweeps floor	70
		Dust mops floor	10
		Empties lint traps	100
		Wet mops floor	70
		Cleans lint from pipes	10
		Cleans lint from drains	10
		Cleans dryer	10

Source: From Hutchins, M., Renzaglia, A., Stahlman, J., & Cullen, M. (1986). *Developing a vocational curriculum for students with moderate and severe handicaps.* Charlottesville, VA: University of Virginia; reprinted with modifications by permission.
[a] See text for further explanation of items in the table.

designing individualized vocational programs for persons with disabilities. A methodology must be developed for evaluating those considerations or variables related to work experience and job placement decisions. Finally, the job skills that require instruction and appear most valuable for obtaining and maintaining employment should be identified. Targeted instructional objectives must be determined with respect to the experiences and/or placements previously selected. Systematic strategies for making job matches, selecting training experiences, and identifying appropriate vocational instructional objectives can reduce the subjectivity with which vocational professionals make decisions and can justify to other professionals, parents, and advocates the vocational training program that is constructed.

Variables to Consider   Vocational training programs may prepare individuals with disabilities for employment either by specifically designing an instructional program for one job or job type or by systematically presenting a range of community-referenced work experiences from which an individual placement is later selected. It is important to determine which approach is appropriate prior to further designing and implementing a vocational program. As already stated, age is the key variable for consideration in such a programmatic decision. Younger individuals (e.g., under 19 years of age), who are most likely participating in an educational program, could potentially benefit from structured vocational instruction across several carefully chosen job types (e.g., dishwashing, housekeeping, janitorial). The training focus should then be narrowed as the individual grows older (e.g., 20–22 years of age) to a specific job type or placement targeted for long-term employment (Hutchins et al., 1986; Pietruski et al., 1985). Older individuals may not be able to afford time spent in systematic job sampling and may need to receive instruction in a carefully selected job type or placement, thus intensifying the need for careful employment selections. Table 3 delineates the variables to consider in making decisions regarding work experiences and job placements for individual trainees. These are discussed in the next several paragraphs.

Community variables that require attention include employment potential and job turnover. In a community-referenced approach, no work experience should be selected if comparable employment opportunities in that job type are not available. The work experiences considered and selected must reflect the community job market. Job turnover information within job types in the community may indicate vocational areas that typically hire and rehire the greatest number of

Table 3.   Variables to consider when selecting work experiences and job placements

Category	Variables	Evaluation with respect to job types		Evaluation with respect to specific employment
		Job sampling approach	Single work experience	Job placement
Community	Employment opportunities available	X	X	X
	Job turnover	X	X	X
Student/client	Physical capabilities	X	X	X
	Sensory capabilities	X	X	X
	Work skills	X	X	X
	Work-related skills	X	X	X
	Environmental factors	X	X	X
Training	Settings available	X	X	
	Materials/equipment available	X	X	
Placement	Wages			X
	Hours			X
	Benefits			X
	Geographic proximity			X

employees and may offer the best chances for employment in the future.

Several *trainee variables* are worthy of evaluation prior to making any training or placement decisions. Physical and sensory capabilities as well as the skills for the disabled individual are often cited as considerations for successful experiences (Connis, Sowers, & Thompson, 1978; Hutchins et al., 1986; Pietruski et al., 1985; Rusch & Mithaug, 1980; Wehman, 1981). Any methodology for identifying potential employment opportunities should assess the possibility for utilizing adaptive equipment or prosthetics on a job if a person's physical or sensory abilities are limited. Identifying creative yet realistic solutions to any physical, visual, auditory, and/or communication impairments should occur early in the job matching process.

An individual's work skills should also be considered in selecting a work experience or job placement. Work skills include specific job task skills, work-related behaviors, and social skills that are requisite for performing any given job responsibilities and successfully integrating into the work force. Prior job experiences, data collected in previous vocational training programs, or initial assessments may offer insights into the individual's current repertoire of vocational abilities. In addition, environmental factors such as possible work hazards, the level of supervision, the presence of coworkers, and equipment use and maintenance are variables that are frequently overlooked but often contribute considerably to a person's job success (Hutchins et al., 1986). Strategies for evaluating these variables should help to place work options in priority order and indicate areas needing training, but should not, on their own, determine employability or vocational potential. Results from systematically collecting data on an individual's skills, abilities, and needs may clarify the choices and minimize training time later.

Locating appropriate settings and materials for instruction are considerations that are unique to work experience training. To maximize generalization of skills, training sites should be carefully identified and selected to reflect the natural working conditions. Materials and equipment should be realistic and not simulated or artificially created.

Additional variables that require special attention when selecting placements include geographic proximity, wages and benefits, and work hours. Placement efforts may not be worthwhile if the business selected is not within a reasonable commuting distance to the individual with disabilities or if no transportation is available. Transportation issues are a variable that can eliminate many employment options, and require careful consideration and often creative solutions.

Supplemental Security Income (SSI) and Medicaid benefits often act as another deterrent to obtaining appropriate employment for a person with handicaps. Prior to job placement, a close evaluation of employment wages and benefits should be conducted with respect to the effects of the job on SSI and Medicaid benefits. This will facilitate a job match that is most beneficial to the prospective employee. Finally, work hours and schedule are an important variable to weigh in order to ensure that the individual can meet the necessary working conditions. Often weekend work, late night shifts, and seasonal employment are not feasible options for a person with disabilities and can cause a lack of family or advocate support, resulting in job termination. In summary, the needs of the individual and the realistic expectations of an employee must be in harmony to facilitate a successful employment experience.

Methods for Selecting Work Experiences and Job Placements Few examples of systematic methodologies for identifying successful training experiences and employment opportunities are available (e.g., Hutchins et al., 1986; Moon, Goodall, Barcus, & Brooke, 1985). A system described by Hutchins et al. (1986) identifies specific considerations regarding both the individual and the work experience or employment site for programs that target a job sampling or job placement approach. Each variable is evaluated systematically using a series of weighted response options. Numerical scores across the different variables allow vocational opportunities to surface in a hierarchical order, permitting an informed professional to present more objective recommendations to the individual and/or interested significant others. Concerns and issues can be resolved prior to placement in order to maximize the success of the job training experience and/or employment.

A second strategy for identifying optimal vocational placements for persons with disabilities by considering client and business characteristics and needs is presented by Moon et al. (1985). Their "Job/Client Compatability" format compares data collected on specific job-related requirements and responsibilities with data obtained from a client screening. The results of the analysis identify the individuals who appear most appropriate to fill the placement position in question.

Considerations for Selecting Target Skills for Training in Work Experiences and/or Job Placements After the selection of work experiences and/or job placements is complete, specific skills must be identified and targeted to receive systematic training. Age and type of approach or program (i.e., job sampling or specific employment) again contribute to the decision-making process (Hutchins et al., 1986).

Individuals who are to sample a range of job experiences or who may be targeted for only one work experience in a specific job type must be able to benefit from skill instruction that generically represents the requisite work responsibilities of all employees within the particular job type. A core skill approach to curriculum, as mentioned earlier, should directly reflect those tasks or skills that can be observed most often in community-based job types. For individuals who have been placed in a specific job opportunity that has been targeted for long-term employment, a core skill approach is not a consideration. Placements demand that the individual acquire the specified tasks of the position, and the skills needed to complete these tasks must be identified for training. However, with an initial placement as well as a work experience, it may be necessary to negotiate with the employer the tasks that are crucial or high priority on the job. If not all tasks are to be performed from the onset, it is imperative to structure the instructional program to target the most important job skills first for training.

Since skills should always represent actual employment opportunities, instruction on skills that cannot be concretely identified, observed, and measured should not appear as instructional

goals. Nor should a vocational training program utilize work stations or introduce job skills that cannot be supported in a community-integrated job.

Paying special attention to strategies and considerations for facilitating the appropriate selection of work experiences and job placements and targeting relevant vocational objectives can only enhance the vocational training program. Systematic procedures for training and placing individuals with disabilities offer a methodology that can be utilized, evaluated and revised to maintain the success of any program.

Training Settings

Once a vocational trainer becomes familiar with the community employment opportunities and the skills needed for gainful employment, he or she must consider the context in which trainees will be taught these skills. A number of setting options for vocational training can be developed, and each program should offer a range of options to meet individual trainee needs. Both agency/school-based and community-based training options should be considered, depending upon the needs of the individuals to be served. However, all training environments should be designed to teach the jobs and skills identified as relevant in the community assessment.

Agency/School-Based Training Sites Any vocational training that is provided on property owned by an adult service agency or public school is considered agency/school based. Vocational trainers can simulate real jobs in these sites or provide experiences alongside actual agency/school employees (e.g., cafeteria workers or janitors).

Simulation is the option most frequently utilized in agency/school sites. However,, simulating real jobs is often difficult and in many cases less effective than other available options. Simulation consists of creating experiences for trainees that resemble, as closely as possible, the demands and requirements of actual jobs. For example, establishing an industrial work station in a work activities program in which students learn to assemble and package a product that is being produced in a local industry is simulation. Similarly, providing instruction in the school cafeteria on skills identified as required by employers who hire food service employees such as buspersons, dish washers, and line servers is also a type of simulation. Simulating the conditions of actual job sites is frequently problematic because characteristics such as large numbers of people, noise, and high volume business are not easily replicated. However, if these conditions are not closely reproduced, many trainees, especially those with moderate and severe handicaps, are likely to have difficulty generalizing to real work settings.

A second agency- or school-based option is to provide experiences alongside actual agency/school employees. Although this option requires less simulation, trainers must be careful to ensure that the skills taught have relevance to similar jobs in the community. For instance, routines or procedures used by agency employees may be unique to that setting and have little generic value. In addition, trainers must actively provide training in these types of experiences; they cannot assume that a trainee will acquire skills by merely observing or accompanying a skilled worker.

School/agency-based sites provide vocational trainers with viable options for training. However, these sites are most appropriate for young students for whom community-based instruction is not always an option (e.g., students under 16 years of age are not allowed to be exposed to certain types of hazards in real worksites), or because of the lack of adequate resources for accessing particular community sites.

Community-Based Settings Most trainees should receive training in community-based vocational sites. The skills selected for training and the context in which those skills are taught must be carefully identified, based on a trainee's past experiences, interests, and skills. Community-based options are training sites available in actual businesses in the community. These options can serve as vocational training, placement, or training and placement sites.

Community-based training sites chosen for training only should be judiciously selected to represent a job *type* or *types* that are likely future employment opportunities for a number of trainees receiving training. The sites are not selected based on their potential for future employment

in that location. Training sites should provide trainers with the opportunity to train the majority of core skills identified in the previously discussed job analyses for a particular job type. For example, if a Ramada Inn is selected to train the skills necessary for employment as a housekeeper, the inn should provide trainers with the opportunity to train the majority of core skills relevant to the range of housekeeping positions available in the community. If for any reason the inn cannot perform this function, it would not be a good candidate for a community-based training site. Community-based training sites should also be able to accommodate groups of trainees (e.g., three to five trainees) at any one time and should remain stable to allow trainees to rotate in and out of the site.

Community-based placement sites are those sites selected specifically because of their potential for future employment for individual trainees. Placement sites should be systematically selected based on individual student skills, interests, and job factors. The potential for on-the-job training should be assessed and negotiated with an employer prior to placing a trainee in the site, as should be the potential for maintenance and follow-up services once a trainee is employed.

Trainees may be placed in community-based placement sites following training in agency-based or community-based training sites or without prior training. However, systematic training must be provided in placement sites regardless of the amount of previous experience a trainee has had in training programs (Rusch & Mithaug, 1980; Wehman, 1981). No more than two trainees should be trained in a placement site at any one time, and in many cases only one trainee will be present in a placement site.

Combination community-based training and placement sites are those sites selected as a placement/employment site for one trainee and a training site for one or two other trainees. These sites must provide the opportunity to train core skills for a particular job type, as well as a future opportunity for paid employment for the trainee being so groomed. This type of community-based option may provide vocational trainers with an alternative to one-on-one instruction for trainees being placed in jobs, and, therefore, would require fewer staff across sites.

Once program options for training have been identified and established, vocational trainers can begin making decisions about the needs of individual trainees. Vocational settings should be selected after considering a number of variables leading to a good trainee job match.

Considerations in Selecting Settings   The identification of appropriate vocational training settings for work experiences may require additional community assessment and cooperative planning among all special service personnel in the community. However, the need for careful planning should not be disregarded; generalization of skills is often difficult for persons with disabilities, thus emphasizing the importance of training in the most natural setting possible (Brown et al., 1976; Rusch & Mithaug, 1980; Wehman, 1981). As previously emphasized, the training sites should reflect the types of work that have been identified in the community as potential employment opportunities when conducting employer interviews during the community assessment process (Hutchins et al., 1986; Pietruski et al., 1985).

Vocational education settings, community colleges, and specific work areas designated for skill training within an appropriate facility can offer some flexibility and temporary solutions to providing a space for early skill instruction and acquisition. However, it is critical that training opportunities be provided within a community business prior to finalizing any decision regarding long-term placement or considering the individual's training program as completed (Hutchins et al., 1986).

In developing and identifying potential training and placement settings, several issues should be discussed with the employer to ensure a more positive working relationship. Negotiations should involve professional staff, employees, the trainee with disabilities, and the family. Areas requiring specific attention and agreement include: 1) the time training will occur, 2) how long the site will be used and how often, 3) space in which instruction can be provided, 4) specific job responsibilities that will be targeted as objectives and how the trainee's work performance will be coordinated with the normal work routine, 5) personnel responsible for training and supervision, 6) expenditures that are required of the employer, and 7) liability or proper insurance coverage (Hutchins et al., 1986). Written agreements should be developed that specify and document the conditions discussed with respect to any of these issues.

Training

Once decisions regarding job experiences, target skills for instruction, and instructional settings have been made and a systematic assessment of an individual trainee's skills in relation to job requirements has been conducted, instruction can be initiated. Trainers should not expect trainees to acquire skills through exposure alone. Skills required to perform successfully on a job must be systematically taught to ensure that the trainee acquires and adequately performs those job skills (Bellamy et al., 1979; Renzaglia et al., 1981; Wehman et al., 1985).

As with specific assessment procedures, training procedures should be delineated prior to initiating training and should be consistent within and across trainers. If task analyses of job skills have been developed for assessment, they should also be used for training. In addition, task analyses should be individualized to accommodate individual trainees' strengths and weaknesses, rate of learning, and need for adaptive devices or task restructuring.

Task analyses provide trainers with the content of instruction. Instructional procedures should be developed to guide trainers in how to teach. Such procedures should identify: 1) the stimuli desired to cue the target skills (e.g., natural cues such as work buzzers or artificial cues such as trainer instructions), 2) the consequences that will be provided for correct responses (reinforcement), 3) the procedures/prompts the trainer will use to facilitate correct performance of the task steps, 4) the method the trainer will use to correct errors, 5) procedures the trainer will use to facilitate maintenance of the skill once it has been acquired, and 6) procedures that will be used to facilitate generalization of skills to real work settings if trained initially in simulation (Bellamy et al., 1979; Renzaglia et al., 1981; Rusch & Mithaug, 1980; Wehman et al., 1985).

Program Format

Date: _____   Student(s): Mike, Jon _____

1. *Specific program objective*:   Given the appropriate setting in Newcomb Hall cafeteria and the appropriate cues ("Wipe the tables," "Wipe the chairs," "Clean the drink station," "Clean the napkin station"), the student will correctly perform the task with 100% accuracy for 5 consecutive daily probes (following the attached task analysis (TA) [Figure 3]).

2. *Rationale*:   This skill is one part of an entire sequence of skills related to competitive employment opportunity.

3. *Student characteristics that:*
   (1) assist: _____
   (2) hinder: _____

4. *Baseline probe procedures*:   Students are taken individually to a specific dining area and given the appropriate cue. Allow 5 seconds for independent initiation of Step 1 in TA. If correctly responds, record (+) and proceed to Step 2, 3, etc. If incorrectly responds, responds with a step out of sequence, or does not respond within 5 seconds, record (−) and discontinue any further steps in the TA. Record all the remaining steps as incorrect (−). Do not prompt or reinforce. Rotate daily probes within the three dining areas correlated with training.

5. *Behavior change procedures*:   After the individual daily probe, training begins. While both students watch, trainer demonstrates all steps in the TA, while verbalizing about the actions. Next both students are simultaneously prompted through the task, giving a verbal prompt (e.g., "Get the rag") at each step. If correctly performed, social reinforcement is given. If incorrectly performed, a verbal and model prompt (e.g., "Get the rag like this") is given, and if correctly completed, give social reinforcement. If incorrect, provide verbal and physical prompt (e.g., "Get the rag" while guiding student with minimum contact). Reinforce with social praise. The students work through each step at the same speed before being given the next verbal cue. Upon completion of this trial, an individual student is given the cue (e.g., "Wipe the table") while the other student watches the performance. Allow 5 seconds for an independent response on Step 1 of TA. If correctly self-initiated, record (+), give social praise, and proceed to Step 2. If incorrect or no response within 5 seconds, provide a verbal, verbal and model, or verbal and physical prompt (described above) as needed. Proceed through all steps in the TA using these procedures. Repeat procedures, alternating the student who performs and the student who observes.

   When one student reaches criterion, probe the skill first, then allow the student to work independently with feedback on the job performed after he or she is finished. Follow the same procedures described above with the student who is still in acquisition, except that he or she will not rotate performing with any other student. If on a previously trained skill the student falls below 100% on 3 out of 5 days, then that skill will be retrained until criterion is reached for 3 consecutive days.

6. *Data collection methods*:   1) *Baseline probe*—Daily individual probes taken prior to training; record (+) for correctly self-initiated response; record (−) for incorrect response, response out of sequence, or no response within 5 seconds; 2) *Intervention*—Record the level of assistance necessary for successful completion of each step (i.e., [+], [V], [M], or [P]). Data are to be kept on the individual trials for each student.

7. *Reinforcement—Type(s) and schedule(s)*: Social praise for all responses and for prompted responses. Reinforcement is not given for a prompted response if the student demonstrates the response twice with a less intrusive prompt. After the student demonstrates one acquisition trial of 100% accuracy for 3 consecutive days, break snack will be contingent on at least one trial being performed perfectly. After 3 consecutive days of two trials performed correctly, the criterion is correspondingly increased in order to receive reinforcement. This procedure is continued until the objective is met. Nonspecific reinforcement may occur for maintenance probes.

   Upon meeting the objective, reinforcement becomes contingent on performing the task correctly on all trials.

8. *Maintenance and generalization procedures*:   Once criterion is met on all skills, probes will occur once a week for a month, then once every 2 weeks for a month, then once a month. On nonprobe days, check results and correct the performance if necessary. Generalization will be trained directly by rotating students through the three different dining areas to work. This rotation occurs at random with a different section used each day.

9. *Criterion to be met for success*:   100% accuracy for five consecutive daily probes.

Figure 4.   Sample instructional program for wiping tables, chairs, and equipment in a cafeteria busing job.

Although some trainees will learn without being systematically taught, this should not be assumed. In fact, even those individuals would learn more quickly and with greater degrees of success with systematic instruction. The range of training procedures from which trainers can select is great and should be conceptualized on a continuum from unintrusive procedures to very intrusive procedures. For example, prompting strategies used to ensure successful performance of target skills may range from picture cues in the work environment to a trainer physically guiding a trainee through the task being taught. Although both of these procedures can be used systematically and consistently, picture cues are much less intrusive than physical guidance. Similarly, when considering reinforcement, the natural reinforcer for work is a paycheck delivered perhaps weekly, and this may be the least intrusive reinforcement procedure. On the other end of the reinforcement continuum may be payment of a quarter for each work unit completed, which can be immediately exchanged for an edible snack (e.g., chips, coffee, etc.). The key is to use the *least intrusive* instructional procedure that is *effective* and to use it consistently and systematically. Figure 4 provides an example of a systematic training program for wiping tables in a cafeteria busing job. The program task analysis appears in Figure 3.

Program evaluation procedures should also be built into the instructional program. An ongoing procedure for evaluating trainee performance should provide trainers with information regarding trainee progress, the need to move on to new skills, or the need to change the instructional program due to inadequate progress. Data collected throughout training should also be used in the decision-making and job-matching process.

SUMMARY

With the growing emphasis on employment in community job sites and the expansion of vocational services to include persons with severe handicaps, traditional rehabilitation strategies must be evaluated and modified to ensure the success of all trainees. A community-referenced approach to program development and training provides an alternative that incorporates decision making, service delivery and ongoing evaluation based on actual employment opportunities in community businesses.

A community-referenced model does not rely on prediction and evaluation of trainee employability or on teaching the general prevocational skills related to work adjustment. Instead, this model assumes employability of all trainees and provides the information needed to directly teach trainees the skills required for actual jobs available. Adoption of this model may help trainers achieve the goal of productive employment for all persons referred for vocational services.

REFERENCES

Bellamy, G. T., Horner, R., & Inman, D. (1979). *Vocational training of severely retarded adults*. Baltimore: University Park Press.

Bellamy, G. T., Rhodes, L., & Albin, J. M. (1986). Supported employment. In W.E. Kiernan & J. A. Stark (Eds.), *Pathways to employment for adults with developmental disabilities* (pp. 129–138). Baltimore: Paul H. Brookes Publishing Co.

Brown, L., Nietupski, J., & Hamre-Nietupski, S. (1976). Criterion of ultimate functioning. In M. Thomas (Ed.), *Hey don't forget about me!* (pp. 2–15). Reston, VA: Council for Exceptional Children.

Connis, R. T., Sowers, J., & Thompson, L. E. (1978). *Training the mentally handicapped for employment: A comprehensive manual*. New York: Human Sciences Press.

Gold, M. (1972). Stimulus factors in skill training of the retarded on a complex assembly task: Acquisition, transfer and retention. *American Journal of Mental Deficiency, 76*, 517–526.

Gold, M. (1974). Redundant cue removal in skill training of retarded adolescents on a complex assembly task: Acquisition, transfer, and retention. *Education and Training of the Mentally Retarded, 9*, 5–8.

Gold, M. (1976). Task analysis of a complex assembly task by the retarded blind. *Exceptional Children, 43*, 78–84.

Hunter, J., & Bellamy, T. (1976). Cable harness construction for severely retarded adults: A demonstration of training technique. *AAESPH Review, 1*, 2–13.

Hutchins, M. P., Renzaglia, A., Stahlman, J., & Cullen, M. E. (1986). *Developing a vocational curriculum for students with moderate and severe handicaps*. Charlottesville, VA: University of Virginia.

Kiernan, W. E., & Stark, J. A. (Eds.). (1986). *Pathways to employment for adults with developmental disabilities*. Baltimore: Paul H. Brookes Publishing Co.

Moon, S., Goodall, P., Barcus, M., & Brooke, V. (1985). *The supported work model of competitive employment for citizens with severe handicaps: A guide for job trainers*. Richmond: Virginia Commonwealth University.

Pietruski, W., Everson, J., Goodwyn, R., & Wehman, P. (1985). *Vocational training and curriculum for multihandicapped youth with cerebral palsy*. Richmond: Virginia Commonwealth University.

Renzaglia, A., Bates, P., & Hutchins, M. (1981). Vocational skills instruction for handicapped adolescents and adults. *Exceptional Education Quarterly, 2*, 61–73.

Renzaglia, A., Wehman, P., Schutz, R., & Karan, O. (1978). Use of cue redundancy and positive reinforcement to accelerate production in two profoundly retarded workers. *British Journal of Social and Clinical Psychology, 17*, 183–187.

Revell, W. G., Kriloff, L., & Sarkees, M. (1980). Vocational evaluation. In P. Wehman & P. McLaughlin (Eds.), *Vocational curriculum for developmentally disabled persons* (pp. 73–93) Baltimore: University Park Press.

Rusch, F. R. (Ed.)., (1986). *Competitive employment issues and strategies*. Baltimore: Paul H. Brookes Publishing Co.

Rusch, F., & Mithaug, D. (1980). *Vocational training for mentally retarded adults: A behavior analytic approach*. Champaign, IL: Research Press.

Rusch, F. R., Schutz, R. P., Mithaug, D. E., Stewart, J. E., & Mar, D. E. (1982). *Vocational assessment and curriculum guide*. Seattle: Exceptional Education.

Schalock, R. L. (1986). Service delivery coordination. In F. R. Rusch (Ed.), *Competitive employment issues and strategies* (pp. 115–127). Baltimore: Paul H. Brookes Publishing Co.

Sowers, J., Thompson, L., & Connis, R. (1979). The food service vocational training program: A model for training and placement of the mentally retarded. In G. T. Bellamy, G. O'Connor, & O. Karan (Eds.), *Vocational rehabilitation of severely handicapped persons: Contemporary service strategies* (pp. 151–205). Baltimore: University Park Press.

Spooner, F., & Hendrickson, B. (1976). Acquisition of complex assembly skills through the use of systematic training procedures: Involving profoundly retarded adults. *AAESPH Review, 1*, 14–25.

Wehman, P. (1981). *Competitive employment: New horizons for severely disabled individuals*. Baltimore: Paul H. Brookes Publishing Co.

Wehman, P., & Hill, J. W. (Eds.). (1979). *Vocational training and placement of severely disabled persons: Project employability* (Vol. 1). Richmond: Virginia Commonwealth University.

Wehman, P., & Hill, J. (1982). Preparing severely handicapped students to enter less restrictive environments. *Journal of the Association for the Severely Handicapped, 7*(1), 33–39.

Wehman, P., Hill, J., & Koehler, F. (1979). Helping severely handicapped persons enter competitive employment. *Journal of the Association for Persons with Severe Handicaps, 4*, 274–290.

Wehman, P., Renzaglia, A., & Bates, P. (1985). *Functional living skills for moderately and severely handicapped individuals*. Austin, TX: PRO-ED.

SECTION II

HUMAN RESOURCE ISSUES:
TRAINING AND MANAGEMENT

Chapter 8

Rehabilitation Management and Supported Employment

Robert McDaniel and Karen Flippo

The management of rehabilitation service delivery programs and systems is currently undergoing substantial change. Numerous developments in corporate management practices are relevant to the human services field and have been adapted to the public and private rehabilitation field. The management of supported employment services in turn calls upon practices emerging in the private business sector. Since relationships with employers is one key factor in the success of supported employment programs, it is apparent that a common understanding of how best to operate the business of rehabilitation employment services will enhance a mutually satisfying relationship among all principal parties.

Several major themes in contemporary management philosophy and practice are being applied in both the private business sector and the human service field. These include:

1. Assessing resource allocations during periods of change to determine the most efficient processes to reach desired objectives relating to the mission and purpose of the organization
2. Considering human resources as investments, and valuing the human aspects in the performance of one's job
3. Combining technology with human competence for greater efficiency in producing goods and services for satisfactory outcomes
4. Monitoring and analyzing results based on specified criteria

Management experts emphasize how today's organizational and systems leaders must be visionaries as well as engineers (Leavitt, 1986; McCormick, 1984). Because of rapid expansion of information and continual discovery of new techniques and approaches in the human services field, it is important to be resourceful and creative in carrying out an agency's mission and purpose. Because of limited resources, the ability to assemble multiple resources to construct a proper framework and then deliver the intended services within the given constraints becomes a valuable skill of any manager. Managers who are able to cultivate a commitment from staff by allowing flexibility and encouraging innovative problem-solving while being politically and fiscally responsible will succeed in today's environment. These are the skills that apply directly to supported employment program management. The application of specific technology itself will not produce successful outcomes. Understanding how supported employment fits into an agency's overall purpose, plus knowing how to foster cooperative and collaborative relationships and how to orchestrate the technology, are the factors that lead to successful supported employment practice.

Following is a look at how supported employment requires the application of contemporary management practices that enable the rehabilitation manager to grasp its unique and common features.

ACCOMMODATING CHANGE
IN THE REHABILITATION SYSTEM

Supported employment is part of the overall purpose and mission of the rehabilitation field, and specifically of the state/federal vocational rehabilitation (VR) program. It is one more adaptation of the original and basic intent of federal legislation that has been in continual existence since 1920. Since the inception of vocational rehabilitation, state/federal VR program managers have had to adapt to innovations, developments, and changes in aspects of the service delivery system. Each change has undergone debate and deliberation, yet the program has continued to focus on its original purpose, which is to assist persons with disabilities to maximize their employment and independence potential. Issues such as which populations are to be served and what services are authorized have been a changing part of VR's long and successful history. The 1943 Rehabilitation Act amendments brought about sweeping changes by broadening the clientele from only the physically disabled population to persons with mental illness and those with mental retardation. In order to accommodate these new classifications of disabilities into the VR system, authorized services had to be broadly defined to include "any services necessary to render a disabled individual fit to engage in a remunerative occupation" (Wright, 1986). As occurred with the 1943 amendments, later with the 1978 amendments, and now with the inclusion of supported employment as an authorized component of the rehabilitation program, the VR program manager has been called upon to enlarge his or her thinking about how the state/federal VR system can be practiced without destroying the basic fiber that has sustained its successful history. Since 1920 the state/federal VR system has been a dynamic program where managers frequently learn to modify procedures with given resources

and manage the change process in conjunction with multiple professional disciplines in a largely bureaucratic structure involving federal, state, and local agencies. As with any long-standing organization, some practices have become somewhat institutionalized, thus limiting the scope of changes the system has been willing to accommodate. Supported employment services represent a departure from the traditional rehabilitation process. In order to make necessary adjustments, the rehabilitation manager must look at supported employment on its own terms, rather than from the traditional rehabilitation orientation. Once the concepts and principles are clearly understood, the rehabilitation manager can translate supported employment practices into existing VR formats by applying the new technologies, strategies, and resources unique to the success of supported employment services.

MANAGING IN
A MULTIAGENCY SYSTEM

The rehabilitation manager is challenged by supported employment to view the person with very severe disabilities, employers, and collaborating human service providers as critical partners, who, when combined with advanced technology and reliable strategies, can produce meaningful outcomes for everyone involved. Like the modern corporate manager, the rehabilitation manager understands that services are not provided in a lineal fashion or in a vacuum. Each element is measured within the overall context of the individual situation. No longer can one agency enforce practices that may appear to benefit only its system. Practices must be implemented and managed in a manner that takes into account the total aspects of the client's life, the employer's needs, and the capacity of the entire service system. A unique feature of supported employment is that multiple forces unite for the common benefit of each consumer and each employer. Policies and procedures can be established only as guidelines, since the specific applications will depend on local and individual circumstances. Flexibility in using human and other resources becomes the major factor in attaining goals for supported employment services. In some respects, managing supported employment services may not call for unique aspects so much as it requires a renewal of principles and approaches grounded in the basic tenets of traditional rehabilitation. It may only require the manager to set aside professionalized and institutionalized practices and return to a former style of treating the consumer individually with creative solutions to reach desired outcomes. The challenge to the manager becomes one of how to assure that proper allocation and application of resources result in specified benefits. Veteran managers see this challenge as fundamentally similar to the demands they have always had to accommodate in the traditional rehabilitation program.

Vocational rehabilitation managers, after all, have always had to draw from a wide range of information and relate it to the VR process. The rehabilitation process throughout has emphasized outcomes and performance standards. In managing supported employment services, the tasks are basically the same, but the service delivery sequence and performance standards may vary from traditional rehabilitation programs. These items are discussed in more detail elsewhere in this chapter. While it may appear that supported employment complicates the rehabilitation process, there are several areas where it proves a convenience to the supervisor by resolving a dilemma assumed to be inherent in the traditional rehabilitation process.

It has been noted that when rehabilitation managers set placement quotas on the number of successful placement closures a rehabilitation counselor is to accomplish, it encourages more noncooperative behavior on the part of the counselor. When the counselor's accountability is based more on case-load difficulty there tends to be more collaborative work (Emener, Luck, & Smits, 1981). With supported employment, the manager can emphasize both placement quotas and severity of disability. By promoting cooperative services, performance standards set by VR can be met. Since supported employment uses a "place in employment and then train" approach, job placement occurs at the beginning. With supported employment training technology and multiple resource utilization, increased results can occur with greater efficiency.

KEY FEATURES OF SUPPORTED EMPLOYMENT RELEVANT TO THE REHABILITATION MANAGER

In application, supported employment is a set of outcomes for persons with severe disabilities. As defined in the 1986 amendments, these outcomes include: 1) paid employment (competitive employment in a meaningful job, not work activities) that enables the person to learn marketable skills at no less than 20 hours a week in an integrated setting; and 2) employment for individuals for whom competitive employment has been interrupted or intermittent as a result of a severe disability and who, because of their handicap, need ongoing support services to perform such work. *Clarification of the definition of supported employment is necessary if the goal of stable, competitive employment is to be achieved.*

To help to ensure job retention, the provider and rehabilitation manager should adopt the "place and train" concept. According to this concept, the client does not have to progress through a sheltered or community continuum to be ready for competitive work or competitive supported placement. Assessment and work adjustment decisions are based on performance at the worksite.

The organization providing supported employment services must have trained staff who find, match, instruct, and provide support services based on the requirements and abilities of the individual. Advocacy and integration are essential to the philosophy of employment services. Provider staff are responsible for seeing that the worker is accepted at the job site and is utilizing appropriate social skills.

Ongoing support is provided on an as-needed basis, and the provider and vocational rehabilitation (VR) personnel identify the monetary and programmatic resources necessary for this support at the time the case is opened.

Productivity and quality standards, employees' interaction, community integration opportunities, wages, part- or full-time employment, length of intensive training, and hours of follow-along services are determined by individual circumstance. Successful supported employment programs are those that have exercised flexibility, creativity, and individuality in their implementation.

THREE STAGES OF MANAGING SERVICE DELIVERY SYSTEMS

The remaining sections of this chapter are organized around the three basic components of any service delivery system. A competent rehabilitation manager supervises each component in order to attain goals that benefit consumers and meet the purpose and objectives of the organization. These components and their relevance to managing supported employment services are:

1. *Inputs to service delivery* The inputs to service delivery include identifying and assessing the needs of the populations appropriately served, securing human and financial resources, and determining relevant conditions, standards, and requirements that must be considered when planning or delivering services.
2. *Processes for delivering services* Processes for delivering services include all activities that need to be consistently applied and the techniques appropriate for those activities, both at the general system level and the individual program level.
3. *Outcomes of service delivery* Service delivery outcomes are the results and benefits, as defined by specific criteria, that are expected to occur as a consequence of the services being delivered. These outcome measures are defined at the systems and individual program levels.

Inputs to the Service Delivery of Supported Employment

The inputs a rehabilitation manager must consider when organizing and planning programs and individual services fall into four categories: 1) legal mandates and public policies; 2) clientele to be served; 3) identifying human resources; and 4) conditions, standards, and

outcome criteria. Each category is explained here in detail.

Legal Mandates and Public Policies Vocational rehabilitation's lead with supported employment was established at the federal level with the 1986 federal Rehabilitation Act amendments. For the first time, supported employment gained statutory authority with specific federal funds authorized for supported employment services expenditures. The U.S. Congress also emphasized that supported employment was not to be vocational rehabilitation's primary form of delivering services. Through statutory and committee report language, supported employment was described as a supplement to the basic vocational rehabilitation program. State vocational rehabilitation administrators and other management staff were clearly given substantial responsibility for carrying out supported employment services. Yet this facet of the VR leadership's duties was recognized as only a portion of their other routine responsibilities. Although some states have initiated laws of their own, the federal laws and regulations will most likely remain the backbone of supported employment. A brief background summary of rehabilitation legislation will place VR's role into perspective.

The state/federal vocational rehabilitation program is one of the longest surviving domestic programs in the United States. Since 1920, it has been valued by Congress as a cost-effective human service that has emphasized placing persons with disabilities into competitive employment. Over the years, it has created administrative and programmatic procedures that have enabled it to respond to changes occurring in the broad disability fields and yet remain focused on its basic aim—achieving competitive employment for persons with employment handicaps. While it has been argued that VR has been selective in accepting which persons it will serve, Congress has reinforced its decisions by continuing to endorse its programs and authorizing steady funding increases while reducing or eliminating many other domestic human service programs. An often quoted national statistic is that given its present level of resources, VR can only serve 1 in 20 persons considered eligible for its services. The addition of supported employment clientele presents a dilemma to the state agency manager and counselor. How can the agency expand its services to a broader population when it cannot serve all the individuals under its existing spectrum of services?

Congress, through the 1986 reauthorization process, made it clear that VR was to serve those persons "with severe handicaps for whom competitive employment has not traditionally occurred" through supported employment. It also, however, limited VR's involvement to "traditional time-limited post employment services." With the definitions and descriptions of authorized services in supported employment, Congress stated that the VR role in supported employment was to be similar to VR's role in delivering its regularly authorized and traditional services. In other words, supported employment was to fit into the familiar and historically successful form of rehabilitation services, yet with a different population from that which VR has typically accepted for employment services.

The federal Rehabilitation Act Amendments of 1986 authorized supported employment services in several sections. State agencies can deliver supported employment services through the basic state grant program (Section 110); through the special demonstration program (Section 311); and through the supported employment formula grant program (Title VI, Part C). The "VI-C" program authorizes supplementary grants to assist states in developing services leading to supported employment. The implications of how this program will affect the vocational rehabilitation manager are highlighted, since the details of how supported employment is to be implemented by VR are now in statuatory language. Some major features are described here.

In order to qualify for federal funds to offer supported employment services under Title VI, Part C, each state must produce a supplemental plan covering a 3-year period. Such a plan would specify the results of a statewide needs assessment identifying the need for supported employment services. The state plan for supported employment services must, by law, provide assurances that an evaluation of rehabilitation potential is provided that describes necessary training and time-limited postemployment services. The

state plan must signify that it will make maximum use of services from other public agencies, private nonprofit organizations, and other appropriate resources in the community to carry out these authorized services. The vocational rehabilitation agency must also demonstrate evidence of collaboration by funding commitments from relevant agencies and community organizations.

Services available under Title VI, Part C, include evaluation of rehabilitation potential, provision of job trainers at the workplace who conduct systematic on-the-job training, job development, and follow-up services. Congress stressed that services authorized under this part of the act are limited to training and traditionally time-limited postemployment services leading to supported employment. Extended, supported employment services are to be provided by other relevant state agencies and private organizations. On an individual client basis, it is this requirement that challenges the VR counselor and district manager. Through collaborative efforts with other sources, VR jointly sponsors, plans, and delivers services.

The VR manager will also benefit from familiarity with other related state and federal laws that affect participants in the supported employment team. Labor laws, Social Security mandates, and other regulations also directly relate to individual program decisions.

Identifying Appropriate Clientele to Be Served The issue of who is appropriate for supported employment services is not so simple as it may appear. Traditional vocational evaluation approaches typically do not produce data that assist the counselor or supervisor in making predictions about persons for whom supported employment is intended. Any information collected from a testing situation that is not based on observations in a natural work setting will not enable the vocational rehabilitation manager or counselor to make a sound decision on acceptance into supported employment services. A major departure from traditional VR eligibility in supported employment is the criterion of predicting the elimination of the client's handicap to employment. For supported employment clients, the continual existence of that "handicap" establishes the need for ongoing support.

Experience to date indicates that vocational rehabilitation's best selections come from sources already familiar to the consumer. Students active in a special or vocational education work training program, persons with a history of work services in facilities or other community service programs, and individuals previously closed as "infeasible" may be the more recognizable candidates for supported employment. One should never assume, merely on the basis of disability severity, that a given person will be a candidate for vocational rehabilitation's role in supported employment. Individual circumstances, particularly the specific job requirements and the possible use of rehabilitation engineering technology, may result in a very severely disabled person being able to retain employment without ongoing support. Consequently, managers must assure that assessment techniques are being conducted that are appropriate for the individual, and the evaluation report must supply useful data on needed supports.

Supported employment is recognized as beneficial to persons with different types of disabilities and employment handicaps. While supported employment has achieved its popularity through demonstration research with persons who have mental retardation, the value of supported employment is also being recognized with other disability groups. One rule of thumb about selection of appropriate populations states that persons who have difficulty transferring learning from one situation to another are likely candidates for supported employment. This is not the only frame of reference, however. For example, if the counselor or supervisors can perceive how having a personal assistant at the work site routinely available to the client in accordance with federal regulations could alleviate employment risks, then that client could be a viable candidate for supported employment. Persons with severe medical problems, persons requiring physical assistance, or persons needing communication help when technical devices are not appropriate may also benefit from supported employment.

It is obvious that the number of people who could appropriately benefit from supported employment far exceeds the resources available to vocational rehabilitation. Through policy and

practice, managers should assure that all levels of disability needs are being served. There are several clues as to whether or not a referral to VR will result in satisfactory gainful employment, regardless of the severity of disability. They are:

1. At the time of referral, has the client had any actual work training experience in a community environment? (This may have occurred as part of a special education program or other adult vocational program.)

2. Based on actual observations in previous assessment or training situations, has the consumer made a choice to be employed? Does the consumer have the endorsement of family or significant others?

3. At the time of referral, do any of the collaborative parties with this particular client know of suitable employment choices for this person?

This information assumes the referral to VR is already involved in some organized service prior to VR being approached. Because of the limited developments in evaluation procedures specifically for candidates for supported employment, it is suggested the VR apply its resources to referrals where the need for long-term support can be documented based on prior services received from other agencies.

Identifying Human Resources in Supported Employment   Determining necessary human resources is best achieved by focusing on the functions to be performed in delivering services. Major functions include the following:

Initial Assessment   Someone must gather materials from work experience programs, situational assessments, transitional employment, and other on-the-job training programs, and conduct interviews with client, parent or guardians, or residential supervisors to ascertain interests and skills.

Job Market Analysis   Someone must perform a job market analysis in the community to determine job openings and business attitudes regarding hiring persons with severe disabilities.

Development of a Plan   The rehabilitation counselor must coordinate the individualized written rehabilitation plan (IWRP) with the consumer, family guardians, agencies providing services, and the case management organization. Short-and long-term goals must be defined and areas of responsibility delineated.

Placement Placement services may be performed by an employment training specialist, special education teacher, or a job developer.

Training Systematic, individualized training is provided by an employment training specialist, lead worker, employer, mobile crew supervisor, or work station supervisor. The rehabilitation counselor monitors progress and problems and makes decisions based on data recorded at the job site regarding appropriateness of the worker/job match.

Ongoing Support Ongoing support usually takes over when the rehabilitation counselor's and job coach's active roles fade. As job stabilization occurs (coach is at the job site 20% or less of the employment time), the case is closed as a code 26 (closed, rehabilitated) and is transferred to another funding source for long-term support. At the time the case is closed, the team involved in the IWRP reconvenes to determine if the job should be retained or if further training is needed. The VR case manager may be involved in seeking other services to assist the person, such as arranging transportation, getting benefits counseling, and/or obtaining financial management assistance. Other funding sources could be sought for less restrictive living options, continuing parent advocacy, peer support, and to assist the worker in accessing integrated social/recreational and community activities.

All personnel from the various agencies involved in the employment process should participate in the following:

1. Identifying joint priorities among agencies
2. Diagnosing the unique competencies of various agencies and establishing patterns of complementary resources
3. Establishing procedures and mechanisms for joint planning and standards of accountability
4. Exchanging ideas on new funding possibilities
5. Planning efforts to educate the community on service needs
6. Developing joint sponsorship of information and referral services
7. Establishing working agreements between agencies to avoid duplication of services
8. Pooling resources to acquire outside consultation and training across agencies
9. Identifying ways for students to get training at an earlier age in environments in which they will function as adults
10. Coordinating eligibility and intake requirements among public schools, vocational rehabilitation, developmental disabilities, and other public or nonprofit sources
11. Defining (using local standards) how to gain access to an appropriate level of employment regardless of functioning capacity
12. Determining how case coordination and case management responsibilities will be accomplished in a multiagency system
13. Defining how state or other public agencies' policies and regulations will be incorporated into the local service operations
14. Establishing a performance review and evaluation system to determine level of success
15. Identifying methods to ensure continuing input from the business community on advising the employment services network system as a whole

Identifying and Securing Financial Resources Combining financial resources of relevant funding sources is inherent in the design of supported employment. The identification of potential resources and the subsequent coordination of those resources becomes a major task for the rehabilitation manager or the designated case manager for individual clients. State and federal agencies authorizing supported employment services have recognized the need to share funds for the benefit of mutual clientele. The basic public agencies typically involved with cost sharing have been the state agencies administering adult services for persons with mental retardation or other developmental disabilities, state departments of education or local education agencies (special education and vocational education), and the state rehabilitation agency.

Other public sources financially contributing to supported employment services include employment development agencies, Job Training Partnership Act authorities, community colleges, adult education, and agencies administering Titles XIX and XX of the Social Security Act. As the disability categories expand in supported employment, other funding agencies will be providing financial assistance.

Rehabilitation facilities and other community-based providers that generate substantial revenue from private sources of contracts can financially contribute to services not supported by VR, and United Way and similar community funds can be allocated for the long-term support costs. Title VII (Parts A and B) funds from the Rehabilitation Act can also be applied to supported employment services if the services comply with approved arrangements. The Centers of Independent Living will most likely become key resources for ongoing support for many supported employment clients. The manner in which facilities and community providers are approached will largely determine their voluntary role in supported employment. For example, an invitation to join the community team for mutual planning and participation typically results in greater involvement. When sparked by equal participation and satisfactory relationships, community sources can often creatively secure funding from local governments and private sources. Diplomacy, clear communications, and considerable time investment on the part of the manager will result in effective negotiations for adequate financial resources.

Because of vocational rehabilitation's legally mandated time-limited role and its need to identify long-term support, rehabilitation agency personnel will need to work cooperatively at the state and local levels with various funding sources. Often the same services are to be provided by several different funding sources, so that agreements that specify the clients' performance criteria, the maximum time for services, or other measures will avoid complications between funding sources when transferring payments or sponsorship from one authority to another. When developing agreements for sharing services and expenses, it is critical to specify the respective areas of responsibilities, the coordination and

decision process, and how implementation will be approved, monitored, and evaluated. The more detailed the financial agreements are at the beginning, the smoother will be the implementation at the local service delivery level.

The cost of a given supported employment program for a specific client will vary, depending on several key factors. Generally, it is VR's role to sponsor the client to the point of job stabilization. (Job stabilization is defined by the cooperating agencies and is usually described in terms of the amount of supervised services a client requires to sustain employment.) Reaching the defined job stabilization level is determined by a combination of current functional skills at the onset of placement, the appropriateness of the assessment information used to select the initial placement, the consistency of preliminary descriptions with actual conditions, and the competency of the service providers. In some states, VR has determined a maximum financial budget per supported employment client. If job stabilization is not met, then the long-term support sources assume the costs from the point at which VR transfers the sponsorship. This is a negotiable arrangement, since the costs to the long-term funding source will likely be increased if the worker has not obtained a certain level of independence in the performance of his or her job.

When estimating the cost of supported employment services, references from other agencies or service providers should be carefully analyzed. It is important to ascertain the types and levels of disabilities served, the primary source of referrals, and previous services the clients have received. The salary ranges of direct service providers and the general overhead costs of the providers will cause the actual service delivery costs to fluctuate. Transportation arrangements and other maintenance needs will also be locally calculated.

Determining the financial needs and acquiring adequate assurances for those funds are often viewed as the most arduous tasks of the rehabilitation manager. Because of the requirement to combine multiple sources of funds into a multiphase comprehensive plan, the manager must devote considerable time to negotiating both programmatic and financial issues simultaneously. Relying on competent community providers who are adept at matching and interrelating funding streams will relieve the rehabilitation manager of much of this labor.

Conditions, Standards, and Outcome Criteria In order for persons with severe disabilities to be employed, personnel of funding agencies, provider organization staff, and family members must believe that the severely disabled person can work. This may be hard for parents who have been told from the time of their child's birth that he or she would probably not progress beyond sheltered programs. Many parents rely upon the stability of the community facility and the federal benefits that sheltered employment maintains. Employment for their son or daughter may be considered a difficult risk to take. For other parents, the chance for their child to gain social acceptance through employment is worth the risks. Support groups may need to be formed to assist parents through the transition.

Provider staff and state agency personnel need to value the outcomes that supported employment programs generate. Individually, personnel must reexamine the reasons they are working in rehabilitation, their own attitudes regarding the employability of persons with severe disabilities, and the purpose and mission of their organization. Visits to employment services programs and attending training sessions will enable staff persons to clarify issues before implementing program objectives.

Gaining employer acceptance of employment partnerships with provider organizations is critical. Employers will have to be convinced of the employment potential of disabled persons and must be confident that provider staff will be able to provide services and training in order to meet employer quality and quantity standards.

Managing the Processes of Supported Employment Services

The State Plan for Supported Employment In addition to the programmatic requirements, such as evaluation of rehabilitation potential and the individualized written rehabilitation plan, the 1986 Rehabilitation Act amendments call for some specific management-related ac-

tivities. The state plan to provide supported employment services is to be based on a statewide needs assessment. The manner in which regional VR managers and district supervisors are involved with this process will be strategic to a cooperative relationship at the local level once VR implements its program. The decision to use Title VI, Part C, funds or a portion of the Section 110 funds will also set the tone for the agency's commitment to serve the population who can benefit from supported employment. Once the needs have been determined locally, the agency will have some idea of the volume of services to which it can respond. The statewide needs assessment instrumentation must be carefully developed to identify the proper criteria from which to determine requirements for long-term employment support. The regional VR manager can expect client advocates to be informed of the state plan procedure policies and will want to be sure that the respective regional needs have been voiced. Because of the needs assessment and public hearing requirements stipulated in the 1986 Rehabilitation Act amendments, the VR manager can assume a greater degree of interest from different groups who believe supported employment is relevant to them. Adequately organized, the state plan process will connect the VR central office functions with field managers and local counselors.

Managing Local Supported Employment Teams One of the major tasks of a rehabilitation manager is to coordinate the local agencies, providers, and consumers and their families involved in supported employment. In coordinating local services, care must be taken to build the team that will set policy and determine implementation strategies. Table 1 lists some characteristics that should be built into the team.

One of the most important duties of the manager and team is to determine how each member is specifically to contribute. Table 2 outlines examples of responsibilities that selected team members may assume.

Evaluating a Potential Vendor of Supported Employment Primary responsibility for servicing, monitoring, and achieving employment outcomes for each client belongs to the VR regional administrator. Prior to vendoring with a community-based organization, the

Table 1. Characteristics of effective team building

1. Members share common values and purpose.
2. Goals are specific, attainable, and measurable; areas of responsibilities and timeliness are clearly delineated.
3. Functions, responsibilities, and authority levels are clarified and agreed upon.
4. Members' individual skills are valued and members are given roles to utilize these skills.
5. Change and conflict are handled openly and are regarded as avenues to opportunity.
6. Risk-taking is encouraged.
7. Meetings are structured to allow for action; team members recognize the importance of continuing action.

ability of that organization to perform its contractual obligations should be carefully investigated. VR administrators should be aware that community providers may be pressed into decisions based on funding priorities before they fully understand the implications and operations of employment services.

Prior to instituting an employment services program, the provider organization should ensure that the following are in place: 1) short- and long-term plans for partial or total conversion to an employment services program; 2) re-

Table 2. Community-supported employment work teams

Participants	Responsibilities
State agency counselors and case managers	Identification of needs Decision making in assessment Job development Case closure and case management Goal planning Provision of support services Monitoring progress and problems at site Funding
Parents or family members of persons with disabilities	Input into interests and skill levels Financial requirements Assistance with transportation Instruction of daily living and social skills
Consultants, trainers	Incorporate needs of those participating in pre- and inservice training curriculum Help team coordinate community training for staff, parents, and state agency personnel
Special education teachers and other vendors of employment services	Provide community job development, assessment, placement, training, and follow-along
Employers	Provide input regarding labor market needs, industry productivity and quality standards, values and attitudes of business community regarding disabled workers
State and local agency administrators and governmental representatives (regional DVR administrator, representatives from special education, community colleges, developmental services, mental health, Private Industry Council, Social Security office—wage and hour division, regional transportation authorities)	Devise service coordination and funding alternatives including definitions of terms and acronyms, provisions for data collection, provisions for training, technical assistance and consultation, specifications for referral procedures, addressing of eligibility criteria, clarification of appeals process
Legislators	Utilize process for drafting legislation for services and rates

Ideally, with participation from all of the above, the team can set goals to:
1. Develop transition procedures between social districts, the VR agency, and adult providers
2. Coordinate service delivery between adult providers to ensure that all persons eligible for employment services have access to these services
3. Develop generic intake procedures, wording of forms, and eligibility criteria
4. Prepare interagency planning documents that distinctly describe and assign responsibility for services and funding
5. Make recommendations or seek funds for services and funding, as necessary
6. Determine realistic service and placement goals for that community, based on information from workers, providers, and employers
7. Develop media campaign on employability for persons with disabilities
8. Assess need for training and technical assistance
9. Compile data on programs, costs, and services, and make policy recommendations to state and federal agencies

sults of a community labor market screening to determine potential for employment and job creation (or a plan to conduct this screening); 3) a programmatic design for approaches (models) to employment services based on the labor market and needs of the persons entering the program; 4) written job descriptions for managers and staff of the employment services programs, an organizational chart clarifying functions and responsibilities, and a plan for providing personnel preparation training; and 5) a history documenting the organization's stability in providing services and its record of community collaboration and networking.

The agreement between the two parties assumes that the provider can obtain paid, meaningful employment for persons with severe disabilities, has skilled staff employed who can assist persons in maintaining those jobs, and can access additional services should it be necessary.

The competitive work environment naturally differs from sheltered settings, necessitating an alteration in the relationship between the VR counselor and the provider. The VR counselor may not be welcome at the job site because of possible interruption of work. Therefore, by vendoring a provider, the VR manager is relinquishing some control. In making decisions, the counselor may have to rely upon periodic visits during lunch hours, written progress notes taken by the job coach, and written employer evaluations. Since the job coach's primary responsibilities at the job site are training, supervision, and advocacy, reporting is difficult. VR personnel and providers may wish to collectively create new forms that will: 1) completely address services listed in the IWRP; 2) accurately reflect progress and problems at the job site; and 3) be used as a training and evaluation tool for the job coach rather than be a cumbersome paperwork burden.

The Individualized Written Rehabilitation Plan (IWRP) Review   The development, execution, and monitoring of the IWRP entail unique adjustments for supported employment services within the state VR structure. As stated earlier, Congress emphasized in the 1986 Rehabilitation Act amendments that VR's role in supported employment is to be conducted within the general format of the VR service delivery system. The IWRP has become the initial document in which procedures appropriate for supported employment are to be described in traditional terms. The VR supervisor and other managers can enhance the supported employment process by recognizing the distinctions between typical IWRP entries and information relevant to supported employment practices.

When the VR manager reviews IWRPs for persons receiving supported employment services, attention should be paid to the fact that most likely the IWRP is only one planning piece in the overall supported employment plan. Ensuring that the development and content of the IWRP reflect coordination and linkages among all responsible participants serves a useful purpose for both the administrative needs of VR as well as the programmatic needs of the client. From the manager's position, the VR counselor retains authority for the development of the IWRP, yet it is clear that the counselor's decisions must be based on a group participation of the various parties that will influence the outcome of services. As the VR counselor and managers are concerned about accountability, it is important to assure that the IWRP content has been negotiated and shared with the other funding sources as well as with the providers who will be implementing the program plan. This negotiation is particularly essential when identifying specific services with projected dates for initiation and completion. Again, while the VR manager may hold the counselor accountable for securing this information, the manager may want to determine if the counselor responded to the recommendations of the supported employment team. If not, the manager may find it helpful to assist the counselor in gaining the team members' approval for the IWRP plan, to help guarantee that the program will work cooperatively for the benefit of the disabled worker and for each service system represented.

Reviewing Client Progress and Adjusting Original Plans   Critical to the success of supported employment is the worker/job match. Yet persons may fail at the job site even if all the components were in place at the time of the compatibility analysis. Termination can be due to a number of factors such as boredom or dissatisfaction with the original job site, layoffs or plant shutdowns, change in management, or behavioral problems.

Prior to a decision being made on continuation of services, the reason for the termination should be identified. It is also important to recognize that nondisabled people generally progress through a series of jobs in their lifetimes, which may be due to career development or termination (firing/resignation). It is unrealistic to expect that a client will be able to find one job and remain there until retirement. Therefore, policies should be determined regarding second and third placements and continued eligibility of service.

Provider's Role in Ensuring Job Retention Responsibility for achieving maintenance and ensuring job retention belongs to the employment training specialist. VR personnel should request that data collected by employment specialists become part of the client's file and be used to measure IWRP objectives. For example, job coaches are trained to break down and teach tasks systematically. In conjunction with training, they are expected to document the levels of prompting required to reach company standards. Included in this recording procedure are data describing the client's ability to perform tasks independently and correctly, attention to task, and productivity levels. Behavior management plans and data describing acquisition of living skills also may be developed, depending upon the needs of the client. Job-coach training programs stress the importance of data collection, not only for reporting intervention hours to funding sources, but also because it assists the coach in making decisions for training. In analyzing the data, the job coach and VR counselor can make objective decisions regarding problems or progress at the job site.

Monitoring Costs VR is usually responsible for costs associated with supported employment in the categories of preplacement, evaluation, and intensive training. Generally, authorization for these costs is time-limited. Variances are seen when cooperative funding is provided for staffing through foundation grants, Joint Training Partnership Act funds, or employer cost sharing. Obviously also affecting costs are the higher levels of assistance and ac-

commodation required by persons who are severely physically, mentally, and emotionally handicapped. These may include costs for adaptations, assistive devices, and transportation, or costs relating to skill level of staff, complexity of the task, and prior work experience of the client. Arrangements for supervision in supported employment models range from 1:1 to 1:8. Whereas the cost for an individual supported jobs approach may be initially expensive because of low ratio, the long-term cost is cheaper because the job coach fades from the site at stabilization. Enclaves and mobile work crews have higher ratios, but supervision may be permanent, especially if it is viewed as a training site by the employer. In a permanent work station, the employer may assume the supervision when the crew becomes stable.

Vogelsberg (1986) reports that competitive training and placement in Vermont costs approximately $6,500 per year per person versus $5,500 for an adult day program. The annual cost for competitive employment training and placement in Virginia is $3,700 per person (Hill, 1984). In Philadelphia, annual per-person costs of traditional day services range from $2,500 to $20,000. The average cost for a vocational program in the same city is $9,000 per person per year. Hill et al. (1986) hypothesize that after 10 years of service, for a person with disabilities, total costs would be $12,907 for supported competitive employment, $47,097 for sheltered workshop services, and $74,441 for adult day programs.

The Virginia Commonwealth University group reports that it will take an average of 129 hours over an average of 19 weeks to fund initial training and stabilization in the individual supported competitive employment approach at an hourly wage of $25. Obviously the number of weeks will vary with each client. Standards being adopted for determining the conclusion of the intensive training phase are based on the on-site intervention by the job coach dropping below 20%. The State of Florida reported that using a $25-per-hour rate to document the levels of training per week will total $3,225 for services delivered over an average of 19 weeks. Several states have implemented a similar guide for service. (California funds this model at $20/hour with an average of 120 hours of intensive training.) Two days after stabilization, funding shifts to other sources. For VR purposes, the number of clients being provided services may remain constant but the agencies providing support will have increased annual costs as more clients progress to follow-up status.

These costs require further investigation before decisions can be made for client-supported employment services. For example, there are ranges in costs of rural versus urban programs, and programmatic costs can vary because of staff salaries. For decision making, the VR case manager must require documentation from the vendors delineating hours and types of services provided. This, coupled with progress notes and evaluation reports, provide information needed to monitor costs.

In any type of cost monitoring, providers must submit data at the beginning of service rather than after programs have run smoothly. If the VR case manager is able to compare costs from several programs in his or her area and thoroughly analyze costs and scope of services, he or she will be able to determine feasibility and continued authorization.

Managing the Outcomes of Supported Employment Services Delivery

Evaluating the Results of Individual Client Services In order to meet the IWRP objectives, the DVR counselor, manager, job coach, and support organization team members must agree on the essential services and environments to be in place for disabled persons. If the objectives are not met, each component of the service delivery process should be evaluated to determine impediments. These may include the inability to find a suitable client/employer match or to purchase additional support services such as a rehabilitation engineer; behavioral problems at the job site; or the inability of staff to train to criterion. Decisions must then be made regarding other options, which may include replacement, retraining, referral to another program, or extension of services. It is important to analyze the situation and personnel thoroughly before deciding to alter the IWRP, especially since supported employment is a new experience for most consumers (client and em-

ployer) and will require a period of adjustment.

When evaluating the appropriateness or success of each placement, the team must have an established method of measuring wages and hours, cost-benefit of the placement, integration opportunities, and overall satisfaction of the consumer.

Evaluating the Outcome of Rehabilitation's Role in Supported Employment As outlined in this chapter, the VR role in supported employment has been defined by Congress. It becomes the responsibility of administrators, managers, and leaders within the state/federal rehabilitation system to determine the value of this role by evaluating the overall outcomes. Establishing acceptable standards of performance for supported employment has been complicated by different definitions, values, and political differences. A major difficulty in reaching consensus on all of the criteria by which supported employment services should be measured is the diversity and flexibility inherent in supported employment's concept and design. The symbiotic structure of the supported employment service system requires managers to assess not only the results of their respective roles, but to determine that the overall system is obtaining the results intended. Much debate about the evaluation or data collection process for supported employment appears to be related to an analysis of values concerning certain variables or criteria. Often these debates center on the individual client or local service level. For the systems manager, the extent of examination of results will be at a more aggregate level.

Following a 12-month national study completed in July 1986, the Berkeley Planning Associates reported a consensus regarding evaluation for six categories of program performance in supported employment (Barker-Toms, 1986). Performance categories included:

1. Meaningful work with measures of employment outcomes such as paid, integrated work in community settings, stability of the employment, full- or part-time status, and the types of businesses involved
2. Compensation related to actual earnings at strategic points and whether or not the worker receives benefits available to nondisabled

workers performing the same or similar job for the business

3. Ongoing support measured by the types of support provided (transportation, self-care, community living, etc.), the location at which the support is provided, and the type of structure in which the support is available

4. Worksite integration measured by the types of supervisory structures (individual or work-crew placements) and presence of nondisabled workers in the immediate work setting

5. Quality-of-life indicators such as type of living arrangements, participation in generic community activities, health status, and exercising of personal choice

6. Community change indicators focusing on who is being served successfully in supported employment, how services are being delivered, the costs, and community response

Not all these items may be directly relevant to VR's role in supported employment, but before VR can assess its value to supported employment, it must focus on the purpose and objectives of the overall supported employment movement. In turn, the indicators of VR's performance within the general supported employment system will need to be translated to the indicators VR traditionally uses to assess and report its accomplishments. In this regard, attention must be directed to the following outcomes:

1. The participant demographics served by VR in the supported employment system, especially notations of the disabling conditions and functioning levels.

2. The aggregate supported employment services provided by VR. Such distinctions as direct on-the-job services and supportive environmental services provided to others who have an impact on the client will be useful to the manager. Documentation of ongoing support levels will substantiate the accuracy in selecting appropriate clients.

3. Financial documentation both for the client and for the funding sources. Financial analysis data for comparison of costs between different service models and for the public disability systems at large have been used as a measure of the value of supported employment.

4. The benefits to clients, including benefits and earnings and other personal or social criteria established as objectives of the supported employment program at the state level.

The emphasis in supported employment on assessing outcomes that include both employment and other measures such as integration entails a slightly different focus from the measures historically emphasized by VR. Although the community employment arrangement may be the same, the fact that services are transferred to another agency makes the actual "employment" status vague. Defining the criteria for job stabilization and performance criteria used to satisfy VR's reporting requirements will be arbitrarily determined between VR and the long-term support agency. Because of the flexibility required to reach that outcome, evaluations focus less on adhering to process and procedure. Federal monitoring and regulations may impose certain procedures, but the rehabilitation manager still needs to be concerned with the "bottom line" for the consumers being served. Before supported employment practices become institutionalized in systems, it is important that consumer-oriented outcome measures be the focal point of performance evaluation. As organizational practices are developed, managers will continually have the opportunity to trace the results of decisions to ensure that they benefit the consumer.

REFERENCES

Allen, B., Biggs, M., Sanford, J., Scarvada, M., & Scott, P. (1987). *Quality indicators in supported employment: A review system.* Unpublished manuscript.

Barker-Toms, L. (1986, July 31). *Development of performance measures for supported employment programs:* *Establishing consensus about recommended data items and developing a data collection strategy.* Berkeley, CA: Berkeley Planning Associates.

Emener, W., Luck, R., & Smits, S. (Eds.). (1981). *Rehabilitation administration and supervision.* Baltimore: University Park Press.

Hill, M, Hill, J., Wehman, P., et al. (1986). *Time limited training and supported employment: A model for redistributing existing resources for persons with severe disabilities*. Richmond: Virginia Commonwealth University, Rehabilitation Research and Training Center, School of Education; and Virginia Department of Mental Health and Mental Retardation.

Langone, J., & Gill, D. (1986, April/May/June). Developing effective vocational programs for mentally retarded persons: Cooperative planning between rehabilitation and education. *Journal of Rehabilitation, 52*(2), 63–67.

Leavitt, H. (1986). *Corporate pathfinders*. Homewood, IL: Dow Jones-Irwin.

McConnell, L. (1986). *If...the future of VR*. Paper presented at Twelfth Insitute on Rehabilitation Issues, October 29–30, 1985, Louisville, KY. Dunbar: West Virginia Research and Training Center.

McCormick, M. (1984). *What they don't teach you at Harvard Business School*. Toronto: Bantam Books.

Parent, W., & Everson, J. (1986, October/November/December). ''Competencies of disabled workers in industry: A review of business literature.'' *Journal of Rehabilitation, 52*(4), 16–23.

Rehabilitation Act Amendments. H.R. 4021, 1986.

Revell, G., Wehman, P., & Arnold, S. (1984). System innovations in response to the congressional mandate to serve severely disabled persons. *Journal of Rehabilitation, 50*(4), 33–38.

Rubin, S., & Rubin, N. (1988). *Contemporary challenges to the rehabilitation counseling profession*. Baltimore: Paul H. Brookes Publishing Co.

Schindler-Rainman, E., & Lippit, R. (1980). *Building the collaborative community—Mobilizing citizens for action*. Riverside, CA: University of California, Riverside.

Smits, S., Decker, R., & Schneider, H. (1982). System innovations in response to the congressional mandate to serve disabled persons. *Journal of Rehabilitation Administration, 6*(1), 15–22.

Vogelsberg, T. (1986). *Competitive and supported employment data systems*. Unpublished manuscript.

Wehman, P., & Kregel, J. (1986). A supported work approach to competitive employment of individuals with moderate and severe handicaps. Richmond: Virginia Commonwealth University, Rehabilitation Research and Training Center, School of Education.

Wright, G. (1986, October 2). *Total rehabilitation*. Boston, 1980. (Conference Report on H.R. 4021, Rehabilitation Act Amendments of 1986.) In *Congressional Record*, Washington, DC: U.S. Government Printing Office.

Chapter 9

Preservice Preparation of Supported Employment Professionals

John Kregel and Paul Sale

One remarkable feature of the supported employment movement is the enthusiasm and optimism with which the initiative has been received by the professional community. Although it has required extensive changes in service delivery models, funding patterns, and a degree of interagency cooperation rarely seen in other social service programs, supported employment in most instances has been embraced by state policymakers and local service providers. Hundreds of supported employment programs are currently operating throughout the nation. While some professionals and family members still voice hesitancy and skepticism, the salient discussion has moved from "Should we implement supported employment programs?" to "How can we implement supported employment programs most effectively and efficiently?"

Despite the clear commitment to supported employment alternatives, the movement is still in its infancy. One of the most urgent problems facing state and local program administrators is an acute lack of qualified personnel to staff the newly emerging programs. Since supported employment programs are just beginning to be fully implemented, it is very difficult to identify specific numbers of personnel necessary at this time. However, all indicators point to a potentially massive labor shortage in this area. Program administrators possess a philosophical and legislative mandate for supported employment activities, and sufficient funding streams are rapidly evolving, but in far too many cases a lack of trained personnel make the delivery of competent supported employment services extremely difficult.

This situation is in many ways similar to the challenge that faced program administrators and institutions of higher education when public school programs attempted to rapidly gear up to serve students with severe and profound handicaps immediately after the passage of the Education for All Handicapped Children Act (PL 94-142) in 1975. When services to a large group of children and adolescents who had previously been excluded from public education were legislatively mandated, program administrators were confronted with developing appropriate service programs, even though hardly any qualified teachers were available to staff the new programs. Colleges and universities were charged with developing new programs and identifying qualified faculty in an extremely short period of time. State agencies had to move quickly to develop credentialing standards for professional staff to work with a group of individuals who possessed very different needs and required qualitatively different types of service programs than other students accommodated in the public schools at that time.

The national supported employment initiative has resulted in the same types of imperatives for institutions of higher education and state agencies. Supported employment programs are designed to serve a group of individuals previously excluded from the rehabilitation system. The services these persons need require competencies—such as a thorough knowledge of systematic instruction strategies and the ability to provide intensive on-the-job training—that at present are generally not included in university training programs for rehabilitation personnel. At the same time, university training programs designed to prepare special educators do not equip professionals with the skills needed to effectively assume roles within the supported employment system. Special education programs generally do not prepare professionals who are able to work effectively with adults, to function successfully in the rehabilitation system, or to perform the job development, job placement, and adult advocacy activities necessary to be successful supported employment specialists.

State and local program administrators are also grappling with changes in personnel roles resulting from the rapid expansion of supported employment programs. A number of new roles are quickly emerging, such as that of job coach, enclave and work-crew supervisor, and other direct service roles. Some states and programs are developing even more specialized roles such as job development specialists or postemployment follow-along specialists. Administrators are frequently struggling to staff new programs with limited guidance as to what skills and experience to look for in new employees, how employees should be supervised and evaluated, or how they may be incorporated into existing state and local personnel systems.

This chapter focuses on the design and development of preservice training programs to prepare personnel to serve in the national supported employment network. First, however, the discussion addresses a critical issue that could potentially affect the overall success of the movement—that of the level of preparation that should be required of supported employment professionals.

The approach described in this chapter focuses on the design of undergraduate and graduate degree programs that prepare highly skilled

supported employment specialists. This strategy has been questioned by some who argue that the skills required by supported employment personnel do not justify attaining an undergraduate or graduate degree and that supported employment programs can be adequately staffed by paraprofessional personnel or by existing personnel who have received limited inservice education. While the present authors agree that a massive inservice training effort is required to meet the immediate needs of newly established programs, they also feel that a total reliance on this strategy is misplaced and shortsighted.

Supported employment personnel must be able to work effectively with consumers who possess limited skill repertoires and for whom traditional service approaches have often not been successful. In addition, supported employment specialists must possess a wide array of highly sophisticated abilities. They must be thoroughly familiar with the employment processes of job development, job analysis, and communicating and negotiating with employers. They must be able to counsel consumers and their families who are contemplating participation in supported employment programs. Also, they must possess in-depth knowledge of systematic instruction strategies such as prompting, reinforcement, task analysis, and data collection in order to provide effective on-the-job training. The breadth and complexity of the skills required, as well as the unique and challenging needs of consumers participating in supported employment programs, argue for preservice instruction in university undergraduate or graduate programs. An overdependence on less-skilled staff in supported employment programs may result in these programs being unable to meet the high expectations placed on them, which may ultimately jeopardize the entire supported employment movement.

The upcoming sections examine the emerging roles required in supported employment programs, followed by a discussion of the specific competencies needed by supported employment specialists. Next, guidelines for implementing training programs that include both classroom and clinical practicum components are included. Finally, the chapter discusses strategies for overcoming existing barriers to implementing effective preservice training programs for supported employment specialists.

PERSONNEL ROLES IN SUPPORTED EMPLOYMENT PROGRAMS

The large-scale development of supported employment programs will generate a variety of new direct service and administrative roles. While great diversity now exists in job titles and job duties among supported employment programs in various locations throughout the country, several specific roles have emerged that appear to exist in sufficient numbers to justify the development of preservice training programs. A number of these roles are described next.

Employment Specialist— Adult Service Programs

Perhaps the key role in the entire supported employment movement is the employment specialist in individual placement models such as supported competitive employment or supported work. This position is also referred to as a job coordinator (Wehman & Kregel, 1985) or a job coach (Wehman & Melia, 1985). The employment specialist must be able to implement all phases of the individual placement model—job development, consumer assessment, job placement, job-site training and advocacy, and long-term follow-along. Employment specialists must possess a wide range of sophisticated competencies, as outlined in the "Preservice Training Curriculum" section following. While some experts recommend that employment specialists be able to perform all facets of the employment process (Moon, Goodall, Barcus, & Brooke, 1986), in some programs around the country more specialized staffing patterns have emerged. Roles have been created for personnel who perform only one component of the individual job placement process, such as job development specialist, job-site training specialist, or follow-along specialist. It has been estimated that as many as 4,000 supported employment specialists will be required to staff existing and emerging programs over the next few years.

Employment Specialists— Public School Programs

Many secondary special education programs serving students with moderate or severe handicaps are also gearing up to provide individual job placement services according to a supported work model. Employment specialists involved in these programs would fill roles very different from those of traditional work-study coordinators or the recently developed roles of vocational special needs personnel. In contrast, employment specialists in public school programs would frequently provide long-term intensive training to students in integrated community-based employment settings. When working in public school settings, employment specialists might in some instances need to possess valid teacher certification for the state in which they are working, and in all cases they will need to possess an in-depth knowledge of transition issues and the transition planning process.

Enclave and Work Crew Supervisors

Enclave-in-industry and work-crew supervisors are the primary titles given to professionals who staff group supported employment options. Enclaves in industry (Rhodes & Valenta, 1985) refer to options in which a small group of individuals with severe disabilities work as a unit within a regular business or industry. Work crews are similar to enclaves in the sense that a small group of individuals are involved in the employment option, but in work crews the group generally moves about the community performing work in several sites in the course of a workday or workweek. Both enclaves and work crews are generally staffed by one or more supervisors, who are responsible for securing and negotiating work contracts, training all workers in the group, and providing permanent supervision at the job-site. Given the nature of these positions, enclave and work-crew supervisors must not only possess excellent consumer training and supervision skills but must also have strong business competencies that allow them to effectively perform the contract negotiation, bidding, and job analysis components of their roles.

Senior Employment Specialists

In many programs, the supported employment or individual job placement program is one of an array of programs supervised by a program manager who may also have responsibility for transitional employment, work adjustment, or sheltered employment programs. In these programs, particularly those with several employment specialists, a specific individual is identified as the senior or lead employment specialist. While still maintaining his or her own active case load, the senior employment specialist may also have responsibility for assisting other employment specialists in solving particular problems, identifying the case loads of all employment specialists in the program, or arranging backup coverage and solving other day-to-day staffing problems. Senior employment specialists must not only be highly qualified job coaches in their own right but must also possess experience in personnel management as well.

Program Managers

In many states, the supported employment initiative has resulted in the development of large numbers of private, not-for-profit service providers that deliver only supported employment services through contract or fee-for-service arrangements. Managers or directors of these programs must possess a wide array of skills, including abilities in procuring not-for-profit status, personnel management, budgeting and finance, and staff training. They must be knowledgeable about supported employment models and strategies, and at the same time must be thoroughly prepared to operate a small business. While at present very few individuals actually possess all the needed skills, the emergence of a group of individuals able to operate private, not-for-profit programs would greatly enhance the rapid development of supported employment services.

Supported Employment
State Agency Personnel

With numerous supported employment programs rapidly emerging, considerable pressure has been placed upon state agency personnel to facilitate and monitor supported employment efforts. State offices of supported employment or other organizational units have been established in many states. While in many instances individuals in existing positions have done a commendable job of educating themselves about supported employment and have taken on supported employment administrative duties in addition to their other responsibilities, it is becoming increasingly clear that there is a need for specialists to fill newly created roles in state and regional agencies. These individuals are needed to coordinate the significant staff development and inservice training programs that are required in each state, to oversee the delivery of technical assistance to operating programs, to design program monitoring and program evaluation systems, and to advocate for the supported employment programs within the state agency and with the state legislature. Without capable and committed state agency leadership, the supported employment movement cannot expect to accomplish its intended purposes for consumers with severe disabilities.

A PRESERVICE
TRAINING CURRICULUM

Required Competencies

The emerging roles of personnel providing supported employment to consumers with severe disabilities require graduates of preservice training programs to achieve a comprehensive set of informational and performance competencies. These required competencies can be grouped into several broad areas, including: 1) philosophical, legal, and policy issues; 2) program development; 3) program implementation; 4) program management; 5) program evaluation; 6) systematic instruction; and 7) transition planning. Each competency area is discussed in more detail in the following sections.

Philosophical, Legal, and Policy Issues Philosophical, legal, and policy issues comprise a broad competency area that serves as a base upon which the preservice professional builds the specific skills required of a supported employment specialist. Specific competencies within this area should address the effects of normalization and deinstitutionalization upon supported employment and the significance of critical issues relative to supported employment such as decent wages, benefits, and integration (e.g., Wehman & Moon, 1986). Knowledge of the purposes, provisions, and significance of legislation and litigation that affect supported employment and transitional programs should also be provided (e.g., see Braddock, 1987). Students should be informed about the different eligibility definitions used by various programs serving disabled individuals (e.g., Special Education, Rehabilitative Services, Social Security Administration, and Administration on Developmental Disabilities). Also included in this competency area is knowledge about the organization, operation, and related services provided by state and local agencies involved with the employment of individuals with disabilities.

Program Development Mastery of competencies within program development imparts skills needed to begin a supported employment program. Specific competencies include the ability to describe an array of supported employment service delivery models potentially available to individuals with disabilities (enclaves, mobile crews, etc.) and to assess the supported employment needs of those individuals through state and local needs assessments. In addition, students should demonstrate abilities related to surveying the local community and analyzing employment trends and opportunities. Competencies within this area should also prepare the student to design and implement comprehensive client assessment procedures at the program and individual level. The student should be required to effectively design, implement, and evaluate programs to educate parents and community members regarding the advantages of supported employment. An awareness of relevant regulations involved in the development of supported employment programs (profit versus not-for-profit organizational status, subminimum wage regulations, etc.) should also be required. The student should futhermore demonstrate a knowledge of the roles of various disciplines in supported employment and an ability to work effectively with professionals from these disciplines in developing comprehensive supported employment programs.

Program Implementation The specific competencies within program implementation are directed to obtaining and maintaining jobs for specific consumers and generally fall within the areas outlined by Moon et al. (1986). Students should demonstrate an ability to perform job development activities including designing and completing comprehensive job analyses on potential job placements. Students should be required to conduct in-depth assessments to include systematic review of consumer records, interviews with consumers and significant others, and observation of consumers in a variety of settings. The ability to perform necessary job placement activities such as arranging for transportation and/or transportation training and explaining the effects of employment on Social Security benefits to the consumer and family members should also be demonstrated within this broad competency area. Students should become competent at designing and implementing systematic instructional strategies to teach clients to independently perform all skills required in a particular vocational setting. Subsequent to this initial skill acquisition, the ability to monitor job performance and provide other follow-along services should also be demonstrated. Skills in providing family support and training services and communicating the results of employment activities to the family should futhermore be acquired through completion of competencies in this broad area. Finally, effective advocacy skills directed toward promoting social interaction between the consumer and coworkers should be evidenced.

Program Management Students graduating from preservice supported employment training programs will often be required to demonstrate skills in program management and administration. Students should acquire an understanding of the major legal issues of significance to a variety of organizational structures (e.g., not-for-profit agencies, local and state governmental agencies) and be able to describe the pertinent regulations and processes for establishing and operating a supported employment program within a variety of organizational structures. The ability to allocate personnel, equipment, transportation, and fiscal resources should be demonstrated. Students should also be skilled in the management of personnel, payroll, and inventories within supported employment programs, including competencies focusing on budgeting and finance. In addition, skills relating to appropriate methods of identifying and evaluating staff development needs of employees within supported employment programs should be acquired. Students should, moreover, demonstrate the ability to design, implement, and evaluate effective public relations programs to publicize the efforts of a supported employment agency.

Program Evaluation Program graduates need to possess skills relative to evaluating individual client progress and overall program effectiveness. Students should demonstrate the ability to evaluate the status of individual consumers through an analysis of wages earned, benefits received, length of employment, job advancement, and job mobility. The ability to design and implement a comprehensive management information system is requisite to tracking consumer progress. In terms of program effectiveness, students should be able to design and implement procedures to measure consumer movement, benefit/cost analysis, parental and employer satisfaction, and other pertinent factors related to the operation of supported employment programs. Students should demonstrate the ability to analyze and synthesize the myriad of evaluation data and prepare reports as required by funding and accreditation agencies.

Systematic Instruction The functional characteristics and styles of learning typically exhibited by consumers for whom supported employment is intended require professionals to possess skills in systematic, behaviorally based instructional programming. Students should be able to use a variety of instructional techniques such as data-based consumer assessment, task analysis, prompting, and reinforcement procedures to teach consumers previously unacquired skill sequences. Similarly, competencies in data collection strategies including rate, proficiency, and duration recording should also be demonstrated by program graduates. Students should be able to utilize a variety of techniques to achieve generalization of skills acquired in the vocational setting across a wide range of residential, community, and recreational settings. Students

should also demonstrate competency in the modification and/or adaptation of tasks and settings to allow consumers with physical and sensory impairments to function as independently as possible. Finally, preservice students should be competent in the design and implementation of a variety of behavior management strategies, including self-management and self-control procedures, to improve and maintain appropriate work performance while reducing inappropriate behaviors that interfere with successful job performance.

Transition Planning Competencies within this content area relate to facilitating the successful movement of a young person with disabilities from secondary special education programs to programs designed to deliver services to adults. Program graduates should be able to design, implement, and evaluate comprehensive educational programs that prepare disabled individuals for independent functioning, and they should be able to identify an array of public school service delivery models that provide comprehensive vocational education to individuals with disabilities. Identification and analysis of skills necessary for success in a variety of postschool environments available to consumers should also be required within this transition area. The ability to work effectively with both educators and adult service professionals in the development and implementation of longitudinal educational and vocational training plans should also be demonstrated. Likewise, students should be able to convey accurate and relevant information regarding guardianship, wills and trusts, and other life-planning activities to families of disabled individuals.

Current special education, vocational education, and vocational rehabilitation training programs do not provide competencies in each of the broad areas just outlined. The professional entering supported employment preservice training *may* already possess some competencies in one or more areas, depending on his or her previous experiences and formal training. For example, professionals from a special education background may already possess skills in systematic instruction. Similarly, professionals from a rehabilitation counseling background may be knowledgeable in vocational rehabilitation legislation affecting disabled persons (Szymanski, Buckley, Parent, Parker, & West-brook, 1988). As another example, special education preservice programs have typically focused on elementary-age students with mild to moderate handicaps rather than on secondary school programming (Kokaska & Brolin, 1985). Likewise, behavioral assessment and training are not covered fully in rehabilitation programs (Szymanski et al., 1988).

Given the range of educational background and practical experiences of students entering supported employment preservice programs, an assessment of existing skills relative to the required training competencies is helpful. Such an assessment should be accomplished early in the training sequence and requires systematically querying the student about courses taken, formal internships/externships completed, inservices and seminars attended, and previous paid and unpaid employment experiences. A structured interview format utilizing an entry competency checklist is one way to obtain the information. An illustrative checklist is provided in Figure 1. The information gleaned from the interview and checklist will allow the student's program to focus on areas in which skills have not been fully developed. A program of didactic and field-based experiences can be developed from the listing of needed competencies.

Didactic Experiences

Content   Renzaglia (1986) and others have noted that personnel delivering supported employment services need grounding in a strong theoretical base from which to make service delivery decisions. This theoretical base should be provided through existing courses in special education and vocational rehabilitation and through courses specifically addressing supported employment issues. The existing curriculum of preservice programs includes courses focusing on: 1) introduction to developmental disabilities; 2) systematic instruction for exceptional individuals; and 3) designing and implementing secondary programming for exceptional students.

Additional courses needed to deliver the informational competencies described in the previous section should cover: 1) an overview of supported employment, including funding issues and varying service delivery models; 2) procedures and techniques for designing and implementing supported employment programs; and 3) management and/or business theory courses. The inclusion of courses in business and management is integral to the comprehensive supported employment curriculum because program graduates will be interacting on a daily basis with business professionals.

Evaluation   The informational competencies gained in the didactic portion of the preservice program can be measured in several ways. Students can convey their mastery verbally through class discussions; structured interviews with the course instructors; and informal and formal presentation to class members, colleagues, and/or panels of experts assembled to evaluate mastery of the competencies. Written products such as literature reviews, position papers, projects, and examinations should also be used in the evaluation process.

Field-Based Experiences

Field-based experiences are a second and equally critical component of an effective preservice supported employment program. The experiences allow the student to transform the theory obtained through the didactic experiences into actual practices. Field-based activities should occur throughout the preservice program and may be acquired in several formats. For example, the experiences may be self-contained in an internship/externship, they may be part of a certain didactic course, or they may be gained through work-study or assistantship activities.

Content   The content of the field experiences will vary among students, based upon their prior education and experience (as indicated by the initial competency assessment discussed earlier) and the student's perceived role upon completion of the training program. In general, however, the content should emphasize: 1) completion of activities related to direct service delivery to consumers and interactions with parents, guardians, and human service personnel; and 2) completion of activities related to the development and management of supported employment programs.

Student: _____ Social Security number: _____

Semester/year admitted: _____   Phone:_____

Program: Full-time _____ Part-time _____   Projected graduation: _____

Educational Background

Degree	Institution	Curriculum	Year completed
_____	_____	_____	_____
_____	_____	_____	_____
_____	_____	_____	_____
_____	_____	_____	_____

Previous Experience in Supported Employment

Position	Employer	Years
_____	_____	_____
_____	_____	_____
_____	_____	_____
_____	_____	_____

Previously Acquired Information Competencies

Degree of completion			Competency area	Remarks/justification
N	P	C		
___	___	___	1. Philosophical, legal, policy issues	_____
___	___	___	2. Program development	_____
___	___	___	3. Program implementation	_____
___	___	___	4. Program management	_____
___	___	___	5. Program evaluation	_____
___	___	___	6. Systematic instruction	_____
___	___	___	7. Transition planning	_____

Previously Completed Field Performance Activities

Degree of completion			Performance activity	Remarks/justification
N	P	C		
___	___	___	1. Client screening and assessment	_____
___	___	___	2. Transitional individualized transition program meetings	_____
___	___	___	3. Job development	_____
___	___	___	4. Job analysis	_____
___	___	___	5. Initial placement preparation	_____
___	___	___	6. Behavior management programming	_____
___	___	___	7. Specific skill instruction	_____
___	___	___	8. Adaptation/modification of settings	_____
___	___	___	9. Ongoing monitoring and follow-along	_____
___	___	___	10. Community needs assessment	_____
___	___	___	11. Proposal and contract development	_____
___	___	___	12. Resource allocation and management	_____
___	___	___	13. Staff/parent education programming	_____

Figure 1. Entry competency checklist. (N = no experience, P = partially acquired, C = completed.)

Field performance activities related to direct service delivery should focus on the following areas:

1. Consumer screening and assessment
2. Individualized Transition Plan (ITP) meetings
3. Job development activities
4. Job analysis activities
5. Preparation for initial consumer placement
6. Design and implementation of behavior management program
7. Specific skill instruction
8. Adaptation/modification of employment settings
9. Ongoing consumer monitoring and follow-along

These areas are generic to all models of supported employment (individual placement, enclaves, mobile crews, and entrepreneurial models). The specific behaviors to be observed under each of the areas will vary according to the model(s) emphasized within the preservice training program. For example, job analysis activities for the individual placement model will not typically include completion of a detailed time motion study. Job analysis for an enclave requires such a study in order to develop a competitive bid for service to the business in which the enclave is to be located. Examples of specific service delivery functions relative to each of the preceding nine areas are presented in Table 1, along with suggested evaluation methods (see next paragraph). Readers should note that these particular behaviors were developed for a program with an emphasis on the individual placement model. Also in Table 1, field-based performance activities related to the development and management of supported employment programs are grouped into the areas of community needs assessment, proposal and contract bid development, resource allocation and management, and staff/parent education program development. The specific student behaviors under each area will vary according to the student's perceived role subsequent to program completion. Again, opportunities to engage in these activities should be provided in a variety of settings and formats; however, these activities generally require student placement with

program managers in supported employment programs, or in state and local mental retardation, education, or rehabilitation agencies. The particular behaviors listed in Table 1 were developed to build student skills at the program or service delivery level as opposed to skills required at the community or state agency management level.

Evaluation Measurement of skills acquired in field-based experiences is accomplished by a variety of methods. Certain skills such as those related to direct instruction, and interactions with professionals and parents, are best evaluated through repeated cycles of observation by a supervisor followed by verbal and written feedback to the student. Assessment of other skills such as job analysis and proposal development can be conducted through evaluation of the written products generated as a result of the related activities. Systematic verbal and written feedback from cooperating professionals with whom the students are placed is also essential and will yield both general and task-specific assessment information to the student and field-based supervisor. Suggestions for methods of evaluation are presented with the listings of the field-based components found in Table 1.

IMPLEMENTING PRESERVICE TRAINING PROGRAMS: A CASE STUDY

The previous sections of this chapter have provided a rationale for the development of preservice supported employment training programs, they have delineated the roles to be filled by program graduates within the national supported employment network, and have provided a detailed discussion of the competencies that should be contained in any effective preservice training program. While to date only a handful of preservice training programs exist (in Massachusetts, Arkansas, California, and Virginia) the urgent need for trained supported employment professionals suggests that many other preservice programs will emerge over the next several years.

The competencies described in this chapter form the basis of the Supported Employment

Table 1. Field-based activities, required student behaviors, and evaluation methodologies

Activity/student behavior	Method of evaluation	
	Observation	Product evaluation
Screening and Assessment		
Obtain and review consumer information/referral form.		X
Review all records (e.g., educational assessments, vocational assessment, medical reports, psychological reports, past work history).		X
Develop a list of questions based on the review of the record (i.e., focus on inconsistencies between and within the records).		X
Interview the consumer and primary caregiver.	X	X
Interview other individuals familiar with consumer's abilities (e.g., teachers, supervisors).	X	X
Observe consumer in several current environments.	X	X
Prepare an assessment report summarizing the results of the consumer assessment.		X
ITP Meetings (Individual Transition Plan)		
Observe first ITP meeting and discuss the meeting with the cooperating professional.		X
Review educational and other relevant data in preparation for a second ITP meeting.		X
Prepare preliminary recommendations relative to the second ITP meeting. Submit those recommendations to the cooperating professional for review.		X
Participate in second ITP meeting to the extent agreed upon with the cooperating professional.	X	
Discuss the ITP with the cooperating professional.	X	X
Job Development		
Screen the local community for specific job openings.		X
Initiate contacts with specific employers, continuing until you locate two who will meet with you.	X	X
Conduct an employer interview explaining the supported work model, its benefits to them, and the consumer's capabilities.	X	X
Job Analysis		
Observe the job site and the worker's responsibilities on the job.	X	
Perform the job yourself.	X	
Interview employer regarding job requirements.	X	
Analyze job/worker compatibility; use data from indicator 1.4 or other Consumer Employment Screening Forms.	X	X
Initial Placement Preparation		
Talk to schools and parents regarding initial placement of consumer.	X	
Identify and place in order of priority all alternatives for transportation to and from the job site.		X
Develop a transportation training program. Provide transportation training on the selected method of transporation.	X	X
Accompany consumer and cooperating professional to Social Security office to establish impact of employment on benefits and procedures relative to reporting wages, and so forth.	X	

(continued)

Table 1. *(continued)*

Activity/student behavior	Method of evaluation	
	Observation	Product evaluation
Explain effects of employment on Social Security benefits to parents and consumer.	X	
Assist the consumer in obtaining the necessary uniforms, medical examinations, and other activities and/or materials prerequisite to employment.		X
Behavior Management		
Identify a potential target behavior needing modification.		X
Define target behavior in measurable terms.		X
Assess the need for behavior management by collecting baseline data (minimum of three data points).	X	X
Determine if the behavior warrants management.		X
Develop an intervention program to manage the consumer's behavior.		X
Implement the intervention program.	X	X
Monitor the intervention program on a weekly basis, modifying as indicated by incoming data.		X
Specific Skill Training		
Task analyze an unacquired skill (#1) for each consumer.		X
Task analyze an unacquired skill (#2) for each consumer.		X
Observe each consumer performing skill #1 and collect baseline data.	X	X
Observe each consumer performing skill #2 and collect baseline data.	X	X
Develop a systematic training program for each consumer for skill #1.		X
Develop a systematic training program for each consumer for skill #2.		X
Implement and systematically evaluate progress of each consumer on skill #1.	X	X
Implement and systematically evaluate progress of each consumer on skill #2.	X	X
Review progress of each consumer on skill #1 and modify instructional program as needed.		X
Review progress of each consumer on skill #2 and modify instructional program as needed.		X
Adaptation/modification		
Review existing data to determine specific problem areas.		X
Evaluate job environments and determine alternatives (e.g., job sharing, adapting equipment).	X	X
Develop and implement modification plans.	X	X
Provide systematic instruction, collecting probe and prompt data.	X	X
Evaluate data weekly, remodifying plans as needed.		X
Monitoring and Follow-Along		
Collect data on consumer performance utilizing the following strategies: frequency, rate, duration, interval time sampling, permanent products.	X	X
Prepare a narrative progress report on consumer's work performance.		X

(continued)

Table 1. *(continued)*

Activity/student behavior	Method of evaluation	
	Observation	Product evaluation
Complete a Progress Report Form detailing the consumer's performance.		X
Verbally interpret progress reports to consumer.	X	
Verbally interpret consumer progress to employer and obtain employer feedback.	X	
Verbally interpret progress reports to consumer's parents/guardians.	X	
Report progress to cooperating agencies (e.g., schools, Department of Rehabilitative Services).	X	
Complete a consumer update form.		X
Obtain a supervisor evaluation form.		X
Community Assessment		
Survey potential consumers of local programs to identify supported employment needs of a consumer population.		X
Analyze employment trends and opportunities in the local community and identify major job clusters and industries to be included in supported employment training.		X
Proposal and Contract Development		
Develop two competitive bids to obtain contracts for enclaves and/or mobile crew programs.		
Prepare a competitive proposal to secure state or federal funding to establish a supported employment program.		
Prepare a proposal to establish vendorship status for a program or agency.		
Resource Allocation and Management		
Complete a project budget for one type of supported employment option that details costs for personnel, travel, consumer salaries and wages, benefits, and overhead.		X
Develop a plan to allocate personnel, equipment, transportation, and fiscal resources within a supported employment program.		X
Operate and maintain a management information system to track consumer's progress within a supported employment program.		X
Prepare a program evaluation report that analyzes consumer's outcomes and the cost-effectiveness of the supported employment program.		X
Staff/Parent Education		
The trainee will design and implement a staff development training program and conduct a minimum of 8 hours of staff development sessions for personnel in a supported employment program.	X	X
The trainee will design and conduct a minimum of 5 hours of parent education activities to improve the participation and address the concerns of parents of individuals in supported employment programs.	X	X

Masters degree program at Virginia Commonwealth University (VCU). The program is designed as a 13-course, 39-credit-hour sequence that awards students a graduate degree through the School of Education. To illustrate the way in which program competencies are woven into a series of didactic and clinical coursework, this section of the chapter provides a case study of an individual student in the program. It describes the skills and experiences the student possessed prior to entering the program, the sequence of courses in the student's program, the clinical experiences in which the student participated, and the student's employment experiences after graduation.

The student in question, referred to here as Mary, came to VCU from a midwestern state to be a full-time student in the Supported Employment Masters program. Previously, Mary had earned an undergraduate degree in rehabilitation and had worked for 3 years in an adult activity center. Although she had not been directly involved in supported employment activities, she had previously been exposed to the concept of supported employment through participation in conferences and seminars. At the same time, she had become disillusioned while attempting to teach what she considered nonfunctional "prevocational" activities to the individuals she worked with in the adult activity center. (Mary's situation is similar to many of the full-time students in the VCU Supported Employment program. Students have entered the program with previous undergraduate training in rehabilitation, special education, or social work. A majority have previously been employed in sheltered workshops, work activity, or day activity centers. While most have been involved in adult service programs, less than half have had any previous work experience in supported employment programs.)

After being admitted to the program and prior to coursework, Mary completed an entry competency checklist in conjunction with her advisor. Based upon the results of this assessment, a program of study was designed for her. Table 2 outlines Mary's program of study. The program contains six core courses designed to provide the student didactic instruction in the program competency areas previously described here. The

Table 2. Example of a supported employment specialist program of study[a]

Program Core (Six Courses)
  Seminar in Developmental Disabilities
  Introduction to Supported Employment
  Developing and Implementing Supported Employment Programs
  Managing Supported Employment Programs
  Teaching Strategies for Persons with Severe Handicaps
  Secondary Programming for Exceptional Students

Externships (Two Courses)
  Externship I: Direct Service
  Externship II: Program Management

Educational Foundations (Three Courses)
  Methods of Educational Research
  Adolescent Growth and Development
  Philosophy of Education

Electives (Two Courses)
  Principles of Public Administration
  Management Theory and Practice

[a] Based on case study (see text) of a student at Virginia Commonwealth University.

Seminar in Development Disabilities (see Table 2) includes instruction in the philosophical, legal, and policy issues integral to the supported employment concept. The Introduction to Supported Employment course covers competencies related to program implementation and is designed to equip the student with skills crucial to future success as employment specialists or crew supervisors. Developing and Implementing Supported Employment Programs deals with developing program competencies such as conducting community surveys, developing parent and family education programs, and working effectively with professionals from other adult service agencies. The course in Managing Supported Employment Programs stresses skills directly involved in program management and evaluation. Systematic instruction competencies are acquired through Teaching Strategies for Persons with Severe Handicaps. Secondary Programming for Exceptional Students provides students an overview of secondary special education programs and specific instruction related to planning and implementing transition programs.

To round out the master's degree, a student must also take three educational foundations courses and two program electives. As shown in Table 2, Mary chose electives in Principles of Public Administration and Management Theory and Practice. She selected these courses because she was interested in pursuing a career as a senior employment specialist or a program manager, positions in which personnel and program management skills would become critically important. Alternative electives chosen by other students have included: Financial Accounting and Fundamentals of the Legal Environment of Business, for individuals interested in establishing and operating small, not-for-profit supported employment corporations; and Behavior Management for Exceptional Individuals and Introduction to Community-Based Instruction, for those preparing for roles as public school employment specialists, in order to emphasize systematic instruction skills useful in working with individuals with severe handicaps.

In addition to didactic coursework, Mary also participated in two "externships" (see Table 2) as part of her training program. Externship I focuses on the acquisition of skills related to the delivery of direct service to consumers, as described in the previous subsection on "Field-Based Experiences." For Externship I, Mary was assigned to an employment specialist working in one of the demonstration projects operated by the VCU Rehabilitation Research and Training Center. This placement allowed her to gain experience in the application of all facets of the supported employment individual placement process. Intensive instruction in the delivery of systematic training at the job site was provided through Mary's participation at a clinical training site operated by the training division of the Research and Training Center.

The purpose of Externship II in the Supported Employment Masters program is to address competencies related to the administration and management of supported employment programs. For her second externship, Mary was placed with the director of the local mental retardation agency. Among her assigned tasks was the development of a supported employment management information system and a program monitoring instrument. She was also able to gain experience in conducting communitywide needs assessments, evaluating supported employment proposals, and in developing staff training activities.

Mary's externship experiences are typical of those of many students in the Supported Employment Masters program. Externship I students are placed in three local supported employment agencies and two different demonstration projects operated by the Rehabilitation Research and Training Center. Externship II students have been placed with local program directors, the state office of supported employment, a local special education supported employment placement program, and the director of the Department of Rehabilitative Services Facilities Office.

After graduation, Mary explored several different options, finally accepting a position as supervisor of supported employment services in a large rehabilitation facility. Other program graduates are filling roles as public school employment specialists, as professionals in university positions providing technical assistance to supported employment programs, and other roles.

SUMMARY

The ultimate success of our nation's efforts to provide meaningful employment opportunities for citizens with severe disabilities depends upon our ability to rapidly train an adequate number of qualified professionals who are able to fill roles in the supported employment movement. Emerging roles include those of direct service providers, program managers, and state agency personnel. While many training needs can be adequately addressed through inservice training efforts, effective preservice programs can also play a critical role in preparing individuals who will possess the range of direct service and management skills required to implement high-quality programs. This chapter has focused on the competencies needed by supported employment professionals. These competencies range from direct service skills such as program implementation, systematic instruction, and transition planning to administrative skills such as program development, management, and implementation.

Building a cadre of skilled supported employment professionals will not occur overnight. While inservice activities must be relied upon now to meet the immediate demands of the new supported employment programs, the human services field must also begin to develop preservice programs that will equip professionals with recently developed technologies. Only a group of highly qualified and motivated supported employment professionals can make our hope for improved employment outcomes for tens of thousands of individuals with severe disabilities a reality.

REFERENCES

Braddock, D. (1987). *Federal policy toward mental retardation and developmental disabilities.* Baltimore: Paul H. Brookes Publishing Co.

Education for All Handicapped Children Act. PL 94–142, 1975.

Kokaska, C., & Brolin, D. (1985). *Career education for handicapped individuals* (2nd ed.). Columbus OH: Charles E. Merrill.

Moon, S., Goodall, P., Barcus, M., & Brooke, V. (1986). *The supported work model of competitive employment for citizens with severe handicaps: A guide for job trainers.* Richmond: Virginia Commonwealth University, Rehabilitation Research and Training Center.

Renzaglia, A. (1986). Preparing personnel to support and guide emerging contemporary service alternatives. In F.R. Rusch (Ed.), *Competitive employment issues and strategies* (pp. 303–316).Baltimore: Paul H. Brookes Publishing Co.

Rhodes, L., & Valenta, L. (1985). Industry-based supported employment: An enclave approach. *Journal of the Association for Persons with Severe Handicaps, 10*(1), 12–20.

Syzmanski, E.N., Buckley, J., Parent, W.S., Parker, R.M., & Westbrook, J.D. (1988). Rehabilitation counseling in supported employment: A conceptual model for service delivery and personnel preparation. In S.E. Rubin & N.M. Rubin (Eds.), *Contemporary challenges to the rehabilitation counseling profession* (pp. 111–133). Baltimore: Paul H. Brookes Publishing Co.

Wehman, P., & Kregel, J. (1985). A supported work approach to competitive employment of individuals with moderate and severe handicaps. *Journal of the Association for Persons with Severe Handicaps, 10*(1), 3–9.

Wehman, P., & Melia, R. (1985). The job coach: Function in transitional and supported employment. *American Rehabilitation, 11*(2), 4–7.

Wehman, P., & Moon, S. (1986). Critical values in employment programs for persons with developmental disabilities: A position paper. *Journal of Applied Rehabilitation Counseling, 18*(1), 12–16.

Chapter 10

Developing Inservice Training Programs for Supported Employment Personnel

Katherine J. Inge, J. Michael Barcus, and Jane M. Everson

The need for well-trained professionals in agencies and organizations charged with managing and implementing supported employment models for individuals with severe disabilities has greatly increased, owing to recent federal legislation and funding priorities for the development of these services. Unfortunately, relatively few preservice programs exist in colleges and universities across the country to prepare professionals to fill the new program management and direct service positions being created by these newly developed supported employment programs. Instead, current staff members who may have never received formal training in supported employment are being called upon to provide management and direct services (Barcus, Everson, & Hall, 1987; Renzaglia, 1986; Will, 1984). These professionals frequently have experience with employment programs of a "train and place" philosophy and/or experiences with persons with severe disabilities, but there is a shortage of professionals who have skills in the supported employment "place and train" approach. New staff with no formal training or experience are therefore needed in unprecedented numbers. Training programs are needed to quickly develop a values, knowledge, and technical skills base in order to facilitate the successful placement of direct service supported employment personnel.

Inservice training is the most logical short-term solution to this pressing need for trained staff, because it can address quickly and efficiently the immediate needs of program managers and service providers. This chapter outlines the planning and implementation of inservice training programs for managers and service providers concerned with one type of supported employment, the supported work model of competitive employment (Wehman & Kregel, 1985; Moon, Goodall, & Wehman, 1985). This model is often referred to as individual placement, supported work, or supported competitive employment. For similar material on other models, the reader is referred to the references and resources at the end of this chapter.

ELEMENTS OF EFFECTIVE INSERVICE TRAINING

Adult Learning Principles

How can the inservice trainer ensure that the instruction provided brings about the necessary changes in values, knowledge, and skills in the participants? An important element in training is the utilization of adult learning principles. Effective inservice trainers are aware that adults learn differently from children or adolescents and that they come to training sessions with their own unique knowledge and experiences (Boyle, 1981; Caffarella, in press; Knowles, 1980). In addition, adults justifiably believe that they have a certain level of competence in their chosen professions and expect that their experiences and knowledge will be valued by inservice trainers. Therefore, participants cannot be viewed merely as recipients of knowledge but, instead, must be allowed to actively participate and must be recognized for the various skills and competencies they bring to the training sessions (Barcus, Everson, & Hall, 1987; Caffarella, in press; McKinley, 1980; Robinson, 1979). If participants are viewed as partners with the inservice provider and as individuals with worthwhile experiences to share, they are more likely to feel comfortable in the learning environment and contribute to as well as benefit from the experience. The following suggestions may prove helpful in developing inservice programs (Barcus, Everson, & Hall, 1987; Caffarella, in press; McDaniel, Flippo, & Lowery, 1986):

1. Actively involve the participants in all planning and follow-up stages of inservice training.
2. Recognize them as partners with the inservice provider during the implementation of inservice training.
3. Incorporate their personal plans and objectives throughout the inservice workshop.
4. Provide a learning atmosphere that makes the participants feel valued and supported.
5. Create an environment of active participation by encouraging participants to discuss their experiences, concerns, and ideas.

Conducting Needs Assessments

One way to actively involve the participants in planning the various stages of inservice training is to conduct a needs assessment prior to the development of inservice materials. By obtaining a baseline of the participants' values, knowledge, and technical skills related to supported competitive employment, the inservice provider can formulate appropriate plans and objectives. If this step is eliminated, the inservice may fail to meet the agency's and participants' needs entirely.

The first step in conducting a needs assess-

ment is to identify the agency(ies) and participants to be involved and determine the value each places on supported employment. Obviously these values will directly influence what services are provided in the community and who is served in the various array of options. The following questions may help the inservice trainer determine the philosophical mind-set of the participants:

1. Do you feel that consumers have the right to work and earn wages?
2. Do you feel that consumers have the right to live independently in the community and to have access to all adult community activities?
3. Within your agency's array of employment services, what do you think is most valuable?
4. What in your agency/community would you like to see changed regarding employment services for persons with disabilities?

Figure 1 offers a needs assessment instrument that can be used to determine the values of an agency and its employees. The assessment will help the inservice provider develop workshop materials as well as enable the participants to target goals for their agencies.

The inservice provider may next want to survey the various agencies operating within the community to determine current employment practices. These practices will directly reflect the values and knowledge base of the agencies and individuals involved in the inservice training. Each agency should be contacted to determine its legislative mandates, perceived mission, types of services provided, eligibility requirements, and individualized planning procedures. The following guidelines should help trainers facilitate this process.

1. Call professionals in the community agencies/organizations to identify the contact person for employment services.
2. Visit sites to meet with the contact persons and to discuss the agency's employment services.
3. Request materials utilized by the agency's employment services (e.g. grant proposals, policy and procedures manuals, local needs

The following statements represent values frequently associated with the employment of individuals who have been labeled severely disabled. Using the Likert-type scale below, first identify where on the scale *your agency's or organization's current practices lie* regarding each of the statements. Place a triangle or some other symbol to be used consistently in the approximate place on the line where your agency's or organization's current practices fall. Next, identify where on the scale *you feel your agency's or organization's practices should lie*. Place a square or some other symbol to be used consistently in the approximate place where you feel your agency or organization's practices should lie. It is likely that several of the statements will reflect discrepancies between how you as a professional value a statement and how your agency's or organization's mission and services value the statement. It is also likely that various professionals from different organizations will place different values on the statements.

The purpose of this activity is to assist participants to more clearly identify their own values and the values they believe their agency or organization holds. Completion of this activity will enable trainers to plan more effective inservice training and will enable participants to target goals for local action plans.

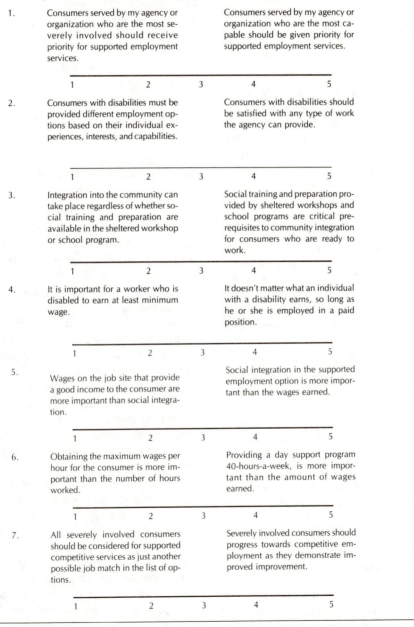

1.   Consumers served by my agency or organization who are the most severely involved should receive priority for supported employment services.

Consumers served by my agency or organization who are the most capable should be given priority for supported employment services.

1   2   3   4   5

2.   Consumers with disabilities must be provided different employment options based on their individual experiences, interests, and capabilities.

Consumers with disabilities should be satisfied with any type of work the agency can provide.

1   2   3   4   5

3.   Integration into the community can take place regardless of whether social training and preparation are available in the sheltered workshop or school program.

Social training and preparation provided by sheltered workshops and school programs are critical prerequisites to community integration for consumers who are ready to work.

1   2   3   4   5

4.   It is important for a worker who is disabled to earn at least minimum wage.

It doesn't matter what an individual with a disability earns, so long as he or she is employed in a paid position.

1   2   3   4   5

5.   Wages on the job site that provide a good income to the consumer are more important than social integration.

Social integration in the supported employment option is more important than the wages earned.

1   2   3   4   5

6.   Obtaining the maximum wages per hour for the consumer is more important than the number of hours worked.

Providing a day support program 40-hours-a-week, is more important than the amount of wages earned.

1   2   3   4   5

7.   All severely involved consumers should be considered for supported competitive services as just another possible job match in the list of options.

Severely involved consumers should progress towards competitive employment as they demonstrate improved improvement.

1   2   3   4   5

Figure 1. Supported employment training values needs assessment.

assessments, manuals for implementation of programs, interagency agreements, staffing flow charts, consumer follow-up studies, staff development plans).

To further assess the participants' community service delivery patterns, it is advisable for the inservice trainer to survey staff development activities, vocational training activities, and paid placement outcomes. The questionnaire presented in Figure 2 may be given to the various agencies' contact persons during the initial site visits. Alternatively, it may be mailed to agency personnel.

Additional information regarding the participants' objectives and knowledge base can be determined by asking them to complete written surveys prior to the training. Surveys can be mailed to the participants and follow-up phone calls should help to fill in any gaps in the information provided. Sample questions may include the following:

1. Describe your definition/understanding of supported employment.
2. Describe any formal training/experience with systematic instructional techniques.
3. Explain your expectations of the training.
4. Describe how you plan to utilize your training.
5. List your personal objectives for this training.
6. List your agency's objectives for supported employment within the next year.
7. Describe your current job and related responsibilities.
8. Describe any interagency efforts related to supported employment in your community.
9. What previous inservice training in the area of supported employment have you participated in? Have these efforts been helpful?
10. Describe the level of support your organization offers concerning the implementation of supported employment.

Finally, it is important to determine each participant's experiences and technical base with the specific supported employment activities, working either as a direct service provider, ad-

ministrator, or a purchaser of supported employment services. The questionnaire presented in Figure 3 may be used to survey participants regarding their experiences with supported employment methodology. It may be utilized either by administrators, contractors of services, or direct service providers.

As much as feasibly possible, planning of inservice should use a combination of the preceeding strategies to obtain information. Combining these strategies will enable the trainer(s) to collect both qualitative and quantitative data that reflect needs in value clarification, knowledge, and technical skills. This process may seem very time-consuming, but it will result in essential preliminary information that should enable the inservice provider to design and implement more effective inservice activities.

Determining Training Goals and Objectives

Based on a thorough assessment of the needs of the targeted trainees, the inservice provider may begin the second stage in inservice planning, that of determining the training objectives of the workshop. The information collected during the needs assessment will assist the trainer in determining: 1) the trainees' current philosophy and values; 2) the trainees' current skill level; 3) the trainees' immediate training needs; and 4) the trainees' long-term training needs. Selection of the most appropriate training objectives and subsequently, the selection of content, sequence of content, and delivery of content will depend upon the assessed needs.

Training objectives focusing on the supported work model of competitive employment fall naturally into the five components of the model (Moon, Goodall, Barcus, & Brooke, 1986). These are: job development, consumer assessment, job placement, job site training and advocacy, and ongoing follow-along. For purposes of illustration in this chapter, a minimum of seven goals with related objectives have been identified from these five components of supported competitive employment. Within each goal, based upon the needs of the participants, the trainer may choose to focus upon philosophy and values, knowledge and general information, and/or technical skills. Figure 4 outlines the three

STAFF DEVELOPMENT: List any presentations, workshops, seminars, and so forth, on supported employment, that your agency has attended/conducted in the past 6 months. Please include on a separate sheet of paper copies of agendas and a brief description of the various inservice programs.

Type of staff development	Dates	No. in-house staff trained	No. parents trained	No. employers	No. staff outside of agency
Examples					

COMMUNITY-BASED VOCATIONAL TRAINING: List any community-based training that your agency has conducted in the past 6 months.

Type of training site	Total no. consumers trained at site	No. consumers paid minimum wage or higher	No. consumers paid substandard wage	No. consumers unpaid	Staff-to-consumer ratio	Staff hours/site per day	No. consumer hours per day on site	Total time on site per consumer
Examples:								

PAID EMPLOYMENT PLACEMENTS: List each consumer that your agency has placed into competitive employment in the past 6 months.

Consumer placed	Date hired	IQ/label	Type of job	Hours worked per week	Total staff hours on site for training	Wages earned per hour	Are wages unsubsidied?	Age of consumer	Is person still employed?	Has this person been contacted in the past 2–4 weeks?
Examples:										

During the previous 6 months:
No. of consumers placed _____
No. of consumers losing jobs _____
No. of jobs refilled after loss _____
No. of consumers replaced after losing first job _____
No. of consumers who received community-based employment
  training prior to placement _____

Figure 2. Staff development and outcomes questionnaire.

broad areas of inservice training in supported employment—philosophy and values, general knowledge, and technical skills. These three areas of focus build on each other and are interdependent components of any inservice program on supported employment. A combination of lectures and activities in each of these three areas will enable trainees to discuss attitudes and beliefs, develop new ideas and skills, and practice and refine new skills.

The role of the inservice trainer is to present information and to facilitate activities and discussions. In planning inservice training, he or she could select from the following seven identified training goals based on the needs of the participants:

Goal 1: Define and examine the philosophy of supported competitive employment

Objective 1.1: To define the supported work model of competitive employment.

Objective 1.2: To discuss the similarities and differences between the supported work model of competitive employment and other

Directions: Please review this form. For each item, rate the frequency with which you or programs you have contracted with for services have engaged in the activity during the past 6 months. Rate all items in both general and specific content areas. Circle *only one number* for each item.
Check one:

| _____ I administer a program offering these types of services. | _____ I have had direct implementation experience. | _____ I have contracted with programs that offer these types of services. |

	More than once/day	Once/ day	2–4 times/ week	Once/ week	2–3 times/ month	Once/ month	Less than once/ month	Not at all
1. Job development	7	6	5	4	3	2	1	0
Conducting community job market screening	7	6	5	4	3	2	1	0
Making specific employer contact	7	6	5	4	3	2	1	0
Conducting employer interview	7	6	5	4	3	2	1	0
Recording sequence of job duties	7	6	5	4	3	2	1	0
Conducting environmental analysis	7	6	5	4	3	2	1	0

Comments: _____
_____
_____

2. Job analysis	7	6	5	4	3	2	1	0
Observing the job site	7	6	5	4	3	2	1	0
Completing the job analyses	7	6	5	4	3	2	1	0

Comments: _____
_____
_____

3. Consumer assessment	7	6	5	4	3	2	1	0
Conducting consumer interview	7	6	5	4	3	2	1	0
Observing consumer	7	6	5	4	3	2	1	0
Interpreting formal evaluations	7	6	5	4	3	2	1	0
Completing task analysis	7	6	5	4	3	2	1	0
Completing employment screening form	7	6	5	4	3	2	1	0

Comments: _____
_____
_____

Figure 3. Experience and needs assessment.

(continued)

4. **Job placement**	7	6	5	4	3	2	1	0
Conducting job compatability analyses	7	6	5	4	3	2	1	0
Accompanying consumer to job interview	7	6	5	4	3	2	1	0

Comments: _____

5. **Job site training**	7	6	5	4	3	2	1	0
Orienting consumer to Job site	7	6	5	4	3	2	1	0
Assessing consumer job skills	7	6	5	4	3	2	1	0
Training for initial skill acquisition	7	6	5	4	3	2	1	0
Advocating for the consumer	7	6	5	4	3	2	1	0
Fading Instruction	7	6	5	4	3	2	1	0

Comments: _____

6. **Follow-along**	7	6	5	4	3	2	1	0
Collecting employer evaluations	7	6	5	4	3	2	1	0
Completing progress reports	7	6	5	4	3	2	1	0
Communicating with parent/guardian	7	6	5	4	3	2	1	0
Conducting on-site visits	7	6	5	4	3	2	1	0
Maintaining phone contact with employers	7	6	5	4	3	2	1	0
Responding to incident reports	7	6	5	4	3	2	1	0
Retraining job skills	7	6	5	4	3	2	1	0

Comments: _____

7. **Data Management**	7	6	5	4	3	2	1	0
Recording intervention time	7	6	5	4	3	2	1	0
Collecting instructional intervention data	7	6	5	4	3	2	1	0
Collecting probe data	7	6	5	4	3	2	1	0
Collecting production data	7	6	5	4	3	2	1	0
Collecting on-/off-task data	7	6	5	4	3	2	1	0
Interpreting data	7	6	5	4	3	2	1	0

Comments: _____

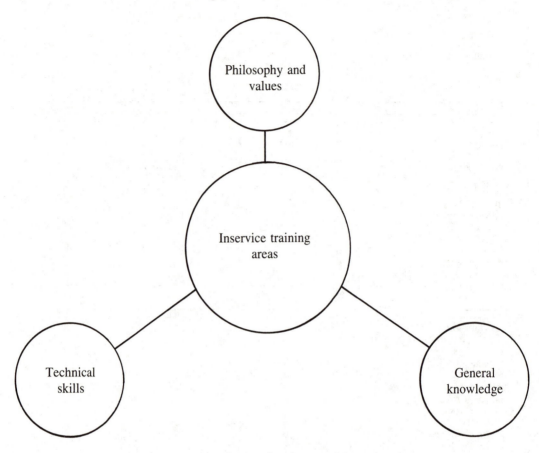

Figure 4. Areas of supported employment training needs.

supported and nonsupported approaches to employment for persons with disabilities.

Goal 2: Define and discuss the job development component of supported competitive employment

Objective 2.1: To describe guidelines for conducting a community job market screening

Objective 2.2: To describe guidelines for making employer contact

Objective 2.3: To describe guidelines for analyzing a job site and specific jobs

Goal 3: Define and discuss the consumer assessment component of supported competitive employment

Objective 3.1: To discuss use of a combination of formal and informal assessment mechanisms:

a. Formal vocational evaluation
b. Parent/consumer/caregiver interviews
c. Consumer observation and behavioral assessment

Goal 4: Define and discuss the job placement component of supported competitive employment

Objective 4.1: To discuss job/consumer match

Objective 4.2: To describe incentives to employers for hiring workers with disabilities

Goal 5: Define and discuss the job-site training and advocacy component of supported competitive employment

Objective 5.1: To describe strategies for use during the orientation and assessment phase of job-site training

Objective 5.2: To describe strategies for use during the skill acquisition phase of job-site training

Objective 5.3: To describe strategies for use during the stabilization phase of job-site training

Objective 5.4: To discuss advocacy with coworkers and supervisors on and off the job-site

Goal 6: Define and discuss the ongoing assessment and follow-along component of supported competitive employment

Objective 6.1: To discuss guidelines for monitoring a worker's progress and maintenance

Objective 6.2: To discuss strategies for intervening with problems and concerns

Goal 7: Discuss program management and implementation issues of supported competitive employment

Objective 7.1: To discuss competencies and characteristics of an employment specialist or job coach

Objective 7.2: To discuss strategies for hiring and supervising employment specialists or job coaches

Objective 7.3: To discuss funding strategies

Determining Inservice Content

After the training goals have been selected based on the needs of the agency(ies) and participants, the inservice provider must determine the content that addresses the identified goals and objectives. Depending on the number and type of goals and objectives selected, the inservice training may be held for several hours or over a period of several days or weeks. Regardless of the length of the sessions, each of the seven goals previously listed merit being addressed, as they include specific content related to supported competitive employment. The following guidelines for content related to each goal are offered to the inservice planner:

Goal 1: Define and Examine the Philosophy of Supported Competitive Employment. Philosophy of the supported work model

may be presented, including a review of the historical evolution of supported employment and the current federal definition. Discussions should focus on project demonstrations, research findings, and legislative action that have resulted in supported employment as a viable option for persons with disabilities. The following topics may be addressed for Goal 1:

1. Employment/underemployment statistics for persons with disabilities
2. Federal definitions of supported employment
3. Legislation related to supported employment
4. Characteristics of each currently accepted model of supported employment (competitive supported jobs, enclave, mobile work crew, and entrepreneurial)
5. Current research information from demonstration projects and research centers
6. Comparison of benefit/cost data for supported employment models and traditional service delivery models (sheltered workshops and day activity centers)
7. Values necessary for implementing a supported employment program

Goal 2: Define and Discuss the Job Development Component of Supported Competitive Employment. When addressing job development for supported competitive employment, the inservice provider should focus on strategies for screening the local community to identify jobs appropriate for the consumer population being served. Emphasis should be placed on strategies for identifying job types currently available, procedures for reviewing available positions within these job types, and guidelines for making employment contacts. The following topics may be addressed for Goal 2:

1. Labor market trends for the future
2. Community job market screening guidelines
3. Environmental analysis guidelines
4. Initial employer contact strategies
5. Job analysis guidelines
6. Employer interview guidelines
7. Job development record keeping
8. Strategies for consumer advocacy

Goal 3: Define and Discuss the Consumer Assessment Component of Supported Competitive Employment. Consumer assessment information should provide a composite picture of the consumer regarding support needs. The process of gathering this information should be clearly explained and contrasted with more traditional assessment procedures. The discussion should include guidelines for conducting interviews and informal observations with consumers, primary caregivers, and current or past teachers/instructors. In addition, strategies for gleaning pertinent information from formal educational, vocational, social, psychological, and medical evaluations should be outlined. And most important, observational and task analytic assessment procedures should be discussed that identify the consumer's strengths and areas where training and support strategies will be necessary. The following topics may be addressed for Goal 3:

1. Guidelines for reviewing formal records
2. Strategies for interviews and informal observations
3. Situational assessment strategies
4. Behavioral task analytic assessment procedures
5. Guidelines for summarizing findings

Goal 4: Define and Discuss the Job Placement Component of Supported Competitive Employment. Two approaches should be explained related to placement of individuals in employment positions. The first method is a job/consumer compatibility process in which a pool of individuals is screened to determine the most appropriate individual for a specific job opening. This process seems most effective when placing individuals with moderate to mild disabilities. The second method is a consumer-specific placement process in which the individual's strengths and support needs are identified before job development is conducted in order to identify a position for the specific individual. This process is frequently needed when placing individuals with severe disabilities. The following topics may be addressed for Goal 4:

1. Key factors that affect job placement
2. Job/consumer-compatibility analysis process

3. Consumer-specific placement process
4. Job interview guidelines
5. Strategies for consumer advocacy

Goal 5: Define and Discuss the Job-Site Training and Advocacy Component of Supported Competitive Employment. Job-site training is the direct instruction of job duties and nonvocationally related skills such as transportation, communication, and appropriate use of breaktimes. Job-site training should be presented in three phases, including orientation and assessment, skill acquisition, and stabilization. Systematic instructional methods and procedures for each phase should be clearly described. The discussion should also include strategies for advocacy or noninstructional intervention. The following topics may be addressed for Goal 5:

Orientation and assessment

1. Strategies for orientation training to the community
2. Strategies for orientation training to the work environment
3. Guidelines for job-duty analysis
4. Guidelines for determining reinforcement

Skill acquisition

1. Procedures for establishing training schedules
2. Techniques for developing job-duty task analyses
3. Procedures for data collection
4. Strategies for systematic instruction
5. Strategies for fading systematic instruction
6. Guidelines for altering instructional programs

Stabilization

1. Strategies for increasing work production to company standards
2. Guidelines for programming naturally occurring cues, contingencies, and reinforcement
3. Strategies for fading employment specialist/job-coach presence from the worksite
4. Strategies for coworker advocacy

Goal 6: Define and Discuss the Ongoing Assessment and Follow-Along Component

of Supported Competitive Employment.
Assessment of a consumer's work performance is an ongoing process from the first day of employment. Daily feedback from training data, observations, and interaction with the employer, coworkers, and family should be reviewed with the participants as important aspects of ongoing consumer assessment. In addition, methods and procedures such as periodic employee evaluations, progress reports, on-site visits, telephone contacts, and parent/guardian questionnaires should be discussed to specify the follow-along component of supported competitive employment. Inevitably, potential job-site problems will be identified, and it is essential to outline guidelines for addressing them. The following topics may be addressed for Goal 6:

1. Guidelines for employee evaluations
2. Procedures for reporting progress
3. Strategies for parent/guardian communication
4. Strategies for solving potential job site problems
5. Procedures for consumer advocacy

Goal 7: Discuss Program Management and Implementation Issues of Supported Competitive Employment. Once participants have had an opportunity to be exposed to the process necessary to implement supported competitive employment, discussion should be directed at the practical, day-to-day issues involved in implementing a supported employment program. The following topics (developed by Mike Barcus, Sherril Moon, Patricia Goodall, and Valerie Brooke) represent common implementation issues faced by programs and may be included when addressing Goal 7.

Program Start-up Issues

1. Attitudes toward supported employment of professionals, parents, and so forth
2. Converting to supported employment program services from more traditional approaches to employment (i.e., sheltered workshops and activity centers)
3. Funding
4. Identifying supported employment model(s) to be implemented

Staffing Issues

1. Developing staff job descriptions
2. Developing recruitment procedures
3. Developing staff training programs
4. Determining staffing patterns and responsibilities

Data management issues

1. Identifying program/system's-level procedures
2. Developing consumer data-collection procedures

Program management

1. Identifying funding sources for initial training and ongoing services
2. Developing interagency collaboration/coordination
3. Identifying host companies
4. Providing technical assistance to employment specialists/job coaches

Consumers

1. Identifying consumers to be served
2. Identifying appropriate employment options for consumers to be served
3. Determining assessment and training procedures
4. Determining/identifying general disincentives to employment (i.e., Social Security, Medicaid)
5. Solving transportation issues

Community

1. Establishing relationships between businesses and service agencies
2. Developing interagency collaboration/coordination
3. Determining effects on existing services
4. Determining long-term effects on consumer/family support services
5. Identifying needs for case management, recreation programs, and appropriate residential options

SELECTING TECHNIQUES FOR DELIVERING INSERVICE CONTENT

The inservice trainer may choose from a number of different techniques when determining strategies for delivering the inservice content. These include lectures, audiovisual materials, group discussions, skits, role-play situations, and fieldwork experience. The selection of strategies should be based on the goals that have been selected for a particular workshop, the characteristics of the inservice participants, the length of the inservice, the experience of the inservice provider, and the location of the inservice.

When selecting techniques based on the goals for the inservice, the trainer needs to consider whether the content area will emphasize values clarification, knowledge, application of technical skills, or a combination of these areas (McDaniel et al., 1986). A lecture may be appropriate for a knowledge content area but inappropriate for a values clarification session. A site visit to a supported employment placement and a group discussion may be more beneficial for values clarification. Figure 5 may be useful in selecting techniques for content related to values clarification, knowledge, and/or application of technical skills.

The characteristics of the inservice participants will also influence the selection of inservice techniques. For example, sessions designed for vocational rehabilitation counselors may focus primarily on the value and knowledge areas of identified goals. In this instance, site visits may be beneficial for values clarification, but fieldwork experiences for training actual ''hands-on'' job placement and training skills may be unnecessary. The vocational counselor might therefore need various activities and/or working-pair situations in which the individuals identify strategies for recognizing appropriate job placement and training strategies. Sessions designed for direct service staff may focus on all three areas—values clarification, knowledge, and application of technical skills. However, technical skills may receive the major focus for each goal and objective, resulting in an emphasis on inservice techniques appropriate to application of technical skills (e.g., case studies, fieldwork experience, role-play situations).

The length of an inservice and the experience of the inservice provider also influence the techniques selected for delivering content. A relatively short session of 1 hour on knowledge related to supported competitive employment may

include a 30-minute lecture with a 5-minute videotape presentation, a 15-minute activity, and a 10-minute large-group discussion. However, a day-long session could include various other techniques. It may be helpful to remember that lectures should be limited to 20 to 30 minutes, followed by a technique that allows the participants to review the material presented (e.g., games, activities, working pairs, role-play situations).

In selecting the techniques to highlight the content presented, the inservice provider should also rely on his or her experience and should use techniques with which he or she is comfortable and familiar. Some presenters may prefer to illustrate a point with a role-play, while others may feel more comfortable with a group discussion activity. The choice of which techniques to use is an individual matter. Figure 6 demonstrates a day-long session focusing on knowledge and technical skills related to the content area of job development.

Finally, the inservice location may have an impact on the various training techniques selected. For example, several small ''break-out'' rooms may be useful for small-group discussions and activities if a large group of participants is being served by an inservice. Community environments must be available if the trainer includes fieldwork experience as a technique. A large room may be necessary if the trainer decides to present formal skits to the participants and so on.

FOLLOW-UP SUPPORT AND TECHNICAL ASSISTANCE

Most inservice trainers readily agree that follow-up support and technical assistance are critical components of inservice training, but they just as quickly point out that this is a luxury that budgets and time often do not permit. Nevertheless, the most effective inservice trainers are committed to providing follow-up support and/or technical assistance and make this an agreed upon part of pretraining planning between the trainer and the sponsoring agency (Barcus, Everson, & Hall, 1987). Pretraining planning between the trainer and the sponsoring agency enables the agency to assume some of the re-

Techniques		Inservice Areas		
		Values Clarification	Knowledge	Application of Technical Skills
Panels	Group of experienced personnel discuss supported employment topics	X	X	
Site visits	Observation of methods being discussed during training	X	X	
Videotapes	May be used for presentation of ideas and practice sessions	X	X	X
Slide shows	Presentation of actual supported employment methods		X	
Group discussion	Five to eight people discuss/exchange ideas on specific topic	X	X	
Working pairs	Two to three people discuss/practice specific information for short time period		X	X
Role-play	"Acting" typical situations related to supported employment	X	X	X
Games/activities	Participants problem solve/practice issues	X	X	X
Skits	Organized presentation of specific situations by trainer(s)	X	X	X
Lecture	Recommended length not to exceed 20–30 minutes		X	
Anecdotes	Examples and experiences of participants and trainers		X	
Case studies	Presentation of a situation for small group to analyze		X	X
Demonstrations	Modeling of procedures and/or process		X	
Written products	Handouts, manuals, newsletters, etc.		X	
Field work	Practice sessions in real-life situations		X	

Figure 5. Techniques for delivering inservice content.

sponsibility for follow-up support and/or technical assistance. For example, the trainer may request that a summary of the training evaluations, including recommendations for future training needs, copies of overheads and handouts, summaries of activities, and additional reading materials and resources be mailed to each of the participants after the training. In addition, the trainer may request that the sponsoring agency organize and facilitate a 6-month follow-up problem-solving session in which the original trainer may or may not participate.

It is the trainer's responsibility to identify and plan for follow-up support and/or technical assistance. One effective way to accomplish this is to lead a wrap-up activity that summarizes

Time	Topic	Suggested techniques
9:00– 9:20 A.M.	Group introduction	*Activity:* "Find Your Other Half." Participants match various supported employment concepts in large-group participation.
9:20– 9:30 A.M.	Brief overview of supported employment	*Slide Show:* "Supported Competitive Employment." Highlights of the model and slides of consumers demonstrating the process.
9:30– 9:50 A.M.	Job market screening	*Lecture:* Guidelines for Job Market Screening.
9:50–10:00 A.M.	Break	
10:00–10:50 A.M.	Job market screening	*Activity:* "Let Your Fingers Do the Walking." Participants practice using the *Yellow Pages* to screen a community job market. *Activity:* "Read the Daily News." Participants practice using the newspaper to screen a community job market.
10:50–11:20 A.M.	Employer contacts	*Lecture:* "Guidelines for Employer Contacts." *Videotape:* "Demonstrating Employer Contacts."
11:20–11:45 A.M.	Employer contacts	*Role-Play:* Participants divide into groups and role-play the guidelines presented in the lecture session.
11:45–12:45 P.M.	Lunch	
12:45– 1:00 P.M.	Employer contacts	*Working Pairs:* "Marketing Bloopers." Participants divide into groups of two to problem solve situations related to employer contacts.
1:00– 2:00 P.M.	Employer contacts	*Fieldwork:* Participants practice employer contacts in the community.
2:00– 2:20 P.M.	Employer contacts	*Large-Group Discussion:* Participants are encouraged to share their recent experiences.
2:20– 2:30 P.M.	Break	
2:30– 2:55 P.M.	Environmental analysis and job-duty analysis	*Lecture:* Guidelines for completing an environmental analysis and job-duty analysis.
2:55– 3:55 P.M.	Environmental Analysis and job-duty analysis	*Fieldwork:* Application of guidelines in a real community setting.
3:55– 4:15 P.M.	Environmental analysis and job-duty analysis	*Large-Group Discussion:* Participants are encouraged to share their recent experiences.
4:15– 4:40 P.M.	Job development summary	*Game:* "What's My Line?" Participants play a game that highlights the principles presented during the day.
4:40– 5:00 P.M.	Wrap-up	*Large-Group Discussion:* Participants can ask questions related to the day's inservice content.

Figure 6. Job development schedule: Sample techniques for an inservice day.

the content and activities of the workshop and enables participants to develop action plans for implementing the material into their individual programs. The format for the action plan should be flexible enough to ensure the development of plans that individuals or groups feel they have the authority to implement, but structured enough to ensure implementation by all participants.

Action plans should include: 1) activities to be completed, 2) person(s) responsible, 3) completion date(s), 4) evaluation mechanism(s), and 5) follow-up support and/or technical assistance needed. Figures 7 and 8 present examples of action plans developed for individuals and agency teams, respectively, at the close of an inservice workshop.

Name: <u>J. Smith, Employment Specialist</u> Development date: <u>1/88</u>

Activity	Person(s) responsible	Timeline/ completion date	Evaluation mechanism	Follow-up support and/or technical assistance
1. Conduct inservice training for staff of Supported Employment Enterprises (SEE)	1. J. Smith and director of SEE[a]	5/88	1. Participant satisfaction evaluation	1. Six-month follow-up workshop
2. Place five individuals in supported competitive work	2. J. Smith and other employment specialists (to be hired)	3/89	2. Training data, placement data, employer satisfaction, parent satisfaction	2. Follow-along from mental retardation case manager(s) SEE staff
3. Identify enclave sites/ negotiate starting date	3. J. Smith	5/89	3. Training data, placement data, employer satisfaction, parent satisfaction	3. Follow-along from mental retardation case manager (e.g., SEE staff)

[a] Supported Employment Enterprises.

Figure 7. Example of individual action plan.

Team Members: <u>M. Bennett</u>   Development date: <u>1/88</u>
              <u>D. Brooks</u>
              <u>B. Snider</u>

Activity	Person(s) responsible	Timeline/ completion date	Evaluation mechanism	Follow-up support and/or technical assistance
1. Conduct needs assessment of local secondary programs.	M. Bennett	8/88	1. Evaluation report	1. Presentation of results to school board
2. Hold inservice training for secondary teachers and workshop providers.	D. Brooks M. Bennett B. Snider	6/88	2. Participant satisfaction evaluation	2. Nine-month follow-up workshop
3. Respond to request for proposal for state supported employment grant.	D. Brooks M. Bennett B. Snider	3/89	3. Formative/ summative as part of grant	

Figure 8. Example of agency action plan.

EVALUATION MECHANISMS

Inservice training should be evaluated using both formative and summative mechanisms. Formative evaluation includes mechanisms for evaluating the training while it is still in progress. This is especially critical during lengthy workshops and may be done informally by individually questioning participants or by leading a short group activity. Formal evaluation might include a survey asking participants to respond to questions such as:

1. Are the objectives of this inservice program being met?
2. Is the information relevant?
3. Are the presentations organized?
4. Are the support materials adequate?
5. Are the activities assisting in covering the inservice content?
6. Would you change anything about this inservice program?
7. Is there any information that has not been covered that you would like to address?

Summative evaluation is completed at the end of the inservice program and should address the following:

1. Participant satisfaction with the workshop
2. Pretest/posttest of knowledge gained
3. Six- to 9-month follow-up of participant satisfaction
4. Application of knowledge/technical skills 6–9 months after the workshop

SUMMARY

This chapter has outlined the steps necessary to develop an inservice training program on supported competitive employment. These steps include conducting a needs assessment, determining inservice goals and objectives, determining the content, selecting techniques for the presentations, providing follow-along, and evaluating inservice effectiveness. This process may seem very time-consuming, but it will enable the inservice provider to design and implement more effective, comprehensive inservice programs.

REFERENCES

Barcus, M., Brooke, V., Inge, K., Moon, S., & Goodall, P. (1987). *An instructional guide for training on a job site: A supported employment resource*. Richmond: Virginia Commonwealth University, Rehabilitation Research and Training Center.

Barcus, M., Everson, J. & Hall, S. (1987). Inservice training in human services agencies and oganizations. In J. Everson, M. Barcus, S. Moon, & M.V. Morton (Eds.), *Achieving outcomes: A guide to interagency training in transition and supported employment* (pp. 1–57). Richmond: Virginia Commonwealth University, Project Transition into Employment.

Boyle, P.G. (1981). *Planning better programs*. New York: McGraw Hill.

Cafferella, R. S. (in press). *Program development and evaluation: A workbook for trainees*. New York: John Wiley & Sons.

Knowles, M. (1980). *The modern practice of adult education: From pedagogy to andragogy*. Chicago: Association Press/Follett.

McDaniel, R. H., Flippo, K., & Lowery, L. (1986). *Telesis: Supported employment resource manual*. San Francisco: University of San Francisco.

McKinley, J. (1980). *Group development through participation training*. New York: Paulist Press.

Moon, S., Goodall, P., Barcus, M., & Brooke, V. (1986).

The supported work model of competitive employment for citizens with severe handicaps: A guide for job trainers (rev. ed.). Richmond: Virginia Commonwealth University, Rehabilitation Research and Training Center.

Moon, S., Goodall, P., & Wehman, P. (1985). *Critical issues related to supported competitive employment: Proceedings from the first RRTC symposium on employment for citizens who are mentally retarded*. Richmond: Virginia Commonwealth University, Rehabilitation Research and Training Center.

Renzaglia, A. (1986). Preparing personnel to support and guide emerging contemporary service alternatives. In F. R. Rusch (Ed.), *Competitive employment issues and strategies* (pp. 303–316). Baltimore: Paul H. Brookes Publishing Co.

Robinson, R. (1979). *An introduction to helping adults learn and change*. Milwaukee: Omnibook Co.

Wehman, P., & Kregel, J. (1985). A supported approach to competitive employment of individuals with moderate and severe handicaps. *Journal of the Association for Persons with Severe Handicaps, 10*(1), 3–11.

Will, M. (1984). OSERS programming for the transition of youth with disabilities: Bridges from school to working life. Washington, DC: U. S. Department of Education, Office of Special Education and Rehabilitative Services.

OTHER RESOURCES

American Society for Training and Development, 1630 Duke St., Alexandria, VA 22313.

Bellamy, G. T., Rhodes, L. E., Mank, D. M., & Albin, J. M. (1988). *Supported employment: A community implementation guide*. Baltimore: Paul H. Brookes Publishing Co.

Bernstein, G. S., & Ziarnik, J. P. (1982). Proactive identification of staff development needs: A model and methodology. *Journal of the Association for the Severely Handicapped*, 7(3), 97–104.

Cafferella, R. S. (1985). A checklist for planning successful training programs. *Training and Development Journal*, 39(3), 81–83.

Fifield, M. G., & Smith, B. C. (Eds.), (1985). *Personnel training for serving adults with developmental disabilities*. Logan: Utah State University Developmental Center for Handicapped Persons.

Friere, P. (1983). *Pedagogy of the oppressed*. New York: Continuum Press.

Houle, C. O. (1972). *The design of education*. San Francisco: Jossey-Bass.

Karan, O. C., & Knight, C. B. (1986). Training demands of the future. In W. E. Kiernan & J. A. Stark (Eds.), *Pathways to employment for adults with developmental disabilities* (pp. 253–269). Baltimore: Paul H. Brookes Publishing Co.

Kiernan, W.E., & Stark, J.A. (Eds.). (1986). *Pathways to employment for adults with developmental disabilities*. Baltimore: Paul H. Brookes Publishing Co.

Laird, D. (1985). *Approaches to training and development* (2nd ed.). Reading, MA: Addison-Wesley.

McLoughlin, C.S., Garner, J.B., & Callahan, M. (1987). *Getting employed, staying employed*. Baltimore: Paul H. Brookes Publishing Co.

Nadler, L. (1985). *The handbook of human resource development*. New York: John Wiley & Sons.

Rusch, F.R. (Ed.). (1986). *Competitive employment issues and strategies*. Baltimore: Paul H. Brookes Publishing Co.

Speakeasy, Inc., 3414 Peachtree Road, NE, Suite 830, Atlanta, GA 30326.

Templeman, T. P., Fredericks, H. D., Bunse, C., & Moses, C. (1983). Teaching research in-service training model. *Education and Training of the Mentally Retarded*, 18(4), 245–252.

Vogelsberg, R. T. (1986). Competitive employment in Vermont. In F. R. Rusch (Ed.), *Competitive employment issues and strategies* (pp. 331–337). Baltimore: Paul H. Brookes Publishing Co.

Wehman, P. (1981). *Competitive employment: New horizons for severely disabled individuals*. Baltimore: Paul H. Brookes Publishing Co.

Wehman, P., & Hill, J. (Eds.). (1985). *Competitive employment for persons with mental retardation: From research to practice*. Richmond: Virginia Commonwealth University, Rehabilitation Research and Training Center.

Weissman-Frisch, N., Crowell, F., & Inman, D. (1980). Inservicing vocational trainees: A multiple perspective evaluation approach. *Journal of the Association for the Severely Handicapped*, 5, 158–172.

William, W. W. & Vogelsberg, R. T. (1980). Comprehensive vocational service model for severely handicapped adults. In *Center for developmental disabilities monograph series*. Burlington, VT: University of Vermont.

Ziarnik, J. P., & Bernstein, G. S. (1982). A critical examination of the effect of inservice training on staff performance. *Mental Retardation*, 20(3), 109–114.

Ziarnik, J. P., Rudrud, E. H., & Bernstein, G. S. (1981). Data vs. reflecting: A reply to Moxley and Ebert. *Mental Retardation*, 19(4), 251–252.

Chapter 11

Critical Performance Evaluation Indicators in Supported Employment

Robert L. Schalock

This chapter is organized around five topical areas related to developing and using critical performance evaluation indicators in supported employment programs. The first area delineates the criteria of supported employment, the goal of which is to promote access to integrated employment settings and decent wages for people traditionally denied both. The second section suggests that program evaluation activities should be viewed in the context of a program's evolutionary phase. The third section outlines a number of proposed critical performance evaluation indicators and suggests that one should select specific performance indicators based on the program's evolutionary phase, the program's objectives, and according to whether the evaluation's primary focus is the participant, the program, or the larger service delivery system. The fourth section provides suggested data processing and analytic strategies that can be used primarily in client- and program-level data collection and analysis. The final section discusses a number of unresolved second-generation program analysis issues that warrant additional research and development. Three of these issues include quality of life, quality of employment, and program analysis/ evaluation.

CRITERIA OF SUPPORTED EMPLOYMENT

Supported employment is usually defined as paid employment in regular (real) work settings in which ongoing support is provided for individuals who have not traditionally experienced competitive employment. This definition implies the presence of four criteria, including employment, integration, ongoing support, and severe disability. The criteria listed in Table 1 can be used to determine whether an individual or program fits the definition of supported employment. The development of data sets (indicators) to measure and report the outcomes from these four criteria is summarized later in the chapter. However, before discussing the data sets, it is important to discuss the significance of a program's evolutionary phase in determining the mind-set with which program personnel approach program evaluation and accountability.

CRITICAL PERFORMANCE EVALUATION INDICATORS WITHIN THE CONTEXT OF A PROGRAM'S EVOLUTIONARY PHASE

Accountability can be understood from two perspectives. The first perspective revolves around the question of ''who is responsible to whom and for what?'' This perspective focuses on a program's heterogeneous constituency and stresses that each constituent has a potentially different criterion for a program's accountability. Program staff and management, for example, may be accountable to the board of directors for such things as participant welfare, licensing,

Table 1. Supported employment criteria

1. *Employment.* Supported employment is employer-paid employment. An individual meets the employment criterion if he or she engages in paid work for at least an average of 4 hours each day, 5 days per week or follows another schedule offering at least 20 hours of work per week. There is no minimum wage or productivity level for supported employment established by this criterion.

2. *Integration.* Work is integrated when it provides frequent daily social interactions with people without disabilities who are not paid caregivers (that is, within an integrated work setting). A simple 3-point rating scale has worked well for this author in evaluating the level of integration. This scale includes: 3 = works along with nonhandicapped workers and has opportunities for integration at breaks and lunch; 2 = no integration during work, but has opportunities for integration at breaks and lunch; 1 = no integration during work, and has no opportunities for integration at breaks or lunch.

3. *Ongoing support.* Supported employment exists only when ongoing support is provided. An individual should be considered to be receiving ongoing support when: 1) public funds are available on an ongoing basis to an individual or service provider who is responsible for providing employment support; and 2) these funds are used for support directly related to sustaining employment. Exemplary support functions include training, assistance, supervision, support, transportation, and case management.

4. *Severe disability.* Supported employment exists when the person served requires ongoing support. Supported employment is inappropriate for persons who would be better served in time-limited preparation programs leading to independent employment. Logical candidates include those individuals who previously have not been served; or who have been served unsuccessfully by vocational rehabilitation because of the lack of ongoing services needed to sustain employment after time-limited rehabilitation services are completed; or who are or may be funded for ongoing services in day programs.

Source: Adapted from Barker, L. T. (1986, July 3l). *Development of performance measures for supported employment programs: Final report.* Berkeley, CA: Berkeley Planning Associates.

accreditation, program compliance with various standards, and participant education/habilitation. The board is accountable to the program for the necessary resources to accomplish the program's goals and objectives and to the public for the provision of services. These multiple perspectives suggest that accountability requirements differ depending on whether one focuses on the participant, the program, or the larger system. This concept is further developed in the next section (Table 2).

The second accountability perspective deals with the program's evolutionary phase. Most education/habilitation programs progress through three distinct phases, diagrammed in Figure 1 and described as follows. Phase I, the Resources phase, corresponds to the initial developmental period and focuses on resources consisting of facilities, clients, staffing, and money. The need and accountability issues during this phase are to develop and maintain the resources necessary to provide habilitative services. The fiscal audit is the primary accountability tool for Phase I organizations. Once programs are developed, however, most see the need to become more refined and systematic in their service delivery. At this point, they evolve into their second evolutionary phase, referred to as the Systematic phase, which involves developing a system to facilitate service delivery, measurabilty, and reportability. During this phase, accountability issues revolve around how well the system is in

Table 2. Supported employment objectives from the perspectives of the participant, program, and system

Participant Level
1. To be employed in an integrated employment environment.
2. To receive equitable compensation (wages) and benefits.
3. To receive appropriate training and ongoing support to maintain employment.

Program Level
1. To obtain the opportunities for supported employment within an integrated employment environment.
2. To lobby for equitable wages and fringe benefits.
3. To provide appropriate training and ongoing support based on maximizing the fit among a person's capabilities, interests, and job requirements.

Systems Level
1. To increase the number of disabled persons employed in integrated employment settings at commensurate wages.
2. To reduce dependence on transfer payments and other services, and to maximize tax contributions.
3. To increase proportion of funding used for supported employment versus day activity programs.

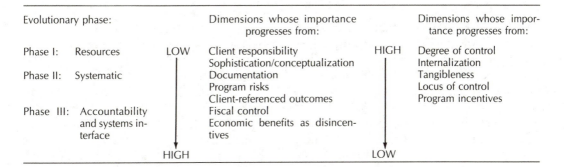

Figure 1.   Importance of various dimensions to program accountability, based on a program's evolutionary phase.

place, and whether or not staff are adhering to the system's policies and procedures. Systems review becomes the mechanism whereby management monitors and evaluates programs and their compliance with the various parameters and criteria established for the system. The program and its system are felt to be accountable if policies and procedures are being followed. It is during the third evolutionary phase, Accountability and Systems Interface, that educational/habilitation programs connect with various public and private sectors of the community and attempt to become more accountable for client-referenced outcomes. This interfacing includes marketing and sales, intersector (public and private programs) agreements, and transitional program plans. Accountability, although a major issue of the third evolutionary phase, is difficult to grapple with at this time because there are numerous external factors over which a program has little or no control; and furthermore, the heterogeneous constituency has different definitions of accountability.

In developing these performance evaluation indicators, it is important also to realize that a program's evolutionary phase has a significant impact on a number of *accountability dimensions*, listed in the two right-hand columns of Figure 1. As shown, some of the accountability dimensions progress from low importance to high importance across evolutionary phases, whereas in some dimensions, the reverse is true. Consider some examples from those dimensions whose importance *increases* from Phase I to Phase III. The dimension involving participants taking responsibility for their growth, development, and rights, for instance, increases as a

program evolves and becomes more systematic and outcome oriented. Similarly, program personnel need to become more sophisticated and better able to conceptualize the dynamic relationships between persons and their multiple environments. A good example of the accountability requirements associated with increased sophistication concerns the skill-training techniques used in the Mid-Nebraska Mental Retardation Services program described in Schalock & Lilley, 1986. During Phase I (about 1970–1972), these techniques included watching and controlling incidental learning. Phase II (1972–1982) incorporated a more systematic approach characterized as precision teaching and prescriptive programming, which included concepts such as acceleration/deceleration cycles and ratio/reinforcement contingencies. Phase III (1982 to present) focuses on applied behavioral analysis, with its emphasis on environmental cures/control, stimulus/response chains, and generalization training. Analogously, the Mid-Nebraska program's behavioral change strategies have also evolved from all-star wrestling, response cost and timeout (Phase I), to deceleration strategies involving differential reinforcement schedules (Phase II), and to gentle teaching (Phase III).

Documentation and fiscal control are other dimensions that intensify, owing both to the trend toward accountability as well as the diminishing resources that many agencies experience. And finally, participant work disincentives increase, owing largely to the income maintenance programs that can be jeopardized if a participant exceeds his or her substantial gainful activity level. Since most persons want to attain the highest level of satisfaction and safety, employment seeking and job placement may well be reduced when tax-free benefits are high.

Figure 1 (right side) also demonstrates that the importance of some accountability dimensions *decreases* from Phase I to Phase III. For example, agencies tend to lose more real and perceived control as they interface with the larger environment. Similarly, an agency's tangibleness decreases as it becomes facility-free. Since success is often the result of interagency processes, the incentives to the specific program tend to decrease. As one might expect, the degree of internalization of program goals and objectives by agency staff also decreases because of the diffusion of roles and responsibilities. Thus, one often sees agencies conducting "back to basics" inservice programs for their personnel to counterbalance the trends toward less perceived control, tangibleness, and internationalization.

Figure 1 also demonstrates graphically a number of built-in accountability conflicts that explain in part why many program pesonnel are sensitive to discussions regarding critical performance evaluation indicators. One obvious example relates to increased participant responsibility versus the agency's emphasis on employment outcomes. As discussed previously, a number of economic benefits, such as Supplemental Security Income (SSI), serve as strong disincentives to postprogram work (Conley, Noble, & Elder, 1986; Walls, Zawlocki & Dowler, 1986). Thus, conflict often occurs between program personnel who stress job placement and participants or families who resist the placement because it might reduce the person's benefits. It is hoped that the permanent enactment of the work incentives provisions [Sections 1619(a) and (b)] of the Social Security Act will resolve much of this conflict. A second conflict occurs when an agency takes several risks in placing persons into less restrictive community environments. One risk relates to the agency's reputation if the placement results in negative results; the second is that the client's replacement may well be a person with greater needs. Many agencies are attempting to resolve this conflict by contracting for specific outcomes and implementing reverse integration programs (Schalock & Keith, 1986). A third conflict deals with agency personnel

who need to be more sophisticated and conceptual in dealing with Phases II and III, yet who find themselves feeling that they are losing control of the program because of its systems-level aspects. Phrases such as, "It's hard to push a rope" and "facilitating services without the person being a client," reflect the complexity of Phase III accountability dimensions. Many agencies attempt to resolve this conflict through marketing and sales of the agency's philosophy, goals, and objectives.

In summary, the multiple dimensions to accountability necessitate a clear understanding of a program's goals, objectives, evolutionary phase, and potential outcome measures. Once these are understood, selecting performance evaluation indicators is facilitated considerably.

SELECTING CRITICAL EVALUATION INDICATORS

Regardless of a program's evolutionary phase, education and (re)habilitation in this country are currently under pressure to be measurable, reportable, and accountable. Unfortunately, many programs have not yet standardized and implemented critical performance evaluation indicators or data collection systems that permit meaningful data analysis and reporting. These two needs are discussed in this section.

Multiple Perspectives on Outcome Data

The potential users of information regarding the outcomes from supported employment include participants, consumer groups, program personnel, state/local administrators, federal/state policymakers and policy analysts who are interested in determining the impact, benefits, and costs of the supported employment initiative. Each group has data needs and accountability criteria. A detailed discussion of these multiple perspectives is found in Schalock and Hill (1986) and Schalock and Thornton (1988). For the purposes of this section, the multiple perspectives have been reduced to three, including participant, program, and system. The respective objectives for supported employment are summarized in Table 2.

Although the three groups' objectives appear somewhat different, a few standardized data sets (indicators) will provide necessary data to meet most of the objectives listed. These *critical* performance evaluation indicators are summarized in the next subsection.

Critical Performance Evaluation Indicators Table 3 summarizes eight indicators or measures that the author and others (Kiernan, McGaughey, & Schalock, 1986; Mank, Rhodes, & Bellamy, 1986; Wehman, Hill, Hill, Brooke, Pendleton, & Britt, 1985) have used to begin evaluating supported employment outcomes. These eight indicators include: 1) participant characteristics; 2) setting prior to placement; 3) employment placement environment; 4) employment data; 5) occupational category; 6) level of integration; 7) hours of job support; and 8) job movement patterns.

It is insufficient, however, to merely identify the critical performance evaluation indicators as was done in Table 3; rather, it is necessary to take the next step, which is to develop a computer-based data processing system that will allow the program to measure and report participant-referenced outcome measures. Strategies for accomplishing this are discussed in the next section.

DATA PROCESSING AND ANALYTIC STRATEGIES

As mentioned previously, data from the proposed performance indicators can be used to meet a number of program accountability requirements, including the program-participant criteria (Table 1) and the multiple perspectives on supported employment objectives (Table 2). The relationships between these proposed supported employment indicators and the various program accountability issues are summarized in Table 4. The table's matrix demonstrates clearly that the specific accountability issue determines which indicators are most important. A reasonable rule at this point is to operationalize and measure all eight indicators, since accountability perspectives and requirements change so quickly.

Several examples illustrate the utility of Table 4's matrix. For instance, to demonstrate that one's program meets the criteria of supported employment (Table 1), data will be needed from

Table 3. Proposed critical performance evaluation indicators in supported employment

1. *Participant characteristic*
   a. Date of birth
   b. Gender
   c. Disability level (5 standardized IQ categories)[a]
   d. Receives SSI/SSDI

2. *Setting prior to placement*
   a. Transitional/training employment
   b. Supported employment
   c. Competitive employment
   d. Sheltered employment
   e. Nonwork (day program)
   f. Unemployed

3. *Employment placement environment* (a, b, or c from #2)

4. *Employment data*
   a. Wages per hour
   b. Average hours per week
   c. Weeks worked since placement
   d. Taxes paid

5. *D.O.T. occupational category*[b]
   a. Professional, technical, managerial
   b. Clerical, sales
   c. Service
   d. Agriculture, forestry, fishing
   e. Processing
   f. Machine trades
   g. Benchwork
   h. Structural work
   i. Miscellaneous
   j. Other

6. *Level of integration*
   a. Works with nonhandicapped people
   b. Limited integration
   c. No integration (See Table 1 for complete definitions.)

7. *Hours of job support*
   a. Training
   b. Assistance
   c. Supervision
   d. Support
   e. Transportation
   f. Case management

8. *Job movement patterns*
   a. Change status with each move to reflect present employment environment (see 2a–2f)
   b. Associate start/stop dates for each movement

[a]IQ below 24 (profound); 25–39 (severe); 40–54 (moderate); 55–69 (mild); 70 or above.
[b]From: U. S. Department of Labor. (1977). *Dictionary of occupational titles.* Washington, DC: Author.

indicators 1, 3, 4, and 6; or to demonstrate that one has met participant-level objectives (Table 2), data from indicators 3, 4, 6, and 7 will be needed; or to demonstrate that one has met

Table 4.   Relationships between supported employment indicators and various program accountability issues

	Accountability Issues			
Indicator (see Table 3)	Participant-program criteria met (Table 1)	Participant's objectives met (Table 2)	Program-level objectives met (Table 2)	Systems-level objectives met (Table 2)
1. Participant characteristics	X		X	X (mainly disability level and transfer payment)
2. Setting prior to placement			X[a]	
3. Employment placement environment	X	X	X	
4. Employment data	X	X	X	X (mainly wages, weeks employed, and taxes paid)
5. Occupational category			X	X[b]
6. Level of integration	X	X	X	
7. Hours of job support		X	X	
8. Job movement patterns			X[a]	

[a]Necessary for process analysis/program description.

[b]Funding pattern changes cannot be obtained from the proposed indicators. This requires analyzing state and federal funding patterns such as recently reported by Braddock (1987).

program-level objectives (Table 2), one will need to summarize across all eight indicators for all of one's (supported employment) clients.

Most programs have microcomputers with a special spread sheet/data-based system such as Lotus that allows for easy analysis of the proposed indicators. The spread sheet format presented in Figure 2 represents a reasonable, inexpensive format for handling the data. The spread sheet can also be used as a data collection form on which program personnel can track their respective clients. Monthly input of the data sheets permits monthly printouts of client-specific data, which can then be aggregated across participants, employment environments, and any critical performance indicators necessary to meet the various accountability perspectives outlined in Table 4. Specific tabular and graphic examples are found in Kiernan, McGaughey, and Schalock (in press).

Systems-level reporting creates a number of unique problems that have not yet been solved. The interesting thing is that data from only three indicators (1, 4, and 5) would meet the major systems-level objectives (see Table 2). The lack of systems-level analysis is explained partly by insufficient client or program-referenced outcome data and the lack of consensus regarding appropriate and obtainable data sets or indicators. However, a major reason for the lack is

the failure to answer the interrogatories of who, what, when, and where in deciding how to proceed. In this regard, three current alternatives might be used to provide systems-level data: state-operated data systems; externally based evaluation contractors; or ongoing sampling procedures. The author's preference is for the latter, provided there is reasonable consensus on the evaluation indicators (data sets) maintained at the program level. Certainly the national survey procedure has provided significant national data bases available for systems-level analysis regarding funding patterns (Braddock, 1987), residential patterns (Lakin, Hill, Bruininks, & White, 1986) and employment outcomes (Kiernan et al., 1986). Using another method, if agencies have data on the proposed indicators, there is no reason why these cannot be submitted to the state center responsible for state planning and evaluation.

To conclude this section on data processing and analytic strategies, a readiness for evaluation assessment is presented in Figure 3, which can help determine whether a program is ready for the impending measurability, reportability, and accountability requirements that are necessary. This instrument helps evaluate the status of each of the eight critical performance evaluation indicators defined in Table 3 and described earlier. Those programs whose self-survey

ID Number	Individual Characteristics					Setting Prior to Placement 3	Placed Into 4	Date of Placement (day/mo.)	Avg. Hours Per Week	Starting Wage Per Hour	Job Title Placed In	Level of Integration 5	Hrs. of Job Support Most Recent Month 6	If Appropriate, Termination Date	Present Employment env. 7
	Date of Birth	Gender	Disability Level 1	Receives											
				SSI 2	SSDI 2										

1. *Disability Level by IQ*
   A. IQ 24 (profound)
   B. IQ 25–39 (severe)
   C. IQ 40–54 (moderate)
   D. IQ 55–69 (mild)
   E. IQ 70 or above

2. *Receives SSI/SSDI*
   Y. Yes
   N. No

3. *Setting Prior to Placement*
   A. Transitional/training employment
   B. Supported employment
   C. Competitive employment
   D. Sheltered employment
   E. Nonwork (day program)
   F. Unemployment

4. *Placed into*
   A. Transitional/training employment
   B. Supported employment
   C. Competitive employment

5. *Level of Integration* (see definitions)
   A. Works with nonhandicapped persons
   B. Limited integration
   C. No integration

6. *Hours of Job Support Most Recent Month*
   Enter number of hours of support for month of September or support for last month worked on this job.

7. *Present Employment Environment*
   A. Transitional/training employment
   B. Supported employment
   C. Competitive employment
   D. Sheltered employment
   E. Nonwork (day program)
   F. Unemployment

Figure 2. Sample spread sheet format for data collection analysis.

Indicator	Subindicator	Self-evaluation of indicator or subindicator				
		Have not thought about (0)	Thought about (1)	Planned (2)	Partially implemented (3)	Fully implemented (4)
1. Participant characteristics	Date of birth Gender Disability level Receive SSI/SSDI					
2. Setting prior to placement						
3. Employment placement environment						
4. Employment data	Wages per hour Average hours/ week Weeks worked since placement Taxes paid					
5. D.O.T. job category						
6. Level of integration						
7. Hours of job support	Training Assistance Supervision Support Case management Transportation					
8. Job movement patterns	Present employment environment Start/stop dates					

Figure 3. Self-survey: Extent of operationalizing and measuring proposed critical supported employment performance evaluation indicators. (D.O.T. = U.S. Department of Labor. (1977). *Dictionary of occupational titles*. Washington, DC: Author.)

results end up primarily with a rating of "4" should be almost ready to begin facing the second-generation issues discussed in the next section.

PROGRAM ANALYSIS ISSUES

Looking toward the future of supported employment, at least three critical issues must be addressed including quality of life, quality of employment, and program evaluation. In discussing these issues here, the author makes two assumptions: first, that the supported employment initiative will continue at the federal, state, and local levels; and second, that the necessary participants continue to provide the opportuni-

ties and long-term support systems that successful supported employment efforts require.

Quality of Life

The concept of quality of life has recently become an important issue in education and (re)habilitation; in fact, it will probably be the overriding issue in these fields in the late 1980s and 1990s. Just as deinstitutionalization, mainstreaming, normalization, and community adjustment were major issues of the 1970s and early 1980s, quality-of-life concerns will provide the impetus over the next decade for improved services and outcomes from education and (re)habilitation programs. James A. Michener in *Chesapeake* (1978) states that "the quality of any human life is determined by the differential experiences which impinge upon it'' (p. 965). Because of the increased variety of work and, it is hoped, living experiences that supported employment affords, it is reasonable to assume that the quality of life of persons in supported employment will be higher than what might otherwise be the case.

Human service professionals are just now beginning to operationalize the concept of quality of life and are attempting to measure it. Current attempts fall generally into one of two approaches that include subjective or objective measures. These measures are summarized in Table 5 (left portion) and are discussed briefly here.

Subjective Measures Operationalizing and measuring a person's quality of life from a subjective perspective requires that one focus on the person's own perceptions and evaluations of his or her life experiences. Within this orientation, one finds two, somewhat complementary, approaches that include psychological well-being and personal satisfaction.

Measuring quality of life by judging *psychological well-being* comes primarily from the area of mental health and is represented by the work of Flanagan (1978), who identified 15 factors defining quality of life. Flanagan grouped these 15 categories into five general dimensions of quality of life, including physical and material well-being; relations with other people; social, community, and civic activities; personal development and fulfillment; and recreation. Table 5 (left column) presents these five general dimensions.

Heal and Chadsey-Rusch (1985) suggest that despite the fact that happiness or satisfaction is an illusive concept that might be difficult to measure due to acquiescence response bias, the evaluation of a person's quality of life is incomplete without an assessment of the person's satisfaction regarding his or her residence, the community environment, friends, time utilization patterns, and services. These *personal satisfaction* variables are presented in Table 5 (bottom left).

Objective Measures The second approach to measuring quality of life uses objective, social indicators such as residential living arrange-

Table 5. Quality of life and quality of employment indicators

QUALITY OF LIFE

SUBJECTIVE APPROACH
1. Psychological well-being[a]
   a. Physical and material well-being
   b. Relations with other people
   c. Social, community, and civic activities
   d. Personal development and fulfillment
   e. Recreation

2. Personal satisfaction[b]
   a. Residential arrangement
   b. Relationships (family, friends, neighbors)
   c. Time utilization (how spends time)
   d. Recreation and leisure activities
   e. Available services
   f. Economic situation

OBJECTIVE APPROACH[c]
1. Mobility
2. Appearance/physical condition
3. Activity level
4. Community involvement
5. Social/recreational activities
6. Individual decision making
7. Living arrangements

QUALITY OF EMPLOYMENT[d]

1. Adequate and fair compensation
2. Safe and healthy working conditions
3. Opportunity to use and develop behavioral capabilities
4. Opportunity for continued growth and security
5. Integrated work, lunch, and break areas
6. Constitutionalism in the work organization (privacy, free speech, equity, and due process)
7. Normal work schedules
8. Variety of jobs
9. Goodness-of-fit between person's interests, capabilities, and job requirements

Sources:
[a]Adapted from Flanagan (1978).
[b]Adapted from Andrews & Withey (1976); Baker & Intagliata (1982); Heal & Chadsey-Rusch (1985).
[c]Adapted from Brown, Diller, Gordon, Fordyce, and Jacobs, (1984); Keith, Schalock, & Hoffman (1986).
[d]Adapted from Schalock & Hill (1986); Walton (1973).

ments, friendship patterns, mobility, and degree of environmental control. For example, Brown, Diller, Gordon, Fordyce, and Jacobs (1984) propose that variables such as mobility, appearance, physical condition, activity level, and community involvement be used to reflect a person's quality of life. Similarly, Keith, Schalock, and Hoffman (1986) suggest that quality of community life is best operationalized by focusing on degree of environmental control, amount of social interaction, and variety of community utilization. Exemplary quality-of-community-life variables that fall under the objective approach are listed in Table 5 (second column). Readers interested in current attempts to measure a person's quality of life are referred to articles by Andrews and Withey (1976), Baker and Intagliata (1982), Heal and Chadsey-Rusch (1985), Keith et al. (1986), and Schalock, Keith, Karan, and Hoffman (in press).

Quality of Employment

In considering quality of life, it becomes apparent that even though one's quality of life is influenced by our job, it is determined even more by such factors as psychological well-being, personal satisfaction, and community living arrangements (see Table 5). Thus, the author proposes that we do not attempt to measure the impact of supported employment on the quality of (work) life, but rather on the *quality of employment*. This impact can be measured by the indicators listed in the right-hand portion of Table 5. Some of these quality-of-employment indicators are already reflected in the proposed supported employment indicators (see Table 3), including employment placement environment, employment data, occupational category, level of integration, hours of job support, and job movement patterns. One additional indicator that the author is convinced will be the focus of much second-generation effort is the last listed in Table 5, namely, the goodness-of-fit between a person's job interests, capabilities, and job (performance) requirements.

In this regard, the current ecological perspective has stimulated a resurgence in studying the effects that environments have upon people. Subspecialities such as social ecology, social psychology, social engineering, systems analysis, and human ecology have joined the older disciplines of sociology and anthropology in addressing the person-environment interaction. This person-environment, or ecobehavioral, perspective has also had an impact on education and (re)habilitation services for handicapped persons by suggesting that:

1. Individuals cannot be separated from their working environments.
2. Both persons and their working environments can be assessed.

3. The congruence between persons and their environments can be quantified.
4. The mismatch between persons and their environments can be reduced through the development of behavioral skills, use of prosthetics, or environmental modification.
5. Persons and environments can be matched to provide optimal opportunity for growth and development.

These ecobehavioral principles have recently been incorporated into work on improving the congruence between persons and their work environments (Schalock & Jensen, 1986). Figure 4 presents a model that reflects this person-environment matching process. The model's premise is that any environmental analysis requires that certain categories of information about a work environment be collected, researched, and analyzed systematically. In reference to this model, an environment might be analyzed according to whether it requires a series of skills to be performed independently, with assistance, or not at all. Those skills that are required (either independently or with assistance) represent the *performance requirements* of that environment. Once the performance requirements are delineated, then a person's *behavioral capability* vis-à-vis those requirements can be evaluated using a similar rating such as: performs the skill independently; performs the skill with assistance; or does not perform the skill. The congruence between these two profiles can then be analyzed through statistical procedures such as *discrepancy* and *goodness-of-fit analyses* (Krejc, Frankforter, & Schalock, 1986). Supported employment efforts may subsequently be directed at improving the quality of the person's employment by *increasing* the congruence through behavioral skill training, prosthetic usage, and/or environmental modification (Schalock & Koehler, 1984).

Program Analysis/Evaluation

The third second-generation issue relates to the underlying theme of this chapter: the need for supported employment performance indicators to meet the increasing demands for program analysis and evaluation. The author is convinced

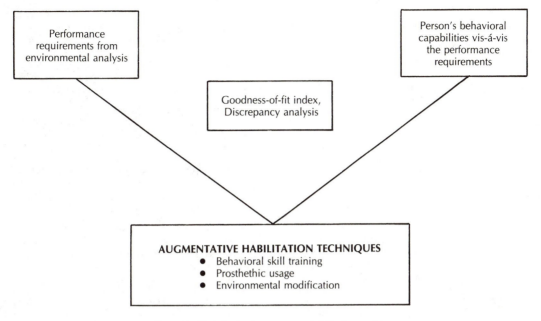

Figure 4. Ecobehavioral assessment-rehabilitation model.

that program analysis in the next decade will be more policy-oriented and that pressure for program accountability will increase, along with measurability and reportability requirements. The three proposed program analysis techniques described next are presented in considerable detail in Schalock and Thornton (1988). The three techniques include process analysis, impact analysis, and benefit-cost analysis. The type of analysis one attempts depends on the questions asked, the complexity of available data, and the sophistication of the analytic effort.

1. *Process analysis.* The analysis of program operations. This describes the program and the general environment in which it operates, including: who is served, what services are provided, how much the service costs, and how the program could be replicated.
2. *Impact analysis.* The analysis of the program's effects. This seeks to determine the difference between the courses of action being considered. In most cases, this is the difference between the current mix of services or actions and what would happen if a new course of action were undertaken.
3. *Benefit-cost analysis.* The analysis of whether a program had impacts that were sufficiently large to justify its costs. This includes analysis of all impacts, not just those that are measured or valued in dollars. The analysis also looks at relative effectiveness and tries to identify alternatives to achieve a given objective at the lowest net cost.

To date, little systematic analysis of supported employment programs has been conducted, owing to the newness of the concept and process. It is hoped that over the next five years, process, impact, and benefit-cost studies will be completed by many of us.

REFERENCES

Andrews, F.R. & Withey, S. B. (1976). *Social indicators of well-being: Americans' perceptions of life quality*. New York: Plenum.

Baker, F., & Intagliata, J. (1982). Quality of life in the evaluation of community support services. *Evaluation and Program Planning, 5*, 69–79.

Barker, L. T. (1986). *Development of performance measures for supported employment outcomes: Final report.* Berkeley, CA: Berkeley Planning Associates.

Braddock, D. (1987). *Federal policy toward mental retardation and developmental disabilities.* Baltimore: Paul H. Brookes Publishing Co.

Brown, M., Diller, L., Gordon, W. A., Fordyce, W.E., & Jacobs, D. F. (1984). Rehabilitation indicators and program evaluation. *Rehabilitation Psychology, 29*(1), 21–35.

Conley, R. W., Noble, J. H., Jr., & Elder, J. K. (1986). Problems with the service system. In: W. E. Kiernan & J. A. Stark (Eds.), *Pathways to employment for adults with developmental disabilities* (pp. 66–84). Baltimore: Paul H. Brookes Publishing Co.

Flanagan, J. C. (1978). A research approach to improving our quality of life. *American Psychologist, 33*, 138–147.

Heal, L. W., & Chadsey-Rusch, J. (1985). The Lifestyle Satisfaction Scale (LSS): Assessing individuals' satisfaction with residence, community setting, and associated services. *Applied Research in Mental Retardation, 6*, 475–490.

Keith, K. D., Schalock, R. L., & Hoffman, K. (1986). *Quality of life: Measurement and program implicators.* Lincoln, NE: Region V Mental Retardation Service.

Kiernan, W. E., McGaughey, M. J., & Schalock, R. L. (1986). *Employment survey for adults with developmental disabilities.* Boston: Developmental Evaluation Clinic, Children's Hospital.

Kiernan, W. E., McGaughey, J. J., & Schalock, R. L. (in press). Employment environments and outcomes for adults with developmental disabilities. *Mental Retardation.*

Krejc, S., Frankforter, T., & Schalock, R. L. (1986). *Person-environmental and discrepancy analysis computer manual.* Hastings, NE: Mid-Nebraska Mental Retardation Services.

Lakin, K. C., Hill, B. K., Bruininks, R. H., & White, C. C. (1986). Residential options and future implications. In: W. E. Kiernan & J. A. Stark (Eds.), *Pathways to employment for adults with developmental disabilities* (pp. 207–228). Baltimore: Paul H. Brookes Publishing Co.

Mank, D. M., Rhodes, L. E., & Bellamy, G. T. (1986). Four supported employment alternatives. In: W. E. Kiernan & J. A. Stark (Eds.), *Pathways to employment for adults with developmental disabilities* (pp. 139–153). Baltimore: Paul H. Brookes Publishing Co.

Matson, J. L., & Rusch, F. R. (1986). Quality of life: Does competitive employment make a difference? In F. R. Rusch (Ed.), *Competitive employment issues and strategies* (pp. 331–337). Baltimore: Paul H. Brookes Publishing Co.

Michener, J. A. (1978). *Chesapeake.* New York: Random House.

Schalock, R. L. & Hill, M. L. (1986). Evaluating employment services. In W. E. Kiernan & J. A. Stark (Eds.), *Pathways to employment for adults with developmental disabilities* (pp. 285–302). Baltimore: Paul H. Brookes Publishing Co.

Schalock, R. L., & Jensen, C. M. (1986). Assessing the goodness-of-fit between persons and their environments. *Journal of the Association for Persons with Severe Handicaps, 11*(2), 103–109.

Schalock, R. L., & Keith, K. D. (1986). Resource allocation approach for determining clients' need status. *Mental Retardation, 24*(1), 27–35.

Schalock, R. L., Keith, K. D., Karan, O. C., & Hoffman, K. (in press). Quality of life measurement: Its use as an outcome measure in human service programs. *Mental Retardation.*

Schalock, R. L., & Koehler, R. S. (1984). *Ecobehavioral analysis and augmentative habilitation techniques.* Hastings, NE: Mid-Nebraska Mental Retardation Services.

Schalock, R. L., & Lilley, M. A. (1986). Placement from community-based mental retardation programs: How well do clients do after 8–10 years? *American Journal of Mental Deficiency, 90*(6), 669–676.

Schalock, R. L., & Thornton, C.V.D. (1988). *Program evaluation: A Field guide for administrators.* New York: Plenum.

U.S. Department of Labor. (1977). *Dictionary of occupational titles.* Washington, DC: Author.

Walls, R. T., Zawlocki, R. J., & Dowler, D. L. (1986). Economic benefits as disincentives to competitive employment. In F. R. Rusch (Ed.), *Competitive employment issues and strategies* (pp. 317–329). Baltimore: Paul H. Brookes Publishing Co.

Walton, R. E. (1973, Fall). Quality of work life: What is it? *Sloan Managment Review, 82*, pp. 11–21.

Wehman, P., Hill, M., Hill, J. W., Brooke, V., Pendleton, P., & Britt, C. (1985). Competitive employment for persons with mental retardation: A follow-up six years later. *Mental Retardation, 23*(6), 274–281.

SECTION III

COMMUNITY-BASED PROGRAMS AND SUPPORTED EMPLOYMENT

Chapter 12

Negotiating Job-Training Stations with Employers

Ian Pumpian, Holly Shepard, and Elizabeth West

This chapter describes strategies for negotiating job-training stations agreements with employers. There are many uses and definitions of the term *job-training station*. This chapter primarily discusses techniques associated with a specific type of training station. Many of these techniques have applications to other job-training development, and placement activities. However, such applications should only be made after careful analysis and planning, consideration of which is beyond the scope of this chapter.

The type of job-training station emphasized in this chapter refers to a training program (e.g., a secondary public school program) that uses the facilities, materials, persons, and/or tasks within a business to teach and assess students' work and related tasks. In this sense, the actual business environment is considered an extension of the classroom. Teachers, counselors, and support staff perform their instructional and evaluation roles within the context of these business environments. In the job-training station development strategies discussed later in this chapter, individual students do not function as employees of the business. Rather, they enter into a trainee/employer relationship as opposed to an employee/employer relationship. A third party such as the school actually coordinates and

provides formal training to the students at the business. Placement in such a business "classroom" is a function and result of specified individualized education and transition plans and objectives. The associated objectives should cover a range of general and specific work skills training. Timelines for completing/reviewing/modifying the objectives should be stated in the objectives. Typically, in school programs for individuals with severe handicaps, placement in such a station may last a semester or an academic year. Other providers may choose to use a work station for more short-term situational assessment. In either case, placement at a station must be based on individual training objectives and a specific data-based training plan. Participation of a student (or students) at a job station is typically delineated in blocks of time across the weekly schedule in a way similar to other subject/curriculum areas and instructional locations.

For a further discussion of the legal parameters surrounding nonpaid training, readers are referred to Pumpian, Lewis, and Engel (1986). For an additional discussion regarding the relationship between training, transition, and placement, readers are referred to Pumpian, West, and Shepard (in press).

This chapter was supported in part by Grant Nos. G0008301455 and G008435102 to the San Diego State University from the U.S. Department of Education, Office of Special Education and Rehabilitative Services.

The section following briefly reviews the purpose of community-based instruction and the benefits of operating the type of job-training station just described. The remainder of the chapter then focuses on specific techniques that have proven useful in negotiating a job-training station with a given employer. The authors have successfully negotiated over 100 job-training stations in businesses in several communities. These stations have all served students with moderate to profound handicaps. The experiences of those negotiations provide the basis for the strategies and techniques offered in this chapter. It is hoped that this discussion will help educators, rehabilitation counselors, and others begin to implement more comprehensive and effective community based vocational training.

One note of caution regarding implementation of the strategies and techniques offered here. Many service providers who have contacted us for information on how to negotiate training station agreements with employers have expressed concern at their inexperience in this area. Therefore, this chapter provides some do's and don't's, as well as examples of the types of statements that could be made to employers. However, the statements are not intended as a script that should be memorized and recited to an employer. Interactions between the employer and the negotiating team, as this chapter underscores, should be fluid and dynamic.

Uses of a Cumulative Vocational Training Record

A cumulative vocational training record (for example, see Pumpian et al., 1981) is a fundamental tool that can be extraordinarily helpful in an individual's transition into employment. Such a record should develop and document at least the following:

1. *A specific listing of vocational skills and interests that have been developed and/or assessed.* This listing is most helpful when evidence of vocational competence can be directly matched to examples of jobs, job descriptions, and job environments that are readily available within the individual's home community. Such a listing should include traditional areas of concern (i.e., productivity, attendance, safety, direction follow-

ing). However, such indicators will be most useful when they are referenced to particular jobs and job environments. Stated another way, it is of limited value to assess a person's general work rate without reference to job tasks and descriptions, since any individual's work rate is almost totally a function of such variables.

2. *A listing of the adaptations and other strategies that have been used to compensate for major skill deficits.* It is assumed that individuals with severe disabilities, despite exemplary training attempts, will continue to manifest specific skill deficits that will present challenges regarding job placement. Good training programs not only teach skills that minimize these deficits, but also consider, develop, use, and evaluate different adaptations. These adaptations should be individually designed to further reduce the significance of skill deficits. Adaptations may be in the form of changes in personnel support/supervision, job description modification, job sharing, creative scheduling, individualized equipment and devices and/or consideration of various payment mechanisms (Baumgart et al., 1982; Nisbet et al., 1983) When considering these adaptations (along with documentation of skills and interests), job-placement personnel will be able to better communicate the marketability of the individual. In one sense, effective job adaptations discovered in training become major components of supported employment plans.

3. *Data reviewing the strengths and needs of the individual.* Documentation through evaluative feedback should be completed not only by education and rehabilitation professionals, but also by employers and employees within the business community. Such data facilitate planning the transition to work. In addition, written feedback from employers serves as an indication of past experience, which is very helpful when talking with a potential employer.

4. *Information pertaining to the aspirations and concerns of the individual and of his or her family members/advocate pertaining to work.* A good training program not only documents these aspirations and concerns,

but demonstrates how they have been incorporated in previous programs. Securing the active involvement of families in vocational training, transition, and placement is critical in attaining vocational success.

Many theories and approaches have been relied upon individually and/or in combination to provide vocational training to individuals with disabilities. However, the methods used should result in a cumulative record that includes at least the preceding information. The extensiveness of the information certainly will be influenced by many factors (e.g., the age of the individual, the number of years in training, changes that have occurred in the training program, the severity of disability). Notwithstanding these factors, a range of prior training experiences (including settings and persons involved) should provide a more complete account of the conditions, circumstances, and resources that will need to be considered to increase the likelihood of a successful job placement. Transition plans are developed to move a person from services focused primarily on training to services focused mainly on job support. Documentation of this range of previous experiences can only enhance the process.

Job-training stations have become one strategy for constructing a considerable part of a cumulative job-training record. The use of the job-training station by training programs provides the opportunity to develop, assess, and document skills, interests, adaptations, concerns, and other support needs. Professionals, employers and family members must all take an active role in helping the individual make the transition into employment. The assumption of this chapter is that the utilization of job-training stations will facilitate the efforts of individuals responsible for the transition to employment.

Educational services for students with severe handicaps should be predominately preparatory in nature. Services should prepare students to participate as actively and meaningfully as possible in all aspects of community and adult life. Therefore, educational services should be evaluated by measuring the degree to which students make the transition from school into normalized work, recreation, community, and living environments. Functional curriculum development

strategies are now being widely used and evaluated in an attempt to enhance the quality of educational services. Utilization of these strategies has resulted in instructional programming in a wide variety of home, work, and other community environments. As already indicated, in the vocational domain, educators are now using actual community businesses as extensions of their classrooms. Many training programs have developed a variety of job-training stations in a number of businesses in their communities. These stations provide educators, counselors, consumers, and others with a basis for developing individualized vocational training programs. The range of stations are designed to: accommodate students of different ages; build and assess students' interests and abilities; facilitate vocational and community integration; and identify instructional and support needs.

The use of any community environment as a classroom extends well beyond the notion of a fieldtrip. When a community environment such as an actual job environment is selected for instructional use, specification of individualized objectives, teaching procedures, and measurement strategies are still fundamental program components. Placement at a job station provides an excellent context not only for functional training, but for situational assessment as well. As already suggested, each selected job-training station should be used in a systematic, ongoing manner to:

1. Identify critical activities and skills required to function there effectively
2. Develop and assess vocational skills and interests in various types of job environments
3. Design individualized instructional programs to teach students to engage meaningfully in those activities
4. Utilize and assess the efficacy of various training and supervising techniques
5. Identify and teach the use of viable alternative performance strategies (Wilcox & Bellamy, 1982) and individualized adaptations (Baumgart et al., 1982)
6. Identify the kinds of support that would be necessary to maintain an individual in a particular job environment

Data related to each of these items are critical

for the development of individualized transition plans that result in the actual movement of individuals from work training to work placement. The use of training stations in the community has been reported useful not only in teaching students valuable job and job-related skills (Brown et al., 1983), but also in gaining the involvement of significant others who will be instrumental in planning, fostering, and otherwise making adult job placement a reality. Specifically, Pumpian et al. (1980) identified the positive impact that skills, attitudes and expectations, and school community-based vocational instruction can have on:

1. Employers and employees
2. Parents, family, and other care providers
3. Other school and adult service providers
4. Funding agencies
5. The community at large

A growing number of consumers, service providers, advocates, and employers are convinced that the majority of individuals with severe handicaps are capable of performing meaningful work in nonsheltered vocational environments (Brown et.al., 1983). Increasing numbers of agencies are providing supported employment service to adults with severe handicaps (Vogelsberg, 1986; Wilcox & Bellamy, 1982). Concurrently, school agencies are now charged with the responsibility to prepare students to work in the community and benefit from supported work services. The better prepared an individual is during school years the more likely he or she will transition from school directly into a community work placement (McCarthy, Everson, Wood-Pietruski, Inge, & Barcus, 1985); and supported work services will be implemented efficiently and effectively (Wehman & Hill, 1985).

Thus, community intensive instruction, including the use of job-training stations, is now regularly occurring within the vocational curriculum domain and provides essential information needed for transition planning.

Many school programs have developed a wide variety of job-training stations in order to provide individualized job and related skill instruction to a student throughout his or her years in public instruction. For example:

1. A student may be placed in one job training station at age 12 for one hour per day and one day per week.
2. Each year that student might be placed at a different station. Each year the number of hours per day and days per week would also increase.
3. When the student has four years left in school, very specific transition planning occurs. Transition objectives will utilize data accumulated from all the training experiences in order to plan and actually transition and place the graduating student into an integrated work environment.

CHARACTERISTICS OF A JOB STATION

There are many kinds and types of definitions used to identify the nature and function of a job-training station. However, only one is presented here. The authors' definition applies to students in real job environments prior to seeking actual job placement, and to students who, due to their age and/or disability, need to have instructional staff present to facilitate implementing the program. Other programs have operated training stations in which instructors are not present daily so that employers and employees execute daily training activities. Although this is desired during transition and placement, it has resulted in exclusion during training of students with more severe disabilities. It also limits the availability of types of sites and jobs. Typical characteristics of the job stations as referred to in this chapter include to following:

1. Students typically are not remunerated although training stipend monies may be used.
2. The station can accommodate the involvement of a small group of students.
3. An instructor is present at the station to operate the program.
4. The training is arranged primarily for the benefit of the student. Students do not displace regular employees and don't substantially affect the employer's profit structure.
5. There is no explicit or implicit expectation that the employer will hire students after the program ends.

6. A vocational training including goals, objectives, and data collection procedures is integrated into the IEP.

Although a "job-training station" is being distinguished as something different from a paid or volunteer job placement, all three should:

1. Focus workers'/trainees' behavior on meaningful work activities.
2. Utilize integrated work environments.
3. Promote interactions between workers/trainees and nonhandicapped coworkers (Breen, Haring, Pitts-Conway, & Gaylord-Ross, 1985.
4. Provide necessary levels of training and support such that the worker/trainee continues to perform meaningful work and work-related skills.
5. Involve the family in planning and implementing programs.
6. Make available information/training/support to employers/coworkers/families as necessary to promote acceptance of trainee/worker.
7. Collect data such that progress is continually monitored, and so that training, support, and transition plans are modified accordingly.
8. Base training and placement decisions upon the individual interests, abilities, and learning needs of the student.

BASIC ORGANIZING STRATEGIES

Organizing Personpower

Developing a community-based vocational training program takes quite a bit of time and energy. A great deal of preparation needs to occur prior to taking the first small group of students to a job-training station. Developing a training station is just one step toward developing the number and variety of sites necessary to accommodate the individual longitudinal needs of all the students enrolled in a program. Therefore, it is necessary to identify and organize resources, including person power, in an effective and efficient manner.

It is recommended that the persons most interested in developing a job training station or enhancing their current community based vo-

cational training program organize themselves as a group. For example, in one school district, a "job-training station task force" was developed with four teachers, one rehabilitation counselor, one parent, and an administrator. The purpose of the task force was to develop one job-training station within two months. The task force developed a regular weekly meeting schedule and then identified, assigned, and reviewed the status of tasks to be completed prior to the next meeting. Shepard, Pumpian, and West (1986) provide more detailed descriptions of the responsibilities, organization, and function of a vocational task force.

Conducting Inventories of Community Businesses

There are many ways to inventory the types of businesses that are prominent in local areas, the trends for future types of jobs, and the ways to prioritize job environments for instructional and placement purposes. Some of this information is infused throughout this chapter, but the authors do recommend that local task forces become familiar with the types of jobs and vocational opportunities existing in their communities, as well as review local job market trends and analyses of their communities.

NEGOTIATING STEPS

The remainder of this chapter describes how to negotiate with a particular business that has been selected as a potential job-training station.

Step 1

Preparation: Getting ready to make the contact At this point, it is assumed that the program staff have organized themselves as a task force. A community business inventory has been initiated and at least one business environment has been selected as a potential job-training station. Preparation for negotiation is an extremely important activity. Basically, the group should review why this particular business was chosen—that is, the characteristics, criteria, and information that were used to select the business. The reasons the business was selected as a potential training environment will be used to prepare for negotiations with the employer. The following questions may assist the task force in preparing their negotiations.

1. *Have other programs been successful either utilizing this type of job environment or performing the types of jobs that most likely occur within that environment?* List these programs and where they are located. It may be valuable to contact an already-participating employer to ask permission to use them as a reference. Prepare them for a possible contact from the prospective employer. Such information will be valuable to share with the potential employer as he or she decides whether to become a job-training station. Training programs across the country should assist each other in helping employers talk to employers.

2. *Is there someone on your staff who has worked in that kind of job environment?* Such a person can be invaluable in planning and participating in the negotiation process. He or she can help identify: typical jobs that could be targeted for training; unique routines the businesses might use; and particular needs the business may regularly have. If nobody on your staff has had such direct experience, try to interview someone who has worked in that type of job environment. Again, the more information you can compile about a specific job environment or kind of job environment, the more information you will have when negotiating with the employer and addressing his or her concerns.

3. *Did you have a contact?* That is, did you select this business because you have an affiliation with someone who is influential there? Interview that person. Try to find out: 1) whom you should contact to set up your meeting; 2) who may be less then cooperative; 3) types of work or work areas that may be of particular interest; 4) whether the business has already expressed interests or concerns that can be addressed in your presentation.

4. *What is the business's public image? What kind of image do they try to project?* Again, the more you understand about that business—their operation, and their current public image or public campaigns—the more your presentation can convince the business that your program will complement their desired public image. Has the business received particularly good or bad press? You may want to bring in news clippings of other businesses who have provided job-training stations, so that the business can get an idea of the sort of public relations that may develop out of such a relationship.

5. *Is it possible to visit the environment beforehand without speaking directly to the employer?* Depending on the type of environment, this may or may not be possible. For example, you can eat in the prospective restaurant or shop in the grocery store or drugstore prior to actually going there. You can note the types of jobs being performed, how busy the environment is and the number of people working there. Obviously, this strategy will not be available to you in a factory or in parts of the store or restaurant not used by consumers of that business.Incidentally, it never hurts to let the employer know that you patronize the business.

6. *What are your scheduling priorities and parameters?* To be prepared for your negotiations from your point of view you must establish what days and hours would be ideal for operating the training station. Keep in mind that these times may not be compatible with the employer's needs.[1] Therefore, you also need to be prepared to discuss parameters. That is, what is the earliest possible time students could arrive at the station? What is the latest possible time students could stay? What is the least and greatest number of students you could bring to the site? Keep in mind the employer might say that he or she has no room for training on

---

[1] By law, the times in which training programs operate must first be based on the needs of the trainee not the employer, Marshall v. Baptist Hospital, 473 F. Supp. (1979). That means you do not arrange to operate your program at times the employer needs you to get a job done and meet work quotas. Contrarily, the authors have not interpreted this to restrict selecting a day or time when the employer may have more space available, as long as training needs can be met then.

Monday and Friday because more employees are needed on those days to prepare for and recover from weekend business. The employer may then say the Tuesday supervisor is pretty rigid, so Wednesday and Thursday may be the ideal days for training.

In conclusion, prepare! Know why you chose the business. Find out as much as you can about the business. Incorporate this information into your presentation.

Step 2

The Contact Team   The task force will be responsible for selecting the members of the contact team that negotiates with a particular employer. It should be realized that the entire task force cannot visit an employer. Instead, a few members will need to represent the task force's interests and the overall program goals.

There are many types of contacts. For example, employers will be contacted at employer breakfasts; program administrators may meet and develop contacts within professional organizations; or administrators may visit the regional offices of a particular business. The contact discussed here, however, deals with a small group of individuals that will actually go to a particular business selected for potential training purposes. The authors have found that at least two individuals should comprise the contact team. In addition, a variety of other roles need to be assumed either by those two people or by one or two others. First, an administrator or somebody with administrative supervisory responsibilities should be on the contact team. The administrator's presence makes it clear to the employer that your proposal represents efforts, policies, and directions of your agency and not just the individual interests of an eager teacher. The employer will, after all, be developing a relationship with a well-respected agency in town. The adminstrator's attendance at the meeting helps to reinforce that image and is more consistent with peer business protocol. There are additional reasons why an administrator should participate. He or she can best provide information and assurances related to liability, insurance, district policies, and other general administrative information. The administrator will also be responsible for dealing with the paperwork connected with the program's as well as the business's needs, and will need to follow up on any unsettled issues regarding board policies, letters of agreement, documentation of insurance and liability issues, and so forth.

The second member of the contact team should be a direct service provider—for example, one of the teachers who may eventually be involved in training and supervision at the worksite. Just as the administrator will be responsible for dealing with policy issues, the teacher will be responsible for dealing with program issues. The teacher can field questions and concerns about the students who will be/might be involved in the training station. The teacher knows the students' range of abilities, past programming efforts, and scheduling priorities and parameters. He or she will also be able to identify the types of jobs and job areas appropriate for training and the process used to develop and implement training programs. The employer will have an opportunity to see the type of person who may be at the business on a regular basis. Thus, the teacher will be able to represent the professionalism that exists within the task force.

In addition to the administrator and direct service provider, other roles need to be represented on the contact team. These roles may be assumed by one of the two members, or additional members may be added. First, it is very helpful to have someone on the contact team who has experience negotiating with employers. Since more community-based programs are now operating across the country, it may be possible to invite an experienced person to be a part of the contact team. This person would be able to model techniques and strategies for the rest of the contact team.

Second, it would be very helpful if one of the team members has had experience working in the type of business being interviewed. This may be the deciding criterion for choosing which teacher serves on the contact team. Employers are typically quick to point out how their business is different from other businesses. For example, a grocery store manager might say, ''I understand that you have worked in hospitals, factories, and restaurants, but the grocery business is very unique, high-paced, and competitive. It is dog eat dog!'' In such a statement the employer not only shows pride in his or her unique business, but also may be expressing reservations about operating a job-training program in that type of business. However, the authors have found that when the employer learns that one of the members of the contact team has had experience in that type of business, an affiliation or bond seems to be created. That is, the employer starts directing his or her comments to that particular person. For example: ''Well, you know what it's like when the produce comes in damaged and the refrigerators are on the blink.'' If the experienced teacher can use this information positively in describing how the training station could operate under such circumstances, the employer is not likely to overwhelm the contact team with information to which they cannot respond.

Third, some programs have found it helpful to involve a local university in developing sites, for a number of reasons. First, affiliation with a university provides the employer the opportunity to associate with two major agencies in the community. Many businesses take pride in having a relationship with such organizations. Second, this leads to a fourth possible team member, that is, a student teacher. Many teachers did not develop skills for negotiating with employers during their training. The authors feel it is very important for student teachers to begin acquiring these kinds of competencies in their training programs.

In conclusion, the authors recommend that no more than four people constitute a contact team. Three individuals are ideal, and two would be acceptable. Under some circumstances one individual may make an initial contact; however, the authors feel there are several advantages to having more than one individual participate in this negotiation. First, two or more individuals can later jointly evaluate the negotiation experience—what seemed to go well, what areas give reason for concern, what agreements were made, and what follow-up should occur. (For example, regarding the latter, should a letter or follow-up telephone call be used to clarify points that seem unclear to the employer?) Second, during the negotiation, the team can pay attention to different aspects of the interaction with

the employer. It is useful to make a mental note of points that seem to most concern the employer. Various members of the contact team may pick up on different verbal statements as well as employers' nonverbal gestures, frowns, and note taking. The more aware the contact team can be of the concerns and interests of the employer, the more the negotiations can relate to these concerns.

Step 3

Setting Up the Meeting: The Initial Contact   The purpose of the initial contact with a business is to arrange a meeting to take place in the near future. The aim at this time is not to negotiate a job-training station agreement. Two major issues must be addressed, regarding which there are no right or wrong answers. Much depends on individual styles and local circumstances.

First, with whom should one try to arrange the meeting? The decision to allow the use of a business as a job-training station is always made at the *top* level of management within the job site. Therefore, the authors have found that the most expedient and successful contacts are those made as close to the top level of management as possible. If one deals initially with lower-level staff, they will eventually have to seek approval for the program from top management, which admits the unfortunate possibility that key program components will be overlooked or misrepresented. If decision makers are not provided information directly, they will tend to evaluate the program in terms of more traditional programs that they may or may not have been directly associated with in the past. To reiterate, then, it is recommended that contact be made with the owner, manager or director in charge. For example, within a hospital, the authors have dealt with the head administrator. In hotels, the initial contact has been the manager; sometimes the head housekeeper is also asked to participate in the meeting if it is already known that a particular area of the business will be targeted for instruction. In stores and restaurants the authors have met with the owner of the franchise. In a large organization such as a university, it would be most appropriate to contact the director of the physical plant to negotiate a job-training station in grounds or building maintenance.

The second thing that must be decided is how to contact a particular business to arrange a meeting. There are at least four general methods to consider: 1) by telephone; 2) in person; 3) by letter; or 4) a combination of these. Again, one is not contacting the business to negotiate the job-training station; one is making an initial contact simply to arrange a 15- to 20-minute meeting with the person or people with whom you wish to negotiate.

The size and type of business will affect the type of contact method you select. The authors have found that in-person contacts are appropriate in places such as grocery stores, restaurants, bowling alleys, or drug stores. Consider the following sample dialogue. You walk into a local grocery store that you have targeted as a potential training station, walk up to an employee and say:

You: "Who is your store manager?"
They: "Mr. Greene."
You: "Is he here?"
They: "Yeah, back by produce."
You: "Thanks a lot." (You walk back to produce section, identify the store manager, walk up to him.)

You: "Hi, Mr. Greene. I am Terry McFarlane for San Diego City Schools."
(Hand him your business card.) "I know I'm catching you at a bad time, I wanted to know if there is a time next week I could sit down with you for 15 minutes or so to share information and ideas about our program."
They: (Mr. Greene may ask you for additional information or say:)
"I'm not hiring" or "I gave at the office."
You: "We are not doing job placement" (or) "This isn't a charity drive. We have just begun some interesting cooperative arrangements with some local businesses. We want to share some of our ideas with you." (If you have a contact, this may be a good time to mention him or her —for example):
You: "Sarah Smith suggested we talk to you."
(Sarah is the agricultural meat inspector for the grocery store and Jake Smith is a teacher on your staff.)
They: "OK, next Tuesday around 10 o'clock."
You: "Great! Next Tuesday at 10 o'clock, we'll look forward to seeing you. If that time becomes a problem, please call." (Get his name and telephone number.)

In a larger corporation and industry, the authors have found that a telephone call is a more appropriate way to make the first contact than an in-person visit. As in the in-person contact, a telephone call may be preceded by or followed up by a letter further explaining the program. When making a telephone call, you may speak first with the secretary of the person with whom you wish to meet. Corporate secretaries typically: 1) screen calls; 2) refer calls to others further down in the administrative structure; 3) have access to the administrator's calendar appointment book. Consider the following example, when attempting to negotiate an initial contact with a local hospital.

They: "Hello, St. Mary's Hospital."
You: "Hello, who is the head administrator at St. Mary's ?"
They: "Mr. Hemostat."
You: "May I speak with Mr. Hemostat's secretary, please?" (At which point the operator will switch you over to the administrative area of the hospital.)
They: "Hello, Mr. Hemostat's office" (or) "Administrative Offices."
You: "Hello, is this Mr. Hemostat's secretary."
They: "Yes it is" (or) "just one second."
You: "This is Dr. Edwards from San Diego State University." (Unfortunately, within corporations, titles denote status and increase your chances of actually setting up the meeting. Therefore try to have a director, professor, principal, or someone with a title before or after his or her name make the call.)
You: "Do you have access to Mr. Hemostat's calendar?"
They: "Yes, I do, what can I help you with?"
You: "I would like to set up a short meeting with Mr. Hemostat." (Again, try to provide as little information as you have to and only provide more information in order to continue toward your goal, that is, to set up a short meeting with Mr. Hemostat.)
They: "What would this meeting be concerning?"
You: "I wanted to discuss a program that I'm involved in with the San Diego Schools."
They: "What kind of program is it?" (Keep in mind the secretary is already attempting to refer you to someone else within the organization who may be more appropriate than his or her boss.)
You: "We are working on a joint program between the San Diego school district and businesses throughout our community."
They: "What kind of program?"

You: "It is designed to improve vocational preparation occurring within our special education program."

They: "If this is a vocational program, I would suggest you contact our head of personnel."

You: "It's not really a job placement program. If you feel it is appropriate to invite the head of personnel to the meeting, that would be great. However, in programs that have been affiliated with other hospitals, we have found that meeting briefly with the head administrator is necessary and can save time down the line."

They: "Well, if this isn't a job placement program, what is it?"

You: "It is a program designed to improve the overall training of students in our program."

They: "Well, if this is a training program, perhaps you should talk to our director of training." (In other words you may need to keep going. For example):

You: "No, this isn't really training in a traditional sense; we develop vocational training through nonpaid work experiences."

They: "Well, perhaps you need to talk with the director of volunteers." (Again, you are going to have to be kind, courteous, and somewhat consistent with the fact that those people would be great to invite to the meeting, but that you feel it is necessary to at least initially meet briefly with the administrator.)

At this point, the secretary has some choices: 1) to say he or she will get back to you after talking with the administrator; 2) to request that you submit a written proposal and that they will get back to you at a later date; or 3) to insist that there is someone else in the organization with whom you should talk. You must then decide whether to push on or agree to his or her suggestions.

They: "How about Tuesday, September 12, at 10 o'clock?"

You: "Fine, I will be coming with two other people." (Inform the secretary of the names and titles of these people. You may also tell him or her that you will need to clear that day with them, and if that time is a problem, you will call back.) "In the meantime, let me give you my name again and my phone number. Thank you so much for your time and I look forward to seeing you on September 12."

If you have made it this far, you have accomplished quite a task. Keep in mind that depending on the type of business and the contact, you may be called back, and the meeting may be canceled or postponed. At worst, you may show up for an arranged meeting only to find that the manager is out of town, is on vacation, or had to deal with an emergency. Keep a stiff upper lip, and do not feel that this is an indictment of your program. Keep in mind that the employer has many concerns that are more important to him or her than your meeting. It is probably a good idea to call to confirm your appointment the day before the meeting. The reader may also wish to refer to Bissonnette and Pimentel (1984), for additional strategies for arranging meetings and dealing with corporate secretaries.

Step 4

The Actual Negotiation   Negotiating a job-training station requires that each member of the contact team demonstrates sophisticated public relations skills. The team is representing your program. The business will, in part, be judging whether they want to affiliate themselves with your program, that is, with you. All members of the contact team must therefore be aware of how they present themselves. Keep in mind that the business is not a social agency; the time the business representatives spend talking with you is time away from operating their business. Try to stay on the topic. The employer does not need to know cute anecdotes about students that have nothing to do with a point in the negotiations. Try to be responsive to the employer's questions and concerns. Help him or her understand how your program deals with, avoids, or attenuates potential problems. Do not spend time pushing a point about which you and the employer already agree. Use those points of agreement to move on to the next point. Be respectful, articulate, and pleasant. Show enthusiasm for what you are doing; it rubs off!

The arrival   Remember, every person in the business environment you have just come to can play an important role in your program's acceptance or rejection. It is likely that upon arrival, you will be asked to wait in the outer office or in a reception area. Be aware that while you are waiting, your conversations, strategizing, and so forth, may be overheard, relayed to others, and possibly misinterpreted. If you meet the person who helped set up the meeting, express your appreciation for his or her assistance.

Handle yourselves and your conversations as professionals.

When introduced to the employer and others participating in the meeting, step forward and introduce yourselves. Shake hands, share business cards, provide eye contact. Thank the participants for their time. This is not the time to be timid or shy.

Beginning the meeting   Keep in mind the employer may have no idea what you want and may make inaccurate assumptions about why you are there. You need to quickly dispel two possible inaccurate assumptions. First, since you are affiliated with a special education program, the employer may assume that you are looking for some sort of charity or handout. Second, since you represented yourself as part of a vocational training program, the employer may assume that you are there pursuing a job placement for an individual. It is important that the employer realize these are not the purposes of your visit. Your opening comments should dispel these notions and set the groundwork for sharing why you are there. You will also want to set a relaxed, yet professional, tone for the negotiations to follow. For example, the authors have used these types of comments to initially break the ice with employers:

> "We are not here to sell lightbulbs for a charity drive. We are not here looking for a job placement, rather we are here to share information about our program and propose some ways we (programs) have been interacting with other businesses in the community."

Defining the population of people you represent   There is some controversy regarding the extent to which an individual's handicaps or limitations should be discussed at the initial meeting. If your program serves individuals with severe handicaps, the authors believe it is important for the employer to realize this so that at a later date there is no question as to whether you have misrepresented your program or your population. Therefore, the authors feel it is important to quickly identify the number of individuals your program serves and the diversity of strengths, skills, and limitations represented. For example:

> "Our programs serve individuals labeled as severely handicapped who are enrolled in the San Diego Unified School District. The school district provides educational programming for approximately 1,000 individuals identified as severely handicapped. Our responsibility is to provide quality educational experiences to each of these individuals. The group is quite diverse in terms of their ages, their individual strengths and interests, as well as the limitations and challenges they need to overcome. A majority of students could be characterized as having significant mental retardation. There are some students in the program who can walk and others who use wheelchairs or other forms of mobility assistance. Some students have very good verbal skills, while others may point to a picture book to communicate. Some of our students require extensive assistance to develop control over their behavior, while other students act exemplarily. Some of our students do not have good oral muscular control and therefore drool, while others have good self-care skills. Some of our students can eat independently; others need help. It really is a diverse group! However, each is entitled to an appropriate education and it is our responsibility to make sure that each has a program designed to prepare him or her to be an active adult in the community. It is obvious we are not interested in bringing all 1,000 of these individuals into your business!"

Brief review of curriculum changes   It is important to provide a short overview of the changes that have occurred in the past several years in services for individuals identified as severely handicapped. Start by saying that in the past there were no community services available; parents either kept their children at home, paid for private services, or segregated them in institutions. Explain that things have changed. For example:

> "Public education is now provided to individuals as a matter of their right. Over the past 10–15 years we have constantly attempted to improve the quality of educational services provided to this group of individuals. As part of that function, we have realized that the major purpose of education is to prepare individuals to lead productive lives in their community. That is, to live, work, and play as part of the community. This has led to some changes in how educational programs have developed. For example, we have realized if we want to teach a student to shop in a grocery store, part of his or her instructional time must be spent in a grocery store. If we want to teach a student to ride on a city bus, instruction must occur in part on city buses. That is, these stores and buses become classrooms for instruction. When we want to teach a student to prepare a simple meal in his or her kitchen at home, homes become expansions

of the classroom. Finally, we are now learning that the best way to teach job and job-related skills is to teach in real business environments. We have had tremendous success developing cooperative training programs with a number of local businesses'' (or you might cite programs elsewhere that have had success with other businesses). ''This brings us to the reason why we are here and to our proposition.''

The proposition   It is important to show the employer that you are knowledgeable about his or her business. This relates to the information used to prepare for your visit. You will need to show that you are aware of type of products produced, clientele involved, the stature of the business in the community, and so forth, to help the employer better formulate an opinion regarding how your program will fit into the business environment. It is also important to show deference. There needs to be a balance between your knowledge about the business and the fact that you are there to seek information that you do not have. For example, tell the employer that you know that no two grocery stores are the same. You are here specifically to find out about some of the particulars and unique characteristics of this store so that your training program can be more responsive to local employer needs. For example:

> ''We suspect that there are excellent training opportunities here facing food products and retrieving grocery carts. We are interested in procedures used to price items to see if adaptations could be made for students. We are also interested in finding out what other training opportunities or future job opportunities may exist, of which we are not aware. We have found it to be tremendously helpful to talk with employers throughout the community about the types of jobs that are done on a regular basis so we can better identify jobs that might be appropriate for individual students.''

Now it is time to present your proposition. It is important to emphasize that the content of your program is probably different from that of other vocational programs he or she may have been involved with in the past. Help the employer realize that owing to the needs of your students, your program has some unique characteristics. Finally, emphasize that these characteristics have been extremely well received by a large number of employers. For example:

''We are interested in using your business environment as our classroom. Let me explain. We propose to use your business as a place to teach a small group of students some specific, meaningful work skills as well as job-related skills. We believe in starting very small in order to make sure the program is successful for all involved. The job station would operate perhaps for 1 to 3 hours a day and 1 to 3 days per week. Two to five students will comprise the station. They will always be accompanied by an instructor. They will be taught to perform the jobs that we all agree upon. We intend to operate our station in a way that may enhance rather than unduly interfere with your business. The instructor will always accompany the students. He or she will be responsible for training, for supervision, for quality control, and for communicating with you and/or your staff regarding work performance, work responsibilities, or work demands. He or she will be responsible for working with your designated staff to identify appropriate training opportunities and to promote interactions. First and foremost, we want to identify jobs that need to be done, that is, meaningful work. We need to identify jobs that are done on a regular basis, but we do not necessarily restrict ourselves to all the requirements of existing job descriptions.''

At this point, you may want to elaborate the preceding statement by providing relevant examples of how students could learn to do important components of a job without learning an entire job title. For example, discuss how students have learned to:

1. Collate papers and prepare mail without performing more complicated skills typically required of clerical staff
2. Stock shelves or retrieve carts without performing other skills required of a typical grocery stocker
3. Affix labels on hospital materials without having responsibilities for actually stocking the nurses' carts
4. Set tables at a limited number of stations without other setup responsibilities in a restaurant

Share the fact that such training of marketable skills has led to new employment opportunities for many students and has also formed a basis for adding new job skills. Use your knowledge and experience to suggest ways students might meaningfully partially participate in the business you have contacted.

Next explain that your students are not to be considered employees of the business. For example:

> "This policy is consistent with the California Education Code State Law for Unpaid Work Experience. Basically, the conditions of unpaid work experiences are that: 1) The student will be involved in a training program in which our staff will be responsible for writing individualized objectives for each participating student and for compiling data related to their progress. 2) None of the students involved in the program can displace a worker; that is, no employee will be fired as a result of our participation. Furthermore, our participation cannot be used to avoid hiring needed personnel. We will be teaching jobs for which employees must be available to do the work if we didn't. Again our primary purpose here is to teach work and work-related skills, so that we may begin to understand conditions under which a particular individual may in the future participate more as an employee than at present. 3) Finally, under the California Education Code, if individuals are involved in an unpaid work experience, the school district will be considered the employer, not the business. Therefore, the school district will be responsible for workmen's compensation insurance. In addition, since this program will function under the supervision of the schools, additional personal liability issues are covered under the school's insurance policy and will not be the direct responsibility of your business. We have a number of examples of letters of agreement that have been drafted by lawyers from businesses as well as school districts that we would be happy to share with you in order to further clarify this matter if in fact the training station is to be developed."

It is now time to review the discussion so far:

> "I'd like to quickly review our proposition and to get your input: 1) First of all, we're talking about starting very small and developing a successful program from the beginning. We would like to propose working 1 to 3 hours a day beginning with 1 to 3 days per week. 2) The program will involve a small number of students (2 to 5). They will be controlled by the school staff. Over time the staff will attempt to facilitate interaction between each trainee and your employees. 3) The students will not be considered employees. If any of these features of our agreement ever need be changed, we would sit down and renegotiate. There is no expectation that anything would change right now. Our hope is that your business would be training grounds for our students, enabling our teachers to

provide a viable and realistic training experience. We want to identify the ways that individuals who have traditionally been unemployed and kept out of the work force may become more a part of that work force."

At this point you might want to show the employer some of the newspaper articles that have resulted from similar programs across the country, or provide a few personal examples. Remember, your stories and examples should not get so wordy and lengthy that you detract from why you are there.

Finally you should discuss what you need from the business. Specifically:

1. *Meaningful work opportunities.* Jobs that need to be performed, that are performed on a regular basis, and that are associated with a routine. Explain that you will be responsible for analyzing the job's components and for teaching the job. You will want to start by assuming responsibilities for a limited number of jobs. You can always increase responsibilities after training begins.

2. *A viable work area.* You need to identify an area that does not eliminate the opportunity for interactions with others, that can accommodate the number of students involved, and is appropriate for the type of work being performed. You should start in one area and spread out students systematically over time in order to facilitate interactions with other workers. Wershing, Gaylord-Ross, and Gaylord-Ross (1985) reviewed various groupings and supervising models for community work training. Remember, you are assuring the employer that you will supervise each student and be responsible for quality control. Be prepared to creatively identify space, since many employers will have concerns about space limitations.

3. *Accessible materials and storage areas.* The employer will be responsible for making sure work materials are available and that you have places to keep jackets, clipboards, and so forth.

4. *A contact person.* The employer will need to identify who in the business will be re-

sponsible for overseeing program activities, answering questions, and communicating concerns. Emphasize that communication is essential if the program is to be responsive to business concerns.

Emphasize the overwhelming success these programs have had. Be prepared to list participating businesses and provide references. Be prepared to discuss how many employees have found this type of program to be extremely acceptable. At first, employees have questioned the purpose of the programs; now they wish the programs had begun sooner. In some cases employees have stated that the program has made their work more interesting and that other businesses would profit from involvement.

Be prepared to repeat that your program involves working with people with very significant handicaps. You are not sure at this point which students will be involved in the program; this will depend on the types of jobs that are identified. However, you can assure the employer that:

1. You can be counted on to be there;
2. The job you agree to perform will get done;
3. Adequate supervision and training will be provided each of the individuals involved;
4. You will be responsive to the concerns communicated to you; and
5. You believe that the individuals you bring to the company will benefit from that training and experience.

You should end by saying, "Well, that's our proposition in a nutshell. We'd like to know what concerns or questions you have, or if there are areas we can further clarify." Various employers at this point will raise a variety of issues from programming to liability to insurance. Your contact team will need to be very sensitive to what concerns the employer may have and then offer reasonable alternatives or reactions to each of these. Again, the purpose of your visit is to negotiate a training station environment. Ensure the employer that your program can be responsive to his or her needs and that you will organize your program to do that. It is certainly possible that you may decide that the business is not an appropriate training environment.

Next steps   The employer will probably give you one of four responses:

1. "I need to talk to so and so and get back to you";
2. "I need to have a written proposal so I can take it to my board (or my colleagues or the owner or the main manager)";
3. "Sounds great, what's next?" or
4. "We are not very interested in having the program at this time. That is, we are rejecting your proposition."

It is important to respond to the employer's statement so as to provide further clarity and increase the likelihood that your program will be accepted and supported. Keep in mind that if the employer wants to get the reactions of other individuals in the business, he or she will not necessarily communicate essential program components (number of hours per day, the nature of ongoing supervision, number of days per week). For instance, the employer may go to a foreman and say, "We have a group of handicapped kids who want to come here and learn job skills. What do you think about that?" The foreman immediately is thinking 20 hours a week and responds, "I don't have room, I don't have the time to supervise, etc." If the employer needs to talk to others, you may want to offer to accompany him or her in order to answer questions that may arise. Ask the employer when you should expect to hear from him or her. Make sure, based on the response you have received from the employer, that you write a follow-up letter that communicates again the components of your program, your appreciation, and your anticipation of their cooperation.

Should the employer say "What's next?" two major components need to be addressed:

1. What paperwork needs to be provided, and what are the outstanding administrative issues? Your administrative representative will take the responsibility for gathering that information and for identifying to whom that information should be provided.
2. What is next pragmatically? There is a need to arrange a meeting with the person(s) responsible for the areas being considered for the training environment. Stress to the em-

ployer that you will want to thoroughly analyze the environment and the types of job possibilities for training. Before teaching the job, you must learn it. You will want to address how the employer feels information about the program should be communicated to the business's employees. Decide whether a formal presentation at a staff meeting is appropriate or whether informal talks are preferred as the teacher analyzes the job environment. Emphasize that the employees should be involved and that you are willing to help in any way in conveying the nature of the program. The employer probably has a good idea of who will be most receptive and who most resistive, as well as of the best way to inform the employees of the program in order to gain their support and reduce, if not eliminate, any rejection of the program. Finally, you will need to meet with the supervisor of the work area in order to agree upon program procedures such as the work schedule, a starting date, arranging the work area, and work responsibilities.

SUMMARY

This chapter has described some rudimentary organizational and tactical procedures for negotiating job-training stations. Readers are urged to keep the following six points in mind while developing and enhancing training opportunities:

1. Many definitions are used to describe the nature and function of a job-training station; the authors have presented only one.
2. Many viable strategies may be used for contacting and negotiating with employers, the authors have presented only a few. The individual styles of each member of the contact team will differ and may not be compatible with the ideas presented here. The suggestions provided here are an outgrowth of the authors' experience in successfully negotiating over 100 job-training stations in several different communities.
3. Certainly local circumstances and opportunities have a direct impact on strategies used to develop vocational programs. Each business environment differs, and these unique differences must be recognized when negotiating with employers.
4. The number of students to be served by a particular program, their ages, and their handicaps will have an impact on the overall program. This chapter's perspective is that of a school program serving a wide age range of students who exhibit a broad range of severely handicapping conditions. The reader may alter the strategies, statements and recommendations suggested here according to the unique circumstances of the populations to be served.
5. Certainly the plans, aspirations, interests, and concerns of each student and his or her family must be brought to bear on the development of community-based training so that individualized vocational training programs can be developed and implemented.
6. Particular strategies for negotiating a job-training station were presented in this chaper. A job-training station is intended to be differentiated from an individual job placement. Strategies for negotiating a job placement for an individual upon completion of a training program will naturally differ from many of the strategies and techniques suggested in this paper. Strategies for negotiating job placements are documented in vocational rehabilitation literature (e.g., the *Performance-based Placement Manual* by Bissonnette and Pimentel, 1984). The authors do recognize a need for job-placement strategies to begin incorporating information regarding transitional and supported employment into the negotiation process.

In summary, individual styles, each business environment, and local circumstances all differ and certainly each student must be treated as an individual. Therefore, it is the reader's responsibility to modify and develop alternative techniques from those presented here as appropriate.

One of the major findings of the federally funded projects the authors have been involved in has been the following: *The most efficient and effective transition processes begin with stu-*

dents whose educational history has included a wide range of functional, age-appropriate curricular activities involving community intensive instruction and instruction in actual job environments. In this way, the sending agency (school) can bring to subsequent individualized education program (IEP) meetings information essential for designing and implementing transition plans. The authors' advice is to start with young clients and involve families, case managers, and adult service providers. If the goal of your program is to help students make the transition from school to integrated work options, involve the community.

REFERENCES

Baumgart, D., Brown, L., Pumpian, I., Nisbet, J., Ford, A., Sweet, M., Messina, R., & Schroeder, J. (1982, Summer). Principal of partial participation and individualized adaptations in educational programs. *Journal of the Association for Persons with Severe Handicaps, 7,* 17–27.

Bissonnette, D., & Pimentel, R. (1984). *Performance-based placement manual.* Chatswork, CA: Milt Wright & Associates.

Breen, C., Haring, T., Pitts-Conway, V., & Gaylord-Ross, R. (1985). The training and generalization of social interactions during breaktime at two job sites in the natural environment. In Joyce Forte, Keith Storey, Alice Wershiry, C.G. Ross, Shep Siegel, Jameson J. Pomies (Eds.), *Community vocational training for handicapped youth* (pp. 1–27). Richmond, CA: Richmond Unified School District.

Brown, L., Ford, A., Nisbet, J., Shiraga, B., VanDeventer, P., Sweet, M., & Loomis, R. (1983). *Teaching severely handicapped students to perform meaningful work in non-sheltered environments.* Unpublished manuscript. University of Wisconsin-Madison.

Marshall vs. Baptist Hospital, 473 F. Supp. 465 (1979).

McCarthy, P., Everson, J., Wood-Pietruski, W., Inge, K., & Barcus, M.(1985). Establishing an individual transition process from school to employment for youth with severe disabilities. In P. McCarthy, J. Everson, S. Moon, & M. Barcus (Eds.), *School to work transition* (pp. 21–42). Richmond: Virginia Commonwealth University.

Nisbet, J., Sweet, M., Ford, A., Shiraga, B., Udvari, A., York, J., Messina, R., & Schroeder, J. (1983). Utilizing adaptive devices. In L. Brown, A. Ford, J. Nisbet, M. Sweet, B. Shiraga, J. York, & R. Loomis (Eds.), *Educational programs for severely handicapped students,* Vol.13, pp.101–145.University of Wisconsin-Madison.

Pumpian, I., Baumgart, D., Shiraga, B., Ford, A., Nisbet, J., Loomis, R., & Brown, L. Vocational training programs (1980). In L. Brown, M. Falvey, I. Pumpian, D. Baumgart, J. Nisbet, A. Ford, J. Schroeder, & R. Loomis (Eds.), *Curricular strategies for teaching severely hand-*

icapped students functional skills in school and nonschool environments (pp. 273–310). Madison, WI: Madison Metropolitan School District.

Pumpian, I., Lewis, L., & Engel, T. (1986). *The criteria used to establish a trainee/employer vs. employee/employer relationship: A review of litigation.* Unpublished manuscript, San Diego State University, San Diego.

Pumpian, I. Shiraga, B., Van Deventer, P., Nisbet, J., Sweet, M., Ford M., & Loomis, R. (1981). A strategy for organizing the cumulative job experience and training records. In L. Brown, D. Baumgart, I. Pumpian, J. Nisbet, A. Ford, A. Donnellan, M. Sweet, R. Loomis, & J. Schroeder (Eds.), *Educational programs for severely handicapped students* (pp.279–327). University of Wisconsin-Madison.

Pumpian, I., West, E., & Shepard, H. (1988). The training and employment of persons with severe handicaps. In R. Gaylord-Ross (Ed.), *Vocational education for persons with special needs* (pp. 355–386). San Francisco, San Francisco State University,

Shepard, H., Pumpian, I., & West, E. (1986). Personnel training: Establishing a job training station task force. In B. Ostertag, I. Pumpian, & R. Gaylord-Ross (Eds.), *An interagency approach to meeting the vocational needs of disabled learners: Final report and personnel training modules.* Sacramento: California State Universities.

Vogelsberg, R.T. (1986). Competitive employment in Vermont. In F.R. Rusch (Ed.), *Competitive employment issues and strategies* (pp. 35–50). Baltimore: Paul H. Brookes Publishing Co.

Wehman, P., & Hill, J.W. (1985). *Competitive employment for persons with mental retardation: From research to practice.* Richmond: Virginia Commonwealth University, Rehabilitation Research and Training Center.

Wershing, A., Gaylord-Ross, C., & Gaylord-Ross, R. (1985). *Implementing a community-based vocational training model: A process of systems change.* Unpublished manuscript, San Francisco State University, San Francisco.

Wilcox, B., & Bellamy, G.T.(1982). *Design of high school programs for severely handicapped students.* Baltimore: Paul H. Brookes Publishing Co.

Chapter 13

Rehabilitation Facilities and Community-Based Employment Services

Joseph F. Campbell

The history of evolving community responses to the vocational rehabilitation needs of disabled individuals largely parallels the history of the traditional sheltered workshop. A limited number of vocational models that have been used to assist the nondisabled population have been replicated in the rehabilitation field. These include on-the-job training (OJT), popularized especially by the former Comprehensive Employment and Training Act (CETA) program and early supported work ventures for welfare populations. Perhaps the increasingly popular supported employment models for severely disabled people is where the two traditions merge in the 1980s.

It would be misleading to view traditional workshops as totally incongruous with the OJT or supported work approaches. A brief examination of rehabilitation facilities across the United States demonstrates numerous cases where job-training practices very similar to supported work have been common since the 1970s. In fact, many of the practices employed today in successful supported work programs are rooted in the more traditional workshop approaches.

This chapter provides a brief historical review of the community workshop's evolution in the United States and focuses specifically on the

rehabilitation facility as a provider of noncenter or community-based employment services. It examines the implications of expanding outside the center into a network of supported worksites in community businesses and of transforming the entire workshop to an industrially integrated network of jobs, in which case the facility-based program would no longer exist.

Finally, this chapter looks at some conversion examples from across the country. The Other Resources section at the end of the chapter provides contact information for readers who wish to learn more about a specific case.

THE REHABILITATION FACILITY: ORIGINS AND EVOLUTION

Among the earliest precursors to the sheltered workshop were the work centers established by St. Vincent de Paul in France in the 16th century for poor people, including those with disabilities (Nelson, 1971). In 1526, Juan Luis Vives published *On the Subvention of the Poor*, hypothesizing that dependent persons should be required to work as a contribution for their support. This thesis is a forerunner to the popular 20th-century rehabilitation economic practice that seeks to reduce the handicapped person's dependency on public welfare sources through the person becoming a worker and, therefore, a taxpayer (Conley 1965; 1973).

According to Obermann (1965), the first actual workshop specifically for handicapped people was established in Paris in 1784. It was a workshop for blind persons developed by Valentine Huay, who was deeply influenced by ''rights-of-man'' issues in prerevolutionary France. This marked the beginnings of vocational rehabilitation as a movement, and led to the ultimate establishment of a sheltered workshop for blind persons in Massachusetts in 1834.

In the early part of the 20th century, the rehabilitation movement sprouted public branches as a result of government legislation and private branches owing to the widespread emergence of not-for-profit organizations in different communities. It was not until mid-century that these separate developments were linked to build a strong, publicly funded network of community programs. However, when the public funding came, it was provided for physical facilities and for day services, and was harnessed directly to the traditional economic treatise that increased productivity and earnings reduce public dependency; therefore, programs were focused heavily on productivity and efficiency, as opposed to issues of integration and normalization.

Early 20th-century laws affecting rehabilitation practices involved a series of state and federal initiatives including the first Worker's Compensation Law in the United States in New York in 1910 (Rubin & Roessler, 1978). The Smith Hughes Act of 1917 established vocational education programs for nondisabled people. Although the Soldier Rehabilitation Act (PL 178), in 1918, is often regarded as the parent of current vocational rehabilitation legislation, it made no provision for the civilian disabled population. Such provisions came 2 years later on June 2, 1920, when the United States passed its first federal vocational rehabilitation law, PL 236, for disabled civilians. This act established a state-federal partnership whereby 50% in matching funds was required from participating states for any federal allocations made. No significant funding was made available for facilities, tuition, or research and development

until 1954. In the 1960s, however, the greatest flow of public resources to community programs took place. By 1968, federal funds required only a 20% match from states, and grants were made available to build new facilities, as opposed to earlier funding for remodeling and expansion (Bitter, 1979).

As one might guess, the first community providers in the early 20th century included organizations like Goodwill Industries, the Salvation Army, and the Easter Seal Society. Other freestanding organizations also participated in these early efforts. Among the first was a program known as Boston Community Workshops.

Many small community-activity-type programs emerged during these years, often supervised by groups of parents of developmentally disabled people. When public funding became available, most of these programs acquired workshop characteristics and eventually took advantage of increasingly available funds for improved buildings and production equipment. During the heightened funding period of the Kennedy-Johnson era (early and mid-1960s), services to mentally retarded and mentally ill consumers increased dramatically (Campbell, 1984).

The need for services in the aftermath of the 1963 Mental Health Act focused new attention on local private community rehabilitation centers. Thousands of deinstitutionalized people, previously served in state schools and mental hospitals, appeared at the doors of local agencies. In the 25 years since the 1963 act, millions of dollars in program service contracts have been made available to sheltered workshops, with the number of facilities growing from 85 U.S. Department of Labor certified workshops in 1948 to more than 5,000 in 1987.

By the mid 1970s, many of these traditional shops had developed sophisticated production facilities that were involved in prime manufacturing or in providing an efficient subcontracting service to local industry. Often the facilities developed a capacity for providing stable, highly paid work opportunities to clients. Also, in many cases, multimillion-dollar government contracts were awarded through the NISH (National Industries for the Severely Handicapped) program, sponsored by the Javitts, Wagner, O'Day Act of 1971. A number of states have replicated this federal set-aside initiative. During the 1960s and 70s, facility operations improved greatly under the influence of the Commission on Accreditation of Rehabilitation Facilities. This national accrediting body developed demanding performance standards for sheltered workshops, which several states required their facilities to adopt.

By 1980, several traditional facilities had successful transitional employment programs (TEP) in place, based in more integrated settings outside the shop (Gerber, 1979; Wehman, 1981). Most of these efforts were seen as extensions of the workshop itself and were not meant to supplant it as a vocational rehabilitation model. For example, some traditional workshops participated in the Projects With Industry (PWI) Program. This program was established with federal funding in 1970 to link disabled workers directly with employers. Ten years after its inception, PWI was providing approximately 100 programs involving more than 5,000 corporations across America. Although the program represented a substantial alternative to the regular workshop-based program, it had a major limitation as a full alternative: the PWI program only serves less disabled clients who have an obvious capacity for competitive employment.

TRADITIONAL REHABILITATION FACILITY AS A SUPPORTED WORK PROVIDER

As of 1987, numerous traditional work centers have established networks of industry-based work opportunities for their clientele. These sites, many of which provide supported work, are usually seen by the sponsoring organizations as added options for their consumers with disabilities. In some instances, organizations have closed down their workshop entirely in favor of an industry-integrated supported work system (Campbell, 1985). Still, some traditional workshop organizations reject the newer supported work models as unstable and threatening to the traditional facility. It is appropriate here to examine briefly

these basic principles that seem to divide these schools of thought.

Early architects of supported work programs often criticized traditional workshops in contrast to their new approaches. Supported work theorists based their case mainly around opportunities for integration in the workplace and higher wages that supported work allows, and cited a variety of studies characterizing traditional facilities as stagnant places to work, with only the slightest hope of graduation to a nonsheltered competitive job. These efforts to identify supported work as more "successful" than the workshop may have contributed to some alienation of traditional providers of vocational services. Some traditionalists feared the new noncenter-based model would render their cherished physical facilities redundant. Other organizations had merged their organizational or corporate identities with their physical centers to the point that they could not easily identify their workshops as service models that, if shed or modified, need not mean the end of their agency or organization. Others saw supported work as a model suited to the more robust economy of the mid-80s, but heralded their workshop as a stable model in times of economic recession.

Principles and Functions

An analysis of what a well-balanced, stable supported employment system should provide suggests that perhaps the traditionalist and the new-age provider can together supply the elements of an ideal system. However, both parties must first accept certain basic principles underlying employment services for severely disabled people and must recognize that the long-term dependency of many clients calls for planned, secure employment supports for decades ahead, in both good and bad economic climates. This latter consideration has been a concern of many parent groups who have watched the illusionary stability of "bricks and mortar" give way to progressive, integrated models.

At the core of supported employment is an identification of the client problem. This problem is identified foremost as unemployment (Campbell, 1985). Local businesses, rather than the human service organizations, are seen as holding the solutions to the unemployment problem. Their workplaces have status, and disabled workers placed there, although with supports, are less likely to be stigmatized. The end result is enhanced perceptions of handicapped people by community members and ultimately enhanced self-perceptions by the disabled individuals themselves.

In the supported work model, the human service organization retains two very important roles. The unemployed client is *linked* to the employer, and the relationship is in turn *supported* by creative program staff. Generally, these varying support methodologies constitute a variety of different types of supported work models. Traditional facilities usually have well-developed industrial contacts and years of subcontract marketing and procurement experience. This would suggest that traditional work centers have at least part of what is needed to build a strong supported work program. The support methodology will vary, however, from that generally provided by traditional workshop staff.

The author's perceptions in discussing these matters with traditional providers across the United States is that direct-care staff and program managers make the adjustment toward industry-based models readily and eagerly. Boards of directors and senior management struggle more with the philosophical issues in most corporations. Therefore, organizational leaders are more apt to become ensnared in discussions of *why* they should change. Even when change is agreed upon, it is sometimes with the anticipation of failure and the expectation of a return to the "old order." Such a lack of clear, value-based commitment to integrated, status-filled employment opportunities can be a certain recipe for failure. Traditional facilities must beware of this tendency to fail with new endeavors if there is a concomitant decision to maintain a workshop. So long as a workshop exists, even as a fallback option, there is less pressure to make programs work outside the facility.

Although traditional facilities are well prepared in many respects to be supported-work providers, they may need very unique and committed leadership to successfully maintain *both* the traditional workshop and supported work

models successfully. For this reason, many organizations are converting entirely to industry-integrated supported work systems.

Models and Practices

Since most traditional centers have, on occasion, sent groups of clients into a host industry on a temporary basis, they will have little difficulty successfully organizing the typical enclave. The enclave arrangement is for a block of labor on a permanent basis. The contract or agreement between the parties is similar to the typical subcontract or temporary work-crew agreement. There may be a requirement by the host industry that the vocational organization provide evidence of liability insurance covering its clients in the industrial worksite. Pricing will often vary from typical subcontract pricing, since workshop overhead is not now a factor and transportation of goods is not necessary. Obviously, pricing should be based on the actual cost of labor, including benefits, administrative overhead, any additional actual costs, and, finally, whatever profit markup the market will bear. An alternative manner of pricing is based on the work-crew approach. In this approach, a dollar amount per hour for either the entire crew or per individual may be agreed upon. Normally, the components of this rate are those described above, including actual costs and a margin for profit.

The author's experience suggests that the traditional approach to productivity measurement is too stringent and that clients who exceed 60% in performance can handle competitive employment. Employers are looking for dependability and quality. High productivity is not always compatible with these traits. Traditional facilities must also recognize the significant weight of data suggesting that clients increase their productivity when they transfer from the workshop to the new environment of the host-industry. Managers must be careful not to lock themselves in at prices that are inadequate to meet the possibility of increased earnings.

Facilities that have provided OJT, PWI, or TEP-type transitional employment services will be experienced in managing a network of individual supported sites. They must make some adjustments, however, in these arrangements to include the more severely disabled consumer in such settings. Whereas the less handicapped individual may be supervised by the host industry with only occasional visits from agency counselors, the more severely disabled client may need an agency staff person present on a full-time basis. This staff involvement, or "job-coaching," as described in the new supported work lexicon, may reduce gradually as the consumer builds more skills and independence.

The ideal supported work system will have a built-in dynamic that moves the client to the most integrated or most normal setting possible (Campbell, 1986). The presence of a continuum, ranging from group to individual placements, while useful for serving an entire range of clients, creates the danger that participants will tend toward the less challenging lower levels. Traditional organizations must guard heavily against this possibility, since they may be overinfluenced by the client's need for security. Some organizations handle this by establishing a strict set of developmental criteria which is used in individual planning and counseling (Incentive Community Enterprises [ICE], 1981). Clients are scored against competencies and then are placed in settings likely to "lock-in" competencies achieved, while individual plans address the next levels of competency on the continuum.

More important is an atmosphere that promotes and supports ambition. Ambition is only present when opportunity is recognized as available. Providers must constantly show their clients what new opportunities for enhanced employment are available. For example, a worker at an enclave might aspire toward upward placement at a different company that is recognized as a "great place to work." Making these opportunities known, and coaching clients to become ambitious for better opportunities, is an important aspect of an employment development program for severely disabled people.

Employment Security without the Workshop

As mentioned previously, organizations that choose to maintain a sheltered workshop may have less motivation or pressure to keep the client working "out" in industry. On the other hand, one could agree that the client has the advantage of the additional option of the workshop model without having to change from one provider agency to another. The author's experience in providing both types of services has been that while the workshop exists, it will tend to get used, perhaps unnecessarily.

It is exceptionally difficult for some supported-work disciples to see the sheltered workshop as a fall-back option. Yet reasonable service planners may recognize that the fall-back concept itself is necessary.

Traditional providers often express concern that temporary employment bonanzas may fizzle and that few potential host industries exist in certain areas. Sometimes parents may see more long-term security in a sheltered workshop than in the relatively unstable small business where their son or daughter is placed. These legitimate security and stability concerns suggest that a supported work program that seeks to serve the entire needs of a community has significant responsibilities. If the traditional facility is not to play a part, then the new program must provide a wide range of options allowing for client movement, loss of jobs, failure of host industries, lack of industry, and ever-changing models. The facility must also have the capacity to address the concerns of family members who seek long-term program security. How can a supported work system address these areas adequately and still maintain the integrated and dynamic qualities that the approach espouses?

Obviously, the greatest protection against unemployment for supported-work participants is the availability of a large reservoir of job opportunities. However, a variety of additional job-security arrangements exist in the absence of the traditional workshop. Many successful organizations operate a continuum of models, including individually coached positions at the most integrated end of the continuum and highly supported enclaves at the more sheltered end. Although the enclaves are geared toward those participants who need a more structured supported environment, they can act as a fall-back location for the more capable client between jobs. It is the author's experience that the development of a continuum should always begin with a couple of enclaves. Without the enclaves in place as a temporary placement location, or as a "security net," clients may spend too many days in their residences. This may be especially valid when dealing with mental health consumers.

Traditional facilities already deal with a range of abilities. For that reason, they are most likely to establish a continuum. They must make certain, however, that clients are not forced unnecessarily to navigate every level. The author has experienced successful competitive placements from the lowest step on a five-step continuum where a host industry recruited clients from an enclave!

Traditional providers have established some unique enclaves that loosely resemble workshop operations, yet maintain heightened integration and keep numbers in keeping with federal mandates. Some such enclaves even use rented space from a host industry—as close as possible to where the action is on the plant floor. Then, when work is not available from the host industry, subcontract work is carried in. Such an enclave provides similar security to the traditional shop and is an excellent fall-back arrangement. Even prime manufacturing can be conducted at these sites. NISH contracts can be handled at selected enclaves.

The author encourages organizations to have a network of such enclaves, ideally using them for disabled clients only when more integrated work is not available. One often forgets that nonhandicapped workers can be hired to keep these back-burner sites available. Ideally the enclave is used during a short transitional period for evaluation and adjustment. Enclaves may be used for long-term employment arrangements where participants are very severely handicapped and where individual placement, or placement in smaller groups, is not feasible.

The small affirmative industry is another model popular with traditional providers where jobs are scarce or where increased levels of employer tolerance are needed for specific clientele. Such affirmative industries, like the enclaves just described, may also provide a significant backup for unexpected days of unemployment or for periods of recession. Typical examples of affirmative industries are mobile janitorial crews, restaurants, bakeries, and even gas stations.

Large affirmative industries operated by rehabilitation facilities, although often highly developed in a business sense, do not meet the basic requirements of a typical supported work program. The affirmative business should hire not more than six or eight clients, and the environmental arrangement should facilitate interaction with the general public. Too often, the affirmative industry concept is confused with a more entrepreneurial type of business established to produce an alternative funding source for the program. If this outcome occurs with an affirmative industry, then it is obviously an added advantage. The true affirmative industry, however, is conceived, planned, and implemented with the primary objective of providing integrated employment to disabled people. More often than not, it may need to be subsidized with program funds rather than proving to be a money-spinner.

What if Models Change . . . Again?!

After the issue of fall-back, traditional facilities' next greatest concern seems to be that of changing models. One often hears concern expressed that supported work may not be a lasting approach. Regardless of how models change, the *organization behind the model* will still be there. In fact, it will be there to pick up with the next popular model, and the next again if necessary. If Sears Roebuck and Company refused to carry a line of merchandise for fear it would not be fashionable forever, the company would soon lose its customers. Our agencies are the businesses or companies behind our models. Our models are our lines of merchandise, which will change appropriately with the times. Parents and advocates in general must be informed that security comes from a well-managed, stable business—not from the bricks and mortar of the workshop model itself.

The distinction between the business behind the model and the model itself suggests that organizations developing supported work programs must pay attention not only to today's creative programming but also to building a secure, well-managed organization. Traditional facilities that have begun providing supported work services have a jump on other service providers in that they have already undergone a model change. They can demonstrate to concerned others that, in spite of changing models, a strong organization remains constant, ready to make the best state-of-the-art services available to its consumers.

The Problem of an Empty Building

Among the greatest challenges to workshop service providers is the issue of an empty or underutilized building. In many cases the physical facilities have been the essence of an agency's identity. Successful capital campaigns have pumped millions of dollars of community funds into new buildings, and often the name of a major donor has been attached to the building. It can be politically difficult to close and sell a building that is named after the deceased member of a prominent community family.

Similarly, there are numerous instances across the country where cities or towns have made HUD funds available to community agencies to build work centers for people with disabilities. In most cases, there is a clear stipulation that the center must be used for the purpose intended or it reverts back to the city or town.

These political issues, though less profound than the intense issues of integration and human dignity, may pose equally serious challenges to managers of traditional rehabilitation facilities. In addressing the political and economic problems posed by an empty building versus responding to the issues of changing service models, managers should recognize that these are, in fact, two separate problems. The problem of providing more integrated employment services to workshop clientele should not go unsolved because of the new problem that the solution might create. The secondary problems require their own solutions, with their own plans and strategies.

Many organizations develop a plan to turn their physical plant into a source of funds. Some organizations sell the building and invest the proceeds. Others rent the entire facility to one company or bring in a number of smaller businesses as tenants and, on occasion, use these as "host" employers. When an agency maintains a worksite in the new tenant's business at the

workshop location, there must be an expectation that some original workshop perceptions may remain. A period of time may need to elapse so that what was seen as a facility for handicapped people can take on a different community profile.

EXAMPLES OF TRADITIONAL ORGANIZATIONS AS SUPPORTED WORK PROVIDERS

In addition to the information provided here, addresses and persons to contact are included in the Other Resources at the end of the chapter.

The Plus Company, Inc., New Hampshire

The Plus Company was established in 1972 and provides services to a cross-section of disabled people in southern New Hampshire and northeast Massachusetts. The organization established its reputation as a provider of quality sheltered employment and work activity services in its two sheltered workshops. In addition, since 1978, the Plus Company has maintained actual placements in industrial settings outside the workshops. These early placements followed the usual TEP model: individual placements with short-term, intermittent supports. These placements, when successful, led to competitive employment.

More recently the organization has developed a network of supported group sites in local businesses, including both manufacturing and service businesses. These arrangements are modeled on a typical work-station-in-industry approach, including enclaves and smaller, more integrated sites. The Plus Company runs a mobile janitorial crew that includes five to six participants. Current plans are to develop this business further. The Plus Company also provides employment services to approximately 125 clientel, 50 of whom are served outside its workshops.

Long-range plans call for maintaining the company's main workshop while engineering its adaptation to a major industrial profit-making venture hiring nondisabled workers, but also including a small number of handicapped employees on the work force. It is interesting to note that the organization has articulated its commitment to the concept that "everyone is deserving of an opportunity to work outside the facility at an *appropriate* community site."

According to Plus Company president Stuart Smith, running the sheltered workshops has helped the organization immensely in the task of establishing supported work settings in community sites. Some areas in which it has helped, according to Smith, include strong business relationships, marketing capacity, knowledge of the state Department of Regulations, transportation experience, and overall busines management experience.

Although the Plus Company is committed to opportunities outside the workshop for all its consumers and is gradually reducing workshop numbers, the management believes the workshop can be useful, particularly in the unfortunate event of a site closing.

AVATRAC, Colorado

AVATRAC established its community workshop in 1966 and added a second facility in 1979. Both facilities are not consolidated while the organization implements a 4-year corporate plan to phase out its workshops entirely.

Although the organization has been decentralizing its work services only since 1986, AVATRAC has provided PWI (Projects with Industry) on a small scale since 1980.

As of early 1987, the organization had already arranged employer connections for 86 supported workers. Fifty-two of these work in individual sites and 34 are in group sites with staff supervision. Altogether, the organization provides employment services to approximately 300 people.

Among industry-based arrangements in AVATRAC's network are the following: a janitorial mobile crew; food court maintenance crew in a shopping mall; a housekeeping crew in a hotel; a car lot crew that provides service to five auto companies; and a group site in a document microfilming company, which handles all document preparation.

Although AVATRAC believes in the total conversion of its workshops to more integrated services, the organization is adamant that managing its workshop facilities has prepared it exceptionally well for the transition to an industry-

based system. AVATRAC's director, Mary Jo Tomsick, suggests that if workshops have been respected by community businesses, they are already ahead in the supported work effort. Tomsick reports that 50% of the membership of their very successful Business Advisory Council for the development of supported work sites comprises past workshop customers.

Elwyn Institute, California

The California Elwyn Insititute has developed a network of noncenter based services called the "Employment Services Network." The network currently serves 75 workers and involves a selection of supported work models, including individual supported placements, mobile janitorial crews, and group sites in industry.

Although the organization runs two large traditional facilities serving 450 clients and plans to maintain its workshops in the immediate future, it has developed a policy that clearly calls for "an increased level of staff and service intervention . . . to provide transitional services, to create an atmosphere of transition, and to maximize client integration." The goal of its Employment Services Network is to shift California Elwyn Institute Programs from the traditional-sheltered model to a transitional-integrated model." Executive Director Joseph Piccari suggests that what his organization has done is "take the two concepts (traditional and industry-based) and integrate them rather than cause them to be at odds with one another."

Dr. Piccari suggests that the experience of working with clients in the workshop setting assisted his staff to become "better placement counselors and better supported employment job coaches."

Incentive Community
Enterprises, Massachusetts

This author is particularly familiar with the Incentive Community Enterprises (ICE) experience in converting four workshops to an industrially integrated employment system, having served as executive director of the agency during the actual transition. ICE is a typical community nonprofit organization, established in 1973. The agency provides services to a cross-section of disabled people, but especially to those with mental health and developmental disabilities. ICE provides employment in integrated settings to approximately 375 people daily throughout western Massachusetts and Connecticut.

In 1981, Incentive Community Enterprises decided that more integrated employment opportunities would better serve its clientele. The board of directors adopted a staff blueprint for replacing its facilities with an industrial continuum ranging from enclave-type settings to employer-supervised individual sites. At the same time, the organization adopted a 3-year plan for the transition.

Six years later, the ICE organization has a highly developed network of industry-based sites with approximately 140 employers. These sites include numerous types of industry and span both urban and rural communities. The ICE system includes a range of employment options featuring elements of all the popular supported work models.

In addition to its creative employment arrangements, ICE, in partnership with the University of Massachusetts, operates an innovative "supported training" program. The hotel school at the university matches college juniors with ICE clients for a two-semester program leading to a special graduation and diploma. In the process, university students, tomorrow's managers in the hospitality industry, are alerted to the potential of people with disabilities, and the ICE clientele acquire top skills as well as the status of attending a university-based program. ICE, using the University of Massachusetts model as a prototype, is negotiating similar supported training arrangements with other public training institutions in western New England.

ICE has phased out all its workshop programs and is committed to maintaining all its services in integrated community settings.

CONCLUSION

This chapter has demonstrated that the traditional agency is a well-qualified organizational unit to provide the more integrated work pro-

grams popular today. It has been emphasized that, in the absence of "the bricks and mortar" of work centers, a stable company or organizational entity is necessary to maintain credibility and to respond to parent fears regarding unstable employment settings. Traditional facilities have in most cases built respected organizations, but they must recognize that radical changes in service delivery methods do not constitute a failure or a rejection of these organizations. Facility managers must face change with a willingness to respond to demands for new models or be prepared to see their organizations become obsolete. Supported work is only one proven method among the many potentially creative approaches for linking disabled people with existing business. It is hoped that numerous approaches will appear as the human services field continues to evolve and as services to disabled people generally become more aligned with those for the population at large.

Many existing traditional facilities have already begun to provide integrated options. Some programs have chosen to convert totally to non-center-based programs, while others have attempted both. Whether or not an agency can successfully provide both services has not been resolved. Generally, the values-base driving an organization's leadership determines whether or not the workshop continues as a fall-back or affirmative industry arrangement. The author's experience suggests that as staff and clientele become exposed to noncenter-based models, the traditional facility becomes less and less acceptable.

Perhaps the entire debate hinges less on the actual mode of employment and more on how one views employment in the individual's life. One must ask what is the primary effect expected of employment, and subsequently choose models and methodologies consistent with this expectation. If our main interest is in providing an opportunity for high earning potential, then a sophisticated pallet manufacturing workshop could perhaps assure good earnings to its sheltered workers. Most supported work disciples, however, see work as a medium that carries the individual to new levels of personal and societal worth and provides a proud answer to the question, "What do you do?" The traditional rehabilitation organization has the capacity to become a powerful community force in establishing disabled people as real workers in real employment settings. Presumably it will rise to the challenge.

REFERENCES

Bitter, J. A. (1979). *Introduction to rehabilitation*. St. Louis: C. V. Mosby.

Campbell, J. F. (1984). *An industrially integrated model versus the sheltered workshop in the vocational rehabilitation of mentally isabled persons*. Ann Arbor: University Microfilms International.

Campbell, J. F. (1985). *Supported work approaches for the traditional rehabilitation facility*. Washington, DC: National Association of Rehabilitation Facilities.

Campbell, J. F. (1986). Concepts and principles related to supported employment. In *Developmental Disability Highlights*. Tucson: Commission on Accreditation of Rehabilitation Facilities.

Conley, R. W. (1965). *The economics of vocational rehabilitation*. Baltimore: Johns Hopkins University Press.

Conley, R. W. (1973). *The economics of mental retardation*. Baltimore: Johns Hopkins University Press.

Gerber, N. M. (1979, February-March). The job worksite: An additional resource in preparing psychiatric clients for job placement. *Journal of Rehabilitation, 45* (1), 39–41.

Incentive Community Enterprises. (1981). *Vocational manual*. Unpublished program manual, Northampton, MA.

Nelson, N. (1971). *Workshops for the handicapped*. Springfield, IL.: Charles C Thomas.

Obermann, C. E. (1965). *A history of vocational rehabilitation in America*. Minneapolis: T. S. Denison & Co.

Rubin, S. E., & Roessler, R. T. (1978). *Foundations of the vocational rehabilitation process*. Baltimore: University Park Press.

Wehman, P. (1981). *Competitive employment: New horizons for severely disabled individuals*. Baltimore: Paul H. Brookes Publishing Co.

OTHER RESOURCES

The following are addresses and contact persons for those organizations mentioned in the chapter:

The Plus Company, Inc., 43 Simon St., Nashua, NH 03060. Contact person: Stuart Smith, President.

AVATRAC, 1930 S. Rosemary St., Denver, CO 80223.

Contact person: Mary Jo Tomsick, Director, Adult Services.

Elwyn Institute, 18325 Mt. Baldy Circle, Fountain Valley, CA 92708. Contact person: Dr. Joseph Piccari, Executive Director.

Incentive Community Enterprises, Inc., 441 Pleasant St., Northampton, MA 01060. Contact person: Susan Keenan-Jabari, Vice President of Employment and Training.

Chapter 14

Organizational Analysis of Values Relative to Supported Work

Walter A. Chernish and Roy Beziat

There are approximately 5,000 sheltered workshops in the United States providing one or more rehabilitation services to adults experiencing disability. The first sheltered workshop opened in Boston in 1905 as Morgan Memorial Cooperative Stores (Beziat, 1984). It was the first Goodwill Industries–type program, and it proved that a work force of people with disabilities could competitively produce goods and provide services to local business and industry. Many community-based rehabilitation facilities continue to do so every day as they bring work from community businesses into the controlled workplace of a sheltered workshop or activity program.

In the 1970s, many sheltered workshops entered into the proprietary manufacture of items to be marketed to middlemen or end-users. In this way facilities created more jobs in sheltered employment, often at higher wages than in the past.

The move to proprietary enterprise was fueled by the availability of large contracts providing opportunities for wages two or three times the minimum wage through the National Industries for the Severely Handicapped program. NISH provides opportunities for sheltered facilities to obtain contracts to provide goods and services to the federal government and the military services. Through NISH contracts, facilities are able to modernize, automate, and upgrade the level of the work performed by their workers, and to pay the highest wages they have ever paid to large numbers of severely handicapped people in a noncompetitive employment setting.

Rehabilitation facilities, in their role as the providers of initial job training and employment opportunities, as the creators of an expanded employment market, and as the sources of steadily increasing wages, are the nation's primary source of nonmedical rehabilitation services (Pacinelli, 1984). In 1985, 28% of all the funds expended by the state-federal program of rehabilitation went to facilities (Rehabilitation Services Administration, 1987).

Facilities have succeeded at what they were created to do—to provide opportunities for people to work and to earn. Advocates who sought to develop organizations that would provide alternatives to homebound adulthood have been rewarded through the establishment of stable, wage-earning alternatives.

The advent of supported employment as an alternative rehabilitation methodology now forces

This chapter is a revised version of a paper that appeared in E. Getzel (Ed.). (1987). *Waves of the future*. Richmond: Virginia Commonwealth University, Virginia Institute for Developmental Disabilities.

rehabilitation facilities to examine their values base to consider inclusion or adoption of a "place-train-follow-along" approach, and to focus upon increased integration of the work force.

TRADITIONAL PROGRAM VALUES

The principal values inherent in traditional sheltered employment programs include:

1. Security: Assurance that the alternative to homebound adulthood will always be there.
2. Gradualism: Change will not be traumatic; it will be evolutionary and controlled, not increasing worker stress.
3. Equity: Whenever possible, all opportunities and rewards will be distributed equally.

These values can be traced to the early desires of parents and family members of young adults with disabilities who had been denied access to schools, public recreation programs, job training, and employment. They were anxious that their children would be provided a secure, consistent vocational opportunity that could not be taken away by government or "professionals."

Times have changed. Public Law 94-142 opened the doors of the public schools to students with disabilities. Section 504 of the Rehabilitation Act of 1973 increased the awareness of the recreation and business communities of their obligation to include those with disabilities. The Carl Perkins Amendments to the Vocational Education Act, passed in 1986, require cooperation between vocational education, special education, and vocational rehabilitation.

The goal of deinstitutionalization has been replaced with the goal of social role valorization. Separate but equal has been replaced by "same."

NEW PROGRAM VALUES

This clarification and redefinition of societal values requires that managers and board members of nonprofit rehabilitation facilities consider a new set of program values:

Severity of disability: The power of the service model and the expense of services should be appropriate for the degree of disability of the consumer.

Variety of employment models: Consumers should exercise options in the choice of work models/ environments.

Hours worked: Total hours worked in any employment model is an indication of that model's success, along with amount of wages and degree of integration.

Level of earnings: The higher the better.

Environmental settings: The environment within which work is performed is as important as the work opportunity itself.

These revised operational values require: 1) physical and social integration in the workplace, 2) equal pay for equal work, and 3) the end of vocational stereotyping, which placed thousands of people experiencing disabilities into entry-level positions in our "food and filth" industries while excluding most other opportunities.

It is important to consider the influence of each of these new operational values in the management of rehabilitation service programs.

Severity of Disability

Values determine what is important, what is possible, and what is impossible. The values an organization exhibits with regard to severity of disability determine which employment opportunities and outcomes will be made available to people with different disabilities and varying degrees of function. More specifically, this set of values will control the availability of alternative programs, the intensity of service, the employment goals and end results, and the total amount of organizational resources dedicated to services for each disability group.

Thousands of severely disabled people languish in "low-level" day programs because productive work is not yet valued for this group. Yet, examples abound of men and women with incredibly severe disabilities who are working in socially integrated settings and earning significant wages.

Factors Involved in Selecting Employment Models

It is no longer appropriate to provide only one type of employment within a community to people with disabilities. These individuals deserve choices. For some people, part-time employment is more likely and beneficial than full-time work. Yet, many organizations only consider full-time employment to be *real* work. As discussed in Chapter 2 of this book, there are numerous models to draw upon in supported employment. The option of job-sharing is just one example of an employment alternative that should be available for less than full-time employment.

Many facilities accept the role of employer of last resort. They provide work that no one else wants to do to people who can find no other work. Neither the worker nor the work is valued in these situations. Other facilities specialize in one or two types of work to become more profitable and reduce their reliance upon public funding. Some specialize in packaging, others in bulk mailing, salvage, or restoration. When rehabilitation facilities consciously limit the types of work available within their walls, they create an obligation to provide more varied alternatives outside. A facility that specializes in the business of mass mailing could provide work crews, enclaves, and individualized training and supported employment in other areas of activity through its community-based programs.

If work and workers are to be valued by the organization, options must be available to provide opportunities to many types of workers experiencing disabilities to perform numerous kinds of work.

Number of Work
Hours and Level of Earnings

Years ago facilities thought they were doing their job if they provided disabled people an alternative to sitting at home. There might be some work, some time for crafts, lunch, recreation, and socialization in each day. The important thing was to fill the day. Many facilities adopted a policy to pay workers for every hour of the workday regardless of the actual hours worked. This was only possible when piece-rated hourly wages were very low. In many activity centers, work is still viewed as inconsequential.

If the number of hours worked is to be valued, there must be enough real hours of real work paying real wages to people valued for the sub-

stantial contribution they can make. Is it better to provide 20 hours of highly sophisticated work at high wages than to provide 40 hours of less sophisticated work at lower wages? This depends upon an organization's values. By the same token, is it better to earn $50 for 10 hours of work or $150 for 40? This values conflict must be resolved between the client and service provider for job satisfaction to occur.

Environmental Settings

The work setting usually reflects how much a worker is valued. For example, compare the office of a company president with that of the janitor in any employment setting. In the private as well as the public sector, the value of a worker may be measured in terms of the square feet of office space provided.

What might be inferred about the value of the work and the worker in a setting where 200 people sit in folding chairs at folding tables inserting plastic spoons into plastic bags? Certainly there is equality, but at a very low level. Neither the work nor the worker can be seen as very important in such a work environment.

Compare that scene to another where workers are busy at a variety of individualized work stations, using power tools, speaking with supervisors. More value is accorded the work as well as the worker. Many sheltered workshops provide these kinds of work environments, but they are still segregated. Only people with disabilities work there.

Supported employment provides a different setting. In supported-work environments, people work in public places and private industries in often highly engineered work spaces. Some of the workers have disablilities, others do not. In enclaves and work crews, people with disabilities are often surrounded by nonhandicapped workers. Other supported work situations do not afford much integration; for instance, the janitorial crew works at night when the building is empty. However, the work environment is open to all, and disability is not a determining factor in the work setting.

All jobs can be said to occur in environments where coworkers are either isolated, segregated, or integrated. The relative degree of isolation, segregation, or integration of the workplace is determined by the tasks that are required to be performed. A monetary value is placed on the job to be performed, based upon degree of difficulty of the tasks, supply of the labor force to perform the tasks, and conditions of the work environment. A greater monetary value may be assigned to jobs requiring higher levels of isolation and segregation from coworkers because of a smaller labor pool willing to perform these jobs (i.e., a second and third shift generally command greater wages than the first shift). The disabled worker, however, has been isolated or segregated from coworkers in the work environment not for reasons of job demand, but because of disability.

The question facing rehabilitation facilities is how to balance the needs of business and industry for qualified workers to perform jobs in isolated and segregated work environments, versus the rehabilitative need to place workers into highly integrated work environments to counter previous employment practices. Decisions must be made by the client and rehabilitative staff at the facility about whether to place a greater value on the job environment or on the monetary outcome that may be achieved in the integrated settings. There is nothing magical about an individualized placement, an enclave, or a mobile work crew. Each can be provided anywhere along a continuum of disability, earnings, integration, or work options. However, each adds to the mix, expands the possibilities, and creates new opportunities.

Tables 1–3 demonstrate a number of employment outcomes for disabled individuals in isolated, segregated, and integrated work environments, respectively. Within each work environment there may be greater or lesser degrees of isolation, segregation, or integration as well as varying levels of compensation. It is incumbent upon facility staff to assess these values in the context of the client and his or her family's needs and interests.

VALUES CLARIFICATION

When considering the implementation of a supported employment program, management must begin at the level of organizational values (Kaplan, 1985). Two types of values exist within organizations. The first type, proposed values, are reflected in the organization's mission statement, or statement of purpose, created at the time of a group's nonprofit incorporation. The second type of values, expressed values, can be identified by examining the outcomes of organizational existence (Greenleaf, 1977).

Proposed Values

The following is a typical mission statement of a facility incorporated in the 1950s or 1960s. "The purpose of the [entity's name] is to provide employment and training to [designation of target disability group] so that they will be employed at their optimal level." The values suggested here were employment and training, and led to organizations that produced the following outcomes:

Separate programs of evaluation, work adjustment, personal adjustment, sheltered employment, and placement

Highly isolated and segregated work settings

Table 1. Organizational values: Isolation versus earnings

Isolated work environment: A work environment that allows few or no interactions with other disabled or nondisabled individuals because of the constraints of the work environment.

HIGH WAGE, HIGH ISOLATION	LOW WAGE, HIGH ISOLATION
Employment situation: Five workers clean five-story office building. Each worker cleans a separate floor. Workers earn $6.00 per hour.	Employment situation: Two workers clean restaurant. One cleans dining room only; one cleans kitchen only. Workers earn $4.00 per hour.

HIGH WAGE, LOW ISOLATION	LOW WAGE, LOW ISOLATION
Employment situation: Five workers clean five-story office building. All workers clean each floor as a crew. Workers earn $5.00 per hour.	Employment situation: Two workers clean restaurant. They clean dining room and kitchen together. Workers earn $3.35 per hour.

Table 2. Organizational values: Segregation versus earnings

Segregated work environment: A work environment that employs people in relatively close proximity to one another, and the disabled individual is excluded from interaction with a significant portion of the nondisabled work force because of the restrictive conditions of the job.

HIGH WAGE, HIGH SEGREGATION	LOW WAGE, HIGH SEGREGATION
Employment situation: Works in manufacturing company employing 50 people. Individual operates stamping machine in room by himself or herself. Worker earns $7.00 per hour.	Employment situation: Works in micrographics company employing 30 people. Works as filmer in room alone. Worker earns $3.35 per hour.
HIGH WAGE, LOW SEGREGATION	**LOW WAGE, LOW SEGREGATION**
Employment situation: Works in sheltered industry that employs 40 people. Works on production line in room with 5 nondisabled persons. Worker earns $6.00 per hour.	Employment situation: Works in bindery employing 25 persons on an assembly line in a room with 4 nondisabled persons. Worker earns $1.68 per hour.

Workers divided into homogeneous ability (productivity) groups

Average worker wages of less than 25% of the minimum wage

Industry average of 20% "down time" (no work to do)

Annual placement of 10% of workers into competitive employment

Creation of 5,000 community sheltered workshops, many of which had long waiting lists for services

Over 80% of the people with disabilities unemployed

Over 25% of the entire direct service budget of the state-federal Program of Vocational Rehabilitation spent in facilities

Expressed Values

The outcomes just listed demonstrated the expressed values of the organizations, the ones that were incorporated into the daily operations of programs. Those values are:

Efficiency through segregation, isolation, and ability grouping (the same as those of the public school system prior to PL 94-142)

Reliance upon manual labor to stretch the hours of work needed to produce products (the same approach used by Mahatma Gandhi in India to combat large-scale unemployment)

Security by not rushing workers through the "rehab process" (the same approach espoused by the gradualists in the Civil Rights movement)

Safety by isolating disabled workers from the rest of the community (the same value that led to the development of mental institutions)

All of this is not to say that sheltered workshops are evil, wasteful, or should be replaced. Rather, each of these values, although in and

Table 3. Organizational values: Integration versus earnings

Integrated work environment: A work environment in which the worker interacts frequently with nondisabled individuals.

HIGH WAGE, HIGH INTEGRATION	LOW WAGE, LOW INTEGRATION
Employment situation: Worker picks up and delivers mail and documents in an office employing 250 persons in 15 divisions. Worker earns $6.00 per hour.	Employment situation: Worker collects tickets from patrons at an amusement park. Worker earns $4.35 per hour.
HIGH WAGE, LOW INTEGRATION	**LOW WAGE, LOW INTEGRATION**
Employment situation: Worker stages material in welding shop for 6 welders. Worker earns $7.00 per hour.	Employment situation: Worker towels cars dry in a car wash with drying crew of 3. Worker earns $3.35 per hour.

of themselves seeming positive, had negative as well as positive consequences. The desire for safety often led to isolation. The desire to fill work hours led to inefficient work methods and low pay. The desire to reduce stress and to provide a secure environment led to the creation of more facilities and the placement into employment of few disabled workers. The section following describes an in-depth evaluation process to help facility staff assess the founding values and outcomes of the programs they operate.

EVALUATION OF ORGANIZATIONAL VALUES AND OUTCOMES

Rehabilitation facilities now, more than ever, are significantly re-examining values, methods, and outcomes, striving to incorporate them into an effective whole. One way human service professionals can conduct this examination is through the completion of an organizational values/outcomes analysis grid. There are several steps in this process.

The first step is to identify and rank the values that the organization wishes to implement through its programs. Values such as the following often emerge: dignity, growth, earnings, freedom of choice, integration, and relationships.

Through a systematic process, the possible values must be collected and then ranked. Ranking is important because almost every organizational decision involves a potential values conflict to some degree. It is helpful for everyone in an organization to know the relative position of important values.

After the ranking is completed, each value must be operationalized, that is, stated in a measurable way. For example, dignity and integration might be defined in terms of items on the PASS evaluation designed by Wolf Wolfensberger (1971). Freedom of choice can be measured by the number of alternative employment programs offered and the number of consumers who try more than one. Earnings can be measured by total wages, or dollars earned for each hour of work (another values decision).

Next, a limited scale must be developed to rate the degree to which each ranked value (as operationalized) has been implemented. If *earnings* was defined as pay per hour, the scale might

rate a 2% increase as a "1," a 4% increase as a "2," and so on (see Table 4).

After the values are operationalized and scales developed, it is helpful to examine the historical performance of the organization to determine the degree to which each value was implemented as well as to develop a baseline against which future program outcomes will be measured. This entire process is a growth-stimulating activity that can bring an organization together in new and exciting ways. The amount of energy the process can generate is amazing. The grid can be used regularly (monthly, quarterly, semi-annually, or whenever) to determine the degree to which each value is affected by program and/or environmental factors.

Even more important, by applying an organization's average program costs for each employment option to the average value outcomes, the organization can assess the cost benefit associated with each value-based outcome. Such analysis can enable the organization to ascertain the degree to which it is applying its resources to implement its values.

The following is an example of organization X's analysis of its values relative to employment outcomes for its disabled clientele. In this example, the board of directors and staff, through a values exploration, identified eight values as important to the organization:

1. Employment options
2. Severity of disability served
3. Integration of worksite
4. Stability of employment
5. Hours worked
6. Wages earned
7. Average hourly rate
8. Direct staff training and intervention hours to achieve earnings

As shown in Figure 1, organization X has operationalized its values by defining in measurable terms what each value means and then ranking the importance of each value, with the lowest rating projecting the highest value to the organization. For example, serving an individual who has multiple disabilities and has an IQ of less than 40 was more valued than serving an individual who has a multiple disability with an IQ of 40 to 70.

Table 4. Organizational value parameters relative to organizational employment outcomes

Rating	*VALUE: Employment options*
1	Competitive employment
2	Supported competitive employment
3	Small business
4	Enclave
5	Mobile work crew
6	Facility-based sheltered employment
7	Activities of daily living

Rating	*VALUE: Severity of disability served*
1	Average IQ 0–40 with multiple disability
2	Average IQ 0–40 with dual disability
3	Average IQ 0–40 with single disability
4	Average IQ 40–70 with multiple disability
5	Average IQ 40–70 with dual disability
6	Average IQ 40–70 with single disability

Rating	*VALUE: Integration of worksite*
1	Employment in an integrated environment in a position requiring a high degree of task dependency and coworker interaction and/or high level of contact with customers
2	Employment in an integrated environment in a position requiring a moderate level of task dependency and coworker interaction
3	Employment in an integrated environment on a shift or position which is relatively isolated; contact with coworkers without disabilities or supervisors is available at lunch or break
4	Employment in an integrated environment on a shift or position that is isolated; contact with coworkers without disabilities or supervisors is minimal
5	Employment in a segregated environment with primarily disabled coworkers

Rating	VALUE: *Stability of employment*
1	Average job lasts longer than 4 years
2	Average job lasts longer than 3 years
3	Average job lasts longer than 2 years
4	Average Job lasts longer than 1 year
5	Average job lasts longer than 6 months

Rating	*VALUE: Hours worked*
1	Average hours worked greater than 2,000
2	Average hours worked greater than 1,500
3	Average hours worked greater than 1,000
4	Average hours worked greater than 500
5	Average hours worked greater than 100

Rating	*VALUE: Wages earned*
1	Average earnings greater than 8,000
2	Average earnings greater than 6,000
3	Average earnings greater than 4,000
4	Average earnings greater than 2,000
5	Average earnings greater than 1,000
6	Average earnings greater than 500
7	Average earnings greater than 250

Rating	*VALUE: Average hourly wage*
1	Average hourly wage greater than $4.00
2	Average hourly wage greater than $3.35
3	Average hourly wage greater than $1.68
4	Average hourly wage greater than $1.00
5	Average hourly wage greater than $0.50

(continued)

Table 4.   (continued)

Rating	VALUE: Direct staff training and intervention hours to achieve earnings
1	Average less than 50 hours
2	Average less than 100 hours
3	Average less than 150 hours
4	Average less than 200 hours
5	Average less than 300 hours
6	Average less than 400 hours
7	Average less than 500 hours

Note: Single disability means consumer has only one diagnosed physical or mental impairment. Dual disability means consumer has two diagnosed physical or mental impairments. Multiple disability means consumer has three or more diagnosed physical or mental impairments.

Organization X then measured its performance in achieving the stated values expressed by the staff and board over the previous 12-month period in order to establish a baseline of current value performance (see Example 2, Period 2). Through systematic measuring of outcomes, organization X can assess its progress toward its stated organizational values.

Example 2, Period 2, demonstrates organization X's achievements 2 years later in meeting its stated values. These are shown in Figure 2. As can be seen, organization X has improved its stated values for consumer options, severity of disability, integration of worksite, hours worked, and wages earned. The organization has not been as successful in improving the values of job stability and direct training and intervention hours in some employment outcomes. The relative importance each of the values holds for the organization would determine if the gains offset the overall decreases. If, for example, integration of the worksite, hours worked, and wages earned were heavily weighted values within organization X, it was very successful in the

Rating Period: July 1, 1983–June 30, 1984

Individuals served	Value rating/ Employment options	Severity of disability	Integration of worksite	Stability of jobs	Hours worked	Wages earned	Hourly wage rate	Direct training and intervention hours
	1 Competitive employment							
10	2 Competitive supported employment	5 IQ 0–55 Dual	1 Complete	4 1 year	3 1040	4 $3,484	2 $3.35	23 150
	3 Small business							
	4 Enclave							
	5 Mobile work crew							
100	6 Facility-based sheltered employment	6 IQ 40–70 Single	5 Segregated	1 4 years	4 500	6 $ 500	4 $1.00	4 200
30	7 Activities of daily living	2 IQ 0–40	5 Segregated	1 4 years	5 None	7 None	5 None	6 400

Figure 1.   Organizational analysis of values relative to employment outcomes: Organization X, Example 1, Period 1. (On a scale of 1–7, the lowest rating corresponds to the highest value to the organization.) (Note: Single disability means consumer has only one diagnosed physical or mental impairment. Dual disability means consumer has two diagnosed physical or mental impairments. Multiple disability means consumer has three or more diagnosed physical or mental impairments.)

Rating Period: July 1, 1983–June 30, 1984

Individuals served	Value rating/ Employment options	Severity of disability	Integration of worksite	Stability of jobs	Hours worked	Wages earned	Hourly wage rate	Direct training and intervention hours
	1 Competitive employment							
30	2 Competitive supported employment	5 / IQ 0–55 Dual	3	2 / 2 years	2 / 1,560	1 / $6,396	4 / $4.10	200
7	3 Small business	6 / IQ 40–70 Single	2 / Moderate	4 / 1 year	2 / 1,900	2 / $7,315	2 / $3.86	3 / 150
12	4 Enclave	3 / IQ 0–40 Single	Isolated	3 / 2 years	3 / 1,560	$4,680	3	3 / 3.00
5	5 Mobile work crew	4 / IQ 40–70 Multiple	2 / Moderate	4 / 1 year	3 / 1,040	5 / $1,768	3 / $1.70	4 / 200
76	6 Facility-based sheltered employment	6 / IQ 40–70 Single	5 / Segregated	1 / 4 years	3 / 1,000	5 / $1,520	4 / $1.25	4 / 180
10	7 Activities of daily living	2 / IQ 0–40 Dual	5 / Segregated	1 / 4 years	5 / 150	7 / $ 75	5 / $ .50	6 / 400

Figure 2. Organizational analysis of values relative to employment outcomes: Organization X, Example 2, Period 2. (On a scale of 1–7, the lowest rating corresponds to the highest value to the organization.) (Note: Single disability means consumer has only one diagnosed physical or mental impairment. Dual disability means consumer has two diagnosed physical or mental impairments. Multiple disability means consumer has three or more diagnosed physical or mental impairments.)

employment outcomes attained. If however, stability of jobs and direct training and intervention hours were heavily weighted values, the organization may view itself as only minimally successful in its employment outcomes.

SUMMARY

This chapter has endeavored to provide a systematic approach to analyzing the values that rehabilitation facilities assign to their programs. Values clarification sharply influences the allocation of staff resources and mission of an organization (Kilmann, 1985). This chapter has demonstrated the importance of a facility's focusing directly upon the critical client employment outcomes, job stability, and severity of disability.

REFERENCES

Beziat, R.E. (1984). *The facility manager of the future*. College Park: University of Maryland Press.

Greenleaf, R.K. (1977). *Servant leadership*. New York: Paulist Press.

Kaplan, A. (1985). Values in decision making. In R. Tannenbaum, N. Margulies, & F. Massarik (Eds.), *Human systems development*. San Francisco: Jossey-Bass.

Kilmann, R. H., (1985). *Gaining control of the corporate culture*. San Francisco: Jossey-Bass.

Pacinelli, R., Kay, H., & Sellars, S. (1984). *Beyond the eighties: The Rehabilitation facility of tomorrow*. College Park: University of Maryland Press.

Rehabilitation Services Administration. (1987). *Annual report to Congress for 1985*. Washington, DC: Author.

Wolfensberger, W. (1971). *Normalization*. Toronto: National Institute on Mental Retardation.

Chapter 15

Rehabilitation Facilities and Supported Employment

Implementation Issues

Terry Bloom Edelstein

As ongoing service providers, rehabilitation facilities are in a position to significantly influence the ways in which future rehabilitation services are to be structured, and can play an intrinsic role in developing supported employment services. Recently, much debate in the rehabilitation community has focused on whether or not rehabilitation facilities were actually providing supported employment services before the term was coined. An equally important question has been whether or not rehabilitation facilities can and should provide supported employment services. Controversy has existed partly because of an ongoing perception on the part of many of these providers that work crews, enclaves, and other types of supported employment are already present in many programs. Others have suggested that rehabilitation facilities are not the appropriate site for initiating supported employment services due to the perception that sheltered programs are too rigid and that staff cannot adapt. Some have viewed facility operations as primarily geared toward production, not rehabilitation. Clearly, the rehabilitation community has been involved in a spirited debate about supported employment.

The question in this author's mind is not so much whether a rehabilitation facility is best suited to manage a supported employment operation, or whether a nonprofit or a for-profit organization would do the job better, but, rather, whether the human service system itself is the appropriate vehicle for providing such services. Is supported employment a natural role for business, or is it a natural extension of the services rehabilitation facilities and others have long been providing?

Whether or not rehabilitation facilities were engaged in supported employment in years past and whether or not their facilities are best equipped to provide supported employment services are not really the issues, since many are now providing these services and breaking new ground in the process. The widespread development of community-based programs run by rehabilitation facilities (i.e., "task teams" doing hotel domestic services, nurse's aide enclaves, individual placements in the hotel and restaurant industry, or custodial work crews) certainly suggests that there are many rehabilitation facilities with the staff and organizational characteristics to effectively operate supported employment.

HISTORICAL PERSPECTIVES

Over the past two decades and, until only recently, professionals and parents encouraged the development and expansion of sheltered employment services. Recent advances in training techniques for severely handicapped adults and philosophical changes toward integration and normalization have resulted in a major push toward more integrated and off-site employment since 1983. This chapter describes some of the events that have most affected the emergence of supported employment within rehabilitation facilities.

Projects with Industry

Many rehabilitation facilities have provided alternative programming for a number of years, serving as the core for Projects with Industry (PWI) programs. When the PWI legislation was first enacted in 1970, rehabilitation facilities took the lead in setting up business advisory councils and offering diverse job-training programs for people with disabilities.

Training programs ranged from food service and custodial maintenance to computer operations. Most training occurred within the rehabilitation facility, followed by placement on the job. A critical element of the placement was backup support from a rehabilitation counselor. Job-seeking skills classes were developed to assist potential employees in handling an interview situation, dressing appropriately for the job, and demonstrating reasonable work behavior. Job clubs were started to support the employee during off-work hours, and such groups afforded disabled employees the opportunity to speak with peers and rehabilitation professionals about the pressures of the job and job-related situations and to work toward solutions. The job clubs also provided regular peer support and a link between previous and current employment. The PWI program has had major success in promoting competitive integrated employment.

While Projects with Industry programs were funded with federal Department of Education, Rehabilitation Services Administration dollars, and the actual number of programs was limited by funding availability, many rehabilitation facilities set up similar training programs funded through their existing state allocations or community donations. These innovative programs greatly increased the number of people served in alternative training programs. Facility-run training programs such as cafeteria operations,

greenhouses, silkscreening, and printing programs flourished. In these models, similar to the PWI model, individuals received training within the rehabilitation facility, followed by competitive job placement and continued support.

To the extent that the Projects with Industry programs emphasize integrated, competitive employment and strong involvement with business, the programs can be viewed as forerunners to supported employment. However, if one precept of supported employment is that work skills are to be learned on the job, then PWI does *not* qualify as an example of supported employment, since most PWI trainees learned their skills in a training setting at the rehabilitation facility. For example, trainees may have learned the requisite skills for food service positions at the six work stations in the rehabilitation facility cafeteria. In some cases they completed "live work" for which they were paid, and in other instances the work was of a training nature and was covered under special U.S. Department of Labor training certificates. Trainees learned real work skills and tasks, but they did not learn them in the employer's environment.

The PWI programs do utilize another component of supported employment, however, that of support services. With the availability of on-the-job counseling and the supports of the job club, PWI programs are a form of employment with supports, meaning that the employee learns the job in a supportive setting, transfers those skills to the employer's work setting, and receives ongoing support as necessary to retain the job.

Transitional Employment Programs

Another alternative employment strategy that has frequently been utilized by rehabilitation facilities, particularly for employees with psychiatric disabilities, has been the Transitional Employment Program (TEP). Patterned after services developed by Fountain House in New York (the originator of the clubhouse model program for serving individuals with psychiatric disabilities), the TEP model incorporated the concepts of prevocational training, simulated work experiences, and finally, on-site employment. The rehabilitation facility developed, for example, a food service operation intended to meet the in-house needs of employees at the facility. Trainees learned the basics of the food service business as they prepared food for and served their peers and facility staff. Once they had learned these skills, they moved to agency-arranged sites in the community. The facility guaranteed to the employer that the job would be done, and a series of workers progressed through this training site. The final step was independent competitive employment in yet another worksite. Typically, no long-term support was provided.

As with PWI, this model offered elements of employment with supports. Employees were trained for community jobs, received support at these jobs, and then moved into competitive employment. While TEP sites were meant to be used on a short-term basis, an employee could move to and from the facility and into a progression of TEP sites without having to make that jump to competitive employment.

Funding Issues

Given the histories of Projects with Industry, of Transitional Employment Programs, and of similar vocational models, it is clear that employment with supports was offered by rehabilitation facilities before the term *supported employment* gained popular usage. These models, however, reflect three critical differences between the way service was provided and the tenets of the supported-employment model. First, the initial training occurred at the rehabilitation facility site, not at the employer's worksite; second, those served needed to be able to enter the competitive job market at a competitive production level; and third, and most crucial, follow-up supports were short-term, not permanent and ongoing. It is in this latter element of long-term, ongoing support that supported employment has broken with rehabilitation models of the past. In so doing, of course, it has departed from traditional reimbursement procedures.

To use the experience of the state of Connecticut as an example, vocational rehabilitation dollars paid for short-term intervention only. A person could receive an evaluation, work adjustment training, on-the-job training, or job-seeking skills, but only in rare instances could the person receive ongoing support services, that

is, long-term postemployment. Most rehabilitation facilities provided short-term follow-up and support services, but few provided ongoing supports and almost none provided daily intervention, if that was the support needed for the person to retain the job. The only way to provide those supports was to do so on an uncompensated basis.

Long-term funding has been provided in Connecticut by the state mental retardation agency from an account known as the "community sheltered workshop" account. Facilities were paid for 5 hours of service a day per person. This funding was used primarily for fixed-site programs serving at least 20 individuals and as many as 300. It has been more cost-efficient for a facility to serve 50 people in one location than to provide service to a much smaller number of persons in several different sites. The more service that was provided via this funding model, the more difficult it became to shift services from this model. With relatively fixed per diem payments covering an established staffing pattern, it seemed impossible, within the existing allocation, to move service recipients into community-based job settings, which also required higher staffing ratios.

While most providers in Connecticut's rehabilitation community have welcomed the concepts of supported employment, funding rigidity imposed by existing statutes, regulations, and policies has partially hindered implementation. The problems in Connecticut are not unlike those in many states facing the same implementation challenges as both public and private sectors struggle to adapt funding structures to enable the expansion of supported employment services. The big challenge for the Connecticut rehabilitation system has been to develop a strategy for shifting service patterns gradually without completely disrupting the existing service system and the lives of the over 3,000 people being served. A further challenge has been to provide services to the 2,000 people in the mental health and mental retardation systems who have been without vocational rehabilitation services in the past.

One partial solution to this dilemma has been additional funding by the Connecticut legislature. The legislature enacted budgets targeted at serving 1,500 people with mental retardation and 500 people with psychiatric disabilities by the end of fiscal year 1988. Partially through a class action lawsuit brought by the Association for Retarded Citizens as well as advocacy efforts in the state, service providers have been able to launch entirely new supported employment programs in addition to those programs already in place.

The policy of Connecticut's mental health department was that these service dollars were to be used for integrated, paid employment opportunities. While utilizing the language of supported employment and recommending the creation of individual sites, work crews, enclaves, and small enterprises, the department clarified that it sought to fund "employment with supports." It wanted the services developed to be creative and flexible and not bound to a specific model. Existing workshop providers were encouraged to offer these new services, but new vendors were also sought. Two years into the program, 13 of the providers have provided workshop services previously, while 26 are new to the provision of work services. Increasingly, community mental health center and psychosocial rehabilitation programs are developing work programs.

Crucial to the success of the state-initiated supported employment program has been the willingness of the state mental health agency to be flexible in funding supported employment services. Early funding was on a per diem basis, but increasingly, funding has been on a grant basis. Rather than being "attendance-driven," it is "client-driven." The state department describes the supported employment programs it funds as being in "a formative and creative state" (Gould & Crompton, 1987).

In the 2 fiscal years in which Connecticut's supported employment account has been operational within the Department of Mental Retardation budget, over 121 projects serving over 1,550 people have been established. Fifty-three provider organizations offer these services, up from the 45 organizations that had provided services under the "community sheltered workshop" account. From the standpoint of rehabilitation facilities, a critical measure is that of how much service rehabilitation facilities are providing. Of the 45 organizations historically providing service, 39 provide supported employment services funded through this new account. The supported employment services that facilities currently offer run the gamut from small enterprises to individual models. In Figure 1, it can be seen that the highest average hourly wage was $4.06. The other wage rates range from $1.57 to $2.11 per hour. While these wages are not sufficient for independent financial support, they do represent major increases in earnings.

ISSUES FOR THE FUTURE

Rehabilitation facilities have made progress in implementing supported-employment projects, but a number of issues must still be confronted, requiring a variety of solutions.

Following is a brief discussion of some of the major issues facing rehabilitation facilities as they continue to initiate community-based employment.

Do Current Supported Employment Models Foster Integration?

While facilities have shown progress in developing all models of supported employment programs, enclaves, small businesses, and work crews are more segregated work options than individual placements. Work crews, with their early morning or evening hours, are the most frequently segregated. However, the extent of their segregation depends on the dynamics of the particular worksite. Not all crews work morning or evening shifts. Many do daytime janitorial, lawn, policing, or service operation functions. However, recent *federal* regulations on supported employment (34 CFR Part 363, The State Supported Employment Services Program; Final regulations [August 14, 1987, p. 30548]) indicate that for those programs receiving federal support, group placements of more than eight clients will not be considered supported employment, nor will group placements in areas where there are no nonhandicapped people. This aspect of the regulations continues to stir professional controversy.

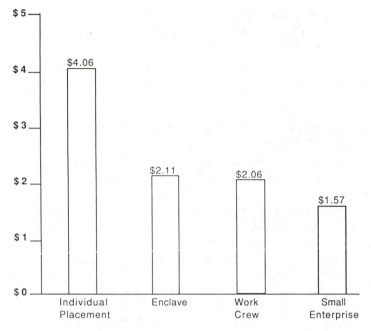

Figure 1. Hourly wages for supported employment by program type in Connecticut, fourth quarter, FY87, April 1–June 30. (Reprinted by permission from Connecticut Department of Mental Retardation, East Hartford.)

Similarly, the degree to which a small business enterprise is a segregated operation depends on the nature of the business and the mix of other company employees. A restaurant is less likely to be segregated than a print shop, but a small print shop that employs a variety of skilled employees and is located on a main street may also be highly integrated. An enclave can be dispersed through a worksite or situated in a separate room. Changes to the Fair Labor Standards Act in 1986 minimized many of the restrictions formerly governing enclaves, so that it is now possible for workers with disabilities to work at the same table with nondisabled workers. Previous federal labor laws had prohibited this.

Are Supported-Work Employees Being Paid a Fair Wage?

To again use Connecticut as an example, figures for the fourth quarter of FY87 (see Figure 1) show that except for those working in individual placements who earned an average of $4.06 an hour, all other workers earned less than the minimum wage, and thus were rated according to the Fair Labor Standards Act. People in enclaves earned an average of $2.11 per hour. Those in work crews earned $2.06 per hour, and those in small business enterprises earned $1.57 per hour (see Figure 1). These work-crew figures are somewhat at odds with figures generated by Connecticut's state-use program, an industrial contracting program comparable to National Industries for the Severely Handicapped, Inc. (National Industries for the Severely Handicapped, Inc., n.d.). In the year ending June 30, 1986, employees in state-use work crews earned a range of $0.25 to $6.00 an hour, with an average wage of $2.34. The wages were bimodal at $3.37 and $4.00 an hour. [The $0.25 wage had been paid in "patient worker" classifications by state agencies. Starting July 1, 1986, these wages had to be paid based on the Fair Labor Standards Act (ConnARF, 1986).]

Are we short-changing employees with disabilities or are we paying a fair wage? If business and industry are desperate for entry-level workers at starting wages of $5.00 an hour, should not employees with disabilities receive the same starting wages, or would this preclude employers from future contractual arrangements with facilities? As the economy flourishes, employers are more likely to pay a higher starting wage; human service professionals, therefore, need to hone their negotiating skills.

How Do We Ensure Health Insurance And Other Benefits?

The higher the wages, the more at risk workers are of losing their Social Security benefits and Medicaid insurance. Workers are quickly exhausting their Trial Work Periods and Extended Periods of Eligibility. Increasingly, they are earning upwards of $800.00 per month. Whereas in the early stages of seeking supported-employment sites, human service professionals were so eager to secure the job site that they failed to focus on the benefit issues, they must now begin to target jobs at sites that pay employee benefits. Workers with disabilities cannot be expected to sacrifice their Medicaid health insurance without being able to secure employer-provided coverage. If employer coverage is not available or is subject to waiting periods, professionals must find ways to make available and fund group insurance or individual insurance coverage.

What Changes Must Be Made in the System to Ensure that Supported Employment Will Work?

From the provider's perspective, the primary challenge is how to implement supported employment on an agencywide basis and yet maintain the basic integrity of the organization. In the myriad of issues to be resolved—including community relations, parent concerns, staffing, and board acceptance—physical plant conversion and finances loom large. Rehabilitation facilities must develop longitudinal business plans addressing their future directions, and they must work with state agency administrators to identify mechanisms to bridge the funding dilemmas.

On a statewide basis, policy-making groups representing the state and the private sectors must review incentives and barriers to the full implementation of supported employment programs. Together, they must develop those systemic changes necessary for full implementation. A prime example is the boundary that must be traversed between short-term and long-term funding support. Too many people are still unable to participate in supported employment programs because there is no guarantee of long-term funding.

REFERENCES

ConnARF. (1987, February 25). *Set aside statistics—FY86.* Connecticut Association of Rehabilitation Facilities.

Connecticut Department of Mental Retardation. (1988). East Hartford: Author.

Former Mental Patients Step Back into the World. (1981). *Practice Digest, 4,* 5–8.

Gould, B., & Crompton, D. (1987, May 21). *Revised policies for funding work services programs.* Connecticut Department of Mental Health.

Knight, L., (1981, March). Aspects of rehabilitation: Fountain House. *Mind Out: The Mental Health Magazine,* No. 4.

National Industries for the Severely Handicapped, Inc. (n.d.). *NISH facts.* Vienna, VA: Author. (2235 Cedar Lane, Vienna, VA 22180).

Projects with industry training manual. (rev. ed.) (1981). Washington, DC: National Association of Rehabilitation Facilities.

SECTION IV

CRITICAL IMPLEMENTATION ISSUES

Chapter 16

Disincentives and Barriers to Employment

William E. Kiernan and Lisa Brinkman

A great deal of discussion has centered on the reasons why people with disabilities are not entering competitive employment. Many of these reasons reflect a belief among human services personnel that there are a number of barriers to employment for such persons (Kiernan & Brinkman, 1985; Whitehead, 1986). This chapter examines the concept of barriers and proposes that, in fact, barriers to employment should be viewed not as immovable obstacles but, in some ways, as signposts identifying issues that need to be addressed if persons with disabilities are to gain access to supported, transitional/training and/or competitive employment.

To analyze a situation by examining its accompanying barriers is to adopt a negative orientation, which reveals why things, in part, have remained unchanged. Webster's *Ninth New Collegiate Dictionary* (1987) defines *barrier* as "a material object or set of objects that separates, demarcates, or serves as a barricade; a factor that tends to restrict the free movement, mingling or interbreeding of individuals or populations." Clearly, in the human services field, there has been a persistent perception that major inhibitors exist to block people from attaining competitive employment. The authors of this chapter, however, propose a more positive approach, one that identifies issues and opportunities rather than barriers.

To examine issues rather than barriers to employment reflects the authors' belief that some of the stumbling blocks to employment for persons with disabilities can be removed; that is, they are negotiable. Webster (*Ninth New Collegiate Dictionary*, 1987) defines *issue* as "a matter that is in dispute between two or more parties; the point at which an unsettled matter is ready for a decision." Thus, an issues orientation rather than a barriers orientation reflects a belief that an opportunity exists for resolving this issue. Webster further defines *opportunity* as "a good chance for advancement or progress." The authors regard changing economic trends, the advances in technology, and the utilization of strategies such as supported employment as promising indicators of progress as persons with disabilities move toward supported, transitional/training, and competitive employment.

In the belief that with change comes opportunity, this chapter examines issues regarding employment for persons with disabilities, discusses the opportunities associated with those issues, and, finally, considers some of the implications from the perspectives of service, training, and technical assistance.

ISSUES AND OPPORTUNITIES IN EMPLOYMENT

Although studies have been done of the issues surrounding employment for persons with disabilities, no *comprehensive* look at the inhibitors to employment has been undertaken. Some specific studies have investigated systemic concerns (Whitehead, 1986), parental apprehensions (Newman, Reiter, Bryen, & Hakim, 1987), staff perceptions, and economic issues (Conley, Noble, & Elder, 1986). What has emerged through the literature is a series of issues often reflecting perceptions, economic factors, and environmental/systemic/training needs.

Two somewhat larger attempts to identify issues in accessing employment deserve mention here. One was a key informant survey conducted by the Developmental Evaluation Clinic (DEC), a University Affiliated Facility at Children's Hospital, Boston (Kiernan & Brinkman, 1985). Using a structured interview format, 27 national experts on the employment of people with disabilities were interviewed in a 1-hour telephone survey. The survey yielded a rank ordering of barriers to employment (see Table 1) as perceived by these experts. Beyond the key informant approach, issues and barriers to employment for adults with developmental disabilities were identified as part of a second national survey on employment of persons with developmental disabilities, also conducted by the DEC (Kiernan, McGaughey, Schalock, & Rowland, in press). Data were collected from approximately 1,000 agencies, facilities, and organizations regarding which issues they felt inhibit access to employment (see Table 2). Although the rank order of the barriers or issues identified is somewhat dif-

Table 1. Barriers to employment for adults with developmental disabilities, identified in key informant survey

1. Economic and benefit disincentives
2. Employer perceptions and attitudes
3. Family beliefs and concerns
4. Staff and professional perceptions
5. Lack of interagency networking and collaboration
6. Transportation
7. Other:
   a. Lack of supported employment options
   b. Restricted work environments
   c. Lack of social and interpersonal skills
   d. Lack of long-term fiscal support through Vocational Rehabilitation
   e. Inappropriate work behaviors on the job
   f. Labor market limitations (high rate of unemployment)
   g. Lack of skills to perform tasks
   h. Lack of transition programs from school to work
   i. Lack of follow-up on the job

Source: From Kiernan and Brinkman (1985).

Table 2. Barriers to employment, as perceived by agencies, facilities, and organizations ($N = 946$)

1. Transportation
2. Lack of appropriate jobs
3. Attitude of employers
4. Financial disincentives
5. High unemployment
6. Lack of social skills
7. Parental concerns
8. Lack of work skills
9. Loss of medical benefits
10. Lack of trained staff
11. Staff perceptions

Source: From Kiernan et al. (in press).

ferent, the actual grouping of the barriers is consistent. One could assume that if a similar survey were done with parents and individuals with disabilities, the rank order again might be different but the core issues would be the same.

The following section examines these issues grouped into the three broad clusters identified earlier—perceptions, economic factors, and environmental/systemic/training needs—and discusses opportunities that may arise in attempting to resolve these issues.

Perceptions

1. Issues Several of the identified issues reflected the perceptions of family members, employers, staff, and persons with disabilities. The perceptions of these various persons directly affect the creation of opportunities for employment, the willingness to seek access to such opportunities, and the actual employability of persons with disabilities.

The family and its role have been identified as central to the success of persons with disabilities as they move toward increased independence from school to work and assimilation into an integrated work setting (McLoughlin, Garner, & Callahan, 1987; Newman et al., 1987). At the same time, parents and family support structures can limit access to competitive employment (Inge, Hill, Shafer, & Wehman, 1987). This role frequently is unintentional and occurs as a result of the family's underestimating the skills and abilities of the disabled person, out of concern for placing him or her at risk socially, emotionally, or financially. The need for a secure environment at times encourages parents to seek sheltered rather than competitive employment. The perceived volatility of the labor market, potential changes in supervisors, reductions in force within industry, relationship with others in the work setting, and travel on public transportation systems all contribute to parental concerns.

Along with the desire for security in the work setting, parents are also anxious to maintain a secure environment from the standpoint of ongoing financial supports and health care benefits. In the past, people with disabilities who became employed frequently lost their entitlements to Social Security and Medicaid, yet received no fringe benefits through their employment (Conley et al., 1986).

The family's overriding concern is often that of securing long-term protection for their disabled family member. As parents themselves age and realize that they will not always be available to provide care, support, and supervision on a day-to-day basis, they tend to seek a more secure environment. For the older parent, there is an increased tendency to seek out those resources that are more stable and guaranteed. This means that they have often settled for security rather than seeking opportunities for increased integration, economic self-sufficiency, and interrelationships within the community.

Employers' perceptions differ from those of the parent and family in that concerns are frequently tied to productivity and appropriate behavior in the workplace, and also reflect lack of knowledge about persons with disabilities (Hasazi, Brody, & Roe, 1985; Maxwell-Hanley, Rusch, Chadsey-Rusch, & Renzaglia, 1986). Employers typically fall into two categories: those who believe that persons with disabilities ought not to be in integrated work settings and those who are supportive of the idea but require assistance if they are to accommodate persons with severe disabilities. Fortunately the latter group is much larger than the former (International Center for the Disabled [ICD], 1987).

Employers may express concerns about insurance and workman's compensation as well as apprehensions about increased rates of injuries on the job (Whitehead & Rhodes, 1986). Some are worried about the adjustment of the disabled worker over time (American Research Group, 1986). Specifically, concerns about job

flexibility or the disabled worker's ability to adapt to changes in supervisors, advances in production methodology, or basic technologic advances have been expressed by employers who have had experience employing persons with disabilities (LaGreca, Stone, & Bell, 1983; Rogers & Stieber, 1985). In many instances the employers' apprehensions are valid, particularly when no interventions are offered for the recently hired or more senior worker with a disability.

Apprehensions about persons with disabilities moving into integrated employment settings are also expressed by human services staff and professionals (Kiernan & Brinkman, 1985). These concerns range from a lack of expectations of individual capacity to a sense of anxiety about the human service employee's own employment status. As with parents and family members, the predominant worry seems to center on the loss of security. Concern over the potential loss of Social Security Supplemental Security Income, Medicaid, and other payment benefits is often voiced by professionals.

Underestimates of a person's capacity and skills reflect a staff perception that the individual can work on only certain types of jobs, if at all. Such a perception can limit the number of job choices available to persons with disabilities. Likewise, restricting one's employment search to "the ultimate job," can limit opportunities. This may reflect the desire for a secure environment or a perception by staff that persons with disabilities should not or cannot change jobs. These expectations place unrealistic demands upon the relationship of the person with disabilities to employment.

Last and most important, the perception of the person with disabilities can be both an asset and a liability in seeking employment. In some instances, apprehension regarding change becomes so significant that the individual chooses not to seek employment. This is characteristic of individuals working in sheltered workshops or participating in day habilitation programs where they have developed friends over the years. Such feelings are not uncommon for all persons. In addition, concerns regarding the loss of cash benefits as well as health care benefits may on occasion interfere with the individual's willingness to move from a publicly supported program to competitive employment (Maxwell-Hanley et al., 1986).

2. Opportunities Concerns about loss of security, isolation, relationships with others, individual capacity, and the uncertainties of change in general can inhibit access to employment by persons with disabilities. A number of options exist for responding to these issues. These include encouraging parents to believe that employment in an integrated work setting can be an appropriate outcome of the educational process (Wehman, Moon, Everson, Wood, & Barcus, 1988). Adoption of concepts such as lifelong learning and career education would encourage parents and educators to develop the expectation that persons with disabilities can make choices and accept the responsibilities associated with the choice (Rusch, 1987). It is this shift away from protecting to expecting that is necessary for parents, professionals, employers, and adults with disabilities. Research on the self-fulfilling prophecy has shown that when limited expectations are placed upon individuals, the end result is likewise limited (Rosenthal & Jacobson, 1968). It is important that expectations for persons with disabilities be adjusted so that independence, integration, and economic self-sufficiency can be encouraged by family, siblings, and educators, even in the disabled person's early years (Governor's Planning Council on Developmental Disabilities, 1987).

Employer apprehensions often reflect a lack of previous experience or in some cases a negative experience in employing a person with a disability. In both situations provision of specific information about accomplishments of persons with disabilities in the workplace can be helpful. This information alone is not sufficient, however. The employer must also feel that sufficient support will be available if problems emerge on the job. Thus, the employment training specialist must act as a resource and a source of support for both the employer and the person with a disability.

Employers will also be more likely to alter their perceptions if they are convinced that the person with a disability can meet their needs. The approach of responding to the employer's needs and providing sufficient support in train-ing the worker with a disability will create an opportunity to demonstrate the abilities and capacities of the worker. This type of encounter, in which a need in the workplace is effectively and efficiently met, is a powerful strategy for changing the perception of the employer.

Specific preservice and inservice training programs for professionals are essential if expectations of persons with disabilities are to be altered (Karan & Knight, 1986). These training programs need to prepare staff to play a supportive role for the adult with disabilities as the movement toward employment progresses. Skills in job coaching, person/environment matching, job modification, behavioral intervention strategies, social skill development, management, and marketing must be developed if human service staff are to effectively and efficiently perform support functions not only for adults with disabilities, but employers and employees as well (Cohen, Patton, & Melia, 1986).

Agencies, organizations, and facilities must adopt a philosophy that facilitates independence, integration, and productivity for persons with disabilities. Such a philosophy would require not just administrative endorsement but also the endorsement of the boards of directors and trustees of the various organizations. This philosophy must be integrated throughout the entire organization, from senior administrative to direct service staff, if changes in perceptions are to be realized.

The apprehensions expressed by adults with disabilities regarding loss of money, health care supports, transportation, and friends must also be responded to. If given the opportunity and accompanying support, most persons with disabilities would choose to have an independent rather than a dependent role in society (ICD, 1986). The concerns just mentioned can be dealt with through accessing the Social Security work incentives, the provision of support by staff not just in skill acquisition but in social integration in the work setting, and an acknowledgment that recreation, leisure, and friendship are as important as a job. The needs of the whole person must be addressed if success is to be realized in the work setting (Kiernan & Stark, 1986).

Alteration of perceptions entails a major change in the attitudes and expectations of persons at all levels: family, professionals, employers, and persons with disabilities. This alteration in attitudes will need to be reflected in educational curricula at all levels, elementary through graduate training. Increased interaction through mainstreaming efforts will, it is hoped, diminish some of the apprehensions regarding persons with disabilities. The adoption of transitional and supported-employment models will provide opportunities for industry to observe the abilities and economic potential of persons with disabilities in increasing productivity and reducing costs (Brannigon, 1986; Terborg & Lee, 1984). Finally, legislative and administrative changes such as those of the Social Security work incentives will introduce major funding supports as persons with disabilities move toward greater independence, integration, and economic self-sufficiency (U.S. Social Security Administration, 1987).

Economic Factors

1. Issues In addition to individual perceptions, a number of economic factors have been identified as inhibiting the employment of persons with disabilities. Most notable are those factors associated with loss of cash and/or medical benefits (Kiernan & Brinkman, 1985). The lack of appropriate jobs and the current unemployment rate in the local community may also limit employment opportunities (Rogers & Stieber, 1985).

As already alluded to in this chapter, a major concern for persons with disabilities in the return to work is the potential loss of Social Security Supplemental Security Income (SSI) and eligibility for Medicaid. In the past when an individual had countable earnings of more than $300 per month (Substantial Gainful Activity—SGA), he or she risked losing eligibility for Social Security by being deemed as no longer having a disability significant enough to impair him or her from engaging in employment at the SGA level.

Concerns about loss of benefits have been well documented over the past several years (Kiernan & Brinkman, 1985; Whitehead, 1986). The potential loss of medical benefits is complicated by the fact that many persons with disabilities who become employed start jobs at the

minimum wage level and do not receive any benefits. By reaching an earnings level above SGA, there is substantial risk for loss of benefits.

Other economic factors such as the level of unemployment in the general area, the lack of available jobs for persons with disabilities, and the shift in this country from a manufacturing to a service-based economy can at times restrict access to employment. When unemployment rates are high, industry can be selective in the individuals they hire. In the past, industry has tended to select the most qualified applicants, frequently on the basis of academic background or previous experience, rather than offering the position to an individual who has limited or no work history or who may require a longer training period initially. In times of low unemployment when the available pool of applicants is more limited, employers are more willing to hire persons with disabilities. A by-product of this latter situation, as noted earlier, is that employers will become more aware of the fact that persons with disabilities can be good workers (ICD, 1986).

The lack of available jobs is generally reflective either of a scarcity of jobs, as seen in some rural settings, or a geographic area that specializes in one product (i.e., steel, automobiles, produce, high tech). In the latter case, the variety of available jobs is limited. In many instances, however, areas that focus on a specific product feature outlying districts that offer a variety of jobs. The issue of lack of jobs can also reflect a lack of effective marketing on the part of the facility or person representing applicants with disabilities as often as it may reflect a true lack of employment opportunity in the area (see also Chapter 17 in this volume).

The expansion of service industry jobs where persons with disabilities will be required to relate to both the customer and other workers and be somewhat flexible in job duties is frequently raised as a problematic issue. This, on occasion, can be viewed as an inhibitor to placing persons who are more severely disabled and who demonstrate less mature work behaviors. In such cases, additional supports may be necessary on site through the use of a job coach who provides direct intervention with the worker and/or support to the line supervisor in responding to performance problems.

2. Opportunities Whereas the economic issues just discussed present major inhibitors to employment, the establishment of the Social Security Administration work incentive programs (see Table 3) goes a long way toward resolving some of the concerns relating to loss of financial and medical benefits for the Social Security Supplemental Security Income recipient. Unfortunately, these same protections are not available to the Social Security Disability Insurance (SSDI) recipient. The extended cash benefits under Section 1619(a) and the threshold point for coverage of medical services under Section 1619(b) are designed to support the efforts of persons with disabilities who enter employment in entry-level positions where minimal benefits are available. These work incentives seek to limit risk in loss of monies or medical payments (U.S. Social Security Administration, 1987). There continue to be some concerns about eligibility redetermination under the work incentive programs. However, the development of permanent incentives such as 1619(a) and 1619(b), effective July 1, 1987, will have a significant impact upon those interested in increasing employment opportunities for adults with disabilities.

The establishment of Section 1619 has somewhat overshadowed the other work incentives available through the Social Security Administration. The use of Impairment Related Work Expenses and Plans for Achieving Self Support are valuable resources for persons with disabilities as they enter employment. Specific services for which a person must pay out of pocket in order to maintain employment may be reduced from the individual's earnings as an impairment-related work expense and thus not counted in earned income. For the SSI recipient, this procedure would allow for the SSI cash payments to be maintained at a higher level. Those SSDI recipients utilizing this incentive may reduce earned income below the SGA level, thereby preserving eligibility for cash and medical benefits. The Plan for Achieving Self Support (PASS) benefits will allow for an accumulation of resources while maintaining eligibility for Social Security.

A great deal of information must be disseminated to parents, rehabilitation professionals, and individuals with disabilities to enable a broad-based understanding of the work incentive initiatives under Social Security. This does not mean that the establishment of the work incentives reduces all of the risks involved, but the incentives do reduce the major inhibitors to employment, particularly among the SSI recipients.

The issues of lack of jobs and high rates of unemployment are macro issues that individual facilities, persons with disabilities, and parents frequently have minimal opportunity to affect. However, as suggested earlier, high rates of unemployment are blamed for lack of employment opportunities for adults with disabilities when in fact the real issue may be a lack of effective marketing and utilization of placement strategies for persons with disabilities. Programs and rehabilitation services must adopt a marketing mode, that is, identify a need in the industry and respond to that need rather than use a selling mode (Kotler, 1980). In the past, specific training programs would develop skills and then place the individual (a selling strategy), while much less, if any, attention was paid to the needs of the customer (a marketing strategy). The movement to a service-based economy requires that the needs of the customer be clearly identified and that the goals of the training program reflect the needs expressed by industry if employment opportunities for adults with disabilities are to be accessed.

In some instances, even though the unemployment rate may be high, this rate may apply to skilled or middle-level employment rather than entry-level positions (Terborg & Lee, 1984). It is important to look at the unemployment rate not as necessarily reflective of all jobs, and therefore examine specific occupational categories and geographic areas.

Where there are few jobs available, opportunities for relocation of individuals with disabilities, as well as more aggressive job engineering, may resolve some of the lack of job opportunities. Where there were high rates of unemployment and few jobs available in inner cities, many companies have developed vans

Table 3. Social Security work incentives (SSI and SSDI programs)

Program	Features
1. 1619(a) (SSI only)	Cash payments continue even though earned income above SGA. Qualifications-1: Disability continues. Meets eligibility rules for income and resources. Those receiving special SSI cash benefits keep their disability status until they are determined to have improved medically or are terminated for a nondisability related reason.
2. 1619(b) (SSI only)	Protects Medicaid benefits when earnings are too high for cash payments but not high enough to offset the loss of Medicaid. Qualifications: Disability continues. Needs Medicaid in order to work. Unable to afford equivalent benefits. Meets all nondisability requirements for SSI payment other than earnings. Uses a threshold concept to measure whether earnings are sufficient to replace SSI and Medicaid benefits lost owing to work; amount varies according to state; based on the amount of earnings that would stop SSI payments and annual per capita Medicaid expenditures for the state.
3. Plans for Achieving (SSI only)	Can help establish or maintain SSI eligibility. Must be written within specific timelines. Can increase SSI payments. Allows individual to set aside income and/or resources for work goal. Income and resources set aside excluded under the SSI income and resources tests.
4. Impairment Related Work Expenses (both SSI & SSDI)	Certain related items and services needed to work can be deducted from earnings in determining substantial gainful activity under SSDI and SSI, and can be excluded from earned income in determining the SSI monthly payment amount. Costs must be paid by the disabled individual. Must first establish SSI eligibility without any deductions for impairment-related work expenses. Impairment-related work expenses can then be excluded to compute payments.
5. Substantial Gainful Activity (SSDI ongoing; SSI eligibility)	Performance of significant physical or mental activities in work for remuneration or profit. Countable earnings of over $300 per month; dollar value of subsidies and impairment-related work expenses subtracted from gross earnings in SGA determination. Applies to the SSDI program; applies to the SSI program only in determining whether initially eligible for SSI payments.
6. Trial Work Period (SSDI only)	Begins with the date claim was filed or month of entitlement, whichever is later. Charges SSDI beneficiary with "service" month for each month earnings exceed $75. Is completed when individual accumulates 9 "service" months (not necessarily consecutive).
7. Extended Trial Work Period (SSDI only)	Reinstatement of SSDI cash payments for up to 15 consecutive months after trial work period completed. No new application is required.
8. Extension of Medicaid Coverage (SSDI only)	Medicaid coverage extended for 24 months. Applies only if termination was due to substantial gainful activity.

and car pools to bring workers to their suburban manufacturing and service centers. Thus, although there may be no jobs available in the immediate vicinity, there may be opportunities to transport individuals to locations that are hiring or to consider relocating the individual to an area where more jobs are available. Although the latter option is an extreme situation, there are certainly occasions where, in seeking residential opportunities as well as employment opportunities, closer proximity to a surburban or urban area may increase employment opportunities and the range of choices available.

Environmental/Systemic/Individual Training Issues

1. Issues Numerous issues related to environmental and systematic areas may inhibit the creation of opportunities for and/or access to employment for adults with disabilities. Among these issues are transportation, limited range of support options, need for follow-along services, staff training, and lack of collaboration.

Transportation is the problem most frequently cited by parents, staff, and persons with disabilities. This issue may be looked at from two perspectives: 1) the lack of available transportation and 2) the inability of the individual to access transportation either because of physical barriers or insufficient skills. The availability of public or private transportation is essential. Many persons with severe disabilities cannot transport themselves; they are dependent upon the assistance of a third party in getting to and from employment. In areas where no public transportation is available, alternative designs will be necessary. In other areas, where transportation may be available, schedules, architectural barriers, or confusing routing systems may inhibit the use of that transportation by persons with disabilities. In the earlier-mentioned national survey of staff in rehabilitation agencies, facilities, and organizations, transportation was ranked as the most significant barrier to accessing employment for persons with disabilities (Kiernan et al., in press). It remains a significant issue when designing employment opportunities.

Additional concerns reflect the limited range of support options that may be available for persons with disabilities. In some instances, this may be a lack of a job coach or support person while the individual is learning a task or maintaining himself or herself in an employment situation. Frequently, the lack of a job coach is a function of limited financial resources for agencies to support job training on site (Hill et al., 1987). When persons with more severe disabilities are placed into supported employment, the role of the job coach becomes more critical. The job coach is not only a trainer on site but also serves as the primary means for facilitating integration of the worker in the company's labor force.

Beyond the on-site needs, there may be periodic social, emotional, or case management issues that must be responded to in supporting an individual who is employed. For certain persons with disabilities, when there are major changes in life circumstances such as a change of residence, a change in the family structure (e.g., marriage, relocation, illness, death), or the loss of a friend, the individual may experience problems in adjusting to the loss, separation, or change. In some instances, this creates difficulties in job performance (Maxwell-Hanley et al., 1986). In addition, changes in supervisors, technology, company location, or lack of job satisfaction may create problems for the person with disabilities who has been employed for a period of time. Intermittent support, particularly in times of transition or change, may be required for the disabled person to maintain his or her job. These supports will be necessary in some instances on an irregular basis for the individual's entire employment history.

Staff training needs, particularly in the roles and functions of staff as they move from sheltered employment, work activities, and day rehabilitation programs into industry settings, are critical. Skills and strategies for reinforcing, supporting, and facilitating integration of the worker with disabilities into the work force within an industry setting will need to be learned by staff who in the past have worked in isolated and protected environments themselves. Staff training in the role of the worker with disabilities in an integrated work setting, in the values of integrated work settings for persons with disabilities, and in strategies for training and supporting individuals is essential. The role of job coaches and of other support staff, as well as of case managers within the community, is an evolving one, requiring a wide variety of skills and experience. The relocation of staff into industry settings creates a potential for staff isolation, lack of connectedness to other rehabilitation staff, and limited opportunities for personal support on the job. Thus, staff development and inservice training will be central. In addition, preservice training programs for persons in university, community college, and in some cases even vocational and comprehensive high school programs must provide graduates with skills in job placement, environmental modification, and training technology.

Interagency collaboration in the areas of shared responsibilities, identified accountability, and resource maximization is essential to develop a comprehensive approach to accessing and supporting adults with disabilities in employment. The issue of the lack of fiscal resources for ongoing support has been viewed as a major concern as the efforts to expand supported employment programs progress (Virginia Commonwealth University [VCU], 1987). Federal regulations, such as those pertaining to the restriction of work in day habilitation programs, have in many ways forced states to limit employment opportunities so as to maximize federal fiscal supports. Coordination, however, pertains not just to fiscal resources but to eligibility criteria, range of services offered, and compatible evaluation procedures, both programmatic and client specific.

2. Opportunities As can be seen, environmental, systemic, and individual training issues are complex and varied. Many of them relate to the adjustment of the individual on the job rather than to the previously noted perceptions or macro economic factors. Thus, the opportunities available for resolving the issues tend to be more oriented specifically toward providing training for staff and the individuals themselves with disabilities; adapting the immediate work and community environments so that persons with disabilities can gain and maintain employment; and modifying eligibility criteria, regulations, and administrative procedures among human service and education agencies.

In the area of transportation, in the absence of available public transportation systems, resources such as vans, car pools and parent-neighbor transportation networking will be required (McLoughlin et al., 1987). Car pools can be arranged either by a job coach, the company itself, or the public transportation agency within the community. The development of a transportation system for a person with disabilities will challenge the creative abilities of the support staff.

When transportation is available, yet is not accessible either because of architectural barriers or lack of individual skills, then specific skill training programs, as well as an effort to increase awareness on the part of the public transportation system, are necessary. Advocating a barrier-free transportation system may be highly appropriate. However, in many instances this is a long-term goal whereas the short-term goal is to arrange for a disabled person's transportation. Thus, the options noted previously could be employed. Where specific skill training and travel training are necessary, the resources of community workers, case managers, parents and siblings, and neighbors will be necessary. Ideally, the actual training procedure should begin considerably before the employment period. However, realistically, in some instances a job opportunity is received with only a day or two's notice. Thus, in the early adjustment period, job coaches, staff, and/or parents may be required to accompany the individual on the public transportation system as he or she goes to and from work.

The limited range of supports available and the need for follow-up and ongoing supports require that there be a state or public service system that allows for the payment of job-coach services and support staff as the individual adjusts to the job. In some states, human service agencies have, through interagency agreements, arranged to provide initial support, as in the vocational rehabilitation system, while other agencies provide ongoing support. Other states have utilized vocational rehabilitation services, other than the traditional Federal-State Vocational Rehabilitation resources, as in the case of state-sponsored sheltered employment, to provide resources for ongoing support in integrated employment settings. Support on an hourly, daily, or flat fee basis can be an option. Finally, resources such as the Job Training Partnership Act (JTPA) and the Private Industry Councils (PIC) can provide ongoing support services for workers with severe disabilities (VCU, 1987).

Industry-sponsored Employee Assistance Programs (EAP) may also be a resource as the individual adjusts to the job. The EAP is an effective tool in assuring maintenance of the individual once the initial training is achieved. The role of the job coach may be more central in initial training and integration to the work setting. An industry sponsored EAP has the capacity to provide support on an ongoing basis. Although such a role is not customary for an EAP, with some orientation to the issues of disability the EAP counselor can be an effective support resource.

As in the design of an individual transportation system, creativity in designing supports for persons on the job will be essential. Job coaches employed by nonprofit organizations as well as coaches trained by agencies but employed by corporations, companies, and industries may provide some assistance. In general, the associated financial support and costs will have to be borne by the nonprofit or public side rather than the industry. Ongoing maintenance on the job may appropriately be supported through industry resources either by training line staff or by providing supports through the employee assistance programs or both.

Rehabilitation staff-training needs reflect modifications both within the inservice and pre-service training programs. Staff need to be instructed in the areas of providing on-site support, supervision, and integration of individuals with disabilities in work settings (Karan & Knight, 1986). Training programs reflecting the role of the job coach and the required skills have emerged at both the master's and bachelor's levels. Some job coaches are trained in community college systems, while others have been trained as a result of the redirection of line staff within sheltered employment settings. As stated earlier, the specific role of the job coach is changing; however, his or her primary functions remain those of providing support on site for the individual

as well as the company. The employment training specialist may serve as a resource to multiple job sites and thus be the middle manager who supports the job coaches in their role of providing one-to-one support.

In addition to the need to address training issues, expanded collaboration and coordination among agencies both in the public and not-for-profit sectors is critical. At the federal level, coordinated activities through the U.S. Department of Education, Office of Special Education and Rehabilitative Services; and the U.S. department of Health and Human Services Administration on Developmental Disabilities have served as the stimulus for creating 27 supported employment statewide initiative projects. Similar collaboration at the state level with the office of vocational rehabilitation, the office of mental retardation/developmental disabilities, the department of education, and employment training programs is necessary.

Last, collaboration at the local level among individual counselors, case managers, job placement specialists, agencies, parents, and persons with disabilities is essential. Collaboration can take two forms: 1) longitudinal support over a lifetime or extended period; and 2) social, recreational, residential, and vocational support structures in a wide variety of areas over a shorter period (Kiernan, 1988). Thus, the role of transition from school to work as well as the assistance of the EAP in maintaining individuals over time will result in a more coordinated approach to services for persons with disabilities as they progress through their employment cycle. There is, moreover, need for coordination and collaboration among the various areas vital to assuring integration of the individual and the community. Most notably, residential, recreational, and work concerns need to be coordinated. For instance, frequently, lack of communication among the day and residential programs leads to difficulties either in the adjustment of the individual to the work setting or in the support of the individual in the residential setting.

As noted early in this chapter, if one views barriers not as immovable obstacles but as issues that can and should be negotiated, many opportunities present themselves. Such opportunities will require changes in perceptions, roles, and responsibilities for parents, professionals, employers, bureaucrats, and most important, adults with disabilities. The final section of this chapter addresses some future perspectives in the areas of service delivery, development of training programs, and provision of technical assistance.

FUTURE PERSPECTIVES

To expand services in the area of employment opportunities for adults with disabilities, a number of specific activities must be undertaken. These include:

The development of a marketing approach focusing upon industry needs

Provision of supports on an ongoing basis to persons with disabilities utilizing a job coach on site

Development of funding to support ongoing services to individuals in integrated employment settings

Expansion of supported and transitional training opportunities for persons with severe disabilities

Reduction in numbers and replacement of individuals who are undergoing transition from school to sheltered employment with graduates of special education who are gaining access to supported, transitional/training, and competitive employment

Provision of supports to parents as the move toward integrated employment opportunities progresses

Support to industries in accessing, maintaining, and expanding employment opportunities for adults with disabilities

Support to line managers in the area of training, supervision, and support to adults with disabilities in the integrated work settings

Support to the individual in facilitating integration into the work setting

These activities will enhance support services to persons with disabilities, their families, and industry. For an expanded employment program for adults with disabilities to be effective, it is necessary to assure support, assistance in integration, and services to industry.

From a training perspective, there is a need to instruct persons with disabilities in the areas of greater independence, choice, and acceptance or responsibility. Beyond the specific training activities for adults with disabilities, there are information-sharing and training needs for parents regarding the existence of various work incentives, the support structures available, benefits to integrated employment opportunities, and assurances that ongoing support will be made available for their son or daughter as they progress toward greater economic and social independence.

Specific inservice training needs for staff relating to values clarification, person-environment matching strategies, utilization of technology in employment, and the role and function of onsite support staff (e.g., job coach, employment training specialist) will be essential. Preservice training packages for job coaches and employment training specialists directed at developing skills in behavior management, environmental accommodation and modification strategies, marketing, organizational behavior, and management skills need to be developed. The presence of a generalist who can appreciate not only industry's needs but the needs both of the individual with disabilities and of his or her parents will assure continued success of the expansion of employment opportunities for adults with disabilities.

Finally, there is a need for technical assistance in facilitating the transition of sheltered employment, work activity, and day habilitation programs toward supported, transitional/training, and competitive employment programs. Technical assistance should be directed not just at the direct service staff but at the managerial staff and board of directors as well. The conversion of existing programs will require mechanisms for ongoing support as programs take a more integrated employment focus. Expansion of the mandates of the program will require a redirection of program goals and objectives. This activity will necessitate an investment in support by the board of directors and senior management. Total agency, facility, or organizational commitment, is required if the agency's mission is to be altered.

CONCLUSIONS

The continued expansion of employment opportunities for adults with disabilities reflects changes in economic trends, advances in employment training technologies, and the increased emphasis upon developing economic self-sufficiency among adults with disabilities. This chapter has examined the issues and described some opportunities that may be available. The improvement of employment opportunities for adults with disabilities will depend heavily upon the personal dedication of a wide range of individuals, including parents, employers, professionals, and most importantly, adults with disabilities. The utilization of work incentives such as those available through the Social Security Administration will be effective only if all individuals involved are convinced that supported, transitional/training, and competitive employment opportunities are more appropriate for persons with disabilities than the more restrictive environments of the past.

REFERENCES

American Research Group (1986). *Survey of New Hampshire employers*. Concord: New Hampshire Developmental Disabilities Council.

Brannigon, M. (1986, September 2). Help wanted: Youth shortages alters Job Market. Opportunities grow for poor, elderly, and handicapped. *Wall Street Journal*.

Cohen, D.E., Patton, S.L., & Melia R.P. (1986, April, May, June). Staffing supported and transitional employment programs: Issues and recommendations. *American Rehabilitation*, 20–25.

Conley, R., Noble, J., & Elder, J. (1986). Problems with the service system. In W.E. Kiernan & J.A. Stark (Eds.), *Pathways to employment for adults with developmental disabilities* (pp. 67–83). Baltimore: Paul H. Brookes Publishing Co.

Govenor's Planning Council on Developmental Disabilities. (1987). *A new way of thinking*. Minneapolis: Author.

Hasazi, S., Brody, G., & Roe, C.A. (1985). Factors associated with the employment status of handicapped youth exiting high school from 1979–1983. *Exceptional Children*, *51*(6), 455–469.

Hill, M.L., Revell, G., Chernish, W., Morell, J.E., White, J., Metzler, H.M.D., & McCarthy, P. (1987). Planning for change: Interagency inititives for supported employment. In P. Wehman, J. Kregel, M. Shafer, & M. Hill (Eds.), *Competitive employment for persons with mental retardation: From research to practice: Vol II* (pp. 189–210). Richmond: Virginia Commonwealth University, Rehabilitation Research and Training Center.

Inge, K.J., Hill, J.W., Shafer, M.S., & Wehman, P.H. (1987). Positive outcomes of competitive employment: Focus upon practical concerns. In P. Wehman, J. Kregel, M. Shafer, & M. Hill (Eds.), *Competitive employment for persons with mental retardation: From research to practice: Vol. II* (pp. 233–253). Richmond: Virginia Commonwealth University, Rehabilitation Research and Training Center.

International Center for the Disabled. (1986). *The ICD survey of disabled Americans: Bringing disabled Americans into the mainstream*, Survey No. 854009. New York: Author.

International Center for the Disabled. (1987). *Employing disabled Americans*. New York: Author.

Karan, O.D., & Knight, C.B. (1986). Training demands of the future. In W.E. Kiernan & J.A. Stark (Eds.),

Pathways to employment for adults with developmental disabilities (pp. 253–270). Baltimore: Paul H. Brookes Publishing Co.

Kiernan, W.E., (1988). Opportunities and options for employment. In S. Pueschel (Ed.), *The young person with Down Syndrome: Transition from adolescence to adulthood* (pp. 155–171). Baltimore: Paul H. Brookes Publishing Co.

Kiernan, W.E., & Brinkman, L. (1985). Barriers to employment for adults with developmental disabilities. In W.E. Kiernan & J.A. Stark, (Eds.), *Employment options for adults with developmental disabilities* (pp. 160–174). Logan: Utah State University Affiliated Facility.

Kiernan, W.E., McGaughey, M. Schalock, R., & Rowland S. (in press). *Employment outcomes for adults with developmental disabilities: A national survey*. Boston: Children's Hospital, Training and Research Institute for Adults with Disabilities.

Kiernan, W.E., & Stark, J.A. (Eds.). (1986). *Pathways to employment for adults with developmental disabilities*. Baltimore: Paul H. Brookes Publishing Co.

Kotler, P. (1980). *Marketing management: Analysis, planning, and control* (4th Ed.). Englewood Cliffs, NJ: Prentice-Hall.

La Greca, A.M., Stone, W.L., & Bell, C.R. (1983). Facilitating the vocational-interpersonal skills of mentally retarded individuals. *American Journal of Mental Deficiency*, 270–278.

Maxwell-Hanley, C., Rusch, F.R., Chadsey-Rusch, J., & Renzaglia, A. (1986). Reported factors contributing to job terminations of individuals with severe disabilities. *Journal of The Association for the Severely Handicapped*, *11* (1), 45–52.

McLoughlin, C.S., Garner, J.B., & Callahan, M. (1987). *Getting employed, staying employed: Job development and training for persons with severe handicaps*. Baltimore: Paul H. Brookes Publishing Co.

Newman, E., Reiter, S., Bryen, D.N., & Hakim S. (1987). *Barriers to Employability of Persons with Handicaps: A Bi-national Study in the United States and Israel*. Project No. J-9-E-3-0172. Philadelphia: Temple University.

Rogers, R.C., & Stieber, J. (1985, September). Employee discharge in the 20th century: A review of the literature. *Monthly Labor Review: Research Summaries*, 35–41.

Rosenthal, R., & Jacobson, L. (1968). *Pygmalion in the classroom*. New York: Holt, Reinhart & Winston.

Rusch, F. R. (Ed.). (1987). *Competitive employment issues and strategies*. Baltimore: Paul H. Brookes Publishing Co.

Sims, R.R. (1983). Kolb's experiential learning theory: A framework for assessing person-job interaction. *Academy of Management Review*, 8 (3), 301–308.

Terborg, J.R., & Lee, T.W. (1984). A predictive study of organizational turnover rates. *Academy of Management Journal* 27 (4), 793–810.

U.S. Social Security Administration. (1987). *A summary guide to Social Security and Supplemental Security In-come for the disabled and blind*. SSA Pub. No. 64-030. Baltimore: Author.

Virginia Commonwealth University. (1987). *Funding supported employment*, 4(1). Richmond: Author.

Webster's Ninth New Collegiate Dictionary. (1987). Springfield: Merriam-Webster, Inc.

Wehman, P., Moon, M.S., Everson, J.M., Wood, W., & Barcus, M.J. (1988). *Transition from school to work: New challenges for youth with severe disabilities*. Baltimore: Paul H. Brookes Publishing Co.

Whitehead, C. (1986, October). *Expanding employment opportunities and options through major barrier removal*. Paper presented at the annual Conference of the Association for The Severely Handicapped, San Francisco.

Chapter 17

Responsive Marketing by Supported Employment Programs

Michael S. Shafer, Wendy S. Parent, and Jane M. Everson

Employers play a central role in the development of all supported employment models. Along with the employee and the supported employment providers, they represent a third leg in the rehabilitation triangle. A determining factor of employment success is the employer's acceptance of the consumer as a productive and contributing member of his or her business. Therefore, the supported employment provider must assume primary responsibility for assuring that the worker is adequately trained and supported to fulfill the needs and expectations of the employer. This role requires supported employment providers to view both employers and individuals with disabilities as consumers of supported employment services. As supported employment consumers, employers represent another market for rehabilitation services that must be recognized by supported employment specialists (Molinaro, 1977).

The recognition of employers as consumers of rehabilitative services has focused great attention upon the importance of marketing these services (Ninth Institute on Rehabilitation Issues, 1982; Perlman, 1983). A distinction should be made here between *marketing* and *selling*; marketing emphasizes responsiveness to the needs of consumers, while selling is typically concerned with the packaging and promotion of products in such a manner that results in wide distribution or sales (Kotler, 1975).

Marketing of rehabilitation services has been conceptualized to include three processes: 1) assessing the needs of potential consumers; 2) tailoring the services to meet consumers' needs; and 3) maintaining long-term relationships with consumers to receive feedback and to provide quality assurances (Young, Rosati, & Vandergoot, 1986). The essential ingredient of effective marketing is *responsiveness*— knowing what consumers want, knowing how to provide what they want, and ensuring that what they received was what they wanted.

This chapter discusses how to develop responsive supported employment plans. While supported employment has many consumers including clients, parents, schools, vocational rehabilitation counselors, and others, this chapter focuses upon the role of supported employment providers in marketing supported employment to employers. Supported employment providers include any organization or agency that provides supported employment services for a targeted group of consumers. The major steps involved in developing an effective marketing strategy (i.e., one that is responsive to both employers

Preparation of this chapter was supported in part by Grant Nos. G008301124, G008430106, and G008430058 from the U.S. Department of Education, Office of Special Education and Rehabilitative Services.

and employees) include: 1) identifying potential markets for supported employment; 2) defining the marketing plan; 3) implementing a marketing plan; and 4) maintaining responsive relationships with employers. This process is described in Figure 1 and is described in detail in the remainder of this chapter. Marketing is a circular process requiring ongoing feedback between the employer, employee, and supported employment provider. A responsive marketing process can be modified by ongoing evaluation to meet the needs of all consumers.

STEP ONE: IDENTIFYING POTENTIAL MARKETS

Recognizing Labor Market Trends

Successful growth in national implementation of supported employment models is dependent upon a number of employer and business-related variables. Paramount among these variables is the health and vitality of the economy, particularly in relation to the individual states and the local labor market. In regions where the unemployment rate is high, the ability to secure existing work opportunities for supported employment consumers may be limited. Failure to identify the economic base of a particular locality or region will ultimately weaken the prospects for supported employment and may result in programs that restrict access to potential jobs or that target locally unavailable positions for employment.

National and Regional Labor Needs A number of resources are available to supported-employment providers to enable them to keep informed of the labor market. Typically, these resources provide information about current labor needs within different industries, projected labor needs for some future period of time, and current unemployment rates for local or regional areas. A representative sample of these resources is listed in Table 1.

Two of the better sources of information for projecting labor market trends are reports issued by the U. S. Department of Labor (DOL) and state employment commissions. These reports provide projections of labor growth needs segmented by geographical region, industry concern, and *Dictionary of Occupational Titles* (DOT) category. For example, recent Department of Labor projections reported that the service-producing sectors of business will account for almost 75% of all new employment positions created nationally between 1982 and 1995 (U.S. Department of Labor, 1984). Businesses such as medical care, business services, professional services, personal services, and nonprofit organizations are predicted to account for more than one of three new jobs over the projection

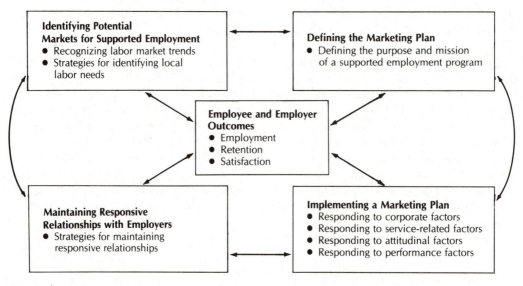

Figure 1. The responsive marketing process.

Table 1. Resources for identifying local labor needs

Supported-employment providers may refer to the following resources for information about the local labor market:

Better Business Bureau
Business and trade newsletters
Chamber of Commerce
City and county employment offices
Clubs and organizations (e.g., Kiwanis, Rotary, Jaycees)
Friends, family, and associates
Local employers
Newspaper classified sections
Private retail groups
Professional journals
State employment commission
Supported-employment providers
Telephone book (Yellow Pages)
Trade associations (e.g., hotel and restaurant)
U.S. Department of Labor
University and college job placement offices
Vocational rehabilitation agencies

period (U.S. Department of Labor, 1984). As a result of this anticipated growth in the service sector, demands for office maintenance and janitorial services are projected to expand 28% between 1982 and 1995, growing from 2.8 million to 3.6 million (Kleiman, 1985). Of equal importance for supported employment providers will be the predicted rapid growth in the food and beverage industry, which is expected to require 1.6 million new cooks and chefs and an additional 2.2 million waiters and waitresses (Kiernan & Stark, 1986). As these positions enjoy expanded growth and demand, so will a variety of peripheral positions such as buspersons, dishwashers, utility staff, and cleaning personnel that are necessary to support this industry's growth.

Local Labor Needs The figures just cited reflect national trends, and as a result their applicability to specific localities may not always be appropriate due to regional economic and labor characteristics. For example, more rural regions of the country that continue to rely upon agricultural industries will not experience the rapid growth in the service areas that is projected nationally. In order to project local and regional employment demands, the supported employment provider should contact various business concerns such as state and regional employment commissions, chambers of commerce, state vocational rehabilitation agencies, as well as private industry trade associations. Each of these sources frequently publishes reports reflecting projected local and regional business growth and labor needs based upon current business and economic activity as well as recent census data. Table 2, for example, depicts projected labor growth within Virginia as well as for the Richmond metropolitan area for the years 1980–1990 (Virginia Employment Commission, 1985). As the table indicates, the three occupations expected to enjoy the greatest amount of growth across the state are clerical positions, professional and technical positions, and service positions, each accounting for over 200,000 new employment opportunities. These figures complement the local projections for the Richmond metropolitan area.

Strategies for Identifying Local Labor Needs

Tapping Existing Resources The preceding section identified several information and data sources to assist the supported employment provider in determining local economic growth and labor needs. The organizations cited (see Table 1) collect and monitor information pertaining to local economic and industry growth patterns and often publish this information in local trade or business newspapers. Supported employment providers can keep informed about local business happenings and trends by subscribing to these publications and perhaps joining the organizations. In addition, as indicated in Table 1, informal networks such as personal acquaintances, friends, and previous employers of the staff can often be valuable sources of information on local labor needs.

Special mention should be made, too, of regional offices of state vocational rehabilitation agencies. Often state rehabilitation offices maintain job banks or accounts with companies expressing a willingness to employ workers with disabilities. Furthermore, representatives or employers from certain companies may serve on select advisory boards for state vocational rehabilitation agencies or governors' panels on employment. Vocational rehabilitation professionals have traditionally placed heavy emphasis upon job development activities and have developed highly efficient and precise methods

Table 2. Local and state employment projections for Virginia, 1980–1990

Occupational group	Richmond metropolitan area			Virginia		
	Total job openings	Openings as a result of growth	Openings as a result of separation	Total job openings	Openings as a result of growth	Openings as a result of separation
Total, all occupations	196,470	81,900	114,570	1,250,740	510,550	740,190
Professional, technical, and kindred	38,670	19,330	19,340	246,560	120,120	126,440
Managers and officials	20,050	7,310	12,740	124,390	44,460	79,930
Sales workers	15,300	5,060	10,240	85,370	29,150	56,220
Clerical workers	44,210	17,650	26,560	261,960	103,270	158,690
Crafts and kindred workers	16,640	6,900	9,740	115,260	46,680	68,580
Operatives	15,230	5,340	9,890	123,960	45,350	78,610
Service workers	37,450	17,150	20,300	233,300	101,970	131,330
Laborers, except farm	8,680	3,100	5,580	56,180	18,490	37,690
Farmers and farm workers	240	70	170	3,790	1,070	2,720

Source: Adapted with permission from Virginia Employment Commission (1985).

for identifying local labor needs and cultivating potential employers (Galloway, 1982). Supported employment providers should cultivate contacts within the established vocational rehabilitation community and attempt to utilize existing vocational rehabilitation resources for identifying potential employment opportunities.

Conducting a Community Job Market Screening   In addition to utilizing existing resources to identify local labor needs, the supported employment provider should also consider conducting a *community job market screening* (Martin, 1986; Moon, Goodall, Barcus, & Brooke, 1986) to identify potential employment opportunities within a given community. This screening should allow the provider to assess the health of a local economy, the markets or industries experiencing greatest growth within the community, and the receptiveness of the local economy to employment of workers with handicaps.

Conducting a thorough community screening in order to identify specific employers, businesses, and job types involves a variety of activities in addition to contacting the information sources previously discussed. The classified section of the local newspaper can provide a reliable source of information for identifying local labor trends. It can also serve as an indicator of the general vitality of the local economy as reflected by the total number of new positions posted as well as the specific labor needs identified by the job listings. By carefully reviewing the classified sections over an extended time period, supported employment providers can assess the general health of the local economy and specific labor market needs. Employment needs can then be classified according to occupational clusters such as food preparation, materials handling, assembly, and maintenance (Sitlington & Easterday, 1985).

The job postings reviewed in the newspapers should be scrutinized to assure that the potential positions are appropriate for the consumer population served by the supported employment program. A number of decision factors must be considered at this initial stage of identification. First, does the position require prior training, experience, or certification that the consumers do not possess? Second, does the position re-

quire cognitive and/or motor activities beyond the abilities of the consumers, given effective and sufficient training and/or job-site modification? Often these determinations will require information that is obtainable only after the completion of an extensive job analysis. However, some job postings, simply by the description or title provided in the posting, will reveal that they are inappropriate for a particular consumer group. For example, although the Silicon Valley region of central California may have extensive want ad postings, the supported employment provider may be less than anxious to initiate job development activities for positions requiring computer programmers or analysts with extensive educational and professional experience.

Employer "Hit List"   As a result of reviewing the classified sections, supported employment providers can develop a "hit list" of companies with whom job development activities should be undertaken. Such a listing may include businesses who appear to have repeated or chronically unmet labor needs, who have a track record for growth and expansion, or who present specific employment opportunities that the supported employment agency wishes to provide its consumers. This listing should be updated regularly, providing a current listing of potential new employers, their location, specific employment opportunities that may be available, and the status of job development activities. For specific guidelines on contacting businesses, the reader is referred to Chapter 12 in this book, as well as Moon et al. (1986) and Barcus, Brooke, Inge, Moon, & Goodall (1987).

STEP TWO: DEFINING THE MARKETING PLAN

Defining the Purpose and Mission of a Supported Employment Program

The preceding section discussed a variety of methods for determining the labor market needs of the locality in which supported employment services are to be marketed. By identifying these community needs, supported-employment providers may begin to more clearly articulate the purpose of their programs, including the employment services to be offered and the targeted consumers of the services. The identification and articulation of a purpose enables the organization to set clear objectives and plan long-range activities. Many sheltered workshops have unclear purposes, which may not directly respond to local need. For example, most sheltered workshops serve as evaluation centers, short-term work adjustment and training facilities, and as long-term employment programs. Such multiple purposes often obscure the mission of an organization, require costly equipment and facilities, and restrict an agency's ability to respond to the local consumers' (employers' and disabled people's) needs.

Identification of a community's labor needs is only one step in defining a supported employment program's mission. Additional variables that must be addressed include the needs of the consumer population for whom supported employment is intended, the reliability and support of funding agencies, and the underlying values or philosophy of the program's administrative leaders. The types of employment opportunities and supported employment services that are to be developed must respond to the specific target. For example, are services needed for a developmentally disabled population or a mentally ill population? Also, programs that provide supported employment services exclusively will have a different mission from programs that provide a broader range of services.

The process of defining the purpose/mission of a supported employment program should focus upon the outcomes that the advisory board or managers have identified based on the local need. The primary outcome that should be realized by any supported employment program is paid employment with individualized levels of support. Many qualitative aspects of this outcome must be considered by a supported employment program when drafting a mission statement. For example, the minimal requirements for acceptable wages, the level of integration that workers must experience, the environmental aspects of the positions that will be accepted, and the range of disabling conditions that may be experienced by potential workers are all issues that must be addressed. When considering these qualitative aspects, supported

employment managers should always remain responsive to the values and needs of their consumers—both employers and individuals with disabilities.

A mission statement should be clear and concise, stating as specifically as possible what services are provided, how these services are to be provided, and what types of consumers may be expected to benefit from these services. For supported employment programs, such a mission statement should specify the type(s) of supported employment services that are provided, the qualitative aspects of employment opportunities, and the intended workers to be served by these services. By articulating such a mission statement, employers, constituents, and service recipients are informed of the supported employment program's operating parameters. Failing to specify a purpose or mission may result in inefficiency, ambiguity, and, worst of all, negative experiences by consumers and employers.

While preparing a mission statement, supported employment providers must recognize that their services are supplied within the business community. The business community and, in particular, the private for-profit business community, operates from a set of values that is sharply different from the values to which most human service providers are accustomed. These former values typically dictate that the activities and goals of a business must maximize the potential for profit generation. While corporations and employers may express community concern and altruism when approached to employ workers with disabilities (Shafer, Hill, Seyfarth, & Wehman, 1987), these expressions and their resulting actions must always be weighed against the need to maintain sufficient profit-making opportunities.

Responding to the profit concerns of the business community requires that supported employment providers assume an orientation that will cultivate demand for their services within the business community. The critical feature of this orientation is recognizing the services that supported employment has to offer to the business community and marketing those services in much the same fashion that insurance, office supplies, building maintenance, or any other service commodity is marketed. While some individuals may argue that marketing is inappropriate, since the base commodity is human beings, the lack of good marketing strategies has been recently identified by employers as a major reason for not employing more workers with disabilities or not utilizing rehabilitative services (Shafer et al., 1987; Young et al., 1986).

A subtle but important distinction must be drawn between marketing the services of supported employment and marketing persons with disabilities. Given the profit concerns with which the business community operates, it is doubtful that many employment opportunities could be developed if service providers simply marketed the skills of persons with disabilities. However, by marketing the skills of these individuals plus the tremendous support services that come with these individuals, employers are provided with a winning proposition. The next section discusses many of the issues that arise when employers are approached to employ workers with disabilities. Many of these issues have the potential to negatively affect employment opportunities. However, supported employment may be marketed in such a manner as to allay employer concerns or fears. By identifying these concerns and remaining responsive to the issues that employers may raise, supported employment providers can respond with factual and knowledgeable information and action, enhancing initial employment opportunities and supported long-term employment retention.

STEP 3: IMPLEMENTING A MARKETING PLAN

After defining a purpose and mission statement, the next step for the supported employment provider is to develop and implement an effective and efficient market plan that responds to the identified labor market needs and meets the identified purpose. This section discusses a variety of factors that may influence a provider's ability to market supported employment services. Many of these factors affect employers when they are deciding to hire new employees, while other factors may affect employment of workers long after they have been employed. The discussion concentrates upon identifying and assessing such factors as the attitudes of employers and the biases or concerns that they express regarding workers with disabilities. Methods by which supported employment providers may respond to facilitate greater employment opportunities are also reviewed.

Responding to Corporate Factors

Obviously, the most prevalent factor motivating employers to hire new workers is to fill or meet existing labor needs. In fact, the need to fill a position was identified as the primary reason for hiring workers with mental retardation by 55% of respondents in a recent survey of employers (Shafer et al., 1987). Similarly, the lack of qualified applicants or even of any applicants has been repeatedly identified as a primary reason why employers do not hire workers with disabilities (Shafer et al., 1987; Young et al., 1986). The paucity of applicants that employers encounter is not strictly limited to rehabilitation-related employment. Recent news accounts have indicated the growing need for entry-level service employees for positions that typically go unfilled. Increasingly, it becomes clear that employment opportunities do exist and that the apparent lack of opportunity may translate into lack of responsive marketing by supported employment providers. While the issue of worker qualification has previously arisen as a factor minimizing employment opportunity, the provision of extended job-site training and supervision that characterizes supported employment effectively negates this argument.

In addition to meeting labor needs, altruism has also been shown to play a significant role in employers' decisions to hire workers with disabilities (Easterday & Dever, 1987; Riccio & Price, 1984; Shafer et al., 1987). Riccio and Price (1984), for example, found that the desire to help persons with disabilities was commonly cited by employers as a reason for hiring them. In addition, the prospect of enhancing public and community relations has been identified as influencing employers to hire workers with disabilities (Easterday & Dever, 1987; Mithaug, 1979; Shafer et al., 1987). Some employers or corporations may view employment of disabled people as part of their corporate responsibility to the community, or at the least, as one means of making the corporate image shine a little brighter within the community (Freedman & Keller, 1981). The Southland Corporation, for example, recently initiated a campaign to employ disabled workers as sandwich makers in their 7–11 stores (Smart, 1987). Similar corporate initiatives have also been recently undertaken by Pizza-Hut, McDonald's Restaurants, Marriott Corporation, Kentucky Fried Chicken, and others.

Supported-employment programs would do well to take advantage of businesses' community spirit and altruism by forging alliances wherever possible with the business community. Traditionally, rehabilitation systems have cultivated such alliances, but typically on the large corporate and impersonal scale (cf., President's Committee on the Handicapped). Alliances between employers and supported employment programs should also be cultivated on the local and personal levels, at the level of the individual employer. For example, including selected employers on the supported employment agency's board of directors is an excellent strategy for involving the business community in the supported employment process and, as a result, making supported employment part of the community. Employers serving on such a board can also be highly effective in securing the participation of other employers by informal word-of-mouth activities as well as by making formal presentations before the chamber of commerce, Kiwanis, Rotary, and other clubs or councils that the business community regularly frequents.

Responding to Service-Related Factors

Supported employment offers a number of desirable service components for employers. Table 3 identifies some of the commonly cited services (with accompanying references) that supported employment may offer to employers beyond services typically provided by rehabilitation agencies.

Two recent investigations surveyed actual employers of workers receiving supported employment to assess the influence that these service components had upon hiring decisions (cf., Easterday & Dever, 1987; Shafer et al., 1987). Both of these studies clearly documented the

Table 3. Supported employment services offered to employers

The following services are among those reported as being offered to employers as a result of their participation in supported employment:

Detailed analysis of job tasks, social skills, and work environment (Martin, 1986; Wehman, 1981).

Screening and matching of worker abilities with job requirements (Moon et al., 1986).

Provision of intensive job-site training of new employee (Barcus et al., 1987; Mank, Rhodes, & Bellamy 1986).

Job completion to meet company standards (Shafer, Hill, et al., 1987).

Production on a fixed-cost basis (Bourbeau, 1985; Rhodes & Valenta, 1985).

Modeling of behavioral training and supervisory techniques (Moon, et al., 1986; Wehman & Melia, 1985).

Modeling of social interactions for coworkers and supervisor (Shafer, 1986).

Coordination of job restructuring, modifications, and adaptations (Mallik, 1979; Pietruski, Everson, Goodwyn, & Wehman, 1985).

Ongoing linkage with community resources (Schalock, 1986).

Systematic and ongoing evaluation of worker performance (Rusch, 1986; Shafer, Kregel, Banks, & Hill, 1987; White & Rusch, 1983).

Intervention by supported employment provider as needed (Moon et al., 1986; Wehman & Kregel, 1985).

Stabilization of job turnover rates (Parent & Everson, 1986; *Rehabilitation Research and Training Center Newsletter*, 1986).

importance of supported employment services in the hiring decision process. Shafer and colleagues surveyed 261 employers in Virginia to assess their perceptions and experiences with workers who have mental retardation. In that investigation, employers were identified who had employed workers with mental retardation while receiving supported-employment services, traditional vocational rehabilitation job placement services, or no special support services. Of interest to the present discussion were the responses of employers when asked to indicate the factors that influenced them to hire mentally retarded workers. The most prevalent response was a belief that these individuals deserved an opportunity to work. In contrast to those employers receiving job placement services, employers who had used supported employment services were found to more frequently identify the provision of follow-along services and assurances that the job would be completed as influencing their hiring decisions.

Similar results were reported by Easterday and Dever (1987), who surveyed 84 employers in the Columbus, Indiana, area to assess the influence of 10 identified "incentives" associated with supported employment. Those incentives most frequently identified by employers as affecting their decisions to hire workers with disabilities included: the probability of regular attendance, ongoing availability of agency personnel to call for assistance, high probability of long-term employment, and on-site training. Clearly, these results indicate that the nature of services that supported employment specialists provide are seen as a "plus" by employers.

An interesting finding from both of these studies is the minor role that some of the traditional employment incentives appear to play in employers' hiring decision process. Specifically, access to the targeted jobs tax credit (TJTC), opportunity to pay subminimum wages, and meeting affirmative action standards have rarely been identified by employers as contributing factors in their decisions to hire workers with disabilities. As noted by Easterday and Dever (1987, p. 9), most businesses involved with supported employment are generally small in size and might view the TJTC and subminimum wage waivers as "little more than unwanted regulatory interference and additional paper work."

Supported-employment providers should emphasize the on-site follow-along services that characterize supported employment when they approach employers or engage in other marketing activities. As is discussed in the following pages, workers with disabilities may be the innocent victims of a host of misconceptions or myths, such as that they are undependable or are poor workers. By emphasizing the intensive and extended nature of supported employment services, employment specialists can effectively address employers' stereotypical attitudes while focusing their attention upon the utilization of supported employment services rather than the simple employment of a disabled worker.

Responding to Attitudinal Factors

Early research into factors affecting the employment of workers with disabilities has typically attempted to correlate the attitudes of employers toward varying types of disabilities with demographic characteristics of the employers and their companies (Cohen, 1963; Hartlage, 1974; Phelps, 1974; Smith, 1981). These studies showed that more favorable attitudes of employers toward hiring people with disabilities was correlated with company size (Hartlage, 1974; Phelps, 1974), the type of product or service provided by the company (Hartlage, 1974; Stewart, 1977), and the educational level of the employer (Cohen, 1963; Phelps, 1974). In addition these studies typically showed that employers were more receptive to employing persons with less severe disabilities. Unfortunately, these studies produced conflicting results, reporting more favorable attitudes from better-educated employers (Phelps, 1974) as well as less-educated employers (Cohen, 1963), or finding no relationship between attitudes and educational level (Hartlage, 1974). Similarly, while some investigators correlated positive hiring attitudes with larger company size (Hartlage, 1974; Phelps, 1974; Posner, 1968), others reported no such relationship (Wolfe, 1961). Much of the research on employers' attitudes was conducted in relation to the provision of traditional, time-limited vocational rehabilitation services. As such, employer's hesitancy to hire workers with more severe disabilities is not surprising considering the fact that these workers would typically not be provided the intensive services that characterize supported employment. The lack of receptivity reported in these studies may in fact be more reflective of employers' attitudes toward the services that accompanied workers with disabilities rather than the workers themselves.

Responding to Performance Factors

In addition to assessing general employer attitudes toward the employment of workers with disabilities, researchers have also attempted to identify specific client characteristics and skills that employers view as critical to employment. Mithaug (1979) for example, surveyed 43 Fortune 500 companies and reported that potential employers were more willing to hire persons with physical handicaps and least likely to employ persons with mental retardation, severe disabilities, or those who are blind. Similarly, Florian

(1978) reported that employers preferred hiring persons who required minimal adjustment and training on the job. Interestingly, a study by E. I. DuPont de Nemours and Company found that individuals with more severe disabilities, who are often rated as "least likely to be hired" by employers, actually performed well on the job (in Steinhauser, 1978).

Researchers have also attempted to identify specific skills that employers deemed important to employment (Mithaug, 1979; Rusch, Schutz, & Agran, 1982; Salzberg, Agran, & Lignuaris-Kraft, 1986). These studies, too, have often produced conflicting results; however, a common thread among many of them appears to suggest that production or work-related behaviors are viewed by employers as most critical to employment. Mithaug (1979) for example, reported that the the three most important behavioral factors affecting hiring decisions included: ability to perform the job, productivity, and absenteeism. Similar results were reported by Smith (1981), who found that employers identified responsibility, cleanliness, punctuality, and social skills as important behavioral considerations. Rusch et al. (1982) identified the ability to verbally recite one's full name, perform basic addition skills, comb one's hair, follow a one-step instruction, and perform repetitive skills to within 25% of the average rate as important behavioral requirements for entry-level employment.

The results of this research provide some general guidelines for curriculum development, but should not be viewed as necessary prerequisites for employment. The repeated demonstrations that many persons with minimal functional skill repertoires are working successfully with supported employment effectively refute many of the findings of this research. One problem of much of this research was a reliance upon *potential* employers of persons with disabilities rather than *actual* employers to assess employer attitudes and hiring practices. For example, Cohen (1963) and Smith (1981) reported results from two of the few published studies in which employers were asked whether they had employed workers with disabilities. As suggested by Bluhm (1977), employer receptivity may be better evaluated by assessing employers' actual experiences rather than drawing inferences from attitudinal statements.

More recent research has attempted to assess performance-related factors affecting employment by surveying employers who have hired workers with disabilities. Interestingly, the majority of the literature pertaining to employers of workers with disabilities does not differentiate between disability types, but typically labels all workers as mentally disabled, physically disabled, or, simply, disabled (Parent & Everson, 1986). The implications of these reports suggest that employers generalize their experiences with employees who have disabilities to be representative of all workers with disabilities.

Research conducted with employers of disabled workers has identified the more salient concerns that employers express when asked to hire workers with disabilities and also provides information about the more subtle, unspoken biases that often affect hiring practices. Although employers may be hesitant to discuss their attitudes and concerns directly, the ability to do so has been shown to positively affect their hiring practices (Dennis, Ebert, & Mueller, 1986). Employment specialists need to be aware of the overt and subtle biases that influence employers' attitudes. By anticipating potential concerns, supported employment providers can respond with factual information and solutions when contacting employers for job placements.

Attendance Employers are often concerned that workers with disabilities will require more time off for doctors' appointments or illness as a result of their disability. Lost time from work by both handicapped and nonhandicapped employees is a costly expense for employers in the form of wages and reduced productivity. In fact, one recent survey of employers identified the promise of regular attendance to be a major incentive affecting their decision to hire a worker with mental retardation (Sitlington & Easterday, 1985). The general consensus of employers who have hired individuals with disabilities is that they are dependable and reliable employees who maintain good attendance records (Parent & Everson, 1986; Ricklees, 1981). A survey by E. I. DuPont de Nemours and Company found that 79% of their

1,452 disabled employees were rated average or above average in attendance when compared with their total workforce (in Nathanson, 1977). In addition, the U.S. Chamber of Commerce reports that individuals with disabilities have better attendance rates than their nonhandicapped coworkers (in Rhodes & Valenta, 1985).

Supported employment responds to employer concerns regarding attendance by providing training and support to facilitate regular attendance and punctuality on the job. This may include training clients to use alarm clocks, to notify employers when ill, to return from breaks on time, and to schedule appointments after work hours. In group employment models such as enclaves or work crews, fluctuations in attendance may be addressed by using replacement workers during the absence of regular members or redistributing work loads. The role of employment specialists is to serve as liaisons and ensure that consumers, family members, or guardians are aware of workers' schedules, company policies, and procedures for handling time off from work.

Employers who have had experiences with supported employment services report greater satisfaction with the attendance of workers with disabilities than other employers of disabled workers who were not receiving these services (Shafer et al., 1987). Specifically, employers who had received supported employment services rated their workers higher on attendance, on time arrival and departure, and on returning from breaks on time than those employers who had received traditional job-placement-only services or no services at all.

Safety Employers rate safety-related concerns as the second most important factor affecting their decisions to hire employees with disabilities (Dennis et al., 1986). Obviously, employers fear the risk of increased accidents, and, in turn, of elevated worker compensation costs. Interestingly, workers with disabilities actually help keep insurance rates down as a result of the reduced frequency of their on-the-job accidents (Nathanson, 1977). According to a study by the U.S. Chamber of Commerce and the National Association of Manufacturers, insurance costs were not affected by hiring work-

ers with disabilities for 90% of the companies surveyed (in "Hiring the Handicapped," 1986). Similar findings were reported in the earlier-mentioned DuPont study which found that 96% of their workers with disabilities demonstrated equal or better safety records when compared to their nonhandicapped employees (in Steinhauser, 1978).

The individualized services of supported employment effectively respond to the safety-related concerns that may arise when employing workers with disabilities. Initially, employment specialists observe job sites, conduct environmental analyses to identify critical skill requirements, and then attempt to "match" these skill requirements with the abilities of potential workers. By matching up potential worker abilities with job skill requirements, the chances of an injury occurring at the job site are reduced. For example, individuals with severe cerebral palsy or other mobility impairments would not be considered for positions requiring extensive movement throughout a job site, entailing difficult mobility requirements such as working on slick tiled floors, or regularly using stairs. In addition to this matching process, systematic instruction, job modifications, and adaptations can be utilized on the job site to reduce hazards and improve performance to meet the employer's needs. Furthermore, on-going monitoring and follow-along services allow employment specialists to provide intervention, should job changes result in increased hazards.

Turnover Employee turnover is a problem frequently reported by employers that results in increased labor costs associated with advertising for vacant positions, interviewing and screening, and training of new employees. In fact, high turnover rates are not uncommon in unskilled, entry level positions; for instance, the National Restaurant Association reports a 400% turnover rate in the restaurant industry (in Kroger, 1979). It is often assumed that employees with disabilities will also experience high turnover. However, recent evidence appears to suggest that workers with disabilities actually display lower turnover rates than their nonhandicapped counterparts. A survey of 1,452 employees with disabilities by the Dupont corporation found that

93% of the employees had remained with the company longer than nonhandicapped employees (in Nathanson, 1977). Other corporations such as Southland, Woodward & Lothrop, McDonald's Restaurants, Quaker Oats, and Marriott have also reported lower turnover among their employees with disabilities (Ricklees, 1981; Smart, 1987).

Supported employment services effectively assist employers in stabilizing their high turnover rates. In fact, 67% of a recent sample of employers using supported employment reported lower turnover rates for their workers with disabilities than for those without handicaps (Shafer et al., 1987). In addition, research on the employment retention of 252 workers with mental retardation who received supported employment services reported lower turnover rates for these workers than for nonhandicapped employees (Wehman, Hill, Hill, Brooke, Pendleton, & Britt, 1985). The average length of employment for these workers was 19 months as compared to less than 5 months for nondisabled workers in comparable positions (Kroger, 1979).

Although supported employment may in fact result in lower turnover, it may be misleading to assume or to market to employers that these services will guarantee lower turnover. Workers with disabilities, like nondisabled employees, should be provided the opportunity for choice in employment and for employment mobility. One advantage of supported employment services that should be stressed to employers is the provision of ongoing services to workers and employers. By maintaining open communication with employers, employees, and family members, supported employment providers can respond to increased job responsibilities that may be required by the employer or desired by the employee. In addition, as employees are promoted within companies or placed into new jobs in other businesses, employment specialists may be able to arrange for replacements for the original jobs. In this way, both the needs of the worker and the employer are met without an interruption in wages or production.

Costs and Adaptations According to surveyed employers, perceived costs by the company are a major factor negatively affecting their hiring decisions regarding disabled workers (Dennis et al., 1986; Steinhauser, 1978). A survey of 300 businesses revealed that employers believe that in general they can accommodate physical disabilities more easily than mental disabilities (Combs & Omvig, 1986). Although employers often anticipate elaborate modifications and increased expenses as a result of hiring workers with disabilities, the need for adaptations and actual costs are frequently minor. In fact, a poll of 2,000 contractors by Pati and Morrison (1982) found costs for reasonable accommodations to be less than $500 per employee for 81% of the businesses surveyed. Another study indicated that costs for making buildings accessible were as little as 1¢ per square foot (Grazulius, 1978). Finally, the Marriott Corporation found the costs of necessary accommodations for developmentally disabled workers to be less than $100 per person in 90% of the cases (Smart, 1987).

Physical adaptations can be purchased commercially from various distributors, such as Prentke Romich Company or TASH, Inc. Other accommodations such as braille labels, hand or foot controls for equipment, ramps and handrails, telephone amplifiers, wooden blocks for elevation of a work station, or rollers added to a desk chair can often be developed and made noncommercially. Rehabilitation engineers can also be consulted to make adaptations, and such services can be paid for through state vocational rehabilitation agencies.

In addition to developing physical adaptations, environmental modifications can be made such as rearranging task sequences or work stations and trading tasks with other workers (Mallik, 1979). For example, stocking and rotating produce in a kitchen may be difficult for a worker with poor discrimination skills or physical limitations. An alternative solution could involve trading a job task with a coworker in exchange for the responsibility of stocking. Another example of adapting a job to meet a worker's needs could include adding colored markings (e.g., colored dots or stars) to time cards for employees having difficulty punching in and out independently.

Supervision A final concern expressed initially by potential employers of workers with disabilities is the perception that these workers require more supervision than other workers. Many employers do not recognize the capabilities of workers with disabilities and perceive of them as requiring extensive supervision and management (Louis Harris and Associates, 1986). Employers who have had experiences hiring workers with disabilities without supported employment services often report that their employees do require more training and supervision (Kroger, 1979; Ricklees, 1981). However, employers of workers receiving supported employment generally report satisfaction with the supervisory needs of their workers, suggesting that the provision of services by employment specialists effectively offsets any additional supervisory needs that disabled workers may display (Hill & Wehman, 1979; Shafer et al., 1987).

Employers may lack experience supervising workers with disabilities and may be unsure how to interact with them. They may respond to this uncertainty by ignoring the worker, providing too much supervision, or treating the employee differently from other coworkers. A function of the employment specialist is to model appropriate and respectful interactions for the employer and to suggest methods of supervision (Wehman & Melia, 1985). At the same time, the employment specialist teaches appropriate social skills to the employee and facilitates interactions with coworkers and customers. The employment specialist serves as a liaison, providing ongoing advocacy activities at the job site that will maximize integration and assure a worker's success.

This section has reviewed many of the factors that practical experience and research have identified as influencing employers' decisions in hiring workers with disabilities. By focusing attention upon the services of supported employment, many, if not all, of the employer concerns that have been discussed here can be confronted within the context of a marketing plan.

Although much of this chapter's discussion has concentrated upon activities related to developing employment opportunities, it must be recognized that a critical aspect of responsive marketing in supported employment is maintaining previously established employment situations. As such, responsive marketing must be perceived as a longitudinal, fluid activity that continually assesses the needs of consumers and modifies service delivery in response to consumers' changing needs. The next section examines some of the strategies effectively used in supported employment to maintain responsive relationships with employers.

STEP 4: MAINTAINING RESPONSIVE RELATIONSHIPS WITH EMPLOYERS

Developing and maintaining responsive relationships with employers is one of the cornerstones of supported employment (Wehman & Kregel, 1985). In sharp contrast to traditional time-limited placement orientation, supported employment implicitly assumes that services will continue to be provided to workers and employers for as long as needed. Wehman and Kregel (1985), for example, discussed the importance of ongoing assessment and extended follow-along services in supported employment. The purpose of the services is to remain responsive to the needs of employers and employees, continually assessing the quality of services that are provided and revising or altering services based upon the information that is received. Whether supported employment is provided through individual placement or group models, the process continues to be relatively similar, remaining knowledgeable and responsive to the needs and desires of employers.

Strategies for Maintaining Responsive Relationships

A variety of strategies may be used to remain responsive to employer needs. For example, maintaining contact with employers by periodic site visits, telephone contact, and regular written evaluations of worker proficiency have been suggested as methods of ongoing assessment (Hill & Wehman, 1979; Moon et al., 1986; Rusch, 1983; Rusch & Mithaug, 1980; Wehman, 1981; Wehman & Kregel, 1985). Typically, these activities may identify skill deficits of workers or environmental factors such as alterations in employee's work duties, schedules, or changes in management. By maintaining regular contact with employees and employers, supported-employment providers can respond to employer needs by providing additional training or support, thereby facilitating long-term employment.

Hill, Hill, and Wehman (1980) provide one of the first illustrations of a supervisor evaluation form, which they used to assess the performance of 23 competitively employed workers who had moderate or severe mental retardation. This form required supervisors (or employers) to respond to a variety of statements regarding their employees' social-vocational behaviors and skill mastery, and the services rendered by the job coach. In general, the results indicated that employers were satisfied with their workers' performance and with the services of the job coach.

Rusch (1983) assessed the validity of supervisor evaluations by comparing written evaluations of worker performance with direct observational measures of the same workers. Eighteen employers in the food service industry, whose employment experience with workers with mental retardation was not reported, viewed randomly presented 1-minute videotape segments of workers busing tables in a university cafeteria. Although the employers were found to moderately agree among themselves in their ratings (interrater reliability), they were also found to rate the same worker differently when viewing a segment more than once (intrarater reliability). While such a finding inspires less-than-desirable faith in the reliability with which employers evaluate worker performance, the inherent validity of employer evaluations cannot be disputed (e.g., employees receiving less than satisfactory evaluations will most likely lose their jobs).

The relationship between employers' evaluations of workers' performance and their employment tenure was recently studied (Shafer, Kregel, Banks, & Hill, 1987). This study sought to compare differences in employers' evaluations across time and between workers who were fired from their jobs versus those who remained employed. The results of that study demonstrated that employers gave workers much higher evaluations during the early stages of employ-

ment, indicating that employers' needs were met best while the level of intervention by employment specialists was the greatest. As job-coaching services were reduced over time, employers rated the performance of their workers lower, particularly with regard to communication, attending to task consistently, and performing comparably to nonhandicapped workers. A second finding of the study was that workers who were subsequently separated from employment were evaluated by their employers significantly lower with regard to attendance and consistency in task performance. Collectively, these findings suggest that the primary need of employers that should be recognized by supported employment providers is that of a reliable and productive work force.

SOME CLOSING CONSIDERATIONS

As this chapter has emphasized, the underlying philosophies and assumptions of responsive marketing are fully embraced by the practices of supported employment. The requirements of developing and maintaining a healthy relationship to the needs of the intended consumer populations, both employers and employees, are unquestionably met in supported employment by attending to general labor market needs, to the specific concerns of employers, and to the ongoing service or training needs important to provide a reliable and productive labor force.

All too often, we have tended to approach the needs of disabled workers and of employers from two separate perspectives in which the needs are identified and resulting marketing strategies are developed in isolation. The net result has often been the perpetuation of developmental or flow-through orientations to vocational rehabilitation, which have rarely led to employment of more severely disabled workers. In contrast, supported employment implicitly assumes that the needs of all of the consumer and constituent groups are assessed simultaneously and are responded to in a coordinated, planned fashion. In so doing, the needs of both the business community and of severely handicapped workers can be met effectively and efficiently.

REFERENCES

Barcus, M., Brooke, V., Inge, K., Moon, S., & Goodall, P. (1987). *An instructional guide for training on a job site: A supported employment resource.* Richmond: Virginia Commonwealth University, Rehabilitation Research and Training Center.

Bluhm, H. P. (1977). The right to work: Employers, employability, and retardation. In C. J. Drew & M. L. Hardman (Eds.), *Mental retardation: Social and educational practices* (pp. 207–215). St. Louis: C. V. Mosby.

Bourbeau, P.E. (1985). Mobile work crews: An approach to achieve long-term supported employment. In P. McCarthy, J. Everson, S. Moon, & M. Barcus (Eds.), *School to work transition for youth with severe disabilities.* (pp. 151–166). Richmond: Virginia Commonwealth University, Project Transition into Employment.

Cohen, J. S. (1963). Employer attitudes toward hiring mentally retarded individuals. *American Journal of Mental Deficiency, 67,* 705–713.

Combs, I. H., & Omvig, C. P. (1986). Accommodation of disabled people into employment: Perceptions of employers. *Journal of Rehabilitation, 52*(2), 42–45.

Dennis, S., Ebert, T., & Mueller, H. (1986). *What employers and employees say about success and failure in the work-place.* Alberta, Canada: Western Industrial Research and Training Center.

Easterday, J. R., & Dever, R. B. (1987). *Severely handicapped youth competing in the labor market: Implementation and effectiveness report from the first two years of Project Complete.* Bloomington: Indiana University.

Ebert, T., & Dennis, S. (1986). *What employers want to know before hiring an individual with a mental handicap.* Alberta, Canada: Western Industrial Research and Training Center.

English, R. W. (1971). *Combating stigma towards physically disabled persons.* Syracuse, NY: Syracuse University.

Florian, V. (1978). Employers' opinions of the disabled person as a worker. *Rehabilitation Counseling Bulletin, 22,* 38–43.

Freedman, S., & Keller, R. (1981). The handicapped in the workforce. *Academy of Management Review, 6*(3), 449–458.

Galloway, C. (1982). *Employers as partners: A guide for negotiating jobs for people with disabilities.* Sonoma, CA: California Institute on Human Services.

Grazulius, C. (1978). Understanding Section 503: What does it really say? *Personnel Administrator, 23*(1), 22–23.

Hartlage, L. C. (1974). Factors affecting employer receptivity toward the mentally retarded. In L. K. Daniels (Ed.), *Vocational rehabilitation of the mentally retarded* (pp. 439–444). Springfield, IL: Charles C Thomas.

Hill, M., Hill, J. W., & Wehman, P. W. (1980). An analysis of supervisor evaluations of moderately and severely mentally retarded workers. In P. Wehman & M. Hill (Eds.), *Vocational training and placement of severely disabled persons* (pp. 84–95). Richmond: Virginia Commonwealth University, Rehabilitation Research and Training Center.

Hill, M., & Wehman, P. (1979). Employer and nonhandicapped co-worker perceptions of moderately and severely retarded workers. *Journal of Contemporary Business, 8*(4), 33–42.

Hiring the handicapped: Overcoming physical and psychological barriers in the job market. (1986). *Journal of American Insurance, 62,* 13–19.

Kiernan, W. E., & Stark, J. A. (Eds.). (1986). *Pathways to employment for adults with developmental disabilities.* Baltimore: Paul H. Brookes Publishing Co.

Kleiman, C. (1985, June 23). Prospective janitors will be cleaning up by 1990. *San Francisco Examiner,* p. 27.

Kotler, P. (1975). *Marketing for nonprofit organizations.* Englewood Cliffs, NJ: Prentice-Hall.

Kroger, W. (1979). Disabled workers are no handicap to business. *National Business, 67*(5), 110–112, 114.

Louis Harris and Associates, Inc. (1986). *The ICD survey of disabled Americans* (Executive Summary). New York: International Center for the Disabled.

Mallik, K. (1979). Job accommodation through job restructuring and environmental modification. In D. Vandergoot & J. Worall (Eds.), *Placement in rehabilitation: A career development perspective* (pp. 143–165). Baltimore: University Park Press.

Mank, D. M. Rhodes, L.E., & Bellamy, G. T. (1986). Four supported employment alternatives. In W. E. Kiernan and J.A. Stark (Eds.), *Pathways to employment for adults with developmental disabilities* (pp. 139–153). Baltimore: Paul H. Brookes Publishing Co.

Martin, J. (1986). Identifying potential jobs. In F.R. Rusch (Ed.), *Competitive employment issues and strategies* (pp. 165–185). Baltimore: Paul H. Brookes Publishing Co.

Mithaug, D. E. (1979). Negative employer attitudes toward hiring the handicapped: Fact or fiction? *Journal of Contemporary Business, 8*(4), 19–26.

Molinaro, D. (1977). A placement system develops and settles: The Michigan model. *Rehabilitation Counseling Bulletin, 21,* 121–129.

Moon, S., Goodall, P., Barcus, M., & Brooke, V. (Eds.). (1986). *The supported work model of competitive employment for citizens with severe handicaps: A guide for job trainers* (rev. ed.). Richmond: Virginia Commonwealth University, Rehabilitation Research and Training Center.

Nathanson, R. (1977). The disabled employee: Separating myth from fact. *Harvard Business Review, 55*(3), 6–8.

Ninth Institute on Rehabilitation Issues. (1982). *Marketing: An approach to placement.* Menomonie: University of Wisconsin-Stout.

Parent, W., & Everson, J. (1986). Competencies of disabled workers in industry: A review of business literature. *Journal of Rehabilitation, 52*(4), 16–23.

Pati, G., & Morrison, G. (1982). Enabling the disabled. *Harvard Business Review, 60*(4), 152–168.

Perlman, L. (1983). Strategies in marketing rehabilitation: A summary of the seventh May E. Switzer seminar. *Journal of Rehabilitation, 49*(1), 14–17.

Phelps, W. R. (1974). Attitudes related to the employment of the mentally retarded. In L. K. Daniels (Ed.), *Vocational rehabilitation of the mentally retarded* (pp. 445–456). Springfield, IL: Charles C Thomas.

Pietruski, W., Everson, J., Goodwyn, R., & Wehman, P. (1985). *Vocational training and curriculum for multihandicapped youth with cerebral palsy.* Richmond: Virginia Commonwealth University, Rehabilitation Research and Training Center.

Posner, B. (1968). *Special report, the President's Committee for Employment of the Handicapped.* Washington, DC: U.S. Government Printing Office.

Rehabilitation Research and Training Center Newsletter. (Vol. 3). (1986). Richmond: Virginia Commonwealth University, Rehabilitation Research and Training Center.

Rhodes, L., & Valenta, L. (1985). Industry-based supported employment: An enclave approach. *Journal of The Association for Persons with Severe Handicaps, 10*(1), 12–20.

Riccio, J. A., & Price, M. L. (1984). *A transitional employment strategy for the mentally retarded: The final STETS implementation report.* New York: Manpower Demonstration Research Corporation.

Ricklees, R. (1981, October 21). Faced with shortages of unskilled labor, employers hire more retarded workers. *Wall Street Journal,* p. 27.

Rusch, F. R. (1983). Evaluating the degree of concordance between employers' evaluations of work behavior. *Applied Research in Mental Retardation, 4,* 95–102.

Rusch, F. R. (Ed.). (1986). *Competitive employment issues and strategies.* Baltimore: Paul H. Brookes Publishing Co.

Rusch, F. R., & Mithaug, D.E. (1980). *Vocational training for mentally retarded adults.* Champaign, Il: Research Press.

Rusch, F.R., Schutz, R.P., & Agran, M. (1982). Validating entry-level survival skills for service occupations: Implications for curriculum development. *Journal of The Association for the Severely Handicapped, 7,* 32–41.

Salzberg, C. L., Agran, M., & Lignuaris-Kraft, B. (1986). Behaviors that contribute to entry-level employment: A profile of five jobs. *Applied Research in Mental Retardation, 7,* 299–314.

Schalock, R. L. (1986). Service delivery coordination. In F. R. Rusch (Ed.), *Competitive employment issues and strategies* (pp. 115–127). Baltimore: Paul H. Brookes Publishing Co.

Shafer, M. S. (1986). Utilizing coworkers as change agents. In F.R. Rusch (Ed.), *Competitive employment issues and strategies* (pp. 225–239). Baltimore: Paul H. Brookes Publishing Co.

Shafer, M. S., Hill, J., Seyfarth, J., Wehman, P. (1987). Competitive employment and workers with mental retardation: An analysis of employers' perceptions and experiences. *American Journal of Mental Retardation, 92*(3), 304–311.

Shafer, M. S., Kregel, J., Banks, P. D., & Hill, M. L. (1987). What's the boss think? An analysis of employer evaluations of workers with mental retardation. In P. Wehman, J. Kregel, M. S. Shafer, & M. L. Hill

(Eds.), *Competitive employment for persons with mental retardation: From research to practice* (Vol. 2, pp. 60–83). Richmond: Virginia Commonwealth University.

Sitlington, P. L., & Easterday, J. R. (1985). *Conducting a labor market trend analysis: Process and results.* Bloomington: Indiana University, Center for Innovation in Teaching the Handicapped.

Sitlington, P. L., & Easterday, J. R. (1986). *An analysis of employer incentive rankings relative to the employment of retarded persons.* Bloomington: Indiana University, Center for Innovation in Teaching the Handicapped.

Smart, W. E. (1987, January 20). Workers with something extra. *Washington Post,* p. E5.

Smith, O. C. (1981). Employer concerns in hiring mentally retarded persons. *Rehabilitation Counseling Bulletin, 24*(2), 316–318.

Steinhauser, C. (1978). Rehabilitation of the handicapped: A boon to employers. *Risk Management, 25*(9), 34–38.

Stewart, D. M. (1977). Survey of community employer attitudes toward hiring the handicapped. *Mental Retardation, 15*(1), 30–31.

U.S. Department of Labor. (1984). *Labor projections for 1995.* Washington, DC: Author.

Virginia Employment Commission. (1985). *Virginia 1990 occupational employment projections.* Richmond: Author.

Wehman, P. (1981). *Competitive employment: New horizons for severely disabled individuals.* Baltimore: Paul H. Brookes Publishing Co.

Wehman, P., Hill, M., Hill, J., Brooke, V., Pendleton, P., & Britt, C. (1985). Competitive employment for persons with mental retardation: A follow-up six years later. *Mental Retardation, 23*(6), 274–281.

Wehman, P., & Kregel, J. (1985). A supported work approach to competitive employment of individuals with moderate and severe handicaps. *Journal of the Association of Persons with Severe Handicaps, 10*(1) 3–11.

Wehman, P., & Melia, R. (1985). The job coach: Function in transitional and supported employment. *American Rehabilitation, 11*(2), 4–7.

White, D. M., & Rusch, E. R. (1983). Social validation in competitive employment: Evaluating work performance. *Applied Research in Mental Retardation, 4,* 343–354.

Wolfe, H. E. (1961). The attitude of small industrial employers toward hiring of former state mental hospital patients. *Journal of Clinical Psychology, 17,* 90–94.

Young, J., Rosati, R., & Vandergoot, D. (1986). Initiating a marketing strategy by assessing employer needs for rehabilitation services. *Journal of Rehabilitation, 52*(2), 37–41.

SECTION V

SUPPORTED EMPLOYMENT
APPLICATIONS WITH
DIFFERENT POPULATIONS

Chapter 18

Supported Employment for Persons with Mental Retardation

Programmatic Issues for Implementation

R. Timm Vogelsberg and Lynda Richard

In 1983 at a statewide conference in Minnesota, Madeleine Will (secretary of the Office of Special Education and Rehabilitative Services of the U.S. Department of Education) made the following comment:

> The most crippling disability of all may not be found among disabled individuals, but instead may be found in the very service system federal and state officials have created to help them. The system is uncoordinated, inconsistent, and often incomprehensible. An estimated 8% of America's gross national product is spent each year on disability programs, yet most of this funding supports dependency . . . . In fiscal year 1983, the Social Security Administration spent 23 billion dollars in support payments that kept many disabled persons from working. Across the street, the Rehabilitation Services Administration spent one billion dollars to restore these same people to employment. And I note and underscore that's a twenty-to-one discrepancy (Will, 1985, p. 79).

Although this statement is now more that 4 years old, it still holds true for the majority of individuals with severe disabilities who are attempting to gain employment in community settings within their respective states.

Service development and placement for individuals with mild disabilities has progressed and time-limited services have advanced to an impressive status in comparison to services 10 years ago. Unfortunately, this development has not been mirrored for individuals with the most severe disabilities.

The 99th U.S. Congress made exemplary efforts to remove existing disincentives and barriers to community employment for individuals with disabilities. Its work in the Rehabilitation Act Amendments (PL 99-506), Education of the Handicapped Act Amendments (PL 99-457), Fair Labor Standards Act Amendments (PL 99-486), Employment Opportunities for Disabled Americans Act (PL 99-643), and the Tax Reform Act (PL 99-514) all contain sections that reduce or remove previous disincentives to employment. The movement at the federal level has been extensive and is widely recognized as progressive. Nevertheless, the 100th Congress still has notable barriers to confront. Issues such as Medicaid-funded day treatment and activity centers remain a challenge to the implementation of supported employment (Laski & Shoultz, 1987).

Acknowledgments: This chapter would not have been possible without the assistance and support of the members, project managers, and staff of the Pennsylvania State Task Force on Supported Employment, and the individual consumers of services who continue to help us understand the mutual benefits of working toward the dream of full community participation.

The work at the federal regulation level must continue if real community services are to flourish and conversion of the existing service system is to occur.

During the past 15 years, at least five areas have received major focus in efforts to expand community integration for individuals with severe disabilities. These areas have included high school curriculum improvement, expanded business incentives, improvement of generic programs that provide transition to employment without special services, improvement of time-limited services such as vocational rehabilitation, and the development of community-integrated time-enduring services (supported employment).

PHILOSOPHICAL UNDERPINNINGS OF SUPPORTED EMPLOYMENT

Integration

Contemporary service development has focused on services in the mainstream of society. Previous attitudes that individuals would benefit from isolated and segregated service options have fallen into disrepute as the success of integrated services has been demonstrated (Heal, Haney, & Novak Amado, 1988; Horner, Meyer, & Fredericks, 1986). Empirical studies of institutional residential settings (Conroy, 1977), deinstitutionalization (Bruininks, Meyers, Sigford, & Lakin, 1981), and facility-based vocational settings (Greenleigh Associates, 1975; Whitehead, 1979) have indicated that individuals with severe disabilities do not grow, move, or prosper within specialized but isolated environments.

On the other hand, repeated examples involving community residential settings (Janicki, Krauss, & Selzer, 1988) and community employment (Rusch, 1986; Vogelsberg, Ashe, & Williams, 1986; Wehman & Hill, 1985; Wehman, Kregel , Shafer, & Hill, 1987) have demonstrated that individuals can and do grow within community settings. The importance of social interaction (Chadsey-Rusch, 1986; Shores, 1987; Vogelsberg, Askin, & Schonfeld, 1987) in addition to simple physical integration has been recognized as a vital contributor to full community participation.

Ecological/Environmental Orientation

Previous service development centered on the individual and on predictive measures to identify preparatory activities for that individual. Contemporary service development also focuses on the individual but heavily emphasizes, as well, the next environment that the individual is expected to occupy. A better understanding of the effect (both positive and negative) of the environment on the individual is emerging. Agencies are providing people with severe disabilities with opportunities in community environments that meet the needs of the individual and provide input for future program development.

Accountable Service Development

As new approaches are initiated, the concept of an accountable service system continues to be explored. Supported employment was established on the basis of empirical evidence of its effective outcomes for individuals, as well as in response to proof that existing traditional service models were both expensive and restrictive. Cost-effectiveness is an economic/business concept previously not widely subscribed to in the human services field, but one that is quickly gaining respect (Ferguson, 1986; Hill, Banks et al., 1987; Hill, Metzler, Banks, & Handrich, 1987; Thornton, 1984). As budgets tighten, accountability and efficiency become focal points for future development. Funding issues are being determined on outcome measures rather than on political or subjective evaluations.

Individual outcomes must be identified, organized, and studied carefully to assure that future programmatic development does not repeat previous mistakes. Quality-of-life issues (Bellamy, Rhodes, Mank, & Albin, 1988; Matson & Rusch, 1986) are finally being recognized for their importance, and programmatic, budgetary, resource-based decisions are being examined carefully. Self-advocacy programs (Gould & Anderson, 1987) are beginning to develop, and their effectiveness is being verified in initiating positive change in people's lives.

The issues of conversion and of downsizing are being increasingly addressed within the adult service delivery system, and there is greater recognition of the importance of direct contact personnel and of reducing administrative levels.

Interagency Approaches

Interagency-directed activities require increased communication and coordination to be successful. If consensus can be gained among state agencies prior to actual project implementation, there will be less confusion and conflict once projects are in place. These activities are time-consuming and entail a certain loss of autonomy by each individual agency.

It is important to keep in mind, however, that the real focus of supported employment programs is to develop an accountable system of service for individuals with severe disabilities. To meet this goal, consensus of all involved state agencies becomes critical. Without real involvement and agreement, the quality and accessibility of the service will be impaired.

If the real focus of these programs is to develop a successful system for individuals with severe disabilities, then consensus developed and enforced by multiple agencies should assist the consumer to receive more effective and coordinated services. Although certain issues must be compromised, the expansion of knowledge, and the coordination of funds and of capable individuals involved in program development as a result of a multiple agency focus are extremely positive benefits.

PROGRAM DEVELOPMENT

In many states a large, sophisticated system of vocational rehabilitation services has assisted persons with mild disabilities to obtain competitive employment. Current vocational technology has proven effective in enabling traditional populations to become part of the work force; however, technology to address the needs of individuals with the most severe disabilities has not yet been fully developed or implemented.

Employment Services

Concurrent with the expansion of the concept of supported employment, existing community employment services must be examined to develop guidelines to improve their efficiency and ability to serve individuals with mild to moderate disabilities. The majority of individuals with mild disabilities do not require the intensive, long-term services of supported employment and can be adequately served through improvement of existing time-limited service models.

Many states have initiated facility surveys and have documented technical assistance and training needs to motivate facilities to implement community-integrated employment. Some states are initiating a financial incentive to facility-based programs for each individual who is placed in a community-based employment setting.

School-Based Employment Preparation

Public school curricula for individuals receiving special education services have traditionally focused on academic development rather than on community skilled development (Lynch, Kiernan, & Stark, 1982). It is now recognized that individuals with moderate to profound disabilities benefit greatly from community skill training prior to leaving public school services (Bates, 1984; Bellamy & Wilcox, 1981; Brown et al., 1981; Everson & Moon, 1987; Rusch & Chadsey-Rusch, in press; Wilcox & Bellamy, 1982; Wilcox & Bellamy, 1987).

Implementing curricula change within middle and high school special education programs is a long-term process that experiences developmental difficulties similar to those of the facility-based program. Change in curricula requires technical assistance, training, and monitoring to be implemented successfully. It also implies the need for a long-term change in university and college curricula to provide highly qualified personnel to work in school-based and community-based vocational settings for individuals with disabilities (Danley & Mellen, 1986).

PENNSYLVANIA STATE TASK FORCE ON SUPPORTED EMPLOYMENT

As a way of exploring new approaches to providing community-integrated vocational services to individuals with severe disabilities in Pennsylvania, a state task force on supported employment was convened in 1985. The charge of the task force was to determine how the state should initiate a plan to implement statewide supported employment projects. A long-term, developmental approach was adopted, including the requirement of a consistent consumer evaluation system that would provide the opportunity to formulate guidelines for statewide implementation of supported employment services for individuals with severe disabilities.

Pennsylvania's approach to the development of supported employment is unique in a number of ways. First of all, the creation of the State Task Force itself is consistent with the importance the state attaches to developing consensus for projects at the state agency level. While other state projects must seek funding from multiple state or local agencies, resulting in varied and diverse expectations, Pennsylvania provides a single stream of funds at the state level. This approach ensures consistent expectations across all involved state agencies and provides an opportunity for long-term support to populations currently without those options.

An additional unique property of the State Task Force is its focus on evaluation and monitoring. It is not uncommon for state agency directors to attend county board meetings or to visit project sites to meet individuals working in community positions. This exposure, evaluation and recognition of project importance is unusual in state government and helps to guarantee that guidelines are appropriately implemented. It also provides the opportunity to identify projects that need assistance while they are in the developmental stage. Typically, state projects are evaluated at the end of their first funding year or funding period. Pennsylvania's supported employment projects are required to submit monthly data in a standardized format that is then compiled and presented quarterly to the State Task Force.

Participating Agencies

The State Task Force consists of eighteen departments, agencies, bureaus, and organizations. Members from each are usually present at monthly meetings. The following is a listing of participating organizations and state agencies:

Department of Public Welfare
  Office of Mental Health
  Office of Mental Retardation
  Bureau of Blindness and Visual Services
Department of Labor and Industry
  Office of Vocational Rehabilitation
  Bureau of Job Training Partnership
Department of Education
  Bureau of Special Education
  Bureau of Vocational Education
Governor's Office of Policy Development
Developmental Disabilities Planning Council
Private Industry Councils
Pennsylvania Association of Rehabilitation Facilities
Pennsylvania Association for Retarded Citizens
Mental Health Association in Pennsylvania
United Cerebral Palsy of Pennsylvania
Pennsylvania Coalition of Citizens with Disabilities

Federal Project

As part of the Task Force's work, a proposal for federal funds was prepared and submitted to the Office of Special Education and Rehabilitative Services in August 1986. This proposal (for $409,000 per year for 5 years), was accepted, and the federal funds are being utilized by the State Task Force to establish three supported-employment technical assistance centers. One is located at the University of Pittsburgh, one at Temple University, and the third in the Central Administrative Office.

State Task Force Definition

The State Task Force identified seven critical criteria for supported employment—agreed to by all members of the Task Force—that fit the federal definition and specify additional components.

Although the federal definition accepts group placements (such as enclaves and mobile work crews in groups of eight people or less), the Pennsylvania State Task Force determined that during the initial years only the one-to-one placement model would be recognized and funded. This decision was made to guarantee that the most independence-producing and integrated model would be established prior to exploring other options. The Task Force did recognize that numerous enclaves and mobile work crews currently exist in Pennsylvania, but was aware of the difficulty of establishing consistent terminology, independence, population definitions, and adequate objective evaluation information among these projects. Concern was also voiced about the problems posed by instituting multiple forms of supported employment when knowledge and expertise in supported employment were extremely limited. The seven critical criteria adopted by the State Task Force are as follows:

1. Real Work in a Real Workplace   The individual must be placed in competitive employment, performing tasks nondisabled employees perform, with the same expectation to be productive that applies to nondisabled workers. The work must not be ''make work'' or charity.
2. Training on the Job Site   Instead of the traditional readiness process of placement after training, *placement and training occur simultaneously*. On-site training occurs in the work environment where performance behaviors are ultimately expected to occur.
3. Substantial Pay   The individual must be paid directly and receive wages *commensurate* with those paid to nondisabled workers for the same or similar work. Wages paid must be sufficient to provide the individual with severe disabilities with self-respect as an employee, coworker, and valued community member.
4. Long-Term Support Services   The individual must receive assistance for whatever period of time is necessary to attain and maintain continued employment. The type and intensity of support required may vary greatly over the course of a work year; however, support must be available when needed. These support services may include, but not be limited to, job training, service coordination, job clubs, transportation, employer/coworker support, and adaptive design assistance. Job-related support services in supported employment are not intended to deal with an individual's 24-hour personal needs, but, rather, to address those needs that focus on the acquisition and maintenance of a position of employment in the community.

5. Industry/Business Integrated   The individual must be placed in employment that is physically and socially integrated (i.e., with access to coworkers, supervisors, and, when appropriate, customers) so that these persons can serve as worker models, peer models, and friends. Early involvement, education, and commitment of employers, supervisors, and coworkers are necessary to facilitate successful integration, placement, and retention.
6. Coordination of Local Service System Resources   It is expected that people with severe disabilities who are receiving supported-employment services will have additional lifetime individual needs requiring sophisticated service coordination and implementation. These include, but are not limited to: social skill training, medical/dental treatment, money management, transportation, family/parent relationships, educational services, self-help skills training, housing considerations, counseling, recreation and leisure skill enhancement, and many others. Effective service coordination must be focused on services outside of work hours that require the application of local generic or specialized, long-term resources.

During initial program development, the supported employment program frequently must assume case management responsibility for the individuals being provided with services. This is not the long-term intent of supported employment, but it is necessary for initial program success while the existing systems adapt to new issues and responsibilities.
7. Consumer and Advocate Involvement   Individuals who are potential employees, together with their family and friends, must be given a significant role in job selection and service organization. This role must be developed to guarantee effective consumer involvement that provides informed consent to service development.

Status of First-Year Projects

In July 1986 five projects (in six counties) were funded to established supported employment.

Each project received approximately $250,000 for the first year to establish the program and maintain continual employment for at least 20 individuals with severe disabilities. As of July 1987, 99 placements of severely disabled individuals had occurred.

An additional six projects were funded in July of 1987. The 6 new projects were selected on a competitive proposal basis and there are now 11 projects serving 13 counties (2 are multiple county projects). It is expected that at least 6 additional projects will be funded each year until supported employment is available statewide to persons with severe disabilities.

Small subsets of the available data on each project are included in Tables 1–4. These tables, representing individual specific outcomes, provide demographics, financial, training and follow-up, and employment-specific information respectively. Individual project information about job development and costs of services is also collected and compiled monthly. The data from these projects, as well as from projects previously established in other states (Illinois, Vermont, Virginia, and Washington) have led to the establishment of project implementation guidelines to attempt to initiate high-quality services focusing on outcomes to individuals rather than on internal adult service processes or political situations.

The data provided by the five projects represent the first 12 months of project implementation. The microcomputer data system used by these projects (Vogelsberg, 1986) allows individual projects to enter data, generate their own reports, and share data as it is being compiled and presented at the state level.

The limits of the 12-month time period make it extremely difficult to draw major conclusions from the data available from these projects. It must be taken into account that certain data, such as that in Table 3, on training and follow-up, are drawn from projects of limited duration. For instance, it must be recognized that Table 3's data represent ongoing training hours and not total number of hours prior to follow-up. Many of the individuals now employed are still in the "on-the-job training phase" and will require additional hours prior to moving into follow-up. The tables represent five separate projects (the Association for Habilitation and Employment of the Developmentally Disabled (AHEDD), Competitive Employment Opportunities (CEO), Private Industry Council/Elwyn Institutes (PIC/

Table 1. Demographic information from five supported employment projects in Pennsylvania, July 1986–July 1987

Project	No. placements/ no. of people/ no. still working	No. women/ no. men	Median/average age	Living arrangement	Supported employment code	
AHEDD	17/16/15 93%	5/11	27/31	9 Nat. family 4 CLA 3 Own apt/home	8 MR 5 CMI 0 BVI	0 Sp. Ed. 1 SPD 3 Other
CEO	21/18/13 72%	10/8	28/37	7 Nt. family 7 Own apt/home 4 Other	7 MR 7 CMI 0BVI	0 Sp. Ed. 5 SPD 2 Other
PIC/ELWYN	12/12/7 58%	4/8	29/32	4 Nat. family 3 CLA 5 Other	2 MR 5 CMI 0 BVI	2 Sp. Ed. 3 SPD 0 Other
OSI	25/24/15 63%	12/12	29/36	9 Nat. family 9 Own apt/home 6 Other	8 MR 10 CMI 2 BVI	1 Sp. Ed. 3 SPD 1 Other
HART	24/19/15 79%	7/12	28/35	8 Nat. family 4 Own apt/home 2 CLA 5 Other	5 MR 11 CMI 0 BVI	3 Sp. Ed. 3 SPD 2 Other
Totals	99/89/65 73%	38/51	28/36	37 Nat. family 23 Own apt/ home 9 CLA (Community Living Arrangement 20 Other	30 MR 38 CMI 2 BVI	6 Sp. Ed. 15 SPD 8 Other

Notes: Data are being verified. See text for explanation of project names, employment codes, and other data.

Table 2. Financial information from five supported employment projects in Pennsylvania, July 1986–July 1987

| Project | Employer assistance | Pay per hour ($) | | Average gross salary/month($) | Average taxes paid/ month ($) |
		Range	Average		
AHEDD	TJTC	3.35–4.00	3.67	367	64
CEO	TJTC	3.35–5.50	3.64	296	54
	5 NARC-OJT				
PIC/ELWYN	TJTC	3.35–4.65	3.93	321	64
OSI	TJTC	3.35–8.93	3.63	337	63
HART	TJTC	3.35–8.65	3.81	411	80
Average	TJTC	3.35–8.93	3.74	349	65
	5 NARC-OJT				

Notes: Data are being verified. See text for explanation of project names, employment codes, and other data.

ELWYN), Occupational Services Incorporated (OSI), and the Hanover Adams Rehabilitation and Training Center (HART)). The following paragraphs briefly explain the findings presented in each table.

Demographic Information Table 1 indicates that 99 placements of 89 individuals have occurred. Sixty-five of these individuals are still working, yielding a 73% retention rate overall. The average age is 36. The majority of the individuals live with their natural families or in their own apartment or home. Thirty of the individuals are classified as mentally retarded (abbreviated in the table as MR), 38 are classified as experiencing chronic mental illness (CMI), 2 experience blindness or visual impairments (BVI), 15 have severe physical disabilities (SPD), 6 are from special education programs (Sp. Ed.), and 8 experience other forms of severely disabling conditions.

Financial Information As shown in Table 2, all of the projects utilize Targeted Jobs Tax Credits (TJTC) with employers, and the average pay per hour is $3.74. Monthly average salary is $349, and the average tax paid is $65.

Training Information As stated earlier, the data must be considered with caution, owing to

the fact that many individuals are still in the "intensive training phase." The total average number of hours per individual per placement as of July 1987 was 112. This number is being utilized to identify the amount of support required by the individual, and as a monitoring number to assist projects to identify individuals who may require more intensive support time to gain supported employment.

Employment Information Table 4 indicates that individuals work part-time (an average of 27 hours per week) and have only been absent or tardy a few times. The present focus for employment positions is to maintain existing service occupations and develop other forms of employment as well.

SUPPORTED EMPLOYMENT GUIDELINES

Supported employment must be recognized as a viable new approach to providing community employment services to persons with severe disabilities. It differs from current vocational programs—which provide a sequence of evaluation training, placement, and follow-up—by combining placement of persons with severe disa-

Table 3. Training information from five supported employment projects in Pennsylvania, July 1986–July 1987

| Project | Average hours/placement | | | | | | | | |
	Evaluation	Service coordination	Job development	Direct training	Indirect training	Observation	Follow-up	Coworker assistance	Total
AHEDD	3	2	4	38	10	33	7	5	102
CEO	3	5	4	40	7	16	8	2	85
PIC/ELWYN	8	6	8	33	20	16	10	5	106
OSI	11	18	3	36	5	22	7	4	106
HART	2	17	34	57	6	37	5	5	163
Average/ placement	6	10	11	41	10	25	7	4	112

Notes: Data are being verified. See text for explanation of project names, employment codes, and other data.

Table 4. Employment information from five supported employment projects in Pennsylvania, July 1986–July 1987

| Project | Averages | | | | |
	Days/week	Hours/week	Hours/month	Absences	Tardiness
AHEDD	5	27	98	2.7	1.9
CEO	4.8	23	77	2.6	1.6
PIC/ELWYN	5	27	81	2.7	3.0
OSI	4.3	25	91	1.6	2.1
HART	5	30	107	2.9	1.4
Average/ placement	4.7	27	91	2.2	2.0

Notes: Data are being verified. See text for explanation of project names, employment codes, and other data.

bilities in competitive jobs with *training on-the-job and long-term support services* to keep them on-the-job. The concept, developed as an alternative to day programs for people with moderate to profound mental retardation, was pioneered by professionals in Virginia (Wehman, 1986), Illinois (Rusch, 1986), Washington (Moss, Dineen, & Ford, 1986), Vermont (Vogelsberg, 1986), and other states and has been documented as an effective service model for individuals with mental retardation. Evidence of effectiveness with other populations is beginning to emerge (Sowers, Jenkins, & Powers, 1987; Vogelsberg & Richard, 1987).

An additional important point is to recognize that many individuals can benefit from community-integrated employment services that are less intensive than supported employment. A continuing issue within service development is the necessity to differentiate between time-limited and long-term services (Powers, 1988; Vogelsberg & Schutz, 1988). Work stations in industry, transitional employment programs, intensive on-the-job training for a short period, job clubs, expanded apprenticeship programs, and other short-term (time-limited) services are but a few of these forms of community-integrated employment that are very successful with individuals who have mild to moderate disabilities. These options should be expanded and improved concurrently with the establishment of supported employment. It must also be noted that the philosophical underpinnings of supported employment (integration, ecological orientation, and accountability) should be integrated into all service development for individuals with disabilities.

Location of Projects

One issue frequently raised by states is the location of projects. Should facility-based programs convert, or is it more efficient to establish private, nonprofit programs that do not have to address existing facility-based conversion issues? Rather than focus on historical issues and potentially negative discussions, an attempt should be made to concentrate on positive outcomes to individuals. Who provides the service (public, private nonprofit, private for-profit, etc.) is irrelevant, so long as the service results in an effective, efficient, and documented improvement in the quality of life of the individual.

Literature on the conversion process is becoming more evident. The reader is referred particularly to the book *Supported Employment: A Community Implementation Guide*, by Bellamy, Rhodes, Mank, and Albin (1988). In this text see specifically the chapters on planning for supported employment, strategies for change for facility-based programs, and developing state leadership in supported employment.

To take again the example of Pennsylvania, a multiagency orientation was initiated at the state, regional, and county levels to deal with the location issue for project implementation. Each county was responsible for identifying the lead agency for funding, and a variety of different locations were funded as a result of this. Projects are now located within a Private Industry Council, a private nonprofit program, and a variety of facility-based programs. The most important issue concerning location is the addition of strong accountability to individual outcomes, based on a multiagency approved monitoring system.

Regarding administrative, reporting, program, and training issues in supported employment, a comprehensive review was undertaken by the authors of previous program development. Findings from this review and from multiagency discussion, and keeping in mind the continual need to focus on consumer outcomes, has resulted in the following guidelines. Some of the guidelines have already been realized in practice, while it is anticipated that others will be implemented in future projects in Pennsylvania.

Administrative-Personnel Issues

Budgets   Budgets must be flexible, separate, and available for audit to determine appropriate use of funds and cost-effectiveness of services.

Program Staff   Program managers, employment training specialists, and job developers must be full-time staff devoted only to supported employment outcomes for individuals. Executive directors of existing agencies may donate time to projects but should not be funded through the project. Donation of time is one indication of conversion of existing funding. At least three full-time staff should be assigned to each project. This will assure that each program will be able to cover training needs and fill in for absences.

Compensation   Supported employment recognizes the value of staff who work directly with consumers. Salaries of employment training specialists must be adequate to demonstrate this value and provide the incentive to retain staff at the direct service level. Existing agency expectations and personnel policies should not restrict the amount of money supported employment staff can receive.

Administrative Involvement   Project managers must be aware of the ongoing responsibilities of the employment training specialists and the importance of one-to-one contact with individuals. It is expected that all project staff will engage in on-the-job training at least once a month to guarantee thorough recognition of the process and to provide relief time for employment training specialists to attend training and/or to take vacations.

Conversion   Projects must accept the expectation that both program directions and financial resources will be converted to supported employment in the future.

Accessibility   Projects should be located in buildings that are architecturally accessible by status-enhancing methods (not by back doors or freight elevators).

Location   Project sites should be separate from other human service facilities. Preferably, projects will be located within easy proximity to employment opportunities (such as an industrial complex).

Service Coordination   The long-range goal of supported employment is to become a functional service that is incorporated into existing services. Recognizing that existing case management and service coordination may not be sufficient to meet the multiple needs of individuals with severe disabilities in community employment, projects must be prepared to provide comprehensive service coordination while they assist in the rebuilding of the existing service system.

Reporting-Written Requirements

Monthly Data   Data on outcomes for each individual placed must be compiled and submitted monthly to a designated Technical Assistance and Monitoring Center.

Quarterly Reports, Final Reports   A written quarterly report must be prepared and submitted to the fiscal agent for dissemination to State Task Force members.

Written Procedures   Written procedures must be developed and implemented in at least the following areas:

1. Parent and advocate communication and support
2. Service coordination and case management
3. Staff scheduling and management of training
4. Consumer:
   a. Involvement and decision making
   b. Referral
   c. Evaluation
   d. On-the-job training
   e. Follow-up services

    f. Long term support

    g. Recreation, leisure, social support

5. Employment effects on all benefits (SSI, etc.)
6. Multi-agency agreements focused on consumer independence
7. Transition from school to work

Program Issues

Interagency Agreements   Local agreements must be prepared in writing and revised each year. These agreements are intended to identify how local programs will work together to gain successful employment outcomes for the individual.

Advisory Boards   A county advisory board must be established and maintained to guarantee that all county agencies are represented and receive ongoing information about the project. Representatives of each of the major agencies must be present on these boards. Most projects also establish a business advisory board to provide input and assist in the development of employment positions within their community.

Role of County Task Force or Advisory Board   The country advisory board will assist in the identification of solutions to systemic issues during project implementation. Projects are expected to analyze and negotiate issues to gain successful placements for individual consumers and to identify systemic barriers. Advisory boards then focus on systemic issues and prepare activities to resolve these issues.

Systemic Issues and Programmatic Issues   Individual projects must deal directly with programmatic issues to gain successful placements. They must also document systemic issues that cannot be resolved at the project level and report this information to their county advisory board for assistance. Frequent documentation of system issues at the county level and then dissemination of this information at the state level will eventually lead to some resolution.

Long-Term Support   Those individuals placed into employment must be guaranteed long-term support to maintain their employment. This support means at least two personal contacts each month (frequently much more), depending upon the needs of the individual.

Integration   Projects must adopt, develop, and implement the philosophy of community integration for all consumers. This includes assistance to the existing service system to identify, develop, and implement appropriate social and leisure activities for individuals who are employed.

Training Issues

Project Manager Meetings   Regional and state manager meetings must be attended by project managers. This is an opportunity for training, sharing of knowledge, and guaranteeing that projects are involved in active movement within the existing service system.

Employment Training Specialists Meetings   Regional employment training specialists meetings must be attended every other month by representatives from each project. The employment training specialists are then expected to disseminate information to other project members.

Inservice Training Sessions   Staff must be allowed release time to attend inservice training sessions. Overnight accommodations will frequently be necessary, a job feature that must be explained to staff during interviewing and hiring. Frequently, project managers substitute for employment training specialists on-the-job to guarantee that staff have the opportunity to receive training.

Internal Staff Training   Project staff who are able to attend training are expected to share valuable training information with other staff who could not attend the sessions. Projects should select individuals for attendance at inservice training sessions, who can assist in internal training.

County Education   Projects must provide educational assistance to local agencies and the private sector to guarantee that the concept of supported employment is understood by all.

SERVICE DESIGN

The most documented form of supported employment continues to be the individual placement on-the-job training approach for individuals classified as severely disabled and mentally retarded (Kiernan & Stark, 1986; McLoughlin, Garner, & Callahan, 1987; Moon, Goodall, & Wehman, 1985; Rudrud, Ziarnik, Bernstein, & Ferrara, 1984; Rusch, 1986; Rusch & Mithaug, 1980; Vogelsberg, 1986; Vogelsberg et al., 1986; Wehman, 1984). From numerous publications, project reports, and conference presentations, a consistent model for program development is emerging.

Many of the previously listed guidelines should be addressed during initial project development. Multiple agencies must be involved to guarantee consistent initiation, implementation, and follow-up of services. Administrative issues must also be addressed from a multiple agency focus. Numerous different approaches are being undertaken to jointly fund positions to guarantee that this focus goes beyond the paper interagency agreement and actually translates into consumer outcomes.

Appropriate Populations for Services

Supported employment is a service approach for the individual with the most severe disability. It is not appropriate for every individual with a disability. The supported-employment candidate must require long-term support in the employment and residential settings. Those individuals who can become independent within a 3- to 6- month training period should be provided with time-limited services rather than the long-term, resource-expensive services of supported employment.

Traditional rehabilitation services have attempted to provide services to multiple populations as their basic thrust, and have then focused "special projects" on more-challenging populations that have not benefited from the traditional approach. Now that supported employment is considered to have moved beyond the "special project" stage and is at the service implementation stage, many states are dealing with the issue of expansion of populations served.

As indicated earlier, the literature concerning service development for individuals with mental retardation is extensive. Unfortunately, literature relating to other populations (individuals with traumatic head injuries, long-term mental illness, severe physical disabilities, etc.) is scarce and frequently conflicting. Perhaps the area of greatest confusion concerns initiating service development for individuals with long-term mental illness. The philosophical and programmatic orientation for this population is still in dispute, and effective models are yet to be empirically verified. Parloff (1986) provides some insight into the existing empirical base for one orientation:

> The general field of psychotherapy—research and practice—now is confronted by an undeniable crisis of credibility, and research evidence has not served to reduce it. Indeed, recent research reports claiming to demonstrate psychotherapy's promiscuously positive effects appear, instead, to have exacerbated latent skepticism and incredulity. (p. 139)

Some new orientations concerning approaches for effective service delivery to persons with long-term mental illness (Selleck, 1987; Wallace, Boone, Donahoe, & Foy, 1985) are beginning to emerge. Many states receiving federal assistance for the development of supported employment have targeted these individuals for inclusion within program development for the coming year.

COMPONENTS OF PROGRAMS

Individual on-the-job training programs consist of four major components focused on community and consumer service development: referral, evaluation and job development, on-the-job training and placement, and follow-up. Figure 1 provides a flow chart of these activities. More detailed information about each stage in the process is available in Vogelsberg (1986) and Vogelsberg et al. (1986).

Referral

Funded projects must establish working relationships with potential referring locations. A local interagency agreement should be prepared between each referring location to guarantee a firm understanding of responsibilities. This agreement, detailing evaluation, support services, individuals responsible, and other areas,

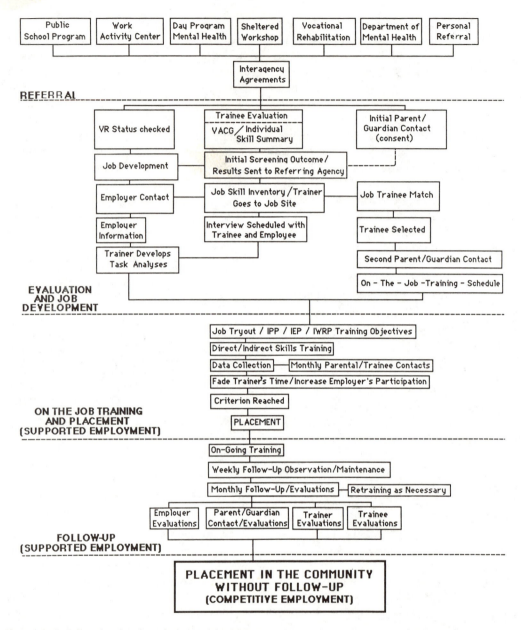

Figure 1. Flow chart of on-the-job employment training programs.

becomes a valuable component for future inter-action and should be revised yearly as each lo-cation gains an in-depth understanding of respective roles for future activities.

Evaluation and Job Development

These activities are focused on the community and the individual. Traditional service delivery has expended large amounts of resources on consumer evaluation and correspondingly small

resources on community evaluation. For ade-quate community job placement to occur, place-ment agencies must have intricate knowledge of the community, of the actual physical and social environment of the position, as well as of the individual.

This does not mean that long-term consumer evaluation is required prior to the actual capa-bility to provide community employment. The most effective evaluation information about an individual with a severe disability comes from actual community placement. Typically, projects in Vermont and Pennsylvania utilize existing (and usually extensive) evaluation information about individuals; they perform their own short-term evaluation of the individual, parent, and service community; and they then provide a placement in a community setting. The actual placement with a full-time employment training specialist results in comprehensive, ongoing performance data in job skills, community skills, and social interaction on the job. This information is continually utilized to determine the next stages within the training paradigm.

Concurrent with individual referrals and evaluation, community positions are being identified and evaluated. The evaluation of the physical and social environment is extremely important prior to the actual placement of the individual. Many difficulties with a specific position can be avoided if the project has an adequate understanding of the actual employment site. Frequently projects will require their employment training specialists or job developers to work the job for a number of days in preparation for the actual placement.

Although many individuals claim that there are not adequate positions available for placement, this has never been documented. Entry-level service occupations are available even in times of high unemployment and in diverse geographic areas of high unemployment (i.e. Pittsburgh, PA; White River Junction, VT; and Anchorage, AK are demonstrating success in placement activities). A present and future concern that does appear to warrant attention, is the future expansion in supported employment to include high-quality nonservice positions.

On-the-Job Training and Placement

Once an individual has been identified and matched to a position, he or she is placed in the position with full-time support from the employment training specialist. This support is intensive and should be available as necessary to maintain the position. If full-time support is not necessary and the individual becomes independent within a short period of time, then the placement agency should take steps to fulfill the continuing need for sophisticated, time-limited, on-the-job training programs.

On-the-job training includes ongoing performance indicators that assist in decision making about the required future levels of support. These performance indicators (typically a task analytic data sheet broken down into components for various job responsibilities that are then graphed and examined) must include social and community survival skills as well. The individual must be able to fit into the social environment and be able to travel, dress, and interact within the community to maintain successful employment.

Once the individual begins to demonstrate a greater level of independence on-the-job, the support of the employment training specialist can be gradually reduced and the follow-up stage can begin. Supported employment was established with the realization that many individuals will require ongoing support. The key component of support is the maximization of independence of the individual, with the guarantee of adequate support to maintain the employment. Frequently, this means reduction of supervision from 100% to 20%–30% over a 6-month period. The amount of supervision needed varies from position to position and from person to person; sometimes support is episodic rather than predictable (as in seasonal variations). It becomes the responsibility of the project to anticipate support needs and to guarantee availability of that support.

Follow-Up: Ongoing Support Services

The distinction between on-the-job training and follow-up support is frequently arbitrary. Many states are identifying the beginning of follow-up services as that time when the individual becomes 80% independent in the position; that is, when the individual is working independently 80% of the time and the employment training specialist is required 20% or less of the time.

Due to present funding mechanisms, it may be necessary to make this distinction. The important aspect from the viewpoint of the consumer and a strong accountable service system is that support should be available as necessary to guarantee ongoing successful employment.

Full-time support must be available if required (e.g, to adapt to a new supervisor, change in job responsibilities, change in residential situation) for job maintenance.

Many excellent sources of more in-depth program implementation activities are available (e.g., Bellamy, Horner, & Inman, 1979; Bellamy, O'Connor, & Karan, 1979; Bellamy et al., 1988; Kiernan & Stark, 1986; Rusch, 1986; Wehman & Hill, 1985; Wehman et al., 1987) and should be reviewed as programs are developing.

SYSTEMIC AND FUTURE ISSUES

The technology for program development of supported employment is readily accessible and is daily becoming more sophisticated. Resources are available concerning high school design and transition from school to work (Wehman, Moon, Everson, Wood, & Barcus, 1987; Wilcox & Bellamy, 1982); functional curriculum (Wehman, Renzaglia, & Bates, 1985; Wilcox & Bellamy, 1987); adult service program development (Vogelsberg & Schutz, 1988); service coordination (MacEachron, Pensky, & Hawes, 1986); parent attitudes (Hill, Seyfarth, Banks, Wehman, & Orelove, 1987); empirical reviews (Rusch, Schutz, & Heal, 1983; Trach & Rusch, in press); and studies verifying individual outcomes for consumers (Agran, Fodor-Davis, & Moore, 1986; Mank & Horner, 1987).

Additional issues for future program development and research on the national level include the need to implement an accountable service system that can demonstrate the improvement of the quality of the lives of the individuals who are supposed to benefit. Although numerous areas need to be addressed, effective multiple-agency service development is one of the most important. The fragmentation and confusion experienced by consumers, parents, and other individuals attempting to gain access to adult services must be resolved. Public Law 94-142 has demonstrated with school-age populations the improvement that can result from co-ordinated services; presumably, similar advances could occur at the adult level.

Second-Generation Issues

Given that program technology has been developed and is available, areas that must be adequately addressed in the future to guarantee ongoing program sophistication include at least the following:

Population similarities and differences in service design
Population severity—integrated services for everyone
Expansion of positions—service plus others
Joint agency funding, combined funding for joint positions
Long-term funding for all populations
Regulations, legislation, right to employment
Removal of federal financial disincentives
Personnel preparation—university and college involvement
Coordinated service delivery (24-hour days, 7 days per week)
Improved quality in time-limited services
Increased access to generic services
Conversion issues
    Funding
    Reduction in size (downsizing)
    Administrative support—reduction in administration
    Direct service personnel salary improvement
    Individual outcome focus—accountability
    Agency role revision—collaboration
    Public school curriculum revision

Although this list appears extensive, the authors' review of the past 10 years' progress in adult service delivery for individuals with severe disabilities reveals that people are benefiting more today from resources than they did previously. The challenge to the service system (education, mental health, mental retardation, developmental disabilities, private sector, etc.), is to maintain this momentum and recognize that the individual, as well as society as a whole, stands to benefit.

REFERENCES

Agran, M., Fodor-Davis, S., & Moore (1986). The effects of self-instructional training on job-task sequencing: Suggesting a problem solving strategy. *Education and Training of the Mentally Retarded, 21,* 273–281.

Anthony, W.A., & Blanch, A. (1986). *Supported employment for persons who are psychiatrically disabled: An historical and conceptual perspective.* Unpublished manuscript, Boston University.

Bates P. (1984). *Vocational curriculum development for persons labeled mentally retarded.* Paper presented at the National Symposium on Employment of Citizens with Mental Retardation, Rehabilitation Research and Training Center, Virginia Commonwealth University, Richmond.

Bellamy, G.T., Horner, R.H., & Inman, D.P. (1979). *Vocational habilitation of severely retarded adults: A direct service technology.* Baltimore: University Park Press.

Bellamy, G.T., O'Connor, G., & Karan, O.C. (1979). *Vocational rehabilitation of severely handicapped persons: Contemporary service strategies.* Baltimore: University Park Press.

Bellamy, G.T., Rhodes, L.E., Mank, D.M., & Albin, J.A. (1988). *Supported employment: A community implementation guide.* Baltimore: Paul H. Brookes Publishing Co.

Bellamy, G.T., & Wilcox, B.L. (1981). *From school to what? Transition services for students with severe handicaps.* Paper presented at the meeting of the Wales/OECD seminar on "The handicapped adolescent," Cardiff, Wales.

Brown, L., Pumpian, I., Baumgart, D., Vandeventer, P., Ford, A., Nisbet, J., Schroeder, J., & Gruenewald, L. (1981). Longitudinal plans in programs for severely handicapped students. *Exceptional Children, 47,* 624–631.

Bruininks, R.H., Meyers, C.E., Sigford, B.B., & Lakin, K.C. (Eds.). (1981). *Deinstitutionalization and community adjustment of mentally retarded people.* Washington, DC: American Association on Mental Deficiency.

Chadsey-Rusch, J. (1986). Identifying and teaching valued social behaviors. In F.R. Rusch (Ed.), *Competitive employment issues and strategies* (pp. 273–288). Baltimore: Paul H. Brookes Publishing Co.

Conroy, J.W. (1977) Trends in deinstitutionalization of the mentally retarded. *Mental Retardation, 15,* 44–46.

Danley, K.S., & Mellen, V. (1986). *Training and personnel issues for supported employment programs which service persons who have a long term mental illness.* Unpublished manuscript, Boston University.

Everson, J.M., & Moon, M.S. (1987). Transition services for young adults with severe disabilities: Defining professional and parental roles and responsibilities. *Journal of the Association for the Severely Handicapped, 12,* 878–95.

Ferguson, P. (Ed.). (1986). *Issues in transition research: Economic and social outcomes.* Eugene: University of Oregon Specialized Training Program.

Gould, M., & Anderson, N. (1987). *Self-advocacy for transition: A preliminary study of student success.* Unpublished manuscript, Maryland Self-Advocacy Training Project, Baltimore.

Greenleigh Associates. (1975). *The role of the sheltered workshop in the rehabilitation of the severely handicapped* (Report to the Department of Health, Education, and Welfare, Rehabilitation Services Administration). New York: Author.

Heal, L.W., Haney, J.I., & Novak Amado, A.R. (Ed.). (1988). *Integration of developmentally disabled individuals into the community* (2nd ed.). Baltimore: Paul H. Brookes Publishing Co.

Hill, J.W., Seyfarth, J., Banks, D.P., Wehman, P., & Orelove, P. (1987). Parent attitudes about working conditions of their adult mentally retarded sons and daughters. *Exceptional Children. 54,* 9–23.

Hill, M.L., Banks, P.D., Handrich, R.R., Wehman, P.H., Hill, J.W., & Shafer, M.S. (1987). Benefit-cost analysis of supported competitve employment for persons with mental retardation. *Research in Developmental Disabilities, 8,* 71–91.

Hill, M.L., Metzler, H.M.D., Banks, P.D., & Handrich, R. (1987). *Evaluating the financial outcomes of supported competitive employment: A consumer's perspective.* Unpublished manuscript, Virginia Commonwealth University, Rehabilitation Research and Training Center, Richmond.

Horner, R.H., Meyer, L.H., & Fredericks, H.D. B. (1986). *Community of learners with severe handicaps: Exemplary service strategies.* Baltimore: Paul H. Brookes Publishing Co.

Janicki, M. P., Krauss, M.W., & Seltzer, M.M. (1988). *Community residences for persons with developmental disabilities: Here to stay.* Baltimore: Paul H. Brookes Publishing Co.

Kiernan, W.E., & Stark, J.A. (Eds.). (1986) *Pathways to employment for adults with developmental disabilities.* Baltimore: Paul H. Brookes Publishing Co.

Laski, F., & Shoultz, B. (1987). Supported employment: What about those in Medicaid-funded day treatment and day activity centers? *TASH Newsletter, 13* (10), 5.

Lynch, K.P., Kiernan, W.E., & Stark, J.A. (1982). *Prevocational and vocational education for special needs youth: A blueprint for the 1980s.* Baltimore: Paul H. Brookes Publishing Co.

MacEachron, A.E., Pensky, D., & Hawes, B. (1986). Case management for families of developmentally disabled clients: An empirical analysis of a statewide system. In J.J. Gallagher & P. M. Vietze (Eds.), *Families of handicapped persons: Research, programs, and policy issues* (pp. 273–287), Baltimore: Paul H. Brookes Publishing Co.

Mank, D.M., & Horner, R.H. (1987). Self-recruited feedback: A cost-effective procedure for maintaining behavior. *Research in Developmental Disabilities, 8,* 91–112.

Matson, J.L., & Rusch, F.R. (1986). Quality of life: Does competitive employment make a difference? In F.R. Rusch (Ed.), *Competitive employment issues and strategies* (p. 331–338). Baltimore: Paul H. Brookes Publishing Co.

McLoughlin, C.S., Garner, J.B., & Callahan, M. (1987). *Getting employed, staying employed.* Baltimore: Paul H. Brookes Publishing Co.

Moon, S., Goodall, P., & Wehman, P. (1985). *Critical issues related to supported competitive employment.* Richmond: Virginia Commonwealth University, Rehabilitation Research and Training Center.

Moss, J.W., Dineen, J.P., & Ford, L.H. (1986). University of Washington Employment Training Program. In F.R. Rusch (Ed.), *Competitive employment issues and strategies* (pp. 77–33). Baltimore: Paul H. Brookes Publishing Co.

Parloff, M.B. (1986). Psychotherapy outcome research. In A.M. Cooper, A.J. Frances, & M. H. Sacks (Eds.). *The personality disorders and neuroses* (pp. 139–154). Philadelphia: J.P. Lippincott.

Powers, M.D. (Ed.) (1988). *Expanding systems of service delivery for persons with developmental disabilities*. Baltimore: Paul H. Brookes Publishing Co.

Rudrud, E. H., Ziarnik, J.P., Bernstein, G.S., & Ferrara, J.M. (1984). *Proactive vocational habilitation*. Baltimore: Paul H. Brookes Publishing Co.

Rusch, F.R. (Ed.) (1986). *Competitive employment issues and strategies*. Baltimore: Paul H. Brookes Publishing Co.

Rusch, F.R., & Chadsey-Rusch, J. (in press). Employment for persons with severe handicaps: Curriculum development and coordination of services. *Focus on Exceptional Children*.

Rusch, F.R., & Mithaug, D.E. (1980). *Vocational training for mentally retarded adults: A behavior analytic approach*. Champaign, IL: Research Press.

Rusch, F.R., Schutz, R.P., & Heal, L.W. (1983). Vocational training and placement. In J.L. Matson & J.A. Mulick (Eds.), *Handbook of mental retardation* (pp. 455–466). New York: Pergamon.

Selleck, B. (1987). *Supported employment for individuals with long term psychiatric disabilities*. Paper presented at South Carolina Conference on Supported Employment, Columbia.

Shores, R.E. (1987). Overview of research on social interaction: A historical and personal perspective. *Behavioral Disorders, 12*, 233–241.

Sowers, J., Jenkins, C., & Powers, L. (1987). *The training and employment of persons with physical disabilities*. Unpublished manuscript, University of Oregon, Eugene.

Thornton, C. (1985). Benefit-cost analysis of social programs: Deinstitutionalization and education programs. In R.H. Bruinicks & K. C. Lakin (Eds.), *Living and learning in the least restrictive environment* (pp. 225–244). Baltimore: Paul H. Brookes Publishing Co.

Trach, J.S., & Rusch, F.R. (in press). Research trends in employment of adolescents with handicaps. In E. Cipani (Ed.), *Child and Youth Services*. Urbana-Champaign: University of Illinois.

Vogelsberg, R.T. (1986). Competitive employment in Vermont. In F.R. Rusch (Ed.), *Competitive employment issues and strategies* (pp. 35–49). Baltimore: Paul H. Brookes Publishing Co.

Vogelsberg, R.T., Ashe, W., & Williams, W. (1986). Community based service delivery in rural Vermont: Issues and recommendations. In R. H. Horner, H. D. Bud, L. H. Meyer, & B. Fredericks (Eds.), *Education of learners with severe handicaps: Exemplary service strategies* (pp. 29–59). Baltimore: Paul H. Brookes Publishing Co.

Vogelsberg, R. T., Askin, B., & Schonfeld, S. (1987). *Physical integration and social interaction of persons with severe disabilities in community and sheltered employment settings*. Unpublished manuscript, Temple University Developmental Disabilities Center, Philadelphia.

Vogelsberg, R.T., & Richard, L. (1987). *Implementation of supported employment for individuals with long term mental illness*. Unpublished manuscript, Temple University Developmental Disabilities Center.

Vogelsberg, R.T., & Schutz, R. (1988). Establishing community employment programs for persons with severe disabilities: Systems designs and resolutions. In M.D. Powers (Ed.), *Expanding systems of service delivery for persons with developmental disabilities* (pp. 127–147). Baltimore: Paul H. Brookes Publishing Co.

Wallace, C.J., Boone, S.E., Donahoe, C.P., & Foy, D.W. (1985). The chronically mentally disabled: Independent living skills training. In D.H. Barlow (Ed.), *Clinical handbook of psychological disorders: A step-by-step treatment manual* (pp. 462–501). New York: Guilford Press.

Wehman, P. (1984). Transition for handicapped youth from school to work. In J. Chadsey-Rusch (Ed.), Conference proceedings from *"Enhancing transition from school to the work place for handicapped youth."* Urbana-Champaign, IL: Office of Career Development for Special Populations, University of Illinois.

Wehman, P. (1986). Competitive employment in Virginia. In F.R. Rusch (Ed.), *Competitive employment issues and strategies* (pp. 23–34). Baltimore: Paul H. Brookes Publishing Co.

Wehman, P., & Hill, J.W. (1985). *Competitive employment for persons with mental retardation: From research to practice—Volume 1*. Richmond: Virginia Commonwealth University, Rehabilitation Research and Training Center.

Wehman, P., Kregel, J., Shafer, M.S., & Hill, M.L. (1987). *Competitive employment for persons with mental retardation: From research to practice—Volume 2*. Richmond: Virginia Commonwealth University, Rehabilitation Research and Training Center.

Wehman, P., Moon, M.S., Everson, J.M., Wood, W., & Barcus, J.M. (1987). *Transition from school to work*. Baltimore: Paul H. Brookes Publishing Co.

Wehman, P., Renzaglia, A., & Bates, P. (1985). *Functional living skills for moderately and severely handicapped individuals*. Austin: PRO-ED.

Whitehead, C.W. (1979). *Sheltered workshop study: A nationwide report on sheltered workshops and their employment of handicapped individuals*. Washington, DC: U.S. Department of Labor.

Wilcox, B., & Bellamy, G.T. (1982). *Design of high school programs for severely handicapped students*. Baltimore: Paul H. Brookes Publishing Co.

Wilcox, B., & Bellamy, G.T. (1987). *The activities catalog: An alternative curriculum for youth and adults with severe disabilities*. Baltimore: Paul H. Brookes Publishing Co.

Chapter 19

Supported Employment for Persons with Autism

Pat McCarthy, Katherine W. Fender, and Don Fender

Nationwide, few people with autism have been placed into competitive employment (K. Fender, 1986; *Job in Operations*, 1986; Juhrs, 1985; Nugent, 1982). It is only recently that the technology and level of support services needed to successfully place and retain a person with autism in a job have been applied. The data in Table 1 illustrate that people with autism can hold productive jobs. Yet, follow-up studies indicate that without appropriate training and support services, these persons cannot maintain employment (DeMeyer et al., 1973; Kanner, 1971; Lotter, 1974; Rutter, Greenfeld & Lockyer, 1967).

The models of supported employment used in assisting adults with autism to enter the work force are the same as those used in serving people who have mental or physical disabilities, such as supported competitive employment (Wehman, 1985), enclaves in industry, mobile work crews, and supported jobs (Mank, Rhodes, & Bellamy, 1986). A key to successful job placement of people with autism is for the rehabilitation professional (e.g. employment specialist or rehabilitation counselor) to be familiar with the syndrome of autism and what it means in terms of how a person learns, so that support services can be molded accordingly.

Autism was first identified by Leo Kanner in 1943 when he studied 11 children who all exhibited the behavior traits of: 1) difficulty relating to others, 2) delayed and/or impaired language, and 3) insistence on sameness as evidenced in ritualistic and/or stereotypic behaviors. Since that time, autism has been defined as a lifelong disorder that "severely impairs the way sensory input is assimilated, causing problems in communication, social behavior and irregularity in learning" (National Society for Autistic Children, 1979). The etiology remains unknown. Although autism was initially identified as an emotional disturbance caused by environmental factors, such as a cold, uncaring mother, it is now hypothesized to be the result of either a biochemical dysfunction (Ritvo, Rabin, Yuwiler, Freeman, & Geller, 1978) or a neurological dysfunction (Mauer & Damasio, 1982; Rutter, 1978).

Although autism is not now viewed as a psychiatric disorder by the Autism Society of America, the *Diagnostic and Statistical Manual of Mental Disorders*, 3rd edition (American Psychiatric Association [APA], 1980, pp. 89–90), referred to as *DSM III*, contains the criteria universally accepted for autism. This manual presents the following diagnostic criteria:

1. onset before 30 months of age;
2. pervasive lack of responsiveness to other people;
3. gross deficits in language development;
4. if speech is present, there are peculiar speech patterns such as immediate and delayed echolalia, metaphorical language, pronominal reversal;

Table 1.   Data from three programs placing persons with autism into employment

Descriptors	Programs		
	CSAAC[a] (Juhrs, 1987)	PIA[b] (Fender, 1987)	TEACCH[c] (Mesibov, 1987)
Supported employment models	Individual and small-group (2–3) placements	Individual placements	Mobile work crews and individual placements
Number of persons placed	60	7	20
Time frame for making placements	6.5 years	1 year	5 years
Average salary	Over $4.00/hr.	$3.75/hr.	$4.00/hr.
Average work (hrs./week)	35	30	20–25
Reasons for job separation	Company moved	Business closed	Breakdown in system
	Client quit owing to lack of work	Layoff due to lack of work	
	Client offered promotion		
Job types	Stock clerk	Grounds maintenance worker	Food service worker
	Quality-control person	Food service worker	Manual laborer
	Library assistant	Motel roomkeeper	Accountant
	Liquor control	File clerk	
	Warehouse worker	Library assistant	
	Bindery worker		
	Printer		
	Electronic assembler		
	Mailing company worker		
	Paper pickers—recycling		
	Lamination specialist		
	T-shirt silkscreening folders		
	Computer cable calibrator		
	Storeroom worker		

[a] CSAAC = Community Services for Autistic Adults and Children, Rockville, Maryland.
[b] PIA = Programs for Individuals with Autism, South Carolina.
[c] TEACCH = Teaching and Educating Children with Autism and Other Communication Handicaps, North Carolina.

5. bizarre responses to various aspects of the environment; e.g. resistance to change, peculiar interest in or attachment to animate or inanimate objects;
6. absence of delusions, hallucinations, loosening of associations, and incoherence as in schizophrenia.

All of these characteristics are exhibited by individuals with autism; however, the patterns and severity of the behaviors will vary. In addition, 75% to 80% of individuals with autism also have mental retardation (Hurley & Sovner, 1983). People who are autistic have difficulties in communication and central coding processes that are generally not experienced by people who have mental retardation only (Rutter, 1978). As a result, they often misinterpret information received through sensory modalities and respond in unusual or distorted ways compared to others of the same mental age.

Most rehabilitation professionals have never encountered a person diagnosed as autistic for several reasons:

1. The *DSM III* classifies autism under the section for childhood disorders. Therefore, most rehabilitation professionals view the autism diagnosis as a syndrome for children only, and generally use the mental retardation or schizophrenia classification, depending on the level of intellectual functioning, for adults who are autistic. Indeed, autism does begin in early childhood; however, it is a chronic disability. A person never outgrows the syndrome. It is important that the rehabilitation professional be aware of the life-span issues and characteristics of autism in order to help the person overcome the language and social challenges specific to autism that go beyond the retardation he or she might experience.

2. Autism is a rare disorder. Generally, it is reported to occur in 4 to 5 persons in every 10,000 (Lotter, 1966; Wing, Yates, Brierley, & Gould, 1976). Even considering the more recently quoted incidence figure of 15 in every 10,000 people (National Society for Autistic Children, 1979), there are only approximately 375,000 people of all ages who are autistic in the United States, or 0.15% of the total population.
3. Most people who are autistic live in institutions as adults (Sullivan, 1977) because of the lack of community resources. The small percentage who live in the community have little or no possibility of being considered eligible for traditional vocational rehabilitation services. Fortunately, this segregated adult life is becoming less common owing to intensive, individualized programming through schools and adult service agencies. Availability of supported employment options, along with semi-independent living arrangements, can be a major factor in changing this dilemma.

Increasingly, rehabilitation professionals, specificially employment specialists, will be serving people with autism as they remain in the community as adults. It is important that the employment specialist be able to identify a person with autism and understand the features associated with the syndrome that have impacts on learning and working. This chapter discusses the cognitive and behavioral characteristics of people with autism, along with implications for employment services. Next, the authors provide recommendations for the employment specialist to follow as he or she and the consumer (i.e., the person obtaining employment services) progress through each step of the supported work model. Finally, the chapter reviews work-related issues.

CHARACTERISTICS ASSOCIATED WITH AUTISM

Communication

Impaired communication is a primary symptom of autism (Faye & Schuler, 1980). Other difficulties related to autism, such as anxious and aberrant behavior, often result from poor expressive and/or receptive communication (Donnellan, Mirenda, Mesaros, & Fassbender, 1984; LaVigna & Donnellan, 1986). Rutter (1978) reports that 50% of people with autism are mute. If verbal speech is present, it is impaired in some manner such as pronoun reversal, abnormal speech tone or rhythm, lack of spontaneous speech, and/or echolalia (APA, 1980). Baltaxe & Simmons (1981) estimated that 75% of people with autism are echolalic. Echolalia is described as the partial or complete repetition of an utterance made by someone else. Echolalia may occur either immediately following the utterance or after a period of time. Prizant and Duchan (1981) describe several categories of echolalia, indicating both interactive (functional) and noninteractive (nonfunctional) forms. They postulate that echolalia often serves several functions for a person, including turn-taking, declaration, yes-answer, request, rehearsal, and self-regulation.

Furthermore, a person with autism generally has poor receptive language skills because of difficulty in processing information. As a result, he or she may become extremely cue-dependent, relying on the speaker's facial expressions to determine the content of the message.

Implications for Employment　In providing job-site training to an employee with autism, the employment specialist will need to address the communication difficulties in order to maximize performance and minimize anxiety induced by confusion or failure of the client. The following recommendations are designed to address these issues.

An employee with autism might need a nonspeech communication system. The employment specialist should conduct a thorough analysis of the job prior to the employee's first workday, in order to identify the components of the job. If the consumer exhibits autism, the employment specialist will need to record all potential receptive and expressive communication requirements of the job. Following the analysis, the employment specialist should determine if the communication requirements exceed the employee's abilities. If so, then a nonspeech system to aid the employee in expressing himself or herself should be developed. The system can take many forms, such as photographs or word communication cards. Figure 1 illustrates possible systems that have been used effectively. The messages contained in the system will be determined by the communication requirements on the job. If, for instance, as part of his job, the employee needs to request supplies from the stockroom or order lunch in the company cafeteria, then specific pictures or sentences would appear in a book or on a board.

The nonspeech system should also address needs in work-related areas. Any person working in a metropolitan location will probably need a card with instructions to the driver on a city bus, explaining where the employee works and requesting assistance from the driver in making connections. Although the employment specialist trains the employee to ride the city bus, the consumer may need the card in the event that he or she misses a bus connection and is unable to request assistance to correct the situation.

Employees with poor receptive language skills often perform better with concrete visual cues. Once the sequence of the duties has been determined, the employment specialist should outline a schedule of responsibilities for the employee. This aid will be particularly important if the employee has difficulty processing auditory information. If the employee has reading skills, the schedule can contain short phrases or sentences; otherwise, pictures or photographs can be used to depict each task (see Figure 2). If job duties change daily, a different schedule should be developed for each day. Some employees may always need the schedule as an aid in recalling the sequence of responsibilities;

however, the schedule can be faded away if the employee learns by rote the steps of the job.

If an employee uses echolalia in a functional manner, it may be beneficial in job training. When the employment specialist is assisting the consumer prior to placement into a job, he or she should determine if the consumer uses functional echolalia as a means of communicating. If the employee uses echolalia in a rehearsal or self-regulatory manner, the employment specialist can train the employee to use verbal mediators, that is, "self talk" to regulate behavior (Schuler & Perez, 1987). For example, the employee can learn to repeat the steps of a complicated task as a way to perform the steps correctly each time. Another example is for the employee to repeat calming phrases such as "slow down and try again," to be used at times when anxiety is building due to confusion about a task.

Social Skills

People with autism do not understand social rules. As a result, they usually present themselves as withdrawn and with stilted or abnormal mannerisms (Wing, 1978). They are not aware of various messages given through body language or voice tone, and take what is said literally, including jokes, irony, or plays on words (Niedringhaus, 1985). They do not have the ability to read emotions and are unable to pick up on subtle behavioral cues from others such as signs of boredom. Rarely do they participate in typical reciprocal dialogue, and will often say things that have no relationship to the conversation or event at hand.

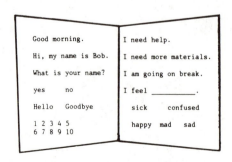

Figure 1.   Expressive communication devices.

1. Ride bus to work

4. Vacuum room

2. Cart to room

5. Clean bathroom

3. Make bed

6. Ride bus home

Figure 2.   Daily written/picture work schedule.

(continued)

Date _____   Staff member present _____

Daily schedule	Work checks
1. Be ready to leave at 10:45 AM and have work schedule and checksheet.	1. When dishes are not coming out of washer, you should put clean dishes, glasses, bowls, etc., away or straighten drying racks or wipe off washing machine.
2. Use toilet and wash hands at Barley & Rye before going to kitchen.	2. When taking things to the food preparation area (big pots, trays, spoons, bowls), take only as many items as you can safely carry.
3. Put on apron and get a rag.	3. Take empty trays off as soon as they are empty.
4. Clock-in, have manager sign card, and put card in back pocket.	4. Put silverware in holders using both hands and work fast. If trays start to back up, place silverware on top of glasses until you have time to catch up.
5. Fix glass of tea and take to work area (1 glass per shift).	5. Always take at least two items at a time to drying rack.
6. Begin work.	
7. When all dishes are finished and Frankie is cleaning up, wipe off counter top—use spray cleaner.	
8. Move rubber mat behind salad-making counter and sweep floor.	
9. Mop floor.	
10. Take trash to dumpster.	
11. Clock-out, have manager sign card.	

Pay-Off

Total checks from daily schedule ☐

Total X's from work checks (subtract) ☐

Total ☐

9 or more = large diet (16 oz) coke and 5 points toward certificate
6–8 = small diet coke (12 oz.) and 4 points toward certificate
3–5 = small diet coke but no points for certificate
Below 3 = nothing

Figure 2.   (continued)

Implications for Employment Employees *with autism will need to be taught appropriate social responses.* Although the employment specialist should generally attempt to identify jobs requiring limited interactions, social demands on a job will need to be evaluated in the initial job analysis. After the employment specialist has determined specific social scenarios at the job site, he or she should systematically teach the employee appropriate responses through task analyses and instruction of social interactions and role-playing (Brady et al., 1984; Liberman, King, DeRisi, & McCann, 1976).

Coworkers need to understand the basis of the unusual responses of the employee with autism. The employment specialist should also concentrate on informally discussing with coworkers the unique way that the person with autism communicates. In addition, he or she should offer suggestions on how the coworkers

can respond effectively to the employee. Through these advocacy efforts, social relationships may be enhanced. However, the employment specialist must be sensitive to the employee's need for time alone to relax during break or lunch and to maintain a balance between socializing and solitude.

Cognition

Kanner's studies (1943) indicated that persons with autism have normal or above-normal intelligence, but may be functionally retarded as a result of their other difficulties. However, more recent research indicates that the majority of persons with autism have mental retardation, with 60% having a measured IQ below 50. Confusion on this issue exists because there is often uneven development across skills (Shea & Mesibov, 1985). A person with mental retardation generally is delayed across all areas. Thus, a person who has a chronological age of 10 but a mental age of 6 has language, social, and cognitive skills of a 6-year-old. However, if the 10-year-old child is autistic with a mental age of 6, he might have the cognitive skills of a 6-year-old, no verbal language, and distorted social skills, and yet be able to read on the level of a 15-year-old. It is sometimes believed that a person with autism is more intelligent than he or she actually is because of an exceptional ability in a particular area, such as remembering dates or playing the piano, which is at a higher level than his or her other skills. Although research indicates that higher intelligence and success on a job do not correlate (Hill et al., 1985), the retardation variable must be considered when determining the techniques to use in training an employee with autism.

Implications for Employment Systematic *instructional techniques must be used in training persons with autism.* Snell (1983) presents several strategies to use when teaching persons who have severe disabilities, including the use of task analyses, data-based decision making, functional and age-appropriate instruction, and prompting. The appropriate use of these techniques is essential in maximizing job performance of the employee with autism.

Persons with autism are concrete learners. People with autism have difficulty with abstract concepts and generally prefer the visual modality rather than the auditory modality for learning. Therefore, new information should be presented in a visual and tangible manner. The picture and word schedules in Figure 2 are examples of how the employment specialist can make task expectations clear to the employee. A similar approach can be used in teaching the steps of a task that might seem simple to most people but is difficult for a person with autism. A task such as opening a combination lock used on the supply closet might be essential in performing a housecleaning job. Yet to a person with cognitive difficulties, the process can be extremely confusing. Visual cues, as shown in Figure 3, provide a concrete, step-by-step explanation to the employee, thus assisting him or her to overcome a potential roadblock to success.

Generalization difficulties are often experienced by persons with autism. As with others experiencing severe disabilities, people with autism have problems generalizing skills (Koegel, Rincover, & Egel, 1982). These difficulties are partially related to the approach used in learning tasks. Persons with autism learn a task as a whole and are not able to separate individual skills and use them in a similar task (Prior, 1979). For example, if the person learns a procedure to clean a mirror as part of cleaning a motel bathroom, he or she might not generalize the procedure to tasks such as cleaning a picture window. The new, yet similar, task will have to be taught as though it is a totally new procedure.

Another characteristic that may be manifested in generalization problems is overselectivity (Rincover & Koegel, 1975), that is, in a multistimuli event, attending to a specific stimulus that might not always be present. When that particular stimulus is absent, the person is unable to perform the task. For example, if the employee meets the floor supervisor on a day when he is wearing a white shirt, the employee may focus on the shirt as the identifying characteristic of the supervisor. As a result, the employee only recognizes the supervisor when he wears white shirts. Another example is responding to something as seemingly insignificant as the distance the trainer stands from the employee during one day's training. Subsequently, the employee might be unable to perform the task if the employment specialist, for example, stands 3 feet away instead of 4. The employment specialist needs to be sure to vary his or her position relative to the employee when training. It is also helpful to periodically introduce a different employment specialist on site so that the presence of the regular employment specialist is not required for the employee to perform the assigned tasks. Owing to the potential for overselectivity, the employment specialist must be conscious about the cues to which the employee is responding and be certain they are appropriate.

Prompt Dependency

A person with autism may appear to lack initiative, even to the extent of waiting for direc-

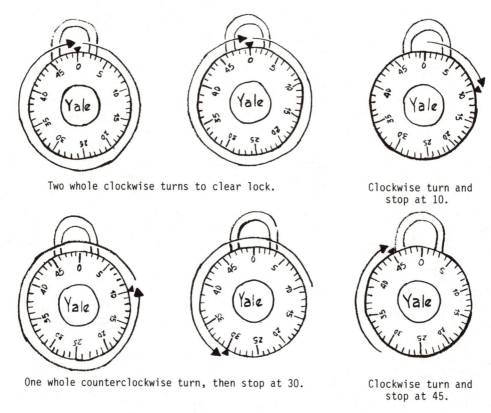

Two whole clockwise turns to clear lock.

Clockwise turn and
stop at 10.

One whole counterclockwise turn, then stop at 30.

Clockwise turn and
stop at 45.

Figure 3. Visual cues for opening a lock with the combination of 10-30-45.

tives to perform each step of a task. Until this reliance on others is overcome, the person will never be able to independently perform a job. This dependency on prompts is generally a learned response (NSAC/NPT Staff, 1981). Through the years, the person has been taught to wait before responding. Examples include a teacher requiring students to raise their hands before taking turns or requiring a student to ask for and then receive verbal permission before going to the restroom. The teacher instills prompt dependency. These procedures are an acceptable part of life. However, a person with autism learns that you must wait for a cue from someone before responding, and the waiting becomes a part of a ritual. Therefore, the sequence leading to a response in a situation such as a pot-scrubbing job becomes: 1) stimulus (several pots in the sink), 2) wait, 3) prompt (employment specialist tells the employee to pick up the scouring pad and scrub the pot), and 4) response (the employee begins scrubbing the pot). The tendency to become prompt dependent is more likely if

the prompt is verbal or gestural, including head nods or glances, than if it is physical, such as holding the employee's hand and guiding it through the motions.

Implications for Employment *During job training, an employee with autism might learn that verbal reinforcement or verbal prompts are part of the task sequence.* Therefore, the employment specialist should be careful about the placement of prompts and reinforcement so that they do not interrupt the proper performance flow. Although least-prompting techniques, in which a person has an opportunity to attempt a step in a sequence before being prompted, are effective in skill development (Moon, Goodall, Barcus, & Brooke, 1986), this method of prompting can be detrimental to the independence of a person who easily becomes prompt dependent. Instead, the prompt needs to be delivered prior to the learner's response.

When an individual with autism is prompt dependent and/or appears to be having difficulties learning a skill, the method of discrete trial training, in which prompts are delivered prior to a response, is effective in lessening the likelihood of the learner becoming prompt dependent (Donnellan-Walsh, Gossage, LaVigna, Schuler, & Traphagen, 1976).

The employment specialist's first step when using the discrete trial format is to do a detailed analysis of the task at hand and to delineate all aspects of the trial format and training steps, as illustrated in Figure 4. Thus, the learning experience is very structured and consistent, as well as specific to the individual's learning needs. This structured teaching format helps avoid any confusion over what is or is not an actual part of the task, and is often referred to as errorless learning.

To implement discrete trial training, the employment specialist should ensure that he or she has the individual's attention before beginning the trial. At that time, the cue to begin should be as clear, succinct, and natural as possible. For example, the natural cue to begin pot scrubbing is the presence of the dirty pots.

Immediately following the cue, the employment specialist should move in to prompt the correct response. The desired response should be operationally defined (i.e., exactly what the employment specialist wants the individual to do following the cue). For example, the response might be: "Pick up the scouring pad with the right hand, hold the pot upside down with the left hand, then begin a clockwise motion with the scouring pad across the bottom of the pot." The employment specialist needs to be aware that he or she should systematically fade the prompts delivered during a discrete trial,

EMPLOYEE'S NAME: _____ EMPLOYMENT SPECIALIST'S NAME: _____

Trial Format	Task Analysis (T.A.)	Training Steps (responses)
S^d: "Clean the mirror" (dirty mirror)	1. Locate materials in cart: Windex, piece of newspaper.	Backward chaining (Prompt 4→ 0)
	2. Take materials to mirror; set on counter.	a. 15.
Prompt levels:		b. 14, 15.
	3. Pick up Windex in dominant hand.	c. 13, 14, 15.
0 independent	4. Spray middle of mirror with Windex, pressing pump twice.	d. 12, 13, 14, 15.
		e. 11, 12, 13, 14, 15.
1 touch shoulder	5. Spray top left corner of mirror, pressing pump once.	f. 10, 11, 12, 13, 14, 15.
		g. 9, 10, 11, 12, 13, 14, 15.
2 touch elbow	6. Spray top right corner of mirror, pressing pump once.	h. 8, 9, 10, 11, 12, 13, 14, 15.
3 touch wrist	7. Spray bottom left corner of mirror, pressing pump once.	i. 7, 8, 9, 10, 11, 12, 13, 14, 15
4 hand over hand	8. Spray bottom right corner of mirror, pressing pump once.	j. 6, 7, 8, 9, 10, 11, 12, 13, 14, 15.
Consequence:	9. Put Windex down on counter.	k. 5, 6, 7, 8, 9, 10, 11, 12, 13, 14, 15.
Correct: 5 min. break	10. Pick up newspaper in dominant hand.	k. 5, 6, 7, 8, 9, 10, 11, 12, 13, 14, 15.
Incorrect: No break	11. Wipe mirror in continuous up and down motion 4 times, top left to bottom left.	l. 4, 5, 6, 7, 8, 9, 10, 11, 12, 13, 14, 15.
Intertrial interval:	12. Wipe mirror in continuous up and down motion 4 times, top middle to bottom middle.	m. 3, 4, 5, 6, 7, 8, 9, 10, 11, 12, 13, 14, 15.
1 day	13. Wipe mirror in continuous up and down motion 4 times, top right to bottom right.	n. 2, 3, 4, 5, 6, 7, 8, 9, 10, 11, 12, 13, 14, 15.
Criteria: Pass | Fail 3 | 3	14. Throw newspaper away.	o. 1, 2, 3, 4, 5, 6, 7, 8, 9, 10, 11, 12, 13, 14, 15.
	15. Return Windex to cart.	

Figure 4. Discrete trial training.

(continued)

Date	T.A. 15		Date	T.A. 15	T.A. 14	T.A. 13			Date	T.A. 15	T.A. 14	T.A. 13						
2/11/87	p^4		2/24/87	p^0	p^4				3/09/87	p^0	p^0	p^4						
2/12/87	p^4		2/25/87	p^0	p^3				3/10/87	p^0	p^0	p^3						
2/13/87	p^3		2/26/87	p^0	p^2				3/11/87	p^0	p^0	p^3						
2/16/87	p^2		2/26/87	p^0	p^2				3/12/87	p^0	p^0	p^2						
2/17/87	p^2		3/02/87	p^0	p^1				3/13/87	p^0	p^0	p^2						
2/18/87	p^1		3/03/87	p^0	p^0				3/16/87	p^0	p^0	p^1						
2/19/87	p^0		3/04/87	p^0	p^0				3/17/87	p^0	p^0	p^1						
2/20/87	p^0		3/05/87	p^0	p^0				3/19/87	p^0	p^0	p^0						
2/23/87	p^0		3/06/87	p^0	p^0	p^4			3/20/87	p^0	p^0	p^0						

Figure 4. *(continued)*

until the individual is responding solely to the natural cue. Prompt levels are outlined in the training format from most intrusive to least intrusive, and are decided for an individual based on his or her learning style. However, verbal prompts are generally not included in the hierarchy. Examples of prompt hierachies are shown in Figure 5. The employment specialist must record data on the success or failure of the trials at each prompt level, to know when to fade to a less-intrusive prompt. For example, after success at a prompt level of hand-over-hand physical prompt, the employment specialist would fade to directed hand guidance, holding the wrist of the employee. Reinforcement is delivered immediately following the correct response. This consequence should be something that is demonstrably reinforcing, as well as something that can be faded to a natural reinforcer. If the person does not perform the step correctly, then he or she is stopped immediately and the trial is started over.

Before moving on to the next instructional unit, the employment specialist must wait a predetermined length of time. This is termed the *intertrial interval* and aids the individual in discriminating between trials. The amount of time in this interval should be paced to meet the individual's needs.

Word/picture schedules and motivational systems can be effective tools in training for initiation. Employees with autism sometimes become reliant on the employment specialist or supervisor to tell them when to respond even after they have learned how to perform a task. A common scenario is for the employee to ap-proach the employment specialist and say: "I am out of materials. Should I go to the storeroom and get more?" Another is for the employee to perform the task, then look at the employment specialist and wait for some form of reinforcement before proceeding with the next task. D. Fender (1983) devised a basic, yet highly effective, self-monitoring system to promote the independence of four workers with autism. He identified five points in the workday when the workers were most likely to seek reassurance or direction. He then designed monitoring cards, as illustrated in Figure 6. The cards served as prompts for initiating behavior, as well as the basis for a motivational system. Prior to entering the job site, the steps on the card were reviewed with each worker, along with an explanation that if each step were self-initiated, the worker would earn a predetermined reinforcer at the end of the workday. The workers carried the cards in their pockets throughout the day as a reminder to self-initiate. At the end of the workday, the employment specialist reviewed the cards and the performance of each worker to determine if the reinforcers were earned. Within a week of implementing the program, all four workers had eliminated the dependency on the employment specialist and were able to initiate job tasks independently.

Ritualistic Behaviors

Ritualistic behavior is a characteristic of autism that can lead to many difficulties on the job if the employment specialist is not aware of the impact it can have on performance. Ritualistic behavior is manifested in different ways, in-

1. **Physical**

Hand on hand

↓

Touch wrist

↓

Touch elbow

↓

Touch shoulder

↓

Stand behind

↓

Stand 3 feet behind

↓

Stand on other side of room

↓

Stand outside of room

2. **Gestural**

Point with finger, full arm extended straight out from shoulder

↓

Point with finger, full arm extended and lowered 30° from shoulder

↓

Point with finger, full arm extended and lowered 45° from shoulder

↓

Point with finger, full arm extended and lowered 60° from shoulder

↓

Point with finger, full arm extended and lowered 75° from shoulder

↓

Point with finger, full arm flat against side of body

↓

Point with knuckle, full arm flat against side of body

↓

Full arm flat against side of body

Figure 5. Examples of prompt hierarchies.

cluding perseveration on a task or insistence by the individual on sameness in routine or organization of the environment (Koegel et al., 1982). Often the routines are self-established, such as insisting on departing a building from the same door through which one entered. Sometimes the individual becomes compulsive about a routine that was established for him or her, such as a specific route to follow on the way to school or work each day. Although someone else decided on the route, the person with autism insists that the same route always be followed with no variations. This insistence on sameness is a means for bringing order into his or her world that otherwise seems confusing for the person with autism.

Implications for Employment *Ritualistic behaviors can be an asset in job performance if considered in job placement and training.* In locating work for a person with the tendency to perseverate, the employment specialist should look for jobs with repetitive tasks such as greasing muffin tins for a large bakery or folding towels in a laundry (McCarthy, 1984). Compulsive behavior resulting from insistence on sameness can be used to advantage on jobs in which an employee must perform a routine exactly the same way each time, such as cleaning motel rooms or following a recipe for preparing pastries at a bakery. Repetitive jobs generally have a high turnover rate because employees become bored. Therefore, employers are looking for workers who are interested and productive in this type of job and who will stay for long periods of time without becoming restless.

If an employee is ritualistic, he or she will often respond quickly to word/picture schedules, as illustrated in Figure 2. Occasionally, these tangible prompts can be faded as the sequence of job duties becomes part of the worker's repertoire of routines.

The disruption of established rituals or routines of a person with autism often leads to aggressive behavior. This reaction occurs when the person feels confused, frustrated, or unable to predict what will happen once the routine has been interrupted. If there is a change in the work schedule, the employment specialist can assist the worker to understand what is happening by indicating the changes on a word/picture schedule. This procedure will provide a concrete cue to the worker. If the days to report to work change regularly, the employment specialist can set up a routine for the employee to help explain the change. The routine could entail marking

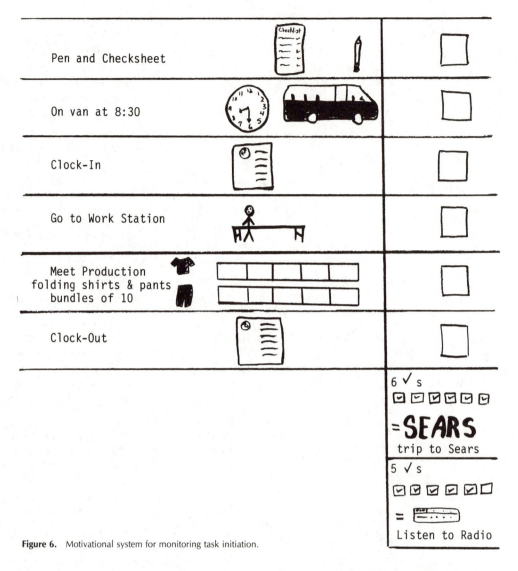

Pen and Checksheet		☐
On van at 8:30		☐
Clock-In		☐
Go to Work Station		☐
Meet Production folding shirts & pants bundles of 10		☐
Clock-Out		☐

6 ✓s
☑ ☑ ☑ ☑ ☑ ☑
=**SEARS**
trip to Sears

5 ✓s
☑ ☑ ☑ ☑ ☑ ☐
=
Listen to Radio

Figure 6. Motivational system for monitoring task initiation.

the calendar days at the beginning of each week to indicate the days to report to work. The employment specialist should also make the schedule of the day as routine as possible, even on jobs in which responsibilities vary daily. For example, a job of being on a housecleaning crew in a large business may entail 15 different cleaning routines. The procedure established would involve routinely checking the board to determine the assignment for that day, then selecting the appropriate word/picture schedule that corresponds to the assignment.

It is also important for the employment specialist to identify any rituals that the worker has established. Often a person with autism will ex-

hibit aggressive behavior for no apparent reason. What has happened is that a ritual has been interrupted. If the rituals are identified, the employment specialist can gradually build the worker's tolerance through systematically reinforcing the worker for calmly handling interruptions in the routine. It is important that the employment specialist address the employee's reactions to the disruption of routines and rituals before fading from the job site.

Disruptive Behaviors

Often associated with people who have autism are behaviors such as hitting, property destruction, head-banging, finger-flipping, rocking, and biting. Although these behaviors are exhibited by many people with autism, it is important to realize that they are not symptoms of autism. Instead, they are responses to the environment, resulting from communication, social, and/or cognitive difficulties (Donnellan et al., 1984). These behaviors are often the major deterrent to a person's being served by a job placement and training program such as a vocational rehabilitation agency. The rationale for exclusion is that the person must overcome these problems before he or she is considered employable. However, employment specialists who have placed people with autism in jobs have found that, in fact, one of the most effective methods for reducing the behaviors is the mere placement of the person in an actual job. For the person with autism, the environment and the reality of the situation have a clear purpose and therefore make sense, and the people surrounding him or her are not exhibiting unusual or disruptive behaviors.

Implications for Employment *In order to reduce a worker's aggressive behavior, the job trainer needs to understand the possible functions the behaviors serve for the person.* Often the behaviors serve to communicate feelings of confusion, boredom, frustration, or lack of control. It is important that the employment specialist analyze the communicative intent of a worker's behavior so that appropriate steps can be taken to remedy the situation. If the person does not have an acceptable means by which to communicate, then the employment specialist should develop a nonverbal or alternative communication system. Even though a person has some speech, he or she may not be able to express thoughts beyond a one-word request; therefore, the system can augment existing speech or be an alternative to speech. Once a communication system is designed, the employment specialist must systematically teach the worker to replace the disruptive behavior with the appropriate response.

The employment specialist must also be sensitive to messages from the worker that in effect state that the worker does not like his or her job and would prefer a different one. Although the person is unable to verbalize job choices during the consumer assessment phase because of an inability to express thoughts and/or the lack of exposure to different occupations, he or she may have strong vocational preferences. Often changing a job will eliminate behavioral difficulties such as refusal to work or tantrums.

The disruptive behaviors may result from a feeling of anxiety or stress. The first week or two on the job, the worker may experience anxiety resulting from an inability to predict what will happen or to understand the expectations placed on him or her. During this time, the employment specialist will need to take extra measures to assist the worker to organize his or her world. Suggestions include: (1) clearly explaining what to expect on the new job, using visual cues; (2) making instructions on the job concrete through written or picture schedules; (3) scheduling frequent, short breaks during the first few days until the worker has adjusted to the stress of the job; (4) explaining unusual circumstances that arise on the job in short, clear statements utilizing visual cues if necessary; (5) providing incentive beyond the natural reinforcement of the paychecks in order to reinforce being attentive and attempting new tasks through concrete motivational systems; and (6) clearly identifying when the employee will receive reinforcers, since he or she may not understand delays in receiving desired events or items. Remember that money is not a direct reinforcer to a person who has never been able to buy anything.

Nonaversive behavioral techniques used during job-site training are effective in reducing or eliminating disruptive behaviors of an employee. The approach often adopted by service providers is that the disruptive behavior must be absent before a person can be placed on a job. However, the results of recent research indicate that nonaversive behavioral techniques can be utilized in reducing or eliminating behaviors after the person has already begun working on the job (McCarthy, 1984; Smith & Coleman, 1986). McCarthy (1984) found the use of a differential reinforcement of low rates of responding (DRL) to be highly effective in eliminating or reducing to an acceptable level high-frequency behaviors, such as talking to one's self or rocking, that were exhibited by four men with autism working on a job site. In assuring success, she designed the DRL procedures with the following components: 1) the criterion for receiving reinforcement was systematically lowered throughout the intervention, based on rate reduction; 2) full-session intervals were used, wherein each interval lasted 1 hour even when the DRL limit was exceeded; 3) response deprivation was considered in the reinforcement schedule for each worker, to assure that contingent reinforcement remained powerful; and 4) tangible monitoring systems were used to provide immediate concrete feedback to the workers on the accumulation of responses within each interval.

Other nonaversive techniques used effectively in community settings to reduce or eliminate disruptive behaviors such as aggression, destruction of property, or self-injury include: 1) differential reinforcement of other behaviors (DRO), 2) differential reinforcement of incompatible or alternate behaviors (DRI and ALT-R), 3) stimulus control, and 4) instructional control (Donnellan, LaVigna, Zambito, & Thvedt, 1985; LaVigna & Donnellan, 1986).

The employment specialist should become familiar with designing and implementing nonaversive behavioral programs before placing into a job a consumer who has a history of aggressive or self-injurious behaviors. Some consumers will exhibit severe aggression toward others or self-injury even when these strategies are used. Instead of concluding that the person is unable to work, the employment specialist should view the behaviors as information to consider in making a decision on an appropriate job placement and the model of support to be adopted. The consumer with severe self-injurious behavior or low-incident, highly explosive behaviors will need to be placed in a job where there is no customer contact and limited exposure to other coworkers. Examples include work in a stockroom or maintenance of recreational facilities such as a golf course or football stadium. With workers who must always have someone available to implement a behavioral program, a supported employment model where the job coach never fades from the site should be utilized. Major points to remember relative to disruptive behaviors are: 1) the behaviors do not have to negate employment success, 2) the elimination or reduction of the behaviors can be addressed

through nonaversive behavioral strategies, and 3) the behavioral strategies can be implemented while the person is on the job.

PHASES OF SUPPORTED WORK MODEL FOR USE WITH PEOPLE WITH AUTISM

The supported work model described by Wehman and Kregel (1985) outlines a systematic approach to job placement, training, and follow-along services. Although the model was developed for individual job placements, it can also be applied to multiple placements within a business, such as an enclave or work stations in industry, if workers are employed in staggered intervals, and if the possible levels of follow-along support include on-going supervision on the job site. When the characteristics of individuals with autism are addressed, the supported work model is an effective approach to successfully placing and retaining these individuals in real work settings. The following section addresses the major considerations of each phase of job training for employment specialists working with persons with autism.

Job Development

Job development involves assessing specific job possibilities in the community. The following points are important to remember when locating jobs for consumers with autism.

1. The most typical approach to job development is to establish a pool of consumers while at the same time searching for jobs without a particular person in mind (Moon et al., 1986). However, a consumer-specific approach is more productive when serving people with autism, due to the varied factors that must be considered for each such consumer. With this approach, the employment specialist evaluates information obtained through the consumer assessment about a particular person, and finds a job that matches that individual's abilities and interests.

2. When conducting a job search for a consumer with autism, the employment specialist should consider jobs requiring minimal

verbal interactions with customers, co-workers, or supervisors. Successful placement with limited communication demands have been made in occupations such as dishwasher in a restaurant (Fender, 1987), assembler in an industry (Nugent, 1982), worker in a stockroom (Juhrs, 1985), proof operator in a bank (Staff, 1986), and maintenance person at a miniature golf course (Fender, 1987).

3. The employment specialist should build on and use to advantage traits that the consumer exhibits. As mentioned earlier, if the employment specialist is locating a job for a person who is quite perseverative or ritualistic, a job requiring performance of repetitive tasks would be ideal. In addition, the employment specialist should attempt to build on any exceptional skills of the person. Examples include finding a job in a mailroom for a person with an excellent memory for number sequences or a quality-control job for a person who notices minute flaws in a product.

4. If the consumer presents severe behavioral challenges such as self-injurious or highly disruptive behaviors, the employment specialist should seek a job that has limited contact with others and well-defined spatial boundaries, to provide structure to the environment.

If the trainer is cognizant of the factors that make the person with autism unique, he or she will be better armed in the job search. Careful job development will enhance the chances for successful job placement and retention.

Consumer Assessment

As with any individual who has disabilities, assessment information is important when attempting to make a job placement for a person with autism. Traditional vocational assessments utilizing paper and pencil or manipulative tasks are generally neither appropriate nor effective when attempting to evaluate the employability of an individual with autism. Situational assessments are more valuable (Halpern & Fuhrer, 1984; Moon et al., 1986), particularly when conducted on a longitudinal basis during the

school years through training on actual job sites. If a school program employs a longitudinal situational assessment approach, the following questions should be answered through systematically recording data and anecdotal notes based on observations during the school years (McCarthy, 1985):

1. Which jobs does the person seem the most self-motivated to perform (i.e., without external motivational systems)?

2. Does the person have a tendency to become prompt dependent?

3. How long does it take the person to learn new tasks, and what level of detail is necessary when developing a task analysis for training purposes?

4. How long can the person continue a task without inappropriate work behaviors occurring at an unacceptable level?

5. Does the person require a motivational system to encourage initiation of tasks, to increase production rate, to slow the pace in order to improve quality, or to remain calm and attentive on a job?

6. What types of permanent or temporary adaptations are needed by the person for independent performance of the task (e.g., behavioral intervention, picture schedule, or adaptive equipment)?

7. What is the reaction of the person to environmental factors such as the number and proximity of coworkers, availability of space on the work site, and intensity of supervision?

8. What is the level of family support toward job placement?

This type of assessment information will enable the employment specialist to more effectively determine abilities and challenges, and hence make a good job-to-consumer match.

Job Placement

Once a job has been identified, it is important to adequately prepare the consumer for a major change in his or her routine. Like any person beginning a new job, a person with autism needs to know as much information as possible about the job, including: 1) what the job is, 2) where it is, 3) what the job entails, 4) names of the supervisor and of some coworkers, and 5) number of employees at the job site. The employment specialist needs to develop concrete ways to provide this information to the consumer. It can be beneficial to role-play with the consumer interactions with his or her supervisor, as well as practice some of the skills required by the job, before the job actually begins, so that the consumer can anticipate what will be expected of him or her.

If at all possible, the employment specialist should work the job before the consumer begins, in order to record the sequence of job duties and develop task analyses. This approach helps the employment specialist avoid teaching an employee routines that later have to be changed.

Job-Site Training

During job training, it is critical that the employment specialist consider the issues discussed earlier in this chapter relative to characteristics of persons with autism. Several strategies for training are offered to overcome the possible barriers to quality job performance posed by these traits. The following points are a consolidation of the primary strategies to consider in order to maximize the success of job-site training.

1. When conducting an initial inventory of duties and responsibilities, the employment specialist needs to identify the communication and social demands of the job. The information obtained should be utilized in developing an appropriate nonverbal communication system if deemed necessary. If social interactions beyond the employee's current level of functioning are identified, the employment specialist should teach the worker how to respond appropriately, through the use of role-playing during nonwork time.

2. If the consumer assessment indicates that the person has difficulty processing information, the employment specialist should make all directives concise and clear. He or she may also use visual cues such as picture/word schedules. These tangible schedules can aid the employee in under-

standing and remembering sequences of tasks as well as predicting changes in the daily routine.

3. Periodic changes in the work routine should be planned and implemented by the employment specialist in order to teach the employee appropriate ways to handle similar situations that may arise at a later time. Even the most routine job may require periodic adjustments. Therefore, the employee must have experiences in dealing with changes in order to develop appropriate coping skills.

4. The issue of prompt dependency is of particular significance when training an employee to work independently. Persons with autism are often rote learners and remember every step of a sequence. Therefore, the employment specialist should ensure that while teaching a task sequence, prompts are not learned as part of the task. It is important to remember that verbal prompts should be avoided, since they are the most difficult to fade.

5. Instruction should be approached systematically throughout training, including the use of: 1) task analyses to identify all steps of each task, 2) systematic prompting and prompt fading, and 3) data-based decision making. A discrete trial format can be used when teaching particularly difficult steps of a task and when the individual is perseverative on a certain step or is prompt dependent.

6. The employment specialist must teach for generalization, since many people with autism are unable to isolate a skill and perform it out of the context in which it was learned. The employment specialist should also be sure that the worker is responding to the correct cues when performing tasks.

7. Often the worker is not intrinsically motivated to initiate and/or perform tasks, nor is he or she able to comprehend the value of a bimonthly paycheck. Therefore, a more immediate external motivational system might need to be employed. It can be used to reduce distractibility, improve performance of tasks, or increase initiation of job duties. The employment specialist should

look for naturally occurring reinforcers in the job setting, such as purchasing coffee or a soft drink at breaktime.

8. Throughout job training, the employment specialist should serve as an advocate for the employee by assisting coworkers to understand the communication and social issues associated with autism. The employment specialist can explain to coworkers how to recognize signs of frustration and confusion and develop ways to assist the employee in communicating effectively.

Follow-Along and Maintenance

Before the employment specialist can be assured that the employee can independently perform the skills necessary, and before the trainer can begin fading from the job, he or she must determine that there is stable performance across time and trainers. Some workers with autism are able to perform all aspects of the job independently; however, they need supervision for monitoring of behavior interventions. The employees are able to earn competitive wages even though they still require the on-site support of an employment specialist. In these situations, a cost-effective approach is to have two or more individuals placed at one site in competitive jobs, but in different locations within the facility. The employment specialist is then responsible for rotating among the workers who otherwise could not be in competitive situations.

Throughout the phases of the supported work model, it is essential that the employment specialist maintain regular communication with the consumer's coworkers and family members/guardian. The person with autism is usually unable to relay work-related information to the appropriate people, owing to impaired communication. Therefore, consistent contact among the employer, family members, and employment specialist is necessary to ensure that the individual continues to perform satisfactorily on the job.

Work-Related Tasks

Work-related tasks are any activities outside of the actual performance of the job that have a bearing on the success of employment (Moon et al., 1986). Some work-related tasks must be performed simultaneously with the job, while others are performed at home or in the community during hours outside the workday. Owing to the severity of their disability, most individuals with autism need assistance in learning effective performance of these tasks that often require initiation of activities and/or communication with people in the community.

For the employment specialist, instruction of the skills involved in work-related tasks is generally more difficult than the actual job-site training because of the essential involvement of family members or of living support professionals in the teaching process. The challenge for the employment specialist is to assess carefully the required work-related skills and to coordinate instructional efforts by all involved professionals and family members.

The numerous work-related tasks may differ, depending on the job or the place where a person lives. For example, if the person lives with his or her family, many of the tasks are probably performed by a family member; thus, it will be less of a priority to teach those skills in the home setting than it would be for a person living in an apartment with minimal support. It does not mean, however, that the tasks now being performed by family members or living support staff should never be taught. Although the priority tasks to be accomplished by the consumer will vary, employment specialists should be aware of a few basic ones, regardless of the job. The following discussion addresses these tasks, along with suggestions for teaching strategies and task modifications.

Getting Ready for Work   Arriving at work on time is essential to the longevity of a job. In order for a person to be prompt regularly, he or she must be able to perform several tasks with ease, particularly if living in an independent or semi-independent setting. The tasks involved in preparing for work in the morning typically include: 1) setting and waking up to an alarm clock, 2) performing a grooming routine, 3) selecting appropriate clothing, 4) preparing, eating, and cleaning up after breakfast, 5) preparing a lunch to take to work, and 6) gathering necessary items to carry to work.

Each of these tasks is complex and is intimately related to job success. Even though family members or living support staff may be available to teach these skills, the employment specialist will need to provide consultation on how to structure the tasks and teach the requisite skills to the individual. In cases where there is no other reliable person to teach the skills, the employment specialist will be directly involved in instruction.

Following are techniques the employment specialist might use when working with an individual with autism:

1. Establish a structured written or picture schedule for all tasks that must be performed from the time the person wakes up until he or she leaves home (see Figure 7). Initially, contingent reinforcement may need to be established for the successful accomplishment of the morning schedule.

2. When gathering items to take to work, the employee will take some things, such as lunch or a bus pass, daily. However, other items such as rain gear are not needed regularly. If the person has difficulty determining when an item is needed, a simple solution is to have him or her carry it daily. Standard items can be carried easily in either a day pack or attaché case, depending on the particular job.

3. If the person has no time concept or tends to be unaware of time, the use of two alarm clocks can be helpful. The first alarm is set for the time to wake up, and the second alarm rings when it is time to leave the house to catch a bus or otherwise get to work on time.

4. Appropriate dress is often a major issue with people who have autism. Not uncommonly, they develop rituals relating to clothing. Examples include always wearing

Time	Activity	Sun.	Mon.	Tues.	Wed.	Thurs.	Fri.	Sat.
Workday, 6:00 A.M. Weekend, 8:00 A.M.	Wake-up when alarm clock rings.							
	Shave and clean razor.							
	Wash face and hands; put on deodorant.							
	Comb hair and brush teeth.							
	Get dressed.							
	Make bed.							
	Eat breakfast.							
	If dishes in dishwasher are clean, put them up.							
	Put all dirty dishes into the dishwasher.							
Workday only	Get bus pass, transfer money and day pack.							
	Leave for bus when living room alarm rings.							
Workday, 9:00 P.M. Weekend, 11:00 P.M.	Undress and put on robe.							
	Throw all dirty clothes into hamper.							
	Shower.							
	Put on clean underwear and pajamas.							
	Comb hair and brush teeth.							
	Set living room clock for 6:55 A.M.							
	Lock all doors.							
	Take medication and record on chart.							
	Set bedroom alarm for 6:00 A.M.							
	Go to bed.							

Figure 7. Self-monitoring schedule for morning and evening routines.

specific clothing on specific days, insisting on wearing winter clothes even though the season has changed to spring or summer, or always wearing a particular style of clothing such as black dress shoes. For many, altering what is possibly a lifelong routine might be very difficult. If a change must be made for the person to be appropriately dressed for work, it can be accomplished most effectively if specific guidelines are developed for the family members or living support staff to follow in assisting the person to make these adjustments. An example that has been successful is the development of a routine to be followed at the beginning of the week in which the person, with assistance from a staff or family member, selects an outfit for each day. The outfits are then placed in sequential order in the closet. Necessary variations in clothing can be made at that time by limiting the item selection.

Money Management/Budget   It is extremely important for a person with autism to learn how to perform tasks associated with money. Often the person just placed on a job has money to manage for the first time in his or her life. A few responsibilities must be addressed.

Depositing a Check   The most appropriate approach to teaching how to deposit a check would be to instruct the person in how to deposit his or her paycheck independently. In addition to providing dignity, this allows the person an opportunity to make acquaintances in his or her local community. If the employment specialist feels that the person will never be able to handle all aspects of the task, other options might include teaching the person portions of the task and assisting where necessary. For example, the person might learn how to fill out his or her deposit slip and then have the living support person accompany him or her to the bank to assist where necessary. The opportunity for socialization with community members is important to building relationships, and only under extreme circumstances should the person not be involved in all aspects of his or her financial matters.

Budgeting   The employment specialist may have to take an active role in assisting the con-

sumer, the family, and/or living support professionals in developing an appropriate budget. The critical issues to be addressed in budgeting are remembering fares for transportation to and from work, notifying the Social Security office about changes in wages, adjusting the budget to reflect variations in Supplemental Security Income (SSI) payments, and planning for emergency money to be carried to work as part of the standard items taken each day in the day pack or attaché case.

Appearing Busy During "Down" Time

Most people develop strategies for looking busy when there is nothing to do on the job. However, the person with autism will often have a difficult time dealing with down time. It is during these times that the person with autism engages in behavior that might seem inappropriate to coworkers. One young man placed on a job at a restaurant enjoyed staring at people. The stare was often accompanied with a smile or odd head movements. The behavior only occurred when the young man had little or no work to do. In order to discourage it, the employment specialist came up with several tasks for him to do when there were no required tasks. The performance of these tasks was included in the employee's motivational program.

Transportation

Regardless of the severity of an employee's disability, he or she should be taught to travel to and from work in the most independent manner possible. In larger cities, the mass transportation system is available. There are many adaptations that will increase the independence of the person with autism. As discussed earlier, the money required for transportation would be a part of the person's weekly budget. In order for the person with limited money skills to develop independence in handling the bus fare, the employment specialist might teach the employee to present a written request to the bank cashier when depositing his or her check, asking for a specific number of quarters, dimes, and nickels. The employee then divides the money into separate containers for bus fare for each workday. The creativity of the employment specialist will be essential if the person lives in a small town without a public transportation system. Although there will be the occasional job where the person is able to walk to work, that is often not an option. Being integrated into community organizations enhances the likelihood that community members will respond to an individual's needs, such as for transportation. For instance, a church member who becomes acquainted with a worker discovers that he or she has a job but is experiencing problems getting to and from work, and volunteers to assist.

Emergencies

There will be times when a person is sick or misses the ride to work. The primary responsibility of the employment specialist regarding these and other events is to forecast possible emergencies, develop specific procedures for the consumer to follow, and then teach the consumer and/or living support personnel to follow these procedures. Adaptations for emergencies include picture/work directions for the consumer to follow in these situations or use of an audio recording for the person to play over the phone if he or she is sick and has no verbal communication skills.

Taking Time Off

As discussed earlier, the person with autism often develops routines that can affect the job. For instance, it might be a long-established routine for the person to visit his parents every other Friday at 3:00 PM. In this case, the employment specialist may be faced with the person wanting to leave at that time, even though the workday lasts until 5:00 PM. The employment specialist needs to clearly and concretely explain the change and, if necessary, help the person request time off. Plans should be developed well in advance so the employee can anticipate the scheduled leave. In addition, the employment specialist

may need to spend time with the parents, emphasizing the seriousness of their son's/daughter's job responsibilites, since the parents may be used to the flexible schedule of a day activity center.

It should be stressed that the employment specialist does not have to be responsible for the employee's entire life. However, by consulting with the employee's family members or the living support staff on job-related issues, the chances of a successful placement and long-term employment are greatly enhanced.

SUMMARY

In 1977, Sullivan reported that 95% of people disabled by autism live their adult lives in institutions. Ten years later, the future of people with autism is beginning to look brighter with the development of services such as supported employment that are designed to increase the chances of continuing community integration and productivity for everyone. The availability of supported employment services is still rare for persons who are autistic. Yet, supported employment holds much promise when the employment specialist carefully considers the particular characteristics associated with the autistic individuals being served. However, the employment specialist will need to use the highest behavioral and instructional technology available to assure job success. It is also essential that the employment specialist develop and maintain close communication with the consumer's family or living support staff throughout the process, to guarantee that the consumer consistently performs all home and community tasks related to work. The knowledge and techniques now available to service providers can help them open the doors to a quality, productive community life for people with autism.

REFERENCES

American Psychiatric Association. (1980). *Diagnostic and statistical manual of mental disorders* (3rd ed.). Washington, DC: Author.

Baltaxe, C.A.M., & Simmons, J. Q. (1981). Disorders of language in childhood psychosis: Current concepts and approaches. In J. Darby (Ed.), *Speech evaluation in psychiatry* (pp. 89–90). New York: Grune & Stratton.

Brady, M. P., Shores, R. E., Gunter, P., McEvoy, M. A., Fox, J. J., & White, C. (1984). Generalization of an adolescent's social interaction behavior via multiple peers in a classroom setting. *Journal of the Association for Persons with Severe Handicaps*, 9(4), 278–286.

DeMeyer, M. K., Barton, S., DeMeyer, W.E., Norton, J. A., Allen, J. E., & Steel, R. (1973). Prognosis in autism:

A follow-up study. *Journal of Autism and Childhood Schizophrenia*, *3*, 199–246.

Donnellan, A. M., LaVigna, G. W., Zambito, J., & Thvedt, J. (1985). A time-limited intensive program model to support community placement for persons with severe behavior problems. *Journal of the Association for Persons with Severe Handicaps*, *10* (3), 123–131.

Donnellan, A. M., Mirenda, P. L., Mesaros, R. A., & Fassbender, L. L. (1984). Analyzing the communicative functions of aberrant behavior. *Journal of the Association for Persons with Severe Handicaps*, *9*(3) 201–212.

Donnellan-Walsh, A. M. Gossage, L., LaVigna, G., Schuler, A. L., & Traphagen, J. (1976). *Teaching makes a difference*. California State Department of Education.

Faye, W., & Schuler, A. L. (1980). *Emerging language in autistic children*. Baltimore: University Park Press.

Fender, D. (1983).[Developing job task initiation skills of workers with autism]. Unpublished raw data.

Fender, K. W. (1986, July–September). Supported employment: Improving the quality of life for individuals with autism. *Newsletter of the South Carolina Society for Autistic Children*, *17*(3), 3. (Available from SCSAC, P.O. Box 684, Effingham, SC 29541).

Fender, K. W. (1987). [South Carolina programs for individuals with autism questionnaire on supported employment for persons with autism]. Unpublished raw data.

Halpern, A. S., & Fuhrer, M. J. (Eds.). (1984). *Functional assessment in rehabilitation*. Baltimore: Paul H. Brookes Publishing Co.

Hill, J. W., Hill, M., Wehman, P., Banks, P. D., Pendleton, D., & Britt, C. (1985). Demographic analyses related to successful job retention for competitively employed persons who are mentally retarded. In P. Wehman & J. W. Hill (Eds.), *Competitive employment for person with mental retardation: From research to practice*. Richmond: Virginia Commonwealth University, Rehabilitation Research and Training Center.

Hurley, A.D., & Sovner, R. (1983, June). Autism. *Psychiatric Aspects of Mental Retardation Newsletter*, *2*(6), 21–24.

Job in operations helps special employee reach potential. (1986, May). *Leader*, *3*(5).

Juhrs, P. D. (1985). *CSAAC vocational program: Overview*. Unpublished manuscript, Community Services for Autistic Adults and Children, Rockville, MD.

Juhrs, P. D. (1987). [Community services for autistic adults and children questionnaire on supported employment for persons with autism.] Unpublished raw data.

Kanner, L. (1943). Autistic disturbances of affective contact. *Nervous Child*, *2*, 217–250.

Kanner, L. (1971). Follow-up study of eleven autistic children originally reported in 1943. *Journal of Autism and Childhood Schizophrenia*, *1*, 119–145.

Koegel, R. L., Rincover, A., & Egel, A. (1982). *Educating and understanding autistic children*. San Diego: College-Hill Press.

LaVigna, G. W., & Donnellan, A. M. (1986). *Alternatives to punishment: Solving behavior problems with non-aversive strategies*. New York: Irvington.

Liberman, R. P., King, L. N., DeRisi, W. J., & McCann, M. (1976). *Personal effectiveness*. Champaign, IL: Research Press.

Lotter, V. (1966). Epidemiology of autistic conditions in young children: I. Prevalence. *Social Psychiatry*, *1*, 124–137.

Lotter, V. (1974). Social adjustment and placement of autistic children in Middlesex: A follow-up study. *Journal of Autism and Childhood Schizophrenia*, *4*, 11–32.

Mank, D. M., Rhodes, L. E., & Bellamy, G. T. (1986). Four supported employment alternatives. In W. E. Kiernan & J. A. Stark (Eds.), *Pathways to employment for adults with developmental disabilities* (pp. 129–153). Baltimore: Paul H. Brookes Publishing Co.

Mauer, R. G., & Damasio, A. R. (1982). Childhood autism from the point of view of behavioral neurology. *Journal of Autism and Developmental Disorders*, *12*(2), 195–205.

McCarthy, P. (1984). *The effects of a differential reinforcement of low rates of responding intervention behaviors of adults with autism during vocational training at a competitive job site*. Unpublished doctoral dissertation, University of South Carolina, Columbia.

McCarthy, P. (1985). *Transition planning leading to employment of youth with autism*. Unpublished manuscript, Virginia Commonwealth University, Rehabilitation Research and Training Center, Richmond.

Mesibov, G. (1987). [North Carolina TEACCH questionnaire on supported employment for persons with autism]. Unpublished raw data.

Moon, S., Goodall, P., Barcus, M., & Brooke, V. (1986). *The supported work model of competitive employment for citizens with severe handicaps: A guide for job trainers* (2nd ed.). Richmond: Virginia Commonwealth University, Rehabilitation Research and Training Center.

National Society for Autistic Children. (1979). *Definition of the syndrome of autism*. Washington, DC: Author.

National Society for Autistic Children/National Personnel Training Grant Staff. (1981). NSAC national personnel training program: Module I. Washington, DC: Author.

Niedringhaus, S. (1985). *A description of the able autistic child and discussion of appropriate education strategies*. Unpublished manuscript, George Washington University.

Nugent, T. (1982, January 21). Autistic and thriving. *The Sun*, (Baltimore), pp. 1, 4.

Prior, M. (1979). Cognitive abilities and disabilities in autism: A review. *Journal of Abnormal Child Psychology*, *2*, 357–380.

Prizant, B. M., & Duchan, A. F. (1981). The functions of immediate echolalia in autistic children. *Journal of Speech and Hearing Disorders*, *3*, 241–249.

Rincover, A., & Koegel, R. L. (1975). Setting generality and stimulus control in autistic children. *Journal of Applied Behavior Analysis*, *8*, 235–46.

Ritvo, E. R. Rabin, K., Yuwiler, A., Freeman, B.J., & Geller, E. (1978). Biochemical and hematologic studies: A critical review. In M. Rutter & E. Schopler (Eds.), *Autism: A reappraisal of concepts and treatment* (pp. 163–183). New York: Plenum Press.

Rutter, M. (1978). Diagnosis and definition. In M. Rutter & E. Schopler (Eds). *Autism: A reappraisal of concepts and treatment*. New York: Plenum.

Rutter, M. (1978). Diagnosis and definition of childhood autism. Journal of Autism and Childhood Schizophrenia, *8*(2), 139–160.

Rutter, M., Greenfeld, D., & Lockyer, L. (1967). A five to fifteen year follow-up study of infantile psychosis: II. Social and behavioral outcomes. *British Journal of Psychiatry*, *113*, 1183–1199.

Schuler, A. L., & Perez, L. (1987, March). The role of social interactions in the development of thinking skills. *Focus on Exceptional Children*, *19*(7), 1–11.

Shea, V., & Mesibov, G. B. (1985). Brief report: The relationship of learning disabilities and higher-level autism. *Journal of Autism and Developmental Disorders*, *15*(4), 1985.

Smith, M. D., & Coleman, D. (1986). Managing the behavior of adults with autism in the job setting. *Journal of Autism and Developmental Disorders*, *16*(2), 145–154.

Snell, M. (Ed.). (1983). *Systematic instruction of the moderately and severely handicapped*, (2nd ed). Columbus, OH: Charles E. Merrill.

Sullivan, R. (1977). *National information and advocacy project for autistic-like persons*. Unpublished manuscript. (HEW Grant No. 54P-71207/1-03).

Wehman, P. (1985). Supported competitive employment for persons with severe disabilities. In P. McCarthy, J.M. Everson, M. S. Moon, & J. M. Barcus (Eds.), *School to work transition for youth with severe disabilities* (pp. 167–182). Richmond: Virginia Commonwealth University, Rehabilitation Research and Training Center.

Wehman, P., & Kregel, J. (1985). A supported work approach to competitive employment of individuals with moderate and severe handicaps. *Journal of Autism and Developmental Disorders*, *16*(3), 295–316.

Wing, L. (1978). Social, behavioral, and cognitive characteristics: An epidemiological approach. In M. Rutter & E. Schopler (Eds.), *Autism: A reappraisal of concepts and treatment* (pp. 27–45). New York: Plenum.

Wing, L., Yates, S., Brierley, L., & Gould, J. (1976). The prevalence of early childhood autism: Comparison of administrative and epidemiology of studies. *Psychological Medicine*, *6*, 89–100.

Chapter 20

Traumatic Brain Injury
Supported Employment and Compensatory Strategies for Enhancing Vocational Outcomes

Jeffrey S. Kreutzer and M.V. Morton

Recent figures indicate that head injury has reached epidemic proportions in the United States. Traumatic head injury is the leading cause of death in persons younger than 45 (MacKenzie et al., 1987). Among all age groups, trauma fatalities are exceeded only by cancer, stroke, and heart disease. Nearly 400,000 new cases are reported annually (Kalisky, Morrison, Meyers, & Von Laufen, 1985), with approximately 44,000 falling within the moderate to severe range. The incidence rate of head injury is double that of cerebral palsy, 6 times that of multiple sclerosis, and 14 times that of spinal cord injury. The estimated number of survivors of moderate to severe head injury is nearly twice that for all the aforementioned afflictions combined (Kurtze, 1982). Overall, an estimated total of 1 million to 1.8 million living Americans have sustained moderate to severe brain injury. The estimated total cost to society is $4 billion per year (Cope & Hall, 1982).

Head injury has been classified into three categories by severity levels, ranging from mild to moderate to severe. Severity levels are based on Glasgow Coma Scores assigned by medical staff on admission to the hospital (Rimel, Giordani, Barth, & Jane, 1982). Many people believe that coma is a dichotomous variable, that patients are *either* in coma or not in coma. However, the level and depth of coma is a continuous variable and can be classified in this manner utilizing Glasgow Coma Scores. Coma scores range from a minimum value of 3 to a maximum value of 15. Higher scores denote higher levels of consciousness, with a score of 15 denoting normal consciousness. Scores less than 6 typically indicate that an individual is entirely unresponsive to environmental stimuli and is in a deep state of coma. The scale includes multiple categories that reflect a patient's ability to respond to verbal commands, to willfully move limbs, normalcy of eye movement, and level of temporal and situational orientation. By consensus, neurosurgeons and researchers classify level of injury on admission as severe, moderate, or mild if Glasgow Coma Scores range from 3–8, 9–12, and 13–15 respectively (Rimel et al., 1982). Research has consistently indicated that more severely injured patients have a significantly worse outcome, particularly in regard to independent living, intellectual, linguistic, and visuomotor skills.

Impairments in intellectual, linguistic, and visuomotor skills contribute to high rates of unemployment for victims of head injury. This chapter describes the typical consequences of head injury, with an emphasis on employment outcome, and examines supported employment and compensatory strategies, focusing on a set of procedures designed to enhance the employability of head injury victims. Three extensive case studies are provided for illustrative purposes.

TRAUMATIC BRAIN INJURY: OUTCOMES

The consequences of moderate and severe head injury can be categorized into six major areas: 1) *functional status*, 2) *neurological and medical status*, 3) *neuropsychological and linguistic status*, 4) *emotional and behavioral status*, 5) *familial status*, and 6) *vocational status*.

Functional status may be defined as ability to carry out activities of daily living (ADL) independently. These activities include eating, toileting, dressing, ambulation, and grooming, among others. The level of ability to carry out these activities determines the extent to which victims of head injury can live independently. Particularly in the early days post injury, many individuals require assistance in carrying out ADL. The primary goal of inpatient rehabilitation is to help injured persons maximize functional status and minimize dependence on others for ADL. Unfortunately, diminished functional status is a long-standing and often permanent consequence of severe head injury.

Impairments in functional status post head injury are well documented. For example, Hall, Cope, and Rappaport (1985) examined functional abilities in a a group of 70 persons with severe head injury at 2, 4, 6, 12, and 24 months post trauma. Disability Rating Scale scores denoting functional status indicated patients were, on the average, severely disabled in the first 4 months postinjury and at least partially disabled throughout the 24-month follow-up-period. Disability severity levels were based on degree of dependence on others. Similar levels of functional impairment in the first 2 years post head injury were reported by Panikoff (1983) and Najenson, Groswasser, Mendleson, and Hackett (1980).

Neurological and Medical Status

Long-term medical and neurological problems postinjury are common. In the largest published study of its kind, Kalisky and colleagues (1985) described the course of medical and neurological problems for a group of 180 victims of severe head injury who were a mean of 42 weeks posttrauma. Fifty-six per cent of the sample had neurological problems, including ventricular dilation (37%) and posttrauma seizures (13%). Additional problems reported for the sample were categorized as gastrointestinal (50%), genitourinary (45%), respiratory (34%), cardiovascular (32%), dermatological (21%), musculoskeletal (21%), and endocrinological (4%). An excellent description of common neurological findings in the early stages postrecovery in severe head injury has been provided by Levin, Benton, & Grossman (1982). Hematomas, cranial nerve injury, hydrocephalus, and seizures are present in a majority of cases.

Neuropsychological and Linguistic Status

Neuropsychologists and speech pathologists have focused on cognitive, intellectual, motor, and linguistic impairments following head injury. Impaired levels of neuropsychological functioning are typically manifested in a wide variety of areas because cortical dysfunction is frequently diffuse. Levin et al (1982) reviewed numerous investigations pertaining to the multiple consequences of head injury. Scores in the defective range on measures of general intellectual ability were related to concomitant impairments in memory, as well as in sustained attention, reasoning, visuoperception, hand-eye coordination, and fine-motor skills. The authors reported that aphasic symptomology is evident in as many as 15% of the head injury population. Most commonly observed are problems associated with visual naming, word association, and language comprehension. Newcombe, Brooks, and Baddeley (1980) also reviewed the head injury outcome literature and found similar patterns of impairment.

Emotional and Behavioral Status

For many years, investigators have acknowledged that physical disability is often accompanied by significant changes in emotional and behavioral status. These changes are often described as manifestations of severe reactive depression. Depression is viewed as a grieving process during which the patient mourns the loss of abilities. In this regard, head injury is certainly not unique. However, head injury is unique in that emotional and behavioral sequelae are a consequence of both the patient's reaction to loss of ability and neurophysiological changes in the brain. Researchers have noted that behavioral and emotional problems cause greater impairments in family and vocational functioning than intellectual and physical disabilities (Newcombe et al., 1980).

Levin et al. (1982) reported behavioral problems related to depression, anxiety, and social withdrawal as being predominant. Lezak (1978) described apathy, silliness, irritability, and either extremely high or low sexual appetite as the most common emotional changes. Similar findings were reported by Maus-Clum and Ryan (1981) in their survey of emotional/behavioral changes as described by family members. Included among problem behaviors reported by more than 50% of family members surveyed were temper outbursts, depression, lack of initiative, and impatience.

Familial Status

Although most head injury researchers have focused on the patient, recent investigations have studied the effects on family members as well. Maus-Clum and Ryan (1981) surveyed reactions of mothers and wives. Anger, depression, annoyance, frustration, and irritability were reported as personal reactions by at least 50% of the sample. Most distressing, 26% of the wives and 36% of mothers reported that they were victims of verbal abuse. Twenty-one percent and 18% of the sample, respectively, reported they had been threatened by physical violence. Spouses of the brain injured were especially affected, and 42% of those sampled reported, "I'm married but don't have a husband." Included among additional concerns expressed were decreased visitation by friends (27%), feeling trapped (42%), feeling married to a stranger (32%), and financial insecurity (58%). Lezak (1978) described similar types of effects on family members and reported feelings of isolation and entrapment to be common as well.

Vocational Status

Because of its clear link to financial status and self-esteem, vocational status has become one of the most important outcome variables in head injury research. Investigators have established that neuropsychological and physical deficits contribute significantly to severely reduced vocational potential. For example, Peck, Fulton, Cohen, Warren, and Antonello (1984) investigated vocational outcome in a group of 60 persons with severe head injury from the Richmond, VA, metropolitan area. Patients were a mean of 3.5 years postinjury, all were comatose at hospital admission, and 82% were between 16 and 40 years of age. Only 13% of the sample had returned to preinjury vocational levels. Thirty-five percent were employed in less demanding or sheltered workshop settings, and 52% were unemployed. Factors most strongly related to vocational adjustment included physical status, thinking efficiency, concentration ability, and motor coordination. Problems with memory, depression, and seizures were reported by 88%, 78%, and 15% of the sample, respectively. Furthermore, 56% reported that they relied on their spouse or other family member as a primary source of income. Disability income was received by 27% of the sample. The authors concluded that significantly diminished status is a common finding even years postinjury, and suggested a need for supplementary rehabilitation programs to reduce symptomatology related to reduced vocational status.

In a 15-year follow-up of 864 Korean War veterans with head injury, Dresser et al. (1973) found a poor vocational prognosis for persons who suffered from aphasia, motor impairment, seizures, and lengthy periods of posttraumatic unconsciousness. Age range of veterans sampled was 30–40 at follow-up, with mean age at time of injury being 22.7 years. Three-fourths of the sample sustained penetrating missile (gunshot) wounds. The remainder had suffered closed head injury. Only 27% of the sample suffered loss of consciousness for a period greater than 1 hour; 43% suffered no loss of consciousness. The investigators discovered a significant relationship between duration of coma and probability of unemployment. Approximately 53%

of the patients who were in coma for more than 6 hours were unemployed. The authors concluded that the primary determinants of employment were preinjury intellectual status, duration of coma, depth of missile penetration, and level of posttraumatic physical and mental disability.

Similarly, Jellinek, Torkelson, and Harvey (1982) completed an investigation of functional, emotional, and occupational status involving a group of 23 persons with brain injury in the Madison, WS area. Values for mean age and time postinjury were 27 and 4 years respectively. Eighty-two percent of the sample were unmarried, and 55% were female. The authors found that 41% of the sample were involved in education or work activity. Unfortunately, no data were provided regarding level of employment, average number of hours worked per week, or type of educational activity. Notably, 68% of the sample were independent in mobility and self-care.

The earliest investigations of vocational status preinjury were carried out in Great Britain and Scotland. Clearly, these countries differ socioeconomically from the United States. However, these investigations provide further insight regarding the long-term consequences of head injury. For example, Weddell, Oddy, and Jenkins (1980) conducted a follow-up study of 31 male and 13 female patients approximately 2 years post-injury. All patients had suffered more than a week of posttraumatic amnesia, were aged 16–39, and lived in the London area. Mean duration of coma was 4.2 weeks. The purpose of the investigation was to determine the quality of occupational, leisure, familial, and social functioning during the 2 months prior to the investigation. Only 5 persons had returned to their former employment, all after absences of more that 6 months. Two were skilled manual laborers, 1 was a teacher, and the remaining 2 were employed in unskilled jobs. Eleven persons returned to work full-time at a reduced capacity. Work resumption occurred at 6–18 months postinjury for this group. Notably, less than half the sample, 20 patients, were reportedly incapable of working. The authors placed considerable emphasis on the fact that parents often sacrificed their own employment to care

for their disabled family member at home. Unemployment was especially attributed to memory dysfunction and personality changes. For example, increased irritability, childishness, and disinhibition were changes commonly reported by family members.

Brooks, McKinlay, Symington, Beattie, and Campsie (1987) recently completed an investigation of employment status within the first 7 years post–head injury. The investigators, who completed their work in Glasgow, followed 98 persons with severe head injury and found a preinjury unemployment rate of 14%. Within the first 4 years postinjury, the unemployment rate was 73%; and within 5 years, 70% of the sample were unemployed. Brooks et al. indicated that there was not a significant change in work status for the sample between 2 and 5 years postinjury. As expected, impairments of cognitive status, personality problems, and behavorial disorders were significant contributors to unemployment. Particularly significant cognitive impairments included deficits in attention, memory, and communication.

Although there are relatively few comprehensive studies of post head injury vocational status, examination of data from the studies described herein yields a number of conclusions. First, the severity and type of injury are determinants of post injury employment potential. Persons with more severe injuries are less likely to return to work. Second, it is reasonable to conclude that less than 50% of persons with moderate to severe injuries, as determined by duration and depth of coma, are likely to return to employment. The likelihood of returning to work at preinjury levels is even smaller, and there are long delays for those who return to work. Finally, high rates of unemployment persist despite the interventions of numerous rehabilitation professionals.

Unfortunately, head injury is a phenomenon that primarily affects young males, typically breadwinners with relatively long life expectancies. The burden of caring for these unemployed individuals often falls on spouses and parents. Families undergo considerable stress, and in many cases, family members sacrifice their own employment to care for the head injured person at home.

STRATEGIES FOR ENHANCING VOCATIONAL OUTCOME

Traditional rehabilitation has not solved the un-employment problems arising from head injury. Victims are clearly in need of additional reha-bilitation strategies to enhance vocational out-come. The need for additional rehabilitation techniques is also critical, considering recent evidence regarding natural recovery processes. Namely, there is little evidence for *spontaneous* (i.e., without treatment) recovery beyond 1 year postinjury. For example, Panikoff (1983) re-viewed the outcome literature and concluded that the greatest proportion of spontaneous re-covery occurs within the first 6 months postin-jury, with little significant change thereafter. In a review of outcome data, Bond (1978) also concluded that the greater part of spontaneous physical and mental recovery occurs within 6 months of injury.

Recent advances in rehabilitation have re-sulted in development and refinement of two important sets of techniques that enhance the employability of persons with head injury. These techniques have been labeled: 1) support em-ployment (Wehman, Kreutzer, Wood, Morton, & Sherron, 1988); and 2) cognitive rehabilita-tion, or compensatory, strategies (e.g., Kreutzer & Boake, 1987).

Supported Employment for the Traumatically Brain Injured

One approach gaining much attention for indi-viduals who have suffered traumatic brain injury is supported employment. The approach merges the best components of behavior rehabilitation technology (Moon, Goodall, & Wehman, 1985) with the most recent advances in medical and neuropsychological rehabilitation (Najenson et al., 1980). Supported employment has been a major initiative of the U.S. Department of Ed-ucation, Office of Special Education and Re-habilitative Services (OSERS) since 1984 (Will, 1984). Most recently, this approach has been defined in the *Federal Register* (May 27, 1987) as,

> paid work in a variety of settings, particularly reg-ular work sites, especially designed for handi-capped individuals: (1) for whom competitive employment has not traditionally occurred; and (2) who, because of their disability, need intensive ongoing support to perform in a work setting. (p. 30546)

A principal underlying theme of supported employment is provision of service at the em-ployment site. The staff person at the job site is often called a job coach or job coordinator (Wehman & Melia, 1985). A second important underlying principal is the provision of services to individuals who have severe handicaps and are in need of special assistance. Characterist-ically, supported employment approaches pro-vide service to persons who would be unlikely to gain or hold employment without *on-site*, *ongoing* professional help. For example, the model has been highly successful with mentally retarded clients with IQs between 20 and 60 who have never worked before or who have consis-tently failed in employment. Virginia Com-monwealth University's Rehabilitation Research and Training Center has been tracking and suc-cessfully providing supported employment ser-vices to persons with retardation for over 9 years (Wehman et al. 1982; Wehman et al., 1985).

Four major program components characterize the supported work model of job placement and retention (Wehman, 1981; Wehman & Kregel, 1985). These components include: 1) job place-ment; 2) job-site training and advocacy; 3) on-going client assessment; 4) job retention and follow-along. Each component is described next.

Program Component 1: Job Placement

Placement of the individual into a job appro-priate to his or her abilities and interests is the first major component of the model. Much has been written about traditional approaches to job placement (e.g., Goodall, Wehman, & Cleve-land, 1983; Vandergoot, 1987). However, within the supported employment model, job place-ment is more than simply assisting an individual to find a job. Major aspects of the placement process include:

1. Matching job needs to client abilities and potential
2. Facilitating employer and client commu-nications
3. Facilitating parent or caregiver communi-cations
4. Establishing travel arrangements or provid-ing travel training

5. Analyzing the job environment to discover potential obstacles

Key Points Regarding Job Placement within the Supported Employment Model First, effective job placement and retention are predicated on an accurate analysis of the work environment characteristics and corresponding job requirements. This process of analysis has been variously referred to as ecological analysis (Wehman, 1981), top-down curriculum (Brown et al., 1979), or job analysis (Vandergoot & Worrell, 1979). Information gathered in the process of analysis is also essential for an appropriate job match, pairing job requirements with client abilities.

Second, suitable job placement can occur with clients who do not possess all the necessary work, cognitive, visuomotor, or social skill competencies for immediate job success. This is a significant departure from traditional job placement approaches, which require the client to be "job ready." Within the supported employment model, the job coach is available on the job site, as necessary, to assist the client in learning job tasks, developing efficient work strategies, and maintaining employment.

Third, within the job placement process, the client is assisted in making arrangements pertaining to ongoing disability benefits, the job interview process, and other procedures not directly related to on-site performance. Traditional employment approaches offer little help in these areas, and the responsibility for making the transition from unemployment to employment is often left entirely to the client or caregiver. Job placement for severely disabled individuals would be impossible or highly unlikely without this type of support, which is provided for or arranged by the job coaches.

Finally, job placement activities are performed by the job coach rather than another individual whose sole responsibility is placement. The coach handles not only placement but all aspects of the supported work model process. A virtue of this approach is continuity across all components of the model. The disadvantage of not having a "placement specialist" is offset by another advantage. The job coach maintains contact with the employer throughout the placement and employment process, allowing development of an important relationship that ensures job retention.

Job Placement as Uniquely Applied to Persons with Brain Injury For persons with head injury, placement decisions should involve considering the type of work the individual has done pre-and postinjury, the type of work the person is interested in doing, the individual's existing skills, and the individual's potential for learning new skills on the job. Unlike many persons with retardation, victims of head injury have often had prior competitive work experience. Prior job experience can be both an advantage and a disadvantage. To some extent, prior work skills are often preserved despite significant injury. Existing skills can facilitate learning a new job as well as maintaining performance. The disadvantage of prior work experience is particularly evident in attempting to place individuals who had high-level positions preinjury. Often, they are left with numerous intellectual, sensory, and motor problems, which prohibit their return to former levels of employment. Issues pertaining to disability acceptance and frustration must often be addressed by the job coach. These issues are especially important in working with individuals, for example, who held professional-level positions preinjury, but who are now barely capable of maintaining simple, entry-level positions. As a rule, the matching process is most difficult for persons who held high-level positions preinjury and who have the greatest levels of postinjury disability.

Regardless of preinjury employment level, head injury typically results in diminished insight, poor self-awareness, and impaired problem-solving ability. These factors contribute to unrealistic expectations regarding suitable employment. Most often, victims of head injury overestimate their abilities and request work that is entirely unsuited to their abilities. Ben-Yishay, Silver, Piasetsky, and Rattok (1987) indicated that poor self-awareness and unrealistic expectations are the primary contributors to high unemployment rates postinjury.

The likelihood of a successful job match and placement can be enhanced by several procedures. Ideally, clients should be encouraged to participate maximally in the placement decision-making processes. Participation often requires direct observation of the job site by the client as well as a series of discussions with the job coach. Client participation promotes greater motivation and job satisfaction. Furthermore, mutual decision making by the job coach and the client facilitates development of rapport, which is essential for job retention. In addition, in the early stages postinjury, victims of head injury often assume childlike roles because of their disabilities and necessary dependence on others. Participation in decision making helps them to resume more normal, adult roles and promotes recovery of self-esteem.

Family members and caregivers should also be encouraged to participate in the job placement process. Family support has been shown to be an important determinant of placement success (MacKenzie et al., 1987; Moon & Beale, 1984). Cooperative family members can help by providing transportation, assisting in the completion of forms and applications, and encouraging the client to accept a suitable position. Conversely, uncooperative family members have the potential to sabotage successful placement. Lack of cooperation is most apparent in situations where family members feel that a particular job selection is "beneath" the patient. Families in higher socioeconomic levels often have difficulty with this issue when the individual with head injury is severely disabled. Certainly, family members should not make the client's decision for him or her. In any case, the job coach should solicit family input.

A comprehensive neuropsychological evaluation is often helpful to the job coach and the client in the job placement process. The evaluation is intended to provide complete information regarding the effects of the client's injury in regard to residual strengths and limitations. Information is provided regarding reading ability, writing skills, arithmetic reasoning, memory, hand-eye coordination, visuoperceptual abilities, and emotional status. Implications regarding the likely manifestation of impairments in the work setting are derived. Furthermore, the evaluation can highlight specific, yet subtle problems, that could interfere with successful placement. For example, difficulties with organization, self-wareness, and problem solving

are hard to measure directly, have serious implications for work performance, and yet are often recognized by the trained neuropsychologist in the context of the evaluation process.

Successful job placement is highly dependent on the job coach's ability to collect accurate information about the client from a variety of sources. Ideally, job selection is made following a series of discussions among the client, family members, the neuropsychologist, and significant other rehabilitation providers.

Program Component 2: Job-Site Training and Advocacy On-the-job training is certainly not a new concept. However, traditional employment models do not provide active professional involvement during the early stages of employment. Rather, training activities are solely provided by employers. At best, vocational rehabilitation personnel may provide brief and infrequent follow-up checks for a short period following initial placement. In short, traditional employment models omit a major step, providing on-site skill training, and other measures to ensure adjustment to the work environment.

The authors' experiences with placement, as well as communication with others using the supported work model, strongly indicate that job-site training and advocacy are essential to the model's success. Two major processes are involved: 1) behavioral training of skills; and 2) advocacy on behalf of the client.

There is scant research regarding the applications of behavioral training to enhancement of vocational skills in nonsheltered or competitive work environments. Rusch and colleagues have clearly been the leaders in this area, and have completed studies related to acquisition of selected work skills (Schutz, Joste, Rusch, & Lamson, 1980), time-telling (Sowers, Rusch, Connis, & Cummings, 1980), time on-task on job (Rusch et al., 1980), reducing inappropriate self-stimulating behaviors (Rusch et al., 1980), and selected communication training (Karlan & Rusch, 1982). Apparently, the technology of behavioral training needs to be extended to nonsheltered work environments with individuals who have traditionally been considered poor candidates for competitive employment.

Clearly, cognitive training, behavioral training, and compensatory instructional strategies, when performed at the job site, can make a significant difference in promoting job acquisition and retention. We have only begun to scratch the surface in this area. Applications of reinforcement principles, manipulation of antecedent stimulus conditions, and use of coworkers as peer trainers are all areas that warrant further investigation.

Client advocacy is a second important feature of Program Component 2. Advocacy involves an active series of interventions by the job coach to enhance skill acquisition and maintenance of performance standards. Advocacy activities often involve client orientation, communication, and counseling. For example, the job coach may be required to assist the client in locating restroom facilities, vending machines, or the employee cafeteria. The coach may be called upon to facilitate communication with parents/caregivers and to provide information regarding job performance. Enhancement of communication between the client and coworkers is often important. Futhermore, the job coach may be called upon to provide counseling regarding required improvements in work behavior, which may be related to physical appearance, social skills, or tardiness.

Job-Site Training and Advocacy as Applied to Persons with Traumatic Brain Injury As stated earlier, individuals with traumatic brain injury may not need extensive direct job training, so much as on-site assistance from the job coach to structure the work environment for success. For example, if the client is especially sensitive to heat or noise, the job coach can work with the employer to reduce the conditions or to place the employee in an alternative setting. If the client becomes irritable, distractible, or confused when working around coworkers, the job coach may arrange to move the person's work station to a less congested area. Ideally, factors that detract significantly from work performance would be accounted for during the job match process. However, if these factors arise following placement, the job coach would be responsible for adapting the work environment to ensure successful job performance.

Development and utilization of adaptive equipment is another area that may require in-tervention on the part of the job coach. Persons with physical disabilities are often unsuccessful in employment because their job lacks the necessary adaptations to enable success. For example, if the production rate for a client required to process papers is too low, the job coach might provide for a jig to make paper handling easier and consequently increase production rates. Consideration must also be given to the issue of accessibility, not only to the worksite but also to break areas and bathrooms.

The use of compensatory strategies is perhaps one of the most important techniques a job coach will use on the worksite. To be effective, strategies must be developed on an individual basis following a thorough examination of the work environment, discussion with the client and employer, and investigation of cognitive and environmental parameters affecting productivity. An example of a compensatory strategy includes careful structuring of a sequence of job tasks through a written list, which allows an individual with severe memory impairment to recall and carry out job responsibilities. The latter portion of this chapter provides a thorough discussion of compensatory strategies used in supported employment.

Feedback to the worker regarding job performance is critical for job success, considering the poor self-awareness often manifested by victims of traumatic brain injury. Feedback is not only essential for maintaining effective employer-employee relationships but is also vital for effective relationships with coworkers. Employers often provide some feedback, but often feedback is inadequate or inappropriate, considering the client's intellectual and memory impairments. Consequently, feedback is often provided by the job coach, and in many cases, the coach works with the employer to enhance the employer's feedback techniques. For example, the individual with brain injury may not realize that it is socially unacceptable to pick up and smoke used cigarettes from an ashtray in the break area. This behavior may contribute to unfavorable impressions, and employers and coworkers may be hesitant to comment on such abnormal behavior. In this instance, the role of the job coach would be to provide feedback to the client in an appropriate way to ensure maintenance of favorable impressions. Often persons with head injury have difficulty accepting feedback, and discussion with the client's neuropsychologist can often be helpful in developing an effective feedback system.

Program Component 3: Ongoing Assessment A major feature that distinguishes supported employment from traditional employment approaches is ongoing assessment. Ongoing assessment is a continuing process of monitoring relevant aspects of the client's work performance. Ongoing assessment immediately follows assessment, and is a frequent and intensive process. As the employee's level of performance improves and stabilizes, ongoing assessment time decreases. In any case, ongoing assessment occurs throughout the client's employment. Conversely, traditional models involve a rehabilitation counselor who places the client and who might check superficially with employers at a later point to assess work performance. In the authors' experience, this superficial assessment process is inadequate because of the numerous problems manifested by victims of head injury.

Typically, there are two major indicators of performance, supervisor evaluation and client data. Although quantifiable data are optimal, in some instances verbal feedback to an on-site staff person may be an appropriate alternative. The amount of assessment data collected is clearly related to such variables as the performance level of the client and the amount of staff available for data collection.

Ongoing Assessment as Applied to Persons with Brain Injury Ongoing assessment is a process requiring communication between the client, job coach, employer, coworkers, and family members. Regular supervisor evaluations provide a variety of information about overall job performance and level of independence, as well as about secondary requirements such as appropriateness of appearance, punctuality, and absenteeism.

Feedback from the client regarding how the job is going and what is needed to work efficiently is important information and is routinely obtained by the job coach. Assessment data allow the job coach to further modify the work environment, coordinate new transportation ar-

rangements, or use different compensatory strategies. Furthermore, assessment allows the job coach to accurately estimate the degree of on-site training that is required and provides time frames for fading the job coach's involvement. Optimally, direct training time decreases as independence increases over time and as the individual becomes stabilized at the worksite.

Assessment data are used by the job coach to establish reasonable goals and timelines to allow the client to plan for success. Feedback to the client can be provided through written goals and discussion of data pertaining to performance levels. Discussion of graphs that depict client performance levels is often helpful, due to the clarity of such formats. Self-awareness can be improved through regular discussions of performance between the coach and client. Progress reports can be reviewed weekly or less frequently, depending on client needs. Progress reports can also be shared with family members to enhance their sense of awareness.

Program Component 4: Job Retention and Follow-Along Although follow-along is frequently referred to in the rehabilitation literature, there is little data regarding optimal types and levels of follow-along to ensure job retention. Relevant variables likely to influence retention, including frequency of employer contact and communication with clients, are rarely discussed in detail. For example, in a recent analysis of data from the Projects with Industry program (Reisner, Haywood, & Hastings, 1983), follow-up was found to be a highly frequent and obviously important activity. Yet, the type and quality of follow-up and concomitant effects on retention were not addressed by the investigators.

In one of the few papers addressing the parameters of follow-along, Hill, Cleveland, Pendleton, and Wehman (1982) list regular on-site visits to employers, phone calls, periodic review of supervisor evaluations, client progress reports, and parent evaluations as mechanisms to promote job retention. Ultimately, the follow-along component of the supported work model may be most critical, since persons with head injury are often at risk of losing their job. Competitive employment for the victims of head injury is essential because of the immediate risk of job loss without a retention plan. Although follow-along has been criticized because of cost factors, Hill, Wehman, Kregel, Banks, and Metzler (1987) provide data that demonstrate cost-effectiveness.

Job Retention and Follow-Along as Applied to Persons with Brain Injury   Follow-along is a proactive process and consists of *early intervention* in problematic areas affecting job performance. By the time an individual is in the follow-along phase of the supported employment model, the job coach should be able to anticipate stressful or confusing situations and intervene before problems become crises. Follow-along is provided throughout the client's employment.

For many victims of brain injury, maintaining employment is far more difficult than finding employment. Often, the client's problems are subtle and surface following the interview and first few days of employment. Factors contributing to difficulty maintaining employment include disinhibition, temper outbursts, memory impairments, slowness, and poor organizational skills. Because of poor self-awareness, clients who have been terminated from several jobs are often unable to explain their failures. Poor self-awareness and memory impairments also contribute to repetition of the same mistakes as individuals move from one job to the next. Consequently, an important role of the job coach is to provide the client with regular feedback on the job, ideally before problems occur.

The follow-along process involves communication with family members as well as with those in the immediate work environment. In some cases, increased independence and improved financial status arising from successful competitive employment can have a negative impact. For example, substance abuse problems may arise for the individual who now has extra spending money and is able to afford a car. Family members are often sensitive to substance abuse issues and are likely to report alcohol abuse or use of illicit drugs to the job coach. The responsible coach is able to arrange for appropriate interventions through the neuropsychologist or community treatment programs such as Alcoholics Anonymous.

Cognitive Rehabilitation or Compensatory Strategies

Cognitive rehabilitation or compensatory strategies are directly applicable to traditional vocational rehabilitation as well as the supported work model. The goal of these strategies is to teach persons with head injury how to live and work more efficiently. Techniques often include personalized checklists and schedules that ensure routine and minimize the effects of memory and attentional failures. Valuable improvements in independent living, academic, and work skills have been brought about through the use of these techniques.

The first step in developing compensatory strategies is completion of a thorough neuropsychological evaluation. The purpose of the evaluation is to determine the person's strengths and weaknesses, particularly in regard to areas with direct implications for work performance. The patient and family are carefully interviewed and a series of tests that measure intellectual, motor, and linguistic skills are administered. The second step is a task analysis, namely a thorough evaluation of the work setting and the step-by-step processes necessary for job completion. The final step involves development of a series of specific instructions and/or materials to be utilized by the patient. These techniques may be utilized either in preparing for work or during the work process.

Following are descriptions of three cases in which compensatory strategies were used to improve the work performance and independent living skills of persons with traumatic head injury.

Case Study I, D.J.   D.J. was a single woman in her mid '30s who was injured in an automobile accident. She was a passenger in the back seat of a compact car that was hit broadside by a tractor trailer truck that reportedly went through a red light. This woman sustained a moderate head injury as well as numerous severe lacerations and broken bones. In addition to resulting significant intellectual and visuoperceptual problems, D.J. suffers constant, excruciating pain from a severe leg injury in the accident. However, she has refused to take pain relief medications because of concerns regarding potential dependency and effects on her cognitive skills. Because of the severity and chronicity of her leg pain, she will require regular physical therapy for the rest of her life.

Prior to her injury, D.J. was employed as a manager of a retail food establishment. Her responsibilities included supervision of employees, payroll computation, inventory taking, and ordering of food products. After several years of inpatient and outpatient rehabilitation, D.J. attempted to return to her former employment on a part-time basis. However, because of problems with arithmetic reasoning, reading comprehension, and memory, she was unable to resume her former managerial responsibilities. Nevertheless, she returned to her former place of employment, working as a stock clerk and cashier. A limousine service funded as a result of litigation transported her.

Several weeks following reemployment, during a psychotherapy session, D.J. indicated that she was becoming increasingly upset and frustrated because of her disability. She explained that she had recently attempted to increase her work schedule from approximately 24 to 40 hours per week. She had also attempted to take on additional responsibilities, shifting from clerical to managerial work. Reportedly, because of fatigue and cognitive impairments, D.J. had failed. Her employer had taken away her newly assumed managerial responsibilities and reassigned her to her former position. Furthermore, D.J. reported an increasing number of problems in carrying out the responsibilities of a volunteer job she had held for more than a year.

D.J. explained that she had served as a volunteer in a home care hospice program for terminally ill patients. Prior to development of the hospice program, many of the patients would have lived out their final days in a hospital. The volunteer group had taken on the responsibility of developing a program that would allow patients the dignity of living at home for the short remainder of their lives. Volunteer responsibilities included family education, liaison with physicians, arranging appointments, providing transportation, arranging for and assessing patients' special needs or requests, and writing reports regarding patient status. D.J. explained that since the accident, she had done extremely

well with all aspects of her job except report writing. Until recently, her supervisors had been patient with her and had overlooked the fact that she completed few reports. This woman expressed apprehension that she was falling farther and farther behind and would eventually be asked to resign. Furthermore, Ms. J. expressed dismay that she had been criticized regarding the quality of the few reports she had completed. She was tearful, since, as she stated, her volunteer work meant a great deal to her, and was perhaps the most valued of her current responsibilities.

While talking with D.J., a clearer picture of her brain-injury-related difficulties emerged. The functional manifestations of her impaired organizational, reading comprehension, and writing skills were apparent. Without professional intervention, she would likely be unable to keep her paying job, be asked to resign from her volunteer position, and would find the request for her resignation personally devastating. She obviously derived a great deal of satisfaction from working with the homebound patients, and her commitment and verbal communication were well respected by volunteer staff and patients.

To test the hypothesis regarding factors underlying her work difficulties, D.J. was assigned to complete a report-writing task during a therapy session. Typically, the drive from D.J.'s rural town took 2 hours and she was driven by a friend because of visual, reaction time, and motor coordination impairments that precluded safe driving. D.J. was asked to write two paragraphs on lined paper and was given a 10-minute time limit. In the first paragraph, she was instructed to write a complete description of her drive to the therapy session. In the second, she was instructed to describe the current weather as completely as possible. No additional structure was provided. With the exception of name changes, the following text was produced by D.J.:

> My trip to Richmond Alice and I had lunch together and we talk while we had lunch The weather was very nice and the sun was shining. It was a very nice day We was late comping here because we went shopping and the time went by before I knew it. Trip there was a nice one with little traffic I did not said much because I was upset.

D.J. labored for the full 10 minutes. Examination of the writing sample revealed a number of problems that also likely affected her ability to write reports for her job. Notably, D.J. did not follow directions to write two separate paragraphs. Her writing was characterized by redundancy, vagueness, grammatical errors, spelling errors, and impoverishment of information. Her failure to write reports on a regular basis probably reflected the inordinate effort required to produce them as well as her embarrassment regarding their quality. Ideally, a sample of her actual reports might have been more useful. For the sake of time and immediate intervention, the sample produced in the therapy session was used to formulate a treatment plan.

To assess D.J.'s ability to respond to structure, her therapist quickly prepared a set of two checklists, using a computer and word processing software. The checklists were designed to help D. J. respond to the two initial assignments she was given to provide information regarding her trip and the weather. A reconstruction of the checklist pertaining to weather appears in Figure 1.

Weather Checklist

Precipitation:
  [ ] snow
  [ ] rain
  [ ] hail
  [ ] sleet
  [ ] none
  [ ] light
  [ ] heavy
Sky:
  [ ] clear
  [ ] partly sunny
  [ ] partly cloudy
  [ ] overcast
Wind:
  [ ] none
  [ ] light breeze
  [ ] very windy
Temperature:
  [ ] very cold
  [ ] chilly
  [ ] comfortable
  [ ] warm
  [ ] hot

Figure 1. Weather checklist designed to assess patient's ability to respond to structured report-writing format. (See case study for D.J., in the text.)

D.J. checked the appropriate items in less than 1 minute, with far less effort than was required in the report writing. The potential value of the checklist format was readily apparent. D. J. had difficulty generating the parameters relevant to each topic area, yet had no problem accurately ascertaining qualitative aspects within each parameter. Further questioning revealed that she was provided with little structure for her patient visit reports. For her next visit, D.J. was asked to bring in the report form she was required to complete following each visit with a hospice patient. Figure 2 is a copy of the form she brought.

The remainder of the form contained additional sets of blanks whereby D.J. could provide "Remarks," the date, and sign her initials.

Clearly, D.J. was not provided with sufficient structure by her supervisors for her volunteer work. She appeared able to respond appropiately, however, when provided with structure. On the basis of discussions with her, a task analysis of the requirements for her reports was completed in the form of a patient visit report (see Figure 3). The task analysis was accomplished by asking D.J. to generate categories of information she felt were required for the report. She was also asked to proved descriptor levels within each category. Emphasis was placed on using her own language as much as possible to make the form "her product" and to ensure preservation of her self-esteem. When difficulties arose, the therapist problem-solved with D.J. and occasionally provided suggestions.

The checklist format enabled D.J. to complete her reports in a timely fashion. Prior to development of the checklist, she had not fully completed a report in more than 5 months. Two weeks following our finalization of the report format, D.J. brought in five appropriately completed reports. The success of the intervention demonstrated not only her ability to work effectively given appropriate structure but also the value of having a computer and word processing software readily available during the therapy session. The computer allowed the patient and therapist to easily design a report format and then quickly assess alternative formats.

An additional set of issues arose when D.J. took on a second part-time job as a nurse's aide.

```
Comment Sheet

                              Hospital Program

Patient: _____

Date: _____

Remarks:
        _____

        _____

        _____

        _____


                                                    Initials: _____
```

Figure 2. Original format for hospice patient visit reports. (See case study for D.J., in the text.)

D.J. requested help preparing a weekly budget. She was now receiving income from two part-time jobs as well as investment income from monies awarded through accident-related litigation. D.J. explained that her income fluctuated from week to week, and she wanted to budget specific amounts of money for a variety of expenses based on percentages she would designate. She was overwhelmed by the record-keeping and financial allocation problems because of impairments in her reasoning and arithmetic processing abilities.

Fortunately, D.J. had a computer at home that was compatible with one used by her therapist. Consequently, she was able to use spreadsheet files generated in the office in her own home. A template (Figure 4) was devised that would automatically calculate amounts to be budgeted, deposited, and paid to various accounts. Flexibility was required, since the amount and sources of income might change on a weekly basis, and since D.J. wanted to be able to alter the percentages of money allotted based on future changes in need.

```
Patient's name: _____                          Date:_____

Completed by: _____

                              Patient Visit Report

Mood?
[ ]  sad         [ ]  angry        [ ]  crying
[ ]  happy       [ ]  scared       [ ]  _____
                                        (other—fill in)

Talking?
[ ]   not at all
[ ]   a little
[ ]   very much

Condition:
A.  Pain?
     [ ]  none
     [ ]  some
     [ ]  much
B.  Hygiene
     1.  Hair combed neatly? [ ]  Yes  [ ]  No
     2.  Clothing clean?     [ ]  Yes  [ ]  No
     3.  Bedding clean?      [ ]  Yes  [ ]  No
```

Figure 3. Sample text from D.J.'s revised, structured patient visit report. (See case study in the text.)

Weekly Budget Calculations

Week of:

Weekly income (enter all income for week)

Nursing:	$0.00
Trust:	0.00
Regina:	0.00
Other 1:	0.00
Other 2:	0.00
Other 3:	0.00
Other 4:	0.00
Other 5:	0.00
Total:	$0.00

Budget	%	Amount to budget
Rent	25	$0.00
Medical care	6	0.00
Clothing/personal	8	0.00
Telephone/utilities	5	0.00
Insurance	10	0.00
Savings	10	0.00
Household/maintenance	5	0.00
Transportation	4	0.00
Vacation/entertainment	5	0.00
Taxes	5	0.00
Food	7	0.00
Church	10	0.00
Other	0	0.00
Totals:	100	$0.00

Figure 4. Template for weekly budget, utilizing spreadsheet software. (See case study for D.J., in the text.)

Weekly Budget Calculations

Week of: May 4, 1987

Weekly income (enter all income for week)

Nursing:	$313.30
Trust:	0.00
Roberta:	84.49
Other 1:	0.00
Other 2:	0.00
Other 3:	0.00
Other 4:	0.00
Other 5:	0.00
Total:	$397.79

Budget	%	Amount to budget
Rent	25	$ 99.45
Medical care	6	23.87
Clothing/personal	8	31.82
Telephone/utilities	5	19.89
Insurance	10	39.78
Savings	10	39.78
Household/maintenance	5	19.89
Transportation	4	15.91
Vacation/entertainment	5	19.89
Taxes	5	19.89
Food	7	27.85
Church	10	39.78
Totals:	100	$397.79

Figure 5. Budget for week of May 4, utilizing spreadsheet software. (See case study for D.J., in the text.)

The checklist was also designed with "automatic checks" to ensure that calculations were performed accurately. As indicated in Figure 5, D.J. would be alerted to inadvertent entry errors if the sum of the "%" column did not equal 100% or if the total amounts in the Weekly Income and the Amount to Budget columns were not equivalent.

D.J. continued to work at her first part-time job and her volunteer job. However, because of problems unrelated to her, she was unable to maintain her second part-time position. She later joined a friend as a partner in a private business and continued to utilize her computer for a variety of purposes, including letter writing, record keeping, and financial management.

Case Study II, S.K. Normal neurological findings in persons with mild injuries are relatively common (Uzzell, 1986). Unfortunately, patients are often confused and frustrated when told by their physicians that there is no medical evidence of brain injury, and yet their perceived intellectual and emotional problems persist. Uzzell has reported that even mild head injuries cause diffuse injury to the brain, resulting in widespread but scattered damage to individual nerve cells. Medical diagnostic techniques including CAT (computerized axial tomography) scan and NMR (nuclear magnetic resonance) are only capable of detecting relatively large areas of damage, which typically includes large blood clots. Very likely, the only appropriate mechanism for medical diagnosis of mild injuries is biopsy, histological examination (microscopic examination of nerve cells following death), or PET scan. The PET (positron emission tomography) scan provides a picture of how brain cells are working, unlike the CT and NMR, which provide a picture reflecting the structure of the brain. Unfortunately, there are less than five PET scanners operating in the United States.

The following case describes intervention strategies prepared for an individual who had difficulty maintaining job performance because of a mild head injury.

S.K. received his injury when his car was hit from behind by another vehicle traveling approximately 45 miles per hour as S.K. was making a left turn. The patient sustained a head injury as a result of hitting his head against the window frame on his car door. In addition, he was in considerable pain as a consequence of back and neck strain resulting from the collision. Because the patient was not unconscious and did not receive any serious cuts or abrasions, he was not hospitalized. Although a Glasgow Coma Score was not obtained, he would most likely have been classified as a mild head injury (Glasgow Coma Score = 12–15). However, both S.K. and his wife observed a number of cognitive and emotional changes that persisted beyond the first week postinjury. Subsequently, the patient made an appointment and was evaluated by a neurologist. The neurological examination and computerized tomography (CT) scan findings were normal. The neurologist assured the patient he was fine and recommended a return to his full working schedule.

S.K. returned to work but noted a significant impairment in work performance relative to preinjury. Problems included consistent tardiness and poor organization, which were also commented on by supervisors. Both S.K. and his wife remained seriously concerned about the possible effects of the injury. A close family friend was a psychiatrist who had considerable experience treating individuals who had sustained head injuries. The psychiatrist recommended that the patient have a neuropsychological evaluation to discern whether perceived changes were attributable to head injury or to psychological and stress-related factors. On examination, the patient reported problems with reading comprehension, memory, attention, and organization. He explained that these problems were particularly troublesome and were affecting his work ability. Prior to the accident he had often been described by his colleagues as the most promising junior member of the firm. Reportedly, he had been confident, punctual, and efficient.

S.K's problems were confirmed by an interview with his wife, who also reported that he had become emotionally labile. At times he would suddenly laugh or cry for no apparent reason. Furthermore, this gentleman had apparently become the subject of jokes at work because of his now relatively poor performance. For example, he had misplaced files, showed up at the wrong time and place for appointments, and had addressed clients by the wrong name. A comprehensive neuropsychological evaluation yielded evidence of impairment of reasoning skills, memory, reading comprehension, and sustained attention, consistent with expected sequelae following mild head injury.

During the first few therapy sessions, S.K. was asked to compose a list of problems he had been having. On several occasions, he was asked to repeat and paraphrase information. In many cases, he was unable to provide a complete summary of the information, confirming the presence of functional memory impairment. Furthermore, at the end of therapy meetings he was often unable to recall many of the important details of the discussion. Consequently, an important initial step was to ask him to carry a notebook and a schedule book, enabling him to record important information. S.K. was initially resistant to carrying a schedule book, and explained that he never had recorded his appointments in the past. However, his resistance faded as he continued to miss appointments. He began to find the appointment book an important compensatory aid.

The next series of meetings focused on putting S.K.'s problems in priority order. To a great extent, his feelings of being overwhelmed were related to the fact that he believed he had a large number of problems, he had not examined them in a systematic fashion, and consequently, he had no plan for specifically addressing them. Initially, S.K. was asked to list all his problems and bring them to his next therapy session. During the next session, Mr. K. and his therapist discussed each problem on the list, with the primary goal of assigning priority order to them.

The problem of arriving to work on time was considered a first priority. Getting to work late each date created severe stress, clearly affected performance evaluations completed by his supervisors, and had a negative impact on his schedule for the remainder of the day.

A task analysis of preparatory activities to be carried out prior to leaving for work was accomplished through in-depth discussions with his therapist. For example, S.K. explained that since his initial injury, his wife had taken over many of the chores. He found he was especially late on mornings in which his wife slept in, when he was required to do chores she usually took responsibility for. S.K. also indicated he had difficulty making decisions regarding clothing selection. This was partly due to the fact that he had lost considerable weight following his accident and many of his clothes no longer fit. He would often spend 10–15 minutes each morning trying to find matching clothing that would fit. Reduced appetite was attributed to loss of his sense of smell, which is especially common following severe head injury, and a general sense of depression.

In completing the task analysis, S.K.'s therapist took copious notes on three separate pads of paper. Earlier, the therapist had requested that the patient get in the habit of taking his own notes. However, S.K. reported that his comprehension and memory of auditory information were not as good when he was required to write at the same time. On one pad the therapist wrote a set of general rules, "Rules for Survival" (Figure 6), to help S.K. organize himself and reduce overall stress levels. Each rule was discussed with the patient as well as with his spouse. The therapist solicited input regarding S.K.'s beliefs pertaining to practicality and potential effectiveness, and the intended purpose of each rule was explained.

On a second notepad, the therapist prepared, again with S.K.'s assistance, a list of tasks to be completed each night before work. The goal was to reduce the number of activities that had to be done in the morning by preparation the evening before. Figure 7 denotes the activities to be completed by S.K. each evening before a workday. The final notepad was used to list activities to be completed in the morning before work (see Figure 8).

The "Rules for Survival" checklist had a number of important purposes. First, the list

---

Rules for Survival

[ ] *Consistency and regularity* are important means of compensating for problems related to memory and confusion. Completing tasks routinely (at the same time and in the same sequence each day) will enhance your memory and reduce overall stress levels.

[ ] There are many ways *to reduce stress in the morning* and ensure that you leave for work on time. Try to organize yourself the evening before. Activities for the night before are organized on your "Night Before—Checklist"; activities to be carried out each morning before work are organized on your "Morning On-Time Checklist." Also, remember to buy a coffeemaker with a timer that you can set the night before.

[ ] *Division of labor.* Decide which chores you will do and which chores your wife will do. Be as consistent as possible in adhering to your chosen responsibilities.

[ ] Try to set *reasonable expectations* for yourself. Expect to make at least some mistakes; we all do.

[ ] Do not be concerned about leaving a mess at home before you leave for work. You can always clean up when you get back home, after work.

[ ] If you must choose between: 1) eating breakfast; or 2) getting to work on time, take choice 2 and skip breakfast. Keep healthy snacks (e.g., fruit, granola bars) in your desk drawer at work in case you miss breakfast.

[ ] Try to work things out as we discussed, so that *you are resonsible for making coffee* and *your wife is responsible for making breakfast.* Ask her to help you by: 1) having breakfast ready at the same time each morning; and 2) warming up your car for you each morning; and 3) feeding cats. Note, establishing breakfast within your routine will help your memory and thereby reduce overall stress levels.

[ ] *Organize your keys, wallet, briefcase, and sunglasses* each night before bed. Keep them in the same place and nearby one another to spare you looking for them in the morning.

[ ] If you are running late for work, don't rush on the ride in by driving fast and/or not being cautious. It is *more important for you to get to work safely* than risk having an accident trying to get there on time.

Figure 6.   Instructions given to S.K. to improve organization and ensure timeliness for work. (See case study in the text.)

Night Before—Checklist

Things to do the night before to make getting out of the house in the A.M. easier:

Clothes:

[ ] Select clothes and shoes.
[ ] Try on clothes to make certain they still fit.
[ ] Check clothes for wrinkles.
[ ] Iron as needed.
[ ] Lay out clothes (in the same area each day) for next AM.

Toiletries:

Lay out items on the vanity for the next day:

[ ] razor
[ ] toothpaste
[ ] hair dryer
[ ] shaving cream
[ ] toothbrush
[ ] after-shave

Coffee:

Lay out items for coffee the next day:

[ ] cream
[ ] cups
[ ] sugar
[ ] spoons

Pick up right before leaving the house in the morning—items:

[ ] wallet
[ ] sunglasses
[ ] coat
[ ] briefcase

Figure 7. Checklist used in the evening by S.K. to ensure timely arrival at work. (See case study in the text.)

served as a memory aid, allowing S.K. to keep a written record of information discussed in therapy, which might otherwise be forgotten. Second, the rules also served, in part, as a contract between the therapist and patient, as well as between the patient and his wife. The patient believed that his wife might have difficulty accepting his suggestions regarding changes in their postinjury routine. Apparently, since the head injury, his wife had assumed a largely maternal role. S.K. indicated that his wife would be more likely to accept the suggested changes if they were provided as "doctor's orders."

During the week following implementation of the checklists, the patient reported significant improvements in punctuality. Reportedly, he began regularly arriving at work on time and he found the remainder of his day to be less stressful. To some extent, his success was attributable to the cooperation of his wife and his employer.

Morning On-Time Checklist

Things to do in the morning to help make getting out of the house in the AM. easier:

[ ] Take shower.
[ ] Put on watch.
[ ] Dry hair.
[ ] Shave.
[ ] Brush teeth.
[ ] Dress.
[ ] Feed cats.
[ ] Eat breakfast/drink coffee.
[ ] Pick up coat, keys, sunglasses, wallet, briefcase.
[ ] Walk to car no later than 7 A.M.

Figure 8. Checklist used in the morning by S.K. to ensure timely arrival at work. (See case study in the text.)

Continued improvements in work performance were attributable to development of an additional number of compensatory strategies and to natural recovery over time.

Case Study III, D.T.   D.T., a married man in his mid '30s, sustained a moderate head injury as a result of a motorcycle accident. He was hit broadside by a car that failed to stop at a stop sign. The patient was hospitalized for less than a week. Within a month postinjury, he had recovered physically and was entirely independent in activities of daily living. However, neuropsychological evaluation revealed that he had numerous cognitive impairments including memory problems, reasoning deficits, and difficulty with organization. In addition, he was extremely frustrated because of his impairments and developed problems controlling his temper. For example, he had a number of altercations while driving. In each case, he felt that he had been wronged by another driver, pulled his car over, and proceeded to assault the driver verbally or physically. On one occasion, he was nearly arrested for beating a young man in a sports car who allegedly had "cut him off." Fortunately for the patient, the young man refused to press charges. The patient reported that he was aware that his actions were inappropriate, yet described his loss of temper as uncontrollable—"something inside me just snaps." Psychotherapy, which also included his wife at times, involved teaching the patient anger management, self-monitoring, and stress reduction techniques.

Because of problems related to memory and organization, D.T. was unable to continue working at the same jobs he had held prior to his injury. He grudgingly gave up free-lance photography and discontinued teaching. D.T. indicated that he was now embarrassed about his teaching skills, and described his classes as disorganized and incoherent. As a consequence, he returned to contracting work, which included painting and home renovation. A major problem for D.T., however, was difficulty organizing his work schedule. Both he and his wife complained that he often took on many more jobs than he could possibly handle. As a consequence, he received many complaints from clients regarding lengthy delays on job completion. In several cases, D.T. had signed contracts with penalty clauses that obligated him to reduce the cost of jobs by a specified amount for each day he went beyond the agreed-upon completion date. Concern was expressed, considering the seriousness of the present situation, that D.T. might not receive any pay for at least several of the jobs he was working on. At one point, his wife calculated his actual hourly pay, including losses, as less than 25 cents per hour.

During a meeting with his therapist, D.T. established that working out a method to improve his timeliness was an immediate priority. As indicated in Figure 9, D.T. was asked to provide, for each job, the name of his client, the number of days expected for completion, and the anticipated completion date. Initially,

after completing the list, D.T. became aware that he had actually agreed to complete a total of 51 days' worth of work for the five clients. When asked what each of his clients was told in regard to estimated time for completion, however, D.T. responded, "2 weeks."

D.T. and his therapist decided it would be helpful for him to keep an ongoing written log using the same format. In addition to completing the log, D.T. also agreed to begin self-monitoring and to abide by the following written rules:

1. New jobs would only be accepted and scheduled on a tentative basis. Specific times and dates would only be set in consultation with his wife or the therapist.
2. The content and quality of record keeping in the log would be reviewed during each of D.T.'s weekly meetings with the therapist.
3. Completion times would be estimated in a liberal fashion, with errors being in the direction of overestimation, rather than underestimation.
4. Because of fatiguability and pain related to overexertion, D.T. would not work on Sundays and would not work more than 10 hours per day.
5. D.T. would only work on one job at a time to reduce problems related to disorganization. He would develop a written plan for each job, including materials needed and sequence of activities prior to initiating each job. Only after completing a scheduled job could he move on to the next scheduled job.

Sleep disturbance is a common result of significant head injury, and D.T. was no exception. Reportedly, he often could not fall asleep until 3:00 AM. Because he rarely felt fresh and rested in the mornings, he often required a nap in the afternoon. Concerns about the effects of D.T.'s sleep disturbance on his cognitive and emotional functioning as well as on his work ability resulted in the development of a behavioral plan to improve sleep patterns. Medications were considered a last alternative because of the patient's preinjury history of substance abuse, the

Work Log

Customer	Expected number of working days	Completion date
J. Smith	12	June 1
L. Stevens	10	June 12
N. Richards	5	June 19
T. Metcalf	1	June 20
M. Robins	9	July 2
Total	27	

Figure 9. Portion of log kept by patient, D.T., to help ensure accurate estimation of job completion times. (See case study in the text.)

fact that patients with head injury are particularly sensitive to the effects of medications, and the likelihood that medication would impair cognitive functioning. D.T. and his wife were therefore given a set of instructions regarding means of improving his sleep patterns (see Figure 10). They were also asked to complete a sleep chart on a daily basis, which depicted the specific hours during which the patient slept.

After several weeks, the sleep plan was reportedly effective. D.T. stated that he was retiring and awakening at the same time each day. In addition, he was sleeping through the night, felt fresh and rested in the mornings, and did not require a nap during the day. As with many victims of head injury, his therapist was concerned about self-awareness and accuracy of self-report. However, a subsequent meeting with D.T.'s wife confirmed the information provided by him.

Application of agreed-upon rules, self-monitoring, and regular meetings to discuss prob-

---

Rules for Good Sleep

1. *Avoid naps* during the day; they make it harder to sleep at night.
2. Try to go to sleep and to wake up at the same time every day, even on weekends.
3. If you go to bed, try to sleep, and spend no more than 15 minutes in bed trying to fall asleep. If you can't sleep, get up and do something (preferably chores).
4. Avoid caffeine and sweets after dinner, they keep you awake.
5. Adjust your sleep hours based on need. For example, if you're not napping during the day and can't ever get to sleep at 11:45 P.M. try readjusting your schedule so that you go to sleep at 12:30 A.M. instead.
6. Regular physical exercise, especially aerobics, will help you to sleep.
7. Try to do something relaxing during the last few hours before bed. Avoid exercising immediately before bedtime.
8. Learn to be sensitive to your stress levels by asking yourself many times during the day, "How much tension am I feeling now?"—or—"How relaxed am I?"
9. Certain foods, including milk and turkey, contain naturally occurring substances that can help you to sleep. However, avoid eating within an hour before bed. Digestion can interfere with sleep.

Figure 10. Written instructions to reduce sleep disturbance in patient, D.T. (See case study, in the text.)

lems and progress resulted in improved work performance. More realistic estimates of job completion times also relieved a great deal of the patient's stress. D.T. has since completed an M.F.A., and although he continues to work as a contractor part-time, he has resumed freelance photography. He has begun to apply for part-time teaching positions. In addition, he and his therapist are developing organizational strategies intended to improve his teaching skills.

SUMMARY AND CONCLUSIONS

Epidemiological research clearly indicates that traumatic head injury has reached epidemic proportions. Incidence rates for head injury are greater than those for cerebral palsy, multiple sclerosis, and spinal cord injury combined. Many victims suffer from long-term impairments in functional, neurological, medical, neuropsychological, and linguistic status. Emotional and behavioral problems are common as well. In addition, family problems often ensue as a consequence of the victim's dependency and concomitant emotional changes. Investigations of postinjury vocational status indicate that unemployment rates within the first 7 years postinjury range as high as 70% for those with moderate and severe injuries. Researchers have demonstrated that the emotional and neuropsychological changes arising from injury are the greatest contributors to reduced employability.

Relatively high unemployment rates for this population strongly suggest that traditional approaches to physical and vocational rehabilitation have been inadequate. To complement existing services and to enhance employment outcome, two approaches have been developed and refined for use with victims of head injury. First, *supported employment* is a unique approach that assists the client to select, obtain, and maintain suitable employment on the basis of his or her interests and abilities. Second, *compensatory strategies* have been developed to help the individual offset intellectual problems that would otherwise interfere with learning job skills and maintaining production levels. Often, compensatory strategies are used in the context of a comprehensive, supported employment program.

Expanded use of supported employment and compensatory strategies promises to enhance

employment outcomes for those with traumatic head injury. Nevertheless, additional research is needed to more clearly define the types of techniques that work best for each unique set of problems.

REFERENCES

Ben-Yishay, Y., Silver, S.M., Piasetsky, E., & Rattok, J. (1987). Relationship between employability and vocational outcome after intensive holistic cognitive rehabilitation. *Journal of Head Trauma Rehabilitation, 2*, 35–48.

Bond, M.R. (1978). *The stages of recovery from severe head injury with special reference to late outcome.* Paper presented at the Third Congress of the International Rehabilitation Medicine Association, Basel, Switzerland.

Brooks, N., McKinlay, W., Symington, C., Beattie, A., & Campsie, B. (1987). Return to work within the first seven years of severe head injury. *Brain Injury, 1*, 5–19.

Brown, L., Branston-McClean, M. Baumgart, D., Vincent, K., Falvey, M., & Schroeder, J. (1979). Using the characteristics of current and subsequent least restrictive environments in the development of curricular content for severely handicapped adults. *AESPH Review, 4*, 407–424.

Cope, N., & Hall, K. (1982). Head injury rehabilitation: Benefit of early intervention. *Archives of Physical Medicine and Rehabilitation, 63*, 433–437.

Dresser, A., Meirowsky, A., Weiss, G., McNeel, M., Simon, G., & Caveness, W. (1973). Gainful employment following head injury: Prognostic factors. *Archives of Neurology, 29*, 111–116.

Federal Register. (May 27, 1987). Volume 52, number 157, 34 CFR Part 363, p. 30546. Washington, DC: U.S. Government Printing Office.

Goodall, P., Wehman, P., & Cleveland, P. (1983). Job placement for mentally retarded individuals. *Education and Training of the Mentally Retarded, 18*, 271–278.

Hall K., Cope, N., & Rappaport, M. (1985). Glasgow Outcome Scale and Disability Rating Scale: Comparative usefulness in following recovery of traumatic head injury. *Achives of Physical Medicine and Rehabilitation, 66*, 35–57.

Hill, M., Cleveland, P., Pendleton, P., & Wehman, P. (1982). Strategies in the follow-up of moderately and severely handicapped competitively employed workers. In P. Wehman & M. Hill (Eds.), *Vocational training and placement of severely disabled persons* (Project Employability, Vol. 3). Richmond: Virginia Commonwealth University.

Hill, M., Wehman, P., Kregel, J., Banks, P.D., & Metzler, M. (1987). Employment outcomes for people with moderate and severe disabilities: An eight year longitudinal analysis of supported competitive employment. *Journal of The Association for Persons with Severe Handicaps, 12*(3), 182–189.

Jellinek, H., Torkelson, R., & Harvey, R. (1982). Functional abilities and distress levels in brain injury patients at long-term follow-up. *Achives of Physical Medicine and Rehabilitation, 63*, 160–162.

Kalisky, Z., Morrison, D., Meyers, C., & Von Laufen, A.

(1985). Medical problems encountered during rehabilitaton of patients with head injury. *Archives of Physical Medicine and Rehabilitation, 66*, 25–29.

Karlan, G., & Rusch, F.R. (1982). Analyzing the relationship between acknowledgement and compliance in a nonsheltered work setting. *Education and Training of the Mentally Retarded, 17*,(3), 202–208.

Kreutzer, J., & Boake, C. (1987). Addressing disciplinary issues in cognitive rehabilitation: Definition, training, and credentialing. *Brain Injury.*

Kurtze, J.F. (1982). The current neurologic burden of illness and injury in the United States. *Neurology, 32*, 1207–1210.

Levin, H.S., Benton, A.L., & Grossman, R.G. (1982). *Neurobehavioral consequences of severe head injury.* New York: Oxford University Press.

Lezak, M.D. (1978). Living with the characterologically altered brain injured patient. *Journal of Clinical Psychiatry, 39*, 592–598.

MacKenzie, E.J., Shapiro, S., Smith, R.T., Siegel, J.H., Moody, M., & Pitt, A. (1987). Factors influencing return to work following hospitalization for traumatic injury. *American Journal of Public Health, 77*, 329–334.

Maus-Clum, N., & Ryan, M. (1981). Brain injury and the family. *Journal of Neurosurgical Nursing, 13*, 165–169.

Moon, M.S., & Beale, A.V. (1984). Vocational training and employment: Guidelines for parents. *Exceptional Parent, 14*(8), 35–38.

Moon, S., Goodall, P., & Wehman, P. (1985). *Critical issues related to supported employment.* Richmond: Virginia Commonwealth University, Rehabilitation Research and Training Center.

Najenson, T., Groswasser, Z., Mendleson, L., & Hackett, P. (1980). Rehabilitation outcome of brain damaged patients after severe head injury. *International Journal of Rehabilitation Medicine, 2*, 17–22.

Newcombe, F., Brooks, D.N., & Baddeley, A. (1980). Rehabilitation after brain damage: An overview. *International Journal of Rehabilitation Medicine, 2*, 133–137.

Panikoff, L.B. (1983). Recovery trends of functional skills in the head-injured adult. *American Journal of Occupational Therapy, 37*, 735–743.

Peck, E., Fulton, C., Cohen, C., Warren, J., & Antonello, J. (1984, February). *Neuropsychological, physical, and psychological factors affecting long-term outcomes following severe head injury.* Paper presented at the annual meeting of the International Neuropsychological Society, Houston.

Reisner, L., Haywood, P., & Hastings, P. (1983). *A review of Projects with Industry projects and effectiveness.* Washington DC: U.S. Department of Education, Rehabilitation Services Administration.

Rimel, R.W., Giordani, B., Barth, J.T., & Jane, J.A. (1982). Moderate head injury: Completing the clinical spectrum of brain trauma. *Neurosurgery, 11*, 344–351.

Rusch, F., Connis, R., & Sowers, J. (1980). The modification and maintenance of time spent using social reinforcement, token reinforcement, and response cost in an applied restaurant setting. *Journal of Special Education Technology*, *2*,(3), 18–26.

Rusch, F.R., Weithers, J.A., Menchetti, B.M., & Schutz, R.P. (1980). Social validation of a program to reduce topic repetition in a nonsheltered workshop setting. *Education and Training of the Mentally Retarded*, *15*, 208–215.

Schutz, R., Joste, K., Rusch, F., & Lamson, D. (1980). Acquisition, transfer, and social validation of two vocational skills in a competitive employment setting. *Education and Training of the Mentally Retarded*, *15*, 306–311.

Sowers, J., Rusch, F., Connis, R.T., & Cummings, L. (1980). Teaching mentally retarded adults to time manage in a vocational setting. *Journal of Applied Behavior Analysis*, *13*, 119–128.

Uzzell, B.P. (1986) Pathophysiology and behavioral recovery. In B.P. Uzzell & Gross (Eds.), *Clinical neuropsychology of intervention* (pp. 3–18). Boston: Martinus Nijhoff Publishing.

Vandergoot, D. (1987). Review of placement research literature: Implications for research and practice. *Rehabilitation Counseling Bulletin*, 30, 243–262.

Vandergoot, D., & Worrell, J.D. (Eds.) (1979) *Placement in rehabilitation: A career development perspective*. Baltimore: University Park Press.

Weddell, R., Oddy, M., & Jenkins, D. (1980). Social adjustments after rehabilitation: A two year follow-up of patients with severe head injury, *Psychological Medicine*, *10*, 257–263.

Wehman, P. (1981). *Competitive employment: New horizons for severely disabled individuals*. Baltimore: Paul H. Brookes Publishing Co.

Wehman, P., Hill, M., Goodall, P., Cleveland, P., Brooke, V., & Pentecost, J. (1982). Job placement and follow-up of moderately and severely handicapped individuals after three years. *Journal of The Association for Persons with Severe Handicaps*, *7*, 5–16.

Wehman, P., Hill, M., Hill, J., Brooke, V., Pendleton, P., & Britt, C. (1985). Competitive employment for persons with menal retardation: A follow-up six years later. *Mental Retardation*, *23(6)*, 274–281.

Wehman, P., & Kregel, J. (1985). A supported work approach to competitive employment of individuals with moderate and severe handicaps. *Journal of the Association for Persons with Severe Handicaps*, *10*(1), 3–11.

Wehman, P., Kregel, J., & Barcus, J.M. (1985). From school to work: A vocational transition model for handicapped students. *Exceptional Children*, *52*(1), 25–37.

Wehman, P. Kreutzer, J., Wood, W., Morton, M., & Sherron, P. (1988, June). Supported work model of competitive employment for persons with traumatic brain injury: Toward job placement and retention. *Rehabilitation Counseling Bulletin*, *31*(4), 298–312.

Wehman, P., & Melia R. (1985). The job coach: Function in transitional and supported employment. *American Rehabilitation*, *11*(2), 4–7.

Will, M.C. (1984). *Supported employment for adults with severe disabilities: An OSERS program initiative*. Washington, DC: U.S. Department of Education.

Chapter 21

Supported Employment for Persons with Severe and Profound Mental Retardation

David Mank and Jay Buckley

The national supported employment initiative for persons with severe disabilities holds unparalleled promise for improving the employment reality for individuals historically denied access to integrated employment (Kiernan & Stark, 1986). This initiative gives individuals with severe disabilities access to paid employment in integrated settings where the supports needed for job success can be provided. The initiative began in part because of increasing dissatisfaction with segregated activity and work programs and because of numerous demonstrations of vocational competence on the part of people previously considered unable to work or lacking in employment potential.

One factor in the recent expansion of integrated employment with long-term support is the failings of the traditional flow-through system of day services for citizens labeled mentally disabled and severely handicapped. The flow-through, or continuum, model assumed that persons would move or graduate from activity centers to sheltered work programs and finally into a competitive job. In reality, few persons moved through the system, and the vast majority of persons with severe and profound mental retardation did not gain access to integrated jobs (Bellamy, Horner, Sheehan, & Boles, 1980; Bellamy, Rhodes, Bourbeau, & Mank, 1986).

Instead, persons with the most severe disabilities in our communities spent years in nonwork or segregated settings with little, if any, hope of change.

A second factor in the development of the supported employment initiative is the increasing number of research and development projects that demonstrate that individuals with severe disabilities can learn complex work skills. Early studies showed that systematic instruction enabled persons with mental retardation to learn detailed tasks (Bellamy, Peterson, & Close, 1975; Crosson, 1966; Gold, 1972; 1973; 1975). Later studies demonstrated that these individuals could perform job tasks at the same production rates (Bellamy, Inman, & Yeates, 1978; Mank & Horner, 1987) and in the same settings (Connis, 1979; Shafer & Brooke, 1985; Sowers, Rusch, Connis, & Cummings, 1980; Wehman, 1981) as nonhandicapped workers. While the ability of individuals labeled with disabilities became undeniably clear, dissatisfaction with our day services increased.

Along with this dissatisfaction is the development of national and state policy affirming the ability and the rights of persons considered severely disabled (Taylor, Biklen, & Knoll, 1987). One of the most important implications of such policy is this: the critical variables for success in integrated employment are *opportunity* and the *support* needed to acquire and keep a job in regular employment settings. Now the widely held and well-supported view is that all persons, regardless of the severity of their disabilities, should have access to integrated employment with long-term support. Even so, there is some risk that those persons with severe and profound mental retardation may not have equal access to supported employment in the months and years to come.

Changing the reality of unemployment and underemployment for persons with severe disabilities will require continued adjustment of federal and state funding and regulatory systems, restructuring the roles and responsibilities of state agency personnel and service providers, new approaches to secondary vocational training and transition, full implementation of recent amendments to the Vocational Rehabilitation Act, and ongoing personnel training and incentives to support these changes. This chapter discusses issues related to providing supported employment for those individuals labeled severely and profoundly mentally retarded. The first section describes recent developments and emerging trends that shape the present context of supported employment. The next section discusses issues that affect the provision of supported employment services for individuals with severe and profound mental disabilities. The last section discusses systemic implementation of support and employment services for these individuals.

THE PRESENT CONTEXT

Recent years have witnessed notable improvements in the awareness and expectations of what is possible in employing persons with severe and profound mental retardation. At the same time, however, questions have been raised about the degree of access afforded to those individuals. Supported employment for persons with severe and profound mental retardation has been, and will continue to be, affected by a number of recent developments. These include demonstrations of innovative employment services for individuals with the most severe disabilities; the need for data describing the implementation of

supported employment; the inclusion of individuals with handicaps other than developmental disabilities; and the expanding role of vocational rehabilitation agencies.

Demonstrations of Innovative Service

A common criticism of the human services field is that program development resources more often lead to the development of isolated instances of high-quality service rather than widespread implementation (Paine, Bellamy, & Wilcox, 1984). It is often said that enough demonstration projects already exist, and that what is needed is a set of clearly articulated procedures for disseminating relevant information and increasing the availability of superior programs. The supported employment initiative is intended to create a profound, system-wide change in the way individuals with disabilities gain access to employment. When the federal initiative was formally launched in 1985, there were examples of high-quality supported employment programs for individuals with disabilities. Some of these programs were providing services to individuals with the most severe disabilities in local communities. Thus, while the initiative seeks to effect systems change, one critical aspect of this change has included the greater development of exemplary services focused on citizens with severe and profound mental retardation.

In many instances the impetus for accepting the challenge of providing support services to individuals with severe and profound mental retardation comes from the commitment of the individual service providers. Armed with consistent belief in the competence of those individuals, and with good technical skills, these programs can serve as resources for their regions, states, and the nation. High-quality supported employment services for persons with severe and profound mental retardation have included individual placement programs and small-group supported employment programs. Programs in states such as Wisconsin, Vermont, Virginia, Washington, Oregon, Minnesota, and California show the opportunity and the promise for widespread development of employment opportunities that include persons with severe and profound mental retardation. Not only do these projects demonstrate the competence of the persons served, but they make clear that supported employment for persons with severe and profound mental retardation can be implemented in a range of industries, in varied communities, and under different economic conditions. A common feature of many of these exemplary programs is a focus on outcomes and quality that exceeds minimum requirements. These voluntary standards promote a commitment to continuous improvement of the supported employment concept and of individual outcomes and benefits.

Model supported employment programs that include individuals with severe and profound mental retardation can promote wider implementation of the concept in at least two ways. First, impetus for serving these most challenging individuals comes from state officials, increasing the likelihood that similar services will be developed on a wider scale. In at least one state, Minnesota, the commitment and resources for developing projects demonstrating that individuals with the most severe disabilities can succeed in integrated employment have come, in part, from the Governor's Council on Developmental Disabilities and the Minnesota Supported Employment Project. Projects are planned for development across the state and not just in a single demonstration site.

A second way to achieve maximum impact from the development of demonstration sites is for state agency personnel to track the accomplishments of exemplary model programs and then ensure that the successes and strategies of these programs are publicized and used as resources. Several state-supported employment projects have arranged for the projects that achieve exemplary outcomes for persons with severe disabilities to serve as training and internship sites.

Need for Data

Although the development of innovative programs has been a major advancement, information about the nature and scope of the implementation of supported employment has only begun to emerge. Federal and state officials, consumer and advocacy groups, provider organizations, and coalitions of researchers from universities across the nation are calling for data

that describe implementation to date (Berkeley Planning Associates, 1986). The available data provide information about only a portion of the total number of individuals receiving supported employment services. Even so, a glimpse of these individuals is available.

Kiernan, McGaughey, and Schalock (1986) conducted a survey designed to document changes in placement patterns of individuals with developmental disabilities, including transitional training, supported employment, and competitive employment. It should be noted that the definitions Kiernan et al. used for *supported* and *competitive employment* are not the same as those in the Developmental Disabilities Act of 1984 (PL 98-507) or the Rehabilitation Act Amendments (PL 99-506). Kiernan et al. collected data from 1,119 rehabilitation facilities serving 160,369 individuals, including 112,996 adults with developmental disabilities. They reported that of the total number, almost 20% were moved out of facilities between October 1, 1984 and September 30, 1985. Of this number, 3.3% were individuals with severe or profound mental retardation.

In 1986 a number of states collaborated to test the feasibility of a voluntary system for collecting and aggregating data on the implementation of supported employment (Supported Employment Information System [SEIS], 1986). These data provide some information about who is served in emerging supported employment programs. Data so far reported provide information on only some of the individuals served to date. From data available on 750 individuals for the fourth quarter of 1986, 45% were considered to have mild mental retardation, 30% were labeled moderately mentally retarded, 9% were labeled severely retarded, and 2% were labeled profoundly retarded (Mank, Buckley, & Smull, 1987).

Given the incomplete nature of available data, this information raises a question without fully answering it. That question is: Are persons with severe and profound mental retardation gaining equal access to supported employment? It is not possible to fully evaluate access to supported employment without more complete data. Until an information system that captures the outcomes of and access to supported employment is made a national, state, and local priority, questions regarding the presence or absence of individuals with severe and profound mental retardation will continue to be posed.

Inclusion of Individuals with Nondevelopmental Disabilities

A major focus of the early developments in supported employment was on individuals with developmental disabilities. In fact, much of the dissatisfaction with the flow-through service system was generated by advocates for persons with severe and profound mental retardation (Bellamy et al., 1980; 1986; Gold, 1972; 1973; 1975; Wehman, Schutz, Bates, Renzaglia, & Karan, 1978). As a result, many approaches for providing supported employment services, as well as emerging training technology and current funding mechanisms, reflect the perceived needs of individuals with developmental disabilities.

The concept of supported employment, that is, long-term support to maintain successful integrated employment, has merit without regard to specific disability labels. For instance, many individuals with long-term mental illness, traumatic brain injury, severe physical disabilities, sensory handicaps, nonintellectual developmental disabilities, severe learning disabilities, and multiple disabilities find sustained employment without support to be difficult at best. Advocates, families, professionals, and federal and state officials are now advocating the inclusion of these individuals in the supported employment initiative.

This emerging demand underscores the tremendous need for supported employment in communities for persons with different disabilities. The fear of advocates for persons with severe and profound intellectual disabilities is that these individuals will be relegated once again to the end of the queue for access to service.

Role of Vocational Rehabilitation

Supported employment has recently been defined as a legitimate employment outcome of vocational rehabilitation (Rehabilitation Act of 1986, PL 99-506). This creates an important difference in access to services through the vocational rehabilitation system in each state. With supported employment as a defined outcome, an important task becomes that of ensuring that the long-term supports needed for many individuals are available through the service system (typically, the mental retardation/developmental disabilities agency in a state). PL 99-506 helps shift the issue and the discussion from "what to do" to "how to do it." The issue is not to define eligibility for services for individuals with severe and profound mental retardation based on expected success with the time-limited support, but to identify the supports needed for successful long-term and integrated employment.

In the context of the vocational rehabilitation system, this presents a number of challenges. These include: 1) disseminating information to vocational rehabilitation professionals about the rapid changes that are occurring in the delivery of service, 2) arranging, funding, supporting, and evaluating the services that individuals in supported employment receive, 3) assuring that the resources for long-term follow-up are provided by sources other than vocational rehabilitation, and 4) providing access to as many individuals as possible.

IMPLEMENTATION ISSUES

Supported employment is a service outcome with three major features: paid work, ongoing support, and integration. The approaches used to generate supported employment outcomes are, and should be, free to vary, based on local opportunity and individual needs. Varied approaches (e.g., enclaves, individual placements, and service crews) have already emerged, and others will be developed in the future. The implementation of any approach demands attention to each outcome of supported employment. Solving implementation issues related to each outcome is required if the initiative is to be successful for persons with severe and profound mental retardation. Employment opportunities must be obtained where payment is fair to the employer and the worker with disabilities. The support provided (training, supervision, advocacy, etc.) must be sufficient for long-term success, and it must be manageable by the support organization. Further, physical and social integration for persons with severe and profound mental retardation should result. Another implementation issue is that of equal access to service. While each implementation area must be addressed for any person deemed appropriate for supported employment, successful implementation in each of these areas may be most critical for developing supported employment options for people with severe and profound mental retardation.

Equal Access

Individuals with severe and profound mental retardation in the United States have had access to day services primarily through the state mental retardation/developmental disabilities systems (Buckley & Bellamy, 1986). In most states, this is an eligibility system rather than an entitlement system. That is, access to service is determined by the availability of the service rather than by the needs of the individual. As a result, most states have waiting lists for day services. Similarly, access to supported employment is limited at present as a direct function of the availability of programs providing these services. This creates difficult decisions about which individuals will receive priority for supported employment services as opportunities develop. Advocates have long argued that persons with severe and profound mental retardation have traditionally been the last to receive existing and new service options and that decisions about access to supported employment must not be decided based on the degree of disability.

The discussion of access to supported employment has led to the development of two different strategies (Bellamy, Rhodes, Mank, & Albin, 1987). Some organizations develop supported employment projects by first serving persons with the most severe disabilities, including people with severe and profound mental retardation. This position holds that such individuals have always been the last in line for improved services, and that the development of supported employment must begin with success for these individuals. Others have argued for first developing options for people considered to be more capable yet still in need of long-term support for employment success. This second strategy has been viewed as an opportunity for agencies

and staff to experience more immediate success, increase confidence, and build a stronger commitment.

Clearly, the question of "where to begin" must be answered, and that the nature of the response will have a significant impact on the individuals served by an agency and the direction of the national initiative. Will (1986), in a presentation to state projects engaged in systems change to supported employment, proposed a nonexclusive approach, termed *heterogeneous staging*. That is, states and agencies should begin by creating community options for the range of persons needing employment with long-term support, including those with the most severe disabilities. This approach has several advantages. First, it delivers the clear message that supported employment is needed and possible for all persons requiring long-term support for employment success. Second, it allows states and agencies to develop competence in meeting a range of needs from the outset. Third, it emphasizes that access to employment will not be determined by the nature of or severity of disability. In this way, access to integrated and supported employment will be determined by our collective ability to develop and support viable community jobs for individuals, rather than according to the perceived "difficulty" of serving a person.

Fair Payment

One objective of supported employment is to provide reasonable jobs with reasonable wages for persons with severe disabilities. For some individuals with such a label, work pace in job settings may be an issue. Definitions of *supported employment* do not set conditions on the wage rate for persons employed. The U.S. Department of Labor (DOL) requires that individuals have access to commensurate wages. Pay based on productivity at the commensurate wage is an acceptable solution. The purpose of this is to ensure that the pace at which an individual works is not a barrier to supported employment. Accordingly, a variety of payment mechanisms are available to ensure that fair payment results for work performed. These payment mechanisms, though far from problem-free (Hagner, Nisbet, Callahan, & Mosely, 1987), make it unacceptable to deny access to supported employment based on the expected rate at which an individual may work.

Those responsible for securing employment for people who may not work at full productivity must become skilled at identifying jobs where high-speed performance is not required. It is important to note, however, that individuals with severe and profound retardation can work at full or near-full productivity; a particular diagnosis does not predict productivity. However, when employment is sought for an individual who is not likely to reach full productivity in the near future, it is still possible to develop jobs that provide fair wages for work performed.

There are individuals with severe and profound mental retardation, or with severe physical disabilities, who may not work at "full productivity" in the near future. The provision to pay based on productivity means that these individuals can obtain and maintain employment. In fact, individuals with such support needs are central to the focus of the origins of supported employment.

Support Structures

Supported employment, by label and definition, is intimately tied to the expectation of stable, integrated employment over time. Definitions of *supported employment* leave open the issue of exactly what kind of support is provided. Recent years have witnessed a wide range of useful approaches for supporting individuals (Gifford, Rusch, Martin, & White, 1984). Even so, data are also available indicating notable loss of jobs for various reasons (Brickey, Campbell, & Browning, 1985; Foss, Walker, Todis, & Lyman, 1986; Hanley-Maxwell, Rusch, Chadsey-Rusch, & Renzaglia, 1986; Hill, Wehman, Hill, & Goodall, 1985; Lagomarcino & Rusch, 1985). This information underscores the need for systematic ways to enable persons with severe disabilities, especially persons with severe and profound mental retardation, to stay employed.

Improvements in strategies for supporting individuals are critical to the long-term success of supported employment. Further, if the methodology for implementing individual support strategies is not further developed and widely publicized, service providers may be less inclined to provide equal access to supported employment for persons with severe and profound mental retardation. This "crisis in confidence" is one of the key issues that may impede the widespread inclusion of these individuals.

Strategies for supporting persons in regular jobs must include approaches for direct support, indirect support, and external supports, and a better understanding of how and when to provide each of these types of assistance. It seems clear that issues remain regarding the *support* in supported employment for persons with severe and profound mental retardation. Several of these are discussed in the paragraphs following.

Support must include direct strategies. A by-product of the research projects and innovative service programs demonstrating that individuals with severe and profound mental retardation can succeed in integrated community environments has been the development of direct instructional strategies. These strategies are founded on the notion that training based in precise behavioral analysis, provided systematically and consistently, and supplemented with individualized maintenance activities, can help individuals overcome the experiential deprivation that typifies the lives of many persons with severe disabilities. The focus of direct strategies must be to build performance in both work and social areas to enable an individual to meet the employer's needs and to participate in the social fabric of the work setting. A number of direct, on-the-job support strategies are available to providers of supported employment. Direct support strategies include: general case programming for the development of enduring and generalizable skills; self-management training for increasing autonomy and adaptability; productivity, rate, and pacing training to ensure that individuals can meet work-flow demands; mobility training for increased access within and around the job site; communication training; and interventions for increasing/developing desired social skills and decreasing undesirable responses. Improvements in teaching technology and individualized intervention have helped make community employment an expectation for significantly more people with severe and profound mental retardation. However, many systematic instructional strategies have been developed in controlled or segregated settings (Mank & Horner, 1987), and relatively few accounts exist of documented procedures for persons with the most severe disabilities in community settings. While it is clear that direct support strategies are needed for employment success, it is equally clear that resources must be devoted to developing systematic procedures for selecting and implementing these strategies effectively, efficiently, and unobtrusively in integrated settings.

Support must include indirect strategies. The data available on job success and job failures suggest that many individuals with severe disabilities keep or lose jobs as a function of non-task-related issues (Brickey et al., 1985; Foss et al., 1986; Greenspan & Shoultz, 1981; Hill et al., 1985; Salzberg, Agran, & Lignugaris-Kraft, 1986). While it has been established that adequate task performance is necessary for long-term success, it is also apparent that long-term job performance depends on more than task proficiency alone. This points out the need for various indirect strategies, that is, strategies not directly related to job training that help to support the employment of individuals in ways that direct training and supervision do not. Indirect strategies must include coworker involvement, supervisor contact, and coordination with an individual's family.

Support must include external strategies. Direct and indirect support strategies tend to focus on features surrounding the specific job setting. In addition, supported employment organizations must often support an individual's employment through coordination with other human service organizations. This may involve coordination among vocational rehabilitation and developmental disability agencies, residential providers, U.S. Social Security Administration personnel, and families and advocates. While not related directly to job sites, failure to coordinate such services can jeopardize employment success (Schalock, 1985).

Support strategies need development. The experience of many highly skilled support organizations, trainers, and researchers has helped to generate a range of strategies and some data on the nature of support for individuals with disabilities placed in integrated jobs (Gifford et al., 1984). However, this work must be viewed as the starting point in the development of an improved support technology for supported employment. The support procedures developed must include a broader range of specific strategies and details on implementation procedures that are workable in local communities.

Support must be tied to integration. Individuals with severe and profound mental retardation cannot be expected to realize meaningful social integration solely because of access to a job in the community. The degree to which social integration is determined by work performance in combination with social skills and cultural adaptation differs in every job. It will depend on the support organization's ability to implement support strategies that foster quality work, social skills, and adaptation to the company's culture. Supporting the employment and the integration of an individual is a process that starts during job development and proceeds through training and ongoing support. The following section discusses issues specifically related to integration in supported employment for persons with severe and profound mental retardation.

Integration

A primary reason for providing individuals with support in regular jobs is the opportunity for contact, interactions, and relationships with coworkers and other community members. Integration may be the single most important quality of supported employment. Because of this, and because individuals with disabilities have traditionally been denied access to environments in which they could interact with nondisabled citizens, integration in supported employment presents a number of issues.

One concern in developing supported employment for individuals with the most severe disabilities is the perception among some program developers that adequate support can only be provided in groups. While grouping individuals indiscriminately may meet some minimum requirements of group size, it all but prohibits full participation. It is argued that job settings that include more than one worker with disabilities threaten integration (Brown et al., 1984; Hagner et al., 1987). This central issue is double-edged. If full integration is perceived as jeopardizing the delivery of needed support, then there is a risk that persons with severe and profound mental retardation will be excluded from supported employment because it is considered "too difficult" or because the individuals are "not ready." Conversely, if supported employment for all or most persons who are labeled as severely or profoundly mentally retarded is considered possible only through group strategies, then integration may well be jeopardized. Solutions to this dilemma can result from a focus on each of the outcomes of supported employment: paid work, integration, and support for long-term success. Solutions will also require careful use of available personnel resources in organizations and better strategies for training and fading support. As a valued outcome and a prime feature of supported employment, integration requires rigorous attention and specific strategies to promote it. The paragraphs following discuss some integration considerations.

Integration requires better definition and measurement. Important features of integration in jobs have been described recently (Brown et al., 1985; Nisbet & Callahan, 1987). There is a continuing need for definition that allows for measurement and for standards of acceptable integration. The current widespread implementation of supported employment without such a definition underscores the need for continued work to operationalize integration in employment settings. Recent attempts to define integration have focused on the nature and extent of interactions on the job and the development of relationships in and around employment settings. Measurement of interactions with nondisabled persons has focused on the nature and extent of contact during working hours (e.g., Storey, Knutson, & Foss, 1987). Measurement of relationships has focused on the forming of social networks (e.g., Gottlieb, 1981; Karan & Knight, 1986; Lakin & Bruininks, 1985). Development is needed in at least these two areas in order to better understand integration and to develop strategies for improving and maintaining integration over time.

Job opportunities should be evaluated relative to their capacity for worthy integration. Depending on certain environmental character-istics, specific jobs developed for persons with severe disabilities can either promote or impede integration. As operational definitions of integration emerge, it will be easier for supported employment organizations to set guidelines about the nature of jobs to be developed. At a minimum, integration can be enhanced by a focus on developing jobs in companies where persons without disabilities are also employed; where work tasks performed by the person with disabilities are the same as or similar to those of other employees; where the daily patterns of work, break, and lunch are the same for disabled and nondisabled employees; and where regular contact with coworkers is a natural part of job duties.

Specific on-the-job strategies are needed to support integration. Developing jobs where there are regular interactions with others helps to enhance the possibility that a particular job setting will provide opportunities for integration. Direct service personnel also need specific strategies for supporting integration on job sites. Such strategies will include developing job-specific social skills, augmented communication systems, and coworker involvement. Supported employment developed as a reaction to the failure of "place and hope" programs; it is ironic that many supported employment programs find themselves placing individuals in jobs and then hoping that integration will occur. Specific strategies are needed that direct service staff can use to promote natural integration on a day-to-day basis.

Systems are needed for tracking integration over time. In the same way that it is important to attend to integration as an individual begins a job, it is also important to ensure that integration continues and expands over time. Job duties change, coworkers change roles, supervisors leave, and daily routines are revised. In these and other situations the pattern of daily work may also change in the nature and extent of contact with others at work. This creates problems for the supported employment specialist. Clearly, methods are needed for tracking what actually occurs in jobs in ways that are not artificial or intrusive.

Again, the main features of supported employment—paid work, support, and integration—each define major opportunities and issues for persons with severe and profound mental retardation. The success of the national initiative for these individuals will depend in part on successful community implementation in each of these areas and on a system that is open, and that indeed invites, continuous improvement in strategies and constant reinforcement of improved implementation. In addition to these substantive local implementation matters, there are also systemic and coordination opportunities and issues in supported employment for persons with severe and profound mental retardation.

SYSTEMIC STRATEGIES

The critical aspect of government and state agency efforts in supported employment is coordination of policy, funding, and services. These areas of government responsibility can support the local efforts of community supported employment programs. More and more persons with severe and profound mental retardation will be referred to supported employment programs. Coordination and definitions of roles, responsibilities, and access are even more important as rehabilitation agencies increase their involvement with individuals with severe disabilities. Persons with severe and profound mental retardation have not typically been considered appropriate for time-limited rehabilitation services. Now that supported employment is a defined outcome of vocational rehabilitation, several steps might be taken to promote supported employment for these individuals. These include: definition of agencies' respective responsibilities and funding conditions; development of a clear process for access to supported employment; flexibility in implementation; and review of collected data. These strategies will be useful for the overall implementation of supported employment and will be related to access for persons with severe and profound mental retardation. The paragraphs following elaborate on these suggestions.

Define Agencies' Responsibility

Supported employment for persons with severe and profound mental retardation will require coordination of services and resources from the state vocational rehabilitation agency and the state mental retardation/developmental disability agency. This necessitates a new working relationship wherein roles and responsibilities are clearly delineated. A number of states have developed agreements between these two agencies to specify responsibilities for initial job development, training, and ongoing support. Such agreements have most often defined job development and initial training as the responsibility of the vocational rehabilitation agency, with ongoing support services provided through the mental retardation agency.

Define Funding Availability and Coordination

In conjunction with definition of agency responsibilities, the availability and use of funding resources must also be detailed. The proposed regulations to amendments in the Vocational Rehabilitation Act of 1986 specify that one criterion for access to supported employment resources through vocational rehabilitation agencies is the availability of long-term support resources through another agency. Definition of this coordination of resources within a state makes it possible for community supported employment programs to plan more effectively to address community needs.

Define the Process for Access

As state-level plans for supported employment develop, it is necessary that a specific process for access to supported employment be defined. Supported employment for persons with severe and profound mental retardation will often involve community programs that have been funded through the state mental retardation agency and may be managed by personnel who are unfamiliar with the process and services of vocational rehabilitation. This, in conjunction with the short history of supported employment projects that are funded by both vocational rehabilitation and the state mental retardation agency, emphasizes the need for a defined process for access that reaches providers and advocates for persons with severe and profound mental retardation.

This plan for access will be facilitated to the extent that local employment councils form and develop plans to analyze employment opportunities, job development, job match, and analysis of support demands. Local employment councils can serve as conduits of information with the major state agencies involved in supported employment. Through this process, state and local planners, providers, and advocates can help realize equal access to supported employment.

Provide Flexibility in Use of Resources

The short history of supported employment for persons with severe and profound mental retardation has not provided a full data base on the range of appropriate costs and needed services. As a result, the actual range of acceptable costs and support services is not clear. This emphasizes a continuing need for flexibility. This flexibility can take several forms. Program funders and developers will need to establish flexible timelines and budgets for program development, job development, intensive training, and the fading of assistance. In addition, more data are needed regarding the amount and intensity of ongoing support that individuals with severe and profound mental retardation will require. Personnel preparation and technical assistance personnel will have to be prepared to respond to requests requiring program content that extends beyond that of the more standard training packages. It is clear that until a greater number of individuals with severe and profound mental retardation are placed, trained, and stabilized in supported employment, our collective ability to plan for their inclusion in the initiative depends on a certain amount of flexibility.

Collect, Report, and Review Data on Implementation

Without regular and ongoing data on the implementation of supported employment, on benefits realized, and on who is served, it will be impossible to measure success and isolate and remedy problems. It will also be impossible to document and address questions about equal access to supported employment. Information systems focused on answering such questions have begun to emerge in a number of states. Coordinated information systems between vocational rehabilitation agencies and long-term funding agencies are being developed and implemented in some locations. Outcome-based information systems are critical for tracking progress and detecting future implementation needs.

SUMMARY

Supported employment as a national initiative holds promise for changing the employment realities of persons with severe disabilities. Supported employment is designed to be nonexclusive and must therefore include those individuals labeled severely and profoundly mentally retarded. For these individuals to have access to integrated employment with long-term support, it will be necessary to address important implementation issues regarding equal access, fair payment, provision of long-term support, and promotion of integration in regular worksites. Further, system needs remain for providing access for these persons and for coordination between vocational rehabilitation and mental retardation agencies.

REFERENCES

Bellamy, G.T., Horner, R.H., Sheehan, M.R., & Boles, S.M. (1982). Structured employment and workshop reform: Equal rights for severely handicapped individuals. *Australian Journal of Special Education*, 6(1), 15–22.

Bellamy, G.T., Inman, D., & Yeates, J. (1978). Evaluation of a procedure for production management with the severely retarded. *Mental Retardation*, 17(1), 37–41.

Bellamy, G.T., Peterson, L., & Close, D. (1975). Habilitation of the severely and profoundly retarded: Illustrations of competence. *Education and Training of the Mentally Retarded*, 10, 174–186. Reprinted in R.M. An-

derson & J.G. Greer (Eds.). (1976). *Educating the severely and profoundly retarded*. Baltimore: University Park Press.

Bellamy, G.T., Rhodes, L. E., Bourbeau, P.E., & Mank, D. M. (1986). Mental retardation services in sheltered workshops and day activity programs: Consumer benefits and policy alternatives. In F.R. Rusch (Ed.), *Competitive employment issues and strategies* (pp. 257–271). Baltimore: Paul H. Brookes Publishing Co.

Bellamy, G.T., Rhodes, L.E., Mank, D.M., & Albin, J.M. (1987). *Supported employment: A community implementation guide*. Baltimore: Paul H. Brookes Publishing Co.

Berkeley Planning Associates. (1986). *Development of performance measures for supported employment programs. Tasks 4 and 5: Availability of existing measures and need for additional measures to address program objectives* (Contract No. 300-85-0138). Washington, DC: U.S. Department of Education.

Brickey, M. P., Campbell, K. M., & Browning, K. J. (1985). A five year follow-up of sheltered workshop employees placed in competitive jobs. *Mental Retardation, 23,* 67–83.

Brown, L., Shiraga, B., York, J., Kessler, K., Strohm, B., Rogan, P., Sweet, M., Zanella, K., VanDeventer, P., & Loomis, R. (1984). Integrated work opportunities for adults with severe handicaps: The extended training option. *Journal of the Association for the Severely Handicapped, 9*(4), 262–269.

Buckley, J., & Bellamy, G.T. (1986). National survey of day and vocational programs for adults with severe disabilities: A 1984 profile. In P. Ferguson (Ed.), *Issues in transition research: Economic and social outcomes* (pp. 1–12). Eugene: Center on Human Development, University of Oregon.

Connis, R.T. (1979). The effects of sequential cues, self-recording, and praise on the job task sequencing of retarded adults. *Journal of Applied Behavior Analysis, 12,* 355–361.

Crosson, J. (1966). The experimental analysis of vocational behavior in severely retarded males. Doctoral dissertation, University of Oregon, Eugene. *Dissertation Abstracts International, 27,* 3304.

Developmental Disabilities Act. PL 98–507. October, 1984.

The Employment Network. (1986). *Supported employment information system* (Grant No. 600–86–3521) Washington, DC: U.S. Department of Education.

Foss, G., Walker, H., Todis, B., & Lyman, G. (1986). *A social competence model for community employment settings.* Eugene: Counseling & Educational Psychology, University of Oregon.

Gifford, J. L., Rusch, F.R., Martin, J. E., & White, D. M. (1984). Autonomy and adaptability: A proposed techology for maintaining work behavior. In N. Ellis & N. Bray (Eds.), *International review of research in mental retardaton* (Vol. 12, pp. 285–314). New York: Academic Press.

Gold, M. (1972). Stimulus factors in skill training of the retarded on a complex assembly task: Acquisition, transfer, and retention. *American Journal of Mental Retardation, 76,* 517–526.

Gold, M. (1973). Research on the vocational habilitation of the retarded: The present, the future. In N. R. Ellis (Ed.), *International review of research in mental retardation* (Vol. 12, pp. 97–147). New York: Academic Press.

Gold, M. (1975). Vocational training. In J. Wortis (Ed.), *Mental retardation and developmental disabilities: An annual review* (Vol. 7, pp. 254–264). New York: Brunner/Mazel.

Gottlieb, B.H. (1981). *Social networks and social support.* Beverly Hills, CA: Sage Publications.

Greenspan, S., & Shoultz, B. (1981). Why mentally retarded adults lose their jobs: Social competence as a factor in work adjustment. *Applied Research in Mental Retardation, 2,* 23–38.

Hagner, D., Nisbet, J., Callahan, M., & Moseley, C. (1987). Payment mechanisms for community employment: Real-

ities and recommendations. *Journal of the Association for Persons with Severe Handicaps, 12*(1), 45–52.

Hanley-Maxwell, C., Rusch, F.R., Chadsey-Rusch, J. H., & Renzaglia, A. (1986). Reported factors contributing to job terminations of individuals with severe disabilities. *Journal of the Association for Persons with Severe Handicaps, 11*(1), 45–52.

Hill, J. W., Wehman, P., Hill, M., & Goodall, P. (1985). Differential reasons for job separation of previously employed mentally retarded persons across measured intelligence levels. In P. Wehman & J. Hill (Eds.), *Competitive employment for persons with mental retardation* (pp. 94–109). Richmond: Virginia Commonwealth University, Rehabilitation Research and Training Center.

Karan, O.C., & Knight, C.B. (1986). Developing support networks for individuals who fail to achieve competitive employment. In F.R. Rusch (Ed.), *Competitive employment issues and strategies* (pp. 241–255). Baltimore: Paul H. Brookes Publishing Co.

Kiernan, W.E., McGaughey, M.J., & Schalock, R.L. (1986). *Employment survey for adults with Developmental Disabilities.* Boston: Developmental Evaluation Clinic, Children's Hospital.

Kiernan, W.E., & Stark, J. A. (Eds.) (1986). *Pathways to employment for adults with developmental disabilities.* Baltimore: Paul H. Brookes Publishing Co.

Lagomarcino, T.R., & Rusch, F. R. (in press). Competitive employment: Overview and analysis of research focus. In V. B. Van Hassett, P.S. Strain, & M. Herson (Eds.), *Handbook of developmental and physical disabilities* (pp. 226–249). New York: Pergamon.

Lakin, K.C., & Bruininks, R.H. (1985). Social integration of developmentally disabled persons. In K. C. Lakin & R. H. Bruininks (Eds.), *Strategies for achieving community integration of developmentally disabled citizens* (pp. 3–25). Baltimore: Paul H. Brookes Publishing Co.

Mank, D. M., Buckley, J., & Smull, M. (1987, June). *Report made on supported employment information system.* Presented at the Rehabilitation Services Administration meeting for State Supported Employment Project Directors, Washington, D.C.

Mank, D. M., & Horner, R. H. (1987). Self-recruited feedback: A cost-effective procedure for maintaining behavior. *Research in Developmental Disabilities, 8*(1), 91–112.

Nisbet, J., & Callahan, M. (1987). Achieving success in integrated workplaces: Critical elements in assisting persons with severe disabilities. In S.J. Taylor, D. Biklen, & J. Knoll (Eds.), *Community integraton for people with severe disabilities* (pp. 184–201). New York: Teachers College Press.

Paine, S.C., Bellamy, G.T., & Wilcox, B. (Eds.). (1984). *Human services that work: From innovation to standard practice.* Baltimore: Paul H. Brookes Publishing Co.

Rehabilitation Act of 1986. October. PL 99–506.

Salzberg, C. L., Agran, M., & Lignugaris-Kraft, B. (1986). Behaviors that contribute to entry-level employment: A profile of five jobs. *Applied Research in Mental Retardation, 7,* 1–16.

Schalock, R.L. (1985). Comprehensive community services: A plea for interagency collaboration. In K. C. Lakin & R.H. Bruininks (Eds.), *Living and learning in the least restrictive environment* (pp. 37–63). Baltimore: Paul H. Brookes Publishing Co.

Shafer, M. S., & Brooke, V. (1985). *The development of punctuality in a mentally retarded worker through self-recording.* Unpublished manuscript, Virginia Commonwealth University, Rehabilitation Research and Training Center, Richmond.

Sowers, J., Rusch, F. R., Connis, R. T., & Cummings, L. E. (1980). Teaching mentally retarded adults to time-manage in a vocational setting. *Journal of Applied Behavior Analysis, 13,* 119–128.

Storey, K., Knutson, N., & Foss, G. (1987). A comparative analysis of social interactions of handicapped workers in integrated work sites. In P. Ferguson (Ed.), *Issues in transition research: Supported work and supported living* (pp. 57–80). Eugene: University of Oregon, Center on Human Development, Specialized Training Program.

Taylor, S.J., Biklen, D., & Knoll, J. (Eds.). (1987). *Community integration for people with severe disabilities.* New York: Teachers College Press.

Wehman, P. (1981). *Competitive employment: New horizons for severely disabled individuals.* Baltimore: Paul H. Brookes Publishing Co.

Wehman, P., Schutz, R., Bates, P., Renzaglia, A., & Karan, O. (1978). Management programs with mentally retarded workers: Implications for developing independent vocational behaviour. *British Journal of Social and Clinical Psychology, 17,* 57–64.

Will, M. (1986, October). *Comments on the national direction of supported employment.* Presented at Rehabilitation Services Administration meeting for State Supported Employment Project Directors, Washington, DC.

Chapter 22

Systems Barriers to Supported Employment for Persons with Chronic Mental Illness

John H. Noble, Jr. and Frederick C. Collignon

The 1986 Amendments to the Rehabilitation Act of 1973 created a new formula grant program of supported employment for persons with severe disabilities. Among the intended beneficiaries are persons with chronic mental illness. Empirical evidence for the cost-effectiveness of the new program is derived primarily from a few fairly well-documented demonstrations of employment for persons with mental retardation and cerebral palsy among the developmentally disabled population (Boles, Bellamy, Horner, & Mank, 1984; Noble & Conley, 1987; Poole, 1985; Rhodes, Ramsing, & Valenta, 1986; Wehman, 1981).

In large part, evidence for the effectiveness of supported employment for persons with mental illness requires an extrapolation from reports of the successes of persons with mental retardation. Given the paucity of hard data on which to rely, state vocational rehabilitation agencies face a considerable challenge as they attempt to expand supported employment services for persons with chronic mental illness. They must come to an understanding of the history, culture, and political constraints of the mental health service system in order to achieve the coordination that will be necessary to provide needed employment services to people with chronic mental illness.

Unlike many other types of disability, chronic mental illness is an unstable condition that presents dramatic risks for the affected individuals themselves and for their communities. Persons with chronic mental illness are stereotyped as older, having spent many years in a mental hospital, and subject to recurring hospitalizations. While this stereotype is true of many persons with chronic mental illness, it does not fit the population of labor force age for whom employment is considered by society an appropriate expectation.

In the postdeinstitutionalized age, the young adult chronically mentally ill patient, as characterized by Pepper and Ryglewicz (1982), shows:

(1) a low rate of hospitalization; (2) a high incidence of use of alcohol and other drugs; (3) a high incidence of suicide attempts as well as of successful suicides; (4) a high incidence of conception of children, who become our next high-risk generation; (5) a sizeable incidence of law violations involving violence; (6) for the majority, a history of mental health treatment before age 18; and (7) for the majority, a high or total degree of financial

This chapter originally appeared as an article in *Psychosocial Rehabilitation Journal, 11*(2), 25–44, October, 1987. Reprinted with permission.

dependence on public assistance programs or on family. (p. 390)

These characteristics necessitate close, continuing coordination of effort by vocational rehabilitation and mental health service providers. Clearly, persons with chronic mental illness cannot be simply referred by the mental health provider to the vocational rehabilitation agency with the expectation that the agency will be able to assume full responsibility for the case.

The necessity for close, continuing coordination by vocational rehabilitation and mental health service providers has potential for creating conflict and systems barriers to the expansion of supported employment opportunities for persons with chronic mental illness. This chapter outlines the dimensions of the problem and suggests possible ways to minimize their impact.

As state and local mental health and vocational rehabilitation agencies begin to cooperate in developing supported employment options in integrated work settings that provide substantial wages for at least 20 hours of work per week, one can anticipate conflicts and systems barriers from the following sources:

1. The unique history and process of deinstitutionalization involving persons with mental illness
2. The politics involved in the financing and delivery of mental health services
3. Societal stereotyping of persons with chronic mental illness
4. Conflicts in philosophy and practice between the "medical" model that underlies much of mental health activities and the vocational rehabilitation model of "human resource investment"
5. Differing traditions of case service documentation and public accountability between the mental health and vocational rehabilitation service system
6. Uncertainty about which supported employment modalities will prove most cost-effective in meeting the needs of people with chronic mental illness with varying symptomatologies and diagnoses

7. The remaining work disincentives in the federal income support and health care programs

DEINSTITUTIONALIZATION POLICY

In essence, deinstitutionalization seeks to safeguard the liberty of citizens whose physical and/or mental impairments limit their capacity to function within the range prescribed by society. The policy of deinstitutionalization calls for maximum restraint by the state when it becomes necessary for it to intervene to protect the life and safety of either the impaired individual or of persons in the surrounding community whose lives and safety may be endangered by that individual.

In its preventive aspect, the policy seeks to minimize inpatient care by taking appropriate steps in the community to assist impaired individuals to function within the prescribed range. In its curative aspect, the policy endeavors to treat and restore to the community as soon as possible persons whose conditions require time-limited inpatient care. In this way, the individual's right to liberty is protected and the needless deterioration caused by prolonged stay in an inpatient facility is avoided.

In general, deinstitutionalization policy has two basic components: 1) movement away from institutional environments as a place in which to provide care and 2) development of alternative living arrangements in the community. Bachrach (1978) characterized deinstitutionalization as "a search for functional alternatives to the mental hospital." The effectiveness of deinstitutionalization policy depends on the development of comprehensive integrated community-based services. Unfortunately, these services have not been provided on a wide scale any place in the United States. Here and there, model programs have been developed that demonstrate the viability and cost-effectiveness of adequate community-based services. The most famous and publicized of these programs are the Fountain House, Horizon House, and Thresholds clubhouse programs in New York, Philadelphia, and Chicago, respectively, and the community outreach and rapid stabilization programs of Madison, WI, and southwest Denver.

Successful deinstitutionalization occurs when there is recognition of the true functions of institutions and provision of alternatives to these functions in the community. The functions of the institution for which alternatives must be provided in the community are shelter, food, clothing, protective oversight, social and recreational opportunities, general health care, treatment of psychiatric symptoms, training of persons with subnormal intelligence and varying degrees of maladaptive behavior, and treatment of alcohol and drug dependency among substance abusers.

Deinstitutionalization fails when communities are not involved in the process and when there is a general lack both of planning and of the specific assumption of designated responsibility by the different levels of government—local, state, and federal. Insufficient funding of community-based services and attempts by one level of government to shift the costs of care to another must also be recognized as additional causes of failure.

In the late 1950s and 1960s, when deinstitutionalization first began, there was a tendency to discharge younger, healthier patients into boarding homes and older, more infirm patients into nursing homes. Nursing homes have been a primary resource within the health care system for the care of deinstitutionalized mentally disabled persons (Denver Research Institute, 1981). Their availability as established sources of federal funding under the Medicare and Medicaid programs and their status as facilities that most approximate the institutional environment made this almost inevitable. Persons accustomed to institutional living are most easily moved from one institutional environment to another. The expansion of nursing home beds under Medicare and Medicaid to supplant more expensive general hospital care for recuperating medical patients provided further incentive. When the loss of revenues caused by the underutilization of general hospital beds reduced transfers of medical patients to nursing homes, nursing homes turned to the long-term care of ex-mental patients (Vladeck, 1980).

The federal takeover in the mid-1970s of state categorical aid programs for poor blind, disabled, and elderly persons created the Supplemental Security Income (SSI) program with its national income support standard, and provided further impetus for deinstitutionalization by giving states an alternative source of financial support for the maintenance of mentally disabled people in the community. Many states have selectively supplemented the basic federal SSI payment in order to pay for board and care arrangements that incorporate service provisions. For example, Virginia paid auxiliary grants in February 1984, averaging $189 per month, to 1,947 disabled people in licensed adult homes. About 30% of these auxiliary grant recipients were expatients and exresidents of state mental health and mental retardation facilities.

Finally, state and county hospitals for persons with mental illness have radically changed in the past 20 years. A variety of factors have improved the treatment capabilities of state hospitals even while the hospitals continue to provide a social control function through civil and criminal commitments and a source of mental health care for the poor. These factors include: technological advances in psychiatry such as use of psychotropic drugs to control psychiatric symptoms; legal reforms; modest improvements in public attitudes toward mental illness; and greatly reduced patient populations with higher staff-to-patient ratios resulting from the deinstitutionalization movement. The future role of state and county mental health facilities in the continuum of services to mentally ill people continues to be a heated topic of debate among professionals, legislators, and the lay public.

Ongoing debates about the wisdom of deinstitutionalization, the shifting of the burden of care to local governments, and uncertainty about the effectiveness of contemporary therapies tend to dissipate the energies of mental health personnel. Indeed, periodic exposés of the inadequacies of services for people with more serious mental illness place public mental health officials in jeopardy, raising questions about their competence and basic motivation.

The following excerpt from one of the more recent exposés (Torrey & Wolfe, 1986) offers

insight into the acrimonious nature of the criticisms leveled against mental health programs
and their administrators:

> Given the enormous economic resources which
> have been poured into the care of the seriously
> mentally ill since 1950, why is the quality of ser-
> vices still so poor in most states? Several answers
> are suggested, including a misunderstanding about
> what causes these diseases . . ., the overselling of
> antipsychotic drugs, a federal-state shell game over
> fiscal responsibility, and over-liberalization of
> commitment laws. But the greatest single reason
> why services for the seriously mentally ill are gen-
> erally so abysmal is the failure of community men-
> tal health centers to accept responsibility for this
> group of patients once their exodus from state hos-
> pitals began over 20 years ago. (p. iii)

Mental health providers within the context of
deinstitutionalization operate defensively within
a highly charged political arena. They are subject to the criticisms of the laity who do not
understand mental illness and fear persons who
are mentally ill, to the criticisms of politicians
who must respond to the expressed fears of constituents who want people with mental illness
removed from their midst, and to the criticisms
of the clients and their families who feel ill-
served by the existing service arrangements and
level of resources.

It is no wonder that the emphasis in mental
health is on survival—both the client's and the
provider's! Within the mental hospital, the focus
is on symptom reduction and the stabilization
of functioning leading to discharge as soon as
possible. Upon discharge, the focus is on stabilization of living arrangements, control of
symptoms, and the processing through the courts
of voluntary and involuntary commitment orders.

Within the institutional tradition, patients—
if they worked at all—worked within a workshop on the grounds of the state or county mental
hospital. In general, work was regarded more
as occupational "therapy" than as a serious productive enterprise. Considering the deficits of
patient functioning that confronted institutional
caregivers, it is understandable that real work
appeared more a remote and distant goal than a
present possibility for patients. In the Maslow-
ian hierarchy of needs, work represented a high
order of function that would become possible

only after the patient had recovered fully or had
made substantial progress toward recovery.

This mind-set has often spilled over into psychiatric outpatient services, where the focus is
again on the control of symptoms and stabilization of living skills at the more basic levels.
Work—if it is considered a possibility at all—
is often attempted only after the patient has made
considerable progress in independent living, rather
than as a normal expectation of daily living.
Indeed, the availability of income support and
of Medicaid coverage for psychiatric outpatient
services has the subtle effect of focusing attention on the client's nonwork-related problems.
Return to work often leads to the loss of Medicaid coverage.

In reaching out to persons with chronic mental
illness, vocational rehabilitation agencies frequently confront a mental health provider culture and clientele whose tradition and instincts
run counter to its own. Work as a value—indeed
as a categorical imperative for normalized living
in a capitalistic society—is something that must
be gradually introduced into the dependency-
oriented mental health service system. Receptivity toward this view will undoubtedly vary.
In some programs, like those of Fountain House,
Horizon House, and Thresholds, work is an integral component. In the more typical psychiatric outpatient programs, however, it may take
longer to establish employment-related linkages
and coordinated service structures.

POLITICAL REALITIES

Chronic mental illness presents challenges that
transcend the usual array of agency and disci-
pline-specific solutions. Clinical services, including medication, income support, housing,
psychosocial rehabilitation, and case management and advocacy are all necessary to sustain
a person with chronic mental illness in the least
restrictive environment. Technical knowledge
about how to do the job is not the problem. As
indicated by Mosher (1983), numerous studies
point the way. Applying what is known in face
of the obstacles is a matter of politics—har-
nessing government as well as professional and
constituency group activities to deploy the necessary technical and monetary resources to im-

plement the approaches that work (Bevilacqua & Noble, 1987).

Politics and the political process intervene in the economy to circumvent market forces in order to assure the financing of specific communal objectives that would not otherwise be met (Musgrave & Musgrave, 1973). There is no natural market for serving persons with chronic mental illness in America, or in any other country for that matter. Thus, government and the political process are the only way to address the needs of this population. In this context, the major obstacles to the application of the relevant technical knowledge stem from government-sanctioned and financed professional education and practices, conflicting program objectives, dysfunctional financing mechanisms, and laws whose emphases swing back and forth between civil liberty and social control.

PROFESSIONAL EDUCATION

The traditional mental health disciplines of medicine, nursing, psychology, and social work largely prepare practitioners for solo private practice where there is money, prestige, and the freedom to be selective in the choice of clients. Professional schools are by nature conservative, offering a curriculum that is responsive to the existing job market and educational consumer interests. Rubin (1979) found that 80% of graduate social-work students aspire to the private practice of psychotherapy within 5 years of graduation. As part of national policy, the National Institute of Mental Health (NIMH) until recently provided training grants to such students. Thus, money considerations and the laissez-faire of government funding have encouraged the mental health disciplines to train and socialize students for a form of practice incapable of responding to the service needs of poor people who cannot afford private practice fees. Graduates in these disciplines neither learn about the appropriate technologies for serving persons with chronic mental illness nor do they gain practice in its use (Bevilacqua & Noble, 1987).

CONFLICTING PROGRAM OBJECTIVES

The service needs of persons with chronic mental illness have never received full attention by any level of government—federal, state, or local. There was an effort during the Carter administration to pay greater attention to this population. NIMH created a small demonstration program of community support. It also drew up a national plan in 1981, which, along with the Mental Health Systems Act of 1980, has never been implemented.

As a matter of national policy, the U.S. Congress has excluded the adult psychiatric population, ages 22–64, from federal support while such persons are undergoing treatment in a free-standing psychiatric facility. Most of these patients are cared for in state mental hospitals, and the federal government did not wish to assume responsibility for financing their care as it did for persons with mental retardation through Title XIX of the Social Security Act. The results of this discrimination are striking. With federal funding, the conditions of care for persons with mental retardation have substantially improved, while they have lagged for persons with chronic mental illness.

State governments, driven more by the imperatives of economy and efficiency in government operations than concern for the effectiveness of coverage of human services (Lynn, 1980), have seized opportunities to balance their budgets by minimizing outlays for the care of persons with chronic mental illness. Cost-shaving is possible because the general population of voters does not care, and persons with chronic mental illness and their families do not have sufficient votes to make a difference.

Local governments, so important to the administration of community mental health programs, are necessarily dependent on state and federal resources. Although dependent on state financial support and sanction, the local community is the place where programs succeed or fail. It is here that the persons with chronic mental illness attain whatever quality of life is possible within the constraints of local government resources and capabilities. The locality is where battles are fought over intergovernmental cost-sharing, discriminatory zoning and employment practices, the appropriateness of voluntary and involuntary commitment procedures, and the like. Local concerns receive great attention in the state legislature, since legislators are ultimately held responsible by their local consitituents. Yet, meager levels of actual state appropriations for community mental health programs are seldom offset by increased local effort. Indeed, every effort is made to avoid local responsibility by shifting the burden of care to programs where the lion's share is paid by the state or federal governments.

Dysfunctional Funding Mechanisms and Decisions

As previously mentioned, the federal government has tried to avoid refinancing state and county mental hospitals. At the same time, state governments have been actively engaged in finding ways to shift the fiscal burden of mental health services onto both the federal and local governments. Enactment of the federal Supplemental Security Income and Medicaid programs has enabled many persons with chronic mental illness to avoid institutional placement as the means of obtaining basic shelter and food. Unfortunately, state governments have not shared with local communities the full measure of savings that have resulted from decreasing mental hospital utilization.

The magnitude of the savings that states have accrued by taking advantage of federal funding is difficult to determine because of the obvious rancor that exists between state and local governments over the issue of mental hospital "dumping" of patients on ill-prepared communities. However, data are available from the State of Virginia to illustrate how much of the problem of local government resistance to community care of persons with mental disabilities is a function of dysfunctional financing mechanisms and decisions. In fiscal year 1974, it cost almost $70 million at $15.63 per person per day to maintain 12,088 persons in Virginia's state institutions. In fiscal year 1984, it would have cost about $400.6 million at $90.80 per person per day to maintain the same number in the face of cost increases over the 10 year span. Instead, it actually cost almost $226 million at $90.80 per day to maintain an average daily census of 6,819 persons. The difference of $174.6 million between what it would have cost and what it actually cost can be construed as savings, of which $103 million (59%) consisted of state

general funds. In fiscal year 1984, the total local government budget for services to persons with mental disabilities was $82 million, of which $61.6 million consisted of state general funds. Thus, there was a difference of $41.4 million in fiscal year 1984 alone between the state general fund's allocation to local community programs and the projected general fund's savings of $103 million resulting from the reduced annual census of 5,269 persons in Virginia institutions (Virginia Department of Mental Health and Mental Retardation, 1985).

Had a greater share of these savings been passed along to the local programs, the capacity and quality of these programs would have been substantially higher. What is more, the in-fighting between state and local mental health officials over state versus local fiscal effort and responsibility, that stood as a systems barrier to more appropriate service delivery at the time, probably would not have existed.

The problem of dysfunctional financing mechanisms and decisions is pervasive throughout the states, and stands as a systems barrier to delivery of appropriate mental health services to persons with chronic mental illness everywhere. It has potential for spilling over and thwarting the supported employment initiative insofar as many persons with chronic illness will need on-going community mental health support to benefit from employment-related services of any kind. To the extent that community mental health services are inadequate for given clients, there is danger of losing the impact of any investment in employment-related services.

CONFLICTING LAWS

The laws governing severe mental illness require that mental health practitioners seek to balance the individual's civil liberties against the need to intervene when the individual's judgment has deteriorated to the point of endangering self or others. Such intervention to protect the individual or society from harm is a form of "social control." Mental health practitioners are held legally responsible for both their treatment and social control functions.

Whereas earlier case law, such as *O'Connor v. Donaldson* (1975) and *Wyatt v. Stickney*

(1971), focused on patients who were wrongfully kept in institutions, deinstitutionalization has led to new case law, such as *Tarsoff v. Regents of the University of California* (1976), which holds mental health practitioners responsible for "wrongful discharge" and a "duty to warn" when ex-patients may cause harm. As stated earlier, the law has alternated between emphasizing civil liberties and stressing the need to exert social control. Most states lack laws that specifically promote treatment and care of persons with chronic mental illness in the community. Indeed, the laws do not adequately describe community and institutional services as parts of a continuum of care. As a result, the courts almost never decide in favor of the least restrictive environment, because judges fail to receive assurances that placement in the community will provide the same level of control as that provided by the institution (Bevilacqua & Noble, 1987).

The lack of legislation emphasizing community support, including nondiscrimination in zoning, employment, insurance, and the like, with specific authorization of involuntary treatment and care of reluctant mentally ill persons in a variety of outpatient settings, can be expected to impede efforts to extend supported work options to persons with chronic mental illness. The vulnerability of mental health practitioners to lawsuits may cause some to hesitate to expose their client to the tensions of the workplace, for fear that the client's decompensation will be construed to be the result of their malpractice. Other mental health practioners may try to shift responsibility for possible harm that may arise from job placement onto the vocational rehabilitation agency that accepts the client for services. If, for any reason, the family of the client is resistant to the client's restoration to work, the defensiveness of the would-be employment service providers—whether a mental health or a vocational rehabilitation agency—can be expected to increase.

SOCIETAL STEREOTYPING

Unfortunately, societal stereotyping stands as the most potent systems barrier to the employment of persons with chronic mental illness.

Laypersons and professionals alike share certain stereotypes about chronic mental illness, including the following:

1. Chronic mental illness is a static condition.
2. Independent living is not feasible.
3. Normalization of lifestyle is not achievable.
4. Dangerousness is always associated with mental illness.
5. The constitutional right to liberty and freedom does not apply to persons with chronic mental illness, because they cannot distinguish right from wrong, reality from hallucinations, and so forth.

These stereotypes embody an overly pessimistic view of what persons with chronic mental illness can achieve in life. Advocates of supported employment for persons with chronic mental illness face the significant challenge of countering these stereotypes. The following truths may help:

1. Chronic mental illness is a continuing condition with numerous "ups" and "downs" and fluctuations in symptomatology and degree of functional limitations.
2. There is need for others to view the treatment and care of each person with chronic mental illness in terms of improved functioning rather than as a cure; the goal is to maintain the individual at as high a functional level as possible in the context of the specific mental disorder.
3. The person with chronic mental illness needs help with the basic necessities of living— shelter, food, clothing, transportation, human support, and employment—none of which is easily handled by the affected individual because of the underlying mental disorder.
4. Persons with chronic mental illness have need for interpersonal support and assistance from other people to the same extent if not more than anybody else.

These truths have significant implications for vocational rehabilitation practice. First and most important, services should be provided if the client can function, despite continuing symptomatology; otherwise, vocational rehabilitation will never begin.

Second, the approach to providing supported employment services to persons with chronic mental illness should not differ significantly from that used in helping persons with other kinds of severe disability. If differences exist, they are differences of emphasis, as described by Anthony, Howell, and Danley (1984):

> More time is needed to go through the process, because of the clients' vocational immaturity. More energy is needed to form a collaborative relationship with clients who are used to having things done *to* and *for* them rather than with them. More alternative vocational environments are needed to allow clients opportunity for reality testing and exploration. More strategies are needed for dealing with stigma against the psychiatrically disabled clients. More effort must be devoted to a deliberate refocusing of the helping process on the client's needed skills and environmental supports rather than focusing on client pathology. (p. 233)

As supported employment programs are developed for persons with chronic mental illness, there is danger that practitioners, molded by current mental health and vocational rehabilitation beliefs and practices, may fail to provide the extra time, energy, creativity, and effort that persons with chronic mental illness will need if they are to succeed in employment. There is danger that service providers, influenced by prevailing negative stereotypes, will focus unduly on psychiatric symptoms and disabilities rather than on client *abilities*.

CONFLICTING INTERVENTION MODELS

The mental health and the vocational rehabilitation systems operate under substantially different assumptions as they seek to influence the lives of their clients. The mental health system tends to view people as sick and in need of medical treatment if they are to recover. The sick person is expected to become a "patient" and to submit to a medically prescribed course of treatment. The vocational rehabilitation system tends to view clients as functionally impaired but capable of surmounting the impairment to achieve specific vocational objectives if assisted through counseling and retraining. In other words, the mental health system follows a "medical" model, while the vocational rehabilitation system is guided by a "human resource investment" model of intervention.

These different models of intervention create both explicit and implicit behavioral expectations for practitioners and clients alike. They also create possible sources of conflict between mental health and vocational rehabilitation practitioners as they undertake collaborative efforts on behalf of shared clients.

Mental health services, for example, whether provided on an inpatient or outpatient basis, direct attention to the signs and symptoms of decompensation (i.e., returning psychosis) and to their control through medication adjustment and reduction of environmental stress. The client is expected to comply with the prescribed medical regimen and, if being treated on an outpatient basis, to report back to the clinic on a regular basis for review and medication adjustment. For persons with severe mental illness who are willing to participate, community-based psychiatric day treatment involving scheduled activities, many of which are "prevocational" in character, augments outpatient services. Mental health services tend to reinforce dependency in clients by virtue of incessant questioning and interpretation of client behavior and emphasis on compliance to avoid decompensation and the return of psychosis.

The vocational rehabilitation model, on the other hand, is grounded in developmental psychology and work adjustment theory. It assumes that behaviors are learned in specific developmental sequences and are autonomously transferable from one setting to another. Accordingly, substantial effort goes into evaluation of the strengths and weaknesses of the individual before the training or other forms of intervention are initiated. This stress on evaluation before intervention is one area where the vocational rehabilitation and mental health models converge. The vocational rehabilitation model typically works toward autonomous client behavior under relatively constant support, instruction, and supervision. It is transitional in outlook, expecting to close the client's case after job placement and stabilization. As such, it sometimes overestimates client capacity for autonomous behavior and offers insufficient ongoing support for persons with severe disabilities after they have been placed on a job.

SUPPORTED EMPLOYMENT

Quite recently, a variant philosophy and set of practices have emerged that are geared to serving persons with severe disabilities who were deemed unsuitable for traditional, time-limited vocational rehabilitation services. The new philosophy of supported employment rejects many of the assumptions of developmental psychology and work adjustment theory. Based on learning theory, behavioral psychology, and applied behavior analysis, it stresses on-the-job training through individualized applied behavior analysis and planning. It recognizes that most persons with severe disabilities are unable to generalize behaviors learned in one setting to another; that behaviors are best taught in settings and under circumstances where they are expected to be performed and rewarded. The philosophy and practice of supported employment provides continuing evaluation along with instruction and other support services on a schedule that varies over time. Initially, support, instruction, and supervision are intensive; they then diminish over time, reaching a stable minimum amount determined by the client's individual need.

As suggested early in the chapter, as mental health and vocational rehabilitation practitioners attempt to coordinate their services, one can predict clashes of philosophy and expectations. Indeed, mental health practitioners may be confused by the ideological differences they currently encounter in the vocational rehabilitation field, which is still experiencing an upheaval regarding its basic processes. Great uncertainty still exists over when to "train first and then place" and when to "place first and then train." Major vested interests hang on how the decision goes in each case, since the entire network of sheltered workshops in the United States was built to accommodate persons who could not benefit from the traditional vocational rehabilitation approach of first providing transitional training and then placing clients in a regular, competitive job.

CASE DOCUMENTATION AND PUBLIC ACCOUNTABILITY

Nowhere are the differences between the mental health and vocational rehabilitation service systems more strikingly revealed than in their methods of case documentation and public accountability. Mental health agencies largely maintain ongoing "process" records for cases, which are seldom closed. If process objectives for clients with chronic mental illness are ever stated, they are diffuse and vary as a function of manifest symptomatology and changing life circumstances. Case management is more often than not directed to crisis resolution and stabilization of the client's role functioning at the most elementary levels. Contacts with a variety of agencies—police, courts, the U.S. Social Security Administration, Medicaid, social services, and vocational rehabilitation—are necessary to secure the client's freedom from incarceration, as well as to obtain medication and medical care, income, shelter, food, clothing, and sometimes even consideration for job training and placement. In consequence, the mental health process record does not disclose an ordered progression of the client's functioning level and need at the time.

Except anecdotally, mental health process records do not figure importantly in either the budgetary or legislative justification process. In many states, except for the inpatient census, little is known about the volume of services. There are often no records of how many clients were served or the number of treatments provided by either inpatient or outpatient programs. Mental health budgets are proposed and defended on grounds of equity (i.e., getting a "fair share" of available federal, state, and local government resources), rather than on grounds of cost-effectiveness. Patient care crises in inpatient, outpatient, or both inpatient and outpatient programs are turned to advantage in arguing for budgetary increases.

In contrast, the vocational rehabilitation record shows a well-documented progression along the pathway to a unitary goal—closure into a regular job, sheltered workshop, self-managed or family business, or homemaker status. If none of these is achieved, the case is closed as "unsuccessful." Client characteristics and earnings before and after case closure are specifically documented. The case record conforms to the specification of a nationwide case closure reporting system that captures the essential steps and costs of the vocational rehabilitation process. The focus on cost-accounting and on the monetary value of specific outcomes is unique among human service agencies. Indeed, the federal Rehabilitation Services Administration, which regulates the activities of the state vocational rehabilitation agencies, provides annual program reports covering such items as the annual volume of cases served, the types and number of case closures, the types and amounts of service expenditures, and the overall benefit-cost ratio that resulted from the investment of public funds. These annual program reports figure prominently in the federal budgetary process and in justifying the program to the congressional committees that oversee its administration by the federal agency and the states.

The radically different case documentation and public accountability expectations of the mental health and vocational rehabilitation systems may create barriers to the expansion of supported employment services to persons with chronic mental illness. If vocational rehabilitation funds are expended, the state vocational rehabilitation agency will undoubtedly feel obligated to obtain detailed documentation on their use. To the extent that mental health agencies become vendors of supported employment services, they may find the vocational rehabilitation case reporting and cost-finding practice nit-picky, distasteful, and onerous. For their part, vocational rehabilitation agencies with a long tradition of standardized reporting are unlikely to react sympathetically to the often-heard rationale used by mental health agencies to defend their own tradition: "The choice is between paper or services; you can't have more of both."

COST-EFFECTIVENESS ISSUES

Considerable uncertainty exists about which of several supported employment options will prove cost-effective for persons with chronic mental illness. As noted in Chapter 2, the major supported employment options that have been tried for persons with mental retardation include: (1) the mobile work-crew model, in which a group of persons with severe disabilities is transported from job site to job site with a supervisor/trainer; (2) the enclave model in which persons with severe disabilities are maintained on a regular worksite with the assistance of a special supervisor/trainer; (3) the job-coach model, in which a trainer/coworker provides support and training to a trainee with a disability for as long as it takes the individual to become proficient on the job; and (4) the specialized training program model, in which persons who would usually be cared for in a day activity program are placed in a heavily work-oriented sheltered workshop on a gainful job. The latter approach is used with people for whom work in a regular worksite is not considered possible because of very severe physical or mental limitations and/or behavioral problems (Boles et al.).

Juxtaposed to these supported employment modalities is the nationally replicated approach pioneered by Fountain House, which provides *transitional* employment opportunities in conjunction with its underlying program of psychosocial rehabilitation, combining residential, social, and vocational programming as well as community outreach services for persons with chronic mental illness. The Fountain House transitional employment program (TEP) provides entry-level jobs in normal places of business that pay at least the minimum wage. No subsidy is provided the employer for the wages paid to the transitional employee. All placements, both individual and group, are designed as transitional, and last from 3 to 9 months. All jobs are allocated by the employer to the psychosocial rehabilitation program, and the responsibility to select candidates to fill the jobs rests with the program. Job failure is viewed as a legitimate experience on the way to eventual successful work adjustment (Fountain House, 1982; Noble, 1984).

Unfortunately, no systematic evidence exists to permit a comparison of the benefits and costs of these alternative approaches to providing employment for persons with chronic mental illness. The extensive economic analysis by the Thresholds program in Chicago (Bond, 1983), based on only 6 months of posttreatment data, showed that competitive employment was positively related to length of program participation and that participation did not lead to a higher rate of hospitalization as a consequence of the increased stress of employment. Unfortunately, the accounting scheme for measuring benefits and costs renders judgment on the benefit-cost ratio impossible, since the basis of comparison was reduced rehospitalization costs ($962 per client) compared to annual earnings ($4,083 per client). Full program costs, including those of the Thresholds program as well as any other program that may have been involved, are needed for a complete accounting.

Rough estimates of the benefits and costs of the Fountain House transitional employment program, involving 1,409 persons with psychiatric disabilities and 604 employers, showed annual earnings in 1983 of $5,225,806 and an average annual cost of providing follow-along services of $1,500 per transitional employee—a 1.5:1 return on the TEP investment (T. Malamud, January, 1984, personal communication with research director of Fountain House).

It will be important to distinguish supported employment from transitional employment modalities in rendering judgments about their relative benefits and costs for persons with chronic mental illness. The conceptual distinction is clear enough: supported employment encompasses programs that are expected to be lifelong, while transitional employment refers to programs that are expected to end after the client becomes proficient on the job. In practice, the distinction is blurred. Some persons in programs usually described as supported employment (e.g. the work-crew and enclave models) are eventually able to move into regular jobs, while some people in programs usually described as transitional (e.g., the Structured Training and Employment Transition Services [STETS] programs [Kerachsky, Thornton, Bloomenthal, Maynard, & Stephens, 1985]) end up requiring long-term assistance or need additional assistance at various times in the course of their life.

The authors believe that the supported employment and transitional employment strate-gies that have been developed in response to the needs of people with severe mental disabilities are all potentially useful and deserve an opportunity to prove themselves. At the same time, it must be acknowledged that the growing acceptance of the supported employment approach is largely based on the well-publicized successes of a relatively small number of demonstration programs. As yet, there has been no rigorous assessment of the benefits and costs of these programs or of the extent to which these successful programs can be widely replicated (Noble & Conley, 1987).

Rigorous documentation of the benefits and costs of alternative forms of employment services for persons with chronic mental illness should be a priority for both the mental health and vocational rehabilitation services systems. With few exceptions (Bond, 1983; Dellario, 1985), the literature is replete with critical comments about how little is known, about what does *not* work, and about how much more attention should be devoted to the topic (Anthony, Cohen, & Farkas, 1982; Anthony et al., 1983; Anthony & Jansen, 1984).

Many elements of both the supported competitive employment model, which has shown such promise for persons with moderate mental retardation (Wehman, 1981), and the Fountain House transitional employment program, address obstacles that prevent persons with chronic mental illness from obtaining and maintaining regular jobs. These elements appear particularly germane in view of Anthony et al.'s (1983) argument that the poor track record of traditional vocational rehabilitation services with psychiatrically disabled clients can be turned around only by forming collaborative relationships with clients who are used to having things done to and for them, by dealing with the stigma of mental illness, and by focusing the helping process on the client's immediately needed skills and environmental supports rather than on pathology. Specifically, needed components include: 1) emphasis on placement in entry-level jobs; 2) using job coaches to find suitable jobs and to provide training in the immediate behaviors and tasks for which wages are paid, and 3) stimulating employers by the use of the Targeted Jobs Tax Credit (TJTC), where necessary, to avoid stereotyping and to encourage hiring a person with a severe disability.

Yet despite the internal logic of this belief, there is a need to document as fully as possible the range of social benefits and costs of the employment service alternatives available for persons with chronic mental illness. The social costs are those that society did not previously bear. Sometimes these costs are entirely borne by a single public agency; sometimes private agencies and individuals share in these costs. Normal living expenses (e.g., food, shelter, clothing and medical care) should not be included as part of the costs of supported and transitional employment programs, since they would be incurred in the presence or absence of the programs.[1]

Ideally, studies of the social benefits and costs of supported employment for persons with chronic mental illness will take into account the earnings of the client, as well as the release of family members and possibly others from caregiving responsibilities and thence to remunerative employment, longer work hours, or attainment of more demanding and higher-paying work. Also important to a full accounting of benefits are the "intangible" effects that work may have on the mood and feelings of persons with disabilities, their families, and others around them. While difficult to measure, these intangible effects are nonetheless important benefits that are often valued by the beneficiaries as much if not more than the earnings that are more easily measured and attributed to the supported employment program.

Still another benefit that may prove critical in justifying the costs of supported employment are possible cost-savings in day activity and other treatment programs that would otherwise have been provided to persons with chronic mental illness. These cost-savings may be as large or larger than the cost of providing the supported work program itself. Even if the earnings of

clients in supported employment programs are less than program costs, other benefits—such as possible savings in the outlays for other programs or the accrual of intangible benefits—could well be more than sufficient to justify the supported employment program on benefit-cost grounds (Noble & Conley, 1987).

It has taken many years to accumulate the amount of data that now exist to justify public expenditures for persons with mental retardation and cerebral palsy. For now, it is politically acceptable to extend supported employment opportunities to persons with chronic mental illness on the basis of ideology, commitment, and the internal logic of the model. In the future, more rigorous evidence may be required. For that reason, the authors argue for the collection of much better program information in order to assess the programs' economic value and to determine which are most cost-effective for persons with chronic mental illness.

To assure strict comparability of data across programs, funding agencies will need to require agencies to adopt a uniform accounting system capable of tracking the benefits and costs that accrue from the time specific clients enter a program until they leave. Future funding decisions to expand and/or contract given types of employment programs for persons with chronic mental illness could then rely on sound evidence of benefits and costs.

Until such information becomes generally available, uncertainty represents a major systems barrier to the expansion of supported employment for persons with chronic mental illness. The conventional economic wisdom reflects the stereotypical thinking of society about the capacities of people with severe disabilities. There is widespread belief among economists that persons with chronic mental illness are incapable of substantial work in integrated employment settings, regardless of how much money is spent trying to accomplish that goal. Negative stereo-

---

[1]See Conley and Noble (1988) for a full discussion of what should and should not be included as a social cost or benefit in a cost-benefit analysis. Income support programs (e.g., Social Security Disability Insurance [SSDI] or Supplemental Security Income [SSI]) and normal medical care, even though paid for by Medicare of Medicaid, are *not* considered as costs but, rather, as ordinary transfer payments taken from the consumption of some members of society for the benefit of others. Only the additional expenditures that society makes as a result of providing a *special* program are appropriately considered in a benefit-cost comparison.

types, unfortunately, weigh heavily in the decisions of government officials, and tend to crowd out information and analysis refuting these stereotypes. Where economic arguments for providing certain kinds of services run counter to the negative stereotypes, they tend to be ignored. Where the economic arguments support these negative stereotypes, they are eagerly grasped and are used to buttress decisions made to satisfy the dominant power interests. This reality argues for implementing the best evaluative research designs possible in order to reduce to a minimum uncertainty about benefits and costs.

Work Disincentives

Last, it is necessary to address the substantial work disincentives that remain in the federal income support and health care programs. The existing system can have a strong effect on the net gain from return to work for many clients who receive income support, health care, and other forms of publicly funded services. The client may only receive a small net increase in income or, in some cases, actually suffer a loss of disposable income. In considering the effects of return to work, the client's total benefit package must be considered—loss of income support, loss of medical care coverage, loss of social services, and discounts/allowances for food and housing costs.

Prior to 1981, the work disincentives for persons receiving Supplemental Security Income under Title 16 of the Social Security Act were extremely potent. An SSI recipient who started working would be placed on a trial work period of 9 nonconsecutive months. At the end of the trial work period, the recipient would be reevaluated and terminated from SSI if considered capable of earning over $300 per month. Since $300 per month is close to the SSI payment rate for individuals and well below the SSI payment rate for couples, and since taxes and normal work expenses would have to be paid out of earnings, there was little incentive for SSI recipients to accept employment unless the position paid considerably more than $300 per month.

Further, SSI recipients prior to 1981 who lost entitlement to cash benefits usually lost entitlement to Medicaid. Continuing health care coverage is often as important, if not more important, to people with severe disabilities, as is receipt of income support payments. Thus, only heroic or fool-hardy persons would risk taking a job that did not pay much more than the minimum wage, that did not provide generous health care coverage for preexisting conditions, and that did not offer an immediately secure future with the firm.

To reduce these work disincentives, Congress approved two special 3-year demonstrations beginning in 1981. One demonstration, incorporated as Section 1619(a) of the Social Security Act, authorized special cash benefits to be paid to working SSI recipients so long as their earnings were below the federal break-even point of twice the monthly SSI payment plus an initial income disregard of $85. To use 1988 figures as an example, SSI payments continued until the breakeven points of $793 per month for an individual and $1,149 per month for a couple were reached (Conley & Noble, 1988).

The other demonstration, incorporated as Section 1619(b) of the Social Security Act, continued Medicaid coverage to some SSI recipients whose return to work resulted in loss of all benefits because their earnings exceeded the break-even point. Medicaid protection is continued if recipients: 1) continue to qualify on the basis of limited assets, 2) would not be able to pay for medical benefits equivalent to Medicaid, and 3) would have difficulty maintaining their employment without such coverage.

Sections 1619(a) and 1619(b) were made permanent by enactment of the Employment Opportunities for Disabled Americans Act of 1986 (P.L. 99-643). This very important piece of legislation also repealed the use of time-limited trial work and extended reentitlement periods for disabled SSI recipients, since these options had become obsolete and confusing under the now permanent provisions of Sections 1619(a) and 1619(b).

These new provisions of law can be expected to help persons with chronic mental illness to receive SSI and Medicaid benefits. However, they still face the demoralizing requirement of proving their incapacity for work that pays the substantial gainful activity (SGA) wage of $300 per month as the condition of eligibility for SSI or SSDI benefits in the first place.

This requirement fosters a defeatist attitude toward work. In the case of persons who have not worked since the onset of their illness, or at any time during their lives, proving incapacity consists of demonstrating that their condition is one in a long list of conditions presumed to show incapacity to earn at the SGA level. In the case of persons who have a work history, or whose conditions are not listed, it is likely to take between 2 months and 1 year to document incapacity to earn at this level to the satisfaction of the Social Security Administration. During this time, the applicant, his or her family, the lawyer, and others are busily engaged in proving that the applicant cannot work. Thus, the application process has very destructive effects on the applicant's morale and willingness to ever try to return to work.

Despite the reductions in work disincentives that have been enacted since 1980, major work disincentives remain in the service system. Among these are:

The SSDI program still makes no provision for reducing benefits gradually as earnings rise and, as a result, many SSDI beneficiaries who return to work face a substantial loss of income.

Although the Section 1619(a) and (b) programs have been made permanent, continuing disability reviews will be required within 12 months after an SSI recipient enters into the Section 1619(b) program. It is unclear the extent to which high earnings will trigger, or incline the persons making the disability evaluation toward, the finding that the recipient is not sufficiently disabled to qualify for continuing SSI payments.

Persons applying for SSI must still prove inability to work at the SGA level of $300 per month, a requirement that places the qualifying conditions for SSI in direct opposition to the intent and purposes of the Section 1619(a) and (b) programs. These programs permit SSI recipients to have earnings up to the federal breakeven point before losing entitlement to SSI payments, and even higher earnings before losing entitlement to Medicaid.

The lack of private health insurability may cause some SSDI beneficiaries to be concerned about the loss of Medicare benefits that occurs by law 3 years after loss of entitlement to cash benefits.

The different rules governing the payment of benefits under the SSDI and the SSI programs also cause serious work disincentives among persons who are eligible for both programs.

Finally, the incomplete knowledge among mental health and vocational rehabilitation providers as to how all of the issues just mentioned impinge on individual clients creates perhaps the greatest systems barrier of all to supported employment for persons with chronic mental illness. Under the ethical principle of "first, do no harm," no responsible service provider is willing to place the interests and well-being of a client in jeopardy. Thus, many persons with chronic mental illness who might benefit from supported employment may be withheld from the opportunity by mental health or vocational rehabilitation providers who are uncertain about how their client may fare under the arcane rules that govern the federal income support, health care, and social services programs.

CONCLUDING REMARKS

This chapter's review has shown how deinstitutionalization policy and community case management have significantly affected mental health services for those with chronic mental illness. Clearly, chronically ill clients are a challenging population to work with. Following are a number of guidelines that may prove helpful in implementing supported employment programs for persons with chronic mental illness:

1. Make placements in more flexible settings with significant flexibility allowed in work schedule and job duties.
2. Complete more extensive job analyses (do the job before making placement); detailed analyses of the psychological aspect of the environment (nature of coworkers and supervisors) will be very helpful.

3. Provide total support to employer (employer hires program, not just client), especially in overcoming stereotypical attitudes.

4. Allocate and expect far more staff intervention time to be required, especially in follow-along time as opposed to "up front" job-site training time.

5. Employment specialists should expect to be completing parts of a client's job for a number of weeks.

6. More systematic intervention and data systems will be required for feedback purposes.

7. Expect more adaptations to the work-schedule, materials, job description, and so forth.

8. Develop early/ongoing communication with parents or other caregivers to ensure attention to medication and related health needs.

9. Provide support systems for job trainers to combat uncertainty/ uneasiness (teamwork approach).

10. Seek and expect an exceptionally strong commitment from trainers, who should have direct mental health experience.

While, of course, a number of these points are important for any type or level of disability, the experience of many employment specialists suggests that success is most likely to result when the program package encompasses all of them.

REFERENCES

Anthony, W., Cohen, M., & Farkas, M. (1982). A psychiatric rehabilitation treatment program: Can I recognize one if I see one? *Community Mental Health Journal*, *18*(2): 83–95.

Anthony, W., Howell, J., & Danley, K. (1984). Vocational rehabilitation of the psychiatrically disabled. In M. Mirabi (Ed.), *The chonically mentally ill: Research and services* (pp. 215–237). Jamaica, NY: Spectrum.

Anthony, W., & Jansen, M. (1984). Predicting the vocational capacity of the chronically mentally ill: Research and policy implications. *American Psychologist*, *39*(5): 537–544.

Bachrach, L. (1978). A conceptual approach to deinstitutionalization. *Hospital and Community Psychiatry*, *29*, 573–578.

Bevilacqua, J., & Noble, J. (1987). Chronic mental illness: A problem in politics. In W. Menninger (Ed.), *The chronic mental patient/II* (pp. 131–147). Washington, DC: American Psychiatric Press.

Boles, S., Bellamy, G., Horner, R., & Mank, D. (1984). Specialized Training Program: The structured employment model. In S. Paine, G. Bellamy, & B. Wilcox (Eds.), *Human services that work: From innovation to practice*. Baltimore: Paul Brookes Publishing Co.

Bond, G. (1983). *Economic analysis of psychosocial rehabilitation*. Unpublished paper, Thresholds program, Chicago.

Conley, R., & Noble, J. (in press). Americans with severe disabilities: Victims of outmoded policies. In J. Goodgold (Ed.), *Handbook of rehabilitation medicine*. St. Louis: C.V. Mosby.

Dellario, D. (1985). *The relationship between mental health and vocational rehabilitation interagency functioning and vocational rehabilitation outcome of psychiatrically disabled persons*. Unpublished paper, University Center of Rehabilitation Research and Training in Mental Health, Boston.

Denver Research Institute.(1981). *Factors influencing the deinstitutionalization of the mentally ill*. Denver: University of Denver.

Fountain House. (1982). *A progress report for 1982*. New York: Author.

Jones, D. (1984, May/June). Donaldson and deinstitutionalization. *Mental Notes*, 2:1.

Kerachsky, S., Thornton, C., Bloomenthal, A., Maynard, R., & Stephens, S. (June, 1985). *Impacts of transitional employment on mentally retarded young adults: Results of the STETS demonstration*. Princeton: Mathematica Policy Research.

Lynn, L. (1980). *The state and human services*. Cambridge: The MIT Press.

Maslow, A. (1954). *Motivation and personality*. New York: Harper & Row.

Mosher, T. (1983). Alternatives to psychiatric hospitalization: Why has research failed to be translated into practice? *New England Journal of Medicine*, *309*: 1579–1580.

Musgrave, R., & Musgrave, P., (1973). *Public finance in theory and practice*. New York: McGraw-Hill.

Noble, J. (1984). Rehabilitating the SSI recipient—Overcoming disincentives to employment of severely disabled persons. In *The Supplemental Security Income Program: A 10-year overview* (pp. 55–102). Washington, DC: U.S. Senate, Special Committee on Aging.

Noble, J., & Conley, R. (1987). Accumulating evidence on the benefits and costs of supported and transitional work for persons with severe disabilities. *Journal of the Association for Persons with Severe Handicaps*, *12*(3), 163–174.

O'Connor v. Donaldson, 422 U.S. 563, 45 L.Ed. 2d 396, 95 S.Ct. 2486 (1975).

Pepper, B., & Ryglewicz, H. (1982). Testimony for the neglected: The mentally ill in the post-deinstitutionalized age. *American Journal of Orthopsychiatry*, *52*(3): 388–392.

Poole, D. (1985). *Supported work services employment project*. Grant no. 90-DD-0065, final report, Sept. 1, 1984–

Oct. 31, 1985. Richmond: Virginia Commonwealth University School of Social Work.

Rhodes, L., Ramsing, K., & Valenta, L. (1986, November 7). *An economic evaluation of supported employment within one manufacturing company*. Paper presented at the 1985 annual TASH conference, San Francisco. Eugene: University of Oregon.

Rosenhan, D. (1973). On being sane in insane places. *Science, 179,* 250–258.

Rubin, A. (1979). *Community mental health in the social work curriculum*. New York: Council on Social Work Education.

Tarsoff v. Regents of the University of California, 17 Cal. 3rd 425, 131 Cal. Reprt. 14, 551 p.2d 334 (1976), 83 A.L.R. 3rd 1166.

Torrey, E., & Wolfe S. (1986). *Care of the seriously mentally ill: A rating of state programs*. Washington, DC: Public Citizen Health Research Group.

Virginia Department of Mental Health and Mental Retardation. (1985, February 6). *Implementing the policy of deinstitutionalization in Virginia: A progress report prepared for the Commission on Deinstitutionlization (SJR 42)*. Unpublished draft report, Richmond.

Vladeck, B. (1980). *Unloving care: The nursing home tragedy*. New York: Basic Books.

Wehman, P. (1981). *Competitive employment: New horizons for severely disabled individuals*. Baltimore: Paul H. Brookes Publishing Co.

Wyatt v. Stickney, 325 F. Supp. 781 (M.D. Ala. 1971).

Chapter 23

Supported Employment for Persons with Physical Disabilities

Wendy Wood

A ccording to a recent study by the U.S. Department of Health and Human Services, an estimated 86% of individuals of working age with severe disabilities are unemployed in the United States. Of those who are employed, only about 2% work full-time (U.S. Department of Health and Human Services, 1982). Many individuals who have significant physical impairments or multiple handicaps (including a physical impairment) fall into the category of "severely disabled" and are included in the large number of unemployed. A large percentage of these individuals are underemployed in sheltered workshops and work activity centers, earning wages of less than $700 per year (U.S. Department of Labor, 1979).

The costs of maintaining disabled adults out of work are high. Approximately 42% of disabled adults are recipients of public support funds such as Supplemental Security Income (SSI) or Social Security Disability Insurance (SSDI) (Bowe, 1986). The cumulative effect of supporting the large numbers of individuals with disabilities over the span of their adult lives is indeed substantial (Hill, Banks, et al.,1987; U.S. Social Security Administration, 1982). In 1985

alone, "the Federal Government spent $62 billion on subsidies, medical care, and other programs for disabled persons, of which more than 93 percent was to support out-of-work individuals with disabilities" (President's Committee on Employment of the Handicapped, 1987, p. 1).

The causes and diagnoses of the different types of motoric impairments are varied and diverse, including: cerebral palsy, muscular dystrophy, multiple sclerosis, rheumatoid arthritis, traumatic brain injury, and spinal cord injury, to name but a few. The resulting disability from any of the many causes of physical handicaps again varies widely, ranging from mild to profound impairment. Terms such as *paraplegia* (paralysis of the lower extremities); *quadriplegia* (paralysis of all four limbs, upper and lower extremities); *hemiplegia* (paralysis of one side of the body affecting one upper and lower extremity); *spasticity* (increased muscle tone and slow movement, which often results in muscle contractions); *athetosis* (fluctuating muscle tone resulting in involuntary movement of the limbs, trunk, and face); and *ataxia* (difficulty with balance and equilibrium, which is most evident in

Acknowledgment: Contributions from Roberta Goodwyn from the Richmond Cerebral Palsy Center are gratefully acknowledged. Ms. Goodwyn was extremely helpful in the development of this chapter.

walking) are just some of the basic descriptors for the many different outcomes of motorically disabling conditions (Inge, 1987).

Individuals may be severely disabled due only to physical impairment, in that their physical handicap severely limits their ability to function independently in one or more of the major life domains such as the work, domestic, recreation, or community environments. This means that they are unable to function in these major environments for everyday living without some assistance or modification made to the environment. Other individuals with physical handicaps may have concomitant handicaps that further complicate their ability to function independently. Accompanying handicaps might include: mental retardation, hearing or vision impairments, emotional disorders, speech and/or communication problems, memory or cognition deficits, learning disabilities, medical or health conditions (e.g., heart conditions, epilepsy, diabetes, respiratory diseases, bladder control problems), and so on.

Vocational education experiences in school and postschool rehabilitation programs have not been effective in providing for successful employment outcomes for individuals with severe physical or multiple handicaps. For one thing, school-sponsored vocational education programs usually offer a generalized curriculum of job and career information but in many cases do not offer specific skill training in selected job skills based on a particular individual's abilities (Pietruski, Everson, Goodwyn, &Wehman 1985). In many cases, the general curricula offered are not even based on the job market of the local community but, rather, reflect the national labor market. Second, these programs and the classroom training materials used are often outdated, as it is impossible for the schools to purchase equipment and keep up with the technology of the real business community. Facility-based rehabilitation training programs have many of the same characteristics of school programs.

The basic characteristics of the supported employment approach enable this model to be used with a diverse group of individuals with severe disabilities, including persons with physical and/or multiple handicaps. First, there are the different models of supported employment (i.e., individual placement, enclave, mobile work crew, or benchwork—see Chapter 2), which provide for varying levels of support to be provided—either continuous intense support and supervision (e.g., enclave model) or intense support during the initial period of placement and training, with support and supervision gradually fading to intermittent, ongoing intervention as needed by the individual (supported competitive employment). Second, supported employment is an individualized approach that provides training and/or resource support according to the needs of a particular individual in a particular employment setting. Even in the group employment models such as enclaves, mobile crews, or benchwork operations, each employee is given individual consideration for placement as well as one-to-one intensive training once the decision for placement is made. Third, supported employment is a postemployment service provision model, so that the training and support services are provided *at and after* the first day of employment at the job site. This eliminates the need for an individual to be able to function independently on the job site (i.e., "ready" for employment) the first day of employment. Fourth, the services are ongoing for as long as the individual is employed. Trained professionals are always available to the consumer or the employer to whatever degree is required in a particular employment situation. In enclave, mobile crew, and benchwork employment programs, a trained supervisor is always on the job site with the disabled employees. With supported competitive employment, an employment specialist will be on the job site continuously at first and then fade off to only intermittent visits once the employee demonstrates an ability to function independently on the job.

This chapter discusses a supported employment approach for helping individuals with different types of physical impairment gain and maintain jobs. Special emphasis is given to the role of the employment specialist (job coach). The employment specialist is primarily responsible for providing the employee with job training to whatever extent training is needed. However, the specialist's ability to gain access to whatever resources or ancillary services are needed to *enable* the individual to be successful in the employment situation is also critically important, especially for individuals with physical or multiple impairments. Job-site training, arranging for adaptations and modifications to compensate for physical and/or cognitive limitations, and accessing other service resources to solve problems are all part of supported employment services for persons with physical handicaps. Selected adaptations and job-site modifications are described later in this chapter. School services with regard to vocational training are also reviewed as an important foundation for successful and desirable employment. School vocational education programs are essential for providing knowledge and exposure to the world of work, and need to provide more specific work experience training in community employment settings. Postsecondary preemployment training programs such as those provided through rehabilitation, college, or technical school programs are suitable services for many individuals with physical handicaps. Supported employment provides additional service alternatives for individuals for whom other vocational options have been unsuccessful. Finally, the chapter discusses decision-making processes for rehabilitation professionals seeking to develop rehabilitation plans for persons with severe physical handicaps.

COMPONENTS OF SUPPORTED COMPETITIVE EMPLOYMENT FOR PERSONS WITH PHYSICAL DISABILITIES

The four basic components of supported competitive employment are: 1) job placement, 2) job-site training/enabling, 3) ongoing assessment, and 4) follow-along for employment retention (Moon, Goodall, Barcus, & Brooke, 1986; Wehman, 1981). This section examines each component in the context of how it applies to individuals with physical disabilities. In many ways, application of the four components of supported competitive employment is similar in theory for individuals with all types of disabling conditions. However, because of the wide variance of individuals with physical handicaps with regard to intellectual functioning, and the prob-

lems associated with mobility impairment, there are specific issues for this population.

Job placement is a process of matching the skills and abilities of a particular individual with the skill requirements of a particular employment situation. Before any individual with a physical disability can be placed into a suitable employment situation, critical information is necessary from two distinct sources. In a supported competitive employment approach, a skilled employment specialist gathers information on consumers first through individual *consumer assessment*, and information on available jobs in the community through a process of *community job market screening*. To work most efficiently, an employment specialist has several (5–10) consumers in mind while involved in the ongoing activity of job development in the community, as Figure 1 illustrates. When a job opening is identified in areas of job-consumer compatability, then a job placement is arranged by the employment specialist.

EMPLOYMENT SPECIALIST

Figure 1. Cartoon drawing representing the process of comparing consumer assessment information and job development information for compatibility analysis.

Consumer Assessment

Individual consumer assessments are necessary in order to gain thorough knowledge of the individuals waiting to be placed. Consumer assessment information is gathered through an uncomplicated process of assessing the skills, abilities, and interests of consumer referrals for supported employment services prior to any attempts at job placement. The process is uncomplicated in that use of formal evaluation instruments such as the VALPAR, SINGER, or other extensive evaluation packages is minimized. These instruments usually succeed in screening individuals out of employment opportunities, rather than providing information useful for identifying jobs for people. Figure 2 is a sample consumer assessment form providing a list of questions that might be used to gather information to consider different employment opportunities for individuals with severe physical and/or multiple handicaps (Pietruski et al., 1985). The assessment areas listed in the figure assist the job placement professional in matching individual skills with specific jobs.

For example, a man in a wheelchair who has good use of one hand, good verbal communication skills, and average intelligence might be able to succeed in a message service job in which he would be required to record messages for answering-service customers. Answering-service systems have become automated by computer technology so that storing and retrieving messages is an efficient process requiring minimal keyboard entry. Oral communication, auditory memory, spelling skills, and the ability to type 20–35 words per minute are basic requirements of a message service position. Other requirements would be a pleasant manner in dealing with service consumers and users and an ability to deal with frustration. On the other hand, a data entry position requiring a production rate of 10,000 keystrokes per hour would not be appropriate for this individual.

Another individual with similar physical characteristics but functioning in the moderate or severe IQ range might be able to succeed in a position filming documents for storage on microfilm or microfiche. In this position the individual would need to have fine motor abilities sufficient to pick up paper documents, use a staple remover, work with tape, unfold paper, and so on. However, this individual, with limited vocabulary, difficult-to-understand speech, no spelling skills, and an inability to respond to callers' requests, would obviously not be appropriate for the message service position.

In assessing individuals with motor impairments, the job placement professional needs to obtain a careful description in behavioral terms of the person's physical capabilities as well as information regarding communication skills, self-care, and independent living skills. General information regarding cognitive abilities such as reading levels, mathematical skills, perceptual abilities, visual acuity, and hearing is also important to gather. Other assessment areas include social and behavioral areas, on-task behavior, physical endurance, parental/family supportiveness, transportation accessibility, and job or career interests (Pietruski et al., 1985). The best ways to compile this information are by direct observation and interview of the individual being assessed, along with supplementing and validating this information by consulting significant others in the individual's life. These significant others might include parents, school personnel, group home or other residential caregivers, personal care attendant, workshop staff, or whomever else may have meaningful contact with the individual being assessed.

Community Job Market Screening

There are four levels of community job market screening for the purpose of gathering information on employment opportunities in a given community. These four levels, 1) community job market analysis, 2) job development and job placement, 3) job analysis, and 4) task analysis, progress from assembling general information about employment opportunities to a microscopic analysis of specific jobs. Table 1 summarizes in sequential order these four levels, each of which is discussed in the paragraphs following.

Community Job Market Analysis   When considering job market screening for individuals with physical or multiple handicaps, the job placement professional must explore a wide variety of job types and levels. Typically, supported competitive employment for individuals

I. Personal data
   A. Name: _____
   B. Address:_____
   C. Date of birth:_____
   D. Parent/guardian name:_____
   E. Evaluation:_____ Date of evaluation:_____

II. Description of student
   A. Disability: _____
   B. Medical needs: _____
   C. Use of upper extremities: _____
      _____
   D. Voluntary head control: _____
   E. Use of lower extremities: _____
      _____
   F. Mobility: _____
   G. Vision/hearing: _____

III. Communication
   A. Oral speech

   5   4   3   2   1
   ....
   Intelligible   Very difficult
   to strangers   to understand

   B. Alternative communication mode: _____
      _____
   C. Follows multiple verbal commands: _____

IV. Adaptive behavior skills: _____
   A. Eating   _____ independent _____ requires assistance
   B. Toileting _____ independent _____ requires assistance
   C. Dressing _____ independent _____ requires assistance
   D. Transportation needs: _____ automobile _____ bus
      _____ van lift _____ ability to board independently
      _____ requires assistance

V. Academic information. (Write a brief description or note approximate grade level.)
   A. Reading skills: _____
   B. Math skills: _____
   C. Perceptual/learning deficits: _____
      _____
   D. Manages/tells time: _____
   E. Manages/uses money: _____
   F. Communicates personal data: _____

VI. Student work interest. (Summarize from student or significant other interview.)
   A. Jobs stated as desirable: _____
      _____
   B. Jobs stated as undersirable: _____

Figure 2. Sample consumer assessment form. *(continued)*

    C. Expressed feelings about work: _____

    D. Limitations stated concerning work: _____

    E. Past work history: _____

VII.   Related vocational skills. (Gather information from teachers and other staff and observations if possible.)
    A. Social skills
       1. With teachers/therapists in authority role: _____

       2. With peers: _____

       3. With family: _____
    B. Appearance/grooming: _____

    C. Describe social skills: _____

    D. Generalization of skills from one task to another similar task:

    E. Perseveration/distractibility: _____

    F. Utilizes the following equipment: _____

    G. Type of prompts needed for learning: _____

    H. Statement of attendance record: _____

    I. Endurance/physical strength: _____

    J. Speed of manipulation/operation of materials/equipment: _____

    K. Level of supervision required: _____

VIII. Other pertinent information: _____

Figure 2. (continued)

with mental retardation has involved job development in service industry areas such as food service, janitorial, housekeeping, and laundry services. These jobs are not appropriate for individuals with mobility impairments, with or without average intelligence, in that all the jobs require mobility and do not make use of the higher cognitive abilities that many of these individuals have.

The issue then becomes one of job development in many different vocations at more than just entry level. Indeed, many individuals with physical handicaps have been in the work force before or had career aspirations prior to an injury

Table 1. A sequential process of community job market screening

Community Job Market Analysis
Checking the business and labor market needs of a local community. What types of businesses and occupations are present?

Job Development
Contacting local business representatives to gather first-hand information on specific jobs.

Job Analysis
Breaking down the workday(s) of a specific job into the separate tasks that are required and gathering information on the actual job requirements, work environment, and so forth, to use in matching with consumer assessment information.

Task Analysis
Breaking down the separate tasks into a step-by-step sequence of the behaviors that are required to complete each task, to be used for training or enabling the individual to do all parts of the job.

Table 2. Jobs identified as potential employment alternatives for persons with physical handicaps in the Richmond, VA, area.

Pharmaceutical Company
  Laser printer operator
  Computer operator

Retail Merchandise Store
  Records management clerk
  Mail order clerk
  Inventory information clerk
  Junior accounting clerk
  Switchboard operator bank

Bank
  Remittance processing technician
  Micrographics clerks
  Mailroom clerk
  Bank tec operator
  Tape library technician
  Photo retrieval clerk

Data Processing Company
  Planetary camera operator

Federal Government Supply Center
  Public voucher

Photo Processing Business
  Photo booth attendant

Microfilm Service
  File preparation clerk
  Planetary camera operator
  Quality control clerk

Insurance Company
  File clerk
  Micrographics clerk

Wholesale Merchandiser
  Inventory clerk
  Accounting clerk
  Data entry operator

Construction Company
  Accounts payable clerk
  Accounts receivable clerk
  Consolidation account clerk

that caused their disability. These individuals, depending on the severity of their handicap after the injury, often want to return to the same or similar positions with the same career goals they held before they became disabled. In addition, physically disabled individuals with average or above-average intelligence will have career interests that must be considered when beginning community job market screening and job development. Table 2 lists jobs, identified through a community screening in Richmond, VA, that have offered employment opportunities to individuals with physical disabilities.

Unfortunately, individuals who have not been exposed to different jobs and occupations may have unrealistic expectations for their employment futures. This problem can be avoided by good vocational education experiences for youth with disabilities, enabling them to explore different career options before making career decisions (Kokaska & Brolin, 1985).

Therefore, before beginning community job market screening for individuals with physical and/or multiple handicaps, it is helpful to do the following:

1. Briefly review the professional literature to find out what vocations have shown promise for individuals with physical handicaps.
2. Conduct a simple follow-up study to see what types of jobs other individuals with phyical handicaps are doing in the local

community. Checking with local rehabilitation professionals and school representatives may facilitate gathering this kind of information.

3. Examine consumer interest survey data from consumer assessments to get an idea of what types of jobs consumers want.

Given a general idea of some vocations that have been successful in the local community and other geographical areas and a notion of the career goals of at least some of the individuals, a community analysis of job possibilities can be initiated. The information gathered in steps 1,

2, and 3 should only provide suggestions for job development, not set limits or boundaries. Human service personnel trying to develop employment opportunities are most limited by the many jobs and business types that are unknown and unexplored.

Job Development and Job Placement

After gathering general information on the labor needs of the local community, the employment specialist begins a process of more specific *job development*. Scanning various resources, such as the telephone Yellow Pages and newspaper want ads, as well as contacting the local chamber of commerce and friends and family members, are effective means for generating a list of businesses and addresses. The employment specialist then begins the ongoing process of contacting business representatives in the community to gather firsthand information on specific jobs.

This process involves getting in touch with business representatives directly and arranging to discuss and observe jobs (see also Chapter 12 in this volume for a detailed discussion on contacting employers). An initial contact can be made by telephone, a written letter, or an in-person "cold call" with no prior notice to the business setting. A skilled employment specialist knows which technique is best for the type of business being considered. Usually a more professional or white collar office setting requires a more formal initial contact (i.e., by letter of introduction or a telephone call). Less professional businesses can be contacted most effectively by simply going to the jobsite and locating the employer-manager or owner. An example of a letter of introduction to a business setting is provided in Figure 3.

Once on the job site, the employment specialist explains how supported employment op-

---

June 1, 1987

Mr. Christopher Simmons
Personnel Director
Nutritional Dietetics Inc.
2012 Main Street
Richmond, VA 27986

Dear Mr. Simmons:

My name is Mary Smith and I work for the Rehabilitation Research and Training Center at Virginia Commonwealth University. It is our organization's goal to obtain competitive employment for persons with disabilities, using the supported employment work model. Supported employment is a way to provide companies with competent, motivated workers. Supported employment services include a careful matching of worker abilities to job requirements; specialized training provided to the new employee by a professional Job Coach on your job site; and follow-up services for as long as the worker is employed at your company to ensure that job performance continues to meet your satisfaction. The Job Coach is available to return to the job site at any time to provide additional training if necessary. Best of all, supported employment services are provided at no cost to you.

We feel that the basic components of supported competitive employment offer a likely approach for improving the employability of these citizens. Furthermore, we believe that returning individuals with disabilities to the work force is essential in providing them with the means to live a more productive and independent life.

I would like to contact you next week to set up an appointment to discuss employment opportunities at your organization. At this time, I would also like to present the supported work model to you in more detail, to show you what it can do for your company. It is only with the cooperation of people in the business and working community that we can provide meaningful employment opportunities for persons with disabilities. I look forward to meeting with you.

Sincerely,

Mary Smith
Supported Employment Specialist

MS/jd

Figure 3.   Sample letter of introduction to a business.

Job title: _____ Date: _____

Contact: _____ Phone: _____

Company: _____

Address: _____

City: _____ State: _____ Zip: _____

I.   Physical requirements
   1. Two hands: yes/no. Notes (modifiable?): _____
       _____

   2. One hand: yes/no. Notes (modifiable?): _____
       _____

   3. Reach: yes/no. Notes (modifiable?): _____
       _____

   4. Mobility: yes/no. Notes (modifiable?): _____
       _____

   5. Lifting/carrying: yes/no. Notes (modifiable?): _____
       _____

II. Communication requirements
   1. Must talk with strangers: yes/no. Specifics: _____
       _____

   2. Must talk with co-workers only: yes/no. Specifics: _____
       _____

   3. Must use telephone: yes/no. Specifics: _____
       _____

   4. Must follow simple instructions: yes/no. Specifics: _____
       _____

III. Academic requirements
   1. Approximate reading level required:
          1.0   2.0   3.0   4.0   5.0   6.0   7.0   8.0   above
       Notes: _____
   2. Writing/typing skills: yes/no. Notes: _____
       _____

   3. Perceptual skills required (e.g., matching, copying, etc.): yes/no.
       Notes: _____
   4. Visual acuity required: yes/no. Notes: _____
       _____

   5. Hearing required: yes/no. Notes: _____
       _____

   6. Time management skills required: yes/no. Notes: _____
       _____

IV. Brief description of job: _____
     _____
     _____

     Entry level: yes/no. Specifics: _____
     _____

     Job duties: repetitive or variable. Specifics: _____
     _____

Figure 4. Sample job analysis form. (GRTC is a public bus system. SPECTRAN is Special Transportation Service [Wheelchair Accessible].)

V.   Brief description of social climate in work environment (check all that apply):

    _____ Friendly, cheerful   _____ Aloof, indifferent

    _____ Busy, relaxed   _____ Busy, tense

    _____ Slow, relaxed   _____ Slow, tense

    _____ Structured, orderly   _____ Unstructured,disorderly

    Other: _____

    Type of dress required: _____

VI. Noted demands of job

    1. Endurance: yes/no. Specifics: _____

    2. Accuracy: yes/no. Specifics: _____

    3. Speed: yes/no. Specifics: _____

        _____

    4. Equipment used: _____

        _____

VII. Other

    1. Accessibility: GRTC   SPECTRAN

        Other: _____

    2. Work hours: _____

    3. Benefits: _____

    4. Architectural barriers: _____

        _____

        _____

VIII. Notes: _____

_____

_____

_____

_____

Figure 4. *(continued)*

erates, as well as benefits to the employer and the person with a disability, and provides examples of other businesses currently employing individuals with supported employment services. Then, if the employer is receptive, the employment specialist inquires about specific job openings within the business. Figure 4 lists questions that might be used to conduct a job analysis for persons with physical disabilities. Important information to collect during the job analysis process includes transportation accessibility and careful attention to employer's standards of performance with regard to quality and productivity.

Job Analysis The information compiled from the consumer assessment, as well as that gathered through the process of job analysis, is used to determine the compatibility of a specific job with the abilities of a specific consumer. A job opening will need to be evaluated from a number of different angels, including availability of transportation, length of workday, fine-motor dexterity required, communication skills required, and so forth. The employment specialist examines all aspects of the job and determines which consumer, from an existing pool of individuals waiting for employment, is best suited for the job in question. Table 3 outlines the functional relationship between the consumer assessment and job analysis information.

The individual with a disability is *not* expected to start off performing all of the job's requirements *without* assistance. If that were the case, supported employment would not be the appropriate service for the particular individual; rather, placement services without job-site assistance would be sufficient. In a supported employment model, the employment specialist

Table 3.   Functional relationship between consumer assessment and job analysis

Consumer abilities	Job requirements
Physical Description Hand use Head control Arm extension Mobility	**Physical Requirements** Hand use Reach Lifting/carrying Mobility
Communication Abilities Oral speech Alternative communication mode Follows multiple commands	**Communication Requirements** Must talk with coworkers Must talk with strangers Must use telephone Must follow instructions

Academic Information
Reading skills
Math skills
Perceptual deficits
Visual acuity
Hearing
Manages/tells time
Communicates telephone number/address
	Academic Requirements
	Approximate reading level
	  required
	Writing/typing skills
	Perceptual skills required
	Visual acuity required
	Hearing required
	Time management skills
	  required

Endurance/Strength Endurance Physical strength Manipulative capabilities Speed of manipulation/operation of materials/equipment	**Demands of Job** Length of workday Lifting requirements Fine-motor skills needed Equipment used for job
Work Behaviors/Responsibility Promptness Completes work on time Ability to work independently Attendance record (school) Appearance Distractibility	**Work Environment** Employee rules Production requirements Degree of supervision Absenteeism policy Dress requirements Distractions in work space

Transportation Needs
Type of transportation needed
Ability to board transportation
  vehicle
Mobility/maneuverabilty
	Accessibility
	Type of transportation
	  available to job site
	Architectural barriers in
	  work environment

Other Work interests Social skills Medical needs Self-help/independent living skills Financial need	**Other** Type of work Social interaction required Provisions for medical assistance Financial incentives

endeavors to help the consumer learn and complete the duties of a particular job by applying reasonable means to close the gap between the consumer's abilities the first day of employment and the abilities ultimately required to meet the employer's standards. The next section of this chapter discusses the process of closing this gap by whatever means are available. Figure 5 is a form that can be used to examine job and consumer characteristics to determine compatibility or appropriateness of a job match.

If a job opening is identified at the time of the job-site visit that appears compatible with a particular individual's abilities and the employer is receptive, then the employment specialist discusses the opening with the employer with special reference to this individual. In this role, the employment specialist acts not only as an advocate and a personnel agent for the disabled consumer but as a human resources agent for the employer. At this time, the employment specialist arranges for a job interview for the consumer. The employment specialist is then responsible for assisting (as needed) the con-

Date: ___/___/___ Company: _____ Job title: _____

Consumer A:	Consumer C:	Consumer E:
Name:_____	Name:_____	Name:_____
SSN: ____/____/____	SSN: ____/____/____	SSN: ____/____/____
Consumer B:	Consumer D:	Consumer F:
Name:_____	Name:_____	Name:_____
SSN:____/____/____	SSN:____/____/____	SSN:____/____/____

Instructions: Indicate whether the factor is critically important for the position in question by placing an "X" in the first column. For factors considered critical to the position, use the following symbols to indicate compatibility in the Consumer column:

  (=) indicates current compatibility between job requirement and consumer ability

  (+) indicates consumer is overqualified in this area

  (− +) indicates the discrepancy can be eliminated by intervention

  (−) indicates a discrepancy without reasonable means of elimination.

Employment factor:	Critical to position	Consumer					
		A	B	C	D	E	F
1. Availability							
2. Transportation							
3. Strength							
4. Endurance							
5. Orienting							
6. Physical mobility							
7. Work rate							
8. Appearance							
9. Communication							
10. Social interactions							
11. No unusual behavior							
12. Attention to task							
13. Sequencing of tasks							
14. Initiation/motivation							
15. Adapting to change							
16. Reinforcement needs							
17. Attitude/support							
18. Financial concerns							
19. Object discrimination							
20. Time awareness							
21. Functional reading							
22. Functional math							
23. Street crossing							

Compatibility: Consumers with negative (−) indication(s) of compatibility in areas critical to this position with no reasonable means of eliminating the discrepancy should not be considered for placement in this position.

Figure 5. Sample compatibility analysis form.

sumer with completing the job application form, arranging for transportation and taking care of other details of the job interview, talking over the position and the financial implications with the consumer and parents or caregivers, and so on, in the event that a placement is made.

If the employer agrees to hire the individual with the disability, the employment specialist negotiates the starting date and makes sure all necessary points are covered between the employer and employee by the first day of employment and on a continuing basis thereafter. The employment specialist provides only so much assistance as is needed by the individual being served, while encouraging the consumer to do whatever he or she can do independently (e.g., fill out the job application or travel to the interview).

Task Analysis Before the first day of employment, the employment specialist thus should complete a thorough *job analysis* of all of the tasks required in the position. From this, a detailed *task analysis* is completed of each different job duty. This step-by-step task analysis is critically important in providing effective services in the job-site enabling component.

Job-Site Enabling

After all of the placement arrangements have been made, the primary objective of the employment specialist is to *enable* the individual with the disability to complete all of the job duties required by the employer to the employer's satisfaction. To accomplish this goal for individuals with severe intellectual deficits, the emphasis is placed on training that utilizes a task analytic approach, applying behavioral and systematic instructional procedures (Barcus, Brooke, Inge, Moon, & Goodall, 1987). Chapter 12 discusses job-site training techniques. For individuals with severe motor impairment who are functioning within the average intelligence range, there is less emphasis on training and more on using modifications, adaptations, and other compensatory strategies to enable the person to perform the duties of the job. The employment specialist may also need to arrange other services for successful employment retention. These may include personal care attendant services, coworker support, and so forth. For individuals with a combination of physical and intellectual deficits, the employment specialist combines job-site training procedures and other enabling procedures. Again, it is important to emphasize that the supported competitive employment model is an individualized approach. The services and the level of intensity are applied according to the particular needs of the individual being served in a particular employment setting.

As suggested earlier, during the process of job/consumer compatibility analysis, the employment specialist examines the gap between the consumer's current abilities and the job requirements and determines if the gap can be closed by implementing job-site enabling intervention strategies. On the first day of employment, strategies of job-site enabling necessary to close that gap are initiated, with new problems identified and solutions formulated as an ongoing process.

Job-site enabling procedures can be categorized into three types: 1) job-site training procedures, 2) job-site modifications/adaptations, and 3) case services coordination. Job-site training procedures were discussed in Chapter 12. Therefore, the remainder of this section emphasizes modifications and adaptations.

Modifications and Adaptations Use of adaptive devices and/or modifications in the work setting can enable an individual with physical disabilities to successfully complete job duties. The role of the employment specialist is to identify motor-related problems and then arrange for solutions to those problems by providing for appropriate and reasonable adaptations or modifications to tasks or equipment.

In considering the use of adaptive devices and modifications, the emphasis is on problem solving to simplify task demands and on choosing adaptations that meet the needs of the individual. If the person can function effectively and safely without special equipment, then he or she may also fit more easily into a standard job setting. However, if adaptive devices improve positioning or reduce fatigue, then long-term employment goals are enhanced by using these devices. Adaptations can include commercially available equipment, devices individually modified for use by a specific person, or homemade adaptations. Modifications can be made to the equipment used in the job task, to the method or sequence of the task, or to the way the person interacts with the task (e.g., altering seating position or the part of the body being used).

Some employment specialists may be skilled in designing and fabricating modifications and adaptive devices. However, in many cases the employment specialist will need the services of other professionals with technical expertise in rehabilitation technology. Two professionals who have specific training in these areas are occupational therapists and rehabilitation engineers (Pietruski et al.,1985).

A registered occupational therapist is a medical professional with at least a bachelor's degree in occupational therapy and clinical experience with individuals with various disabilities. His or her training includes activity analysis (analyzing what a person must do physically and psychologically to complete a task); modifying functional daily activities based on a person's abilities and limitations; and designing, fabricating, or prescribing simple adaptive equipment.

Rehabilitation engineers are engineers with additional training in problem solving, designing, and fabricating devices and equipment specifically to meet the needs of persons with disabilities. Their expertise is essential when off-the-shelf commercial modifications are inadequate or unavailable. They are especially helpful as consultants for specific situations and are usually contacted through state departments of vocational rehabilitation (VR) services. Persons do not need a degree in rehabilitation engineering to be talented in design and application of rehabilitation technology.

Although it is necessary to individualize when choosing adaptations based on the person's specific physical impairments, a few general guidelines should be considered. As with nondisabled workers, the disabled worker's posture greatly affects his or her ability to perform by influencing endurance, reaching (or range of motion), muscle tone, comfort, and in some cases, coordination. Because of the importance of posture on motor control, it is essential to assess and improve a worker's seating before attempt-

ing to modify finer control such as hand usage or head control.

In assessing posture, an important guideline is to maintain the hips and knees at 90° angles with feet flat on the floor or supported with a footrest. This is the typical posture of someone typing or "sitting up straight." In this position the worker has the stability in the lower body that is necessary to use the hands well.

It is also important to provide lower back support in the person's chair. Support of the lower back reduces fatigue as well as enhancing more upright posture, factors that greatly affect performance of job tasks.

Another important consideration is proper placement of equipment and of job supplies. Visual work, such as a computer monitor, should be at eye level or slightly below. Avoid making the worker look upward to work, as this increases neck extension, which in turn increases whole body extension, increases fatigue, and decreases eye-hand efficiency.

Many individuals with physical handicaps have difficulty using one or both hands. Position the individual's work and/or equipment to his or her less-involved side. Some individuals cannot cross their hands over to their other side; some cannot get either or both hands to their midline. These points are important to consider when positioning written work or a computer terminal.

Some individuals, especially those with poor coordination, will need to fix or stabilize their arms in order to accomplish fine-motor tasks. Elevating the work surface may be advantageous for some individuals, in that stress is relieved in shoulder muscles, while others may benefit from a lower than normal surface so that they can work with their elbows straight for increased stability.

Efficiency in hand usage also varies with the position of the rest of the body and the position of the task. If the shoulder, trunk, or hips are not well supported, the arms and hands will not be stable for fine-motor performance. Likewise, the worker may be able to grasp, reach, or use both hands together, but may not be able to perform these movements at the same time or in combination. Therefore, skill in one task may not indicate the ability to transfer this skill to other settings without modifications.

Just as good positioning and seating adaptations are prerequisites to success in work tasks, another essential component for many disabled persons is the application of appropriate adaptive devices to aid in specific job tasks. Devices are used primarily to enable a person to perform independently in situations in which he or she would otherwise need help.

Choosing specific devices involves analyzing the worker's movements, abilities, and problems in completing the task. Much like a job is analyzed in formulating the task analysis for the job itself, the interaction of the worker and the task is analyzed in order to formulate a plan for task or equipment modification.

In addition to the staff's analyzing the task and figuring out how they would accomplish it themselves, it is necessary for them to observe the worker attempting the same task. Consider some of the following questions:

1. What are the visual demands of the task? Can the worker see the work adequately? Can the worker change his or her focus from equipment to worksheet without reversing or dropping digits? If not, the worker may need devices to minimize the visual demands of the task.

2. What is his or her position as the task is attempted? Is the task feasible from this position?

3. At which step does the individual have difficulty? Is this an essential step, or can it be bypassed or modified?

4. Does the task require a physical ability the individual does not and will never have? If so, can the task be modified or an adaptive device added that is acceptable to the employer?

5. Are all the steps in the task analysis necessary and arranged in the most efficient manner for completion by the worker?

6. Are there perceptual components of the task (as well as physical demands) that are hindering the worker? Perceptual components include motor-planning, sequencing, memory, figure-ground, visual focusing, and attending skill. If there are hindering components, an adaptive device

will not alter these problems, but adapting the perceptual demands of the task may help.

7. Does the task require both hands? If so, in what position, and how close to the body, or how far to the side?

8. Is strength of grasp *and* positioning of both hands required? Does the worker have the necessary grasp strength; could a device substitute?

9. If only one hand is needed, how much grasp strength is necessary, and in what position? A worker may be able to use one or both hands close to the body, but may have much more difficulty if he or she needs to reach out.

10. Can the worker supinate his or her forearm? (To supinate is to turn the wrist so the palm is upward; most manipulative tasks require the hand turned at least half way.) Many individuals with severe physical disabilities cannot do this, and therefore must compensate with other movement, or the situation must be modified.

11. Does the individual have enough range of motion to reach all supplies or equipment? If not, can these be rearranged?

12. Can the worker use his or her nondominant hand as an assist? If not, can a device be designed to compensate?

13. Is the worker compensating for lack of normal movement with abnormal postures or with excessive effort? Either way, he or she will not be able to do the task for long.

14. If special equipment could simplify the task, does the individual have the skill to use the equipment? Could he or she learn? There are many alternate ways to enter information into a computer, but the individual would need to learn additional skills such as typing with a headpointer, using morse code, scanning with single switch input, or using an optical indicator.

15. In the long term, will it be most efficient to change the task (to one the worker can do independently), to change the worker (by teaching him or her the difficult steps), or to change the equipment (by modifying

or using adaptive devices)? These considerations are an important part of the job enabling process that is performed by the employment specialist during the initial period of intervention at the job site.

Standard, nonadapted work supplies and equipment are encouraged when appropriate and possible, allowing the worker to adapt these to himself or herself. This enables the worker to fit into various work settings without conspicuously bringing a set of special equipment along. However, in many cases adaptive devices or modifications to equipment are required, whether they are simple and homemade or expensive and commercially produced. A list of commercially available equipment sources is provided in the Appendix at the end of this chapter.

Services Coordination   In implementing a supported work approach for persons with physical handicaps, some services may be required to achieve a successful employment situation that the employment specialist is unable to provide directly. Indeed, arranging for adaptations or modifications will, in some cases, require utilizing others for service provision. Therefore, the employment specialist becomes actively involved in services coordination using services and/or resources that are available through other individuals or other agencies. For example, a particular consumer is hired for a job, and arrangements are made for transportation to be provided for persons in wheelchairs. However, the consumer's home, because of lack of need prior to the job placement, is not equipped with a wheelchair ramp, so the individual cannot leave and re-enter the residence independently. Therefore, the special transportation service denies services because it is beyond their responsibilities to assist persons out of or back into houses or other buildings. To arrange for the consumer to be able to use the special transportation service, the employment specialist must obtain whatever resources are available to build a ramp. The first choice, if the individual is a client of vocational rehabilitation services, is to contact the rehabilitation counselor. If financially eligible, the rehabilitation counselor can arrange for a licensed contractor to build a suitable wheelchair ramp according to approved specifications. Other services that an employment specialist may need to coordinate include personal care attendant services, coworker support arrangements, individual or family counseling/therapy, change of residence assistance, and special transportation assistance. Employment has such a major impact on the life of an individual that it is impossible to avoid a considerable ripple effect in all other life domains.

However, once the decision is made for a placement, the employment specialist must provide services directly or locate other service provision agencies to solve whatever problems are impeding or complicating job stability. Table 4 is a list of the services that might be necessary for supported employment for persons with physical disabilities.

In short, job-site enabling is a process of problem solving or gap closing. During the period of examining consumer assessment information and job analysis information, the employment specialist compares each facet of the consumer's abilities on the first day of employment with the ultimate requirements of the job. He or she must determine that the gaps or problems can be solved through application of any of the available strategies or resources before the placement decision is made. Feasibility and consideration of what is reasonable with regard to expense of service provisions, time commitment required, and the outcome and benefits for the individual should be considered. Consumer satisfaction is, of course, the primary consideration.

On-Going Assessment   Continuous monitoring of the individual's ability to perform the job duties is important. The employment specialist keeps regular checks with employer and consumer throughout her or his employment. Assessment techniques during initial training or enabling activities involve daily recording of observational data, including task analytic assessment and production rate recording. As the worker begins to demonstrate proficiency performing the various job duties and behaviors, the employment specialist begins the gradual process of fading from the jobsite. Assessment is critical during the fading period to make sure that the worker is able to perform job duties to the employer's standards without intervention

Table 4. Model components and services provided by employment specialist—rehabilitation engineering services team for consumer with physical disabilities

Model components	Services provided
Job development	• Community job market screening • Development of a responsive marketing program • Specific employer contact • Job analysis/environmental analysis
Consumer assessment	• Assessment of individual's gross- and fine-motor abilities • Assessment of individual consumer's vocational interests • Assessment of individual consumer's transportation, attendant care, and other support service needs
Job placement	• Match of consumer's abilities and job requirements • Communication with Social Security office (as needed) • Assistance with transportation planning and training (as needed) • Counseling with parents, caregivers, family, and/or consumer (as needed) • Assistance with job interview • Assistance with financial planning, implications of employment
Job-site enabling	• Assessment of consumer's current skills, training needs, job modification needs, and support needs • Provision of systematic and behavioral training on job and job-related skills • Provision of adaptive equipment and job-site modifications • Completion of job requirements while consumer is being trained and job site is being modified • Ongoing assessment of skill acquisition, production, employer satisfaction, consumer satisfaction, and appropriateness of adaptive equipment and job-site modifications • Advocacy between consumer, coworkers, and employer • Referrals/contacts with community agencies/organizations • Advocacy between consumer and family or caregivers
Follow-along	• Periodic assessment of employer/consumer satisfaction, productivity, appropriateness of adaptive equipment and job-site modifications, and employment specialist intervention time • Implementation of systematic plan for reducing staff intervention time • Assistance in replacing consumer in new job (as needed) • Assistance with retraining/job-site modifications (as needed)

or assistance from the employment specialist. By continuing to collect observational data and to solicit feedback from the work supervisor, the employment specialist is able to gauge his or her fading rate. If performance measures stay at an acceptable level and less intervention time is required, then the appropriateness of decreasing intervention time is confirmed. In the event that a problem arises, an increase of intervention time is warranted.

Follow-Along Services

Persons with severe physical handicaps will continue to require support services during their employment lifetime. Levels of intensity and frequency will vary, however. For example, assume that a 36-year-old man is employed and being served by a supported competitive employment program. He can perform all of his required work duties. However, during periodic times every 2–3 months, the employment specialist may need to schedule job-site intervention in order to help the worker achieve the necessary production standards, especially during high volume work periods. Otherwise, only intermittent monthly contacts are necessary.

Another situation may involve a worker who needs ongoing intervention perhaps twice a month to deal with social skills associated with stressful situations in the employment setting. Visiting twice a month to provide counseling to an individual to facilitate his or her interactions with coworkers may seem extravagant. However, the expense of repeating job development, re-placement into another position, and retraining usually outweighs the expense of ongoing semimonthly intervention. The benefits of retaining employment are obvious for both the individual with the disability and society in general.

Follow-along services are provided as an on-going service to prevent small or infrequent problems from interrupting employment retention. If management or equipment change, the employment specialist will be able to return for short intervals to provide the assistance necessary to help the worker achieve maximum performance again. This component of the supported work model of competitive employment is, to a large degree, responsible for employers' receptiveness to hiring persons with severe disabilities (Shafer, Hill, Seyfarth, & Wehman, 1987). In the long run, it is more cost efficient to provide ongoing follow-along services that prevent frequent turnover. Having to go back through the entire service cycle because a minor issue caused an employment termination is much more costly and time consuming. For persons with mental retardation or developmental disabilities, the interagency model makes vocational rehabilitation responsible for funding the job placement and job-site training/enabling periods through his or her stabilization on the job. Stabilization is achieved when employment specialist intervention time levels off and does not significantly change for a 30- to 60-day period (Hill et al., 1987). At this point, the community service agency providing for day support services (typically work activity, sheltered employment, case management services) takes over responsibility for the long-term follow-along supported employment services (i.e., local mental health and mental retardation services or developmental disabilities agencies). Unfortunately, there is not a readily available agency or funding source for long-term follow-along services for persons with physical disabilities or traumatic brain injury. Some states are currently examining this funding and services discrepancy, and looking at possible solutions for the dilemma.

Supported employment is being recognized as an important service alternative for persons with all types of disabilities, not just mental retardation. As more and more persons with severe disabilities are able to achieve gainful employment through this approach, demands will be placed on state and federal programs to amend funding and service discrepancies. Parents, consumer advocacy groups, and professionals can facilitate this process by documenting the needs in their communities. Groups such as United Cerebral Palsy and the National Head Injury Foundation are already putting political pressure on legislators and policymakers to fill in services gaps.

One solution to the lack of a follow-along service agency would be to alter the vocational rehabilitation (VR) system from a time-limited service provision agency to an ongoing service provision agency. Virginia is one state that has considered this option. In this plan, all vocational and employment services would begin and remain the responsibility of VR. A more appropriate plan would involve despecializing the mental health, mental retardation, and developmental disabilities agencies so that all disability groups that need community support services could use that service system. Both vocational rehabilitation and special education are time-limited service provision agencies offering services to all disability groups. The discrepancy occurs for those persons whose disabilities are severe enough for them to require ongoing community support, but because of their particular diagnosis, they are excluded from taxpayer supported public services. Parents and, in some cases, individuals with physical disabilities or disabilities due to injuries that occurred past the age of 22, are paying taxes to support an agency that excludes them from services that they may need but are ineligible for because they have the wrong disability label. Public advocacy and political lobbying are necessary to correct this discrepancy.

CASE STUDY: ERIC[1]

What follows is a case study of a person with physical impairments and cognitive deficiencies that occurred as a result of a traumatic injury to the brain.

---

[1]This case study was originally reported in Wehman, P., Wood, W., Everson, J., Goodwyn, R., & Conley, S. (1988). *Vocational education for multihandicapped youth with cerebral palsy.* Baltimore: Paul H. Brookes Publishing Co.

Employee Characteristics

Eric is a 26-year-old man who was injured in a car accident at age 21. His accident left him traumatically brain injured (TBI), with resulting physical handicaps and cognitive deficits. Eric has right side hemiplegia with no use of his right upper extremity, and left hand ataxia with an absence of fine movement and slow gross movement. His ambulation is difficult with poor balance, difficulty stopping, and a pronounced limp in his gait. Eric also has brittle diabetes requiring a special diet, daily blood sugar checks, and insulin injections as needed. Eric tires easily, has poor short-term memory, and experiences problems processing information.

Following the injury, Eric received vocational rehabilitation that included a vocational evaluation and theraputic services such as physical and occupational therapy. He received independent living skills training in areas of cooking, transportation, and budgeting.

He expressed an interest in computer programming to his rehabilitation counselor, who then enrolled him in an introductory course in data processing at a local college. He experienced a good deal of difficulty in completing his course assignments satisfactorily and on time so he decided to discontinue his coursework in computers and information management. Eric, however, continued to be interested in the field of data processing and computer operations, but lacking any other options, worked as a volunteer for a short period at a local hospital. Later, through a neighbor, Eric was able to work part-time doing data entry a few hours each week when there was enough work.

Employment Record

Four and one-half years after his injury, Eric was referred for supported employment services. After assessing Eric's skills and interests, and screening the local community job market, the supported employment job coach (employment specialist) arranged for him to become employed as an order entry operator for a pizza delivery business. Eric's job duties consisted of taking incoming calls from customers ordering pizzas and routing the order to the appropriate distribution center via a computer terminal. The employment specialist started with Eric the first

day of employment and provided the major portion of training, advocacy, and service coordination for a 7-week period to enable Eric to perform the job duties to the employer's satisfaction. At the beginning of the 7th week, the employment specialist began to fade her intervention from the employment setting. By the 12th week, intervention time was less than 20% of the time that Eric was at the jobsite.

Problems Presented and Nature of Intervention

There were minimal problems with acquiring the skill. Eric reached 100% accuracy by the second week of employment. However, because of physical limitations, Eric was unable to work fast enough to meet the required production rate. Factors that contributed to his slow speed were an inability to press the shift key with other keys simultaneously, periods of increased extraneous movement caused by his ataxia, and generally poor fine motor skills. Also, Eric displayed frustration when correction procedures were implemented by the employment specialist.

The employment specialist did not spend a great deal of time training skill acquisition. Instead, she spent a large part of her time analyzing problems related to productivity and then coordinating services with others to solve them. In the capacity of services coordinator, the employment specialist arranged for an occupational therapist to visit the employment setting and together (employment specialist, O.T.R., and Eric) they discussed changes and adaptations that would help to increase Eric's work speed. One adaptation was a wooden lap board built to fit Eric's chair in order to better position him in his workspace. The lap board was designed by the O.T.R. and built by a friend of a staff member. Three different lap boards were built from scrap wood before the final one was accepted as optimal for Eric's working position. The materials and labor were volunteered, but an estimate of the cost was figured at $64.50. A city map was laminated and tabs were added to the edges of the pages to make page turning easier. Finally, a shift key switch was added to allow upper case keying with just one hand. A person with skills comparable to that of a rehabilitation engineer was contracted for $50 to visit the employment setting, to design the shift key device, and to fabricate it. The O.T.R. was employed by the same organization that provided the employment specialist, and thus there was no additional charge for her service. However, she spent just under 4 hours in consultation on the job site with Eric. If the occupational therapist had billed for this service, the fee would have been approximately $240 (4 hours × $60 hour). Eric had also been receiving services from another occupational therapist who also visited the employment setting and was involved in the discussion of adaptive devices. Her time was paid through Eric's insurance policy.

During the time that adaptations were being planned and fabricated, the employment specialist completed part of the work for Eric in order to keep the production rate within acceptable limits. This is part of the supported employment service guaranteed to the employer.

To help Eric with short-term memory prob-

lems, a memo that provided a list of important steps to remember when taking orders was mounted above and to one side of Eric's work station. During the training period, the employment specialist worked with Eric on learning the basic routine of the work activity. However, there were often exceptions that called for changes in the basic routine (e.g., if a customer ordered 10 or more pizzas, he or she was given a 10% discount). The memo pad assisted Eric in responding to the exceptions by providing written cues. When Eric was unsure of the sequence of steps to complete the order, he referred to the memo pad.

Eric's frustration when corrected decreased as he improved in his job duties. Another problem that arose, however, was frequent request for special considerations that were related in some way to his disability (i.e., his diabetes). Eric started checking his blood sugar levels from three to four times each day. He also asked for a longer lunch break and requested to have his

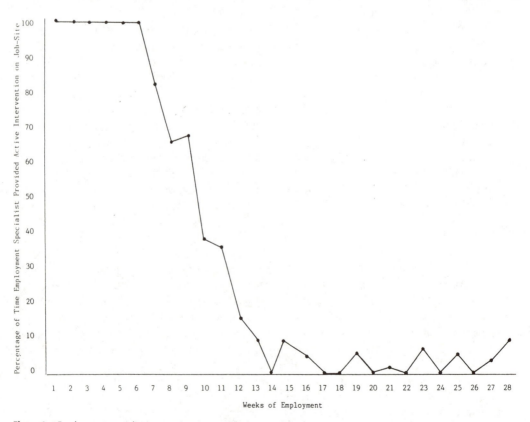

Figure 6. Employment specialist intervention time on job-site.

break right in the middle of the day (at the peak ordering time for pizza deliveries) when other employees were required to wait until the peak hour was over. Again, the special consideration was requested because of his diabetic condition. He also asked if the rest of the employees could be instructed in emergency care techniques for diabetics. Some of these requests were viewed as reasonable, and some were seen as demands for too much special treatment. Eric was encouraged to approach his supervisor with all such requests. The employment specialist worked with the employer on treating Eric as any other employee.

Length of Employment Specialist Intervention Time

The employment specialist provided full-time job-site intervention for the initial 6 weeks of Eric's employment. This equalled just over 150 hours of trainer intervention time. Fading began in the 7th week of job-site training and gradually decreased over the next 5 weeks. By the 13th week of training, trainer intervention had decreased to 1.5 hours. Initial training required the most employment specialist intervention, totaling 150 hours. The fading period shows a gradual reduction of intervention time until stabilization was achieved with 2 hours or less required per week by the 19th week. Figure 6 provides an illustration of the employment specialist intervention time.

Outcome Measures

Eric was employed at $4.15 per hour for 20 hours per week. After 26 weeks of employment, he earned over $2,100 in wages and paid over $400 in taxes. He began to remove some of the adapations made to the computer as his arm and hand coordination greatly improved after extended practice of his job duties. It is possible that Eric's entire performance improved as he gained confidence and became more familiar with work duties. After a conversation with his employer, Eric initiated plans to resume community college coursework in areas designed to enhance his potential earnings. He is also exploring possibilities of moving out of his family's home.

The Role of Education in Preparation for Employment

Public education programs serving youth with physical handicaps have a responsibility to provide for awareness of and experience with different occupational choices. Access to vocational education programs that expose students to different types of jobs and career options is important to help students develop career interests and goals. Students without intellectual deficits may well choose professional career goals that require post secondary education and training. However, students with multiple handicaps may not benefit from college or technical training and may choose to enter the work force immediately after public school. For both groups, exposure to work options prior to graduation will better enable them to make choices and decisions before they enter the adult service system.

During the intermediate school years when students are between the ages of 10 and 16, vocational awareness and exposure to different jobs is important (Wehman, Wood, Everson, Goodwyn, & Conley, 1988). Discussing different types of work, inviting visitors from the working community to talk about jobs, and most important, taking field trips to job sites are all ways to provide awareness and exposure during these years.

School staff need to spend time developing general work habits such as being on task, having a neat appearance, and responding to criticism. General work habits are best taught in the context of actual work skills (Wehman & Pentecost, 1983). Learning to use a computer, operate a copy machine, use a calculator, and file documents are all tasks that can be taught in classroom settings. Actual work skills and related work behaviors that may lead to a marketable trade and related work behaviors can also be developed, such as working independently for a prescribed period of time, being responsible for work materials, and completing work tasks with appropriate quality and an acceptable production rate. Teachers need to promote independence in work tasks and work-related behaviors because they are important requirements for successful employment.

At the secondary school level one can truly assess the success or failure of the vocational experiences provided in the earlier years. More time should be spent on vocational education at the secondary level. At least five additional areas need to be emphasized, at this level, along with continued reinforcement of the activities and suggestions already mentioned. These five areas include:

1. *Focus on increasing or improving production rates.* The speed at which students work in vocational training and initial employment situations will directly affect their employability and attractiveness to potential employers.

2. *Focus on improving the quality of job performance.* The accuracy and care with which a job is completed will influence the likelihood of job retention, assuming, of course, that work proficiency, work speed, and general work skills are adequate. Objectives in this area should be set to eventually achieve the employer's or industry's quality standards.

3. *Focus on increasing the student's endurance and stamina.* Increasing the number of work hours for secondary level students over a period of weeks will go far toward promoting improved employability in adulthood. School-sponsored employment training should require students to complete a series of job tasks without stopping for more than a brief period.

4. *Focus on providing vocational experiences in natural or real life environments.* Too often, secondary level students receive vocational and other education services in highly protected classroom and center environments. This service delivery pattern leads to the students' inability to generalize vocational skills learned at the school or to interact with nonhandicapped individuals in the natural workplace. These critical deficits are usually best overcome by providing training in natural work environments outside the classroom and/or by actually plac-

ing the students into part-time or full-time jobs and then providing job-site training in a supported work model (Wehman & Kregel, 1985; Wehman, Moon, Everson, Wood, & Barcus, 1988).

5. *When placement is not possible, do not let students graduate without a transition plan into an adult vocational service program that will provide necessary follow-through.* A transition plan should list service options available for the student in the community, identify an advocate (such as a rehabilitation counselor or case manager), and describe strategies for ensuring a smooth change from school to adult-based programs (Wehman, Moon, Everson, Wood, & Barcus, 1988).

REHABILITATION PLANNING DECISION RULES FOR THE REHABILITATION COUNSELORS

Supported competitive employment and other supported employment models such as enclaves and mobile crews are simply additional alternatives for rehabilitation professionals to consider when developing individualized written rehabilitation plans (IWRPs) for persons with severe physical disabilities. They are *not* replacements for long-standing rehabilitation programs or service options that have served many persons with disabilities for years. Some questions that are helpful to consider when evaluating supported employment services for a particular individual are the following:

1. Following completion of any of the currently available employment *preparation* or training programs, will the disabled person be able to succeed in an employment situation independently? The individual must be able to transfer general skills and behaviors to a specific environment and set of conditions. If yes, then supported employment is not the appropriate service. If no, then supported employment is appropriate.

2. If assistance is provided to locate a job for the disabled individual (i.e., job placement

services), will he or she be able to learn the job without undue hardship on the employer in a reasonable amount of time? If yes, then placement services may be adequate. If no, then supported employment services may be appropriate.

3. Has the individual been employed with repeated and frequent terminations of employment? If yes, then there may be a need for support services on the job site (i.e., as with supported employment).

4. Has the individual been involved in preemployment training, readiness, work hardening, work adjustment, or other programs for extended time periods without achieving the desired outcome of gainful employment? If yes, then supported employment may be an appropriate service to consider.

SUMMARY

Supported employment has not yet been extensively demonstrated for persons with severe physical or multiple handicaps. However, neither have traditional rehabilitation practices demonstrated achievement of meaningful outcomes for the majority of these individuals. Adding supported employment as another service model alternative may provide success for many of the persons who have not met with success with the more traditional service approach of "train and place." By individualizing the delivery of professional support through the employment specialist and by providing support and training at and after placement, the particular problems that have prevented job retention in the train and place model can be addressed and solved.

REFERENCES

Barcus, M., Brooke, V., Inge, K., Moon, S., & Goodall, P. (1987). *An instructional guide for training on a job site: A supported employment resource*. Richmond: Virginia Commonwealth University, Rehabilitation Research and Training Center.

Bowe F. (1986). *Disabled in 1985: A portrait of disabled adults*. Hot Springs: University of Arkansas.

Hill, M.L., Banks, P.D., Handrich, R.R., Wehman, P.H., Hill, J.W., & Shafer, M.S. (1987). Benefit-cost analysis of supported competitive employment for persons with mental retardation. *Research in Developmental Disabilities*, 8,(1), 71–89.

Hill, M.L., Hill, J.W., Wehman, P., Revell, G., Dickerson, A., & Noble, J.H. (1987). Supported employment: An interagency funding model for persons with severe disabilities. *Journal of Rehabilitation*, 53,(3), 13–21.

Inge K.J. (1987). Atypical motor development. In F.P. Orelove & D. Sobsey, *Educating children with multiple disabilities: A transdisciplinary approach* (pp. 43–65). Baltimore: Paul H. Brookes Publishing Co.

Kokaska, C.J., & Brolin, D.E. (1985). *Career education for handicapped individuals*. Columbus, OH: Charles E. Merrill.

Moon, M.S., Goodall, P.A., Barcus, J.M., & Brooke, V.A. (1986). *The supported work model of competitive employment: A guide for job trainers*. Richmond: Virginia Commonwealth University, Rehabilitation Research and Training Center.

Pietruski, W.W., Everson, J.M., Goodwyn, R., & Wehman, P. (1985). *Vocational training and curriculum for multihandicapped youth with cerebral palsy*. Richmond: Virginia Commonwealth University.

President's Committee on Employment of the Handicapped (1987). *Out of the market: A national crisis*. Washington, DC: United States Government Printing Office.

Shafer, M.S., Hill, J.W., Seyfarth, J., & Wehman, P. (1987). Competitive employment and workers with mental retardation: An analysis of employers' perceptions and experiences. *American Journal of Mental Retardation*, 92 (3), 304–311.

U.S. Department of Health and Human Services, Social Security Administration. (1982). *1978 survey of disability and work*. Washington, DC: United States Government Printing Office, Office of Research and Statistics.

U.S. Department of Labor. (1979). *Sheltered workshop study, Vol. 2: Study of handicapped clients in sheltered workshops and recommendations of the Secretary*. Washington, DC: U.S. Department of Labor, Employment Standards Administration.

U.S. Social Security Administration. (1982, November). *Report on transitional employment for mentally retarded SSI recipients and vocational rehabilitation demonstrations*. Bethesda, MD: Author.

Wehman, P. (1981). *Competitive employment: New horizons for severely disabled individuals*. Baltimore: Paul H. Brookes Publishing Co.

Wehman, P., & Hill, J.W. (1982). Preparing severely handicapped students for less restrictive environments. *Journal of the Association for Severely Handicapped*, 7(3), 33–39.

Wehman, P., & Kregel, J. (1985). A supported work approach to competitive employment of individuals with moderate and severe handicaps. *Journal of The Association for Persons with Severe Handicaps*, 10(1), 3–11.

Wehman, P., Moon, M.S., Everson, J.M., Wood, W., & Barcus, J.M. (1988). *Transition from school to work: New challenges for youth with severe disabilities*. Baltimore: Paul H. Brookes Publishing Co.

Wehman, P., & Pentecost, J. (1983). Facilitating employment for moderately and severely handicapped youth. *Education and Treatment of Children*, 6, 69–80.

Wehman, P., Wood, W., Everson, J., Goodwyn, R., & Conley, S. (1988). *Vocational education for multihandicapped youth with cerebral palsy*. Baltimore: Paul H. Brookes Publishing Co.

Appendix

Equipment Source List

Access to Computers for the Physically
  Handicapped
Prentke Romich Company
8769 Township Rd. 513
Shreve, OH 44676-9421

Closing the Gap
P.O. Box 68
Henderson, MN 56044

Maryland Computer Services, Inc.
  Newsletter
MCS Headquarters
2010 Rock Spring Rd.
Forrest Hill, MD 21050

Metro Telemarketing Systems of Tidewater,
  Inc.
C. Rober Freed
441 S. Independence Blvd. #1
Virginia Beach, VA 23452

*Personal Computers for the Physically
  Disabled: A Resource Guide*
Apple Computers, Inc.
10260 Bandley Dr.
Cupertino CA 95014

Phonic Ear, Inc.
250 Camino Alto
Mill Valley, CA 94941

Prentke Romich Company
8769 Township Rd, 513
Shreve, OH 44676-9421

TASH, Incorporated
70 Gibson Dr.
Unit 1
Markham, Ontario L3R 2Z3

Trace Research and Development Center
  for the Severely Communicatively
  Handicapped
University of Wisconsin-Madison
314 Waisman Center, 1500 Highland Ave.
Madison, WI 53707

Trinformation Systems, Inc.
3132 S. E. Jay St.
Stuart, FL 33494

Index